A Reader's Guide to

Shakespeare

A READER'S GUIDE TO
Shakespeare

Also published as *Magill's Choice: Shakespeare*

JOSEPH ROSENBLUM

BARNES
&NOBLE
BOOKS
NEW YORK

Frontispiece: William Shakespeare, engraved by Martin Droeshout, from the title page to the 1623 First Folio. *(Library of Congress)*

Also published as *Magill's Choice: Shakespeare*

Original essays appeared in the following sets, edited by Frank N. Magill: *Great Lives from History: British and Commonwealth Series* (1987), *Critical Survey of Poetry: English Language Series* (Revised Edition, 1992), *Masterplots II: Poetry Series* (1992), *Critical Survey of Drama: English Language Series* (Revised Edition, 1994), and *Masterplots: Revised Second Edition* (1996), *Cyclopedia of World Authors* (Revised Third Edition, 1997); new material has been added.

This edition published by Barnes & Noble, Inc.,
by arrangement with Salem Press, Inc.

1999 Barnes & Noble Books

ISBN 0-7607-1494-0 *casebound*
ISBN 0-7607-1495-9 *paperback*

Printed and bound in the United States of America

99 00 01 02 MC 9 8 7 6 5 4 3 2 1
99 00 01 02 MP 9 8 7 6 5 4 3 2 1

FG

Publisher's Note

A Reader's Guide to Shakespeare compiles a wide range of essays on the life and works of the most famous English playwright of all time, William Shakespeare (1564-1616). A basic part of the curriculum, Shakespeare's plays—still being introduced to students, from middle school through college, four centuries after their composition—have never lost their popularity, and succeeding years have witnessed hundreds of new theatrical productions as well as a constantly growing list of film adaptations that have kept audiences riveted to the plays' enduring themes of love, human relationships, responsibility, tolerance, and the lessons of history. The impact of Shakespeare's sometimes difficult language on modern English speech also attests to the Bard's influence. Even those unfamiliar with *Romeo and Juliet, As You Like It, Macbeth, Hamlet, King Lear,* or the sonnets have probably heard and used expressions from these classic works: "star-crossed lovers," "All the world's a stage," "Out, damned spot," "To be or not to be?," "more sinned against than sinning."

The volume is divided into three parts: "Biography" first presents a time line of those events in Shakespeare's life of which we are reasonably certain. There follow three essays focusing on his life from three different viewpoints: as man, as dramatist, and as poet. "The Plays" offers an essay on each of the plays, including a play newly attributed to Shakespeare, *Edward III*, each between 2,000 and 2,500 words, each presenting a plot summary ("The Story") and an analysis ("Critical Evaluation") of the play, and each ending with a targeted, annotated list of secondary sources for more in-depth study. Similarly, the final section contains separate analyses of "The Poetry": *A Lover's Complaint, The Passionate Pilgrim, The Phoenix and the Turtle, The Rape of Lucrece, Venus and Adonis,* an overview of the 154 sonnets, and individual essays on fourteen of the more famous sonnets.

Throughout the text, more than fifty famous quotations from Shakespeare's plays appear as separate boxed elements, in which the famous words are cited by play, act, scene, and line, and are fully explained within the context of the play's plot. At the end of the volume, a "Quotation Index" (immediately preceding the "Subject Index") will link readers to these discussions and assist them in identifying the exact source of the quotation.

Additional aids to study appear at the front of the volume: Three listings of Shakespeare's works—an "Alphabetical List of Works," a "Categorized List of Works," and a "Chronological List of Works"—appear after the introduction. Here, the dates that follow the abbreviations "pr." and "pb." indicate, respectively, years of first production and first publication. Appendices include a thirty-thousand-word "Bibliography," which has been updated by its author, Joseph Rosenblum; this listing of sources organizes the plethora of major Shakespeare editions and studies into useful categories. For those interested in the history of trends and fashions in Shakespeare studies, Rosenblum's "Brief History of Shakespeare Studies" precedes the bibliography. Next, a "Character Index" directs readers to essays covering famous characters from the plays. Finally, following the "Quotation Index" mentioned above, the comprehensive "Subject Index" lists plays, poems, people, and concepts likely to be of interest to those learning about Shakespeare for the first time.

List of Contributors

Edward C. Adams
Independent Scholar

Stanley Archer
Texas A&M University

Kenneth John Atchity
Occidental College

Bryan Aubrey
Independent Scholar

Nicholas Birns
New School for Social Research

Robert G. Blake
Elon College

Harold Branam
University of Pennnsylvania

Bill Delaney
Independent Scholar

Sandra K. Fischer
State University of New York—Albany

Edward E. Foster
University of San Diego

John L. Grigsby
Tennessee Technological University

James Hale
Central Washington University

Susan Henthorne
White Pines College

John R. Holmes
Franciscan University of Steubenville

Muriel B. Ingham
San Diego State University

Shakuntala Jayaswal
University of New Haven

David L. Kubal
State University of California, Los Angeles

R. T. Lambdin
University of South Florida

James Livingston
Northern Michigan University

Russell Lord
Plymouth State College

Andrew Macdonald
Loyola University

Gina Macdonald
Loyola University

Brian L. Mark
California State University, Fullerton

Bernard E. Morris
Independent Scholar

Thomas Amherst Perry
East Texas State University

H. Alan Pickrell
Emory & Henry College

Joseph Rosenblum
University of North Carolina, Greensboro

Gary F. Waller
Wilfrid Laurier University

Robert F. Willson, Jr.
University of Missouri—Kansas City

CONTENTS

The Poetry

Introduction

William Shakespeare, greatest of English poets and dramatists, was born at Stratford-upon-Avon in 1564 and died there in 1616. The biographical data—though sufficient to demolish the Baconian and other heresies, which have posited various others, including Sir Francis Bacon, as the true author of Shakespeare's works—are not helpful in other respects. The view that Shakespeare attended Stratford Grammar School, though inherently probable, remains a surmise, and little is known of his activities prior to 1590, save that he married Anne Hathaway in 1582 and had three children by her.

Most of Shakespeare's working life was spent in London, and allusions, friendly and otherwise, show that by 1592 he was a dramatist of recognized achievement. Francis Meres, in his review of 125 English authors, *Palladis Tamia: Wit's Treasury* (1598), virtually establishes that his supremacy in comedy, tragedy, and narrative poetry was generally acknowledged, and this view is endorsed by later testimony, notably that of contemporary playwright and poet Ben Jonson. From 1594 on, Shakespeare was associated exclusively with the Lord Chamberlain's company, which became the King's company in 1603. This was the most stable and prosperous of the Elizabethan dramatic companies. It built the Globe Theatre in 1599 and acquired the Blackfriars private theater in 1608.

So far as can be ascertained, Shakespeare's career as a dramatist covers the period c. 1590 to c. 1612. His early years show him working in all categories: Chronicle histories are a conspicuous feature of the years 1590-1599, and they reflect England's self-awareness at a time when the threat from Spain was still acutely felt. The same period saw the maturing of his comic genius, through such minor masterpieces as *Love's Labour's Lost* and *A Midsummer Night's Dream* to the three great comedies, *The Merchant of Venice*, *Much Ado About Nothing*, and *As You Like It*. Two early tragedies, *Titus Andronicus* and *Romeo and Juliet*, promise far more than they actually perform, and *Julius Caesar*, though flawless in conception and execution, lacks urgency and depth. By the end of the century, Shakespeare's achievement had equaled, but not surpassed, that of England's greatest writer to that time, the fourteenth century poet Sir Geoffrey Chaucer. The foremost lesson so far learned was that human and poetic truth, as embodied in Shakespeare's most famous fictitious character, Falstaff, is greater than the historical truth of his depictions of Prince Hal (Henry V) and Hotspur (Henry Percy).

After 1600, Shakespeare bade farewell to romantic comedy in the incomparable *Twelfth Night*, and he appears to have devoted one or two years to earnest contemplation of both life and art. *Hamlet* is the first of the great tragedies and also the first of a group of deeply contemplative dramas, often referred to as "problem plays," comprising *Troilus and Cressida*, *All's Well That Ends Well*, and *Measure for Measure*, which furnish an ample background to Shakespeare's whole output. When the tragic hero emerges again in *Othello*, his appeal is more directly emotional than Hamlet's, and this impassioned conception prevails in *King Lear* and *Macbeth*. In these titanic masterpieces, humanity's response to the workings of a relentless and malign destiny is explored and exploited to the full, and the terrible logic of the action is communicated in language of ever-increasing urgency and intensity. *Antony and Cleopatra*, despite its superlative poetry, fails to secure a comparable tragic effect, but looks forward to the regenerative pattern of the late romances. *Timon of Athens* is excessive in its pessimism and was left unfinished, but *Coriolanus* triumphantly affirms Shakespeare's capacity for recovery. Though outwardly uninviting in both matter and manner, its emotional impact proves terrific, and its psychology is penetrating.

The plays of Shakespeare's final period are dramatic romances that present improbable persons and incidents and draw freely upon the musical and spectacular elements popular in the court masques of the period. In these plays, the themes of atonement and reconciliation, earlier treated in *All's Well That Ends Well* and *Measure for Measure*, are coordinated in a general pattern of regeneration symbolized by the heroines. *Pericles* and *Cymbeline* are uncertain in their handling of complicated plot material, but *The Winter's Tale* is magnificent and intense and *The Tempest* confers perfection on these endeavors. *Henry VIII*, last of the canonical plays, is thought to have been written in collaboration with another prolific playwright, John Fletcher. *The Two Noble Kinsmen* purports to be the product of the same partnership, although the alleged Shakespearian scenes have been disputed by many competent critics. Attempts to claim other dramatic works of the period for Shakespeare have, in the main, proved abortive, though it has now been established, beyond reasonable doubt, that *The Book of Sir Thomas More* (British Museum manuscript Harley 7368) contains three pages of his work in autograph. The early history play *Edward III*, first attributed to Shakespeare in 1656, has also been added to the canon. Thematically, structurally, and historically, it is closely related to the second tetralogy.

The seventeenth century poet John Dryden justly claimed that Shakespeare "was the man who of all Modern, and perhaps Ancient Poets, had the largest and most comprehensive soul." He is the supreme interpreter of human relationships, the supreme percipient of human frailties and potentialities. It is often alleged that he is no philosopher, that his mind is neither mystical nor prophetic, that the beatific vision of the great Italian epic poet Dante is beyond his scope. Even so, his thought, governed by the Christian Neoplatonism of his day, is earnest and profound, and his writings as a whole reveal a consistent, coherent, and possibly distinctive philosophical system. The comedies move ultimately to an acute awareness of the mutability of human affairs, and this sense of time's implacability is crystallized in the sonnets and communicated, with inexpressible poignancy, in *Twelfth Night*.

In the historical plays the curse that falls upon the commonwealth through the deposition and murder of an anointed king is pursued through successive manifestations of violence and anarchy, of which the character Falstaff is made finally the most potent symbol, until expiation is complete in Henry Tudor. Here the manipulation of history is determined by a clearly ordered conception of political morality no less than by an artistic conscience. The same outlook is more flexibly presented in *Hamlet*, and Ulysses' great exposition of degree in *Troilus and Cressida* summarizes the acquired political wisdom of a decade. But there is no break in continuity, and Ulysses' speech is equally applicable to the great tragedies, in which Shakespeare contemplates the chaos that ensues when "degree is suffocate."

Cognate with the doctrine of degree, and informing the histories and tragedies at all stages, is the concept of absolute justice. Portia, in *The Merchant of Venice*, pleads that mercy is above justice, and this is exemplified, in strenuous and practical terms, in *Measure for Measure*. The conflict between justice and mercy is a conspicuous feature of the great tragedies, notably *King Lear*, and is ultimately resolved, in its tragic context, in *Coriolanus*, when the hero spares Rome and gains his greatest victory—that over himself. *Cymbeline* and *The Winter's Tale*, albeit artificially, plunge into chaos comparable to the chaos of the tragedies, but the resolution now is in terms of reconciliation and regeneration instead of sacrifice and waste. Music, the prime function of the Creation, becomes increasingly prominent in these final romances, each of which looks clearly toward the harmony and unity of the Golden Age. The Platonic vision of the Many and the One, which informs these plays and carries them nearly into mysticism, though dramatically new, is something which Shakespeare had earlier achieved in certain of the sonnets and in the concentrated intricacy of *The Phoenix and the Turtle*, published in Robert Chester's *Loves Martyr* in 1601.

Criticism has often erred in emphasizing particular aspects of Shakespeare's art. With him, action, thought, character, and language are not separable elements; and our response, in theater and study alike, must be to a complex unity in which dramatic conceptions are simultaneously natural and poetic, and language, unique and infinitely creative. The greatest Shakespeare critics—Dryden, Samuel Johnson, Samuel Taylor Coleridge, and A. C. Bradley—can always be read with profit and delight, and the enormous mass of twentieth century criticism contains much that is of value; but if we have ears to hear and a heart to understand, we shall always find that Shakespeare is his own best interpreter.

Alphabetical List of Works

THE PLAYS

All's Well That Ends Well, pr. c. 1602-1603

Antony and Cleopatra, pr. c. 1606-1607

As You Like It, pr. c. 1599-1600

The Comedy of Errors, pr. c. 1592-1594

Coriolanus, pr. c. 1607-1608

Cymbeline, pr. c. 1609-1610

Edward III, wr., pr. c. 1589-1595

Hamlet, Prince of Denmark, pr. c. 1600-1601

Henry IV, Part I, pr. c. 1597-1598

Henry IV, Part II, pr. 1598

Henry V, pr. c. 1598-1599

Henry VI, Part I, wr. 1589-1590, pr. 1592

Henry VI, Part II, pr. c. 1590-1591

Henry VI, Part III, pr. c. 1590-1591

Henry VIII, pr. 1613 (with John Fletcher)

Julius Caesar, pr. c. 1599-1600

King John, pr. c. 1596-1597

King Lear, pr. c. 1605-1606

Love's Labour's Lost, pr. c. 1594-1595 (revised 1597 for court performance)

Macbeth, pr. 1606

Measure for Measure, pr. 1604

The Merchant of Venice, pr. c. 1596-1597

The Merry Wives of Windsor, pr. 1597 (revised c. 1600-1601)

A Midsummer Night's Dream, pr. c. 1595-1596

Much Ado About Nothing, pr. c. 1598-1599

Othello, the Moor of Venice, pr. 1604 (revised 1623)

Pericles, Prince of Tyre, pr. c. 1607-1608

Richard II, pr. c. 1595-1596

Richard III, pr. c. 1592-1593 (revised 1623)

Romeo and Juliet, pr. c. 1595-1596

The Taming of the Shrew, pr. c. 1593-1594

The Tempest, pr. 1611

Timon of Athens, pr. c. 1607-1608

Titus Andronicus, pr., pb. 1594

Troilus and Cressida, pr. c. 1601-1602

Twelfth Night: Or, What You Will, pr. c. 1600-1602

The Two Gentlemen of Verona, pr. c. 1594-1595

The Two Noble Kinsmen, pr. c. 1612-1613 (with John Fletcher)

The Winter's Tale, pr. c. 1610-1611

THE POETRY

A Lover's Complaint, 1609

The Passionate Pilgrim, 1599 (miscellany with poems by Shakespeare and others)

The Phoenix and the Turtle, 1601

The Rape of Lucrece, 1594

Sonnets, 1609

Venus and Adonis, 1593

Categorized List of Works

THE PLAYS

The Histories (in historical sequence):
King John, pr. c. 1596-1597
Edward III, wr., pr. c. 1589-1595
Richard II, pr. c. 1595-1596
Henry IV, Part I, pr. c. 1597-1598
Henry IV, Part II, pr. 1598
Henry V, pr. c. 1598-1599
Henry VI, Part I, wr. 1589-1590, pr. 1592
Henry VI, Part II, pr. c. 1590-1591
Henry VI, Part III, pr. c. 1590-1591
Richard III, pr. c. 1592-1593 (revised 1623)
Henry VIII, pr. 1613 (with John Fletcher)

The Comedies:
All's Well That Ends Well, pr. c. 1602-1603
As You Like It, pr. c. 1599-1600
The Comedy of Errors, pr. c. 1592-1594
Love's Labour's Lost, pr. c. 1594-1595 (revised 1597 for court performance)
Measure for Measure, pr. 1604
The Merchant of Venice, pr. c. 1596-1597
The Merry Wives of Windsor, pr. 1597 (revised c. 1600-1601)
A Midsummer Night's Dream, pr. c. 1595-1596
Much Ado About Nothing, pr. c. 1598-1599
The Taming of the Shrew, pr. c. 1593-1594

Troilus and Cressida, pr. c. 1601-1602
Twelfth Night: Or, What You Will, pr. c. 1600-1602
The Two Gentlemen of Verona, pr. c. 1594-1595

The Tragedies:
Antony and Cleopatra, pr. c. 1606-1607
Coriolanus, pr. c. 1607-1608
Hamlet, Prince of Denmark, pr. c. 1600-1601
Julius Caesar, pr. c. 1599-1600
King Lear, pr. c. 1605-1606
Macbeth, pr. 1606
Othello, the Moor of Venice, pr. 1604 (revised 1623)
Romeo and Juliet, pr. c. 1595-1596
Timon of Athens, pr. c. 1607-1608
Titus Andronicus, pr., pb. 1594

The Romances (Tragicomedies):
Cymbeline, pr. c. 1609-1610
Pericles, Prince of Tyre, pr. c. 1607-1608
The Tempest, pr. 1611
The Two Noble Kinsmen, pr. c. 1612-1613 (with Fletcher)
The Winter's Tale, pr. c. 1610-1611

THE POETRY
A Lover's Complaint, 1609
The Passionate Pilgrim, 1599 (miscellany with poems by Shakespeare and others)
The Phoenix and the Turtle, 1601
The Rape of Lucrece, 1594
Sonnets, 1609
Venus and Adonis, 1593

Chronological List of Works

THE PLAYS

wr., pr. c. 1589-1595	*Edward III*
wr. 1589-1590, pr. 1592	*Henry VI, Part I*
pr. c. 1590-1591	*Henry VI, Part II*
pr. c. 1590-1591	*Henry VI, Part III*
pr. c. 1592-1593 (rev. 1623)	*Richard III*
pr. c. 1592-1594	*The Comedy of Errors*
pr. c. 1593-1594	*The Taming of the Shrew*
pr., pb. 1594	*Titus Andronicus*
pr. c. 1594-1595	*The Two Gentlemen of Verona*
pr. c. 1594-1595 (rev. 1597)	*Love's Labour's Lost*
pr. c. 1595-1596	*Romeo and Juliet*
pr. c. 1595-1596	*Richard II*
pr. c. 1595-1596	*A Midsummer Night's Dream*
pr. c. 1596-1597	*King John*
pr. c. 1596-1597	*The Merchant of Venice*
pr. c. 1597-1598	*Henry IV, Part I*
pr. 1597 (rev. c. 1600-1601)	*The Merry Wives of Windsor*
pr. 1598	*Henry IV, Part II*
pr. c. 1598-1599	*Much Ado About Nothing*
pr. c. 1598-1599	*Henry V*
pr. c. 1599-1600	*Julius Caesar*
pr. c. 1599-1600	*As You Like It*
pr. c. 1600-1601	*Hamlet, Prince of Denmark*
pr. c. 1600-1602	*Twelfth Night: Or, What You Will*
pr. c. 1601-1602	*Troilus and Cressida*
pr. c. 1602-1603	*All's Well That Ends Well*
pr. 1604 (rev. 1623)	*Othello, the Moor of Venice*
pr. 1604	*Measure for Measure*
pr. c. 1605-1606	*King Lear*
pr. 1606	*Macbeth*
pr. c. 1606-1607	*Antony and Cleopatra*
pr. c. 1607-1608	*Coriolanus*
pr. c. 1607-1608	*Timon of Athens*
pr. c. 1607-1608	*Pericles, Prince of Tyre*
pr. c. 1609-1610	*Cymbeline*
pr. c. 1610-1611	*The Winter's Tale*
pr. 1611	*The Tempest*
pr. c. 1612-1613	*The Two Noble Kinsmen* (with John Fletcher)
pr. 1613	*Henry VIII* (with Fletcher)

THE POETRY

BIOGRAPHY

Biographical Time Line

Apr. 23?, 1564	Shakespeare is born in Stratford-upon-Avon, Warwickshire, England.
1571	Enters grammar school.
1582	Marries Anne Hathaway, eight years his senior.
1583	Daughter Susanna is born.
1585	Twins Hamnet and Judith are born.
1592	Shakespeare is working in London as an actor and playwright.
1593-1594	The London stage is closed during a plague epidemic; Shakespeare writes poetry.
1594	The theaters reopen; Shakespeare acquires a partnership in a new theater company, the Lord Chamberlain's Men.
1595	Begins writing the sonnets, tracing his friendship with a young man and a romance with a "Dark Lady."
1596	Shakespeare's father John is granted a hereditary coat of arms.
1596	Shakespeare's son Hamnet, age eleven, dies.
1597	Shakespeare purchases New Place in Stratford-upon-Avon.
1599	Shakespeare's company builds the Globe Theatre.
1603	King James I renames Shakespeare's company the King's Men.
1607	Shakespeare's daughter Susanna marries physician John Hall.
1608	The King's Men acquires the Blackfriars Theatre and the services of collaborating playwrights Francis Beaumont and John Fletcher. Their "cavalier" style—light, witty comedies—becomes popular, perhaps hastening Shakespeare's retirement.
1608	Susanna and John have a daughter, Elizabeth, Shakespeare's first grandchild.
1613	Shakespeare retires completely to Stratford-upon-Avon; with John Heminge, a partner in the King's Men, and William Johnson, the host of the Mermaid Tavern, he purchases the gatehouse of the Blackfriars priory for London visits.
Feb. 10, 1616	Younger daughter Judith marries Thomas Quiney.
Mar. 25, 1616	Shakespeare makes out his last will and testament, leaving most of his estate to Susanna, a substantial amount of money to Judith, and his "second best bed" to wife Anne.
Apr. 23, 1616	Shakespeare dies and is buried in Holy Trinity Church, Stratford-upon-Avon.

An engraving of William Shakespeare done from the Chandos portrait.
(Library of Congress)

The Man

William Shakespeare was born in Stratford-upon-Avon, Warwickshire, England, descended from tenant farmers and landed gentry. His traditional birth date, April 23, 1564, is conjectural. Baptism was on April 26, so April 23 is a good guess—and a tidy one, since that date is also St. George's Day as well as the date of Shakespeare's own death.

One of Shakespeare's grandfathers, Richard Shakespeare of Snitterfield, rented land from the other, Robert Arden of Wilmcote. Shakespeare's father, John, moved to nearby Stratford-upon-Avon, became a prosperous shop owner (dealing in leather goods) and municipal officeholder, and married his former landlord's youngest daughter, Mary Arden. Thus Shakespeare—the third of eight children but the first to survive infancy—was born into a solidly middle-class family in a provincial market town.

During Shakespeare's infancy, his father was one of the town's leading citizens. In 1557, John Shakespeare had become a member of the town council and subsequently held such offices as constable, affeeror (a kind of assessor), and chamberlain (treasurer); in 1568, he became bailiff (mayor) and justice of the peace. As the son of a municipal officer, the young Shakespeare was entitled to a free education in the town's grammar school, which he probably entered around the age of seven. The school's main subject was Latin studies—grammar and readings drilled into the schoolboys year after year. The Avon River, the surrounding farmlands, and the nearby Forest of Arden offered plenty of opportunities for childhood adventures.

When Shakespeare was a teenager, his family fell on hard times. His father stopped attending town council meetings in 1577, and the family's fortunes began to decline. Matters were not improved in 1582 when Shakespeare, at the age of eighteen, hastily married Anne Hathaway, the twenty-six-year-old daughter of a farmer from the nearby village of Shottery; she presented him with a daughter, named Susanna, approximately five months later. In 1585, the couple also became the parents of twins, Hamnet and Judith. As was then customary, the young couple probably lived in his parents' home, which must have seemed increasingly crowded.

The next mention of Shakespeare is in 1592, when he was an actor and playwright in London. His actions during the seven-year interim have been a matter of much curious speculation, including unproved stories of deer poaching, soldiering, and teaching. It may have taken him those seven years simply to break into and advance in the London theater. His early connections with the theater are unknown, although he was an actor before he became a playwright. He might have joined one of the touring companies that occasionally performed in Stratford-upon-Avon, or he might have gone directly to London to make his fortune, in either the theater or some other trade. Shakespeare was a venturesome and able young man who had good reasons to travel—his confining family circumstances, tinged with just enough disgrace to qualify him to join the disreputable players. The theater was his escape to freedom; he therefore had strong motivation to succeed.

A mid-eighteenth century view of Stratford-upon-Avon showing the town dominated by Trinity Church, where Shakespeare is buried. (Library of Congress)

Life's Work

The London theater, in Shakespeare's day, was composed of companies of men and boys (women were not allowed on the Renaissance English stage but were played by young men or boys). These actors performed in public playhouses roughly modeled on old innyards. The theaters were open to the air, had balconies surrounding the pit and stage, and held from two to three thousand people. A group known as the University Wits—John Lyly, George Peele, Thomas Lodge, Robert Greene, Thomas Nashe, and Christopher Marlowe—dominated the drama. Shakespeare learned his art by imitating these Oxford and Cambridge men, but for him they were a difficult group to join. They looked down on most actors and on those playwrights, such as Thomas Kyd, who had not attended a university. Shakespeare offended on both counts, and Robert Greene expressed his resentment in the posthumously published book *Greene's Groatsworth of Wit Bought with a Million of Repentance* (1592), which included a famous warning to three fellow "gentlemen" playwrights:

> Yes, trust them [the players] not: for there is an upstart crow, beautified with our feathers, that with his *Tiger's heart wrapt in a player's hide*, supposes he is as well able to bombast out a blank verse as the best of you: and being an absolute *Johannes Factotum*, is in his own conceit the only Shake-scene in a country.

Greene's literary executor, Henry Chettle, later printed an apology for this slur on Shakespeare, with its pun on his name and its parody of a line from *Henry VI, Part*

III. Upon meeting him, Chettle found Shakespeare's "demeanor no less civil than he, excellent in the quality he professes. Besides, divers of worship have reported his uprightness of dealing, which argues his honesty, and his facetious grace in writing, that approves his art."

Actually, Greene's judgment of Shakespeare's early work is more accurate. The early plays are far from excellent; they include some of the most slavish imitations in Renaissance English drama, as Shakespeare tried his hand at the various popular modes. The interminable three-part history play *Henry VI* (1589-1592), as Greene notes, makes bombastic attempts at Marlowe's powerful blank verse. In *The Comedy of Errors* (c. 1592-1594), based on Plautus' *Menaechmi*, and in the Senecan tragedy *Titus Andronicus* (c. 1593-1594), Shakespeare showed his ability to copy Roman models down to the smallest detail, even if he did lack a university degree. Apparently, he also lacked confidence in his own imagination and learned slowly. *Richard III* (c. 1592-1593), however, showed promise in the malignant character of Richard, while *The Taming of the Shrew* (c. 1593-1594) offered its rambunctious love-fight.

Despite their imitative nature and many other faults, Shakespeare's early plays—notably the *Henry VI* plays—were popular onstage, but his greatest early popularity came from two long narrative poems, *Venus and Adonis* (1593) and *The Rape of Lucrece* (1594). Shakespeare wrote these two poems during the two years that the plague closed down the London theaters. He dedicated the poems to a patron, the young Henry Wriothesley, third Earl of Southampton, who may have granted him a substantial monetary reward in return. In any event, when the

Shakespeare's birthplace, on Henley Street in Stratford-upon-Avon, is now a museum that draws thousands of visitors annually. (Library of Congress)

theaters reopened in 1594 the acting companies were almost decimated financially, but Shakespeare was in a position to buy or otherwise acquire a partnership in one of the newly reorganized companies, the Lord Chamberlain's Men. Henceforth, Shakespeare earned money not only from the plays he had written or in which he acted but also from a share of the profits of every company performance. The financial arrangement seemed to inspire his creative efforts, for he set about writing the plays that made him famous, beginning with *Romeo and Juliet* (c. 1595-1596) and going on to the great history plays and comedies, including *Richard II* (c. 1595-1596), the two-part *Henry IV* (c. 1597-1598), *Henry V* (c. 1598-1599), *A Midsummer Night's Dream* (c. 1595-1596), *The Merchant of Venice* (c. 1596-1597), *Much Ado About Nothing* (c. 1598-1599), *As You Like It* (c. 1599-1600), and *Twelfth Night: Or, What You Will* (c. 1600-1602).

A fanciful depiction of a gathering of Shakespeare and some of his notable contemporaries, including Francis Beaumont (standing, third from left), John Fletcher (seated, with head on hand), Sir Francis Bacon (next to Fletcher, in hat), Ben Jonson (seated to right of Bacon), Shakespeare (center, in upholstered chair), Sir Walter Raleigh (standing to right of Shakespeare, in feathered hat), Shakespeare's patron the third Earl of Southampton (standing to right of Raleigh and looking at Shakespeare), and Thomas Dekker (far right). (Library of Congress)

At about the time Shakespeare wrote *Romeo and Juliet* and *Richard II*, he probably also began his great sonnet sequence, not published until 1609. The 154 sonnets, tracing a friendship with a young man, sometimes called the "Fair Youth," and a romance with a "Dark Lady," raise the question of how Shakespeare lived when he was away from Stratford, where his wife and children presumably remained. The young man might be a patron—perhaps Southampton, though other names have also been proposed—and the Dark Lady strictly imaginary, created to overturn the sonnets' trite Petrarchan conventions. Other speculations favor a more personal interpretation, seeing an actual *ménage à trois* of the poet, the Fair Youth, and the Dark Lady. All the questions raised by the sonnets remain open, and the only evidence about how Shakespeare spent his spare time in London indicates that he sometimes frequented taverns (notably the Mermaid) with his fellow playwrights and players.

Evidence also indicates that he remained in close contact with Stratford-upon-Avon, to which he probably returned as frequently as possible. He used his earnings from the theater to install himself as the town's leading citizen, buying New Place as a family residence in 1597 and thereafter steadily amassing other land and

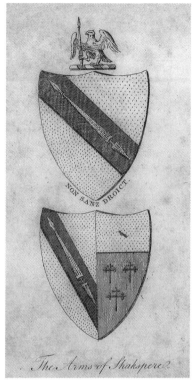

The hereditary coat of arms granted to Shakespeare's father in 1596, possibly at his son's behest. (Library of Congress)

property. In 1596, his father John was granted a hereditary coat of arms (or his son may have purchased it for him) and thus became a gentleman, a status he had never achieved on his own. Unfortunately, also in 1596, Shakespeare suffered a setback when his son, Hamnet, died at the age of eleven. Shakespeare's affection for his two remaining children, Susanna and Judith, may be reflected in the witty, saucy, but lovable heroines of his great comedies.

Shakespeare's company in London prospered. In 1599, it stopped renting theaters and built its own, the Globe, which increased company profits. The company was a favorite of the reigning monarchs, who paid well for special performances at court—first Elizabeth I and then, after 1603, James I, who loved the theater even more and renamed Shakespeare's company the King's Men. The company also began performing most of the plays of Ben Jonson, who ranked second only to Shakespeare and who excelled at satiric comedy. Shakespeare turned to tragedy, first writing *Julius Caesar* (c. 1599-1600) and *Hamlet, Prince of Denmark* (c. 1600-1601) and then—one after another—*Othello, the Moor of Venice* (1604), *King Lear* (c. 1605-1606), *Macbeth* (1606), and *Antony and Cleopatra* (c. 1606-1607).

Yet even during this period—perhaps the high point in the history of Western drama—Shakespeare's company had its problems. One was the competition of the boys' companies, which performed in the private theaters—small indoor theaters that charged higher admission and appealed to a more exclusive audience than the public theaters. In 1608, the King's Men acquired one of the private theaters, the Blackfriars, plus the services of two playwrights who wrote for it, the collaborators Francis Beaumont and John Fletcher. With their light, witty comedy and melodramatic tragicomedy, represented by such plays as *The Knight of the Burning Pestle* (1607), *Philaster: Or, Love Lies A-Bleeding* (c. 1609), and *A King and No King* (1611), Beaumont and Fletcher introduced a new "cavalier" style into Renaissance English drama that ultimately eclipsed even Shakespeare's popularity and perhaps hurried his retirement. It is uncertain whether they or Shakespeare introduced tragicomedy, but Shakespeare's final complete plays are in this fashionable new mode: *Pericles, Prince of Tyre* (c. 1607-1608), *Cymbeline* (c. 1609-1610), *The Winter's Tale* (c. 1610-1611), and *The Tempest* (1611). After Beaumont married an heiress and stopped writing plays in 1612 or 1613, Shakespeare collaborated with Fletcher, and possibly others, on *Henry VIII*, *The Two Noble Kinsmen*, and *Cardenio* (now lost), all performed during 1612-1613.

New Place, the Stratford home to which Shakespeare retired in 1613; the building was demolished in 1759. (Library of Congress)

By 1608, when his productivity dropped to one or two plays per year, Shakespeare may have spent part of each year in Stratford-upon-Avon. In 1607, his elder daughter had married Dr. John Hall, the local physician, and in 1608, with the birth of their daughter, Elizabeth, Shakespeare became a grandfather. Around 1613, he retired completely to Stratford-upon-Avon, though he also joined John Heminge, a partner in the King's Men, and William Johnson, the host of the Mermaid Tavern, in purchasing the gatehouse of the Blackfriars priory, probably for London visits. On February 10, 1616, his younger daughter, Judith, at the age of thirty-one, married Thomas Quiney, a member of another prominent Stratford family. On March 25, 1616, Shakespeare made out his last will and testament, leaving most of his estate to Susanna, a substantial amount of money to Judith, and his "second best bed" to Anne. He died on April 23, 1616, and was buried in Holy Trinity Church, Stratford-upon-Avon.

In 1623, Shakespeare's surviving partners in the King's Men, John Heminge and Henry Condell, published a collection of his plays now known as the First Folio. The portrait included in the First Folio depicts Shakespeare with a short mustache, large, staring eyes, and an oval face accentuated by his high, balding forehead and the remaining hair that almost covers his ears. The bust erected above his grave is similar, except that he has a goatee and the balding has progressed further. The First Folio portrait resembles a soulful intellectual, while the Stratford bust suggests a prominent burgher.

Achievement and Influence

The two portraits of Shakespeare portray the two parts of his nature. On the one hand, he possessed immense intellectual curiosity about the motives and actions of people. This curiosity, plus his facility with language, enabled him to write his masterpieces and to create characters who are better known than some important figures in world history. On the other hand, reflecting his middle-class background, Shakespeare was himself motivated by strictly bourgeois instincts; he was more concerned with acquiring property and cementing his social position in Stratford than he was with preserving his plays for posterity. If his partners had not published the First Folio, there would be no Shakespeare as he is known today: still acted and enjoyed, the most widely studied and translated writer, the greatest poet and dramatist in the English and perhaps any language.

Besides his ability to create a variety of unforgettable characters, there are at least two other qualities that account for Shakespeare's achievement. One of these is his love of play with language, ranging from the lowest pun to some of the world's best poetry. His love of language sometimes makes him difficult to read, particularly for young students, but frequently the meaning becomes clear in a well-acted version. The second quality is his openness, his lack of any restrictive point of view, ideology, or morality. Shakespeare was able to embrace, identify with, and depict an enormous range of human behavior, from the good to the bad to the indifferent. The capaciousness of his language and vision thus help account for the universality of his appeal.

Shakespeare's lack of commitment to any didactic point of view has often been deplored. Yet he is not entirely uncommitted; rather, he is committed to what is human. Underlying his broad outlook is Renaissance Humanism, a synthesis of Christianity and classicism that is perhaps the best development of the Western mind and finds its best expression in his work. This same generous outlook was apparently expressed in Shakespeare's personality, which, like his bourgeois instincts, defies the Romantic myth of the artist. He was often praised by his fellows, but friendly rival and ferocious satirist Ben Jonson said it best: "He was, indeed, honest, and of an open and free nature," and "He was not of an age, but for all time."

Harold Branam

For Further Study

Alexander, Peter. *Shakespeare's Life and Art*. London: Nisbet, 1939, reprint 1961. A short but much-admired critical biography, treating Shakespeare's life in relation to his work.

Bradbrook, Muriel C. *Shakespeare, the Poet in His World*. London: Weidenfeld and Nicolson, 1978. An excellent study by one of the leading scholars and critics of Renaissance English drama.

Chute, Marchette. *Shakespeare of London*. New York: E. P. Dutton, 1949. The most readable of the popular biographies, based on documents contemporary to Shakespeare.

Frye, Roland Mushat. *Shakespeare's Life and Times: A Pictorial Record*. Princeton, N.J.: Princeton University Press, 1967. Introduces the most important information about Shakespeare through 114 illustrations and captions of one to three paragraphs each.

Halliday, F. E. *Shakespeare and His World*. New York: Charles Scribner's Sons, 1956. A short introduction containing the essential facts and 151 illustrations.

Quennell, Peter. *Shakespeare: A Biography*. New York: World Publishing Co., 1963. A fine critical biography, scholarly and readable.

Reese, M. M. *Shakespeare: His World and His Work*. Rev. ed. New York: St. Martin's Press, 1980. A full, well-written introduction to Shakespeare's life, the drama which preceded his, the Elizabethan stage, and his art.

Schoenbaum, Samuel. *Shakespeare's Lives*. 2d ed. New York: Oxford University Press, 1991. Not a biography per se, but rather an evaluation of the portraits of Shakespeare, the contemporary references, the legends, and the many biographies written about him up to 1970. Fascinating but dense reading. An important scholarly reference work.

_____. *William Shakespeare: A Compact Documentary Life*. New York: Oxford University Press, 1977. A scholarly biography that scrupulously examines the facts, documents, and myths of Shakespeare's life, supported by the author's considerable knowledge of previous biographies.

The Dramatist

Few dramatists can lay claim to the universal reputation achieved by William Shakespeare. His plays have been translated into many languages and performed on amateur and professional stages throughout the world. Radio, television, and film versions of the plays in English, German, Russian, French, and Japanese have been heard and seen by millions of people. The plays have been revived and reworked by many prominent producers and playwrights, and they have directly influenced the work of others. Novelists and dramatists such as Charles Dickens, Bertolt Brecht, William Faulkner, and Tom Stoppard, inspired by Shakespeare's plots, characters, and poetry, have composed works that attempt to re-create the spirit and style of the originals and to interpret the plays in the light of their own ages. A large and flourishing Shakespeare industry exists in England, America, Japan, and Germany, giving evidence of the playwright's popularity among scholars and laypersons alike.

A Playwright for All Time

Evidence of the widespread and deep effect of Shakespeare's plays on English and American culture can be found in the number of words and phrases from them that have become embedded in everyday usage: Expressions such as "star-crossed lovers" are used by speakers of English with no consciousness of their Shakespearean source. It is difficult to imagine what the landscape of the English language would be like without the mountain of neologisms and aphorisms contributed by the playwright. Writing at a time when English was quite pliable, Shakespeare's linguistic facility and poetic sense transformed English into a richly metaphoric tongue.

Working as a popular playwright, Shakespeare was also instrumental in fusing the materials of native and classical drama in his work. *Hamlet*, with its revenge theme, its ghost, and its bombastic set speeches, appears to be a tragedy based on the style of the Roman playwright Seneca, who lived in the first century A.D. Yet the hero's struggle with his conscience and his deep concern over the disposition of his soul reveal the play's roots in the native soil of English miracle and mystery dramas, which grew out of Christian rituals and depicted Christian legends. The product of this fusion is a tragedy that compels spectators and readers to examine their own deepest emotions as they ponder the effects of treacherous murder on individuals and the state. Except for Christopher Marlowe, the predecessor to whom Shakespeare owes a considerable debt, no other Elizabethan playwright was so successful in combining native and classical strains.

Shakespearean characters, many of whom are hybrids, are so vividly realized

The Jansen Portrait of Shakespeare. (Reprinted by permission of The Folger Shakespeare Library)

that they seem to have achieved a life independent of the worlds they inhabit. Hamlet stands as the symbol of a man who, in the words of the famous actor Sir Laurence Olivier, "could not make up his mind." Hamlet's name has become synonymous with excessive rationalizing and idealism. Othello's jealousy, Lear's madness, Macbeth's ambition, Romeo and Juliet's star-crossed love, Shylock's flinty heart—all of these psychic states and the characters who represent them have become familiar landmarks in Western culture. Their lifelikeness can be attributed to Shakespeare's talent for creating the illusion of reality in mannerisms and styles of speech. His use of the soliloquy is especially important in fashioning this illusion; the characters are made to seem fully rounded human beings in the representation of their inner as well as outer nature. Shakespeare's keen ear for conversational rhythms and his ability to reproduce believable speech between figures of high and low social rank also contribute to the liveliness of action and characters.

In addition, Shakespeare excels in the art of grasping the essence of relationships between husbands and wives, lovers, parents and children, and friends. Innocence and youthful exuberance are aptly represented in the fatal love of Romeo and Juliet; the destructive spirit of mature and intensely emotional love is caught in the affair between Antony and Cleopatra. Other relationships reveal the psychic control of one person by another (of Macbeth by Lady Macbeth), the corrupt soul of a seducer (Angelo in *Measure for Measure*), the twisted mind of a vengeful officer (Iago in *Othello*), and the warm fellowship of simple men (Bottom and his followers in *A Midsummer Night's Dream*). The range of emotional states manifested in Shakespeare's characters has never been equaled by succeeding dramatists.

These memorable characters have also been given memorable poetry to speak. In fact, one of the main strengths of Shakespearean drama is its synthesis of action and poetry. While Shakespeare's poetic style is marked by the bombast and hyperbole that characterize much of Elizabethan drama, it also has a richness and concreteness that make it memorable and quotable. One need think only of Hamlet's "sea of troubles" or Macbeth's daggers "unmannerly breech'd with gore" to substantiate the imagistic power of Shakespearean verse. Such images are also worked into compelling patterns in the major plays, giving them greater structural unity than the plots alone provide. Disease imagery in *Hamlet*, repeated references to blood in *Macbeth*, and allusions to myths of children devouring parents in *King Lear* represent only a few of the many instances of what has been called "reiterated imagery" in Shakespearean drama. Wordplay, puns, songs, and a variety of verse forms, from blank verse to tetrameter couplets—these features, too, contribute to the "movable feast" of Shakespeare's style.

In a more general sense, Shakespeare's achievement can be traced to the skill with which he used his medium—the stage. He created certain characters to fit the abilities of certain actors, as the role of Falstaff in the *Henry IV* and *Henry V* plays so vividly demonstrates. He made use of every facet of the physical stage—the trapdoor, the second level, the inner stage, the "heavens"—to create special effects or illusions. He kept always before him the purpose of entertaining his audience, staying one step ahead of changes in taste among theatergoers. That both kings and tinkers were able to find in a Shakespearean play something to delight and instruct them is testimony to the wide appeal of the playwright. No doubt the universality of his themes and his deep understanding of human nature combined to make his plays so popular. These same strengths generate the magnetic power that brings large audiences into theaters to see the plays today.

Growth of the Dramatist

William Shakespeare was born in Stratford-upon-Avon, England, probably on or near April 23, 1564. His father was John Shakespeare, a glovemaker and later bailiff (or mayor) of the town; his mother was Mary Arden, the daughter of a well-to-do landowner in nearby Wilmcote. His parents had eight children; William was the oldest. Although no records exist to prove the fact, Shakespeare probably began attending a Stratford grammar school at six or seven years of age. There, he studied Latin grammar, literature, rhetoric and logic for between eight and ten hours a day, six days a week. William Lily's largely Latin text, *A Short Introduction of Grammar* (1527), was the staple of the course, but Shakespeare also read Cicero, Plautus, Terence, Vergil, and Ovid. Many of these authors influenced the playwright's later work; Ovid in particular was a favorite source of material, used in such plays as *A Midsummer Night's Dream* and *Romeo and Juliet*. Shakespeare probably knew very little of other languages, although he does exhibit an understanding of French in such plays as *Henry V* and *All's Well That Ends Well*. (The sources for most, if not all, of the plays existed in English translations published during Shakespeare's lifetime.)

A roughly contemporary view of Shakespeare's London, by Wenceslaus Hollar (1647), looking north across the Thames from Southwark. The Globe Theatre is in the center; the flag indicates a performance day. (Reprinted by permission of The Folger Shakespeare Library)

Shakespeare may have left school around 1577, the year in which his father fell on hard times. Legend says the young man worked as a butcher's apprentice, but there is no proof to support this notion. His marriage to Anne Hathaway of Shottery took place in 1582; she was eight years his senior and pregnant at the time of the wedding. Whether Shakespeare felt obliged to marry her or simply took pity on her unfortunate predicament is yet another matter for speculation. Their first child, Susanna, was born in May, 1583, and in 1585, twins named Hamnet and Judith were born to the young couple. (It is interesting to note that by 1670, the last of Susanna's descendants died, thereby ending the Shakespeare family line.)

There is no evidence concerning Shakespeare's activities between 1585 and 1592. Legend asserts that he was forced to leave Stratford in order to escape punishment for poaching deer on the estate of Sir Thomas Lucy, one of Stratford's leading citizens. Another popular story has Shakespeare taking a position as schoolmaster at the grammar school, where he supposedly improved his Latin. None of these accounts can be substantiated by fact, yet they continue to seduce modern readers and playgoers. One intriguing suggestion is that Shakespeare joined a troupe of professional actors that was passing through Stratford in 1587. This company, called the Queen's Men, may have been in need of a new performer, since one of their members, William Knell, had been murdered in a brawl with a fellow actor.

Shakespeare and the London Stage

In 1592, Robert Greene, a playwright and pamphleteer, attested Shakespeare's presence in London in a sneering remark about the young upstart whose "tiger's heart [is] wrapt in a player's hide." This reference is a parody of a line from one of Shakespeare's earliest plays, *Henry VI, Part III*. Greene's "Shake-scene in a country" is clearly Shakespeare, who by this date was identifiable as both an actor and a playwright. Greene's remark also implies that the uneducated upstart had probably served an apprenticeship of a few years revising old plays, a practice that was common in this period. By 1594, Shakespeare had become a member of the Lord Chamberlain's Men, who were then performing at the Theatre in Shoreditch, to the north of the city. He continued as a member of this essentially stable company, which constructed the Globe Theatre in 1599 and, in 1603, became the King's Men, until he retired from the stage in 1611 or 1612. In part because of the popularity of Shakespeare's plays and in part because of the strong support of Elizabeth and James I, the company achieved considerable financial success. Shakespeare shared in that success by acquiring a one-tenth interest in the corporation. By 1596, he was able to purchase a coat of arms for his father, and in the next year, he acquired the second-best house in Stratford. This degree of prominence and success was unusual for someone in a profession that was not highly regarded in Renaissance England. Robert Greene, Shakespeare's harsh critic, died a pauper, a condition that was typical of many Elizabethan playwrights.

Actors and playwrights were in fact regarded as entertainers whose companions were bearbaiters, clowns, and jugglers. Confirmation of this fact comes from evidence that some public theaters were used both for plays and for bearbaiting and bullbaiting. After 1590, moreover, the playhouses had to be constructed in the Bankside district, across the Thames from London proper. City fathers afraid of plague and opposed to public entertainments felt that the Bankside, notorious for its boisterous inns and houses of prostitution, was the fitting locale for "playing" of all kinds. Indeed, theatrical productions were not regarded as high art; when plays were published, by the company or by individual actors, apparently no effort was made to correct or improve them. As has already been pointed out, Shakespeare himself never corrected or took to the printer any of the plays attributed to him. Poetry was valued as true literature, and there is considerable evidence that

Shakespeare hoped to become a recognized and respected poet like Sir Philip Sidney or Edmund Spenser. His poems of the early 1590's (*Venus and Adonis* and *The Rape of Lucrece*) were immensely popular. Still, Shakespeare chose to become a public entertainer, a role that he played with convincing brilliance.

The company to which this best of the entertainers belonged was relatively small—fifteen or twenty players at most. The actors were generally well known to the audience, and their particular talents were exploited by the playwrights. Richard Burbage, the manager of Shakespeare's company for many years, was renowned for his skill in acting tragic parts, while William Kemp and Robert Armin were praised for their talents as comic actors. Shakespeare composed his plays with these actors in mind, a fact borne out by the many comedies featuring fat, drunken men such as Sir John Falstaff (of the *Henry IV* and *Henry V* plays) and Sir Toby Belch (of *Twelfth Night*). Shakespeare could not compose his works for an ideal company; he suited his style to the available talent.

Since his company was underwritten to some degree by the government, Shakespeare and his fellows were often called upon to perform at court: thirty-two times during Elizabeth's reign and 177 times under James I. The king and queen did not venture to the Theatre or the Globe to mingle with the lower classes, depending instead on the actors to bring their wares to them. *Macbeth* was written as a direct compliment to James I: Banquo, the brave general treacherously murdered by the villainous hero, was one of James's ancestors. Shakespeare had to change the facts of history to pay the compliment, but the aim of pleasing his and the company's benefactor justified the change.

There were no women actors on Shakespeare's stage; they made their appearance when Charles II returned to the throne in 1660. Young boys (eleven to fourteen years old) played the female parts, and Shakespeare manipulated this convention with considerable success in his comedies, where disguises created delightful complications and aided him in overcoming the problem of costuming. The lady-disguised-as-page device is worked with particular effect in such plays as *As You Like It*, *Twelfth Night*, and *Cymbeline*.

Since there were few actors and sometimes many parts, members of the company were required to double (and sometimes triple) their roles. The effect of this requirement becomes evident when one notes that certain principal characters do not appear in consecutive scenes. One should likewise remember that performance on the Elizabethan stage was continuous; there was no falling curtain or set change to interrupt the action. No scenery to speak of was employed, although signs may have been used to designate cities or countries and branches may have been tied around pillars to signify trees. The absence of scenery allowed for a peculiar imaginative effect. A place on the stage that had been a throne room could within a few seconds become a hovel hiding its inhabitants from a fierce storm. Shakespeare and his contemporaries could thereby demonstrate the slippery course of Fortune, whose wheel, onstage and in real life, might turn at any moment to transform kings into beggars.

The apronlike stage jutted out into an area called "the pit," where the "groundlings," or those who paid the lowest admission fee (a penny), could stand to watch

Part of an early seventeenth century panoramic view of London, looking north from the South Bank of the Thames, with the bear-baiting garden visible in the foreground. Many of the structures shown, including the original St. Paul's Cathedral, were destroyed in the Great Fire of 1666. (Reprinted by permission of The Folger Shakespeare Library)

heroes perform great deeds. The octagon-shaped building had benches on the two levels above the pit for customers willing to pay for the privilege of sitting. Although estimates vary, it is now generally believed that the Globe could accommodate approximately twenty-five hundred people. The design of the stage probably evolved from the model of innyards, where the traveling companies of actors performed before they took up residence in London in the 1570's. On either side of the stage were two doors for entrances and exits and, at the back, some kind of inner stage behind which actors could hide and be discovered at the right moment. A trapdoor was located in the middle of the apron stage, while above it was a cupola-like structure that housed a pulley and chair. This chair could be lowered to the stage level when a *deus ex machina* (literally, a "god from a machine") was required to resolve the action. This small house also contained devices for making sound effects and may have been the place from which the musicians, so much a part of Elizabethan drama, sent forth their special harmonies. The little house was called "the heavens" (stars may have been painted on its underside), while the trapdoor was often referred to as "hell." For Shakespeare's Globe audience, then, the stage was a world in which the great figures of history and imagination were represented doing and speaking momentous things.

In 1608, the King's Men purchased an indoor theater, the Blackfriars, which meant that the company could perform year-round. This theater was located within the city proper, which meant that a somewhat more sophisticated audience attended the plays. Seating capacity was approximately seven hundred; there was no pit to stand in, and there is some evidence that the stage machinery was more elaborate than the equipment at the Globe. Some historians therefore argue that the plays written after 1608—*Cymbeline*, *Pericles, Prince of Tyre*, *The Winter's Tale*, *The Tempest*—were composed especially for performance at the Blackfriars. These tragicomedies or romances teem with special effects and supernatural characters, and this emphasis on spectacle differentiates them from Shakespeare's earlier comedies. While such a theory is attractive, at least a few of these plays were also performed at the supposedly "primitive" Globe.

By 1608, Shakespeare had achieved the fame and recognition for which he had no doubt hoped. He was in a position to reduce his output to one or two plays per year, a schedule that probably allowed him to spend more time in Stratford with his family. In 1611, he left London for Stratford, returning from time to time to see plays performed at both theaters and possibly to engage in collaborative efforts with new playwrights such as John Fletcher. His last play, *Henry VIII*, was a collaboration with Fletcher; it was produced on June 29, 1613, a fateful day for the Globe. A spark from one of the cannon shot off during the performance set the thatched roof on fire and burned the building to the ground.

From 1613 until his death in 1616, Shakespeare led the life of a prosperous citizen in his native town. No doubt the happiest moment of this period came with the marriage of his daughter Judith in 1616. One of the persistent legends about the cause of the playwright's death is that he celebrated too vigorously at the reception with his friends Ben Jonson and Michael Drayton and contracted a fatal fever. Whatever the cause, Shakespeare died on April 23, 1616, and was buried in Holy

Trinity Church. His epitaph gives no hint of the poetic strength that marked his plays, but it does express a concern common among men of his age:

> Good friend for Jesus sake forbear
> To dig the dust enclosed here.
> Blessed be the man that spares these stones
> And cursed be he that moves my bones.

The History Plays

William Shakespeare began his career as a playwright by experimenting with plays in the three genres—comedy, history, and tragedy—that he would perfect as his career matured. The genre that dominated his attention throughout his early career, however, was history. Interest in the subject as proper stuff for drama was no doubt aroused by England's startling victory over Spain's vaunted navy, the Armada, in 1588. This victory fed the growing popular desire to see depictions of the critical intrigues and battles that had shaped England's destiny as the foremost Protestant power in Europe.

This position of power had been buttressed by the shrewd and ambitious Elizabeth I, England's "Virgin Queen," who, in the popular view, was the flower of the Tudor line. Many critics believe that Shakespeare composed the histories to trace the course of destiny that had led to the emergence of the Tudors as England's greatest kings and queens. The strength of character and patriotic spirit exhibited by Elizabeth seem to be foreshadowed by the personality of Henry V, the Lancastrian monarch who was instrumental in building an English empire in France. Since the Tudors traced their line back to the Lancastrians, it was an easy step for Shakespeare to flatter his monarch and please his audiences with nationalistic spectacles that reinforced the belief that England was a promised land.

Whatever his reasons for composing the history plays, Shakespeare certainly must be seen as an innovator of the form, for which there was no model in classical or medieval drama. Undoubtedly, he learned much from his immediate predecessors, however—most notably from Christopher Marlowe, whose *Edward II* (pr. c. 1592) treated the subject of a weak king nearly destroying the kingdom through his selfish and indulgent behavior. From Marlowe, Shakespeare also inherited the idea that the purpose of the history play was to vivify the moral dilemmas of power politics and to apply those lessons to contemporary government. Such lessons were heeded by contemporaries, as is amply illustrated by Elizabeth's remark upon reading about the life of one of her predecessors: "I am Richard II."

Shakespeare's contribution to the history-play genre is represented by two tetralogies (that is, two series of four plays), each covering a period of English history. He wrote two other plays dealing with English kings, *King John* and *Henry VIII*, but they are not specifically connected to the tetralogies in theme or structure. *Edward III*, written sometime between 1589 and 1595, is, on the other hand, closely related to the second tetralogy in theme, structure, and history. Edward III is the grandfather of Richard II, and his victories in France are repeated by Henry V. Muriel Bradbrook has pointed out the structural similarities between *Edward III* and *Henry V*. Like the second tetralogy as a whole, *Edward III* deals with the education of the prince. King Edward, like Prince Hal, at first neglects his duties and endangers the realm by placing personal pleasure above his country's needs. The Countess of Salisbury begins his education in responsibility, and Queen Philippa completes the process by teaching him compassion. By the end of the play Edward has become what Shakespeare calls Henry V, "the mirror of all Christian kings."

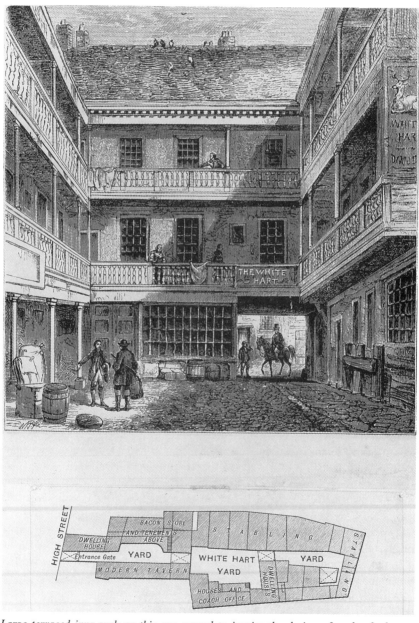

Large terraced inns such as this one served to inspire the design of early playhouses. (Reprinted by permission of The Folger Shakespeare Library)

The first tetralogy concerns the period from the death of Henry V in 1422 to the death of Richard III at the Battle of Bosworth Field in 1485. Although he probably began this ambitious project in 1588, Shakespeare apparently did not compose the plays according to a strict chronological schedule. *Henry VI, Part I* is generally considered to have been written after the second and third parts of the Henry story; it may also have been a revision of another play. Using details from Raphael Holinshed's *Chronicles of England, Scotland, and Ireland* (1577) and Edward Hall's *The Union of the Two Noble and Illustre Families of Lancaster and York* (1548)—his chief chronicle sources for the plays in both tetralogies—Shakespeare created in *Henry VI, Part I* an episodic story of the adventures of Lord Talbot, the patriotic soldier who fought bravely to retain England's empire in France. Talbot fails and is defeated primarily because of a combination of intrigues by men such as the Bishop of Winchester and the indecisiveness of young King Henry VI. Here, as in the other history plays, England appears as the central victim of these human actions, betrayed and abandoned by men attempting to satisfy personal desires at the expense of the kingdom. The characters are generally two-dimensional, and their speeches reveal the excesses of Senecan bombast and hyperbole. Although a few of the scenes involving Talbot and Joan of Arc—as well as Talbot's death scene, in which his demise is made more painful by his having to witness a procession bearing his son's corpse—aspire to the level of high drama, the play's characters lack psychological depth, and the plot fails to demonstrate the unity of design that would mark Shakespeare's later history plays. Joan's nature as a strumpet-witch signals the role of other women characters in this tetralogy; Margaret, who will become England's queen, helps to solidify the victory that Joan cleverly achieves at the close of *Henry VI, Part I*. Henry V's French empire is in ruins and England's very soul seems threatened.

Henry VI, Part II represents that threat in the form of what might be called "civil-war clouds." The play focuses on the further degeneration of rule under Henry, whose ill-considered marriage to the French Margaret precipitates a power struggle involving the two houses of York and Lancaster. By eliminating wise Duke Humphrey as the chief protector of the king, Margaret in effect seizes control of the throne. In the meantime, however, a rebellion is broached by Jack Cade, the leader of a group of anarchist commoners. This rebellion lends occasion for action and spectacle of the kind that is lacking in *Henry VI, Part I*; it also teaches a favorite Shakespearean lesson: The kingdom's "children" cannot be expected to behave when their "parents" do not. Scenes involving witchcraft, a false miracle, and single combat seem to prove that the country is reverting to a primitive, chaotic state. Though the uprising is finally put down, it provides the excuse for Richard, Duke of York, and his ambitious sons to seize power. York precipitates a vengeful struggle with young Clifford by killing his father; in response, Clifford murders York's youngest son, the Earl of Rutland. These murders introduce the theme of familial destruction, of fathers killing sons and sons killing fathers, which culminates in the brutal assassination of Prince Edward.

As *Henry VI, Part III* begins, England's hopes for a strong successor to weak King Henry are dashed on the rocks of ambition and civil war. When Henry himself is murdered, one witnesses the birth of one of Shakespeare's most fascinating villain-heroes, Richard, Duke of Gloucester. Although Richard's brother Edward becomes king and restores an uneasy peace, Shakespeare makes it clear that Richard will emerge as the political force of the future. Richard's driving ambition also appears to characterize the Yorkist cause, which, by contrast with the Lancastrian, can be described as self-destructive on the biblical model of the Cain and Abel story. While one is made to see Richard's wolfish disposition, however, Shakespeare also gives him a superior intellect and wit which help to attract one's attention and interest. Displaying touches of the irony and cruelty that will mark his behavior in *Richard III*, Richard declares at the close of *Henry VI, Part III*: "See how my sword weeps for the poor king's death."

In order to present Richard as an arch-villain, Shakespeare was obliged to follow a description of him that was based on a strongly prejudiced biographical portrait written by Sir Thomas More. More painted Richard as a hunchback with fangs, a beast so cruel that he did not flinch at the prospect of murdering the young princes. To More—and to Shakespeare—Richard must be viewed as another Herod; the imagery of the play also regularly compares him to a boar or hedgehog, beasts that know no restraint. Despite these repulsive features, Richard proves to be a consummate actor, outwitting and outperforming those whom he regards as victims. The most theatrical scene in the play is his wooing of the Lady Anne, who is drawn to him despite the knowledge that he has killed her husband (Prince Edward) and father-in-law, whose corpse she is in the process of accompanying to its grave. Many of the audacious wooing tricks used in this scene suggest that one of the sources for Richard's character is the Vice figure from medieval drama.

Richard III documents the breakneck pace and mounting viciousness of Richard's course to the throne. (Steeplechase imagery recurs throughout, culminating in the picture of Richard as an unseated rider trying desperately to find a mount.) He arranges for the murder of his brother Clarence, turns on former supporters such as Hastings and Buckingham, whom he seemed to be grooming for office, and eventually destroys the innocent princes standing in his path. This latter act of barbarism qualifies as a turning point, since Richard's victories, which have been numerous and easily won, now begin to evaporate at almost the same rate of speed. While Richard moves with freedom and abandon from one bloody deed to another, he is hounded by the former Queen Margaret, who delivers curses and prophecies against him in the hope of satisfying her vengeful desires. She plays the role of a Senecan fury, even though her words prove feeble against her Machiavellian foe. Retribution finally comes, however, in the character of the Lancastrian Earl of Richmond, who defeats Richard at Bosworth Field. On the eve of the battle, Richard's victims visit his sleep to announce his fall, and for the first time in the play, he experiences a twinge of conscience. Unable to respond by confessing and asking forgiveness, Richard fights fiercely, dying like a wounded animal that is finally cornered. With Richmond's marriage to Elizabeth York, the Wars of the Roses end, and England looks forward to a prosperous and peaceful future under Henry Richmond, founder of the Tudor line.

Whether Shakespeare wrote *King John* in the period between the first and second tetralogies is not known, but there is considerable support for the theory that he did. In the play, he depicts the career of a monarch who reigned into the thirteenth century and who defied papal authority, behavior that made him into something of a Protestant hero for Elizabethans. Shakespeare's John, however, lacks both the dynamism and the charisma of Henry V; he is also guilty of usurping the throne and arranging for the death of the true heir, Arthur. This clouded picture complicates the action and transforms John into a man plagued by guilt. Despite his desire to strengthen England and challenge the supremacy of Rome, John does

Elizabeth I, Queen of England during Shakespeare's time, in a 1579 depiction known as the Sieve portrait. The flower of the Tudor line, England's "Virgin Queen" was descended from the Lancastrians, her personality foreshadowed in Henry V's strength of character. Many believe that Shakespeare wrote his history plays in part to trace the course of destiny that led to the emergence of the Tudors as England's greatest kings and queens. (Reprinted by permission of The Folger Shakespeare Library)

not achieve either the dimensions of a tragic hero or the sinister quality of a consummate villain; indeed, his death seems anticlimactic. The strongest personality in the play belongs to Faulconbridge the Bastard, whose satiric commentary on the king's maneuvering gives way to patriotic speeches at the close. Faulconbridge speaks out for Anglo-Saxon pride in the face of foreign challenge, but he has also played the part of satirist-onstage throughout much of the action. Something of the same complexity of character will be seen in Prince Hal, the model fighter and king of the second tetralogy. In *King John*, Shakespeare managed only this one touch of brilliant characterization in an otherwise uninteresting and poorly constructed play. He may have been attempting an adaptation of an earlier chronicle drama.

Shakespeare began writing the second tetralogy, which covers the historical period from 1398 to 1422, in 1595. The first play in this group was *Richard II*, a drama which, like the *Henry VI* series, recounts the follies of a weak king and the consequences of these actions for England. Unlike Henry, however, Richard is a personage with tragic potential; he speaks the language of a poet and possesses a self-dramatizing talent. Richard invites his fall—the fall of princes, or *de casibus virorum illustrium*, being a favorite Elizabethan topic that was well represented in the popular *A Mirror for Magistrates* (first published under Elizabeth I in 1559, although printed earlier under Queen Mary)—by seizing the land of the deceased John of Gaunt to pay for his war preparations against Ireland. This dubious act brings Henry Bolingbroke, Gaunt's son, rushing back from France, where he had been exiled by Richard, for a confrontation with the king. The result of their meeting is Richard's sudden deposition—he gives up the crown almost before he is asked for it—and eventual death, which is so movingly rendered that many critics have been led to describe this as a tragedy rather than a political play. Such a reading must overlook the self-pitying quality in Richard; his actions rarely correspond to the quality of his speech. Yet there has been little disagreement about Shakespeare's achievement in advancing the history-play form by forging a world in which two personalities, one vacillating, the other resourceful, oppose each other in open conflict. *Richard II* likewise qualifies as the first play in which Shakespeare realizes the theme of the fall by means of repeated images comparing England to a garden. Richard, the gardener-king, has failed to attend to pruning; rebels, like choking weeds, grow tall and threaten to blot out the sun. Because Bolingbroke usurps the crown and later arranges for Richard's death, however, he is guilty of watering the garden with the blood of England's rightful—if foolish—ruler. The result must inevitably be civil war, which is stirringly prophesied by the Bishop of Carlisle as the play draws to a close: "The blood of English shall manure the ground,/ And future ages groan for this foul act."

The civil strife that Carlisle predicted escalates in *Henry IV, Part I*. Bolingbroke, now King Henry IV, is planning a crusade in the midst of a serious battle involving rebels in the north and west of Britain. This obliviousness to responsibility is clearly motivated by Henry's guilt over the seizing of the crown and Richard's murder. It will take the courage and ingenuity of his son, Prince Hal, the future Henry V, to save England and to restore the order of succession that Shakespeare

Elizabeth I in a gem-encrusted ceremonial costume. (Library of Congress)

and his contemporaries saw as the only guarantee of peaceful rule. Thus, *Henry IV, Part I* is really a study of the rise of Hal, who in the opening of the play appears to be a carefree time waster, content with drinking, gambling, and carousing with a motley group of thieves and braggarts led by the infamous coward Sir John

Falstaff. Using a kind of Aristotelian mode of characterization, Shakespeare reveals Hal as a balanced hero who possesses the wit and humanity of Falstaff, without the debilitating drunkenness and ego, and the physical courage and ambition of Henry Hotspur, the son of the Earl of Northumberland and chief rebel, without his destructive choler and impatience.

The plot of *Henry IV, Part I* advances by means of comparison and contrast of the court, tavern, and rebel worlds, all of which are shown to be in states of disorder. Hal leaves the tavern world at the end of the second act with an explicit rejection of Falstaff's fleshly indulgence; he rejoins his true father and leads the army in battle against the rebels, who are unable to organize the English, Welsh, and Scottish factions of which they are formed. They seem to be leaderless—and "fatherless." Above all, Hal proves capable of surprising both his own family and the rebels, using his reputation as a madcap to fullest advantage until he is ready to throw off his disguise and defeat the bold but foolish Hotspur at Shrewsbury. This emergence is nicely depicted in imagery associated by Hal himself with the sun (punning on "son") breaking through the clouds when least suspected. Falstaff demonstrates consistency of character in the battle by feigning death; even though Hal allows his old friend to claim the prize of Hotspur's body, one can see the utter bankruptcy of the Falstaffian philosophy of self-preservation.

In *Henry IV, Part II*, the struggle against the rebels continues. Northumberland, who failed to appear for the Battle of Shrewsbury because of illness, proves unable to call up the spirit of courage demonstrated by his dead son. Glendower, too, seems to fade quickly from the picture, like a dying patient. The main portion of the drama concerns what appears to be a replay of Prince Hal's reformation. Apparently Shakespeare meant to depict Hal's acquisition of honor and valor at the close of *Henry IV, Part I*, while *Part II* traces his education in the virtues of justice and rule. Falstaff is again the humorous but negative example, although he lacks the robustness in sin that marked his character in *Part I*. The positive example or model is the Lord Chief Justice, whose sobriety and sense of responsibility eventually attract Hal to his side. As in *Part I*, Shakespeare adopts the structure of a medieval morality play to depict the rejection of the "bad" angel (or false father) and the embracing of the "good" one (or spiritual father) by the hero. The banishment of Falstaff and his corrupt code takes place during the coronation procession. It is a particularly poignant moment—to which many critics object, since Hal's harshness seems so uncharacteristic and overdone—but this scene is well prepared for by Hal's promise, at the end of act 2 in *Part I*, that he would renounce the world and the flesh at the proper time. The example of Hal's father, whose crown Hal rashly takes from his pillow before his death, demonstrates that for the king there can be no escape from care, no freedom to enjoy the fruits of life. With the Lord Chief Justice at his side, Hal prepares to enter the almost monklike role that the kingship requires him to play.

It is this strong and isolated figure that dominates *Henry V*, the play that may have been written for the opening of the Globe Theatre. (Until 1599, Shakespeare's company performed at a theater located north of the river in Shoreditch.) Appropriately enough, the Chorus speaker who opens the play asks if "this wooden O" can "hold the vasty fields of France," the scene of much of the epic and episodic action. Hal shows himself to be an astute politician—he outwits and traps the rebels Scroop, Cambridge, and Grey—and a heroic leader of men in the battle scenes. His rejection of Falstaff, whose death is recounted here in tragicomic fashion by Mistress Quickly, has transformed Hal's character into something cold and unattractive. There is little or no humor in the play. Yet when Hal moves among his troops on the eve of the Battle of Agincourt, he reveals a depth of understanding and compassion that helps to humanize his character. His speeches are master-pieces of political rhetoric, even though Pistol, the braggart soldier, tries to parody them. "Once more into the breach, dear friends, once more . . ." introduces one of the best-known prebattle scenes in the language.

An artist's conception of a performance by Shakespeare (onstage, far left) and his company at the court of Elizabeth I. Although Shakespeare's early connections with the theater are unknown, by 1592 he was an actor in London. (Library of Congress)

With the defeat of the French at Agincourt, Hal wins an empire for England, strengthening the kingdom that had been so sorely threatened by the weakness of Richard II. Both tetralogies depict in sharp outline the pattern of suffering and destruction that results from ineffective leadership. In Henry VII and Henry V, one sees the promise of peace and empire realized through the force of their strong, patriotic identities. At the close of *Henry V*, the hero's wooing of Katherine of France, with its comic touches resulting from her inability to speak English, promises a wedding that will take place in a new garden from which it is hoped man will not again fall. The lesson for the audience seems to be that under Elizabeth, the last Tudor monarch, England has achieved stability and glory, and that this role of European power was foreshadowed by the victories of these earlier heroes. Another clear lesson is that England cannot afford another civil war; some capable and clearly designated successor to Elizabeth must be chosen.

Shakespeare's last drama dealing with English history is *Henry VIII*, which is normally classed with romances such as *The Tempest* and *Cymbeline*. It features none of the military battles typical of earlier history plays, turning instead for its material to the intrigues of Henry's court. The play traces the falls of three famous personages, the Duke of Buckingham, Katherine of Aragon, and Cardinal Wolsey. Both Buckingham and Queen Katherine are innocent victims of fortune, while Wolsey proves to be an ambitious man whose scheming is justly punished. Henry seems blind and self-satisfied through much of the play, which is dominated by pageantry and spectacle, but in his judgment against Wolsey and his salvation of Cranmer, he emerges as something of a force for divine justice. The plot ends with the christening of Elizabeth and a prophecy about England's glorious future under her reign. Shakespeare's audience knew, however, that those atop Fortune's wheel at the close—Cranmer and Anne Bullen, in particular—would soon be brought down like the others. This last of Shakespeare's English history plays, then, sounds a patriotic but also an ironic note.

The Comedies

Of the plays that are wholly or partly attributed to Shakespeare, nearly half have been classified as comedies. In addition, many scenes in plays such as *Henry IV, Part I* and *Romeo and Juliet* feature comic characters and situations. Even in the major tragedies, one finds scenes of comic relief: the Porter scene in *Macbeth*, the encounters between the Fool and Lear in *King Lear*, Hamlet's inventive punning and lugubrious satire. There can be little doubt that Shakespeare enjoyed creating comic situations and characters and that audiences came to expect such fare on a regular basis from the playwright.

In his first attempt in the form, *The Comedy of Errors*, Shakespeare turned to a source—Plautus, the Roman playwright—with which he would have become familiar at Stratford's grammar school. Based on Plautus' *Menaechmi* (second century B.C.), the comedy depicts the misadventures of twins who, after several incidents involving mistaken identity, finally meet and are reunited. The twin brothers are attended by twin servants, compounding the possibilities for humor growing out of mistaken identity. Considerable buffoonery and slapstick characterize the main action involving the twins—both named Antipholus—and their servants. In one hilarious scene, Antipholus of Ephesus is turned away from his own house by a wife who believes he is an impostor. This somewhat frivolous mood is tempered by the presence of the twins' father in the opening and closing scenes. At the play's opening, Egeon is sentenced to death by the Duke of Ephesus; the sentence will be carried out unless someone can pay a ransom set at one thousand marks. Egeon believes that his wife and sons are dead, which casts him deep into the pit of despair. By the play's close, Egeon has been saved from the duke's sentence and has been reunited with his wife, who has spent the many years of their separation as an abbess. This happy scene of reunion and regeneration strikes a note that will come to typify the resolutions of later Shakespearean comedy. Providence appears to smile on those who suffer yet remain true to the principle of family.

Shakespeare also unites the act of unmasking with the concept of winning a new life in the fifth act of *The Comedy of Errors*. Both Antipholus of Syracuse, who in marrying Luciana is transformed into a "new man," and Dromio of Ephesus, who is freed to find a new life, acquire new identities at the conclusion. The characters are, however, largely interchangeable and lacking in individualizing traits. Types rather than full-blown human beings people the world of the play, thus underscoring the theme of supposing or masking. Shakespeare offers a gallery of familiar figures— young lovers, a pedantic doctor, a kitchen maid, merchants, and a courtesan—all of whom are identified by external traits. They are comic because they behave in predictably mechanical ways. Dr. Pinch, the mountebank based on Plautus' *medicus* type, is a good example of this puppetlike caricaturing. The verse is designed to suit the speaker and occasion, but it also reveals Shakespeare's range of styles; blank verse, prose, rhymed stanzas, and alternating rhymed lines can be found throughout the play. This first effort in dramatic comedy was an experiment using numerous Plautine elements, but it also reveals, in the characters Egeon and Emilia, the playwright's talent for humanizing even the most typical of characters and for creating life and vigor in stock situations.

In *The Taming of the Shrew*, Shakespeare turned to another favorite source for the theme of transformation: Ovid's *Metamorphoses*. He had already used this collection for his erotic poems *Venus and Adonis* and *The Rape of Lucrece*; now he plundered it for stories about pairs of lovers and the changes effected in their natures by the power of love. In *The Taming of the Shrew*, he was also improving upon an earlier play which dealt with the theme of taming as a means of modifying human behavior. Petruchio changes Kate's conduct by regularly praising her "pleasant, gamesome" nature; by the end of the play, she has been tamed into behaving like a dutiful wife. (Her sister Bianca, on the other hand, has many suitors, but her father will not allow Bianca to marry until Kate has found a husband.) The process of taming sometimes involves rough and boisterous treatment—Petruchio withholds food from his pupil, for example—as well as feigned madness: Petruchio whisks his bride away from the wedding site as if she were a damsel in distress and he were playing the role of her rescuer. In the end, Kate turns out to be more pliant than her sister, suggesting that an ideal wife, like a bird trained for the hunt, must be instructed in the rules of the game.

Shakespeare reinforces the theme of transformation by fashioning a subplot featuring a drunken tinker named Christopher Sly, who believes he has been made into a lord during a ruse performed by a fun-loving noble and his fellows. The Sly episode is not resolved, since this interlude ends with the play's first scene, yet by employing this framing device, Shakespeare invites a comparison between Kate and Sly, both of whom are urged to be "better" than they thought they were.

The Two Gentlemen of Verona takes a comic tack that depends less on supposing than on actual disguise. Employing a device he would later perfect in *As You Like It* and *Twelfth Night*, Shakespeare put his heroine Julia in a page's outfit in order

Shakespeare's patron, the Earl of Southampton, in a portait painted sometime after 1620.
(Reprinted by permission of The Folger Shakespeare Library)

to woo her beloved Proteus. The main theme of the comedy is the rocky nature of love as revealed in male friendship and romantic contest. Valentine, Proteus' friend, finds him to be fickle and untrue to the courtly code when Proteus tries to force his affections on Silvia, Valentine's love. Although Proteus deserves worse punishment than he receives, he is allowed to find in Julia the true source of the romantic love which he has been seeking throughout the play. These pairs of lovers and their clownish servants, who engage in frequent bouts of punning and of horseplay, perform their rituals—anatomizing lovers, trusting false companions—in a forest world that seems to work its magic on them by bringing about a happy ending. As in the other festive comedies, *The Two Gentlemen of Verona* concludes with multiple marriages and a mood of inclusiveness that gives even the clowns their proper place in the celebration. The passion of love has led Proteus (whose name, signifying "changeable," symbolizes fickleness) to break oaths and threaten friendships, but in the end, it has also forged a constant love.

After this experiment in romantic or festive (as opposed to bourgeois) comedy, Shakespeare next turned his hand to themes and characters that reflect the madness and magic of love. *Love's Labour's Lost* pokes fun at florid poetry, the "taffeta phrases [and] silken terms precise" that typified Elizabethan love verses. There is also a satiric strain in this play, which depicts the foiled attempt of male characters to create a Platonic utopia free of women. The King of Navarre and his court appear ludicrous as, one by one, they violate their vows of abstinence in conceits that gush with sentiment. Even Berowne, the skeptic-onstage, proves unable to resist the temptations of Cupid. As if to underscore the foolishness of their betters, the clowns and fops of this comic world produce an interlude featuring the Nine Worthies, all of whom overdo or distort their roles in the same way as the lover-courtiers have distorted theirs. (This interlude was also the playwright's first attempt at the play-within-the-play.) When every Jack presumes to claim his Jill at the close, however, Shakespeare deputizes the princess to postpone the weddings for one year while the men do penance for breaking their vows. The women here are victorious over the men, but only for the purpose of forcing them to recognize the seriousness of their contracts. Presumably the marriages to come will prove constant and fulfilling, but at the end of this otherwise lighthearted piece, Shakespeare interjects a surprising note of qualification. Perhaps this note represents his commentary on the weight of words, which the courtiers have so carelessly—and sometimes badly—handled.

In *A Midsummer Night's Dream*, Shakespeare demonstrates consummate skill in the use of words to create illusion and dreams. Although he again presents pairs of young lovers whose fickleness causes them to fall out of, and then back into, love, these characters display human dimensions that are missing in the character-types found in the earlier comedies. The multiple plots concern not only the lovers' misadventures but also the marriage of Duke Theseus and Hippolyta, the quarrel between Oberon and Titania, king and queen of the fairy band, and the bumbling rehearsal and performance of the play-within-a-play *Pyramus and Thisbe* by Bottom and his companions. All of these actions illustrate the themes of love's errant course and of the power of illusion to deceive the senses. The main action, as in *The Two Gentlemen of Verona*, takes place in a wood, this time outside Athens and at night. The fairy powers are given free rein to deceive the mortals who chase one another there; Puck, Oberon's servant, effects deception of the lovers by mistakenly pouring a potion in the wrong Athenian's eyes. By the end of the play,

The Globe Theatre as it looked in 1616, after it was rebuilt following the fire of 1613, in a detail from Claes Jansz Visscher's panoramic view of London, Londinum Florentisima Britanniae Urbs *(c. 1625).* (Reprinted by permission of The Folger Shakespeare Library)

however, the young lovers have found their proper partners, Oberon and Titania have patched up their quarrel, and Bottom, whose head was changed into that of an ass and who was wooed by the enchanted Titania while he was under this spell, rejoins his fellows to perform their tragic and comic interlude at the wedding reception. This afterpiece is a burlesque rendition of the story of Pyramus and Thisbe, whose tale of misfortune bears a striking resemblance to that of Romeo and Juliet. Through the device of the badly acted play-within-the-play, Shakespeare instructs his audience in the absurdity of lovers' Petrarchan vows and in the power of imagination to transform the bestial or the godlike into human form. In design and execution, *A Midsummer Night's Dream*, with its variety of plots and range of rhyme and blank verse, stands out as Shakespeare s most sophisticated early comedy.

The Merchant of Venice shares bourgeois features with *The Taming of the Shrew* and *The Two Gentlemen of Verona*, but it has a much darker, near-tragic side, too. Shylock's attempt to carve a pound of flesh from the merchant Antonio's heart has all the ingredients of tragedy: deception, hate, ingenuity, and revenge. His scheme is frustrated only by the superior wit of the heroine Portia during a trial scene in which she is disguised as a young boy judge. Requiring Shylock to take nothing more than is specified in his bond, while at the same time lecturing him on the quality of mercy, Portia's speeches create the elements of tension and confrontation that will come to epitomize the playwright's mature tragedies. With the defeat and conversion of Shylock, the pairs of lovers can escape the threatening world of Venice and hope for uninterrupted happiness in Belmont, Portia's home. Venice, the scene of business, materialism, and religious hatred, is contrasted with Belmont (or "beautiful world"), the fairy-tale kingdom to which Bassanio, Antonio's friend, has come to win a fair bride and fortune by entering into a game of choice involving golden, silver, and leaden caskets. Though the settings are contrasted and the action of the play alternates between the two societies, Shakespeare makes his audience realize that Portia, like Antonio, is bound to a contract (set by her dead father) which threatens to destroy her happiness. When Bassanio chooses the leaden casket, she is freed to marry the man whom she would have chosen for her own. Thus "converted" (a metaphor that refers one back to Shylock's conversion), Portia then elects to help Antonio, placing herself in jeopardy once again. Portia emerges as Shakespeare's first major heroine-in-disguise, a character-type central to his most stageworthy and mature comedies, *Twelfth Night* and *As You Like It*.

Much Ado About Nothing likewise has a dark side. The main plot represents the love of Claudio and Hero. Hero's reputation is sullied by the melodramatic villain Don Juan. Claudio confronts his supposedly unfaithful partner in the middle of their wedding ceremony, his tirade causing her to faint and apparently expire. The lovers are later reunited, however, after Claudio recognizes his error. This plot is paralleled by one involving Beatrice and Benedick, two witty characters who in the play's beginning are set against each other in verbal combat. Like Claudio and Hero, they are converted into lovers who overcome selfishness and pride to gain a degree of freedom in their new relationships. The comedy ends with the marriage of Claudio and Hero and the promise of union between Beatrice and Benedick.

A central comic figure in the play is Dogberry, the watchman whose blundering contributes to Don Juan's plot but is also the instrument by which his villainy is revealed. His behavior, especially his hilariously inept handling of legal language, is funny in itself, but it also illustrates a favorite Shakespearean theme: clownish errors often lead to happy consequences. Like Bottom in *A Midsummer Night's Dream*, Dogberry and his men are made an important part of the newly transformed society at the end of the play.

As You Like It and *Twelfth Night* are widely recognized as Shakespeare's wittiest and most stageworthy comedies; they also qualify as masterpieces of design and construction. In *As You Like It*, the action shifts from the court of Duke Frederick, a usurper, to the forest world of Arden, the new "court" of ousted Duke Senior. His daughter Rosalind enters the forest world in disguise, along with her friend Celia, to woo and win the young hero Orlando, forced to wander by his brother Oliver, another usurping figure. Although his florid verses expressing undying love for Rosalind are the object of considerable ridicule, Orlando earns the title of true lover worthy of Rosalind's hand. She proves successful in winning the support of the audience by means of her clever manipulation of Orlando from behind her mask. His inept poetry and her witty commentary can be taken "as we like it," as can the improbable conversions of Oliver and Duke Frederick that allow for a happy ending. Two characters—Touchstone, the clown, and Jacques (pronounced JAYK weez), the cynical courtier—represent extreme attitudes on the subjects of love and human nature. Touchstone serves as Rosalind's protector and as a sentimental observer, commenting wistfully and sometimes wittily on his own early days as a lover of milkmaids. Jacques, the trenchant commentator on the "Seven Ages of Man," sees all this foolery as further evidence, along with political corruption and ambition, of man's fallen state. He remains outside the circle of happy couples at the end of the play, a poignant, melancholy figure. His state of self-centeredness, it might be argued, is also "as we like it" when our moods do not identify so strongly with youthful exuberance.

Twelfth Night also deals with the themes of love and self-knowledge. Like *As You Like It*, it features a disguised woman, Viola, as its central figure. Motifs from other earlier Shakespearean comedies are also evident in *Twelfth Night*. Viola and Sebastian are twins (a motif found in *The Comedy of Errors*) who have been separated in a shipwreck but, unknown to each other, have landed in the same country, Illyria. From *The Two Gentlemen of Verona*, Shakespeare took the motif of the disguised figure serving as page to the man she loves (Duke Orsino) and even playing the wooer's role with the woman (Olivia) whom the duke wishes to marry. Complications arise when Olivia falls in love with Viola, and the dilemma is brought to a head when Orsino threatens to kill his page in a fit of revenge. Sebastian provides the ready solution to this dilemma, but Shakespeare holds off introducing the twins to each other until the last possible moment, creating effective comic tension. The play's subplot involves an ambitious and vain steward, Malvolio, who, by means of a counterfeited letter (the work of a clever servant named Maria), is made to believe that Olivia loves him. The scene in which Malvolio finds the letter and responds to its hints, while being observed not only by the theater audience but also by an audience onstage, is one of the funniest stretches of comic pantomime in drama. When Malvolio attempts to woo his mistress, he is thought mad and is cast in prison. Although he is finally released (not before being tormented by Feste the clown in disguise), Malvolio does not join the circle of lovers in the close, vowing instead to be revenged on all those who deceived him. In fact, both Feste and Malvolio stand apart from the happy company, representing the dark, somewhat melancholy clouds that cannot be dispelled in actual human experience. By this stage in his career, Shakespeare had

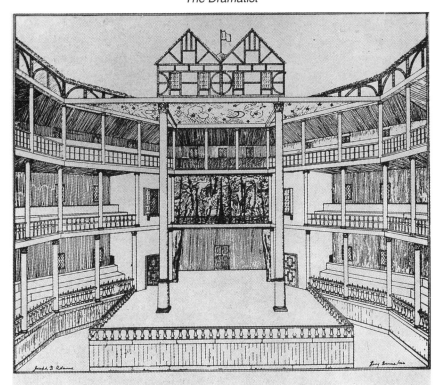

CONJECTURAL RECONSTRUCTION OF THE INTERIOR OF THE GLOBE
The curtains to the rear stage are open; the curtains to the upper stage are closed; the "music rooms," occupied by the playhouse orchestra, are represented as above the upper stage; the "painted heavens" over the stage are adorned with stars, moon, and clouds; the "huts" are supported by the columns resting on the stage.

A reconstruction of the interior of the Globe Theatre from Joseph Quincy Adams, A Life of Shakespeare *(1923).* (Reprinted by permission of The Folger Shakespeare Library)

acquired a vision of comedy crowded by elements and characters that would be fully developed in the tragedies.

The Merry Wives of Windsor was probably composed before Shakespeare reached the level of maturity reflected in *As You Like It* and *Twelfth Night*. Legend suggests that he interrupted his work on the second history cycle to compose the play in two weeks for Queen Elizabeth, who wished to see Falstaff (by then familiar from the history plays) portrayed as a lover. What Shakespeare ended up writing was not a romantic but instead a bourgeois comedy that depicts Falstaff attempting to seduce Mistress Ford and Mistress Page, both wives of Windsor citizens. He fails, but in failing he manages to entertain the audience with his bragging and his boldness. Shakespeare may have been reworking an old play based on a Plautine model; in one of Plautus' plays, there is a subplot in which a clever young man (Fenton) and his beloved manage to deceive her parents in order to get married. This is the only strain of romance in the comedy, whose major event is the punishment of Falstaff: He is tossed into the river, then singed with candles and pinched by citizens disguised as fairies. Critics who see Falstaff as the embodiment of Vice argue that this punishment has symbolic weight; his attempted seduction of honest citizens' wives makes him a threat to orderly society. Regardless of whether this act has a ritual purpose, the character of Falstaff, and the characters of Bardolph, Pistol, and Justice Shallow, bear little resemblance to the comic band of *Henry IV, Part I*. In fact, *The Merry Wives of Windsor* might be legitimately seen as an interlude rather than a fully developed comedy, and it is a long distance from the more serious, probing dramas Shakespeare would soon create.

All's Well That Ends Well and *Measure for Measure* were composed during a period when Shakespeare was also writing his major tragedies. Because they pose questions about sin and guilt that are not satisfactorily resolved, many critics have used the terms "dark comedies" or "problem plays" to describe them. *All's Well That Ends Well* features the familiar disguised heroine (Helena) who pursues the man she loves (Bertram) with skill and determination. The play differs from the earlier romantic comedies, however, because the hero rejects the heroine, preferring instead to win honor and fame in battle. Even though Helena is "awarded" the prize of Bertram by the King of France, whom she has cured of a near-fatal disease, she must don her disguise and pursue him while undergoing consider able suffering and hardship. In order to trap him, moreover, she must resort to a "bed trick," substituting her body for that of another woman whom Bertram plans to seduce. When Bertram finally assents to the union he bears little resemblance to comic heroes such as Orlando or Sebastian; he could be seen in fact as more a villain (or perhaps a cad) than a deserving lover. The forced resolution makes the play a "problem" for many critics, but for Shakespeare and his audience, the ingenuity of Helena and the multiple marriages at the close probably satisfied the demands of romantic comedy.

Measure for Measure has at the center of its plot another bed trick, by which a patient and determined woman (Mariana) manages to capture the man she desires. That man, Angelo, is put in the position of deputy by Duke Vincentio at the opening of the action. He determines to punish a sinful Vienna by strictly enforcing its laws against fornication; his first act is to arrest Claudio for impregnating his betrothed Juliet. When Isabella, Claudio's sister, who is about to take vows as a nun, comes to plead for his life, Angelo attempts to seduce her. He asks for a measure of her body in return for a measure of mercy for her brother. Isabella strongly resists Angelo's advances, although her principled behavior most certainly means her brother will die. Aided by Vincentio, disguised as a holy father, Isabella arranges for Mariana to take her place, since this woman is in fact Angelo's promised partner. Thus, Angelo commits the deed that he would punish Claudio for performing. (Instead of freeing Claudio, moreover, he sends word to have him killed even after seducing his "sister.") Through another substitution, however, Claudio is saved. In an elaborate judgment scene, in which Vincentio plays both duke and holy father, Angelo is forgiven—Isabella being required by the duke to beg for Angelo's life—and marries Mariana. Here, as in *All's Well That Ends Well*, the hero proves to be an unpunished scoundrel who seems to be in fact rewarded for his sin, but the biblical "Judge not lest ye be judged" motivates much of the action, with characters finding themselves in the place of those who would judge them and being forced to display mercy. Some critics have argued that this interpretation transforms Duke Vincentio into a Christ figure, curing the sins of the people while disguised as one of them. Whether or not this interpretation is valid, *Measure for Measure* compels its audience to explore serious questions concerning moral conduct; practically no touches of humor in the play are untainted by satire and irony.

The Romances

For about four years following the writing of *Measure for Measure*, Shakespeare was busy producing his major tragedies. It is probably accurate to say that the problem comedies were, to a degree, testing grounds for the situations and characters he would perfect in the tragedies, but in the later years of his career, Shakespeare returned to writing comedy of a special kind: tragicomedy or romance. The four plays usually referred to as "the romances" are *Pericles*, *Cymbeline*, *The Winter's Tale*, and *The Tempest*. Three of these portray situations in which fathers are separated from daughters, then are rejoined through some miraculous turn of fortune. Except for *The Tempest*, the events cover many years and involve travel to exotic locales by the heroes and heroines. Sharp contrasts between the court and pastoral settings vivify the theme of nature as the ideal teacher of moral values. In *Pericles*, *Cymbeline*, and *The Winter's Tale*, the plots move inexorably toward tragedy, but through some form of intervention by Providence—or in some cases, by the gods themselves—happiness is restored and characters are reunited. All the plays witness the power of faith as instrumental in the process of regeneration; the loyal counselor or servant is a regular character-type in the plays. The general outlook of the romances is optimistic, suggesting that man is indeed capable of recovering from the Fall and of creating a new Paradise.

Pericles recounts the adventures of a good king who seems hounded by fortune and forced to wander through the Mediterranean. The plot is faintly reminiscent of that of *The Comedy of Errors*, suggesting that Shakespeare was returning to tested materials from his earliest comedies. During a storm at sea, Pericles' wife, Thaisa, apparently dies in childbirth and is set ashore in a coffin. He then leaves his daughter Marina in the care of a scheming queen, who tries to have her murdered. Instead, Marina is captured by pirates and eventually is sold to a brothel owner. After many years of lonely sojourning, Pericles is finally reunited with his daughter; later, through the offices of a doctor figure named Cerimon, they find Thaisa in the temple of Diana at Ephesus, where she has been resting for years. Throughout, the sea represents both a threatening and a peaceful force; Marina's name points to the theme of the sea as a great restorative power. She "cures" her father aboard a ship.

Cymbeline, set in ancient Britain, recounts the misfortunes of its characters against the background of the Roman invasion of England. The tragicomedy has strong patriotic overtones, but it does not qualify as a history play such as those in the two tetralogies. The play depicts the moral education of Posthumus, the hero, whose desire to marry Imogen, Cymbeline's daughter, is frustrated by his low birth. While in exile in Italy, Posthumus brags to an Italian acquaintance, Iachimo, that his beloved would never consider deceiving him. Thus challenged, Iachimo visits Imogen's room while she sleeps and, through a clever ruse involving a ring and a

Richard Burbage, one of the leading actors of Shakespeare's day and an important early interpreter of his plays. (Reprinted by permission of The Folger Shakespeare Library)

birthmark, convinces Posthumus that he has slept with her. As a result of numerous plot turns, one of which calls for Imogen to disguise herself as a page, the two lovers are finally reunited when Iachimo confesses his sin. Comingled with this strain of plot is another involving two sons of Cymbeline who have been reared in the rugged world of caves and mountains by an old counselor banished by the king. (He originally kidnapped the boys to seek revenge against Cymbeline.) In a climactic scene brought about by the Roman invasion, the mountain-men heroes are reunited with their father and sister, whom all believed was dead. So complex is the plot that many readers and audiences have found the play confusing and sometimes unintentionally humorous. The characters are not fully developed, and it is difficult to determine just what is the central story. Here, too, spectacle overpowers dialogue and characterization, with little or no attention paid to plausibility. Shakespeare seems preoccupied with demonstrating the healthfulness of pastoral life, the patriotic spirit of Englishmen, and the melodramatic quality of evil. Clearly, this agenda of themes and values places one in a comic world that is distinct from the one that typifies the mature comedies.

In *The Winter's Tale*, Shakespeare again explores the motif of the daughter separated from her father, but in this play, the father, King Leontes, must be seen as a potentially tragic figure. His jealousy leads him to accuse his wife, Hermione, of unfaithfulness with his friend and fellow king Polixenes. When Leontes confronts her, even after consultation of the oracle indicates her honesty, she faints and apparently expires. Leontes banishes the child Perdita, who is his daughter but whom he refuses to acknowledge because of his suspicions, and the third act ends with a loyal servant depositing the baby on the shore of Bohemia to be favored or destroyed by Fortune. (A bear pursues and kills the servant, thus destroying any link between Leontes' court and the baby.) Perdita, "the lost one," is found and reared by a shepherd; as sixteen years pass, she grows into a kind of pastoral queen, revealing those traits of goodness and innocence that Shakespeare associates with the Golden Age. When Polixenes repeats Leontes' sin by banishing his son Florizel for falling in love with a lowly shepherdess, the couple, with the help of a rejected servant still loyal to Leontes, returns to Sicilia to seek the aid of the now repentant king. Through a series of revelations and with the help of the old shepherd. Perdita's identity is discovered, she and Florizel are married, and the two kings are reunited in friendship. As a final tour de force, Hermione, who has been hidden away for the whole time by another loyal servant, comes to life as a statue supposedly sculpted by a famous artist. As in the other romances, some divine force has obviously been operating in the affairs of men to bring about this happy reunion of families, friends, and countries.

The Winter's Tale comes closer than the romances to a realistic treatment of emotion, with all of its destructive possibilities, and to a more nearly honest vision of the pastoral world. Autolycus the clown, for example, pretends to be nothing other than a successful thief, "a snapper-up of unconsidered trifles."

The Tempest is the only romance in which father and daughter are together from the beginning. It also possesses the only plot that observes the classical unities of time and place. Many commentators believe that the play represents Shakespeare's greatest dramatic achievement, blending together beautiful verse, richly realized characters, and the moving wonders of the imagination. There can be no question that *The Tempest* is a refined and elevating statement of the themes of Providence and of order and degree. Prospero, the Duke of Milan, exiled by his usurping brother Antonio, vows to punish both Antonio and his chief supporter, King Alonso; the two are aboard a ship sailing near the island on which Prospero and his daughter Miranda reside. Using magical power and the aid of a spirit named Ariel, Prospero apparently wrecks the ship, saving all the voyagers but supposedly drowning Ferdinand, Alonso's son. Once on the island, the party is tormented by disorienting music and distracting sights, especially when Prospero's brother Antonio attempts to convince Alonso's brother Sebastian to kill him and seize the crown. Another rebellion is attempted by Caliban (his name an anagram for "cannibal"), the half-human, half-bestial servant of Prospero. Both rebellions fail, but instead of punishing his victims further, Prospero, moved by the compassion displayed by Ariel, decides to give up his magic and return to civilization. The decision proves crucial, since Prospero was on the verge of becoming a kind of Faust, forgetting his identity as a man. When he acknowledges Caliban, "this thing of darkness," as his own, one realizes that this gesture betokens an internal acceptance of the passions as a legitimate part of his nature. Instead of revenging himself on Alonso, Prospero allows Ferdinand to woo Miranda in a mood and manner that recall Eden before the Fall. It should also be noted that Prospero creates a marriage masque featuring Iris, Ceres, and Juno, at the close of which he delivers the famous "Our revels now are ended" speech. Some critics claim that Prospero's words constitute Shakespeare's farewell to the stage, but there is considerable evidence that he continued to write plays for at least another year.

The Two Noble Kinsmen was probably one of the plays composed during that period. It is not included in the First Folio (published 1623); it appeared in print in 1634 and bearing a title page ascribing the comedy to John Fletcher and William Shakespeare. Although collaboration was common among Elizabethan and Jacobean playwrights, it was not a form of composition in which Shakespeare regularly engaged. Since *Henry VIII* was also most likely a collaborative effort, there seems to be compelling evidence that Shakespeare was enjoying a state of semiretirement during this period. Based on Geoffrey Chaucer's "The Knight's Tale" (from his *Canterbury Tales*), *The Two Noble Kinsmen* depicts the love of Palamon and Arcite for Emilia in a polite and mannered style that can easily be identified with Fletcher's other work. The play is similar to the other romances in its emphasis on spectacle: It opens with a magnificent wedding ceremony before the Temple of Hymen, and there are excursions to the shrines of Mars and Diana as well. However, there are no scenes of regeneration involving fathers and daughters, no emphasis on the forgiveness of sin. If this was Shakespeare's last play, it shows him returning to old sources for oft-told tales; his interest in developing new comic forms had obviously waned. On the whole, the romances represent a more sophisticated but less playful and inventive style than that of the character-oriented comedies, such as *Twelfth Night* and *Much Ado About Nothing*.

The Tragedies

Titus Andronicus was the earliest—and clumsiest—of Shakespeare's attempts at tragedy. The plot no doubt came from the Roman poet Ovid, a school subject and one of the playwright's favorite Roman authors. From Seneca, the Roman playwright whose ten plays had been translated into English in 1559, Shakespeare took the theme of revenge: The inflexible, honor-bound hero seeks satisfaction against a queen who has murdered or maimed his children. She was acting in retaliation, however, because Titus had killed her son. Titus' rage, which is exacerbated by the rape and mutilation of his daughter Lavinia, helps to classify him as a typical Senecan tragic hero. He and the wicked queen Tamora are oversimplified characters who declaim set speeches rather than engaging in realistic dialogue. Tamora's lover and accomplice, the Moor Aaron, is the prototype of the Machiavellian practicer that Shakespeare would perfect in such villains as Iago and Edmund. While this caricature proves intriguing, and while the play's structure is more balanced and coherent than those of the early history plays, Titus' character lacks the kind of agonizing introspection shown by the heroes of the major tragedies. He never comes to terms with the destructive code of honor that convulses his personal life and that of Rome.

An exterior view of the Globe Theatre, as shown in H. E. Conklin's 1935 scale-model reconstruction. (Library of Congress)

With *Romeo and Juliet*, Shakespeare reached a level of success in characterization and design far above the bombastic and chaotic world of *Titus Andronicus*. Based on a long narrative and heavily moralized poem by Arthur Brooke, this tragedy of "star-crossed lovers" excites the imagination by depicting the fatal consequences of a feud between the Veronese families of Montague and Capulet. Distinguished by some of Shakespeare's most beautiful poetry, the style bears a strong resemblance to that of the sonnets: elaborate conceits, classical allusions, witty paradoxes, and observations on the sad consequences of sudden changes of fortune. Some critics have in fact faulted the tragedy because its plot lacks the integrity of its poetry; Romeo and Juliet come to their fates by a series of accidents and coincidences that strain credulity. The play also features abundant comic touches provided by the remarks of Romeo's bawdy, quick-witted friend Mercutio and the sage but humorous observations of Juliet's nurse. Both of these "humor" characters (character-types whose personalities are determined by one trait, or "humor") remark frequently, and often bawdily, on the innocent lovers' dreamy pronouncements about their passion for each other. With the accidental murder of Mercutio, whose last words are "A plague on both houses!" (referring to the feuding families), the plot accelerates rapidly toward the catastrophe, showing no further touches of humor or satire. The tireless Friar Lawrence attempts, through the use of a potion, to save Juliet from marrying Paris, the nobleman to whom she is betrothed, but the friar proves powerless against the force of fate that seems to be working against the lovers. Although it lacks the compelling power of the mature tragedies, whose heroes are clearly responsible for their fate, *Romeo and Juliet* remains a popular play on the subject of youthful love. The success of various film versions, including Franco Zeffirelli's 1968 feature film, with its teenage hero and heroine and its romantically moving score, proved that the play has a timeless appeal.

At least three years passed before Shakespeare again turned his attention to the tragic form. Instead of treating the subject of fatal love, however, he explored Roman history for a political story centering on the tragic dilemma of one man. In *Julius Caesar*, he could have dealt with the tale of the assassination of Caesar, taken from Plutarch's *Parallel Lives* (A.D. 105-115, translated 1579), as he did with material from English history in the chronicle dramas he had been writing in the 1590's. That is, he might have presented the issue of the republic versus the monarchy as a purely political question, portraying Caesar, Brutus, Cassius, and Antony as pawns in a predestined game. Instead, Shakespeare chose to explore the character of Brutus in detail, revealing the workings of his conscience through moving and incisive soliloquies. By depicting his hero as a man who believes his terrible act is in the best interest of the country, Shakespeare establishes the precedent for later tragic heroes who likewise justify their destructive deeds as having righteous purposes.

The tragic plot is developed by means of irony and contrast. Cassius, jealous of Caesar's achievements, seduces Brutus into taking part in the conspiracy by appealing to his idealism. This political naiveté stands in sharp contrast to Antony's Machiavellianism, which is so brilliantly demonstrated in his crowd-swaying funeral oration ("Friends, Romans, countrymen, lend me your ears . . ."). Antony's transformation from playboy to power broker displays Shakespeare's belief that the historical moment shapes the natures of great men. Caesar appears to be a superstitious, somewhat petty figure, but in typical fashion, Shakespeare makes his audience see that, just as the conspirators are not free of personal motives such as jealousy, so Caesar is not the cold and uncompromising tyrant they claim he is. With the visit by Caesar's ghost to Brutus' tent on the eve of the final battle at Philippi, Shakespeare foreshadows the ultimate revenge of Caesar in the character

Copyright 1935
H. ERNEST CONKLIN

The cut-away interior view of H. E. Conklin's 1935 scale-model reconstruction of the Globe Theatre. (Library of Congress)

of his grandson, Octavius, who emerges as a strong personality at the close of the play. Brutus and Cassius quarrel before the end, but they nevertheless achieve a kind of nobility by committing suicide in the Roman tradition. For Brutus, the events following the assassination demonstrate the flaw in his idealism; he could not destroy the spirit of Caesar, nor could he build a republic on the shifting sand of the populace. In *Julius Caesar*, one witnesses a tragedy that is both politically compelling and morally complex.

While the revenge theme is an important part of *Julius Caesar*, it dominates the action of *Hamlet*. Learning from his father's ghost that Claudius, the new king, is a brother-murderer and a usurper, the hero sets out passionately to fulfill his personal duty by destroying the villain-king. Like Brutus, however, Hamlet is a reflective man, given to "saucy doubts" about the veracity of the ghost, about the effect on his soul of committing regicide, and about the final disposition of Claudius' soul. As a result, Hamlet delays his revenge—a delay that has preoccupied audiences, readers, and critics for centuries. Numerous reasons have been proposed for the delay: Hamlet is melancholic; his morality does not condone murder; he is a coward; he is secretly envious of Claudius for murdering his "rival" for his mother's affections. These explanations, while appealing, tend to shift attention away from other, equally significant elements in the play. Hamlet's soliloquies illustrate the range of Shakespearean blank verse and provide the means for exploring character in detail. The play's trap motif can be seen to represent effectively the doomed, claustrophobic atmosphere of the play. Indeed, those who deliberatively set traps in the play—Polonius, Claudius, Laertes, Hamlet—find that those traps snap back to catch the "inventor." Hamlet's relationships with Ophelia and with Gertrude amply reveal his self-destructive belief that his mother's marriage to Claudius has tainted his own flesh and transformed all women into strumpets. Throughout the action as well, one becomes aware that Shakespeare is using the theatrical metaphor "All the world's a stage" to illustrate the way in which deceit and corruption can be masked. In another sense, Hamlet's behavior is that of a bad actor, one who either misses his cues (as in the accidental murder of Polonius) or fails to perform when the audience expects action (as in his behavior following the play-within-the-play). There is a good deal of reflection on death and disease in *Hamlet* as well; the hero's preoccupation with these images seems to mirror the sickness of the state and of his own enterprise. When Hamlet finally acts, however, he does so in the role of an avenger and scourge. He murders Claudius after the king has arranged for Laertes to slay him in a duel and after the queen has fallen dead from a poisoned drink intended for Hamlet. With Hamlet's death, the kingdom reverts to the control of young Fortinbras, whose father Hamlet's father had killed in another duel. Though Fortinbras stands as a heroic figure, one cannot help but observe the irony of a situation in which the son, without a struggle, inherits what his father was denied.

In *Troilus and Cressida*, one encounters another kind of irony: satire. This strange play, which may have been composed for a select audience, possibly of lawyers, was placed between the histories and tragedies in the First Folio. The dual plot concerns the political machinations among the Greeks during their siege of Troy and the tortured love affair between Troilus and the unfaithful Cressida. There are no epic battles in the play; indeed, the murder of Hector by a band of Achilles' followers might easily be viewed as cowardly or ignominious at best. Much of the political action consists of debates: Hector argues eloquently that Helen should be sent back to Menelaus; Ulysses produces many pithy arguments urging the reluctant Achilles to fight. Many of these scenes, moreover, end in anticlimax, and action is often frustrated. Throughout, Thersites, the satirist-onstage, bitterly attacks the warring and lecherous instincts of men; even the love affair between Troilus and Cressida seems tainted by the general atmosphere of disillusion. Although the two lovers share genuine affection for each other, one cannot ignore the truth that they are brought together by Pandarus and that their passion has a distinctly physical quality. When Cressida proves unable to resist the advances of Diomedes, Troilus becomes a cuckold like Menelaus; his bitterness and misogyny push one toward Thersites' assessment that the "argument" of the war "is a whore and a cuckold." Still it is possible to see tragic dimensions in the characters of both Hector and Troilus—one the victim of treachery in war, the other the victim of treachery in love.

Although probably written after the other major tragedies, *Timon of Athens*

A 1660's engraving of a playhouse stage illustrating various stock characters; Shakespeare's Sir John Falstaff and Mistress Quickley ("Hostes") are visible in the left foreground. (Reprinted by permission of The Folger Shakespeare Library)

Ex dono Willi. Iaggard Typographi. aº 1623

Mr. WILLIAM

SHAKESPEARES

COMEDIES,
HISTORIES, &
TRAGEDIES.

Publiſhed according to the True Originall Copies.

Martin Droeshout ſculpſit London.

LONDON

Printed by Iſaac Iaggard, and Ed. Blount. 1623.

The title page of the 1623 First Folio, featuring the well-known engraving of Shakespeare by Martin Droeshout. The epigraph on the facing page reads: "This Figure, that thou here seest put,/ It was for gentle Shakespeare cut;/ Wherein the [en]Graver had a strife/ with Nature, to out-doo the life;/ O, could he but have drawn his wit/ As well in brasse, as he hath hit/ His face, the Print would then surpasse/ All, that was ever writ in brass./ But since he cannot, Reader, looke/ Not on his Picture, but his Booke." (Reprinted by permission of The Folger Shakespeare Library) shares a number of similarities with *Troilus and Cressida*. Here again is an ironic vision of humanity, this time in a social rather than martial setting. That vision is expanded by the trenchant comments, usually in the form of references to sexual disease, of Apemantus, another cynical choric commentator. In addition, Timon appears to be a tragic rather than misanthropic figure only if one sees him as the victim of his idealistic reading of humankind. When those on whom he has lavishly bestowed gifts and money consistently refuse to return the favor, Timon then becomes a bitter cynic and outspoken satirist. This exploding of a naive philosophy or political idea, with its attendant destructive effect on the believer, would seem to be the basis for tragedy in a character like Brutus or Hamlet, but even Hamlet fails to achieve the degree of misanthropy that typifies Timon's outlook. Although he is loyally followed to the end by his servant Flavius, moreover, he dies alone and not as a result of someone else's direct attack. One cannot say that the hero acquires a larger view of humanity or of himself as the result of his experience; he simply seems to swing from one extreme view to its opposite. A comparison of Timon with more sympathetic "railers" such as Hamlet and Lear shows how narrow and shallow are his character and the dimensions of the play. The fragmented nature of the text has led some critics to question Shakespeare's authorship, but it is probably closer to the truth to say that this was an experiment that failed.

An experiment that clearly succeeded is *Othello, the Moor of Venice*, an intense and powerful domestic tragedy. Based on an Italian tale by Giraldi Cinthio, the story concerns a Moor, a black man who is made to believe by a treacherous, vengeful ensign that his new Venetian bride has cuckolded him with one of his lieutenants, Cassio. In a rage, the Moor suffocates his bride, only to discover too late that his jealousy was unfounded; rather than face the torture of a trial and his own conscience, he commits suicide as he bitterly accuses himself of blindness. In its simple outline, this story has the appearance of a crude melodrama, but Shakespeare brilliantly complicates the play's texture through skillful manipulation of scenes, characters, and language. He also creates a world with two distinct symbolic settings: Venice and Cyprus. In Venice, Othello shows himself to be a cool, rational captain, deserving of the respect he receives from the senators who send him to Cyprus to defend it from the Turks. Once Othello is on the island, however, Iago begins to chip away at the hero's veneer of self-control until he transforms him into a terrifyingly destructive force. Iago's success depends not only on his close contact with Othello on the island but also on the generally held opinion that he, Iago, is an "honest man." He is thus able to manipulate all the central characters as if he were a puppeteer. These characters share information with Iago that he later uses to ensnare them in his web, as when Desdemona begs him to find some way to reinstate Cassio in Othello's favor. Iago is especially adept at using the handkerchief Othello gave to Desdemona but which she dropped while trying to ease her husband's headache. When Iago's wife Emilia dutifully hands her husband this handkerchief, he easily makes Othello believe that Desdemona gave it to Cassio as a love token. Although some critics have ridiculed Shakespeare for depending so heavily on one prop to resolve the plot, they fail to note the degree of psychological insight Shakespeare has displayed in using it. The handkerchief represents Othello's wife's honor and his own; she has given both away, in Othello's mind, as if they were trifles.

This play features a hero whose reason is overwhelmed by the passion of jealousy—"the green-eyed monster," in Iago's words. This theme is realized through numerous sea images, by which Shakespeare likens Othello's violent reaction to a storm or tidal wave that drowns everything in its path. Like Shakespeare's other great villains, Iago is a supreme individualist, acknowledging no authority or power beyond himself. That this attitude was a copy of the fallen angel Satan's would not have escaped the attention of Shakespeare's audience, which no doubt interpreted the plot as a replay of the Fall of Man. It may be especially important to perceive Iago as another Satan, since commentators have suspected the sufficiency of his motive (he says he wants revenge because Othello passed over him in appointing Cassio as his lieutenant). The extreme evilness of Iago's nature and the extreme purity of Desdemona's have led others to claim that Shakespeare was simply intent on fashioning a contemporary morality play for his audience. Such a reading tends to simplify what is in fact a thoroughgoing study of the emotions that both elevate and destroy man. As Othello discovers before his suicide, he was one "who loved not wisely but too well"; one might observe ironically that it was Iago, and not Desdemona, whom he loved "too well."

If Othello's tragedy results from the corrosive disease of jealousy, the hero of *King Lear* suffers from the debilitating effects of pride and self-pity. When the play opens he is in the process of retiring from the kingship by dividing his kingdom into three parts, basing his assignment of land on the degree of affection mouthed by each of the three daughters to whom he plans to assign a part. Cordelia, his youngest and favorite, refuses to enter into this hollow ceremony, and Lear responds by suddenly and violently banishing her. Left in the hands of his evil and ambitious daughters Goneril and Regan, Lear quickly discovers that they plan to pare away any remaining symbols of his power and bring him entirely under their rule. This theme of children controlling, even destroying, their parents is echoed in a fully developed subplot involving old Gloucester and his two sons, Edmund and Edgar. With Cordelia and Edgar cast out—the former to live in France, the latter in disguise as Poor Tom—Lear and Gloucester suffer the punishing consequences of their sins. Lear runs mad into a terrible storm, accompanied by the Fool, a witty and poignant commentator on the unnaturalness of his master's decision; there, Lear goes through a "dark night of the soul" in which he sees for the first time the suffering of others whom he has never regarded. Gloucester, who is also lacking insight into the true natures of his sons, is cruelly blinded by Regan and her husband and cast out from his own house to journey to Dover. On the way, he is joined by his disguised son, who helps Gloucester to undergo a regeneration of faith before he expires. Cordelia performs a similar task for Lear, whose recovery can be only partial, because of his madness. After Cordelia is captured and killed by the forces of Edmund, whose brother conquers him in single combat, Lear, too, expires while holding the dead Cordelia in his arms.

This wrenching ending, with its nihilistic overtones, is only one of the elements that places this play among the richest and most complex tragedies in English.

Lear's blindness, which is expertly represented in image clusters dealing with sight and insight, leads to cataclysmic suffering for his family and the state. More than any other Shakespearean tragedy, *King Lear* also succeeds in dramatizing the relationship between the microcosm, or little world of man, and the macrocosm, or larger world. One sees how the breakdown of the king's reason and control leads to the breakdown of control in the state and in nature. At the moment when Lear bursts into tears, a frightening storm breaks out, and civil war soon follows. Images of human suffering and torture likewise crowd the action, the most compelling of which is the representation of the hero tied to a "wheel of fire" and scalded by his own tears as the wheel turns. The Wheel of Fortune emblem is clearly evoked by this image, revealing Shakespeare's purpose of depicting the king as another fallen prince

The 1612 Ashbourne Portait of Shakespeare depicts the playwright in his late forties, four years before his death. (Reprinted by permission of The Folger Shakespeare Library)

brought low by his own mistakes and by the caprice of the goddess. That Lear has created the circumstances of his own fall is underscored by the antic remarks of his companion the Fool, the choric speaker who early in the play tries to keep Lear's mind from cracking as he comes to realize how wrong was the banishment of Cordelia. The Fool speaks in riddles and uses barnyard analogies to make the point that Lear has placed the whip in the child's hand and lowered his own breeches. Gloucester must learn a similar lesson, although his dilemma involves a crisis of faith. Lear must strip away the coverings of civilization to discover "unaccommodated man," a discovery he begins to make too late; just as he realizes that Cordelia represents those qualities of truth and compassion that he has been lacking, she is suddenly and violently taken from him.

Macbeth treats the *de casibus* theme of the fall of princes, but from a different perspective. Unlike Lear, Macbeth is a usurper who is driven to kill King Duncan by the witches' prophecy, by his own ambition, and by his wife's prompting. Once that deed is done, Macbeth finds himself unable to sleep, a victim of conscience and guilt. Although Lady Macbeth tries to control his fears, she proves unsuccessful, and her influence wanes rapidly. Evidence of this loss of power is Macbeth's plot to kill Banquo, his fellow general, to whom the witches announced that he would be the father of kings. During the climactic banquet scene, Duncan's ghost enters, invisible to the other guests, to take Macbeth's place at the table; when the host reacts by raging and throwing his cup at the specter, the celebration is broken up and the guests scatter. Immediately, Macbeth rushes to the witches to seek proof that he is invincible. They tell him that he will not be conquered until Birnam Wood comes to Dunsinane and that no man born of woman can kill him. They also show him a procession of eight child-kings, all of whom represent Banquo's descendants, including the last king, who is meant to be James I. (This procession has helped many critics to conclude that *Macbeth* was written as an occasional play to honor James, who became the company's protector in 1603.)

Seeking to tighten his control of Scotland and to quiet his conscience, Macbeth launches a reign of terror during which his henchmen kill Lady Macduff and her children. Macduff, exiled in England with Duncan's son Malcolm, learns of this vicious deed and spearheads an army that returns to Scotland to destroy the tyrant. In the final battle, which commences with the attacking army tearing down branches from trees in Birnam Wood to camouflage its advance, Macbeth discovers that his nemesis, Macduff, "was from his mother's womb/ Untimely ripped." Thus standing alone (Lady Macbeth commits suicide) and defeated, Macbeth represents himself as a "poor player" who has had his moment onstage and is quickly gone. This use of the theatrical metaphor looks back to the world of *Hamlet* at the same time that it underscores the villain-hero's role as an impostor king. Macbeth is also depicted as a Herod figure (recalling Richard III) when he murders the innocent children of Macduff in an obsessive fit brought on by the realization that he is childless and heirless. Two strains of imagery reinforce this perception, featuring recurring references to blood and to children. When Macbeth kills Duncan, he describes his blood as "gilding" his flesh, suggesting that the king is God's anointed representative on earth. Shakespeare also depicts Macbeth's nemesis as a bloody child; this image hints at the strength-in-innocence theme that dominates the latter part of the play. That is, as Macbeth grows into the "man" that Lady Macbeth claimed he should be, he becomes more destructive and less humane, the caricature of a man. Macduff, on the other hand, in tears over the brutal murder of his wife and children, emerges as a stronger and more compassionate man because he has shown himself capable of deep feeling. The bloody-babe image might also be defined as a Christ emblem, with the attendant suggestion that Macduff comes to free the land from a tyrant's grasp by spreading a philosophy of goodness and mercy. If the play was written to honor James I, it might also be argued that the comparison between his reign and that of Christ was intended. Whatever the intention of these image patterns, they help one to trace the transformation in Macbeth's character from battlefield hero to usurping tyrant, a transformation brought about by the powerful motive of ambition.

Written soon after *Macbeth*, *Antony and Cleopatra* again traces the complex psychological patterns of a male-female relationship. Like Lady Macbeth, Cleopatra appears to control and direct the behavior of her man, Antony, but as the play progresses, she, too, begins to lose power. Unlike Lady Macbeth, Cleopatra outlasts her love, gaining from Antony's death the spirit and stature of rule that was not evident throughout much of the play. Indeed, most of the action involves quarrels between these two mature but jealous and petulant lovers as they struggle to escape the harsh political world created by Octavius Caesar, Antony's rival. Angered by Antony's reveling in Egypt and later by his desertion of Caesar's sister Octavia, whom Antony married only to buy time and an unsteady truce, Octavius begins to move against Antony with a powerful army and navy. During a first encounter between the two forces, in which Antony foolishly decides to fight at sea and also depends on Cleopatra's untested ships, Antony leaves the field in pursuit of the retiring Cleopatra. Angered by her withdrawal and his own alacrity in following her, Antony rages against his "serpent of old Nile" and vows to have nothing further to do with her, but Cleopatra's pull is magnetic, and Antony joins forces with her for a second battle with Caesar. When a similar retreat occurs and Antony finds Cleopatra apparently arranging a separate peace with one of Caesar's representatives, he has the messenger beaten and sent back to Octavius with a challenge to single combat. These wild and desperate moves are commented on by Enobarbus, associate of Antony and choric voice; after the threat of single combat, Enobarbus leaves his master to join forces with Octavius. (Overcome by remorse, however, Enobarbus dies on the eve of battle.)

Believing that Cleopatra has killed herself, Antony decides to commit suicide and calls upon his servant Eros to hold his sword so that he can run himself on it. Instead, Eros kills himself, and Antony must strike the blow himself. Still alive, he is carried to the monument where Cleopatra has decided to take up residence. There, Antony expires, "a Roman, by a Roman/ Valiantly vanquished." Almost immediately, Cleopatra's character seems to change into that of a noble partner; her elegant speeches on Antony's heroic proportions are some of the most powerful blank verse in the play. It is also clear that she intends to escape Octavius' grasp,

Workers apply finishing touches to the restored Globe Theatre shortly before its 1996 reopening. (Reuters/Michael Crabtree/Archive Photos)

knowing that he intends to parade her and her children before a jeering Roman crowd. Putting on her royal robes and applying the poison asps to her breast, Cleopatra hurries off to join her lover in eternity.

This complicated story is brilliantly organized by means of placing in balance the two worlds of Rome and Egypt. While Rome is presented as a cold, calculating place, reflective of the character of Octavius, Egypt stands out as a lush paradise in which the pursuit of pleasure is the main business of the inhabitants. This contrast is particularly telling because Antony's status as a tragic hero depends on one's seeing him as caught between the two worlds, at home in neither, master of neither. Water and serpent imagery dominate the play, creating a picture of Cleopatra as a Circe figure or a spontaneously generated creature that has seduced the once heroic Antony. Although this is the Roman view of the "gypsy" queen, Shakespeare requires his audience to appreciate her infinite variety: She is beautiful and playful, demanding and witty, cool and explosive. On the other hand, the assessment of Octavius as a puritanical, unfeeling man of destiny is also oversimplified; his reaction to Antony's death reveals genuine emotion. At the close of the play, one realizes that Antony and Cleopatra's vast empire has been reduced to the size of her monument—Caesar must attend a while longer to make this discovery himself. Antony and Cleopatra, however, have found a world of love that Octavius could never enter, and the tragedy is as much concerned with tracing the boundaries of that empire as it is with marking the triumphs of Octavius.

While reading the story of Antony and Cleopatra in Plutarch's *Parallel Lives*, to which the play reveals a number of similarities, Shakespeare found another Roman figure whose career he saw as appropriate matter for tragedy: Coriolanus. Composed in the period between 1607 and 1608, *Coriolanus* dramatizes the career of a general in the age of Republican Rome. He proves to be a superhuman figure in battle, earning his name by single-handedly subduing the town of Corioles and emerging from its gates covered in blood. (This birth image has a mixed meaning, since the blood is that of his victims.) Unfortunately, Coriolanus refuses to humble himself before the Roman plebeians, whom he despises, as a requirement for holding the office of consul. Indeed, many of his bitter comments about the fickleness and cowardice of the populace remind one of characters such as Thersites and Apemantus. Such contempt and condescension make it hard to identify with Coriolanus, even though one is made aware that the Roman crowd is set against him by the jealous and ambitious tribunes, Brutus and Sicinius. Driven by his pride and anger, Coriolanus challenges the citizens' rights and is subsequently banished. He then joins forces with his former enemy Aufidius, and the two of them lead an army to the very gates of Rome. Coriolanus' mother comes out to plead with her son to spare Rome—and his family—in the most emotional scene of the play. Deeply moved by his mother's arguments, Coriolanus relents and urges his companion to make peace with their enemy. Aufidius agrees but awaits his opportunity to ambush his partner, whom he regards as a lifelong enemy. In a masterstroke of irony, Coriolanus is brought down by the citizens of the very town—Corioles—that he conquered in acquiring his name. Because the play is so heavily laden with swatches of Coriolanus' vitriol and instances of irony such as the final one, it is difficult to classify this tragedy with those in which the heroes present richly complex characters. If Hamlet, Othello, Macbeth, and Lear possess tragic flaws, those flaws are only a part of their complicated makeup. Coriolanus, on the other hand, can be understood only in terms of his flaw, and the character and play are therefore one-dimensional.

There is little argument, however, that Shakespeare's tragedies constitute the major achievement of his career. These dramas continue to appeal to audiences because their stories are intriguing; because their characters are fully realized human beings, if somewhat larger than life; and because their poetic language is metaphorically rich. Shakespeare possessed a profound insight into human nature and an ability to reveal what he found there in language unequaled in its power and beauty.

Robert F. Willson, Jr.

Updated by John R. Holmes and Joseph Rosenblum

For Further Study

Bloom, Harold, ed. *Shakespeare: The Tragedies*. New York: Chelsea House, 1985. A collection of influential scholarly articles by various Shakespeare authorities, originally published between 1930 and 1983. These esssays cover a wide variety of themes and approaches to Shakespeare's major tragedies. Bloom's introduction glosses major trends in Shakespeare criticism in the twentieth century. Bibliography.

Bradley, A. C. *Shakespearean Tragedy*. London: Macmillan, 1904. A seminal work that has influenced virtually all subsequent discussion of Shakespearean tragedy. Reproduces Bradley's college lectures at the University of Oxford and other British universities, beginning with "The Substance of Shakespearean Tragedy" and continuing with a lecture on tragic construction and two lectures each on *Hamlet*, *Othello*, *King Lear*, and *Macbeth*.

French, Marilyn. *Shakespeare's Division of Experience*. New York: Summit, 1981. A groundbreaking feminist analysis of Shakespeare's entire canon, this book takes gender-based discussion of Shakespeare beyond character roles to an analysis of the way Shakespeare, as a representative of his time, saw the world in male-female polarities. French also suggests ways in which Shakespeare transcended those poles.

Granville-Barker, Harley. *Prefaces to Shakespeare's Plays*. 4 vols. Princeton, N.J.: Princeton University Press, 1947. Offers the equivalent of a small book on each of Shakespeare's plays, each of which functions as a "preface" in the original sense of an essay giving readers what they need to know in order to understand or interpret a particular work.

Harbage, Alfred. *William Shakespeare: A Reader's Guide*. New York: Farrar, Straus, 1963. A basic resource for new Shakespeare students. Each play is introduced with a few pages of interpretive suggestions. Then the play is summarized scene by scene, with further interpretations interwoven. These introductory chapters on Shakespeare's words and verse techniques are valuable to those approaching the plays for the first time.

Spurgeon, Caroline F. E. *Shakespeare's Imagery and What It Tells Us*. Cambridge, England: Cambridge University Press, 1935. This pioneer work on Shakespeare's imagery is an ideal starting point for anyone interested in that important aspect of his art. In addition to a demonstration of the patterns of imagery in each of Shakespeare's plays, Spurgeon offers appendices of color-coded charts demonstrating these patterns in works by both Shakespeare and his contemporaries.

The Poet

Shakespeare wrote some of the greatest love poems in English. His short erotic narratives, *Venus and Adonis* (1593) and *The Rape of Lucrece* (1594), were typical examples of fashionable literary genres. Other minor poems include contributions to the miscellany *The Passionate Pilgrim* (1599) and *The Phoenix and the Turtle*, written for a collection of poems appended to *Loves Martyr* (1601), an allegorical treatment of love by Robert Chester. All of these pale alongside Shakespeare's sonnets, which, in an age of outstanding love poetry, attain a depth, suggestiveness, and power rarely duplicated in the history of humankind's passionate struggle to match desire with words.

One of William Shakespeare's great advantages as a writer was that, as a dramatist working in the public theater, he was afforded a degree of autonomy from the cultural dominance of the court, his age's most powerful institution. All over Europe, even if belatedly in England, the courts of the Renaissance nation-states conducted an intense campaign to use the arts to further their power. The theater, despite its partial dependency on court favor, achieved through its material products (the script and the performance) a relative autonomy in comparison with the central court arts of poetry, prose fiction, and the propagandistic masque. When Shakespeare briefly turned to Ovidian romance in the 1590's and, belatedly (probably also in the 1590's), to the fashion for sonnets, he moved closer to the cultural and literary dominance of the court's taste—to the fashionable modes of the Roman poet Ovid, the Italian Renaissance poet Petrarch, and the Neoplatonists—and to the need for patronage. Although the power of the sonnets goes far beyond their sociocultural roots, Shakespeare nevertheless adopted the culturally inferior role of the petitioner for favor, and there is an undercurrent of social and economic powerlessness in the sonnets, especially when a rival poet seems likely to supplant the speaker in the sonnets. In short, Shakespeare's nondramatic poems grew out of and articulated the strains of the 1590's, when, like many ambitious writers and intellectuals on the fringe of the court, Shakespeare clearly needed to find a language in which to speak—and that was, necessarily, given to him by the court.

What he achieved within this shared framework, however, goes far beyond any other collection of poems in the age. Shakespeare's occasional poems are unquestionably minor, interesting primarily because he wrote them; his sonnets, on the other hand, constitute perhaps the language's greatest collection of lyrics. They are love lyrics, and clearly grow from the social, erotic, and literary contexts of his age. Their greatness, however, lies in their power to be read again and again in later ages, and to raise compellingly, even unanswerably, more than merely literary questions.

Early Poetry

In his first venture into public poetry, Shakespeare chose to work within the generic constraints of the fashionable Ovidian verse romance. *Venus and Adonis* appealed to the taste of young aristocrats such as the Earl of Southampton, to whom this poem was dedicated. It is a narrative poem in six-line stanzas, mixing classical mythology with surprisingly (and incongruously) detailed descriptions of country life, designed to illustrate the story of the seduction of the beautiful youth Adonis by the comically desperate aging goddess, Venus. The poem's story is relatively static, with too much argument to make it inherently pleasurable reading. Its treatment of love relies on Neoplatonic and Ovidian commonplaces, and it verges—unlike Christopher Marlowe's later poem *Hero and Leander* (1598), to which Shakespeare's poem is a fair but decidedly inferior fellow—on moralizing allegory, with Venus as flesh and Adonis as spiritual longing. The poem's articulation of the nature of the love that separates them is abstract and often unintentionally comic—although Shakespeare's characterization of Venus as a garrulous, plump matron brings something of his theatrical power to enliven the poem. The poem was certainly popular at the time, going through ten editions in as many years, possibly because its early readers thought it fashionably sensual.

The Rape of Lucrece is the "graver labor" which Shakespeare promised to Southampton in the preface to *Venus and Adonis*. Again, he combines a current poetical fashion—the complaint—with a number of moral commonplaces, and writes a novelette in verse: a melodrama celebrating the prototype of matronly chastity, the Roman lady Lucrece and her suicide after she was raped. The central moral issue—that of honor—at times almost becomes a serious treatment of the psychology of self-revulsion, but the decorative and moralistic conventions of the complaint certainly do not afford Shakespeare the scope of a stage play. There are some fine local atmospheric effects which, in their declamatory power, occasionally bring the directness of the stage into the verse.

The Phoenix and the Turtle is an allegorical, highly technical celebration of an ideal love union: It consists of a funeral procession of mourners, a funeral anthem, and a final lament for the dead. It is strangely evocative, dignified, abstract, and solemn. Readers have fretted, without success, over the exact identifications of its characters. Its power lies in its mysterious, eerie evocation of the mystery of unity in love.

The Sonnets

Probably more human ingenuity has been spent on Shakespeare's sonnets than on any other work of English literature. In his outstanding edition entitled *Shakespeare's Sonnets* (1978), Stephen Booth briefly summarizes the few facts that have led to a plethora of speculation on such matters as text, authenticity, date, arrangement, and, especially, biographical implications. The sonnets were first published in 1609, although numbers 138 and 144 had appeared in *The Passionate Pilgrim* a decade before. Attempts to reorder the sonnets have been both varied and creative, but none represents the "correct" order. Such attempts simply fulfill an understandable anxiety on the part of some readers to see narrative continuity rather than variations and repetition in the sonnets. The so-called story "behind" the sonnets has, as Booth puts it, "evoked some notoriously creative scholarship": speculation on the identity of the young man, or Fair Youth, mentioned in many of the first 126 sonnets, of Mr. W. H., to whom the sequence is dedicated by the printer; of the so-called Dark Lady of Sonnets 127-154; and of the rival poet of some of the earlier sonnets. All of these matters have filled many library shelves. Such speculations—which reached their peak in critics and readers wedded to the sentimental Romantic insistence on an intimate tie between literary and historical "events"—are in one sense a tribute to the power of the sonnets.

The sonnets are, nonetheless, among the greatest love poems in the English language, and they provide a crucial test for the adequacy of both the love of poetry and the sense of the fascinating confusion which makes up human love. In a sense, the sonnets are as "dramatic" as any of Shakespeare's plays inasmuch as their art concerns the drama of love, beauty, time, betrayal, insecurity, and joy. Each sonnet is like a little script, with (often powerful) directions for reading and enactment, with textual meanings that are not given but made anew in every performance, by different readers within their individual and social lives. What Sonnet 87 terms "misprision" may stand as the necessary process by which each sonnet is produced by each reader.

It is conventional to divide the sonnets into two groups: Sonnets 1-126, purportedly addressed or related to a young man, sometimes referred to by scholars as the "Fair Youth," and sonnets 127-154, to the so-called Dark Lady. Such a division is arbitrary at best; within each group there are detachable subgroups, and without the weight of the conventional arrangement many sonnets would not seem to have a natural place in either group. Sonnets 1-17 (and perhaps 18) are ostensibly concerned with a plea for a young man to marry; but even in this group, which many readers have seen to be the most conventional and unified, there are disruptive suggestions that go far beyond the commonplace context.

What may strike contemporary readers, and not merely after an initial acquaintance with the sonnets, is the apparently unjustified level of idealization voiced by many of the sonnets—an adulatory treatment of noble love which, to a post-Freudian world, might seem archaic, no matter how comforting. The continual self-effacement of the anguished lover, the worship of the "God in love, to whom I am confined" (110), the poet's claim to immortalizing "his beautie . . . in these blacke lines" (63)—such idealizations are all born out of a world of serene affirmation. Some of the most celebrated sonnets, such as "Shall I compare thee to a summer's day" (18) or "Let me not to the marriage of true minds" (116), may even seem cloyingly affirmative, their texts seemingly replete, rejecting any subtextual challenges to their idealism.

In the two hundred years between the time of Petrarch, the Italian poet credited with the development of the sonnet form, and Shakespeare's Elizabethan England, the sonnet had evolved into an instrument of logic and rhetoric. Under Shakespeare's pen, however, the sonnet, with its three quatrains and a concluding couplet, allowed especially for the concentration on a single mood. The Shakespearean sonnet is held together less by the apparent logic of many of the sonnets (for example, the "when . . . then" pattern) than by the invitation to enter into the dramatization of a brooding, sensitive mind. The focus is on emotional richness, on evoking the immediacy of felt experience. Shakespeare uses many deliberately generalized epithets, indeterminate signifiers and floating referents which provoke meaning from their readers rather than providing it. Each line contains contradictions, echoes, and suggestions which require an extraordinary degree of emotional activity on the part of the reader. The couplets frequently offer a reader indeterminate statements, inevitably breaking down any attempt at a limited formalist reading. The greatest of the sonnets—including 60 and 129, as well as many others—have such an extraordinary combination of general, even abstract, words and unspecified emotional power that the reader may take it as the major rhetorical characteristic of the collection.

In particular lines, too, these poems achieve amazing power by their lack of logical specificity and emotional open-endedness. As Booth points out, many lines show "a constructive vagueness" by which a word or phrase is made to do multiple duty—by placing it "in a context to which it pertains but which it does not quite fit idiomatically" or by using phrases which are simultaneously illogical and amazingly charged with meaning. He instances "separable spite" in Sonnet 36 as a phrase rich with suggestion; another example is the way in which the bewilderingly ordinary yet suggestive epithets sit uneasily in the opening lines of Sonnet 64. Often a reader is swept on through the poem by a syntactical movement that is modified or contradicted by associations set up by words and phrases. There is usually a syntactical or logical framework in the sonnet, but so powerful are the contradictory, random, and disruptive effects occurring incidentally as the syntax unfolds that to reduce the sonnet to its logical framework is to miss the most amazing effects of these extraordinary poems.

Shakespeare was writing at the end of a very long tradition of using lyric poems to examine the nature of human love, and there is a weight of insight as well as of rhetorical power behind his collection. Nowhere in the Petrarchan tradition are the extremes of erotic revelation offered in such rawness and complexity. Critic Northrop Frye once characterized the sonnets as a kind of "creative yoga," an imaginative discipline meant to articulate the feelings that swirl around sexuality. Most of the conventional themes of traditional poetry are the starting points for the sonnets—the unity of lovers (36-40), the power of poetry to immortalize the beloved (18, 19, 55), contests between eye and heart, beauty and virtue (46, 141), and shadow and substance (53, 98, 101). Like Petrarch's *Rime* (c. 1327) or Sir Philip Sidney's *Astrophil and Stella* (1591), Shakespeare's sonnets contain the basis for a schematic account of commonplace Renaissance thinking about love. However, to limit them to the construction of such an account would be to nullify their extraordinary power of creation, the way they force recognition, horror, or joy from their readers.

After half a century of existentialist writing, readers in the late twentieth century understood that one of the most urgent subjects of the sonnets is not the commonplaces of Renaissance thinking about love, nor even the concern with the power of art, but what Sonnet 16 calls our "war upon this bloody tyrant Time." It is no accident that the "discovery" of the sonnets' concern with time and mutability dates from the 1930's, when the impact of philosophers such as Sören Kierkegaard, Friedrich Nietzsche, and the existentialists, including Martin Heidegger, was starting to be widely felt in England and America. The sonnets' invitation to see humanity's temporality not merely as an abstract problem but as part of inherent human nature—what Heidegger terms man's "thrownness," the sense of being thrown into the world—seems central to a perception of the sonnets' power. Unpredictability and change are at the heart of the sonnets—but it is a continually shifting heart, and one that conceives of human love as definable only in terms of such change and finitude. The sonnets avoid the transcendentalism of Geoffrey Chaucer beseeching his young lovers to turn from the world, or of Edmund Spenser rejecting change for the reassurance of God's Eternity and His providential guidance of time to a foreknown, if mysterious, end. Shakespeare's sonnets, rather, overwhelm readers with questions and contradictions. In Sonnet 60, for example, time is not an impartial or abstract background. Even where it is glanced at as a pattern observable in nature or humankind, it is evoked as a disruptive, disturbing experience that cannot be dealt with as a philosophical problem. Some sonnets portray time as a sinister impersonal determinant; some thrust time at the reader as an equally unmanageable force of unforeseeable chances and changes, what Sonnet 115 calls man's "million'd accidents."

In Sonnet 15, it may be possible to enter into an understandable protest against time destroying its own creations (a common Renaissance sentiment), and to accede to a sense of helplessness before a malignant force greater than the individual human being. When the sonnet tries, however, by virtue of its formally structured argument, to create a consciousness that seeks to understand and so to control this awareness, the reader encounters lines or individual words that may undermine even the temporary satisfaction of the aesthetic form. Such, for example is the force of the appalling awareness that "everything that grows/ Holds in perfection but a little moment." What is the application of "everything" or the emotional effect of the way the second line builds to a seemingly replete climax in "perfection" and then tumbles into oblivion in "but a little moment"? The sonnet does not and need not answer such questions. In a very real sense it cannot answer them, for readers can only acknowledge time's power in their own contingent lives. What is shocking is not merely the commonplace that "never-resting time leads summer on/ To hideous winter, and confounds him there" (5) but that each reading fights against and so disrupts the logical and aesthetic coherence of the reader's own sense of change and betrayal.

To attempt criticism of the sonnets is, to an unusual extent, to be challenged to make oneself vulnerable, to undergo a kind of creative therapy, as one goes back and forth from such textual gaps and indeterminacies to the shifting, vulnerable self, making the reader aware of the inadequacy and betrayal of words, as well as of their amazing seductiveness. Consider, for example, Sonnet 138. When one falls in love with a much younger person, does one inevitably feel the insecurity of a generation gap? What is more important in such a reading of the sonnets is the insistence that age and youthfulness are not important in themselves. It is the insistence itself that is important, not the mere fact of age—just as it is the anxiety with which a man or woman watches the wrinkles beneath the eyes that is important, not the wrinkles themselves. The note of insistence, in other words, is not attached merely to the speaker's age; it stands for an invitation to participate in some wider psychological revelation, to confess the vulnerability that people encounter in themselves in any relationship that is real and growing, and therefore necessarily unpredictable and risky. Without vulnerability and contingency, without the sense of being thrown into the world, there can be no growth. Hence the poet invites the reader to accept ruefully what the fact of his age evokes—an openness to ridicule or rejection. The sonnet's insistence on being open to the insecurity represented by the narrator's age points not merely to a contrast between the speaker and his two lovers but, more important, to a radical self-division.

This is especially so in the Dark Lady sonnets, where there is a savage laceration of self, particularly in the fearful exhaustion of Sonnet 129, in which vulnerability is evoked as paralysis. At once logically relentless and emotionally centrifugal, Sonnet 129 generates fears or vulnerability and self-disgust. Nothing is specified: The strategies of the poem work to make the reader reveal or recognize his or her own compulsions and revulsions. The poem's physical, psychological, and cultural basis forces one to become aware of an awful drive to repress words because they are potentially so destructive.

Even in the seemingly most serene sonnets there are inevitably dark shadows of insecurity and anxiety. In Sonnet 116, for example, the argument is that a love that alters with time and circumstance is not a true love but a self-regarding love. The poem purports to define true love by negatives—what it is *not*—but if those negatives are deliberately negated, the poem that emerges may be seen as the dark, repressed underside of the apparently unassailable affirmation of a mature, self-giving, other-directed love. If lovers admit impediments, and play with the idea that love is indeed love which "alters when it alteration finds," that it is an "ever-fixed mark" and, most especially, that love is indeed "time's fool," then the poem connects strikingly and powerfully with the strain of insecurity about the nature of change in human love that echoes throughout the whole collection. Such apparent affirmations may be acts of repression, an attempt to regiment the unrelenting unexpectedness and challenge of love. There are poems in the collection which, although less assertive, show a willingness to be vulnerable, to reevaluate constantly, to swear permanence within, not despite, transience—to be, in the words of Saint Paul, deceivers yet true. Elsewhere, part of the torture of the Dark Lady sonnets is that such a consolation does not emerge through the pain.

In short, what Sonnet 116 represses is the acknowledgment that the only fulfillment worth having is one that is struggled for and that is independent of law or compulsion. The kind of creative fragility that it tries to marginalize is that evoked in the conclusion to Sonnet 49, when the poet admits his vulnerability: "To leave poor me thou hast the strength of laws,/ Since, why to love, I can allege no cause." This is an affirmation of a different order—or rather an acknowledgment that love must not be defined by repression and exclusion. Lovers can affirm the authenticity of the erotic only by admitting the possibility that it is not absolute.

Love has no absolute legal, moral, or causal claims; nor, in the final analysis, can love acknowledge the bonds of law, family, or state—or if finally they are acknowledged, it is because they grow from love itself. Love moves by its own internal dynamic; it is not motivated by a series of external compulsions. Ultimately it asks from the lover the *nolo contendere* of commitment: Do with me what you will. A real love—that is to say, an altering, bending, *never* fixed and unpredictable love—is always surrounded by, and at times seems to live by, battles, plots, subterfuges, quarrels, and irony. At the root is the acknowledgment that any affirmation is made because of, not despite, time and human mortality. As Sonnet 12 puts it, having surveyed the fearful unpredictability of all life, lovers must realize that it is even "thy beauty" that must be questioned. At times this thought "is as a death" (64), a "fearful meditation" (65)—that even the most precious of all human creations will age, wrinkle, fade, and die. Just how can one affirm in the face of that degree of reality?

Under the pressure of such questioning, the affirmation of Sonnet 116 can therefore be seen as a kind of bad faith, a false dread—false, because it freezes lovers in inactivity when they should, on the contrary, accept their finitude as possibility. Frozen in the fear of contingency, which Sonnet 116 so ruthlessly represses in its insistent negatives, readers may miss Shakespeare's essential insight that it is in fact the very fragility of beauty, love, poetry, Fair Youth, and Dark Lady alike that enhances their desirability. Paradoxically, it is precisely because they are indeed among the wastes of time that they are beautiful; they are not desirable because they are immortal but because they are irrevocably time-bound. One of the most profound truths is expressed in Sonnet 64: "Ruin hath taught me thus to ruminate/ That Time will come and take my love away./ This thought is as a death, which cannot choose/ But weep to have that which it fears to lose." The power of such lines goes far beyond the serene platitudes of Sonnet 116. At his most courageous, human beings do not merely affirm, *despite* the forces of change and unpredictability which provide the ever-shifting centers of life; on the contrary, we discover our greatest strengths *because* of and within our own contingency. To accept rather than to deny time is to prove that our deepest human life ultimately does not recognize stasis but always craves growth, and that fulfillment is built not upon the need for finality—for being "ever fixed"—but on the need to violate apparent limits, to push forward or die.

Against a sonnet such as 116, some sonnets depict love not as a serene continuation of life but rather as a radical reorientation. Readers are asked not to dismiss fears of limitation but to affirm them. It is in the midst of contingency, when meditations are overwhelmed by the betrayals of the past, while "I sigh the lack of many a thing I sought,/ And with old woes new wail my dear Time's waste" (Sonnet 30), that love may open up the future as possibility, not as completion—so long as one accepts that it is time itself that offers such possibility, not any attempt to escape from it.

The typical Renaissance attitude toward time and mutability was one of fear or resignation unless, as in Spenser, the traditional Christian context could be evoked as compensation; but for Shakespeare the enormous energies released by the

Renaissance are wasted in trying to escape the burden of temporality. The drive to stasis, to repress experiences and meanings, is a desire to escape the burden of realizing that there are some transformations which love cannot effect. Ultimately, it is impossible to get inside a lover's soul no matter how much the flesh is seized and penetrated. The drive to possess and so to annihilate is a desire derived from the old Platonic ideal of original oneness, which only Shakespeare among the Renaissance poets seems to have seen as a clear and fearful perversion. It certainly haunts the lover of the Dark Lady sonnets, and we are invited to stand and shudder at the speaker's Augustinian self-lacerations. In Sonnet 144 the two loves "of comfort and despair,/ Which like two spirits do suggest me still" are not just a "man right fair" and a "woman, colour'd ill"; they are also aspects of each lover's self, the two loves that a dualistic mind cannot affirm and by which people may be paralyzed.

Throughout this discussion of the sonnets, what has been stressed is that their power rests on the seemingly fragile basis not of Shakespeare's but of their readers' shifting and unpredictable experiences. They are offered not in certainty but in hope. They invite affirmation while insisting that pain is the dark, visceral element in which human beings must live and struggle. Many of the Dark Lady sonnets are grim precisely because the lover can see no way to break through such pain. What they lack, fundamentally, is hope. By accepting that, for a time, "my grief lies onward and my joy behind" (Sonnet 50), the lover may be able, however temporarily, to make some commitment.

Sonnet 124 is particularly suggestive, categorizing love as "dear"—meaning costly—not only because it is "fond" (beloved) but also because it is affirmed in the knowledge of the world. Moreover, while it "fears not Policy" it is nevertheless "hugely politic." It is as if love must be adaptable, cunning, even deceptive, aware of the untrustworthiness of the world from which it can never be abstracted: "it nor grows with heat, nor drowns with showers." Finally, the poet affirms with a strong and yet strangely ironic twist: "To this I witness call the fools of Time,/ Which die for goodness, who have liv'd for crime." As Stephen Booth notes, Sonnet 124 "is the most extreme example of Shakespeare's constructive vagueness," its key the word "it," which, "like all pronouns, is specific, hard, concrete, and yet imprecise and general—able to include anything or nothing." The pronoun "it" occurs five times, each time becoming more indeterminate, surrounded by subjectives and negatives: In this sonnet "composed of precisely evocative words in apparently communicative syntaxes which come to nothing and give a sense of summing up everything, the word *it* stands sure, constant, forthright, simple and blank." The blankness to which Booth points has been filled very specifically by generations of readers to force the poem into a repressive argument like that of Sonnet 116. For example, the key phrase "the fools of time" is usually glossed as local, historical examples of political or religious time servers—but the phrase contains mysterious reverberations back upon the lovers themselves. There is a sense in which human beings are *all* fools of time. When Sonnet 116 affirms that "Love's not Time's fool," it betrays a deliberate and fearful repression, an unwillingness to acknowledge that Love is not able to overcome Time; time is something that can be fulfilled only as it presents opportunity and possibility to us. People rightly become fools—jesters, dancers in attendance on Time, holy fools before the creative challenge of human finitude—and men are fulfilled sexually, existentially, only if they submit themselves, "hugely politic," to the inevitable compromises, violence, and disruption which is life. Men "die for goodness" because in a sense they have all "lived for crime." People are deceivers yet true; the truest acts, like the truest poetry, are the most feigning.

The twelve-line Sonnet 126 is conventionally regarded as the culmination of the first part of the sequence. Its serenity is very unlike that of 116. It acknowledges that, even if the Fair Youth is indeed Nature's "minion," even he must eventually be "rendered." Such realism does not detract from the Youth's beauty or desirability; it in fact constitutes its power.

Whether one considers the Fair Youth or the Dark Lady sonnets, whether one attempts to see a "hidden" order in the sonnets, or even if one wishes to see a story or some kind of biographical origin "within" them, their greatness rests on their refusal to offer even the possibility of "solutions" to the "problems" they raise. They disturb, provoke, and ask more than merely "aesthetic" questions; read singly or together, they make readers face (or hide from) and question the most fundamental elements of poetry, love, time, and death.

Gary F. Waller

For Further Study

Burgess, Anthony. *Shakespeare.* London: Jonathan Cape, 1970. A prolific novelist, linguist, and literary analyst, Burgess here presents an attractive, copiously illustrated, and immensely readable volume. Although many of his insights are conjectural, he is tremendously persuasive. A highly recommended first reference, though the bibliography is limited. The index is useful.

Campbell, Oscar James, and Edward G. Quinn. *The Reader's Encyclopedia of Shakespeare.* New York: Thomas Y. Crowell, 1966. The most comprehensive single-volume reference, this illustrated work remains unsurpassed. Not only does it arrange an immense array of Shakespeare topics in alphabetic order, but it also includes excerpts of the full range of literary criticism and surveys of stage history. The most widely used reference by both experts and amateurs.

Donno, Elizabeth Story. "The Epyllion." In *English Poetry and Prose, 1540-1674,* edited by Christopher Ricks. New York: Peter Bedrick Books, 1987. This brief introductory survey provides the best basic approach to Shakespeare's mythological poems, placing them securely in their contemporary literary context. Includes basic documentary notes and a complete bibliography of all relevant materials. The volume is fully indexed.

Hulse, Clark. *Metamorphic Verse: The Elizabethan Minor Epic.* Princeton, N.J.: Princeton University Press, 1981. Hulse surveys with great learning and enlightening insights the entire range of the Elizabethan mythological poem. Shakespeare's narrative poems are examined in detail and integrated with their literary and cultural backgrounds. Contains sound notes, a complete bibliography, and a thorough index.

Reese, M. *M. Shakespeare: His World and His Work.* Rev. ed. London: Edward Arnold, 1980. Reese's essays on various aspects of Shakespeare, his life, his background, and his writings, constitute one of the best introductions to these topics available in one volume. Although they are best for intellectual and cultural backgrounds, they offer illuminating comments on the poetry. The directions for further reading are helpful.

Roche, Thomas P., Ir. *Petrarch and the English Sonnet Sequences.* New York: AMS Press, 1986. This is a comprehensive study of the phenomenon of the Elizabethan sonnet sequence, considered primarily from the point of view of its source in Petrarch. It covers the subject completely, and its consideration of Shakespeare's sonnets is unrivaled. The bibliographical apparatus is complete.

_____. "Shakespeare and the Sonnet Sequence." In *English Poetry and Prose, 1540-1674,* edited by Christopher Ricks. New York: Peter Bedrick Books, 1987. The title of this excellent introductory essay is misleading. In fact it is almost entirely about Shakespeare's sonnets, and the material is concisely presented and rewarding. The bibliographical material is excellent for beginners.

Wilson, John Dover, ed. *The Sonnets.* 2d ed. New York: Cambridge University Press, 1967. The introductory essay of twenty-four pages and the notes and commentary are simply the best ever done on this poetry. The bibliographical material is dated but sound.

THE PLAYS

All's Well That Ends Well

Type of plot: Comedy: problem play
Time of plot: Sixteenth century
Locale: France and Italy
First performed: c. 1602-1603; first published, 1623

Principal characters

THE KING OF FRANCE
BERTRAM, the Count of Rousillon
COUNTESS OF ROUSILLON, his mother
HELENA, the Countess' ward
PAROLLES, a scoundrel, Bertram's follower
A WIDOW OF FLORENCE
DIANA, her daughter

The Story

Bertram, the Count of Rousillon, had been called to the court to serve the King of France, who was ill of a disease that all the royal physicians had failed to cure. In the entire country the only doctor who might have cured the king was now dead. On his deathbed he had bequeathed to his daughter Helena his books and papers describing cures for all common and rare diseases, among them the one suffered by the king.

Helena was now the ward of the Countess of Rousillon, who thought of her as a daughter. Helena loved young Count Bertram and wanted him for a husband, not a brother. Bertram considered Helena only slightly above a servant, however, and would not consider her for a wife. Through her knowledge of the king's illness, Helena at last hit upon a plot to gain the spoiled young man for her mate, in such fashion as to leave him no choice in the decision. She journeyed to the court and, offering her life as forfeit if she failed, gained the king's consent to try her father's cure on him. If she won, the young lord of her choice was to be given to her in marriage.

Her sincerity won the king's confidence. She cured him by means of her father's prescription and, as her boon, asked for Bertram for her husband. That young man protested to the king, but the ruler kept his promise, not only because he had given his word but also because Helena had won him over completely.

When the king ordered the marriage to be performed at once, Bertram, although bowing to the king's will, would not have Helena for a wife in any but a legal way. Pleading the excuse of urgent business elsewhere, he deserted her after the cere-

69

mony and sent messages to her and to his mother saying he would never belong to a wife forced upon him. He told Helena that she would not really be his wife until she wore on her finger a ring he now wore on his and carried in her body a child that was his. He then stated that these two things would never come to pass, for he would never see Helena again. He was encouraged in his hatred for Helena by his follower, Parolles, a scoundrel and a coward who would as soon betray one person as another. Helena had reproached him for his vulgar ways, and he wanted vengeance on her.

Helena returned to the Countess of Rousillon, as Bertram had commanded. The countess heard of her son's actions with horror, and when she read the letter he had written her, restating his hatred for Helena, she disowned her son, for she loved Helena like her own child. When Helena learned that Bertram had said he would never return to France until he no longer had a wife there, she sadly decided to leave the home of her benefactress. Loving Bertram, she vowed that she would not keep him from his home.

Disguising herself as a religious pilgrim, Helena followed Bertram to Italy, where he had gone to fight for the Duke of Florence. While lodging with a widow and her daughter, a beautiful young girl named Diana, Helena learned that Bertram had seduced a number of young Florentine girls. Lately he had turned his attention to Diana, but she, a pure and virtuous girl, would not accept his attentions. Then Helena told the widow and Diana that she was Bertram's wife, and by bribery and a show of friendliness she persuaded them to join her in a plot against Bertram. Diana listened again to his vows of love for her and agreed to let him come to her rooms, provided he first gave her a ring from his finger to prove the constancy of his love. Bertram, overcome with passion, gave her the ring, and that night, as he kept the appointment in her room, the girl he thought was Diana slipped a ring on his finger as they lay in bed together.

News came to the countess in France and to Bertram in Italy that Helena had died of grief and love for Bertram. Bertram returned to France to face his mother's and the king's displeasure, but first he discovered that Parolles was the knave everyone else knew him to be. When Bertram held him up to public ridicule, Parolles vowed he would be revenged on his former benefactor.

When the king visited the Countess of Rousillon, she begged him to restore her son to favor. Bertram protested that he really loved Helena, though he had not recognized that love until after he had lost her forever through death. His humility so pleased the king that his confession of love, coupled with his exploits in the Italian wars, won him a royal pardon for his offense against his wife. Then the king, about to betroth him to another wife, the lovely and wealthy daughter of a favorite lord, noticed the ring Bertram was wearing. It was the ring given to him the night he went to Diana's rooms; the king in turn recognized it as a jewel he had given to Helena. Bertram tried to pretend that it had been thrown to him in Florence by a high-born lady who loved him. He said that he had told the lady he was not free to wed, but that she had refused to take back her gift.

At that moment, Diana appeared as a petitioner to the king and demanded that Bertram fulfill his pledge to recognize her as his wife. When Bertram tried to pretend that she was no more than a prostitute he had visited, she produced the ring he had given her. That ring convinced everyone present, especially his mother, that Diana was really Bertram's wife. Parolles added to the evidence against Bertram by testifying that he had heard his former master promise to marry the girl. Bertram persisted in his denials. Diana then asked for the ring she had given to him, the ring which the king thought to be Helena's. The king asked Diana where she had gotten the ring. When she refused to tell on penalty of her life, he ordered her taken to prison. Diana then declared that she would send for her bail. Her bail was Helena,

---

"Our remedies oft in ourselves do lie, which we ascribe to heaven"

All's Well That Ends Well, Act I, scene i, lines 231-232

Bertram, young Count of Rousillon, departs from his home for service at the court of France. Behind him remain his mother and her ward, the lovely and accomplished Helena, daughter of a physician. While living in the Countess' home, Helena has fallen in love with Bertram but believes that their difference in rank makes her love hopeless. Parolles, a servant and follower of Bertram, tells her, before he follows his master, to pray to Heaven and marry a good husband and use him well, but Helena is not planning to follow his advice.

> *Helena.* Our remedies oft in ourselves do lie,
> Which we ascribe to heaven. . . .
> Impossible be strange attempts to those
> That weigh their pains in sense, and do suppose
> What hath been, cannot be. . . .
> But my intents are fixed, and will not leave me.

---

now carrying Bertram's child within her, for it was she, of course, who had received him in Diana's rooms that fateful night. To her Diana gave the ring. The two requirements for becoming his real wife being now fulfilled, Bertram promised to love Helena as a true and faithful husband. Diana received from the king a promise to give her any young man of her choice for her husband, the king to provide the dowry. Thus the bitter events of the past made sweeter the happiness of all.

Critical Evaluation

All's Well That Ends Well is one of William Shakespeare's plays that defies easy genre classifications and is often grouped under such categories as dark comedy or problem play. Though more comic than tragic, these plays contain troublingly dark aspects or resolutions whose very glibness causes unease. Some of these plays received very little attention until the twentieth century, when the unflagging interest in Shakespeare caused critics to turn to the less familiar works in his canon. The modern interest in these more difficult plays is also quite natural because modern literature often focuses on uncertainty, ambiguity, irony, unstable characters, and mixed moods. Those aspects of Shakespeare's plays which may have puzzled his contemporaries and repelled even his greatest fans invite creative attention from modern readers and audiences.

Among such plays, *All's Well That Ends Well* presents several distinctive problems of interpretation. The history of the critical reception of this play, though covering many other aspects, identifies fairly clearly three key subjects of controversy: the active character of Helena, the surprisingly ungracious character of Bertram, and the bed-trick to which the heroine turns in order to win back her reluctant husband, a trick which raises grave questions about the moral center of the play.

One way that scholars have tried to ease their discomfort about issues in the play is to consider the folk tradition underlying the plot. Several have noted that tales of women who endured much hardship for love and of wives who were sorely tested were extremely popular. Stories about women who manipulated events in order to get what they wanted often presented such women in a favorable light. That Shakespeare might have wanted to preserve this point of view for those in his audience not familiar with the folk tradition seems likely, given his depiction of the older characters in the play. Unlike traditional comedies, where the older people are obstructions to the younger ones, in *All's Well That Ends Well*, Helen has the support of the Countess and of the King. Such support serves two purposes. Within the plot, it allows Helena to concentrate her efforts on winning Bertram, and the approval of the older characters places Helena in a positive light, subtly persuading the audience to accept her desires and actions favorably.

These differences from other comedies give rise to controversies in interpretation. On the one hand, Helena can be seen as the agent of a double healing action in the play. She effects the physical cure by healing the king and then spiritually "cures" Bertram of his immaturity and brings about his acceptance of responsibility as an adult male. This interpretation is not far from the love-conquers-all scenario found in most romantic comedies. It may be considered merely a pleasant change that the woman, rather than the man, is the active pursuer who resorts to doing all that is necessary to achieve her desire. The basic underlying plot of traditional comedy remains intact.

A closer scrutiny of this, however, reveals that the gender change creates a much messier play. Innumerable questions about Helena's motivations and behavior come to mind. In the first act alone, Helena mentions several times, in her soliloquy and in speaking to the Countess, that she is deeply conscious of the class difference between Bertram's position in society and her own. Yet she decides to try to win him anyway. Having used her personal knowledge and skill inherited from her physician father to get Bertram, only to find that he does not want her, she then exacerbates her initial mistake in judgment by continuing to pursue him. She lies to those who care about her, pretending to take a pilgrimage when she is actually on her way to find Bertram in Italy. When she gets there, she is willing to pay to degrade herself to substitute for Diana. Though it is quite conventional for comic characters—and more often, their servants—to resort to all manner of guile and deception to overcome obstacles, it has seemed troubling to some critics over the

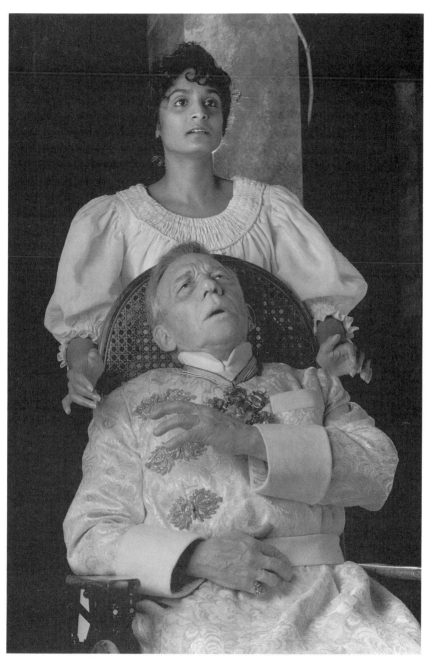

The King of France (Sandy McCallum) is comforted by Helena (Luck Hari) in a scene from the Oregon Shakespeare Festival's 1992 production of All's Well That Ends Well. *(Christopher Briscoe, courtesy of the Oregon Shakespeare Festival by permission of the Actors' Equity Association)*

years that it is a woman who determines the man she wants and then sets out to get him by any means available.

The object of all her travails is another source of unease in the play because Bertram is such an unattractive male character. Granted that his position in the beginning is pitiable, since he is forced by the king into a marriage he does not want, his subsequent actions seem both reprehensible and inconsistent. He behaves in a hateful manner, taunting Helena with two impossible tasks, running away to war, and abandoning his mother, estate, and country to escape his wife. He seduces young women, and then, as in the case of Diana, denies responsibility for his behavior, casting aspersions on their characters. His repentance and newfound love for Helena upon hearing of her death is, at the very least, patently insincere, and, at best, a mysteriously sudden and inconsistent change of heart. This young man, with so few discernible attractive personality traits, seems to have little but noble birth to recommend him. Helena's determination to have him anyway is sometimes interpreted to mean that she is a social climber. This motivation links her to Parolles, one of Shakespeare's great comic creations, morally questionable but theatrically vital to the comic atmosphere of the play. This viewpoint alone makes the play unusual, for though other characters in Shakespeare's plays have attempted to move up in class, Helena is the only one who succeeds, to general approval.

From being a simple comic tale of sturdy and faithful love surviving all obstacles, the meaning of *All's Well That Ends Well* thus begins to shift and waver, starting with the ambivalence of the title. The play can only ironically be said to end well, when the heroine has tricked the hero into staying with her. That the hero cannot distinguish between Diana, the woman he obstensibly desires, and Helena, the wife he has rejected, is unromantic, at the very least. Instead of sounding like a simple exclamation of relief that troubles have been successfully endured, the title can take on a more morally ambiguous shade: that all—including the means—is justified by the end.

The concept that merit, as in the case of Helena's independent and courageous spirit, counts as much as or more than the inherited position of Bertram seems startlingly modern. That and the combination of comic and puzzling characterizations make *All's Well That Ends Well* one of Shakespeare's more thought-provoking plays.

"Critical Evaluation" by Shakuntala Jayaswal

For Further Study

Adams, John F. *"All's Well That Ends Well*: The Paradox of Procreation." *Shakespeare Quarterly* 7, no. 3 (Summer, 1961): 261-270. Includes a discussion of the human worth and the nature of honor in the play. Stresses the importance of the bed-trick in understanding the play.

Charlton, H. B. "The Dark Comedies." In *Shakespearian Comedy*. London: Methuen, 1938. Approaches the comedy from the point of view of the older people and their role in the play. Useful for discussions of characters.

Cole, Howard C. *The All's Well Story from Boccaccio to Shakespeare*. Urbana:

University of Illinois Press, 1981. A unique source for tracing the different versions of the basic story, starting with Giovanni Boccaccio's *Decameron* (1348-1353). Detailed discussions include a chapter on Shakespeare's handling of the tale.

Lawrence, William Witherle. "*All's Well That Ends Well.*" In *Shakespeare's Problem Comedies*. London: Macmillan, 1931. One of the earliest, and most influential, studies to connect the play with the narrative and dramatic traditions preceding it. Explains the basic folktale underlying the plot.

Zitner, Sheldon P. *All's Well That Ends Well*. New York: Harvester Wheatsheaf, 1989. An excellent critical introduction to many aspects of the play. Considers the stage history, critical reception, sources, and the main critical issues of the play. A good starting point for study.

Antony and Cleopatra

Type of plot: Tragedy
Time of plot: c. 30 B.C.E.
Locale: Egypt and parts of the Roman Empire
First performed: c. 1606-1607; first published, 1623

Principal characters

MARK ANTONY,
OCTAVIUS CAESAR, and
LEPIDUS, triumvirs who ruled Rome
ENOBARBUS and
EROS, Antony's friends
SEXTUS POMPEIUS, the leader of the party opposed to Octavius Caesar
CLEOPATRA, the Queen of Egypt
OCTAVIA, Caesar's sister and Antony's wife
CHARMIAN and
IRAS, Cleopatra's attendants

The Story

After the murder of Julius Caesar, the Roman Empire was ruled by the noble triumvirs Mark Antony, Lepidus, and Octavius (Caesar's nephew). Antony, having been given the Eastern sphere to rule, had gone to Alexandria and there he had seen and fallen passionately in love with Cleopatra, Queen of Egypt. She was the flower of the Nile, but she had also been the mistress of Julius Caesar and many others. Antony was so enamored of her that he ignored his own counsel and the warnings of his friends. As long as he could he also ignored a request from Octavius Caesar that he return to Rome. Sextus Pompeius, son of Pompey the Great, and a powerful leader, was gathering troops to seize Rome from the rule of the triumvirs, and Octavius Caesar wished to confer with Antony and Lepidus. At last the danger of a victory by Sextus Pompeius, coupled with the news that his wife Fulvia was dead, forced Antony to leave Egypt and return to Rome.

Because Antony was a better general than either Lepidus or Octavius, Pompeius was confident of victory as long as Antony stayed in Egypt. When Pompeius heard that Antony was returning to Rome, he was reduced to hoping that Octavius and Antony would not mend their quarrels but continue to fight each other as they had in the past. Lepidus did not matter, since he sided with neither of the other two and cared little for conquest and glory. Pompeius was disappointed, however, for Antony and Octavius joined forces in the face of common danger. To seal their renewed friendship, Antony married Octavia, Octavius' sister, through whom each was bound to the other. Pompeius' scheme to keep Antony and Octavius apart had failed, but he still hoped that Antony's lust for Cleopatra would entice him back to Egypt. To stall for time, he sealed a treaty with the triumvirs. Antony, accompanied by his new wife, went to Athens to deal with matters relating to the Empire. There word reached him that Lepidus and Octavius had waged war in spite of the treaty they had signed and that Pompeius had been killed. Octavius next seized Lepidus on the pretext that he had aided Pompeius. Now the Roman world had but two rulers, Octavius and Antony.

Antony could not resist the lure of Cleopatra. Sending Octavia home from Athens, he hurried back to Egypt. By so doing, he ended all pretense of friendship between him and Octavius. Both prepared for a battle that would decide who was to be the sole ruler of the world. Cleopatra joined her forces with Antony's. Antony's forces were supreme on land, but Octavius ruled the sea and lured Antony to fight him there. Antony's friends and captains, particularly loyal Enobarbus, begged him not to risk his forces on the sea, but Antony was confident of victory and he prepared to match his ships with those of Octavius at Actium. In the decisive hour of the great sea fight, however, Cleopatra ordered her fleet to leave the battle and sail for home. Antony too left the battle, disregarding the duty he had toward his honor, and because he had set the example for desertion, many of his men went over to Octavius' forces.

Antony was sunk in gloom at the folly of his own actions, but he was drunk with desire for Cleopatra and sacrificed everything, even honor, to her. She protested that she had not known that he would follow her when she sailed away, but Antony had reason to know she lied. Yet he could not tear himself away.

Octavius sent word to Cleopatra that she might have anything she asked for if she would surrender Antony to him. Knowing that Octavius was likely to be the victor in the struggle, she sent him a message of loyalty and of admiration for his greatness. Antony, who saw her receive the addresses of Octavius' messenger, ranted and stormed at her for her faithlessness, but she easily dispelled his fears and jealousy and made him hers again. After his attempt to make peace with Octavius failed, Antony decided to march against his enemy again. At this decision, even the faithful Enobarbus left him and went over to Octavius, thinking Antony had lost his reason as well as his honor. Enobarbus was an honorable man, however, and shortly afterward he died of shame for having deserted his general.

On the day of the battle, victory was in sight for Antony despite overwhelming odds. Once again, though, the Egyptian fleet deserted him. With the defeat of Antony, Octavius became master of the world. Antony was like a madman and thought of nothing but avenging himself on the treacherous Cleopatra. When the queen heard of his rage, she had word sent to him that she was dead, killed by her own hand out of love for him. Convinced once more that Cleopatra had been true to him, Antony called on Eros, his one remaining follower, to kill him so that he could join Cleopatra in death, but Eros killed himself rather than his beloved general. Determined to die, Antony fell on his own sword. Even that desperate act was without dignity or honor, for he did not die immediately and could find no one

---

"Age cannot wither her, nor custom stale her infinite variety"

Antony and Cleopatra, Act II, scene ii, lines 240-241

These famous lines are frequently employed today to convey a compliment not only to or about a woman, but, with the substitution of a few words, about any skill or talent. Thus, by changing the feminine pronouns to masculine, a very accurate comment is made on Shakespeare himself. Enobarbus, friend of Mark Antony and officer in his forces, describes the beauty and fascination of Cleopatra, Queen of Egypt. He is in Rome, where he and Antony have recently arrived from Egypt, and is talking to two fellow officers, one of whom suggests that now Antony must desert her.

> *Enobarbus.* Never; he will not:
> Age cannot wither her, nor custom stale
> Her infinite variety: other women cloy
> The appetites they feed, but she makes hungry
> Where most she satisfies. . . .

---

who loved him enough to end his pain and misery. While he lay there, a messenger brought word that Cleopatra still lived. He ordered his servants to carry him to her. He died in her arms, each proclaiming eternal love for the other.

When Octavius Caesar heard the news of Antony's death, he grieved. Although he had fought and conquered Antony, he lamented the sorry fate of a great man turned weakling and ruined by his lust. He sent a messenger to assure Cleopatra that she would be treated royally, that she should be ruler of her own fate. The queen learned, however, as Antony had warned her, that Octavius would take her to Rome to march behind him in his triumphant procession, where she, a queen and mistress to two former rulers of the world, would be pinched and spat upon by rabble and slaves. To cheat him of his triumph, she put on her crown and all her royal garb, placed a poisonous asp on her breast, and lay down to die. Charmian and Iras, her loyal attendants, died the same death. Octavius Caesar, entering her chamber, saw her dead, as beautiful and desirable as in life. There was only one thing he could do for his onetime friend and the dead queen: He ordered their burial in a common grave, together in death as they had wished to be in life.

Critical Evaluation

In his tragedies, William Shakespeare rose to dramatic heights seldom equaled. *Antony and Cleopatra* surely belongs to the greatest of his tragedies for its staggering scope; as one of Shakespeare's three "Roman plays," it covers the entire Roman Empire and the men who ruled it. Only a genius could apply such beauty of poetry and philosophy to match the powerful events: A man born to rule the world is brought to ruin by his weaknesses and desires; deserted by friends and subjects, he is denied a noble death and must attempt suicide, but bungles even that.

The tragedy is grimly played out, and honor and nobility die as well as the man.

In *Antony and Cleopatra*, Shakespeare did not bind himself with the Aristotelian unities. He moves swiftly across the whole of the civilized world with a panorama of scenes and characters, creating a majestic expanse suitable to the broad significance of the tragedy. The play is Shakespeare's longest. It is broken up into small units, which intensify the impression of rapid movement. Written immediately after Shakespeare's four great tragedies—*Hamlet, Prince of Denmark* (c. 1600-1601), *Othello, the Moor of Venice* (1604), *King Lear* (c. 1605-1606), and *Macbeth* (1606)—it rivals them in tragic effect though it has no plot that Aristotle

Shakespeare's version of the story of Antony and Cleopatra was not the first, nor would it be the last: Hollywood has portrayed the queen of Egypt as an alluring vamp, from Claudette Colbert, pictured here in a scene from Cecil B. DeMille's 1934 film Cleopatra, *to Elizabeth Taylor in Joseph L. Mankiewicz's 1963 version.* (Courtesy of The Museum of Modern Art, Film Stills Archive)

would recognize. Shakespeare took the story of *Antony and Cleopatra* from a translation of Plutarch but refashioned it into a complex rendering of a corruption that ennobles as it destroys. The play may lack the single, poignant representative character of the great tragedies, but it extends its significance by taking the whole world for its canvas.

As a tragic figure, Antony leaves much to be desired. His actions are little more than a series of vacillations between commitment to a set of responsibilities that are his by virtue of his person and office and submission to the overpowering passion that repeatedly draws him back to Cleopatra's fatal influence. His nobility is of an odd sort. He commands respect and admiration as one of the two omnipotent rulers of the world, but the audience is only told of his greatness; they do not see it represented in any of his actions. In fact, he does not really do anything until his suicide—and that he does not do efficiently. His nobility is attested by his past deeds and by his association with the glories of Rome, and Shakespeare frequently reminds the audience of it, but Antony does not demonstrate this quality in the play.

There is another impediment to Antony's tragic stature: He is too intelligent and aware of what he is doing. As Mark Van Doren has noted, he lives "in the full light of accepted illusion." He is not duped; Cleopatra is not Antony's Iago. Nor is there any self-deception; Antony does not pretend that his love for Cleopatra is more than it is.

Yet that love is sufficiently great to endow Antony with the nobility he salvages. It is not simply that he is a hero brought to disgrace by lust, although that much is true. Viewed from another angle, he is a hero set free from the limits of heroism by a love that frees him from a commitment to honor, allowing him instead to give his commitment to life. Of course, his liberation is also his humiliation and destruction. Both noble and depraved, both consequential and trivial, Antony finds new greatness in the intense passion that simultaneously lays him low.

"I have immortal longings in me"

Antony and Cleopatra, Act V, scene ii, lines 283-284

Cleopatra is alone in her tomb with her attendants and the Roman guards. She is the captive of Octavius Caesar. Her lover and husband, Mark Antony, is dead by his own hand after a disgraceful defeat. Her dreams of ruling Rome jointly with him are also dead. Caesar, impervious to her charms, promises her a future, but she sees through his scheme. She realizes she is no match for him, and that he desires to exhibit her in his triumph in Rome. Cleopatra decides to die a noble death rather than endure such humiliation. She arranges for a poisonous snake, an asp, to be brought to her in a basket of figs. When it bites, it brings quick, painless death.

> *Cleopatra.* Give me my robe, put on my crown, I have
> Immortal longings in me. Now no more
> The juice of Egypt's grape shall moist this lip.
> Yare, yare, good Iras; quick. Methinks I hear
> Antony call. . . .

Cleopatra is an equally complex character, but her complexity is less the result of paradox than of infinite variation. Throughout the first four acts she lies, poses, cajoles, and entices, ringing manifold changes on her powers to attract. Yet she is not a coarse temptress, not a personification of evil loosed upon a helpless victim. As her behavior in the last act reminds the audience, she is also an empress. Cleopatra too is swept along by overwhelming passion. She is not only a proud queen and conniving seducer but a sincere and passionate lover. Despite her tarnished past, her plottings in *Antony and Cleopatra* are dignified through the underlying love. Like Antony, she is not the sort of character who challenges the universe and transcends personal destruction. Rather, her dignity lies somewhere beyond, or outside, traditional heroism.

The complexity of Cleopatra is most apparent in the motivation for her suicide. Certainly one motive is the desire to avoid the humiliation of being paraded through Rome by the victorious Octavius Caesar. If that had been all, however, she would be nothing more than an egoistic conniver. More important, she is also motivated by her sincere unwillingness to survive Antony. The two motives become intertwined, since the humiliation of slavery would also extend to Antony, whose failures left her vulnerable, and taint his reputation. This mixture of motives is a model of the way in which the two lovers are at once each other's undoing and salvation. Their mutual destruction springs from the same love that provides both with their antiheroic greatness. Love is lower than honor in the Roman world, but it can generate an intensity that makes heroism irrelevant. Antony is too intelligent, Cleopatra too witty, and their love too intricate for ordinary tragedy.

The structure of the plot departs from the tragic norm. There is almost none of the complication and unraveling that are expected in tragedy. Rather, the action moves in fits and starts through the forty-two scenes of the play. Although the action of the play must extend over a long period of time, the quick succession of scenes suggests an unsteady hurtling toward the fatal conclusion. The helter-skelter quality is reinforced by the language of the play. Few speeches are long and there are many abrupt exchanges and quick, wide-ranging allusions. Shakespeare often uses feminine endings and spills the sense over the ends of lines in a metrical reflection of the nervous vitality of the play. Thus, plot and language spread the drama over the entire world and hasten its progress toward the inevitable conclusion.

"Critical Evaluation" by Edward E. Foster

For Further Study

Bloom, Harold, ed. *Modern Critical Interpretations: William Shakespeare's "Antony and Cleopatra."* New York: Chelsea House, 1988. Bloom's concise anthology of major Shakespeare criticism of the 1970's and 1980's judiciously samples postmodernist, new historicist, feminist, and deconstructionist discussions of *Antony and Cleopatra*. See especially the essays by Jonathan Dollimore, Linda Bamber, and Laura Quinney.

Charney, Maurice. *Shakespeare's Roman Plays*. Cambridge, Mass.: Harvard University Press, 1961. Chapter 3, the centerpiece of Charney's influential book, brilliantly analyzes the imagery of *Antony and Cleopatra*; Charney gives particular attention to the imagery that clusters around the Egypt-Rome polarity, thereby constituting it as a complex central theme.

Granville-Barker, Harley. *Prefaces to Shakespeare*. Vol. 1. Princeton, N.J.: Princeton University Press, 1946. Granville-Barker's prefaces remain timeless monuments to a golden age of Shakespearean scholarship and theatrical performance.

The preface to *Antony and Cleopatra* offers valuable insights into staging and characterization from the perspective of an influential stage director and critic.

Riemer, A. P. *A Reading of Shakespeare's "Antony and Cleopatra."* Sydney, Australia: Sydney University Press, 1968. A monograph-length, lucid introduction to the background of the play and its plot, characterization, and dramatic structure. Also contains a very useful chapter that discusses important criticism of the play during the early and mid-twentieth century.

Traversi, Derek. *Shakespeare: The Roman Plays*. Stanford, Calif.: Stanford University Press, 1963. In chapter 3 of this classic study, Traversi offers a methodical, analytical commentary on *Antony and Cleopatra*. Sees the play as a profound work of art that in its spaciousness, episodic form, and morally ambivalent valuations of Rome and Egypt escapes traditional definitions of tragedy.

As You Like It

Type of plot: Comedy
Time of plot: Middle Ages
Locale: Forest of Arden, France
First performed: c. 1599-1600; first published, 1623

Principal characters

DUKE SENIOR, a banished duke
FREDERICK, his brother and usurper of his dominions
AMIENS and
JAQUES, lords attending on the banished duke
OLIVER,
JAQUES, and
ORLANDO, sons of Sir Rowland de Boys
ADAM, a servant to Oliver
TOUCHSTONE, a clown
ROSALIND, the daughter of Duke Senior
CELIA, the daughter of Frederick

The Story

A long time ago, the elder and lawful ruler of a French province, Duke Senior, was deposed by his younger brother, Frederick. The old duke, driven from his dominions, fled with several faithful followers to the Forest of Arden. There he lived a happy life, free from the cares of the court and able to devote himself at last to learning the lessons nature had to teach. His daughter, Rosalind, had remained at court as a companion to her cousin Celia, the daughter of the usurping Duke Frederick. The two girls were inseparable, and nothing her father said or did would make Celia part from her dearest friend.

One day, Duke Frederick commanded the two girls to attend a wrestling match between the duke's champion, Charles, and a young man named Orlando, who was a special object of Duke Frederick's hatred because he was the son of Sir Rowland de Boys, who had been one of the banished duke's most loyal supporters. When Sir Rowland died, he had charged his oldest son, Oliver, with the task of looking after his younger brother's education, but Oliver had neglected his father's charge. The moment Rosalind laid eyes on Orlando she fell in love with him, and he with her. She tried to dissuade him from an unequal contest with a champion so much more powerful than he, but the more she pleaded the more determined Orlando was to distinguish himself in his lady's eyes. In the end he completely conquered his antagonist and was rewarded for his prowess by a chain from Rosalind's neck.

When Duke Frederick discovered his niece's interest in Sir Rowland's son, he immediately banished her from the court. Rosalind disguised herself as a boy and set out for the Forest of Arden, accompanied by Celia and the faithful Touchstone, the jester. Orlando had also found it necessary to flee because of his brother's harsh treatment. He was accompanied by the faithful servant Adam, an old man who willingly turned over his life savings of five hundred crowns for the privilege of following his young master.

"All the world's a stage"

As You Like It, Act II, scene vii, line 139

Duke Senior, in the Forest of Arden with his lords Jaques, Amiens, and others, is about to eat when they are interrupted by the entrance of Orlando, who has been driven from his home by his greedy oldest brother. Orlando demands and is given food, but he will not eat until he summons his "old poor man" Adam. At his departure, Duke Senior remarks, "This wide and universal theatre/ Presents more woeful pageants than the scene/ Wherein we play in." Jaques then responds:

> *Jaques.* All the world's a stage,
> And all the men and women merely players.
> They have their exits and their entrances,
> And one man in his time plays many parts,
> His acts being seven ages.

Jaques goes on to describe the "seven ages of man," from infancy to old age, in one of the most famous passages in Shakespeare. The idea of the world's being a stage was common in Shakespeare's time. The French poet Du Bartas (*Divine Weekes and Workes*, 1578) had said that "The World's a stage, where God's omnipotence,/ His justice, knowledge, love, and providence/ Do act the parts." Thomas Heywood, in his *Apology for Actors* (1612), and Thomas Middleton, in *A Game of Chess* (1624, Act V, scene i), used the same idea. Shakespeare himself used this metaphor throughout his plays, notably in *Macbeth* (Act V, scene v, lines 24-25) and *The Tempest* (Act V, scene i, lines 153ff.).

Orlando and Adam set out for the Forest of Arden, but before they had traveled very far they were both weary and hungry. While Adam rested in the shade of some trees, Orlando wandered into that part of the forest where the old duke was, and came upon the outlaws at their meal. Desperate from hunger, Orlando rushed upon the duke with a drawn sword and demanded food. The duke immediately offered to share the hospitality of his table, and Orlando blushed with shame over his rude manner. He would not touch a mouthful until Adam had been fed. When the old duke found that Orlando was the son of his friend, Sir Rowland de Boys, he took Orlando and Adam under his protection and made them members of his band of foresters.

Rosalind and Celia also arrived in the Forest of Arden, where they bought a flock of sheep and proceeded to live the life of shepherds. Rosalind passed as Ganymede, Celia, as her sister Aliena. They encountered real Arcadians—Silvius, a shepherd, and Phebe, a dainty shepherdess with whom Silvius was in love. The moment Phebe laid eyes on the disguised Rosalind, she fell in love with the supposed young shepherd and would have nothing further to do with Silvius. Disguised as Ganymede, Rosalind also met Orlando in the forest, and twitted him on his practice of writing verses in praise of Rosalind and hanging them on the trees. Touchstone displayed the same willfulness and whimsicality in the forest that he had shown at court, even in his love for Audrey, a country girl whose sole appeal was her unloveliness.

One morning, as Orlando was on his way to visit Ganymede, he saw a man lying asleep under an oak tree. A snake was coiled about the sleeper's neck, and a hungry lioness crouched nearby ready to spring. He recognized the man as his own brother, Oliver, and for a moment he was tempted to leave him to his fate. Then he drew his sword and killed the two animals. In the encounter, he himself was wounded by the lioness. Because Orlando had saved his life, Oliver repented and the two brothers were joyfully reunited.

His wound having bled profusely, Orlando was too weak to visit Ganymede, and he sent Oliver instead with a bloody handkerchief as proof of his wounded condition. When Ganymede saw the handkerchief, the supposed shepherd promptly fainted. The disguised Celia was so impressed by Oliver's concern for his brother that she fell in love with him, and they made plans to be married on the following day. Orlando was overwhelmed by this news and a little envious, but when Ganymede came to call upon Orlando, the young shepherd promised to produce the lady Rosalind the next day. Meanwhile Phebe came to renew her ardent declaration of love for Ganymede, who promised on the morrow to unravel the love tangle of everyone.

Duke Frederick, enraged at the flight of his daughter, Celia, had set out at the head of an expedition to capture his elder brother and put him and all his followers to death. On the outskirts of the Forest of Arden he met an old hermit who turned Frederick's head from his evil design. On the day following, as Ganymede had promised, with the banished duke and his followers as guests, Rosalind appeared as herself and explained how she and Celia had posed as the shepherd Ganymede and his sister Aliena. Four marriages took place that day with great rejoicing between Orlando and Rosalind, Oliver and Celia, Silvius and Phebe, and Touchstone and Audrey. Frederick had been so completely converted by the hermit that he resolved to take religious orders and straightway dispatched a messenger to the Forest of Arden to restore his brother's lands and those of all his followers.

Critical Evaluation

William Shakespeare took most of the plot of *As You Like It* from a popular novel of the period, Thomas Lodge's *Rosalynde* (1590). What he added was dramatic characterization and wit. The play, a splendid comedy on love and life, is compounded of many elements, the whole set to some of Shakespeare's loveliest poetry. *As You Like It* more than fulfills the promise of its title. Its characters are, for the most part, wonderfully enamored of love, one another, and themselves. The play has freshness and vitality and, although adapted from an older story full of artifice, suggests a world of spontaneity and life.

As You Like It is often called a pastoral comedy because it employs the conventions of pastoral literature. Beginning in the third century B.C.E. and popular in the late sixteenth century, pastoral literature enabled poets, novelists, and dramatists to contrast the everyday world's fears, anxieties, disloyalties, uncertainties, and tensions with the imagined, mythical world where peace, longevity, contentment, and fulfillment reigned. Each age develops its own manner of describing lost happiness, far removed from the normal toil of human existence; the pastoral was the dominant vision in the late sixteenth century.

In the pastoral, the mythic, lost world is set in a simple, rural environment, which then becomes the image of all things desirable to honest people. *As You Like It* is typical of this convention and contains two contrasting worlds: the world of the court and the rural world—in this case the Forest of Arden. The court is inhabited by corrupt men such as Duke Frederick and Oliver. It is not significant that the gentle banished duke, Orlando, Rosalind, and Celia also once resided there. Rather, as the play develops, the court is the natural home of the wicked and ambitious. The audience is not shown the degeneration of Duke Frederick and Oliver; they are naturally wicked, and the court is their proper milieu.

The elder duke, Orlando, Rosalind, and Celia, on the other hand, are naturally good and the forest their natural milieu. If the court represents elaborate artifice, ambition, avarice, cruelty, and deception, the forest represents openness, tolerance, simplicity, and freedom. Rather than developing complex characters such as Hamlet, who like most humans has good and bad characteristics, pastorals apportion good and bad traits to separate characters, an allocation that imposes a necessary artifice upon the play and colors all actions, from falling in love to hating or helping a brother. A play such as *As You Like It* does not present natural behavior. On the other hand, by his adroit use of the conventions and artifice, Shakespeare achieved a remarkable exploration of love and its attendant values.

In the opening scene, Orlando, who has been denied an education and kept like an animal by his brother, is seen to be naturally good and decent. Talking to his brother Oliver, Orlando says, "You have train'd me like a peasant, obscuring and hiding from me all gentleman-like qualities. The spirit of my father grows strong in me, and I will no longer endure it: therefore allow me such exercises as may become a gentleman. . . ." Oliver, as naturally wicked as Orlando is naturally decent, says, "for my soul—yet I know not why—hates nothing more than he." Logic has no necessary place in this world. Love, however, does.

Love is a natural part of the pastoral world. Practically at first glance, Rosalind and Orlando are in love. Shakespeare's magic in *As You Like It* is to take the contrived love that is the expected part of the pastoral convention, and make of it a deeply felt experience that the audience can understand. Shakespeare manages this not only through the extraordinary beauty of his language but also through the structure of his play.

As You Like It is full of parallel actions. Orlando and Rosalind meet and immediately fall in love. Silvius and Phebe are in love. Touchstone meets Audrey in the forest, and they fall in love. At the end of the play Celia meets the reformed Oliver, and they fall in love just as quickly as Rosalind and Orlando had at the beginning of the play. The love match at the play's end nicely sets off the love match at the beginning.

Each love pairing serves a particular purpose. The focus of the play is primarily upon the Rosalind-Orlando match. Rosalind is the more interesting of the pair, for while she recognizes the silliness of the lover's ardor, she is as much a victim as

Henry Ainley (left) appears as the exiled duke with Laurence Olivier as Orlando in the 1936 British film version of As You Like It, *one of the earliest film adaptations of Shakespeare's plays.* (Courtesy of The Museum of Modern Art, Film Stills Archive)

those she scorns. In Act IV, while in boy's disguise, she pretends to Orlando that his Rosalind will not have him. He says, "Then . . . I die." Her response pokes fun at the expiring love: "No, faith, die by attorney. The poor world is almost six thousand years old, and in all this time there was not any man died in his own person, videlicet, in a love-cause. . . . Men have died from time to time and worms have eaten them, but not for love." She can toy with Orlando in her disguise as Ganymede, yet she is completely dominated by her strong passion, which is a part of the love experience. Rosalind's and Orlando's passion, however, is more refined than the passion the others experience.

Touchstone, in his quest for Audrey, exemplifies the earthier side of love. He at first wants to marry her out of church so that he can, once he tires of her, claim their marriage was invalid. The kind of love he represents is physical passion. The Phebe-Silvius pairing shows yet another face of love, that of the typical pastoral lover hopelessly in love with a fickle mistress. He sighs on his pillow and breaks off from company, forlornly calling out his mistress' name. Touchstone's and Silvius' kinds of love are extreme versions of qualities in Rosalind's love. In the comedies Shakespeare often used this device of apportioning diverse characteristics to multiple characters rather than building one complete character. Without Touchstone, love in the play might have been too sentimental to take seriously. Without Silvius, it might have been too crude. With both, love as exemplified by Rosalind and Orlando becomes a precious balance of substance and nonsense, spirituality and silliness.

Curious things happen in *As You Like It*. Good men leave the honorable forest to return to the wicked court. Wicked men who enter the forest are converted in their ways. At the end of the play, Oliver, who came to the Forest of Arden to hunt down his brother Orlando, gives his estate to Orlando and marries Celia, vowing to remain in the forest and live and die a shepherd. Duke Frederick came to the Forest of Arden in order to kill his brother. Meeting "an old religious man" in the forest, Duke Frederick "was converted/ Both from his enterprise and from the world." He too gives up his estate and his crown to his brother. The forest, the pastoral world, has the power to convert.

Why, then, do the elder duke, Orlando, and Rosalind elect to return to the court, home of wickedness? They do so because *As You Like It* is ultimately not a fairy tale but an expression of humanly felt experiences. The forest is a cleansing and regenerative experience, a place to which to retire to renew simplicity, honesty, and virtue. It is not, however, a permanent retreat. Good men stained by labor and trouble in their everyday world in the end must participate in that world. If they retreat to the pastoral world to renew themselves, they must return in the end to the community to take on the responsibilities all must face.

"Critical Evaluation" by Brian L. Mark

For Further Study

Halio, Jay L., ed. *Twentieth Century Interpretations of "As You Like It."* Englewood Cliffs, N.J.: Prentice-Hall, 1968. Includes essays by Helen Gardner, John Russell Brown, Marco Mincoff (on Lodge's *Rosalynde* as the source), and the editor (on time and timelessness in Arden). Also includes an introduction and bibliography.

Jenkins, Harold. *"As You Like It." Shakespeare Survey* 8 (1955): 40-51. Mainly concerned with the structure of the play, this essay notes the dearth of big theatrical scenes and causally linked events, which are replaced by a more complex design that emphasizes comic juxtapositions.

Knowles, Richard. "Myth and Type in *As You Like It*." *English Literary History* 33 (1966): 1-22. Discusses the many mythical allusions in *As You Like It* that make the literal action reverberate beyond itself. Hercules is the dominant mythological figure, whom by analogy Orlando resembles. Biblical overtones are also discussed.

Leggatt, Alexander. *Shakespeare's Comedy of Love*. London: Methuen, 1974. Leggatt shows how the forest scenes provide an imaginative freedom to explore ideas and play roles. Partisan laughter against any one character in the play is discouraged, for the audience is reminded of the partiality of any single perspective.

Young, David. *The Heart's Forest: A Study of Shakespeare's Pastoral Plays*. New Haven, Conn.: Yale University Press, 1972. Young reviews the pastoral tradition and its salient characteristics, so important in this play, and shows how Shakespeare explored and exploited the medium of pastoral drama in *As You Like It* and other plays, including *The Winter's Tale* (c. 1610-1611) and *The Tempest* (1611). A deliberate self-consciousness, he says, pervades *As You Like It*, whose atmosphere of artifice and hypothesis is fostered by extensive use of "if," and whose major theme is self-knowledge.

The Comedy of Errors

Type of plot: Comedy
Time of plot: First century B.C.E.
Locale: Greece
First performed: c. 1592-1594; first published, 1623

Principal characters

SOLINUS, Duke of Ephesus
AEGEON, a merchant of Syracuse
ANTIPHOLUS OF EPHESUS and
ANTIPHOLUS OF SYRACUSE, twin brothers, sons of Aegeon and Aemilia
DROMIO OF EPHESUS and
DROMIO OF SYRACUSE, twin brothers, attendants of above twins
AEMILIA, Aegeon's wife
ADRIANA, wife to Antipholus of Ephesus
LUCIANA, Adriana's sister
A COURTESAN

The Story

According to the laws of the lands of Ephesus and Syracuse, it was forbidden for a native of one land to journey to the other; the penalty for the crime was execution or the ransom of a thousand marks. Aegeon, a merchant of Syracuse who had recently traveled to Ephesus, was to be put to death because he could not raise the thousand marks. When Solinus, Duke of Ephesus, heard Aegeon's story, he gave the merchant one more day to raise the money.

It was a sad and strange tale Aegeon told. He had, many years earlier, journeyed to Epidamnum. Shortly after his wife joined him there she was delivered of identical twin boys. Strangely enough, at the same time and in the same house, another woman also bore identical twin boys. Because that woman and her husband were so poor that they could not provide for their children, they gave them to Aegeon and his wife Aemilia, to be attendants to their two sons. On the way home to Syracuse, Aegeon and his family were shipwrecked. Aemilia and the two children with her were rescued by one ship, Aegeon and the other two by a different ship, and Aegeon did not see his wife and those two children again. When he reached eighteen years of age, Antipholus, the son reared by his father in Syracuse, grew anxious to find his brother, so he and his attendant set out to find their twins. Aegeon had come to Ephesus to seek them.

Unknown to Aegeon, Antipholus and his attendant, Dromio, had just arrived in

Ephesus. There a merchant of the city warned them to say that they came from somewhere other than Syracuse, lest they suffer the penalty already meted out to Aegeon. Antipholus, having sent Dromio to find lodging for them, was utterly bewildered when the servant returned and said that Antipholus' wife waited dinner for him. What had happened was that the Dromio who returned to Antipholus was Dromio of Ephesus, servant and attendant to Antipholus of Ephesus. Antipholus of Syracuse had given his Dromio money to pay for lodging, and when he heard a tale of a wife about whom he knew nothing he thought his servant had tricked him and asked for the return of the money. Dromio of Ephesus had been given no money, however, and when he professed no knowledge of the sum Antipholus of Syracuse beat him soundly for dishonesty. Antipholus of Syracuse later heard that his money had been delivered to the inn.

A short time later, the wife and sister-in-law of Antipholus of Ephesus met Antipholus of Syracuse and, after berating him for refusing to come home to dinner, accused him of unfaithfulness with another woman. Not understanding a word of what Adriana said, Antipholus of Syracuse went to dinner in her home, where Dromio was assigned by her to guard the gate and allow no one to enter. Thus it was that Antipholus of Ephesus arrived at his home with his Dromio and was refused admittance. So incensed was he that he left his house and went to an inn. There he dined with a courtesan and gave her the gifts he had intended for his wife.

In the meantime, Antipholus of Syracuse, though almost believing that he must be the husband of Adriana, fell in love with her sister Luciana. When he told her of his love, she called him an unfaithful husband and begged him to remain true to his wife. Dromio of Syracuse was pursued by a kitchen maid whom he abhorred but who mistook him for the Dromio of Ephesus who loved her.

Even the townspeople and merchants were bewildered. A goldsmith delivered to Antipholus of Syracuse a chain meant for Antipholus of Ephesus and then tried to collect from the latter, who in turn stated that he had received no chain and accused the merchant of trying to rob him.

Antipholus and Dromio of Syracuse decided to leave the seemingly mad town as soon as possible, and the servant was sent to book passage on the first ship leaving the city. Dromio of Syracuse brought back the news of the sailing to Antipholus of Ephesus, who by that time had been arrested for refusing to pay the merchant for the chain he had not received. Antipholus of Ephesus, believing the servant to be his own, sent Dromio of Syracuse to his house to get money for his bail. Before Dromio of Syracuse returned with the money, however, Dromio of Ephesus came to Antipholus of Ephesus, naturally without the desired money. Meanwhile Dromio of Syracuse took the money to Antipholus of Syracuse, who had not sent for money and could not understand what his servant was talking about. To make matters worse, the courtesan with whom Antipholus of Ephesus had dined had given him a ring. Now she approached the other Antipholus and demanded the ring. Knowing nothing about the ring, he angrily dismissed the woman, who decided to go to his house and tell his wife of his betrayal.

On his way to jail for the debt he did not owe, Antipholus of Ephesus met his wife. Wild with rage, he accused her of locking him out of his own house and of refusing him his own money for bail. She was so frightened that she asked the police first to make sure that he was securely bound and then to imprison him in their home so that she could care for him.

"There is something in the wind"

The Comedy of Errors, Act III, scene i, line 69

This is one of Shakespeare's most bizarre and incredible comedies. Aegeon, an old merchant from Syracuse, and his wife Aemilia had twin sons, both named Antipholus and provided with twin slaves, both named Dromio. Because of a shipwreck, the members are separated, Aegeon taking with him to Syracuse a son (Antipholus of Syracuse) and one Dromio, Aemilia taking with her to Ephesus one Antipholus (Antipholus of Ephesus) and one Dromio. The comedy of errors results when the Syracusan son is summoned home by Dromio of Ephesus. He is assumed by his brother's wife to be her husband. When the real husband reaches home, he is denied admittance because presumably he is already inside. After repeatedly explaining his identity and repeatedly being denied admittance, Antipholus of Ephesus observes that there is something wrong:

> *Antipholus of Ephesus.* There is something in the wind, that we cannot get in.
> *Dromio of Ephesus.* You would say so master, if your garments were thin.

At the same time Antipholus and Dromio of Syracuse were making their way toward the ship that would carry them away from this mad city. Antipholus was wearing the gold chain. The merchant, meeting them, demanded that Antipholus be arrested. To escape, Antipholus of Syracuse and his Dromio fled into an abbey. To the same abbey came Aegeon, the duke, and the executioners, for Aegeon had not raised the money for his ransom. Adriana and Luciana also appeared, demanding the release to them of Adriana's husband and his servant. Adriana, seeing the two men take refuge in the convent, thought they were Antipholus and Dromio of Ephesus. At that instant a servant ran in to tell Adriana that her husband and Dromio had escaped from the house and were even now on the way to the abbey. Adriana did not believe the servant, for she herself had seen her husband and Dromio enter the abbey. Then Antipholus and Dromio of Ephesus appeared before the abbey. Aegeon thought he recognized the son and servant he had been seeking, but they denied any knowledge of him. The confusion increased until the abbess brought from the convent Antipholus and Dromio of Syracuse, who instantly recognized Aegeon. Then all the mysteries were solved. Adriana was reunited with her husband, Antipholus of Ephesus, and his Dromio had the kitchen maid once more. Antipholus of Syracuse was free to make love to Luciana, and his Dromio too was freed. Still more surprising, the abbess turned out to be Aegeon's wife, the mother of the Antipholus twins. So the happy family was together again. Lastly,

Antipholus of Ephesus paid his father's ransom and brought to an end all the errors of that unhappy day.

Critical Evaluation

William Shakespeare was not always the master playwright that he became in his later life. When he first began writing plays, he did not have the mastery of plot, character, concept, and language for which he was to be universally praised. In 1592, he was a young playwright with a historical trilogy and a classical tragedy to his credit; he was just beginning to explore and perfect his craft. *The Comedy of Errors* is an early experiment with comedy, and his enthusiasm for the experiment is clear in his writing.

Shakespeare followed the example of most playwrights of the Elizabethan era by adapting other plays and sources to make his dramas. This in no way detracts from his genius because what he adapted he made distinctively his own.

Most of *The Comedy of Errors* derives from *Menaechmi* (*The Twins Menaechmi*), by the classical Roman playwright Plautus, who lived from c. 254 B.C.E. to 184 B.C.E. Act III, scene i of the play originates from another work by Plautus, *Amphitruo* (*Amphitryon*). Both of these plays concern mistaken identity, which Shakespeare adapted for the crux of his plot as well. Just as Shakespeare adapted Plautus, Plautus apparently drew from an unknown Greek playwright. It was said of Plautus that his special genius was for turning a Greek original into a typically Roman play with typically Roman characters. Similarly, Shakespeare, like Plautus, set the play in ancient Ephesus, and used some of Plautus' situations, but Shakespeare's characters are typically and recognizably of Shakespeare's Elizabethan age.

Shakespeare changed the framework of the plot, making it much more romantic and accessible to popular tastes. In Shakespeare's version, the twins' father, Aegeon, is introduced in the midst of his search for his wife and other son, separated from him by shipwreck. This story line, demonstrating husbandly and paternal devotion, was appealing to the audience. Shakespeare then created the servant twins (Dromios) to add to the fun of the mistaken identity plot. In so doing he doubled the amount of action. He also introduced Luciana, sister of the wife of Antipholus of Ephesus, and thus provided a love interest for Antipholus of Syracuse. Out of the Plautine cast of nine, Shakespeare retained six of the original characters and developed many more of his own.

In addition, Shakespeare changed the characters to fit the tastes of his audience. Plautus' twins are extremely one-dimensional characters. Both are self-centered, callous young men whose only interest was in the gratification of their animal appetites. It is difficult to feel any sympathy or empathy for them. In Shakespeare's play, however, the twins are simply callow youths whose characters are not yet completely formed. They are not amoral, as are Plautus' twins. They are simply naïve.

The relationship between Shakespeare's Antipholus of Ephesus and his wife was much more appealing to Elizabethan audiences than that relationship as depicted by Plautus would have been. Shakespeare's Antipholus does not steal his wife's jewelry and gowns to give to a courtesan. In fact, he dines with the courtesan and gives her his wife's presents only out of revenge at being shut out of his house and being given the impression that his wife was entertaining another man. There is a moral dimension to Shakespeare's play that is lacking in Plautus'.

Like Plautus', Shakespeare's play is a farce, filled with fast-paced action and dialogue, peopled with eccentric characters, and developed by improbable, exaggerated situations. It was the most elementary of the comic arts—the comedy of situation, rather than the comedy of character or theme. Shakespeare's later comedies would develop the more difficult styles.

"We'll pluck a crow together"

The Comedy of Errors, Act III, scene i, line 83

In the street in front of his house in Ephesus, Antipholus loudly demands admittance for himself, his friends Angelo and Balthazar, and his servant Dromio. Antipholus does not know that his shipwrecked twin brother, Antipholus of Syracuse, accompanied by his servant, Dromio of Syracuse (twin of Dromio of Ephesus), has come to Ephesus to search for his long-lost brother, and that Adriana, his wife, has discovered her husband's twin at an inn and has angrily brought him home to dinner, assuming him to be her husband. In a comical dialogue filled with double meanings, Antipholus of Ephesus calls for a crowbar to gain admittance to his own home.

> *Dromio of Ephesus.* . . . I pray thee let me in.
> *Antipholus of Ephesus.* Well, I'll break in. Go borrow me a crow.
> *Dromio of Ephesus.* A crow without feather, master, mean you so?
>   For a fish without a fin, there's a fowl without a feather.
>   If a crow help us in sirrah, we'll pluck a crow together.
> *Antipholus of Ephesus.* Go get thee gone; fetch me an iron crow.

Even in this elementary comedy, Shakespeare shows talent enough to draw some basic characterization and suggest polarities of characters. The younger twin from Syracuse is, stereotypically, more timid than his arrogant older brother. Luciana is gentler and shier than her sister. The eccentrics, the courtesan and Doctor Pinch, are each separately and strikingly developed.

Shakespeare's experiments with language and poetry betray his apprenticeship. There is a noticeable simplicity and repetition of diction. The play's accomplishment and fluency augur what the mature Shakespeare would later produce. The poetic passages of wooing that he created for the Syracuse twin and Luciana anticipate *Romeo and Juliet* (1594-1595). Dromio of Ephesus' punning description of his twin's wife, the slattern Nell, in geographic terms, is a masterpiece of comic overstatement, as is the bawdy, double entendre that enriches the scene in which Ephesus is denied access to his home and wife. All of these touches are strokes of genius and wit.

Shakespeare's later romantic comedies are foreshadowed by the dignified characters of Aegeon and Aemilia: Their lifelong devotion and eventual reunion elevate the farce to a higher level of comedy. Their plot resolution not only incorporates the plot and subplots but also unites all the characters. This plot development anticipates the festive communion that is the goal of all of Shakespeare's later romantic comedies.

Shakespeare probably set out to write the perfect Roman-style play. It observes two of Aristotle's unities. It is set in one locale, and it takes place in the span of a day's time. Shakespeare added subplots, however, to complement and complicate the main plot. Plautus would never have broken the third unity. Shakespeare also handles his exposition tritely (Solinus asks Aegeon what brought him to Ephesus), and as a result, the first act moves slowly. Once the playwright moves into the plot complications of Act II, the action and humor never slow until the conclusion.

The characters are shallowly developed, the plot is improbable, and the comedy is developed primarily through situation, but *The Comedy of Errors* has proved to be a play that delights audiences. Shakespeare wrote more thought-provoking plays than this one, plays that were more sensitive and profound, and plays peopled with better-developed characters, but *The Comedy of Errors* remains a fun romp, written in excellent pentameter.

"Critical Evaluation" by H. Alan Pickrell

For Further Study

Baldwin, Thomas Whitfield. *On the Compositional Genetics of "The Comedy of Errors."* Champaign: University of Illinois Press, 1965. Likens Shakespeare to the Dromios, awed by their change from the rural to the urban.

Berry, Ralph. *Shakespeare and the Awareness of the Audience.* New York: St. Martin's Press, 1985. Discusses the "dark underside" of the play, which enriches and compliments the comedy. Argues that Aegeon may be more important to the plot structure than he seems to be.

Colie, Rosalie L. *Shakespeare's Living Art.* Princeton, N.J.: Princeton University Press, 1974. Colie sees the plays as experiments with the craft of writing plays. Discusses Shakespeare's improving on Plautus.

Dorsch, T. S., ed. *The Comedy of Errors.* Cambridge: Cambridge University Press, 1988. This edition features a comprehensive introductory essay, with a brief look at history, sources, characters, and plot.

Tillyard, E. M. W. *Shakespeare's Early Comedies.* New York: Barnes & Noble Books, 1965. One of the most noted of Shakespeare's commentators points out that Shakespeare probably did not read the Roman original for the play; the commentator focuses on a translated manuscript.

Coriolanus

Type of plot: Tragedy
Time of plot: Third century
Locale: Rome, Corioles, and Antium
First performed: c. 1607-1608; first published, 1623

Principal characters

CAIUS MARTIUS CORIOLANUS, a noble Roman
TITUS LARTIUS and
COMINIUS, generals against the Volscians
MENENIUS AGRIPPA, a friend of Coriolanus
TULLUS AUFIDIUS, a general of the Volscians
SICINIUS VELUTUS and
JUNIUS BRUTUS, tribunes of the people
VOLUMNIA, the mother of Coriolanus
VIRGILIA, the wife of Coriolanus

The Story

Caius Martius, a brilliant soldier, was attempting to subdue a mob in Rome when he was summoned to lead his troops against the Volscians from Corioles. The Volscians were headed by Tullus Aufidius, also a great soldier and perennial foe of Martius. The hatred the two leaders had for each other fired their military ambitions. Martius' daring as a warrior, known by all since he was sixteen, led him to pursue the enemy inside the very gates of Corioles. Locked inside the city, he and his troops fought so valiantly that they overcame the Volscians. Twice wounded, the victorious general was garlanded and hailed as Caius Martius Coriolanus.

On his return to Rome, Coriolanus was further proclaimed by patricians, consuls, and senators, and he was recommended for the office of consul, an appointment wholeheartedly approved by the nobles. Because the citizens too had to vote on his appointment, Coriolanus, accompanied by Menenius Agrippa, went to Sicinius and Brutus, the plebeian tribunes, to seek their approval.

The people had long held only contempt for Coriolanus because of his arrogance and inhumane attitude toward all commoners. Although coached and prompted by Menenius to make his appeal as a wound-scarred soldier of many wars, Coriolanus could not bring himself to solicit the citizens' support but instead demanded it. He was successful in this with individuals he approached at random on the streets, but Brutus and Sicinius, who represented the common people, were not willing to endorse the elevation of Coriolanus to office. They voiced the opinions of many citizens when they accused Coriolanus of insolence and of abuses such as denying the people food from the public storehouses. Urging those citizens who had voted for him to rescind their votes, Brutus and Sicinius pointed out that his military prowess was not to be denied but that this very attribute would result in further suppression and misery for the people. Coriolanus' ambitions, they predicted, would lead to his complete domination of the government and to the destruction of their democracy.

Menenius, Cominius, and the senators repeatedly pleaded with Coriolanus to approach the tribunes civilly, and Volumnia admonished him that if he wanted to realize his political ambitions he must follow their advice. Appealing to his responsibility as a Roman, Volumnia pointed out that service to one's country was not shown on the battlefield alone and that Coriolanus must use certain strategies and tactics for victory in peace as well as in war.

Coriolanus misconstrued his mother's suggestions. She had taught him arrogance, nurtured his desires in military matters, and boasted of his strength and of her part in developing his dominating personality. Coriolanus now inferred that his mother in her older years was asking for submissiveness and compliance. Although he promised Volumnia that he would deal kindly with the people, it was impossible for him to relent, even when his wife, Virgilia, who had never condoned his soldiership, lent her pleas to those of the group and appealed to his vanity as a capable political leader and to his responsibility as a father and husband.

Coriolanus' persistence in deriding and mocking the citizens led to an uprising against him. Drawing his sword, he would have stood alone against the mob, but Menenius and Cominius, fearing that the demonstration might result in an overthrow of the government, prevailed upon him to withdraw to his house before the crowd assembled. Coriolanus misinterpreted the requests of his friends and family that he yield to the common people, and he displayed such arrogance that he was banished from Rome. Tullus Aufidius, learning of these events, prepared his armies to take advantage of the civil unrest in Rome.

Coriolanus, in disguise to protect himself against those who wanted to avenge the deaths of the many he had killed, went to Antium to offer his services to Aufidius against Rome. When Coriolanus removed his disguise, Aufidius, who knew the Roman's ability as a military leader, willingly accepted his offer to aid in the Volscian campaign. Aufidius divided his army in order that he and Coriolanus each could lead a unit, thereby broadening the scope of his efforts against the Romans. In this plan, Aufidius saw the possibility of avenging Coriolanus' earlier victories over him; once they had taken Rome, Aufidius thought, the Romans' hatred for Coriolanus would make possible his dominance over the arrogant patrician.

The Romans heard with dismay of Coriolanus' affiliation with Aufidius; their only hope, some thought, was to appeal to Coriolanus to spare the city. Although Menenius and Cominius blamed the tribunes for Coriolanus' banishment, they went as messengers to the great general in his camp outside the gates of Rome. They were unsuccessful, and Cominius returned to inform the citizens that in spite of old friendships, Coriolanus would not be swayed in his intentions to annihilate the city. Cominius reported that Coriolanus refused to take the time to find the few grains who were his friends among the chaff he intended to burn.

Menenius, sent to appeal again to Coriolanus, met with the same failure. Coriolanus maintained that his ears were stronger against the pleas than the city gates were against his might. Calling the attention of Aufidius to his firm stand against the Romans, he asked him to report his conduct to the Volscian lords. Aufidius promised to do so and praised the general for his stalwartness. While Coriolanus vowed not to hear the pleas of any other Romans, he was interrupted by women's voices calling his name. The petitioners were Volumnia, Virgilia, and young Martius, his son. Telling them that he would not be moved, he again urged Aufidius to observe his unyielding spirit. Then Volumnia spoke, saying that their requests for leniency and mercy were in vain, since he had already proclaimed against kindliness, and that they would therefore not appeal to him. He had also made it impossible for them to appeal to the gods: They could not pray for victory for Rome because such supplication would be against him, and they could not pray for his success in the campaign because that would be to betray their country. Volumnia proclaimed that she did not seek advantage for either the Romans or the

---

"Like an eagle in a dovecote"

Coriolanus, Act V, scene vi, line 115

Caius Martius, Roman general, leads his forces against the Volscians and defeats them near Corioles, their capital. He is given the surname Coriolanus by his troops and returns home in triumph. Martius, now Coriolanus, despises the Roman rabble, and they hate him. When the Senate rewards him by nominating him as consul, he reluctantly exhibits himself in the Forum, shows his wounds, and solicits votes as tradition demands. The people give him their support but, as he is preparing to leave, the fickle public, led by two dissident tribunes, turns on him, fearful he will take away their liberties. Incapable of tact, flattery, or compromise, Coriolanus is banished. Bitterly, he joins his old enemies; and their leader, Aufidius, amazed at Rome's ingratitude, accepts him as his equal. They march on Rome, sweeping all in their way, but Aufidius resents Coriolanus' popularity with the Volscians and swears vengeance. Coriolanus is finally dissuaded from sacking Rome by his mother and wife, who intercede for the city, and he agrees to make peace between the two nations. Now, at Corioles, Aufidius accuses Coriolanus of treason and of making a disgraceful peace. He is inciting the Volscians against Coriolanus, and the latter, incapable of cajolery, flares out in anger and pride, referring to his initial victory over them, and seems to invite death.

> *Coriolanus.* Cut me to pieces Volsces; men and lads,
>   Stain all your edges on me. Boy! False hound!
>   If you have writ your annals true, 'tis there,
>   That like an eagle in a dovecote I
>   Fluttered your Volscians in Corioles.
>   Alone I did it, boy!

Volscians but asked only for reconciliation. She predicted that Coriolanus would be a hero to both sides if he could arrange an honorable peace between them.

Finally moved by his mother's reasoning, Coriolanus announced to Aufidius that he would frame a peace agreeable to the two forces. Aufidius declared that he too had been moved by Volumnia's solemn pleas and wise words. Volumnia, Virgilia, and young Martius returned to Rome, there to be welcomed for the success of their intercession with Coriolanus. Aufidius withdrew to Antium to await the return of Coriolanus and their meeting with the Roman ambassadors, but as he reviewed the situation, he realized that peace would nullify his plan for revenge against Coriolanus. Moreover, knowing of the favorable regard the Volscians had for Coriolanus, he felt he had to remove the man who had been his conqueror in war and who might become his subduer in peace. At a meeting of the Volscian lords, Aufidius announced that Coriolanus had betrayed the Volscians by depriving them of victory. In the ensuing confusion, he stabbed Coriolanus to death. Regretting his deed, he then eulogized Coriolanus and said that he would live forever in men's memories. One of the Volscian lords pronounced Coriolanus the most noble corpse that was ever followed to the grave.

Critical Evaluation

Coriolanus, one of Shakespeare's three "Roman plays," first appeared in 1607 or 1608. It marked a vision quite distinct from and unlike the earlier great tragedies *Hamlet* (1600-1601), *King Lear* (1605-1606), and *Macbeth* (1606), which retain their appeal as much for their differences as for their likenesses to later ages. *Coriolanus*, on the other hand, remains modern in a number of significant ways. For one thing, there are no noble kings in the quasi-democratic society being portrayed, no amusing comic interludes with clowns and jesters that epitomize the jolly side of English sensibility, no fundamentally decent great men marred only by one tragic flaw, no declamatory soliloquies, no uplifting philosophical or poetic musings, no reassurances of a better future after the tragic hero's downfall. Instead, the landscape not only reflects the pessimism of Jacobean London but also distressingly resembles that of the twentieth century. The play presents a proudly democratic and secular society marred by the corrosive effects of established wealth in tandem with rigid social class divisions, a populace easily distracted by concerns of the moment and appeals to narrow self-interest (which allow rabble-rousers and charlatans to use their false rhetoric to great effect), a guns-or-butter debate that pits military preparedness against social welfare, and a fundamental question about the role of the exceptional individual in a supposedly egalitarian society. These remained the concerns of later ages as well, and they give *Coriolanus* a political and social resonance with twentieth century audiences that is not the case in those great Shakespearean tragedies that focus more exclusively on questions of individual morality.

Three related themes have particular resonance. In a society that at least tips its hat toward egalitarian ideals, the character of Coriolanus is a Shakespearean version of a figure that the philosopher Friedrich Nietzsche would later call the *Übermensch*, or superman. Known as the "overreacher" to the Elizabethans, this

Derrick Lee Weeden as the triumphant Coriolanus in a 1996 production of Coriolanus.
(Andrée Lanthier, courtesy of the Oregon Shakespeare Festival by permission of the Actors'
Equity Association)

was a figure the Renaissance regarded with fear and fascination both in literature—as in Christopher Marlowe's characters Doctor Faustus and Tamburlaine and
in John Milton's Satan—and in real life, as in such figures as Sir Francis Drake and
Sir Walter Raleigh. These Renaissance overreachers took advantage of the new
freedoms of their liberated age to accomplish wonders but in doing so shook the
foundations of their society, which, though initially valuing what they represented,
usually ended by destroying them. A Macbeth, Lear, or Richard III might temporarily threaten the state as a result of personal ambition, foolishness, or corruption,
but these figures were not, like Coriolanus, a barely contained force whom those
around him tolerated for his usefulness but never ceased to regard nervously.
(Othello comes closest to this description, but he is a basically good man led astray
by personal weakness.) The dilemma William Shakespeare develops in *Coriolanus*
anticipates the historical situations of individuals with a will to dominate, generals
who accomplish what society wanted and who then turn on their own people with
ferocity. Such strong personalities are needed in crisis but dangerous any other
time, and from Napoleon to Adolf Hitler, Joseph Stalin to Mao Zedong, society has
been terrorized by such figures. Whether we agree with those critics who regard
Coriolanus as a play about politics or see it, as Algernon Charles Swinburne did,
as a "drama of individuality" focused on an outsized hero, the problem is timeless.

As perhaps nowhere else in his works, Shakespeare in *Coriolanus* ties the
character of his hero to his upbringing. This is in contrast to the way he explores
the forces that shape Prince Hal in the *Henry IV* (1597-1598) and *Henry V*
(1598-1599) series, where it is shown how little power they had over the prince.
Here, Shakespeare looks at Coriolanus' nature as peculiarly male rather than as
simply natural for a great warrior, and in the scenes with his mother, Volumnia, and
his wife, Virgilia, he suggests the power of upbringing. Volumnia, a stalwart Roman
matron, is fiercely masculine in her martial virtues and has proudly raised Coriolanus in this model of manhood. Virgilia, more conventionally feminine, deplores
her husband's violent ways and their influence on their son. Few other Shakespearean heroes have their natures so linked to environment, and nowhere else, save in
the frothy problems of the comedies, is the gender difference confronted so
directly. As with the superman type, the male ego in its purest untamed form has
practical uses for guarding the city, but Shakespeare asks what is to be done with
it during peacetime. The easy answer, and the one the Romans first choose, is exile,
but this backfires when Coriolanus thereupon embraces the worst enemy of those
who had rejected him. Critic John Holloway called Coriolanus a typical "scapegoat
figure," a disturbing influence in the society to be symbolically driven out to
restore peace. Yet such figures cannot easily be pushed into the desert permanently,
as were biblical scapegoats. Those like Coriolanus must be accepted as part of
society itself, to be endured or dealt with.

Another concern in the play that had surfaced during Shakespeare's Renaissance and continues to be relevant is that of mob psychology. It would be several
generations before the English Civil War and almost two hundred years before the
terrors of the French Revolution, but fear of mob rule was endemic in Britain since
the earliest days of Elizabeth I's rule, during Shakespeare's childhood. This fear

runs through *Coriolanus*, balancing the equally abhorrent specter of rule by an undisciplined general teetering on the edge of manic fury. The play offers no solution to this Hobson's choice between governance by the whim of the "many-headed multitude" and that by aristocratic contempt for the concerns of the commonality, but it establishes the problem. The world of *Coriolanus* exemplifies the dilemma between distrust of the failed values of a self-serving aristocracy and distrust in the alternative, the passions of a "democratic" mob, and it explores that problem in connection with ambition, social stratification, and gender roles. Shakespeare's entire tragic canon illuminates human nature as no other dramatist's has done, but in *Coriolanus* he also provides insight into the problems of an age that was just beginning.

"Critical Evaluation" by Gina and Andrew Macdonald

For Further Study

Barton, Anne. "*Julius Caesar* and *Coriolanus*: Shakespeare's Roman War of Words." In *Shakespeare's Craft: Eight Lectures*, edited by Philip H. Highfill, Jr. Carbondale: Southern Illinois University Press, 1982. Barton points out that in a world dependent on verbal rhetorical persuasion, Coriolanus' distrust of language alienates and isolates him, as does his personal use of language without regard to audience response.

Crowley, Richard C. "*Coriolanus* and the Epic Genre." In *Shakespeare's Late Plays: Essays in Honor of Charles Crow*, edited by Richard Tobias and Paul Zolbrod. Athens: Ohio University Press, 1974. Argues that *Coriolanus* merges tragedy and epic and has at its heart the conflict between mercy and honor.

McAlindon, T. "*Coriolanus*: An Essentialist Tragedy." *Review of English Studies* 44 (November, 1993): 502-520. Rather than as a metaphor for England's problems, McAlindon regards *Coriolanus* as a political tragedy of class conflict and manipulation of power in a realistic, historically specific society.

McKenzie, Stanley D. "'Unshout the Noise That Banish'd Marcius': Structural Paradox and Dissembling in *Coriolanus*." *Shakespeare Studies: An Annual Gathering of Research, Criticism, and Reviews* 18 (1986): 189-204. Argues that in a world of chaotic reversals, betrayals, and paradoxes where only the adaptable survive, Coriolanus' unchanging consistency dooms him.

Miller, Shannon. "Topicality and Subversion in William Shakespeare's *Coriolanus*." *Studies in English Literature, 1500-1900* 32, no. 2 (Spring, 1992): 287-310. Discusses *Coriolanus'* intricate structure of topical references and draws parallels with the career of James I, early seventeenth century issues of authority and monarchy, and other conflicts and contradictions of Shakespeare's age.

Rackin, Phyllis. "*Coriolanus*: Shakespeare's Anatomy of 'Virtus.'" *Modern Language Studies* 13, no. 2 (Spring, 1983): 68-79. Interprets *Coriolanus* as a cautionary illustration of the narrow, exclusive inadequacy of the Roman ideal. The hero's Roman virtues ironically are the vices that doom him.

Cymbeline

Type of plot: Romance or tragicomedy
Time of plot: First century B.C.E.
Locale: Britain, Italy, and Wales
First performed: c. 1609-1610; first published, 1623

Principal characters

CYMBELINE, the King of Britain
THE QUEEN, Cymbeline's wife
CLOTEN, the queen's son by a former husband
IMOGEN, Cymbeline's daughter by a former marriage
POSTHUMUS LEONATUS, Imogen's husband
PISANIO, a servant of Posthumus
IACHIMO, an Italian braggart
BELARIUS, a banished lord
GUIDERIUS and
ARVIRAGUS, Cymbeline's sons, reared by Belarius
CAIUS LUCIUS, a Roman ambassador

The Story

Gullible Cymbeline and his conniving queen intended that his daughter Imogen should marry his stepson Cloten. Instead, Imogen chose the gentle Posthumus and secretly married him. In a fit of anger, the king banished Posthumus, who fled to Italy after promising to remain loyal and faithful to his bride. As a token of their vows, Imogen gave Posthumus a diamond ring that had belonged to her mother; in turn, Posthumus placed a bracelet of rare design on Imogen's arm.

In Rome, Posthumus met Iachimo, a vain braggart who tried to tempt Posthumus by appealing to his sensuality. Posthumus, not to be tempted into adultery, told Iachimo of his pact with Imogen and of the ring and bracelet they had exchanged. Iachimo scoffingly wagered ten thousand ducats against Posthumus' ring that he could seduce Imogen.

Iachimo went to Britain with letters to which he had forged Posthumus' name, which persuaded Imogen to receive him. Using ambiguous implications and innuendo, Iachimo played on her curiosity about her husband's faithfulness. When that failed to win her favor, he gained access to her bedroom in a trunk which, he had told her, contained a valuable gift he had bought in France that was intended for the Roman emperor; he had asked that the trunk be placed in her chamber for safekeeping. While Imogen slept, he noted the details of the furnishings in the room, took the bracelet from her arm, and observed a mole on her left breast.

Back in Italy, Iachimo described Imogen's room to Posthumus and produced the bracelet, which he said Imogen had given him. Incredulous, Posthumus asked Iachimo to describe some aspect of Imogen's body as better proof of his successful seduction. Iachimo's claim that he had kissed the mole on Imogen's breast enraged Posthumus. He sent a letter to Pisanio, commanding that the servant kill Imogen, and a letter to Imogen asking her to meet him in Milford Haven. Pisanio was to kill Imogen as they traveled through the Welsh hills.

On the journey Pisanio divulged the real purpose of their trip when he showed Imogen the letter ordering her death. Unable to harm his master's wife, Pisanio instructed her to dress as a boy and join the party of Caius Lucius, who was in Britain to collect tribute to the Emperor Augustus and who was soon to return to Rome. Then Imogen would be near Posthumus and could try to disprove Iachimo's accusations against her. Pisanio also gave Imogen a box containing a restorative, which the queen had entrusted to him ostensibly in case Imogen became ill during her trip. The queen actually thought the box contained a slow-acting poison, which she had procured from her physician; he, suspecting chicanery, had reduced the drug content so that the substance would do no more than induce a long sleep. Pisanio took leave of his mistress and returned home.

Dressed in boy's clothing, hungry, and weary, Imogen came to the mountain cave of Belarius, who had been banished from Cymbeline's court twenty years earlier and had kidnapped Guiderius and Arviragus, Cymbeline's infant sons. In Wales, the two boys had been brought up to look upon Belarius as their father. Calling herself Fidele, Imogen won the affection of the three men when she asked shelter of them. Left alone when the men went out to hunt food, Imogen, worn out and ill, swallowed some of the medicine that Pisanio had given her.

Cymbeline, meanwhile, had refused to pay the tribute demanded by Rome, and the two nations prepared for war. Cloten, who had been infuriated by Imogen's coldness to him, tried to learn her whereabouts. Pisanio hoped to trick her pursuer and showed him the letter in which Posthumus asked Imogen to meet him at Milford Haven. Disguised as Posthumus, Cloten set out to avenge his injured vanity.

In Wales, he came upon Belarius, Arviragus, and Guiderius while they were hunting. Recognizing him as the queen's son, Belarius assumed that Cloten had come to arrest them as outlaws. He and Arviragus went in search of Cloten's retinue while Guiderius fought with and killed Cloten. Guiderius then cut off Cloten's head and threw it into the river. Returning to the cave, the three men found Imogen, as they thought, dead, and they prepared her for burial. Benevolent Belarius, remembering that Cloten was of royal birth, brought his headless body for burial and laid it near Imogen.

When Imogen awoke from her drugged sleep, she was grief-stricken when she saw lying nearby a body dressed in Posthumus' clothing. Sorrowing, she joined the forces of Caius Lucius as the Roman army marched by on their way to engage the soldiers of Cymbeline.

Posthumus, who was a recruit in the Roman army, now regretted his order for

Imogen's death. Throwing away his uniform, he dressed himself as a British peasant. Although he could not restore Imogen to life, he did not want to take any more British lives. In a battle between the Romans and Britons, Posthumus vanquished and disarmed Iachimo. Cymbeline was taken prisoner and rescued by Belarius and his two foster sons. These three had built a fort and, aided by Posthumus, had so spurred the morale of the fleeing British soldiers that Cymbeline's army was victorious.

Since he had not died in battle, Posthumus identified himself as a Roman after Lucius was taken, and he was sent to prison by Cymbeline. In prison, he had a vision in which Jove assured him that he would yet be the lord of the Lady Imogen. Jove ordered a tablet placed on Posthumus' chest. When Posthumus awoke and found the tablet, he read that a lion's whelp would be embraced by a piece of tender air and that branches lopped from a stately cedar would revive. Shortly before the time set for his execution, he was summoned to appear before Cymbeline.

"Death will seize the doctor too"

Cymbeline, Act V, scene v, lines 29-30

King Cymbeline of Britain, dominated by his wicked queen and her arrogant son, Cloten, refuses to pay tribute to Rome. As a result, Rome makes preparations to invade Britain. Meanwhile, Cloten, pressing an odious suit for the hand of Imogen, his step-sister, follows her when she flees the court. He comes to grief, and the queen, his mother, hears nothing further from him. During the Roman invasion, the queen goes mad over the disappearance of Cloten. Now just as Cymbeline is victorious over the invaders, word is brought by Cornelius, a physician, that the queen is dead.

> *Cornelius.* Hail great King,
>   To sour your happiness, I must report
>   The Queen is dead.
> *Cymbeline.* Who worse than a physician
>   Would this report become? But I consider
>   By medicine life may be prolonged, yet death
>   will seize the doctor too. How ended she?

In Cymbeline's tent, the king conferred honors upon Belarius, Guiderius, and Arviragus and bemoaned the fact that the fourth valiant soldier, so poorly dressed, was not present to receive his reward. Cornelius, the physician, told Cymbeline that the queen had died after her villainies. Lucius pleaded for the life of Imogen, still dressed as a boy, because of the page's youth. Pardoned, Imogen asked Iachimo to explain his possession of the ring he wore. As Iachimo confessed having lied to win the ring from Posthumus, Posthumus entered and identified himself as the murderer of Imogen. When Imogen protested against his confession, Posthumus struck her. Pisanio then identified Imogen to keep Posthumus from striking her

Cloten (Don Burroughs, left) and his servant Pisanio (Sandy McCallum) from the 1993 Oregon Shakespeare Festival production of Cymbeline. *(Christopher Briscoe, courtesy of the Oregon Shakespeare Festival by permission of the Actors' Equity Association)*

again. The truth disclosed, Belarius understood his foster sons' affinity for Imogen. Posthumus and Imogen, reunited, professed to remain devoted to each other for the rest of their lives.

After Guiderius confessed to the murder of Cloten, Cymbeline ordered him bound, but he stayed the sentence when Belarius identified himself and the two young men. Cymbeline then blessed his three children who stood before him. A soothsayer interpreted Jove's message on the tablet left on Posthumus' chest. The lion's whelp was Posthumus, the son of Leonatus, and the piece of tender air was Imogen. The lopped branches from the stately cedar were Arviragus and Guiderius, long thought dead, now restored in the king's love. Overjoyed, Cymbeline made peace with Rome.

Critical Evaluation

Cymbeline, together with *The Winter's Tale* (1610-1611) and *The Tempest* (1611), belongs to William Shakespeare's final period of writing. These last three plays are marked by their mood of calmness, maturity, and benevolent cheerfulness; a kind of autumnal spirit prevails. This is not to say that *Cymbeline* lacks villains, traumatic events, or scenes of violence—the play contains all these elements—but that the tone is serene in spite of them. *Cymbeline* may be classified as a tragicomedy to distinguish it from such more dazzling predecessors among Shakespeare's comedies as *Love's Labour's Lost* (1594-1595) and *Twelfth Night: Or, What You Will* (1600-1602), which have roguish heroes and heroines, dialogues filled with witty and sparkling repartee, and plots abounding in mischievous scheming and complications. The main characters in *Cymbeline*, by contrast, are remarkable for their virtue rather than their cleverness, wit, or capacity for mischief; Posthumus is a model of earnestness and fidelity, and Imogen is the picture of purity and wifely devotion. The text is memorable not for the brilliance and sparkle of its dialogue, but for its moving poetry. Much of the plot consists of the trials and sufferings of the good characters, brought on by the scheming of the bad ones. However, the play ends as comedy must, with the virtuous rewarded and the wicked punished.

In the plot of *Cymbeline*, Shakespeare combined two lines of action: the political-historical story line of the British king preparing for war with Rome, and the love story of Imogen and Posthumus. For the historical background, Shakespeare once again used Raphael Holinshed's *Chronicles of England, Scotland, and Ireland* (1577). Finding, however, that Cymbeline, a descendant of King Lear, was too dull to provide for interesting drama, he took the liberty of assigning to that king the refusal to pay the Roman tribute, which action Holinshed had attributed to Cymbeline's son Guiderius. In this way, he enlivened the plot with a war, which was resolved in a peace treaty at the end. Imogen's story, however, provides the primary interest in *Cymbeline*, a love story centering on a wager between a cunning villain and a devoted husband regarding the faithfulness of the absent wife; for this story Shakespeare was indebted to one of the tales in Giovanni Boccaccio's *Decameron* (1349-1351). In addition to the two main story lines, the plot of *Cymbeline* contains many characters traveling in disguise and cases of mistaken identity. In a subplot of Shakespeare's invention, the story is further complicated with the consequences of Belarius having abducted and subsequently reared the king's infant sons in Wales. Such elements lend a certain extravagance to the plot of *Cymbeline*.

Cymbeline bears many resemblances to previous plays of Shakespeare. The figure of the gullible king influenced by his wicked queen reminds one of *Macbeth*, as does the scene of supernatural intervention, the ghosts of Posthumus' family, and the tablet bearing a prophecy. Iachimo does not approach *Othello*'s villain, Iago, in malignancy, but nevertheless calls to mind Othello's tormentor through his cunning strategies and his manipulation of Posthumus' capacity for jealousy. Likewise, the scenes of Imogen's travels disguised as a boy and her eventual reunion with her lost brothers are reminiscent of Viola's similar adventures in *Twelfth Night: Or, What You Will*. Perhaps most important, however, is the relation it bears to that final masterpiece, *The Tempest*.

For Further Study

Bergeron, David M. "*Cymbeline*: Shakespeare's Last Roman Play." *Shakespeare Quarterly* 31, no. 1 (Spring, 1980): 31-41. Traces the historical and political factors at work in the play.

Frye, Northrop. *A Natural Perspective: The Development of Shakespearean Comedy and Romance*. New York: Columbia University Press, 1965. Frye puts the play in the context of other late romances. The most interesting commentary available on the role of Imogen and on the visions experienced by Posthumus toward the end of the play.

Hieatt, A. Kent. "*Cymbeline* and the Intrusion of Lyric." In *Unfolded Tales: Essays on Renaissance Romance*, edited by George M. Logan and Gordon Teskey. Ithaca, N.Y.: Cornell University Press, 1989. Hieatt displays *Cymbeline*'s relationship to Edmund Spenser's sonnet sequence "The Ruins of Rome" and other treatments of the theme of historical inheritance in the frame of lyricism. A major reinterpretation of the play and a valuable commentary.

Miola, Robert S. *Shakespeare's Rome*. Cambridge, England: Cambridge University Press, 1983. Places *Cymbeline* in the context of Shakespeare's Roman plays. Emphasizes how Shakespeare's portrait of Britain has an ambiguous relationship to the Roman imperial legacy.

Parker, Patricia. "Romance and Empire: Anachronistic *Cymbeline*." In *Unfolded Tales: Essays on Renaissance Romance*, edited by George M. Logan and Gordon Teskey. Ithaca, N.Y.: Cornell University Press, 1989. Speculates on what has always been one of the most vexing issues surrounding *Cymbeline*, the fact that half of it seems set in ancient Roman times and the other half in the Italian Renaissance of Shakespeare's lifetime. Parker also traces the influence on the play of Vergil's *Aeneid* (29-19 B.C.E.), particularly as regards the roles of oracles, prophecy, and kingship.

Edward III

Type of plot: Historical
Time of plot: 1340-1356
Locale: England and France
First performed: wr., pr. c. 1589-1595; first published, 1596

Principal characters

EDWARD III, King of England
EDWARD, Prince of Wales, his son
JOHN, King of France
COUNTESS OF SALISBURY, loved by King Edward
EARL OF WARWICK, her father

The Story

King Edward III was preparing to enforce his claim to the throne of France when the Duke of Lorraine came from the French ruler, King John, ordering Edward to go to France to swear allegiance for his (Edward's) dukedom of Guyenne. Edward promised to come in force, but before he could invade France he had to repel the Scots under King David, who had attacked England and were besieging the castle of the Countess of Salisbury.

As soon as Edward and his army approached the countess' castle, the Scots fled. Edward immediately fell in love with the countess. He wanted to pursue the Scots, but she entreated him to stay. Now, instead of the Scots' besieging the countess in enmity, Edward besieged her in love. When she resisted him, he engaged her father, the Earl of Warwick, and a writer, Lodowick, to woo her. Edward was so distracted that he could not pay attention to the preparations for war against France. When his son appeared and the king recognized in the youth the features of his queen, Philippa, he determined to leave the countess to attack France. News that the countess was approaching quickly banished this resolution.

The countess told Edward that if he wanted to win her, he would have to kill the queen and Salisbury, so she and the king would be free to marry. Edward agreed. She then told him that her husband lived within her heart; she was prepared to kill herself rather than yield to Edward. Recognizing his folly at last, the king relented and set off for France.

At the battle at Crecy (which actually occurred in 1356 but which Shakespeare stages before Poitiers, fought in 1340) King Edward sent his son to lead the troops while the king remained with the reserves. Urged to help his son at a crucial point in the battle, Edward refused so that the prince could gain confidence in his own abilities. The Black Prince triumphed, and the king knighted him. Then the prince pursued the fleeing French, while the king headed toward Calais.

Prince Edward, with eight thousand men, found himself surrounded by sixty thousand French troops. King John sent a herald offering peace if the prince would agree to be held for ransom. The prince rejected this offer, as he did the proposal to flee made by the Duke of Normandy and the prayerbook of Philip. Despite the odds, the English triumphed at Poitiers and captured the King of France and his two sons.

Prince Edward took his prisoners to Calais, which had surrendered to the English after the citizens recognized that further resistance was pointless. Angered by the city's earlier defiance, King Edward demanded that six burghers be surrendered to him for execution. Queen Philippa persuaded him to relent, and the king in turn convinced her to forgive Copeland, who had captured King David but refused to surrender him to her, insisting on presenting the Scots ruler to Edward himself. The play ends with the triumphant entry of the Black Prince.

Critical Evaluation

Edward III was first published anonymously in 1596. In 1656 the booksellers Richard Rogers and William Ley ascribed the play to Shakespeare in an unreliable list appended to Thomas Goffe's *The Careless Shepherdess*. This list also credited Shakespeare with plays by Christopher Marlowe and Thomas Heywood. Edward Capell was the first Shakespeare scholar to attribute the play to Shakespeare. Though the play was excluded from all the seventeenth century folios and from the 1986 Oxford University Press Shakespeare, the editors of the latter, Stanley Wells and Gary Taylor, have since joined Eric Sams and others in agreeing that the play is canonical.

The date of composition remains more controversial. Shakespeare alludes to the Spanish Armada (1588) in describing the naval battle of Sluys (1340). This topical reference suggests that the play may have been composed as early as 1589. Echoes of the sonnets and of *The Rape of Lucrece* (1594), on the other hand, imply that the work may have been written in the early 1590's. The play also refers to war between Austria and Turkey, which began in June, 1593. In March of that year Thomas Deloney registered for publication his ballad "Of King Edward III and the Fair Countess of Salisbury," the subject of the first two acts of *Edward III*. The theaters were closed because of plague from mid-1592 to early 1594. Perhaps Shakespeare wrote *Edward III* during this interval.

The sources of the play are typically Shakespearean: Raphael Holinshed's *Chronicles of England, Scotland, and Ireland* (1577; 2d ed., 1587), William Painter's *The Palace of Pleasure* (1566), and Jean Froissart's *Chroniques* (1513; *Chronicles*, 1523-1525), along with Ovid and Plutarch. Roger Prior has suggested that the author of *Edward III* used Henry Carey, Lord Hunsdon's copy of Froissart; Shakespeare belonged to Lord Hunsdon's acting company from its inception in 1594.

Another characteristically Shakespearean touch is the insertion of humor into a serious situation. In *The Palace of Pleasure* Edward employs a letter-writer to assist him with his attempted seduction of the Countess of Salisbury. Shakespeare transforms this figure into a slow-writing sonneteer who composes only two lines of poetry, both unsatisfactory for the king's purpose because they conjure up images of constancy and chastity. *Edward III* contains lines that also appear in the sonnets. If the play is quoting the poems rather than the reverse, the king's use of these images in speaking to his poet would heighten the humor for those who had read the verses in manuscript.

Among the play's concerns are those occupying Shakespeare in the early 1590's. One of these is the relationship between sexuality and the abuse of power, treated in *Titus Andronicus* (1594) and *The Rape of Lucrece*. Edward III's lust prompts him to consent to the murders of her husband, a faithful subject, and the queen. Only the countess' Lucrece-like determination to kill herself rather than suffer dishonor recalls Edward to his better self.

Another theme of *Edward III* is that of conflicting loyalties, a subject treated in *The Book of Sir Thomas More*, in which Shakespeare had a hand and which may date from as early as 1593. The Countess of Salisbury is torn between obedience to her monarch and obedience to her husband, as well as her vow of loyalty to Edward and her vow to God to be faithful to the count. When Edward orders Warwick to assist in the seduction of the countess, the earl must choose between fidelity to his king and fidelity to his daughter. Later in the play, King John and his son Charles must decide whether to honor a pledge made to the Count of Salisbury or to override that promise for reasons of state.

In each case those in authority learn morality from their subjects and choose properly. Shakespeare thereby introduces another theme, especially important in the second tetralogy: the education of princes. Edward III must learn to control his passions. The Countess of Salisbury teaches him to curb his lust, and Queen Philippa later educates him in overcoming anger. Instead of imitating the tyrannical Tarquin, Edward becomes a model ruler. Edward III teaches his son to scorn danger and death. King John learns the importance of keeping one's word and that prophecies can be misleading. He had been told that he would penetrate England as far as the English advanced into France, but he did not consider that he would do so as a prisoner.

Shakespeare would develop this theme of education in his treatment of Richard II and Prince Hal. The former, like King John, puts too much faith in language, and he learns too late that he has wasted time. Hal, who first appears in *Henry IV*, also begins as a waster of time, as one who, like Edward III at the beginning of his play, pursues personal pleasure when he should be devoting his attention to matters of state. Both reform at the end of Act II and reach the pinnacle of glory in conquering France.

Though Shakespeare's history plays thus depict English victories, they are not blind celebrations. Talbot's triumphs in *Henry VI, Part I* culminate in his death, and the whole of the first tetralogy portrays English losses in France and civil war at home. Though the second tetralogy ends with Henry V's victory at Agincourt and his marriage to Katherine, daughter of the French king, thereby ensuring that the French crown will go to their son, the epilogue to *Henry V* reminds the audience of the events to follow under the hapless Henry VI. In *Edward III* the tragic tone is muted, but Shakespeare's audience would know that the Black Prince who captured King John never would reign, and that his son Richard would prove, like Henry VI, a poor monarch who would lose his crown and his life. The Scottish invasion of England also calls into question the English invasion of France. Why is the one condemned and the other glorified? Henry V's invasion will also appear problematic; Shakespeare renders the justification offered for it highly convoluted and questionable. In *Edward III* Shakespeare refers to the English fleet as "the proud Armado of King Edward's ships," which sail in the formation of "the hornéd circle of the moon," calling to mind the name and battle formation of the Spanish fleet of 1588—hardly a flattering reference and again questioning the legitimacy of Edward's actions. Though an early play, *Edward III* contains the seeds that would mature into greater works to follow.

Joseph Rosenblum

For Further Study

Metz, G. Harold, ed. *Sources of Four Plays Ascribed to Shakespeare*. Columbia: University of Missouri Press, 1989. In addition to presenting Shakespeare's major sources for *Edward III*, Metz provides a useful introduction surveying the critical debate about the play's authorship.

Muir, Kenneth. "A Reconsideration of *Edward III*." *Shakespeare Survey* 6 (1953): 39-48. Muir examines the language and image patterns in the play. He finds particularly close resemblances between *Edward III* on the one hand and *Henry V* and *Measure for Measure* on the other. He concludes that if Shakespeare did not write *Edward III* he was deeply influenced by the work.

Osterberg, V. "The 'Countess Scenes' of *Edward III*." *Shakespeare Jahrbuch* 65 (1929): 49-91. Argues that in 1594 the Chamberlain's Men acquired a play about Edward III by Christopher Marlowe, Thomas Kyd, and Robert Greene. Shakespeare already had been working on a poem about the Countess of Salisbury. He added this material to the old play and hastily revised the rest to produce the present text of the play.

Sams, Eric, ed. *Shakespeare's "Edward III": An Early Play Restored to the Canon*. New Haven, Conn.: Yale University Press, 1996. Sams has been one of the leading advocates for Shakespeare's authorship of the play. In addition to presenting the text here, he offers an extended argument for Shakespearean attribution.

Westersdorf, Karl P. "The Date of *Edward III*." *Shakespeare Quarterly* 16 (1965): 227-231. The play was registered in the *Stationers' Register* on December 1, 1595, and was published the next year. It alludes to the Armada, especially regarding the formation of the English ships. Present at the Battle of Sluys was the English ship the *Nonpareil*, which fought the Spanish in 1588. Given these references and the patriotic spirit that Westersdorf finds in the work, he thinks that the play probably dates from 1589-1590.

Hamlet, Prince of Denmark

Type of plot: Tragedy
Time of plot: c. 1200
Locale: Elsinore, Denmark
First performed: c. 1600-1601; first published, 1603

Principal characters

HAMLET, the Prince of Denmark
THE GHOST, Hamlet's father, the former King of Denmark
CLAUDIUS, the present king
GERTRUDE, Hamlet's mother
POLONIUS, a courtier
OPHELIA, his daughter
LAERTES, his son
HORATIO, Hamlet's friend

The Story

Three times the ghost of Denmark's dead king had stalked the battlements of Elsinore Castle. On the fourth night Horatio, Hamlet's friend, brought the young prince to see the specter of his father. Since his father's untimely death two months earlier, Hamlet had been grief-stricken and exceedingly melancholy. The mysterious circumstances surrounding the death of his father perplexed him, and his mother had married Claudius, the dead king's brother, much too hurriedly to suit Hamlet's sense of decency.

That night, Hamlet saw his father's ghost and listened in horror when it told him that his father had not died from the sting of a serpent, as had been reported, but that he had been murdered by his own brother, Claudius, the present king. The ghost added that Claudius was guilty not only of murder but also of incest and adultery. The spirit cautioned Hamlet to spare Queen Gertrude, his mother, and leave her punishment to heaven.

The ghost's disclosures should have left no doubt in Hamlet's mind that Claudius must be killed, but the introspective prince was not quite sure that the ghost was his father's spirit and he feared it might have been a devil sent to torment him. Debating with himself the problem of whether or not to carry out the spirit's commands, Hamlet swore his friends, including Horatio, to secrecy concerning the appearance of the ghost. He also told them not to consider him mad if from then on he were to act strangely.

Claudius was facing not only the possibility of war with Norway, but also, much worse, his own conscience, which had been much troubled since his hasty marriage to Gertrude. It worried him that the prince was so melancholy, for he knew that he resented the marriage and he feared that Hamlet might try to take his throne away from him. The prince's strange behavior and wild talk made the king think that perhaps Hamlet was mad, but he was not sure. To learn whether Hamlet's manner and actions were caused by madness or ambition, Claudius commissioned two of Hamlet's friends, Rosencrantz and Guildenstern, to spy on the prince. Hamlet saw through their clumsy efforts, however, and confused them with his answers to their questions.

Polonius, the garrulous old chamberlain, believed that Hamlet's behavior resulted from lovesickness for his daughter, Ophelia. Hamlet, meanwhile, became increasingly melancholy. Rosencrantz and Guildenstern, as well as Polonius, were constantly spying on him. Even Ophelia, he thought, had turned against him. The thought of deliberate murder was revolting to him, and he was plagued by uncertainty as to whether the ghost represented good or evil. When a troupe of actors visited Elsinore, Hamlet saw in them a chance to discover whether Claudius was guilty. He planned to have the players enact before the king and the court a scene resembling the one that, according to the ghost, had taken place the day the old king died. By watching Claudius during the performance, Hamlet hoped to discover the truth for himself.

His plan worked. Claudius became so unnerved during the performance that he walked out before the end of the scene. Convinced by the king's actions that the ghost was right, Hamlet had no reason to delay in carrying out the wishes of his dead father. Even so, he failed to take advantage of the first chance to kill Claudius when, coming upon the king in an attitude of prayer, he could have stabbed him in the back. Hamlet refrained because he did not want the king to die in a state of grace.

When the queen summoned Hamlet to her chamber to reprimand him for his insolence to Claudius, Hamlet, remembering what the ghost had told him, spoke to her so violently that she screamed for help. A noise behind a curtain followed her cries, and Hamlet, suspecting that Claudius was eavesdropping, plunged his sword through the curtain, killing old Polonius. Fearing an attack on his own life, the king hastily ordered Hamlet to England in company with Rosencrantz and Guildenstern, who carried a warrant for Hamlet's death. The prince discovered the orders and altered them so that the bearers should be killed on their arrival in England. Hamlet then returned to Denmark.

Much had happened in that unhappy land during Hamlet's absence. Ophelia, rejected by Hamlet, her former lover, had gone mad and later drowned herself. Laertes, Polonius' hot-tempered son, had returned from France and collected a band of malcontents to avenge the death of his father. He thought that Claudius had killed Polonius, but the king told him that Hamlet was the murderer and persuaded Laertes to take part in a plot to murder the prince.

Claudius arranged for a duel between Hamlet and Laertes. To allay suspicion of foul play, the king placed bets on Hamlet, who was an expert swordsman. At the same time, he had poison placed on the tip of Laertes' weapon and put a cup of poison within Hamlet's reach in the event that the prince became thirsty during the duel. Gertrude, who knew nothing of the king's treachery, drank from the poisoned cup and died. During the contest, Hamlet was mortally wounded with the poisoned rapier, but the two contestants exchanged foils in a scuffle, and Laertes himself received a fatal wound. Before he died, Laertes was filled with remorse and told Hamlet that Claudius was responsible for the poisoned sword. Hesitating no longer, Hamlet seized his opportunity to act, and fatally stabbed the king before himself dying.

"To thine own self be true"

Hamlet, Act I, scene iii, line 78

Of all the lines in a great and famous speech from *Hamlet*, the one beginning "to thine own self be true" is perhaps most commonly recalled and used as one of the most meaningful proverbs in the English language. Polonius, chief councilor to Denmark's King Claudius, gives his son Laertes this sage advice as the young man patiently waits for his talkative father to complete his lengthy speech and bid him farewell before the son sets sail for France. The scene has come to epitomize the timeless exchange between a wise father, anxious to impart the lessons he has learned across the years, and a son who is probably not listening in his anticipation of the voyage upon which he is about to embark.

> *Polonius.* Yet here Laertes? Aboard, aboard, for shame!
> The wind sits in the shoulder of your sail,
> And you are stay'd for. There—my blessing with thee!
> And these few precepts in thy memory
> Look thou character. Give thy thoughts no tongue,
> Nor any unproportion'd thought his act.
> Be thou familiar, but by no means vulgar. . . .
> Give every man thy ear, but few thy voice. . . .
> Costly thy habit as thy purse can buy,
> But not express'd in fancy, rich, not gaudy. . . .
> Neither a borrower nor a lender be,
> For loan oft loses both itself and friend. . . .
> This above all, to thine own self be true,
> And it must follow, as the night the day,
> Thou canst not then be false to any man.
> *Laertes.* Most humbly do I take my leave, my lord.

Critical Evaluation

Hamlet has remained the most perplexing, as well as the most popular, of Shakespeare's tragedies. Whether considered as literature, philosophy, or drama, its artistic stature is universally admitted. To explain the reasons for its excellence in a few words, however, is a daunting task. Apart from the matchless artistry of its language, the play's appeal rests in large measure on the character of Hamlet

Hamlet (Laurence Olivier) and Queen Gertrude (Eileen Herlie) in a scene from the 1948 British film version of Shakespeare's Hamlet, *which won an Oscar for Best Picture and for Olivier as Best Actor.* (Courtesy of The Museum of Modern Art, Film Stills Archive)

himself. Called upon to avenge his father's murder, he is compelled to face problems of duty, morality, and ethics, which have been human concerns through the ages. Yet the play has tantalized critics with what has become known as the Hamlet mystery, that of Hamlet's complex behavior, most notably his indecision and his reluctance to act.

Freudian critics have located his motivation in the psychodynamic triad of the father-mother-son relationship. According to this view, Hamlet is disturbed and eventually deranged by his Oedipal jealousy of the uncle who has done what, we are to believe, all sons long to do themselves. Other critics have taken the more conventional tack of identifying as Hamlet's tragic flaw the lack of courage or moral resolution. In this view, Hamlet's indecision is a sign of moral ambivalence that he overcomes too late.

Both of these views presuppose a precise discovery of Hamlet's motivation. However, Renaissance drama is not generally a drama of motivation either by psychological set or moral predetermination. Rather, the tendency is to present characters with well-delineated moral and ethical dispositions who are faced with dilemmas. It is the outcome of these conflicts, the consequences, that normally hold center stage. What Shakespeare presents in *Hamlet* is an agonizing confrontation between the will of a good and intelligent man and the uncongenial role— that of avenger—that fate calls upon him to play.

The role of avenger is a familiar one in Renaissance drama. In the opening description of Hamlet as bereft by the death of his father and distressed by his mother's hasty marriage, Shakespeare creates the ideal candidate to assume such a role. Hamlet's despondency need not be Oedipal to explain the extremity of his grief. His father, whom he deeply loved and admired, is recently deceased and he himself seems to have been robbed of his birthright. Shakespeare points to Hamlet's shock at Gertrude's disrespect to the memory of his father rather than his love for his mother as the source of his distress. Hamlet's suspicion is reinforced by the ghostly visitation and the revelation of murder.

If Hamlet had simply proceeded to act out the avenger role assigned to him, the play would have lacked the moral and theological complexity that provides its special fascination. Hamlet has, after all, been a student of theology at Wittenberg, and his knowledge complicates the situation. His accusation of incest is not an adolescent excess but an accurate theological description of a marriage between a widow and her dead husband's brother. Moreover, Hamlet's theological accomplishments do more than exacerbate his feelings. For the ordinary avenger, the commission from the ghost of a murdered father would be more than enough, but Hamlet is aware of the unreliability of otherworldly apparitions and consequently reluctant to heed its injunction to perform an action that is objectively evil. In addition, the fear that his father was murdered in a state of sin and is condemned to hell not only increases Hamlet's sense of injustice but also, paradoxically, casts further doubt on the reliability of the ghost's exhortation, for perhaps the ghost is merely an infernal spirit goading him to sin.

Hamlet's indecision is therefore not an indication of weakness but the result of his complex understanding of the moral dilemma with which he is faced. He is unwilling to act unjustly, yet he is afraid that he is failing to exact a deserved retribution. He debates the murky issue and himself becomes unsure whether his behavior is caused by moral scruple or cowardice. His ruminations are in sharp contrast with the cynicism of Claudius and the verbose moral platitudes of Polonius, just as the play is in sharp contrast with the moral simplicity of the ordinary revenge tragedy. Through Hamlet's intelligence, Shakespeare transformed a stock situation into a unique internal conflict.

Hamlet believes that he must have greater certitude of Claudius' guilt if he is to take action. The device of the play-within-a-play provides greater assurance that

Claudius is suffering from a guilty conscience, but it simultaneously sharpens Hamlet's anguish. Seeing a re-creation of his father's death and Claudius' response stiffens Hamlet's resolve to act, but once again he hesitates when he sees Claudius in prayer. Here Hamlet's inaction is not the result of cowardice or even perception of moral ambiguity but rather of the very thoroughness of his commitment, for, having once decided on revenge, he wants to destroy his uncle body and soul. It is ironic that Hamlet is thwarted this time by the combination of theological insight with the extreme ferocity of his vengeful intention.

That Hamlet loses his mental stability is clear in his behavior toward Ophelia and in his subsequent meanderings. Circumstance has enforced a role whose enormity has overwhelmed the fine emotional and intellectual balance of a sensitive, well-educated young man. Gradually, he is shown regaining control of himself and arming himself with a cold determination to do what he has decided is the just thing. Yet, even then, it is only in the carnage of the concluding scenes that Hamlet finally carries out his intention. Having concluded that "the readiness is all," he strikes his uncle only after he has discovered Claudius' final scheme to kill him and Laertes.

The arrival of Fortinbras, who has been lurking in the background throughout the play, superficially seems to indicate that a new, more direct and courageous

---

"To be, or not to be, that is the question"

Hamlet, Act III, scene i, line 55

Hamlet has learned from the Ghost of his father the terrible story of the latter's murder by his brother, Claudius, who has usurped the crown and married the murdered King's widow, Hamlet's mother. The Ghost has made Hamlet swear to avenge the crime, and Hamlet has undertaken to assassinate Claudius. Now, conscious of the terrible duty that he, a scholar rather than a man of action, has taken upon himself, he muses on the possibility of suicide as an escape from his task. Is it better to endure quietly what fortune brings or to contend against it? Or is it better still to end one's life and thus to evade the problem altogether?

> *Hamlet.* To be, or not to be, that is the question:
> Whether 'tis nobler in the mind to suffer
> The slings and arrows of outrageous fortune,
> Or to take arms against a sea of troubles,
> And by opposing, end them. To die, to sleep—
> No more, and by a sleep to say we end
> The heart-ache and the thousand natural shocks
> That flesh is heir to; 'tis a consummation
> Devoutly to be wished. To die, to sleep—
> To sleep, perchance to dream—ay, there's the rub,
> For in that sleep of death what dreams may come,
> When we have shuffled off this mortal coil,
> Must give us pause. . . .

---

order will prevail in the place of the evil of Claudius and the weakness of Hamlet. Yet Fortinbras' superiority is only superficial. He brings stasis and stability back to a disordered kingdom but does not have the self-consciousness and moral sensitivity that destroy and redeem Hamlet.

Gerald Else has interpreted Aristotle's notion of *katharsis* (catharsis) to be not a purging of the emotions but a purging of the moral horror, pity, and fear ordinarily associated with them. If that is so, then Hamlet, by the conflict of his ethical will with his role, has purged the avenger of his bloodthirstiness and turned the stock figure into a self-conscious hero in moral conflict.

"Critical Evaluation" by Edward E. Foster

For Further Study

Bowers, Fredson Thayer. *Elizabethan Revenge Tragedy, 1587-1642*. Reprint. Princeton, N.J.: Princeton University Press, 1966. A full discussion of revenge tragedy and its connections to the central action of *Hamlet*. Bowers' historical account of the conventions of revenge tragedy provides an illuminating context for the play.

Grene, Nicholas. *Shakespeare's Tragic Imagination*. New York: St. Martin's Press, 1992. The chapter on *Hamlet* attempts to revise and question some of the Christian interpretations of the play. Also of value is Grene's connecting *Hamlet* to the play that preceded it in Shakespeare's oeuvre, *Julius Caesar* (c. 1599-1600).

Prosser, Eleanor. *"Hamlet" and Revenge*. Stanford, Calif.: Stanford University Press, 1967. Prosser uses an historical approach to try to answer such central questions as the Elizabethans' attitude toward revenge, the nature of the father's ghost, and regicide.

Shakespeare, William. *Hamlet*. Edited by Harold Jenkins. London: Methuen, 1982. Considered by many to be the best edition of the play, its notes are clear and thorough, and Jenkins includes a number of longer notes that discuss such controversies as those surrounding Hamlet's "To be, or not to be" speech. Also includes an excellent discussion of the sources for the play and earlier criticism on it.

Watts, Cedric. *Hamlet*. Boston: Twayne, 1988. Includes a stage history and a critical history that provide some of the contexts for *Hamlet*. The discussion is intended to preserve the play's mystery rather than offering another solution to the so-called Hamlet problem.

Wilson, John Dover. *What Happens in Hamlet*. 3d ed. Cambridge, England: Cambridge University Press, 1951. Wilson attempts to resolve all of the unsolved questions in the play by a close analysis of the text. Suggests plausible answers for some of the problems but fails to resolve the most important ones.

Henry IV, Part I

Type of plot: Historical
Time of plot: 1403
Locale: England
First performed: 1592; first published, 1598

Principal characters

HENRY IV, first Lancastrian English king
PRINCE HAL, Henry's son and successor-to-be
HENRY PERCY, SR.,
HENRY PERCY, JR., or HOTSPUR,
THOMAS PERCY,
EDMUND MORTIMER, and
OWEN GLENDOWER, noblemen and enemies of the king
SIR JOHN FALSTAFF, friend of Prince Hal

The Story

After he forced the anointed king, Richard II, to relinquish his crown, Henry Bolingbroke became King of England in 1399 as Henry IV. Within only a few years Henry IV himself began to face challenges to his kingship when the nobles who had supported him against Richard II began to defy the new king and aspire to the throne. Henry Percy, Jr., or Hotspur, defeated, on behalf of Henry IV, the invading army of Douglas of Scotland in northern England, but Hotspur then refused to subordinate himself to the king's authority and turn his Scottish prisoners over to the king. Realizing the threat of revolt by Hotspur and other nobles affiliated with him, Henry IV postponed his planned trip to the Holy Land and began to make preparations to confront the challenge of Hotspur and his allies. Among these were Owen Glendower, Welsh leader and alleged magician, who captured the Earl of March, and Edmund Mortimer, who had been sent by the king to defeat Glendower. Angry because he had been Richard II's chosen successor, Mortimer joined with Glendower, marrying his daughter and aligning himself with her father, with Hotspur, and with Hotspur's father, Henry Percy, Sr. Also allied with Hotspur were the Scotsmen under Douglas, whose defeat but retention by Hotspur had precipitated the conflict. Realizing the serious threat represented by such a powerful alliance, Henry IV began to gather his forces to protect his throne.

Notably absent from the king's supporters was his own son, Prince Hal, who was occupied with drunken revelry with the prankster Sir John Falstaff and Falstaff's thieving cohorts. Hal did not, however, join in the highway robbery performed by Falstaff and his friends, being content to play a joke on Falstaff by accosting the robbers, his friends, and frightening them away, then returning the stolen money to its owners. Hal's enjoyable antics were terminated by a summons from his father, and upon being chastised for his waywardness, Prince Hal promised that he would atone for his inattention to matters of state by killing his father's most determined enemy, Hotspur.

Victor Buono as Sir John Falstaff (left) bows in jest to Prince Hal (Kristoffer Tabori), the future king of England, in a production of Henry IV, Part I *at Los Angeles's Mark Taper Forum.* (Jay Thompson, courtesy of the Mark Taper Forum)

At the same time that King Henry IV was developing a new alliance with his son and Falstaff, who was allowed to organize a troop of foot soldiers, the powerful alliance in opposition to the king was beginning to unravel. First, Hotspur's father, Henry Percy, Sr., sent notice that he could not bring his troops to Shrewsbury, the anticipated place of battle, because he was ill. Angry and undaunted as befitting his name, Hotspur insisted on continuing with the planned confrontation, stating his intention to kill Prince Hal personally. Next came the news that Owen Glendower was not going to help in the fight against the king because of supernatural premonitions of failure. Hotspur still persisted, despite Edmund Mortimer's also staying in Wales, in obedience to his father-in-law.

The day of battle arrived with appropriately tempestuous weather. Armed conflict became certain when Thomas Percy, Earl of Worcester, decided not to tell Hotspur of the king's final offer of amnesty if the nobles disbanded their troops, reaffirmed subordination and allegiance to Henry IV, and returned to their homes. Falstaff, meanwhile, asserted his belief (in no one's hearing) that honor was not worth fighting for and that he would avoid actual fighting if at all possible. The battle began, with Douglas killing Blount, one of the nobles supporting Henry IV. Falstaff arrived to denounce Blount's death as the predictable result of fighting for honor and, in his opinion, vanity. Hal then ran to Falstaff, to borrow Falstaff's sword for use in the battle, but found that Falstaff's scabbard contained only a bottle of wine. After rescuing his father from danger in a fight with Douglas by forcing Douglas to withdraw, Hal then met Hotspur.

In his prideful exuberance preceding the fight with Hal, Hotspur complained about Hal's nonexistent military record and bemoaned that killing Hal would not increase his own fame. Hal responded by promising to elevate his military reputation by killing Hotspur, and the battle began. While Hal and Hotspur were courageously struggling, Douglas encountered Falstaff, and rather than fight, Falstaff fell down and faked death, thus surviving Douglas' onslaught. Meanwhile, Hal defeated and killed Hotspur, and then saw Falstaff lying still and apparently dead. Hal bemoaned his old friend's death and departed, upon which Falstaff arose and proceeded to stab the dead Hotspur, in preparation for his planned contention that he killed the famous military leader. Hal then returned, listened to Falstaff's fabrication, and laughed and promised to lie to help his old friend conceal his cowardice if he could. Finally, Hal returned to his father and obtained the release of Douglas, the Scottish leader, because of Douglas' valor. The Shrewsbury battle solidified the reign of Henry IV as the first Lancastrian king of England; Prince Hal redeemed himself with his valor.

Critical Evaluation

Henry IV, Part I contributed considerably to Shakespeare's fame. It has been successful in production from the date of its first performance until the present and is widely regarded as among the best of Shakespeare's history plays. Essentially, Shakespeare created a new type of drama by his use of historical materials (such as Raphael Holinshed's *Chronicles of England, Scotland, and Ireland*, 1577) to depict patriotically events of English history. Shakespeare helped to authenticate English historical and cultural tradition while at the same time altering and enhancing historical materials to create works of art. Shakespeare's histories are not factually precise; they are dramas.

Shakespeare's artistic embellishment is evident in the play in a number of ways.

One of the most important is his creation of a structural symmetry lacking in the original, factual material that leaves the reader with a clear impression of the opposing forces involved in Henry's struggle to keep his crown. Shakespeare was also one of the first dramatists to integrate comic subplots into otherwise serious plays, as a way to entertain his heterogeneous audience and to unify his plays' themes. In *Henry IV, Part I*, the comic subplot of Falstaff and his cohorts (not really

---

"Discretion is the better part of valor"

Henry IV, Part I, Act V, scene iv, line 122

The king's son, Prince Hal (destined to become King Henry V) and Hotspur finally meet on the battlefield. The aging and rotund Falstaff, who with his low-life friends has been drinking companion to Prince Hal, stands and watches them fight. At that moment Falstaff is attacked by one of Hotspur's men. Falstaff, to save his own skin, falls down as if dead. Hal kills Hotspur and then exits after having looked at Falstaff and concluded that he is dead. Falstaff, Shakespeare's greatest comic creation, then rises and comments on his philosophy of life.

> *Falstaff.* I am no counterfeit; to die is to be a counterfeit, for he is but the counterfeit of a man, who hath not the life of a man; but to counterfeit dying, when a man thereby liveth, is to be no counterfeit, but the true and perfect image of life indeed. The better part of valour is discretion, in the which better part I have saved my life. . . .

---

a part of English history) achieves all of these purposes. As humor, Falstaff's comments and actions enliven the play, such as his hacking and damaging his sword in order to support his preposterous story of valiant resistance to attack, when in fact he ran away at the very first sign of danger, as the audience is well aware. The Falstaff subplot serves to unify the play and elucidate its themes. Falstaff is the embodiment of misrule, cowardice, and fun. Shakespeare juxtaposes him and others who are his opposite, such as the valiant Hotspur and the serious, worried Henry IV. Falstaff is also parallel to Hotspur in their efforts to forcibly take that which others possess, in Falstaff's case the money of travelers on the highway and in Hotspur's case the kingship of Henry IV. On another level, however, Hotspur and Falstaff contrast; Falstaff is notoriously cowardly and is convinced that honor is only a word. Hotspur is the opposite, prone to anger and violence and so honor-crazed that he bemoans Prince Hal's lack of military reputation because he sees killing Hal as unlikely to sufficiently enhance his own status. This juxtaposition is astutely symbolized in Act V of the play, when Hotspur lies dead on stage because of excess interest in honor while Falstaff lies beside him, alive but exposed as equally excessive in cowardice. That juxtaposition of extremes also enables Shakespeare to convey a central theme of the play, the nature of true honor, represented by Hal, who embodies the happy medium between Falstaff and

Hotspur. Hal, unlike Hotspur, enjoys diversions and humor, but not to the drunken, cowardly excess of his friend Falstaff. Hal is admirably courageous in defending his father and his kingdom from Hotspur, but unlike Hotspur is not in constant conflict with even allies as a result of excessive pride and militancy.

Shakespeare also creates structural parallels and contrasts in the plot as a way to delineate the qualities of his characters and as a way to integrate symbolism into the play. For example, important paralleling is done of King Henry IV and Prince Hal. Alike in their ultimate devotion to defense of their rule from rebellious nobles, they are opposites too. King Henry is reserved, in contact only with a chosen few in his aristocratic, military circle. Thus, he is not a well-loved king and must constantly fight to retain power. Hal, however, is regularly in enjoyable, intimate contact with all levels of English society, ranging from barmaids like Mistress Quickly (whose name speaks for itself) to the aristocratic, military group of his father. Thus, it seems clear, Hal will eventually be a popular king. King Henry decides to postpone his trip to the Holy Land in favor of military defense of his kingship, a clear hint that he is not a particularly peaceful ruler but rather one prone to respond violently to violent challenge, regardless of religious commitments. In contrast, Prince Hal engineers the release of Douglas, the Scottish leader who has fought vigorously against the king and Hal, preferring leniency to the fate his father imposes at the play's end upon Worcester and Vernon: death. In fact, one could say that Hal is forgiving of Douglas' transgressions, a clear indication of a subtle level of biblical symbolism in the play. Like the Old Testament God, Henry IV is wrathful and violent, leading by brute force, but like Christ, Hal is devoted to the commoners of the realm and is forgiving of those who oppose him (with the exception of Hotspur, who had to be dealt with by violence).

Thus, Shakespeare creates an artistic and structural symmetry in *Henry IV, Part I* via subplots, parallels, and contrasts that achieves interrelated purposes of audience entertainment, character clarification, symbolic integration, and thematic expression. Such complex compression gives the play a multiplicity in unity that has helped to generate its enduring appeal.

John L. Grigsby

Bibliography:

Baker, Herschel. Introduction to *Henry IV, Part I*, by William Shakespeare. In *The Riverside Shakespeare*, edited by G. Blakemore Evans. Boston: Houghton Miflin, 1974. Brief introduction to the play, with explanation of Shakespeare's use of his sources, his different levels of plotting, and use of humor.

Bevington, David. Introduction to *Henry IV, Part I*, by William Shakespeare. New York: Oxford University Press, 1987. General introduction to the play. Discusses its performance history, its sources, its major characters, its structural unity, and its politics.

Cohen, Derek. "The Rite of Violence in *I Henry IV*." *Shakespeare Survey* 38 (1985): 77-84. A detailed analysis of Hotspur as structural center of the play, explaining his evolution from comic to heroic and then to tragic figure.

Fehrenbach, Robert J. "The Characterization of the King in *I Henry IV*." *Shake-*

speare Quarterly 30 no. 1 (Winter, 1979): 42-50. Contends that a focus upon King Henry is crucial to comprehension of Shakespeare's use of indirect characterization.

Levin, Lawrence. "Hotspur, Falstaff and the Emblem of Wrath in *I Henry IV*." *Shakespeare Studies* 10 (1977): 43-65. Analyzes the relationship between Hotspur and Falstaff, contending Falstaff is a visual representation of the wrath that controls Hotspur.

Henry IV, Part II

Type of plot: Historical
Time of plot: 1405-1413
Locale: England
First performed: 1597; first published, 1600

Principal characters

KING HENRY IV
HAL, the Prince of Wales
JOHN OF LANCASTER, another son of the king
EARL OF WESTMORELAND, a member of the king's party
EARL OF NORTHUMBERLAND, enemy of the king
SIR JOHN FALSTAFF, a riotous old knight
SHALLOW, a country justice
THE LORD CHIEF JUSTICE, judge of the King's Bench
MISTRESS QUICKLY, hostess of the Boar's Head Tavern in Eastcheap

The Story

After the battle of Shrewsbury many false reports were circulated among the peasants. Northumberland believed for a time that the rebel forces had been victorious, but his retainers, fleeing from that stricken field, brought a true account of the death of Hotspur, Northumberland's valiant son, at the hands of Prince Henry, and of King Henry's avowal to put down rebellion by crushing those forces still opposing him. Northumberland, sorely grieved by news of his son's death, prepared to avenge that loss. Hope for his side lay in the fact that the archbishop of York had mustered an army, because soldiers so organized, being responsible to the church rather than to a military leader, would prove better fighters than those who had fled from Shrewsbury field. News that the king's forces of twenty-five thousand men had been divided into three units was encouraging to his enemies. In spite of Northumberland's grief for his slain son and his impassioned threat against the king and Prince Henry, he was easily persuaded by his wife and Hotspur's widow to flee to Scotland, there to await the success of his confederates before he would consent to join them with his army.

Meanwhile, Falstaff delayed in carrying out his orders to proceed north and recruit troops for the king. Deeply involved with Mistress Quickly, he used his royal commission to avoid being imprisoned for debt. With Prince Henry, who had paid little heed to the conduct of the war, he continued his riotous feasting and jesting until both were summoned to join the army marching against the rebels.

King Henry, aging and weary, had been ill for two weeks. Sleepless nights had taken their toll on him, and in his restlessness he reviewed his ascent to the throne and denied, to his lords, the accusation of unscrupulousness brought against him by the rebels. He was somewhat heartened by the news of Glendower's death.

In Gloucestershire, recruiting troops at the house of Justice Shallow, Falstaff flagrantly accepted bribes and let able-bodied men buy themselves out of service. The soldiers he took to the war were a raggle-taggle lot. Prince John of Lancaster, taking the field against the rebels, sent word by Westmoreland to the archbishop that the king's forces were willing to make peace, and he asked that the rebel leaders make known their grievances so that they might be corrected.

When John and the archbishop met for a conference, John questioned and criticized the archbishop's dual role as churchman and warrior. The rebels announced their intention to fight until their wrongs were righted, so John promised redress for all. Then he suggested that the archbishop's troops be disbanded after a formal review; he wished to see the stalwart soldiers that his army would have fought if a truce had not been declared.

His request was granted, but the men, excited by the prospect of their release, scattered so rapidly that inspection was impossible. Westmoreland, sent to disband John's army, returned to report that the soldiers would take orders only from the prince. With his troops assembled and the enemy's disbanded, John ordered some of the opposing leaders arrested for high treason and others, including the archbishop, for capital treason. John explained that his action was in keeping with his promise to improve conditions and that to remove rebellious factions was the first step in his campaign. The enemy leaders were sentenced to death.

News of John's success was brought to King Henry as he lay dying, but the victory could not gladden the sad old king. His chief concern lay in advice and admonition to his younger sons, Gloucester and Clarence, regarding their future conduct, and he asked for unity among his sons. Spent by his long discourse, the king lapsed into unconsciousness.

Prince Henry, summoned to his dying father's bedside, found the king in a stupor, with the crown beside him. The prince, remorseful and compassionate, expressed regret that the king had lived such a tempestuous existence because of the crown and promised, in his turn, to wear the crown graciously. As he spoke, he placed the crown on his head and left the room. Awaking and learning that the prince had donned the crown, King Henry immediately assumed that his son wished him dead in order to inherit the kingdom. Consoled by the prince's strong denial of such wishful thinking, the king confessed his own unprincipled behavior in gaining the crown. Asking God's forgiveness, he repeated his plan to journey to the Holy Land to divert his subjects from revolt, and he advised the prince, when he should become king, to involve his powerful lords in wars with foreign powers, thereby relieving the country of internal strife.

The king's death caused great sorrow among those who loved him and to those who feared the prince, now Henry V. A short time before, the Lord Chief Justice, acting on the command of Henry IV, had alienated the prince by banishing Falstaff and his band, but the newly crowned king accepted the Lord Chief Justice's explanation for his treatment of Falstaff and restored his judicial powers.

Falstaff was rebuked for his conduct by Henry V, who stated that he was no longer the person Falstaff had known him to be. Until the old knight learned to correct his ways, the king banished him, on pain of death, to a distance ten miles away from Henry's person. He promised, however, that if amends were made Falstaff would return by degrees to the king's good graces. Undaunted by that reproof, Falstaff explained to his cronies that he yet would make them great, that the king's reprimand was only a front, and that the king would send for him and in the secrecy of the court chambers they would indulge in their old foolishness and plan the advancement of Falstaff's followers. Prince John, expressing his admiration for Henry's public display of his changed attitude, prophesied that England would be at war with France before a year had passed.

"Uneasy lies the head that wears a crown"

Henry IV, Part II, Act III, scene i, line 31

Despite Henry IV's victory at Shrewsbury, at which battle Henry Percy (Hotspur) was slain by Prince Hal, the rebellion continues. King Henry finds that the affairs of the world have made sleep impossible, and he broods on the fact that all the world except himself lies asleep:

> *King Henry.* Canst thou, o partial sleep, give thy repose
> To the wet sea's son in an hour so rude,
> And in the calmest and most stillest night,
> With all appliances and means to boot,
> Deny it to a king? Then, happy low, lie down,
> Uneasy lies the head that wears a crown.

Critical Evaluation

The third play in William Shakespeare's second tetralogy, *King Henry IV, Part II* is based on Raphael Holinshed's *Chronicles of England, Scotland, and Ireland* (1577) and on an anonymous Elizabethan drama, *The Famous Victories of Henry V*. It offers a collection of well-rounded characters for whose creation Shakespeare makes slender use of his sources. The drama resolves the conflict, carried over from *King Henry IV, Part I*, between the king and rebellious nobles. In its essence this conflict is one of local versus national rule. The second play also continues the character development of Prince Hal as an ideal future king. The denial of characters' expectations, marked by sudden dramatic reversals, represents a unifying motif of the drama.

Retaining the main plot of the rebellion and the subplot involving Falstaff and his companions from *Henry IV, Part I*, the drama limits action in favor of rhetoric. To the panoply of characters surrounding the king from *Henry IV, Part I*, Shakespeare adds the astute and farsighted Warwick as an adviser and the upright Lord Chief Justice as another father figure for Prince Hal. Additions also enhance the subplot involving Falstaff. He is furnished, in *Henry IV, Part II*, with a spirited young boy as a page, with the histrionic, swaggering Pistol, and with the sharp-tongued Doll Tearsheet. In a further strand in the subplot, Justice Shallow, his cousin Silence, and Shallow's servants serve as humorous country bumpkins who willingly play into Falstaff's hands.

Rumors of battles linger through much of the drama, but they prove to be only rumors. As the rebels regroup under the able archbishop of York following their loss at Shrewsbury, the king's divided army prepares to move against the centers of rebel strength, Wales and York, arousing expectations of decisive battles. The threat of battle in Wales simply evaporates as the king learns the news that Glendower, the Welsh leader, has died. In the north, Prince John entices the rebels into a deceptive truce and sends their leaders to summary execution. The crushing of rebel power consolidates the king's rule, yet ironically he is too ill to enjoy the fruits of his victory. The action seems subdued and anticlimactic, the elimination of the rebel threat and the consolidation of regal power pave the way for an orderly succession.

Instead of vivid action, the play offers rhetorical confrontations to strengthen the dramatic conflict and to help resolve the two poles that influence Prince Hal: his father and Falstaff. In one of many indications that the fat knight will be rejected, Falstaff freely expresses his indiscreet opinions of other characters—Justice Shallow, Prince John, and Hal—in soliloquies. His comments on others are less extensive but no less indiscreet. In two early scenes, encounters between Falstaff and the Lord Chief Justice foreshadow the major rhetorical confrontations involving Hal. Falstaff, who has escaped punishment for theft only because he holds a military commission, attempts to intimidate the Lord Chief Justice, who has sought to admonish him about his thievery. To the Lord Chief Justice, Falstaff pretends that he is deaf. This joke turns on Falstaff, who hears but fails to understand what others are saying. To the Lord Chief Justice Falstaff intimates that the king is dying, that Hal will become king, and that as Hal's friend Falstaff will have important influence. Unmoved by any personal threat, the Lord Chief Justice demonstrates his commitment of law as an ideal.

The scene foreshadows Hal's three great rhetorical confrontations in the drama: with the king, his real father; with the Lord Chief Justice, a just and wise father figure; and with Falstaff, a parody of a father figure who must be rejected. In Act IV, scene iv, Hal is summoned to his dying father's bedside. The king's doubts about him are reinforced when Hal, thinking his father dead, removes the crown from a pillow to meditate on the pain and grief it has brought. Regaining consciousness, the king notices that the crown is missing and concludes that Hal has seized it prematurely. When the prince returns, the king denounces him for ingratitude, citing numerous examples from the past, but this sense of personal injury gives way to a more important concern—the future of the nation under Hal's rule. He fears that Hal will recklessly give power to Falstaff and others like him. As a consequence, the national unity that the king has achieved will degenerate into riot and anarchy. In an eloquent response, Hal convinces the king that he has been mistaken about Hal's intentions. He assures the king that he will follow the king's example, not Richard's. Following the speech, the king, now more confident, advises Hal to rely on the wise counselors who have served him and to involve the country in a foreign war in order to promote unity.

Following the king's death, his counselors and Hal's brothers fear impending chaos. In order to reassure them, Hal addresses the Lord Chief Justice, who is convinced that he has the most to lose. Of his three confrontations, this is the only one that Hal deliberately manages; the other two are either unexpected or opportunistic. Assuming the role of an injured party, Hal demands that the Lord Chief Justice explain his earlier decision to send Hal to prison. The Lord Chief Justice recounts the episode in detail and argues that authority and justice demanded Hal's punishment. Pointedly, he asks Hal to explain how his sentence was unjust. The king's response, moving in its dignity, affirms to the Lord Chief Justice that he had been correct, confirms him in his office, retains him as counselor, and assures those present that Hal will follow the example of his father.

"Thy wish was father . . . to that thought"

Henry IV, Part II, Act IV, scene v, line 93

After the defeat of the rebellious barons, King Henry gathers his sons around him. Then he falls into a fit of apoplexy and is laid in a bed. Prince Hal, the future king, comes in and sits beside his father, whom he thinks dead. Seeing the crown on the bed beside the king, Hal begins to meditate on his coming reign. He promises himself that nothing will force the crown from him. He will pass "this lineal honor" on to his successor. He then steps into another room, wearing the crown. King Henry wakes and misses it. When told that Hal is wearing it, Henry thinks that Hal can hardly wait to ascend the throne. Hal explains that he believed his father to be dead: "I never thought to hear you speak again." King Henry replies with a warning that the responsibilities of the crown constitute a mixed blessing:

> *King Henry.* Thy wish was father, Henry, to that thought,
> I stay too long by thee, I weary thee.
> Dost thou so hunger for mine empty chair,
> That thou wilt needs invest thee with my honours,
> Before thy hour be ripe? O foolish youth,
> Thou seek'st the greatness that will overwhelm thee.

The third confrontation is arranged by Falstaff, who has rushed from Gloucestershire to London after hearing of Hal's succession. Arriving in time for the coronation procession, Falstaff thrusts himself forward and addresses the king with impudent familiarity: "God save thee, my sweet boy!" Hal coldly turns aside and directs the Lord Chief Justice to speak to Falstaff. The move astonishes Falstaff, who believes that the Lord Chief Justice will be punished for his transgressions, and he again directs his speech to Hal. Speaking as king, Henry V denounces Falstaff as a misleader of youth and banishes him from the royal presence.

Incredulous at this reversal and denial of his expectation, Falstaff thinks the king will send for him in private, but even Justice Shallow discerns the finality of the king's tone. By the play's end, Hal has convinced the skeptics of his ability to rule.

"Critical Evaluation" by Stanley Archer

For Further Study

Ornstein, Robert. *A Kingdom for a Stage*. Cambridge, Mass.: Harvard University Press, 1972. In a critical study that includes all of Shakespeare's history plays, Ornstein devotes a chapter to *Henry IV, Part II*. He describes Hal's development and his rejection of Falstaff.

Pearlman, Elihu. *William Shakespeare: The History Plays*. Boston: Twayne, 1992. A valuable scholarly overview of the histories. The chapter on *Henry IV, Part II* is divided into numerous brief analyses of characters and themes.

Porter, Joseph A. *The Drama of Speech Acts*. Berkeley: University of California Press, 1979. Analyzes speech and oratory in the second tetralogy. A chapter on *Henry IV, Part II* explores the contrasts between Falstaff's speech and Hal's.

Tillyard, E. M. W. *Shakespeare's History Plays*. London: Chatto & Windus, 1944. Strong on historical interpretation, Tillyard's study explores the important themes of the second tetralogy. Traces the growth and development of Hal's character.

Traversi, Derek Antona. *Shakespeare: From "Richard II" to "Henry V."* Stanford, Calif.: Stanford University Press. A close reading of the second tetralogy includes a chapter on *Henry IV, Part II* that emphasizes character development and style.

Henry V

Type of plot: Historical
Time of plot: Early fifteenth century
Locale: England and France
First performed: c. 1598-1599; first published, 1600

Principal characters

HENRY V, the King of England
CHARLES VI, the King of France
PRINCESS KATHARINE, his daughter
THE DAUPHIN, his son
MONTJOY, a French herald

The Story

Once the toss-pot prince of Falstaff's tavern brawls, Henry V was now king at Westminster, a stern but just monarch concerned with his hereditary claim to the crown of France. Before the arrival of the French ambassadors, the young king asked for legal advice from the archbishop of Canterbury. The king thought he was the legal heir to the throne of France through Edward III, whose claim to the French throne was, at best, questionable. The archbishop assured Henry that he had as much right to the French throne as did the French king, and both he and the bishop of Ely urged Henry to press his demands against the French.

When the ambassadors from France arrived, they came not from Charles, the king, but from his arrogant eldest son, the Dauphin. According to the ambassadors, the Dauphin thought the English monarch to be the same hot-headed, irresponsible youth he had been before he ascended the throne. To show that he considered Henry an unfit ruler with ridiculous demands, the Dauphin presented Henry with tennis balls. Enraged by the insult, Henry told the French messengers to warn their master that the tennis balls would be turned into gun stones for use against the French.

The English prepared for war. The Dauphin remained contemptuous of Henry, but others, including the ambassadors who had seen Henry in his wrath, were not so confident. Henry's army landed to lay siege to Harfleur, and the king threatened to destroy the city and its inhabitants unless it surrendered. The French governor had to capitulate because help promised by the Dauphin never arrived. The French—with the exception of King Charles—were alarmed by the rapid progress of the English through France. King Charles, however, was so sure of victory that he sent his herald, Montjoy, to Henry to demand that the English king pay a ransom

132

to the French, give himself up, and have his soldiers withdraw from France. Henry was not impressed by this bold gesture.

On the eve of the decisive battle of Agincourt, the English were outnumbered five to one. Henry's troops were on foreign soil and riddled with disease. To encourage them, and also to sound out their morale, the king borrowed a cloak and in this disguise walked out among his troops, from watch to watch and from tent to tent. As he talked with his men, he told them that a king is but a man like other men, and that if he were a king he would not want to be anywhere except where he was, in battle with his soldiers. To himself, Henry mused over the cares and responsibilities of kingship. He thought of himself simply as a man who differed from other men only in ceremony, itself an empty thing.

Henry's sober reflections on the eve of a great battle, in which he thought much English blood would be shed, were quite different from those of the French, who were exceedingly confident of their ability to defeat the enemy. Shortly before the conflict began, Montjoy again appeared to give the English one last chance to surrender. Henry, who was not discouraged by the numerical inferiority of his troops, again refused to be intimidated. As he reasoned in speaking with one of his officers, the fewer troops the English had, the greater would be the honor to them when they won.

The following day the battle began. Under Henry's leadership, the English held their own. When French reinforcements arrived at a crucial point in the battle, Henry ordered his men to kill all their prisoners so that their energies might be directed entirely against the enemy before them. Soon the tide turned. A much humbler Montjoy approached Henry to request a truce for burying the French dead. Henry granted the herald's request, and at the same time learned from him that the French had conceded defeat. Ten thousand French had been killed, and only twenty-nine English.

The battle over, nothing remained for Henry but to discuss with the French king terms of peace. Katharine, Charles' beautiful daughter, was Henry's chief demand, and while his lieutenants settled the details of surrender with the French, Henry made love to the princess and asked her to marry him. Though Katharine's knowledge of English was slight and Henry's knowledge of French little better, they were both acquainted with the universal language of love. French Katharine consented to become English Kate and Henry's bride.

"The Story" by James Marc Hovde

Critical Evaluation

Henry V is the last play in the cycle in which William Shakespeare explores the nature of kingship and compares medieval and Renaissance ideal rulers. In *Henry IV, Part I*, Hal (the nickname by which Henry was known in his youth) soliloquizes that his roguish behavior, which so disturbs his father and the court, is policy—a temporary ploy soon to be discarded, after which he will astonish and delight his critics. True to that promise, Hal becomes the perfect English king, a true representative of all of his people, one who understands his own vices and virtues and those of his citizens. His youthful escapades have taught him a deep understanding of the human nature of the citizens he must rule, making him wise beyond his years.

Henry V, Shakespeare's summarizing portrait of what a good king should be, acts in the best Elizabethan tradition. The archbishop of Canterbury's description in Act I, scene i, confirms him as well rounded, a man of words and of action, a scholar, diplomat, poet, and soldier. He can "reason in divinity," "debate of commonwealth affairs," "discourse of war" or of music, and "unloose the Gordian knot of policy . . . in sweet and honeyed sentences." Unlike his father, who was tortured by self-recrimination, Henry V is sure of his authority, power, and ability. Proud of his country and followers, he attributes his successes to God's leadership. Unlike Richard II, Henry V keeps fears and worries private. He stays attuned to his

In the 1989 film version of Henry V, *Kenneth Branagh as King Henry (center) leads England and his brothers, Gloucester (Simon Sheperd, left) and Bedford (James Larkin, right), into battle against France.* (Courtesy of The Museum of Modern Art, Film Stills Archive)

subjects' undercurrents of feelings, as when he walks among them in disguise instead of relying on censored reports. His effective spy system ferrets out traitors, whom he disposes of swiftly and violently. His earlier experiences help him to distinguish loyal subjects and good soldiers from the disloyal and incompetent; in Act IV, scene i, he rejects flattery but values blunt honesty. Moreover, he surrounds himself with good advisers whose advice he follows. He is generous to friends and supporters, rewards loyalty, and in his St. Crispin's speech he calls those who fight by his side "brothers" no matter what their rank or class. Above all, Henry V is flexible, able to be a king in war and a king in peace and capable of gentle mercy as well as harsh justice. His leniency to enemy villagers wins their hearts, but he is merciless to French captives who broke the rules of war, killing English baggage boys.

As a model king, Henry V is, above all else, politic, a follower of Niccolò Machiavelli's principles as enunciated in *The Prince* (1513) and able to manipulate language and people to attain his country's welfare. The opening action demonstrates Machiavellian policy consummately managed. As a new, untried king with a youthful reputation for riotous living, Henry V must secure his throne, extend his power, and improve his reputation while he still has youth, vigor, and political support. At the same time, he must take his subjects' minds off the internal conflicts, rebellions, and usurpations that had plagued his father's reign and he must unite diverse English factions. The quickest, most effective way to achieve these ends is to do as his father advised: "busy giddy minds with foreign quarrels." the French, by contemptuously dismissing Henry V as an effeminate wastrel fit only for the tennis courts, provide the perfect common enemy.

Henry's forceful yet poetic retorts to French insults couple powerful rhetoric with personal magnetism, and his threat to confiscate church property motivates its representatives to find religious and legal justifications for a foreign war. Thus England has not only "means and might" but a righteous "cause": ousting a usurper. The attack on France will be a holy war, fully backed by holy church and legal precedent: "God for Harry, England, and Saint George!" Extending England's legal claims in the tradition of Edward III reminds Henry's subjects and his European critics of his glorious ancestry and evokes English patriotism. Here, Henry V effectively employs Machiavellian strategies; his forceful rhetoric demonstrates good policy and good kingship. His warning to Harfleuer, for example, paints such a grim picture of death and destruction, of raped maidens and skewered infants, that fearful town officials surrender peacefully.

The victorious battle at Agincourt, the play's crux, proves Hal's right to rule England. Shakespeare carefully avoids mentioning the main historical reason for victory, the fact that the English battle methods of foot soldiers with long bows were superior to the medieval French methods of single armored knights waging hand-to-hand combat. He chooses instead to attribute the victory to a glorious English king whose rhetoric and personal valor was able to inspire common men to brave deeds against impossible odds. The French Dauphin and his nobles provide the antithesis to Hal's good English king, for they are vain, arrogant and overconfident, willing to leave the battle to servants and to flee at the first real opposition; they are disorganized and quarrelsome, whereas, thanks to Henry V's leadership, the English fight as an organized "band of brothers," their hearts "in the trim," "warriors for the working-day" ready for God to "dispose the day."

Act V shows Henry V as the complete hero king. The first four acts having demonstrated Henry's virtues in war, Act V shows a more casual Henry, commanding but at ease, a king for peace. It also demonstrates what a hero king can bring

---

"Once more unto the breach"

Henry V, Act III, scene i, line 1

King Henry V (Prince Hal in the *Henry IV* plays) and his soldiers have departed from England, leaving her "guarded with grandsires, babies, and old women," to conquer France. The English are laying siege to Harfleur. Henry, his noblemen, and soldiers, approach the walls of the city with scaling ladders. Henry spurs them to battle.

> *Henry.* Once more unto the breach, dear friends, once more;
> Or close the wall up with our English dead.
> In peace, there's nothing so becomes a man,
> As modest stillness, and humility.
> But when the blast of war blows in our ears,
> Then imitate the action of the tiger;
> Stiffen the sinews, summon up the blood,
> Disguise fair nature with hard-favoured rage.

---

to England: a peace treaty with provisions for lands, power, title, and honor, as well as an attractive queen whose intelligence and proud spirit make her worthy to carry on both royal lines. A "conqu'ring Caesar," Hal tempers justice with mercy, restores order and harmony, and strengthens political bonds through a royal marriage that weds nations and provides a new garden, sullied but mendable, for England's royal gardener, the king, to cultivate and make profitable. Henry does not bargain away what was gained in the field but stays firm. He shows another facet of his rhetoric and understanding of psychology when he adopts the appealing role of a blunt solider, unused to wooing, to win a hesitant princess who does not wish to be forced into a loveless political marriage.

Henry V purposefully lends weight to the Tudor myth of divine right and reflects glory on Henry's descendant, Elizabeth I. Henry's victories confirm his (and by extension Elizabeth's) God-given right to power. Elizabethan audiences were meant to understand that the qualities and blessings of Henry V had been passed on to Elizabeth by right of birth. Moreover, Henry V provides a model of good kingship: The harsh realities of political life demand both action and thought, mercy and justice, war and peace. A good king uses whatever tools available to attain order, harmony, peace and prosperity, for good ends justify the means.

"Critical Evaluation" by Gina Macdonald

For Further Study

Berger, Thomas L. "Casting 'Henry V.'" *Shakespeare Studies: An Annual Gathering of Research, Criticism, and Reviews* 20 (1987): 89-104. Emphasizes that understanding the Elizabethan custom of multiple acting roles helps readers make thematic, ironic, comic, and aesthetic connections in the play.

Cook, Dorothy. "'Henry V': Maturing of Man and Majesty." *Studies in the Literary*

Imagination 5, no. 1 (April, 1972): 111-128. Argues that the play demonstrates Henry's responsibility and personal maturity, his political and military virtues in Acts I and II and his private virtues in the final acts. The play's structural pattern alternates triumphs and reversals and uses a quickening pace, multiple plotting contrasts, and a psychologically effective dramatic balance.

Kernan, Alvin. "The Henriad: Shakespeare's Major History Plays." *The Yale Review* 59, no. 1 (October, 1969): 3-32. Concludes that the tetralogy records "the passage from the Middle Ages to the Renaissance and the modern world" and depicts Henry V as a consummate politician with a clear-cut public role that is necessitated by his desire to rule well.

Rabkin, Norman. "Rabbits, Ducks, and *Henry V*." *Shakespeare Quarterly* 28, no. 3 (Summer, 1977): 279-296. Rabkin argues the "fundamental ambiguity" of the play: Henry as both model Christian monarch and brutal Machiavel, a ruthless, expedient, manipulative ruler with spiritual and political virtues. This mature duality makes Henry V a good but inscrutable king.

Thayer, C. G. "The Mirror of All Christian Kings." In *Shakespearean Politics: Government and Misgovernment in the Great Histories*. Athens: Ohio University Press, 1983. Argues that the pragmatic, responsible Henry V is Shakespeare's model for a Renaissance monarch. Ruling more by personal achievement than by divine right, he reflects the kind of kingship considered ideal in 1599.

Henry VI, Part I

Type of plot: Historical
Time of plot: 1422-1444
Locale: England and France
First performed: c. 1592; first published, 1598

Principal characters

KING HENRY VI
DUKE OF GLOSTER, uncle of the king and Protector of the Realm
DUKE OF BEDFORD, uncle of the king and Regent of France
HENRY BEAUFORT, bishop of Winchester, afterward cardinal
RICHARD PLANTAGENET, who becomes Duke of York
JOHN BEAUFORT, Earl of Somerset
EARL OF SUFFOLK
LORD TALBOT, a general, afterward Earl of Shrewsbury
CHARLES, THE DAUPHIN, afterward King of France
THE BASTARD OF ORLEANS, a French general
MARGARET OF ANJOU, afterward married to King Henry
JOAN LA PUCELLE, also known as Joan of Arc

The Story

The great nobles and churchmen of England gathered in Westminster Abbey for the state funeral of King Henry V, hero of Agincourt and conqueror of France. The eulogies of Gloster, Bedford, Exeter, and the bishop of Winchester, profound and extensive, were broken off by messengers bringing reports of English defeat and failure in France, where the Dauphin, taking advantage of King Henry's illness, had raised a revolt. The gravest defeat reported was the imprisonment of Lord Talbot, general of the English armies. Bedford swore to avenge his loss. Gloster said that he would also hasten military preparations and proclaim young Prince Henry, nine months old, King of England. The bishop of Winchester, disgruntled because the royal dukes had asked neither his advice nor aid, planned to seize the king's person and ingratiate himself into royal favor.

In France, the Dauphin and his generals, discussing the conduct of the war, attempted to overwhelm the depleted English forces. Although outnumbered and without leaders, the English fought valiantly and tenaciously. Hope of victory came to the French, however, when the Bastard of Orleans brought to the Dauphin's camp a soldier-maid, Joan La Pucelle, described as a holy young girl with God-given visionary powers. The Dauphin's attempt to trick her was unsuccessful, for she recognized him although Reignier, Duke of Anjou, stood in the Dauphin's place. Next she vanquished the prince in a duel to which he had challenged her in an attempt to test her fighting skill.

The followers of the Duke of Gloster and the bishop of Winchester rioted in the London streets, as dissension between church and state grew because of Winchester's efforts to keep Gloster from seeing young Henry. The mayor of London declaimed the unseemly conduct of the rioters.

When the English and the French fought again, Lord Salisbury and Sir Thomas Gargrave, the English leaders, were killed by a gunner in ambush. Meanwhile Lord Talbot, greatly feared by the French, had been ransomed in time to take command of English forces in the siege of Orleans. Enraged by the death of Salisbury, Talbot fought heroically, on one occasion with La Pucelle herself. At last the English swarmed into the town and put the French to rout. Talbot ordered Salisbury's body to be carried into the public market place of Orleans as a token of his revenge for that lord's murder.

The countess of Auvergne invited Lord Talbot to visit her in her castle. Fearing chicanery, Bedford and Burgundy tried to keep him from going into an enemy stronghold, but Talbot, as strong-willed as he was brave, ignored their pleas. He whispered to his captain, however, certain instructions concerning his visit.

On his arrival at Auvergne Castle the countess announced that she was making him her prisoner in order to save France from further scourges. Talbot proved his wit by completely baffling the countess with double talk and by signaling his soldiers, who stormed the castle, ate the food and drank the wine, and then won the favor of the countess with their charming manners.

In addition to continued internal strife resulting from Gloster's and Winchester's personal ambitions, new dissension arose between Richard Plantagenet and the Earl of Somerset. Plantagenet and his followers chose a white rose as their symbol, Somerset and his supporters a red rose, and in the quarrel of these two men the disastrous Wars of the Roses began. In the meantime Edmund Mortimer, the rightful heir to the throne, who had been imprisoned when King Henry IV usurped the crown some thirty years before, was released from confinement. He urged his nephew, Richard Plantagenet, to restore the family to the rightful position the Plantagenets deserved. Youthful King Henry VI, after making Plantagenet Duke of York, much to the displeasure of Somerset, was taken to France by Gloster and other lords to be crowned King of France. In Paris, Talbot's chivalry and prowess were rewarded when he was made Earl of Shrewsbury.

In preparation for the battle at Rouen, La Pucelle won Burgundy over to the cause of France by playing upon his vanity and appealing to what she termed his sense of justice. The immaturity of the king was revealed in his request that Talbot go to Burgundy and chastise him for his desertion. The Duke of York and the Earl of Somerset finally brought their quarrel to the king, who implored them to be friendly for England's sake. He pointed out that disunity among the English lords would only weaken their stand in France. To show how petty he considered their differences he casually put on a red rose, the symbol of Somerset's faction, and explained that it was merely a flower and that he loved one of his rival kinsmen as much as the other. He appointed York a regent of France and ordered both him and Somerset to supply Talbot with men and supplies for battle. Then the king and his party returned to London.

The king's last assignment to his lords in France was Talbot's death knell; Somerset, refusing to send horses with which York planned to supply Talbot, accused York of self-aggrandizement. York, in turn, blamed Somerset for negligence. As their feud continued, Talbot and his son were struggling valiantly against

---

"Choked with ambition"

Henry VI, Part I, Act II, scene v, line 124

Edmund Mortimer, now old, has been imprisoned in the Tower of London since losing in his fight with Henry IV over succession to the English throne. Richard Plantagenet, Duke of York and Mortimer's nephew, visits him and asks the story of Mortimer's imprisonment. Mortimer recounts the unjust holding of the throne by the House of Lancaster (Henry's family) when the crown should have gone to the House of Mortimer. When Richard raves against these injustices, Mortimer advocates caution, for the House of Lancaster is "like a mountain, not to be moved." After Mortimer dies, Richard comments on his unjust fate, imposed by the ambitious Lancastrians. Ironically, however, the House of Mortimer and Richard are equally ambitious.

> *Richard.* Here dies the dusky torch of Mortimer,
> Choked with ambition of the meaner sort.
> And for those wrongs, those bitter injuries,
> Which Somerset hath offered to my house,
> I doubt not but with honour to redress.

Ambition and its consequences are themes of many of Shakespeare's plays, especially the history plays and tragedies such as *Macbeth*.

---

the better-equipped and larger French army at Bordeaux. After many skirmishes Talbot and his son were slain, and the English suffered tremendous losses. Flushed with the triumph of their great victory, the French leaders planned to march on to Paris.

In England, meanwhile, there was talk of a truce, and the king agreed, after a moment of embarrassment because of his youth, to Gloster's proposal that Henry accept in marriage the daughter of the Earl of Armagnac, a man of affluence and influence in France. This alliance, designed to effect a friendly peace between the two countries, was to be announced in France by Cardinal Beaufort, former bishop of Winchester, who, in sending money to the pope to pay for his cardinalship, stated that his ecclesiastical position gave him status equal to that of the loftiest peer. He threatened mutiny if Gloster ever tried to dominate him again. The king sent a jewel to seal the contract of betrothal.

The fighting in France dwindled greatly, with the English forces converging for one last weak stand. La Pucelle cast a spell and conjured up fiends to bolster her morale and to assist her in battle, but her appeal was to no avail, and York took her prisoner. Berated as a harlot and condemned as a witch by the English, La Pucelle pleaded for her life. At first she contended that her virgin blood would cry for vengeance at the gates of heaven. When this appeal failed to move York and the Earl of Warwick, she implored them to save her unborn child, fathered, she said variously, by the Dauphin, the Duke of Alencon, and the Duke of Anjou. She was condemned to be burned at the stake.

In another skirmish the Earl of Suffolk had taken as his prisoner Margaret, daughter of the Duke of Anjou. Enthralled by her loveliness, he was unable to claim her for himself because he was already married. He finally struck upon the notion of wooing Margaret for the king. After receiving her father's permission to present Margaret's name to Henry as a candidate for marriage, Suffolk went to London to petition the king. While Henry weighed the matter against the consequences of breaking his contract with the Earl of Armagnac, Exeter and Gloster attempted to dissuade him from following Suffolk's suggestions. Their pleas were in vain. Margaret's great courage and spirit, as described by Suffolk, held promise of a great and invincible offspring.

Terms of peace having been arranged, Suffolk was ordered to conduct Margaret to England. Suffolk, because he had brought Margaret and Henry together, planned to take advantage of his opportune political position and, through Margaret, rule youthful Henry and his kingdom.

Critical Evaluation

This play is the first in a trilogy of plays about the reign of King Henry VI of England, and the story is continued in a fourth play, *Richard III* (c. 1592-1593). The series of plays depicts the Wars of the Roses, which was civil warfare in England arising out of a dispute about the rightful succession to the throne. The theme of the series, an important and practical one to William Shakespeare's Elizabethan audience, is the necessity for a strong and secure monarchy to ensure the peace and prosperity of the realm. *Henry VI, Part I* deals with events leading up to the war.

The play can be confusing to read for a number of reasons, one of which is that it portrays disunity. The society it reflects is confused, inconsistent, and disorderly. In addition, the events shown in the play occurred over a period of many years, but in the play are telescoped down to fit into two or three hours. Consequently, the action tends to be fast-paced, unevenly developed, and sometimes disjointed. There are many short scenes and complete reversals of fortune in the war. The historical details are sometimes distorted and not always fully consistent. The cast of characters is very large, and several of them are central to the action of the play, but no single one of them dominates the play as a whole. Finally, a number of conflicts are presented, the causes of which are complex. An audience may be helped along by abridgment and stagecraft; audiences and readers alike benefit from an understanding of the play's historical background.

Joan of Arc (Terri McMahon) is condemned to burn at the stake in the Oregon Shakespeare Festival's 1992 production of the first part of Henry VI. (Christopher Briscoe, courtesy of the Oregon Shakespeare Festival by permission of the Actors' Equity Association)

After the death of the strong and popular Henry V, the English face two problems: the resurgence of unity and fighting spirit among the French, who seek to reestablish France's sovereignty, and the disintegration of England, lacking an effective leader. The Duke of Bedford makes a gloomy prophecy at the funeral of Henry V, "Posterity, await for wretched years," which is fulfilled during the course of the play in the emergence of a power struggle between the Duke of Gloster and the bishop of Winchester and in the ultimately disastrous quarrel between Richard Plantagenet and the Earl of Somerset.

Winchester is portrayed as a corrupt, power-hungry bishop who buys his elevation to cardinal and who seeks to overthrow the rightful, secular authority of the Protector. This can be seen as anti-Roman Catholic propaganda, a politically orthodox, patriotic bias widely shared by the Elizabethan audience. The dispute between Richard and Somerset is more complex. They are motivated by the desire for power and influence as well as by envy and mutual dislike. In Richard's case, he seems to be more than a mere opportunist. The dying Edmund Mortimer establishes his position, and right seems to be on Richard's side in his claim to the house of York, and perhaps the English throne. Richard is more developed and more ambiguous than most of the characters in the play. Audiences see in him not only imperative ambition but also a more thoughtful judgment, as in the scene in which Henry unwisely puts on a red rose and Richard chooses to hold his tongue.

The situation of the English armies fighting in France, poorly provisioned and equipped, lacking reinforcements, and close to mutiny, is a consequence of the dissension among the nobles at home, and to some extent a parallel to it. Leadership, values, and focus are generally absent, and replaced by uncertainty and self-interest.

Lord Talbot is an example of how an English leader should be. He is courageous and strong, loved by his own people and feared by his enemies. In the incident with the countess of Auvergne, audiences see he is charming but nobody's fool. He is loyal, optimistic and God-fearing. Talbot, like England, is betrayed and brought to ruin by the self-serving discord among the English nobility.

The portrayal of the French is unflattering. Their success in battle is the result of problems in the English ranks rather than to any virtue of their own, and the English blame it on French sorcery. Any pretensions the French have to valor are undercut. The Dauphin, Charles, for example, proclaims that he prefers to die rather than run; the next thing the audience sees him do is flee, complaining bitterly of the cowardice of his men. The scenes about the French are often comic, with Shakespeare mocking the French as effete blusterers whose main interest is in making love.

Many critics have objected to the playwright's version of Joan of Arc, but in this play, with its clear anti-French, anti-Catholic bias, the portrayal is hardly surprising. Even the French characters undermine Joan's holiness with lust and wise-cracking innuendo. The play shows her to be whore, hypocrite, sorceress, and liar. All these attributes of a characterization were presumably popular with an Elizabethan audience.

In the final act, the alliance between Margaret of Anjou and the Earl of Suffolk, the arrangements for the marriage between Henry and Margaret, and Suffolk's vow to use his influence with her to control the king and the realm form a strong link with the next play in the trilogy. *Henry VI, Part I*, written early in Shakespeare's career, lacks the stature of the later plays. Its structure is loose and episodic. The characters are generally impelled by one dominant characteristic and lack the subtlety of Shakespeare's later characterizations. The verse does not achieve the fluency and grandeur seen in the later plays. Critics have disputed whether the play was written by Shakespeare alone, or even whether Shakespeare wrote any of it at all. Modern scholarship tends to attribute the play entirely to Shakespeare, however, and to find in its vigor the greatness that the playwright would later show in abundance.

"Critical Evaluation" by Susan Henthorne

For Further Study

Berry, Edward I. "*1 Henry VI:* Chivalry and Ceremony." In *Patterns of Decay: Shakespeare's Early Histories*. Charlottesville: University Press of Virginia, 1975. Addresses some of the issues raised by earlier critics. Concludes that the play needs to be read in sequence, not alone.

Bevington, David. "The First Part of King Henry the Sixth." In *William Shakespeare: The Complete Works*, edited by Alfred Harbage. Rev. ed. New York: Viking Press, 1969. Examines the functions of the characters. Considers multiple authorship theories and date of composition.

Blanpied, John W. *Time and the Artist in Shakespeare's English Histories*. Newark: University of Delaware Press, 1983. Examines how the playwright transforms historical material into drama. Contains a chapter on *Henry VI, Part I* that sees the play as flawed and immature, but one from which Shakespeare learned about his craft.

Saccio, Peter. *Shakespeare's English Kings: History, Chronicle, and Drama*. New York: Oxford University Press, 1977. Contains a section on the play recounting Shakespeare's sources. Includes genealogical charts and maps.

Tillyard, E. M. W. *Shakespeare's History Plays*. London: Chatto & Windus, 1944. Argues against multiple authorship theories, claiming the structure of the play shows clear signs of Shakespeare's style.

Henry VI, Part II

Type of plot: Historical
Time of plot: 1444-1455
Locale: England
First performed: c. 1590-1591; first published, 1594

Principal characters

KING HENRY VI
DUKE OF GLOSTER (HUMPHREY), his uncle
CARDINAL BEAUFORT, great-uncle of the king
RICHARD PLANTAGENET, Duke of York
EDWARD and
RICHARD, York's sons
DUKE OF SOMERSET, leader of the Lancaster faction
DUKE OF SUFFOLK, the king's favorite
EARL OF SALISBURY, a Yorkist
EARL OF WARWICK, a Yorkist
MARGARET, Queen of England
ELEANOR, Duchess of Gloster
JACK CADE, a rebel

The Story

The Earl of Suffolk, having arranged for the marriage of King Henry VI and Margaret of Anjou, brought the new queen to England. There was great indignation when the terms of the marriage treaty were revealed. The contract called for an eighteen-month truce between the two countries, the outright gift of the duchies of Anjou and Maine to Reignier, Margaret's father, and omission of her dowry. As had been predicted earlier, no good could come of this union, since Henry, at Suffolk's urging, had broken his betrothal to the daughter of the Earl of Armagnac. However, Henry, pleased by his bride's beauty, gladly accepted the treaty and elevated Suffolk, the go-between, to a dukedom.

The voices were hardly still from the welcome of the new queen before the lords, earls, and dukes were expressing their ambitions to gain more control in affairs of state. The old dissension between the Duke of Gloster and Cardinal Beaufort continued. The churchman tried to turn others against Gloster by saying that Gloster, next in line for the crown, needed watching. The Duke of Somerset accused the cardinal of seeking Gloster's position for himself. These high ambitions were not exclusively the failing of the men. The Duchess of Gloster showed great impatience with her husband when he said he wished only to serve as Protector of the Realm. When she saw that her husband was not going to help her ambitions to be queen, the duchess hired Hume, a priest, to traffic with witches and conjurers in her behalf. Hume accepted her money, but he had already been hired by Suffolk and the cardinal to work against the duchess.

Queen Margaret's unhappy life in England, her contempt for the king, and the people's dislike for her soon became apparent. The mutual hatred she and the duchess had for each other showed itself in tongue lashings and blows. The duchess, eager to take advantage of any turn of events, indulged in sorcery with Margery Jourdain and the notorious Bolingbroke. Her questions to them, all pertaining to the fate of the king and his advisers, and the answers which these sorcerers had received from the spirit world, were confiscated by Buckingham and York when they broke in upon a seance. For her part in the practice of sorcery the duchess was banished to the Isle of Man; Margery Jourdain and Bolingbroke were executed.

His wife's deeds brought new slanders upon Gloster. In answer to Queen Margaret's charge that he was a party to his wife's underhandedness, Gloster, a broken man, resigned his position as Protector of the Realm. Even after his resignation Margaret continued in her attempts to turn the king against Gloster. She was aided by the other lords, who accused Gloster of deceit and crimes against the state; but the king, steadfast in his loyalty to Gloster, described the former protector as virtuous and mild.

York, whose regency in France had been given to Somerset, enlisted the aid of Warwick and Salisbury in his fight for the crown, his claim being based on the fact that King Henry's grandfather, Henry IV, had usurped the throne from York's great-uncle. Suffolk and the cardinal, to rid themselves of a dangerous rival, sent York to quell an uprising in Ireland. Before departing for Ireland, York planned to incite rebellion among the English through one John Cade, a headstrong, warmongering Kentishman. Cade, under the name of John Mortimer, the name of York's uncle, paraded his riotous followers through the streets of London. The rebels, irresponsible and unthinking, went madly about the town wrecking buildings, killing noblemen who opposed them, and shouting that they were headed for the palace, where John Cade, the rightful heir to the throne, would avenge the injustices done his lineage. An aspect of the poorly organized rebellion was shown in the desertion of Cade's followers when they were appealed to by loyal old Lord Clifford. He admonished them to save England from needless destruction and to expend their military efforts against France. Cade, left alone, went wandering about the countryside as a fugitive and was killed by Alexander Iden, a squire who was knighted for his bravery.

Gloster, arrested by Suffolk on a charge of high treason, was promised a fair trial by the king. This was unwelcome news to the lords, and when Gloster was sent for to appear at the hearing, he was found in his bed, brutally murdered and mangled. Suffolk and the cardinal had hired the murderers. So was fulfilled the first prophecy of the sorcerers, that the king would depose and outlive a duke who would die a violent death.

Shortly after Gloster's death the king was called to the bedside of the cardinal, who had been stricken by a strange malady. There King Henry heard the cardinal confess his part in the murder of Gloster, the churchman's bitterest enemy. The cardinal died unrepentant. Queen Margaret became more outspoken concerning affairs of state, especially in those matters on behalf of Suffolk, and more openly contemptuous toward the king's indifferent attitude.

At the request of Commons, led by Warwick and Salisbury, Suffolk was banished from the country for his part in Gloster's murder. Saying their farewells, he and Margaret declared their love for each other. Suffolk, disguised, took ship to leave the country. Captured by pirates, he was beheaded for his treacheries and one of his gentlemen was instructed to return his body to the king.

In London, Queen Margaret mourned her loss in Suffolk's death as she caressed his severed head. The king, piqued by her demonstration, asked her how she would react to his own death. Evasive, she answered that she would not mourn his death; she would die for him. The witch had prophesied Suffolk's death: She had said that he would die by water.

"Thrice is he armed that hath his quarrel just"

Henry VI, Part II, Act III, scene ii, line 233

The Duke of Suffolk, who has had Humphrey, Duke of Gloster, in his keeping, has ordered two murderers to kill Humphrey. The Earl of Warwick has reported that the "commons" (the mass population), wanting their leader, Humphrey, are ready to revolt. Humphrey is slain. King Henry is almost maddened by this unjust homicide. Warwick accuses Suffolk of the murder. These two step outside to fight. Henry believes that victory will come to the innocent, a belief underlying the medieval and Renaissance practice of trial by combat, and with us today in our conviction that God aids the innocent.

> *Henry.* What stronger breastplate than a heart untainted!
> Thrice is he armed that hath his quarrel just;
> And he but naked, though locked up in steel,
> Whose conscience with injustice is corrupted.

Returning from Ireland, York planned to gather forces on his way to London and seize the crown for himself. He also stated his determination to remove Somerset, his adversary in court matters. The king reacted by trying to appease the rebel by committing Somerset to the Tower. Hearing that his enemy was in prison, York ordered his army to disband.

His rage was all the greater, therefore, when he learned that Somerset had been restored to favor. The armies of York and Lancaster prepared to battle at Saint Albans, where Somerset, after an attempt to arrest York for capital treason, was slain by crookbacked Richard Plantagenet, York's son. Somerset's death fulfilled the prophecies of the witch, who had also foretold that Somerset should shun castles, that he would be safer on sandy plains. With his death the king and queen fled. Salisbury, weary from battle but undaunted, and Warwick, proud of York's victory at Saint Albans, pledged their support to York in his drive for the crown, and York hastened to London to forestall the king's intention to summon Parliament into session.

Critical Evaluation

Like the first play of the Henry VI trilogy, this play contains a large cast of characters and continues the coverage of the conflict between the houses of York and Plantagent known in history as the Wars of the Roses. The time span covered in the second play is much shorter than that covered in the first, but the second play's action sprawls, covering a wide range of events. The depiction of a number of nobles, many of them hypocritical and self-serving, who group and regroup, deceive and dissemble, creates a potentially bewildering situation for the reader, requiring close attention. There are many threads of the narrative that are carried over from *Henry VI, Part I*, and a prior reading of that play enhances understanding of this one. More consistently than the preceding play, however, *Henry VI, Part II* explores its major thematic material: the consequences throughout the realm of an ineffectual monarch.

The animosity between the Duke of Gloster and Cardinal Beaufort is one of the basic conflicts in the first part of the play. This conflict divides the other nobles into factions. Gloster, who has been the Protector of the Realm since the infant Henry became king, displays genuine concern for the welfare of the realm rather than self-interest. He refuses to join in his wife's ambitious hopes for his advancement. All he wants is to guide the young, unworldly king and protect him from harmful influences that would adversely affect England. Gloster's downfall lies in his assumption that he commands the loyalty of many of the other nobles, whom he believes share his own right-minded support of the king. Gloster, virtuous and loyal, is betrayed by everyone. Even those who have respect for him have their own agenda to pursue. His short-sightedness is a flaw, a failure in responsibility, because it has the tragic consequence of leaving the inadequate king and England itself vulnerable to the destructive effects of others' self-interest.

The Duke of York is the contrast to Gloster. His fortunes wax as Gloster's wane. His cynicism is the opposite of Gloster's naïve goodness. York supports factions and chooses friends solely on consideration of who will serve his purpose best. York sides with Gloster against the cardinal at first because York believes it will help his cause, but later he allies himself with the cardinal and even his old enemies the dukes of Somerset and Suffolk in the plot to get rid of Gloster. He enjoins the support of the earls of Salisbury and Warwick because they will be useful to him when he makes his claim to the throne. The plot he hatches of using Jack Cade to foment rebellion against the king is based on the deception of the rebels. York is a Machiavellian villain—so named for the author of a political treatise, *The Prince* (1513), by Niccolò Machiavelli; as a character type, the Machiavellian villain appears frequently in drama of the sixteenth century. For York, as for the author of *The Prince*, the end justifies the means. York is fully conscious of his own villainy, which he communicates to the audience, disclosing his plans and his motives.

King Henry is a virtuous man, pious and dutiful, but these virtues are not enough. He seems unable to understand that the terms of his marriage weaken his kingdom. He willingly surrenders hard-won territories in France. He remains blind to the true nature of his queen, who diminishes him personally with her scorn for his passive religiosity and with her relationship with Suffolk. Henry recognizes the cardinal's malice against Gloster and is not fooled by the queen, Suffolk, York, and the cardinal when they band together and declare Gloster to be personally ambitious to the point of treason, but he is quite helpless to save Gloster. He is unwilling or unable to exert his authority and impotently rails against what he rightly sees as a tragedy.

It is not only the nobility which is affected by the lack of a strong ruler. The populace is also in disorder. Saunder Simpcox, the imposter who falsely claims that his sight has been miraculously restored to him, shows that honesty and right values have become distorted. Although Gloster shrewdly sees the truth of the matter and deals with it swiftly, the king, as usual, is helpless.

The Jack Cade rebellion occurs after Gloster's death and the king is without genuine support. The whole episode is full of cynicism. The commoners lack faith in all leadership and authority. They have no illusions about Cade, seeing through his false claims to noble birth. Cade's ambitions are absurd, his logic clearly false, him promises beyond all that is possible. He is a caricature. Underlying this grotesque veneer is a more sinister truth. Cade and his rebels have might but no judgment, and they abuse whatever power they gain. Their rebellion violates the established political and moral orders. Ironically, it is a vision of an England that has vanished, the strong England of Henry V's time, that brings the rabble to its senses. Alexander Iden, who ultimately kills Cade, represents the right values. He lives a serene life, content with his lot. The Cade rebellion is a precursor of the civil war to come, and illustrates William Shakespeare's contention that society consists of interdependent strata arranged in a hierarchy. If the harmony of this structure is perverted at any level, all levels will suffer the consequences.

As a drama, *Henry VI, Part II* is superior to *Henry VI, Part I*. Its characterizations are subtler. There are a number of well-executed comparisons and parallels. The self-serving rebellions of Cade and York help to provide a dramatic unity and coherence that do not occur in the linear, historical narrative. The verse is generally better both in terms of metrical fluency and imagery. There is some fine prose dialogue in the Jack Cade scenes, in which the abuse of language parallels the abuse of political power. This early play does not achieve the stature of Shakespeare's later history plays, but it is worthy of attention.

"Critical Evaluation" by Susan Henthorne

For Further Study

Berry, Edward I. "2 *Henry VI:* Justice and Law." In *Patterns of Decay: Shakespeare's Early Histories*. Charlottesville: University Press of Virginia, 1975. Analyzes the play in the context of the whole of the trilogy. Addresses in the footnotes some of the negative criticism of earlier critics and recommends other critical analyses.

Blanpied, John W. *Time and the Artist in Shakespeare's English Histories*. Newark: University of Delaware Press, 1983. A chapter on *Henry VI, Part II* finds the play superior to *Henry VI, Part I*. Analyzes structure and characters.

Saccio, Peter. *Shakespeare's English Kings: History, Chronicle, and Drama*. New York: Oxford University Press, 1977. Contains a section on Henry VI discussing the history as recounted in Shakespeare's sources, as understood by twentieth century scholarship, and as it is dramatized in the plays. Includes genealogical charts and maps.

Tillyard, E. M. W. *Shakespeare's History Plays*. London: Chatto & Windus, 1944. Praises the structure of *Henry VI, Part II*, defending it against negative criticism.

Turner, Robert K., and George Walton Williams. "The Second and Third Parts of King Henry the Sixth." In *William Shakespeare: The Complete Works*, edited by Alfred Harbage. Rev. ed. New York: Viking Press, 1969. Useful introductory essay analyzes sources and style of the two plays, comparing them with Shakespeare's later history plays.

Henry VI, Part III

Type of plot: Historical
Time of plot: 1455-1471
Locale: England and France
First performed: c. 1590-1591; first published, 1595

Principal characters

KING HENRY VI
EDWARD, the prince of Wales, his son
LOUIS XI, the King of France
RICHARD PLANTAGENET, the Duke of York
EDWARD, York's son, afterward King Edward IV
EDMUND, York's son, the Earl of Rutland
GEORGE, York's son, afterward the Duke of Clarence
RICHARD, York's son, afterward the Duke of Gloster
LORD HASTINGS, of the Duke of York's party
THE EARL OF WARWICK, a king-maker
MARGARET, the Queen of England
LORD CLIFFORD, Margaret's ally
LADY GREY, afterward Edward IV's queen
LADY BONA, the sister of the Queen of France

The Story

In the House of Parliament, the Duke of York, his sons, and the Earl of Warwick rejoiced over their success at Saint Albans. Riding hard, the Yorkists had arrived in London ahead of the routed king, and Henry, entering with his lords, was filled with consternation when he saw York already seated on the throne, to which Warwick had conducted him. Some of the king's followers were sympathetic toward York and others were fearful of his power; the two attitudes resulted in defection in the royal ranks. Seeing his stand weakened, the king attempted to avert disorder by disinheriting his own son and by pledging the crown to York and his sons, on the condition that York stop the civil war and remain loyal to the king during his lifetime.

Annoyed by the reconciliation and contemptuous toward the king because of her son's disinheritance, Queen Margaret deserted the king and raised her own army to protect her son's rights to the throne. The queen's army marched against York's castle as York was sending his sons to recruit forces for another rebellion. York's sons had persuaded their father that his oath to the king was not binding because his contract with the king had not been made in due course of law before a magistrate.

In a battle near Wakefield, Lord Clifford and his soldiers killed Rutland, York's young son, and soaked a handkerchief in his blood. Later, as he joined Margaret's victorious army, which outnumbered York's soldiers ten to one, Lord Clifford gave York the handkerchief to wipe away his tears as he wept for his son's death. York's sorrow was equaled by his humiliation at the hands of Margaret, who, after taking him prisoner, put a paper crown on his head that he might reign from the molehill where she had him placed to be jeered by the soldiers. Clifford and Margaret stabbed the Duke of York and beheaded him. His head was set on the gates of York.

Hearing of the defeat of York's forces, Warwick, taking the king with him, set out from London to fight Queen Margaret at Saint Albans. Warwick's qualities as a general were totally offset by the presence of the king, who was unable to conceal his strong affection for Margaret, and Warwick was defeated. Edward and Richard, York's sons, joined Warwick in a march toward London.

King Henry, ever the righteous monarch, forswore any part in breaking his vow to York and declared that he preferred to leave his son only virtuous deeds, rather than an ill-gotten crown. At the insistence of Clifford and Margaret, however, the king knighted his son as the prince of Wales.

After a defiant parley, the forces met again between Towton and Saxton. The king, banned from battle by Clifford and Margaret because of his antipathy to war and his demoralizing influence on the soldiers, sat on a distant part of the field lamenting the course affairs had taken in this bloody business of murder and deceit. He saw the ravages of war when a father bearing the body of his dead son and a son with the body of his dead father passed by. They had unknowingly taken the lives of their loved ones in the fighting. As the rebel forces, led by Warwick, Richard, and Edward approached, the king, passive to danger and indifferent toward his own safety, was rescued by the prince of Wales and Margaret before the enemy could reach him. He was sent to Scotland for safety.

After a skirmish with Richard, Clifford fled to another part of the field, where, weary and worn, he fainted and died. His head, severed by Richard, replaced York's head on the gate. The Yorkists marched on to London. Edward was proclaimed King Edward IV; Richard was made Duke of Gloster, and George, Duke of Clarence.

King Edward, in audience, heard Lady Grey's case for the return of confiscated lands taken by Margaret's army at Saint Albans, where Lord Grey was killed fighting for the York cause. The hearing, marked by Richard's and George's dissatisfaction with their brother's position and Edward's lewdness directed at Lady Grey, ended with Lady Grey's betrothal to Edward. Richard, resentful of his humpback, aspired to the throne. His many deprivations resulting from his physical condition, he felt, justified his ambition; he would stop at no obstacle in achieving his ends.

Because of their great losses, Margaret and the prince went to France to appeal for aid from King Louis XI, who was kindly disposed toward helping them maintain the crown. The French monarch's decision was quickly changed at the appearance of Warwick, who had arrived from England to ask for the hand of Lady

Bona for King Edward. Warwick's suit had been granted, and Margaret's request denied, when a messenger brought letters announcing King Edward's marriage to Lady Grey. King Louis and Lady Bona were insulted; Margaret was overjoyed. Warwick, chagrined, withdrew his allegiance to the House of York and offered to lead French troops against Edward. He promised his older daughter in marriage to Margaret's son as a pledge of his honor.

"Live we how we can, yet die we must"

Henry VI, Part III, Act V, scene ii, line 28

With his last breath, Warwick, maker of kings, dies in the service of the House of Lancaster. From fast friend of the Duke of York, he becomes foe when the young King Edward marries Lady Grey instead of Bona, sister to the Queen of France. Warwick switches his allegiance to King Henry VI after he is told that Edward, who succeeded his father as usurper of Henry's throne, has married Lady Grey out of lust, thereby making a fool of Warwick, who had gone to France to plead for the hand of the Lady Bona for his king. Edward has no intention of giving up his crown, and Warwick is mortally wounded in battle between the two houses and their supporters.

> *Warwick.* For who lived king, but I could dig his grave?
> And who durst smile when Warwick bent his brow?
> Lo, now my glory smeared in dust and blood!
> My parks, my walks, my manors that I had,
> Even now forsake me; and of all my lands
> Is nothing left me, but my body's length.
> Why, what is pomp, rule, reign, but earth and dust?
> And live we how we can, yet die we must.

At the royal palace in London, family loyalty was broken by open dissent when King Edward informed his brothers that he would not be bound by their wishes. Told that the prince was to marry Warwick's older daughter, the Duke of Clarence announced that he intended to marry the younger one. He left, taking Somerset, one of King Henry's faction, with him. Richard, seeing in an alliance with Edward an opportunity for his own advancement, remained; he, Montague, and Hastings pledged their support to King Edward.

When the French forces reached London, Warwick took Edward prisoner. The king-maker removed Edward's crown and took it to crown King Henry once again, who had, in the meantime, escaped from Scotland only to be delivered into Edward's hands and imprisoned in the Tower. Henry delegated his royal authority to Warwick and the Duke of Clarence, in order that he might be free from the turmoil attendant upon his reign.

Richard and Hastings freed Edward from his imprisonment. They formed an army in York; while Warwick and Clarence, who had learned of Edward's release, were making preparations for defense, Edward, marching upon London, again seized King Henry and sent him to solitary confinement in the Tower.

Edward made a surprise attack on Warwick near Coventry, where Warwick's forces were soon increased by the appearance of Oxford, Montague, and Somerset. The fourth unit to join Warwick was led by Clarence, who took the red rose, the symbol of the House of Lancaster, from his hat and threw it into Warwick's face. Clarence accused Warwick of duplicity and announced that he would fight beside his brothers to preserve the House of York. Warwick, a valiant soldier to the end, was wounded by King Edward and died soon afterward. Montague was also killed.

When Queen Margaret and her son arrived from France, the prince won great acclaim from Margaret and the lords for his spirited vow to hold the kingdom against the Yorkists. Defeated at Tewkesbury, however, the prince was cruelly stabbed to death by King Edward and his brothers. Margaret pleaded with them to kill her too, but they chose to punish her with life. She was sent back to France, her original home. After the prince had been killed, Richard of Gloster stole off to London, where he assassinated King Henry in the Tower. Again he swore to get the crown for himself.

The Yorkists were at last supreme. Edward and Queen Elizabeth, with their infant son, regained the throne. Richard, still intending to seize the crown for himself, saluted the infant with a Judas kiss, while Edward stated that they were now to spend their time in stately triumphs, comic shows, and pleasures of the court.

Critical Evaluation

In *Henry VI, Part III*, which belongs to William Shakespeare's tetralogy of history plays dealing with the political upheaval that followed Henry Bolingbroke's overthrow and murder of Richard II, England continues to suffer the evils of civil strife and social disorder arising from the battles between the houses of York and Lancaster known as the Wars of the Roses. Shakespeare's general purpose in this series of plays is to reassert the power of Providence, to glorify England, and to suggest the nature of her salvation; only with the restitution of the rightful heir to the throne at the end of *Richard III* will England be able to bind her wounds and enjoy peace once again.

Henry VI, Part III is a powerful study of disorder and chaos; the play interweaves a cohesive body of imagery and symbolism with the action of its plot to create a strong unity of impression centering on the theme of anarchy and disunity. Chaos prevails on all levels of society, from the state, to the family, to the individual. At the highest level of authority and social organization—the throne—anarchy has replaced traditional rule. The king, who must be the center of political strength and embody the sanctity of social duty, oath, and custom, is instead the essence of weakness; Henry not only yields the right of succession to York, but eventually abdicates in favor of Warwick and Clarence. Whenever he attempts to intervene in events, his weak voice is quickly silenced; finally he is silenced permanently, and his murder represents the ultimate overturning of political order and rejection of the divine right upon which his rule was founded.

Contrasted to Henry, the representative of rightful power, is Richard, who in this play becomes the epitome of total anarchy. Richard murders the prince, the king, and his brother Clarence, boasting later, "Why, I can smile, and murder while I smile"; he scornfully disregards any form of moral obligation and eventually falls victim to unreasoning fears and nightmares.

The primary social bond, that of the family in a state of dissolution. Again, the malady begins at the level of the king; Henry disinherits his own son, the rightful heir, thus causing his wife Margaret to cut herself off from him, sundering their marital bond. York's three sons become hopelessly divided by their conflicting ambitions. In Act II, scene v, Shakespeare shows, by means of the morality tableau, that the same family breakdown prevails among the common people as well. Simultaneously with its presentation of political and social chaos, the play dramatizes the disruption that is occurring in individuals' morality. Hatred, ambition, lust,

Members of the House of York in the Oregon Shakespeare Festival's production of the conclusion of Henry VI *(clockwise from upper left): George (Remi Sandri), Edward (Robert Lisell-Frank), Richard (Michael J. Hume), young Rutland (Adam Michael Hogan, sitting on knee), and York (Rick Hamilton, seated).* (Christopher Briscoe, courtesy of the Oregon Shakespeare Festival by permission of the Actors' Equity Association)

and greed are the keynotes, while duty, trust, tradition, and self-restraint are increasingly rare.

Henry VI, Part III thus depicts a society in the throes of anarchy and war, a society where kings surrender their duties, fathers and sons murder each other, and brothers vie for power at any cost. Yet the play contains an occasional feeble ray of light, such as Henry's weak protests against the cruelty of the usurpers, his pleas for pity for the war's victims, and his ineffectual calls for an end to the conflict and a restoration of peace and order. These scattered flickers, dim as they are, along with several prophecies planted throughout the play, foreshadow the coming hope, the resolution of conflict, and the return of peace and rightful authority which will follow in *Richard III*.

For Further Study

Evans, Gareth Lloyd. *The Upstart Crow: An Introduction to Shakespeare's Plays*. London: J. M. Dent and Sons, 1982. A comprehensive discussion of the dramatic works of William Shakespeare. While emphasis is on critical reviews of the plays, there are also discussions of sources, as well as material on the circumstances which surrounded the writing of the plays.

Leggatt, Alexander. *Shakespeare's Political Drama: The History Plays and the Roman Plays*. New York: Routledge, 1988. A discussion of Shakespeare's history plays, dealing with English history from the reign of King Henry II to that of Henry VIII, as well as three plays dealing with Roman history: *Julius Caesar* (1599-1600), *Antony and Cleopatra* (1606-1607), and *Coriolanus* (1607-1608).

Pierce, Robert B. *Shakespeare's History Plays: The Family and the State*. Columbus: University of Ohio Press, 1971. A general discussion of Shakespeare's history plays. The three plays on King Henry VI are discussed in a relatively positive way but are still generally treated as experimental.

Ribner, Irving. *The English History Play in the Age of Shakespeare*. London: Methuen, 1965. A revised edition of the 1957 work first published in the United States by Princeton University Press. A discussion of history plays in the Elizabethan era of English drama, including a discussion of Shakespeare's contributions in the field. The development of the form through the period is discussed, and its sources are considered.

Shakespeare, William. *The Third Part of King Henry VI*. Edited by Andrew S. Cairncross. Cambridge, Mass.: Harvard University Press, 1964. Part of the *Arden Shakespeare* series. This volume contains more than sixty pages' worth of introductory notes, including discussion of the various original texts, the sources of the play, and a critical evaluation of the work, as well as genealogical tables.

Henry VIII

Type of plot: Historical
Time of plot: 1520-1533
Locale: England
First performed: 1613; first published, 1623

Principal characters

KING HENRY VIII
THOMAS WOLSEY, cardinal of York and lord chancellor of England
CARDINAL CAMPEIUS, papal legate
CRANMER, the archbishop of Canterbury
DUKE OF BUCKINGHAM
DUKE OF SUFFOLK
DUKE OF NORFOLK
GARDINER, the bishop of Winchester
THOMAS CROMWELL, Wolsey's servant
QUEEN KATHERINE, wife of Henry, later divorced
ANNE BULLEN, maid of honor to Katherine, later queen

The Story

Cardinal Wolsey, a powerful figure at court during the reigns of Henry VII and Henry VIII, was becoming too aggressive. Wolsey was of humble stock, which fact accentuated his personal qualities. He had lacked the advantages of family and ancestral office, and his political prominence was entirely the result of his own wisdom, manner, and persistence. Unscrupulous in seeking his own ends, he had ruthlessly removed obstacles in his climb to power.

One such hindrance to his ambitious designs was the Duke of Buckingham, accused of high treason. When Buckingham was brought before the court for trial, Queen Katherine, speaking in his defense, protested against the cardinal's unjust taxes and informed the king of growing animosity among his people because he retained Wolsey as his adviser. Wolsey produced witnesses, among them Buckingham's discharged surveyor, who testified to Buckingham's disloyalty. The surveyor swore that, at the time of the king's journey to France, the duke had sought priestly confirmation for his belief that he could, by gaining favor with the common people, rise to govern England. In his long and persistent testimony the surveyor played upon earlier minor offenses Buckingham had committed, and he climaxed his accusation with an account of the duke's assertion that he would murder the king in order to gain the throne.

In spite of Katherine's forthright protestations against Wolsey in his presence, her repeated contention that the testimony against Buckingham was false, the accused man was found guilty and sentenced to be executed. The duke, forbearing toward his enemies, recalled the experience of his father, Henry of Buckingham, who had been betrayed by a servant. Henry VII had restored the honor of the family by elevating the present duke to favor. One difference prevailed between the two trials, the duke stated; his father had been unjustly dealt with, but he himself had had a noble trial.

Wolsey, fearing reprisal from Buckingham's son, sent him to Ireland as a deputy; then, incensed and uneasy because of Katherine's open accusations, he pricked the king's conscience with questions regarding his marriage to Katherine, who had been the widow of Henry's brother. Wolsey furthered his cause against Katherine by arousing Henry's interest in Anne Bullen (Bolyen), whom the king met at a ball given by the cardinal.

The plan followed by Wolsey in securing a divorce for Henry was not a difficult one. In addition to his evident trust of Wolsey, the king felt keenly the fact that the male children born to him and Katherine in their twenty years of marriage had been stillborn or had died shortly after birth. Consequently, there was no male heir in direct succession.

The cardinal's final step to be rid of his chief adversary at court was to appeal to the pope for a royal divorce. When Cardinal Campeius arrived from Rome, Katherine appeared in her own defense. Wolsey once more resorted to perjured witnesses. Requesting counsel, Katherine was told by Wolsey that the honest and intelligent men gathered at the hearing were of her choosing. Cardinal Campeius supported Wolsey's stand.

In speeches of magnificent dignity and honesty, Katherine denounced the political treachery that had caused her so much unhappiness. Later, however, Katherine, expelled from the court and sequestered in Kimbolton, was able to feel compassion for Wolsey when informed that he had died in ill-repute; her undying devotion to Henry was indicated in her death note to him. Altruistic to the last, she made as her final request to the king the maintenance of the domestics who had served her so faithfully. Her strength to tolerate the injustices she had endured lay in her trust in a Power which, she said, could not be corrupted by a king.

Ambition overrode itself in Wolsey's designs for power. His great pride had caused him to accumulate greater wealth than the king had. The cardinal also used an inscription, *Ego et Rex meus*, which subordinated the king to the cardinal, and had a British coin stamped with a cardinal's hat. These, among many other offenses, were of little importance compared with Wolsey's double-dealing against the king in the divorce proceedings. Wolsey feared that Henry would marry Anne Bullen instead of seeking a royal alliance in France, so Wolsey asked the pope to delay the divorce. When his letter was delivered by mistake to the king, Wolsey, confronted with the result of his own carelessness, showed the tenacious character of the ambitious climber. Although he realized that his error was his undoing, he attempted to ingratiate himself once more with the king.

He could not save himself. He could instigate the unseating and banishment of subordinates and he could maneuver to have the queen sequestered, but Henry wished no meddling with his marital affairs. Repentant that he had not served God with the effort and fervor with which he had served the king, Wolsey left the court, a broken man. He was later arrested in York, to be returned for arraignment before Henry. He was saved the humiliation of trial, however, because he died on the way to London.

"Fling away ambition"

Henry VIII, Act III, scene ii, line 440

Cardinal Wolsey, an overly ambitious and unscrupulous divine, is adviser to King Henry VIII of England. Not content with amassing wealth and having the ear of the king, he connives secretly for an alliance with France and urges the king to divorce Katherine of Aragon, who has been his wife for twenty years. Wolsey hopes the king will then marry a French princess to cement the alliance. The king, however, falls in love with Anne Bullen, a Protestant. Alarmed at this turn, Wolsey requests the pope to delay the divorce. A copy of this letter and an accounting of Wolsey's wealth—enough to make a king jealous—fall into Henry's hands. Confronted with the king's wrath, these evidences of his double-dealing, and the loss of his offices, Wolsey meditates on the precarious nature of ambition, and then speaks a touching farewell to his servant Cromwell.

> *Wolsey.* Cromwell, I charge thee, fling away ambition.
> By that sin fell the angels; how can man then,
> The image of his Maker, hope to win by it?
> Love thyself last, cherish those hearts that hate thee;
> Corruption wins not more than honesty.
> Still in thy right hand carry gentle peace,
> To silence envious tongues. Be just and fear not;
> Let all the ends thou aim'st at be thy country's,
> Thy God's, and truth's. Then if thou fall'st, O Cromwell,
> Thou fall'st a blessed martyr.
> Had I but served my God, with half the zeal
> I served my King, he would not in mine age
> Have left me naked to mine enemies.

Henry, shortly after the divorce, secretly married Anne Bullen. After Wolsey's death she was crowned queen with great pomp. Cranmer, the new archbishop of Canterbury, became Henry's chief adviser. Jealousy and rivalry did not disappear from the court with the downfall of Wolsey. Charging heresy, Gardiner, bishop of Winchester, set out to undermine Cranmer's position with the king. Accused as a heretic, Cranmer was brought to trial. Henry, trusting his favorite, gave him the royal signet ring which he was to show to the council if his entreaties and reasoning failed with his accusers. Cranmer, overcome by the king's kindness, wept in gratitude.

As he stood behind a curtain near the council room, the king heard Gardiner's charges against Cranmer. When Gardiner ordered Cranmer to the Tower, stating that the council was acting on the pleasure of the king, the accused man produced the ring and insisted upon his right to appeal the case to the king. Realizing that they had been tricked by a ruse that Wolsey had used for many years, the nobles were penitent. Appearing before the council, Henry took his seat at the table to condemn the assemblage for their tactics in dealing with Cranmer. After giving his blessings to those present and imploring them to be motivated in the future by unity and love, he asked Cranmer to be godfather to the daughter recently born to Anne Bullen.

At the christening Cranmer prophesied that the child, Elizabeth, would be wise and virtuous, that her life would be a pattern to all princes who knew her, and that she would be loved and feared because of her goodness and her strength. He said that she would rule long and every day of her reign would be blessed with good deeds.

Critical Evaluation

Henry VIII is the last of William Shakespeare's histories, in terms of both time of composition and the date of its setting. It is very different from Shakespeare's earlier history plays such as *Henry V* or *Richard III*. First of all, the events of the play were much closer to those of Shakespeare's own time. Henry VIII had died only eighteen years before Shakespeare was born, and his daughter Elizabeth, whose birth is hailed at the end of the play, was herself Shakespeare's patron. Shakespeare had to treat certain political themes that might still have current relevance more gingerly than he would events that had occurred two or three centuries before. At the same time the playwright must have felt more emotion in writing about the recent monarchs of the House of Tudor than remote, long-dead kings; this emotion clearly shows through in the play's final scene.

Another difference between *Henry VIII* and the rest of the history plays is its genre. By the time of the play's composition, Shakespeare had written several of his most successful late romances, including *Cymbeline* (c. 1609-1610), *The Winter's Tale* (c. 1610-1611), and *The Tempest* (1611). The modes of treatment used by Shakespeare in these plays were also applied to *Henry VIII*. This is particularly demonstrated by the way the play does not end tragically, but amid joy and reconciliation. The way the overall pattern of the plot predominates over action and narrative is another marked differentiation between this history play and its predecessors.

King Henry himself displays this pattern in the play. He does not so much dominate the action as coordinate it. All the actions of the major characters are in reference to him. All the participants in political intrigue wish to gain his ear or influence. Although he is personally involved in the play's events, as is evidenced by his divorce from Katherine and remarriage to Anne spurring the drama's action, he is always somewhat above the fray, an image of the play's wish for harmony.

If there is tragedy in *Henry VIII*, it is not that of the king himself, but Cardinal Wolsey, much as it is Brutus, not the title character, who is the tragic figure in

Shakespeare's *Julius Caesar* (c. 1599-1600). The audience sees Wolsey at the height of his power and intrigue as he successfully maneuvers against Buckingham, and suspects that the wheel of fate is about to turn against him. Unlike Shakespeare's earlier tragic protagonist Macbeth, Wolsey does not get to stir up serious trouble regarding the authority of his king; he is apprehended before his plans go too far. Even though Wolsey is sentenced to death, Shakespeare, with his characteristic late insights into the mixed nature of much human motivation, gives Wolsey's character a graceful and sympathetic turn as he goes to his end. In Wolsey's final speech, the audience can see inside his own thought processes, such that they do not necessarily think he has been well motivated from the beginning, but they do perceive that he has faced his demise in a spirit of Christian humility and self-knowledge.

Scholars have speculated that *Henry VIII* was influenced by the masques prominent in the Jacobean court of the early 1600's. These masques, which integrated music and ceremony into the pattern of drama, prized a kind of serenity and a pleasing overall composition. For all the historical material and political jostling of the play, there is also a stateliness and a gravity that raise the play above the level of chronicle and controversy.

There is controversy in abundance in the historical material of which the play is composed. The reign of Henry VIII was the most eventful period of English history. At the beginning of his reign, England was a minor country in an overwhelmingly Catholic Europe. At its end, England was a rising power of the North, a bulwark of Protestantism, and a pioneer in maritime exploring and trade. This development is shown in the play. At the beginning, Henry meets with the King of France at Field of Cloth of Gold. This lavish and splendid occasion, eloquently described in the opening dialogue between Norfolk and Buckingham, celebrates Henry's sovereignty. He is, however, one European crowned head in the company of another. At the end of the play, Henry, for better or for worse, has set England on its own course in control of its own destiny. His divorce from Katherine of Aragon, potentially the most pettily personal of issues, has been developed into a metaphor for wresting control of law and morality away from the Pope and into the power of the English crown. At the end of the play, when the prophecies are made concerning Elizabeth, it is mentioned that her successor shall "make new nations," a possible reference to the English colonization of Virginia which was occurring as Shakespeare was writing the play. The path of English history had been changed forever.

The English Reformation, that is to say England's religious changeover from Catholicism to Protestantism, is not at the center of Shakespeare's play. Neither a polemicist nor an ideologue, Shakespeare was concerned to honor the grandeur of the English royal family and the society for which it stood. Though Shakespeare's positive portraits of Cranmer, the archbishop of Canterbury, and the accused heretic Cromwell show that his sympathies lie with Protestantism, the play's spiritual heart is not sectarian. Cranmer's response of providential joy to the birth of Elizabeth is less political or religious than a kind of miraculous wonder reminiscent of the endings of Shakespeare's late romances. Elizabeth's birth, like

Leontes' reunion with his daughter and heir Perdita in *The Winter's Tale*, signifies that there is a bright future ahead for the world of the play. The unusually auspicious portents that arrive with the birth of the child operate to soothe the tensions and rivalries that have just transpired and open the way for a calmer, more serene era. Shakespeare may have just been trying to flatter the royal family and Elizabeth's successor James. Most likely, however, Cranmer's speech represents the genuine praise of the playwright for the society that had fostered his talent.

"Critical Evaluation" by Nicholas Birns

For Further Study

Donoghue, Denis. *The Sovereign Ghost: Studies in Imagination*. Berkeley: University of California Press, 1976. Emphasizes how Shakespeare portrays artistic as well as political order in *Henry VIII*.

Frye, Northop. *A Natural Perspective: The Development of Shakespearean Comedy and Romance*. Ithaca, N.Y.: Columbia University Press, 1965. Discusses the providential nature of Elizabeth's birth at the end of the play and the manner in which the prophecy at her birth causes the play to function as a romance as much as a history.

Hamilton, Donna B. *Shakespeare and the Politics of Protestant England*. Lexington: University Press of Kentucky, 1992. Argues that Shakespeare's presentation of Henry VIII is a reflection on the religious controversies of Shakespeare's day. Valuable in glimpsing the political issues behind Shakespeare's negative portrayal of Wolsey.

Kermode, Frank. "What There Is to Know About Henry VIII." In *Shakespeare: The Histories*, edited by Eugene M. Waith. Englewood Cliffs, N.J.: Prentice-Hall, 1965. Seizes on essential elements of *Henry VIII* for an understanding of the play's place in Shakespeare's canon. A good starting place.

Richmond, Hugh M. *King Henry VIII*. Manchester: Manchester University Press, 1994. An informative treatment of the relationship between the historical King Henry VIII and Shakespeare's character. Discusses the role of Protestantism and English nationalism in Shakespeare's portrait of the king.

Julius Caesar

Type of plot: Tragedy
Time of plot: 44 B.C.E.
Locale: Rome
First performed: c. 1599-1600; first published, 1601

Principal characters

JULIUS CAESAR, dictator of Rome
MARK ANTONY, his friend
MARCUS BRUTUS, a conspirator against Caesar
CAIUS CASSIUS, another conspirator against Caesar
PORTIA, wife of Brutus and Cassius' sister
CALPURNIA, Caesar's wife

The Story

At the feast of Lupercalia all Rome rejoiced, for the latest military triumphs of Julius Caesar were being celebrated during that holiday. Yet tempers flared and jealousies seethed beneath the public gaiety. Flavius and Marallus, two tribunes, coming upon a group of citizens gathered to praise Caesar, tore down their trophies and ordered the people to go home and remember Pompey's fate at the hands of Caesar.

Other dissatisfied noblemen discussed with concern Caesar's growing power and his incurable ambition. A soothsayer, following Caesar in his triumphal procession, warned him to beware the Ides of March. Cassius, one of the most violent of Caesar's critics, spoke at length to Brutus of the dictator's unworthiness to rule the state. Why, he demanded, should the name of Caesar have become synonymous with that of Rome when there were so many other worthy men in the city?

While Cassius and Brutus were speaking, they heard a tremendous shouting from the crowd. From aristocratic Casca they learned that before the mob Mark Antony had three times offered a crown to Caesar and three times the dictator had refused it. Thus did the wily Antony and Caesar catch and hold the devotion of the multitude. Fully aware of Caesar's methods and the potential danger that he embodied, Cassius and Brutus, disturbed by the new turn of events, agreed to meet again to discuss the affairs of Rome. As they parted, Caesar arrived in time to see them, and suspicion of Cassius entered his mind. Cassius did not look contented; he was too lean and nervous to be satisfied with life. Caesar much preferred to have fat, jolly men about him.

Cassius' plan was to enlist Brutus in a plot to overthrow Caesar. Brutus himself was one of the most respected and beloved citizens of Rome; if he were in league against Caesar, the dictator's power could be curbed easily. It would, however, be difficult to turn Brutus completely against Caesar, for Brutus was an honorable man and not given to treason, so that only the most drastic circumstances would override his loyalty. Cassius plotted to have Brutus receive false papers that implied widespread public alarm over Caesar's rapidly growing power. Hoping that Brutus might put Rome's interests above his own personal feelings, Cassius had the papers secretly laid at Brutus' door one night. The conflict within Brutus was great. His wife Portia complained that he had not slept at all during the night and that she had found him wandering, restless and unhappy, about the house. At last he reached a decision. Remembering Tarquin, the tyrant whom his ancestors had banished from Rome, Brutus agreed to join Cassius and his conspirators in their attempt to save Rome from Caesar. He refused, however, to sanction the murder of Antony, which was being planned for the same time—the following morning, March 15—as the assassination of Caesar.

"Beware the ides of March"

Julius Caesar, Act I, scene ii, line 18

As the play begins, the citizens of Rome are enjoying a holiday for two reasons; not only is it the Lupercalia, a holiday, but also it is a day of festivities to celebrate Caesar's victory over Pompey, an erstwhile rival for political power. The proud, triumphant Caesar, en route to the holiday's games and ceremonies, is hailed by a soothsayer who twice gives him the sinister warning to beware March 15 (the "ides" of March). Today, this saying has come to mean any kind of warning or premonition.

> *Caesar.* Who is in the press that calls on me?
> I hear a tongue shriller than all the music
> Cry Caesar. Speak; Caesar is turned to hear.
> *Soothsayer.* Beware the ides of March.
> *Caesar.* What man is that?
> *Brutus.* A soothsayer bids you beware the ides of March.
> *Caesar.* Set him before me, let me see his face. . . .
> What sayst thou to me now? Speak once again.
> *Soothsayer.* Beware the ides of March.
> *Caesar.* He is a dreamer, let us leave him.

On the night of March 14, all nature seemed to misbehave. Strange lights appeared in the sky, graves yawned, ghosts walked, and an atmosphere of terror pervaded the city. Caesar's wife, Calpurnia, dreamed she saw her husband's statue with a hundred wounds spouting blood. In the morning, she told him of the dream and pleaded with him not to go to the Senate that morning. When she had almost convinced him to remain at home, one of the conspirators arrived and persuaded the dictator that Calpurnia was unduly nervous and that the dream was actually an omen of Caesar's tremendous popularity in Rome, the bleeding wounds a symbol of Caesar's power extending out to all Romans. The other conspirators arrived to allay any suspicions Caesar might have of them and to make sure that he attended the Senate that day.

In the 1953 film version of Julius Caesar, *Marlon Brando as Mark Antony (right) prepares to lay the dead body of the assassinated Julius Caesar before the Roman citizens as one of the assassins, Brutus (James Mason, center), apprehensively looks on.* (Courtesy of The Museum of Modern Art, Film Stills Archive)

As Caesar made his way through the city, more omens of evil appeared to him. A paper detailing the plot against him was thrust into his hands, but he neglected to read it. When the soothsayer again cried out against the Ides of March, Caesar paid no attention to the warning.

In the Senate chamber, Antony was drawn to one side. Then the conspirators crowded about Caesar as if to second a petition for the repealing of an order banishing Publius Cimber. When he refused the petition, the conspirators attacked him, and he fell dead of twenty-three knife wounds.

Craftily pretending to side with the conspirators, Antony was able to reinstate himself in their good graces. In spite of Cassius' warning, he was granted permission to speak at Caesar's funeral after Brutus delivered his oration. Before the populace, Brutus frankly and honestly explained his part in Caesar's murder, declaring that his love for Rome had prompted him to turn against his friend. The mob cheered him and agreed that Caesar had been a tyrant who deserved death. Then Antony rose to speak. Cleverly and forcefully, he turned the temper of the crowd against the conspirators by explaining that even when Caesar was most tyrannical, everything he did was for the people's welfare. The mob became so enraged over the assassination that the conspirators were forced to flee from Rome.

The people's temper gradually changed and they split into two camps. One group supported the new triumvirate of Mark Antony, Octavius Caesar, and Aemilius Lepidus. The other group followed Brutus and Cassius to their military camp at Sardis.

At Sardis, Brutus and Cassius quarreled constantly over various small matters. In the course of one violent disagreement, Brutus told Cassius that Portia, despondent over the outcome of the civil war, had killed herself. Cassius, shocked by this news of his sister's death, allowed himself to be persuaded to leave the safety of the camp at Sardis and meet the enemy on the plains of Philippi. The night before the battle, Caesar's ghost appeared to Brutus in his tent and announced that they would meet at Philippi.

At first, Brutus' forces were successful against those of Octavius. Cassius, however, was driven back by Antony. One morning, Cassius sent one of his followers, Titinius, to learn if approaching troops were the enemy or Brutus' soldiers. When Cassius saw Titinius unseated from his horse by the strangers, he assumed that everything was lost and ordered his servant Pindarus to kill him. Actually, the troops had been sent by Brutus; rejoicing over the defeat of Octavius, they were having rude sport with Titinius. When they returned to Cassius and found him dead, Titinius also killed himself. In the last charge against Antony, Brutus' soldiers, tired and discouraged by events, were defeated. Brutus, heartbroken, asked his friends to kill him. When they refused, he commanded his servant to hold his sword and turn his face away. Then Brutus fell upon his sword and died.

Critical Evaluation

The first of William Shakespeare's so-called Roman plays—which include *Coriolanus* (c. 1607-1608) and *Antony and Cleopatra* (c. 1606-1607)—*Julius Caesar* also heralds the great period of his tragedies. The sharply dramatic and delicately portrayed character of Brutus is a clear predecessor of Hamlet and Othello. With *Titus Andronicus* (1594) and *Romeo and Juliet* (c. 1595-1596), *Julius Caesar* is one of the three tragedies written before the beginning of the sixteenth century. It is, however, more historical than Shakespeare's four great tragedies—*Hamlet* (c. 1600-1601), *Othello* (1604), *Macbeth* (1606), and *King Lear* (c. 1605-1606)—being drawn in large part from Sir Thomas North's wonderfully idiomatic translation of Plutarch's *Lives of the Noble Grecians and Romans* (1579). A comparison of the Shakespearean text with the passages from North's chapters on Caesar, Brutus, and Antony reveals the remarkable truth of T. S. Eliot's statement: "Immature poets borrow; mature poets steal." In instance after instance, Shakespeare did little more than rephrase the words of North's exuberant prose to fit the rhythm of his own blank verse. The thievery is brilliant.

Shakespeare's originality, found in all his historical plays, is similar to that of

---

"Friends, Romans, countrymen, lend me your ears"

Julius Caesar, Act III, scene ii, line 78

Mark Antony, young friend of the murdered Caesar, has been forced to appear friendly with Brutus and the rest of the assassins of his mentor. He swallows his anger and professes sympathy for their deed, but in his heart he swears vengeance on them. To gain his goal he needs an opportunity to sway the populace of Rome. He asks the assassins for the opportunity to speak the funeral oration over Caesar's body. Brutus, trusting Antony, grants this request but reserves the right to speak to the crowd first. When Brutus finishes, the crowd believes him and his fellow assassins to be honorable men and the murder of Caesar to have been just. Then Antony begins his speech:

> *Antony.* Friends, Romans, countrymen, lend me your ears.
> I come to bury Caesar, not to praise him.
> The evil that men do, lives after them,
> The good is oft interred with their bones;
> So let it be with Caesar. The noble Brutus
> Hath told you Caesar was ambitious;
> If it were so, it was a grievous fault. . . .
> He was my friend, faithful and just to me;
> But Brutus says he was ambitious
> And Brutus is an honorable man. . . .
> When the poor have cried, Caesar hath wept;
> Ambition should be made of sterner stuff:
> Yet Brutus says he was ambitious,
> And Brutus is an honorable man.

By the end of Antony's speech, he has revived sympathy for the dead Caesar and has shown Brutus and the other assassins to be despicable murderers. The fickle crowd cries for vengeance. Antony's speech is a model of oratory skill: He makes the crowd question the supposed crimes of Caeser and instead persuades them of the assassins' guilt—all while asserting that Brutus and the other conspirators are "honorable men."

---

the great classical Greek playwrights Aeschylus, Sophocles, and Euripides. They too faced a dramatic challenge very unlike that of later writers, who came to be judged by their sheer inventiveness. Just as the Greek audience came to the play with full knowledge of the particular myth involved in the tragedy to be presented, the Elizabethan audience knew the particulars of events such as the assassination of Julius Caesar. Shakespeare, like his classical predecessors, had to work his dramatic art within the restrictions of known history. He accomplished this by writing "between the lines" of Plutarch, offering insights into the minds of the characters that Plutarch does not mention and which become, on the stage, dramatic motivations. An example is Caesar's revealing hesitation about going to the Senate because of Calpurnia's dream, and the way he is swayed by Decius into going after all. This scene shows the weakness of Caesar's character in a way not found in a literal reading of Plutarch. A second major "adaptation" by Shakespeare is a daring, dramatically effective telescoping of historical time. The historical events associated with the death of Caesar and the defeat of the conspirators actually took three years; Shakespeare condenses them into three tense days, following the unity of time (though not of place).

Although prose is used in the play by comic and less important characters or in purely informative speeches or documents, the general mode of expression is Shakespeare's characteristic blank verse, which consists of five stressed syllables, generally unrhymed. The iambic pentameter, a rhythm natural to English speech, has the effect of making more memorable lines such as Flavius' comment about the commoners, "They vanish tongue-tied in their guiltiness," or Brutus' observation, "Men at some time are masters of their fates." As in most of his tragedies, Shakespeare follows a five-part dramatic structure, consisting of the exposition (to Act I, scene ii), complication (Act I, scene ii, to Act II, scene iv), climax (Act III, scene i), consequence (Act III, scene i, to Act V, scene ii), and denouement (Act V, scenes iii to v).

The main theme of *Julius Caesar* combines the political with the personal. The first deals with the question of justifiable revolutions and reveals with the effectiveness of concentrated action the transition from a republic of equals to an empire dominated by great individuals such as Antony, influenced by the example of Caesar himself, and Octavius, who comes into his own at the end of the play. The personal complication is the tragedy of a noble spirit involved in matters it does not comprehend. Despite the title, Brutus, not Caesar, is the hero of this play. It is true that Caesar's influence motivates Mark Antony's straightforward and ultimately victorious actions throughout the play and accounts for his transformation from an apparently secondary figure into one of stature. It is, however, Brutus, as he gradually learns to distinguish ideals from reality, who captures the sympathy of the audience. Around his gentle character, praised at last even by Antony, Shakespeare weaves the recurrent motifs of honor and honesty, freedom and fortune, ambition and pride. Honor as it interacts with ambition is the theme of Brutus' speech to the crowd in the forum: "As Caesar loved me, I weep for him; as he was fortunate, I rejoice at it; as he was valiant, I honour him, but, as he was ambitious, I slew him." After the deed, Brutus comments, "Ambition's debt is paid." One of the great, dramatically successful ironies of the play is that Antony's forum speech juxtaposes the same two themes: "Yet Brutus says he was ambitious/ and Brutus is an honourable man." By the time Antony is finished, the term "honour" has been twisted by his accelerating sarcasm until it has become a curse, moving the fickle crowd to call for death for the conspirators.

The conjunction of Brutus and Antony in this scene reveals the telling difference between their dramatic characterizations. Whereas Caesar may have had too much ambition, Brutus has too little; Brutus is a man of ideals and words, and therefore he cannot succeed in the arenas of power. Cassius and Antony, in contrast, are not concerned with idealistic concepts or words such as honor and ambition; yet there is a distinction even between them. Cassius is a pure doer, a man of action, almost entirely devoid of sentiment or principle; Antony is both a doer of deeds and a speaker of words—and therefore prevails over all in the end, following in the footsteps of his model, Caesar. To underline the relationships among these characters and the themes that dominate their actions, Shakespeare weaves a complicated net of striking images: the monetary image, which creates tension between Brutus and Cassius; the tide image ("Thou are the ruins of the noblest man/ That ever lived in the tide of times") connected with the theme of fortune; the star image (Caesar compares himself, like Christopher Marlowe's Tamburlaine, to a fixed star while Cassius says, "The fault, dear Brutus, is not in our stars,/ But in ourselves, that we are underlings"); and the image of wood and stones used to describe the common people by those who would move them to their own will.

In yet another way, *Julius Caesar* marks the advance of Shakespeare's artistry in its use of dramatic irony. In this play, the Shakespearean audience itself almost becomes a character in the drama, as it is made privy to knowledge and sympathies not yet shared by all the characters on the stage. This pattern occurs most notably in Decius' speech interpreting Calpurnia's dream, showing the ability of an actor to move men to action by well-managed duplicity. The pattern is also evident when Cinna mistakes Cassius for Metellus Cimber, foreshadowing the mistaken identity scene that ends in his own death; when Cassius, on two occasions, gives in to Brutus' refusal to do away with Antony; and, most effectively of all, in the two forum speeches when Antony addresses two audiences, the one in the theater (who know his true intentions), and the other the Roman crowd whose ironic whimsicality is marked by its startling shift of sentiment. The effect of the irony is to suggest the close connection between functional politics and the art of acting. Antony, in the end, defeats Brutus—as Bolingbroke defeats Richard II— because he can put on a more compelling act.

"Critical Evaluation" by Kenneth John Atchity

For Further Study

Bloom, Harold, ed. *William Shakespeare's "Julius Caesar."* New York: Chelsea House, 1988. Nine essays on various aspects of the play by distinguished Shakespeare critics of the 1970's and 1980's, Marjorie Garber's essay on the significance of dreams and Michael Long's on the social order are particularly worthwhile.

Bonjour, Adrien. *The Structure of "Julius Caesar."* Liverpool, England: Liverpool University Press, 1958. Sensitive, illuminating monographic study that sees *Julius Caesar* as a drama of divided sympathies. Brutus and Caesar are both heroic, both wrong; opposing motives and antithetical themes from the texture of the play as well as a balanced inner structure.

Dean, Leonard F., ed. *Twentieth Century Interpretations of "Julius Caesar."* Englewood Cliffs, N.J.: Prentice-Hall, 1968. Informative collection of short articles by leading mid-twentieth century Shakespeare critics. Dean's introduction gives an overview of earlier criticism. Various articles provide character studies, analyze language, and supply literary-historical background.

Thomas, Vivian. *"Julius Caesar."* London: Harvester Wheatsheaf, 1992. Concise study of *Julius Caesar* that reflects various postmodernist approaches to Shakespeare while also providing a thorough analysis of the play's stage history, style, and relationship to its principal source, Plutarch's *Lives of the Noble Grecians and Romans*. Includes an extensive bibliography.

Traversi, Derek. *Shakespeare: The Roman Plays*. Stanford, Calif.: Stanford University Press, 1963. Chapter two of this classic study focuses on the moral and political themes of *Julius Caesar*. Following the text closely and in detail, Traversi probes the interplay of contrasting personalities and motives that generated a political tragedy with universal significance.

King John

Type of plot: Historical
Time of plot: Early thirteenth century
Locale: England and France
First performed: c. 1596-1597; first published, 1623

Principal characters

JOHN, the King of England
PRINCE HENRY, his son
ARTHUR OF BRETAGNE, the king's nephew
WILLIAM MARESHALL, the Earl of Pembroke
GEFFREY FITZ-PETER, the Earl of Essex
WILLIAM LONGSWORD, the Earl of Salisbury
HUBERT DE BURGH, the Chamberlain to the king
ROBERT FAULCONBRIDGE, an English baron
PHILIP FAULCONBRIDGE, his half brother, the natural son of King Richard I
CARDINAL PANDULPH, the papal legate
LEWIS, the Dauphin of France
ELINOR, King John's mother
CONSTANCE, Arthur's mother
BLANCH OF CASTILE, King John's niece

The Story

King John sat on the throne of England without right, for the succession should have passed to Arthur of Bretagne, the fourteen-year-old son of King John's older brother. John and Elinor, his mother, prepared to defend England against the forces of Austria and France, after Constance of Bretagne had enlisted the aid of those countries to gain the throne for her son Arthur.

As John and Elinor made ready for battle, Philip Faulconbridge, the natural son of Richard the Lion-Hearted by Lady Faulconbridge, was recruited by Elinor to serve John's cause in the war. Faulconbridge, weary of his half brother's slights regarding his illegitimacy, willingly accepted the offer and was knighted by King John.

The French, Austrian, and British armies met at Angiers in France, but the battle was fought with words, not swords. To John's statement that England was ready for war or peace, King Philip of France answered that, for the sake of justice, France would fight for Arthur's place on the throne. When Elinor accused Constance of self-aggrandizement in seeking the throne for her son, Constance accused her mother-in-law of adultery. Faulconbridge and the Archduke of Austria resorted to a verbal volley.

Lewis, the Dauphin of France, halted the prattle by stating Arthur's specific claims, which John refused to grant. The citizens of Angiers announced that they were barring the gates of the city to all until they had proof as to the actual kingship. The leaders prepared for a battle.

After excursions by the three armies, heralds of the various forces appeared to announce their victories to the citizens of Angiers, but the burghers persisted in their demands for more definite proof. At last, Faulconbridge suggested that they destroy the city walls and continue to fight until one side or the other was conquered. Arrangements for the battle brought on more talk, for the citizens suggested a peace settlement among the forces and promised entrance to the city if Blanch of Castile were affianced to the Dauphin of France.

John gladly offered certain provinces as Blanch's dowry, and it was agreed that the vows should be solemnized. Faulconbridge analyzed John's obvious motive: It was better to part with some parcels of land and keep the throne than to lose his kingdom in battle.

Constance, displaying the persistence and tenacity of a mother who wished to see justice done to her child, doubted that the proposed alliance would succeed; she wished to have the issue settled in battle. Her hopes rose when Cardinal Pandulph appeared to announce John's excommunication because of his abuse of the Archbishop of Canterbury. John, unperturbed by the decree of excommunication, denounced the pope. The alliance between France and England, the outgrowth of Lewis and Blanch's marriage, could not stand, according to Pandulph, if France hoped also to avoid excommunication. King Philip wisely decided that it would be better to have England as an enemy than to be at odds with Rome.

His change of mind made war necessary. The battle ended with the English victorious. Faulconbridge beheaded the Archduke of Austria. Arthur was taken prisoner. When Hubert de Burgh pledged his unswerving support to the king, John told him of his hatred for Arthur. He asked that the boy be murdered. Grieved by her separation from Arthur, Constance lamented that she would never see her son again. Even in heaven, she said, she would be denied this blessing because Arthur's treatment at the hands of the English would change him from the gracious creature he had been. Pandulph, unwilling to let John have easy victory, persuaded Lewis to march against the English forces. The cardinal explained that with Arthur's death—and news of French aggression would undoubtedly mean his death—Lewis, as Blanch's husband, could claim Arthur's lands.

In England, Hubert de Burgh had been ordered to burn out Arthur's eyes with hot irons. Although Hubert professed loyalty to John, he had become attached to Arthur while the boy was in his charge. Touched by Arthur's pleas, he refused to carry out King John's orders. After hiding Arthur in another part of the castle, he went to tell John of his decision. On his arrival at the palace, however, he found Pembroke and Salisbury, in conference with the king, pleading for Arthur's life. The people, they reported, were enraged because of John's dastardly action; they threatened to withdraw their fealty to the cruel king. John's sorrow was increased by the information that a large French army had landed in England and that Elinor was dead. Faulconbridge, who had been collecting tribute from monks, appeared with Peter of Pomfret, a prophet. When Peter prophesied that John would lose his crown at noon on Ascension Day, John had Peter jailed and ordered his execution if the prophecy were not fulfilled.

Told of Hubert de Burgh's refusal to torture Arthur, the king, overjoyed, sent his chamberlain in pursuit of Pembroke and Salisbury to tell them the good news. Arthur, however, fearful for his welfare, had attempted escape from the castle. In jumping from the wall, he fell on the stones and was killed. When Hubert overtook the lords and blurted his tidings, he was confronted by information and proof that Arthur was dead. Pembroke and Salisbury sent word to John that they could be found with the French.

"Tedious as a twice-told tale"

King John, Act III, scene iv, line 108

Philip, King of France, has been beaten by John, King of England, who has fortified his French conquests and sailed for England. Constance, mother of Arthur, complaining to Philip about the loss of her son, is going mad with grief over her tragedy. She curses peace and wishes that her feeble hand were strong enough to shake the very earth. When she leaves, beside herself with anguish, Philip, fearing some "outrage," follows her. Lewis, the dauphin, summarizes his own opinion as well as that of Constance in these lines:

> *Lewis.* There's nothing in this world can make me joy.
> Life is as tedious as a twice-told tale,
> Vexing the dull ear of a drowsy man;
> And bitter shame hath spoiled the sweet world's taste
> That it yields naught but shame and bitterness.

Harried at every turn—deserted by his nobles, disowned by his subjects, attacked by his former ally—John, on Ascension Day, surrendered his crown to Cardinal Pandulph, thus fulfilling Peter's prophecy. He received it back only after he had acknowledged his vassalage to the pope. In return, Pandulph was to order the French to withdraw their forces. Opposed to such arbitration, however, Faulconbridge secured John's permission to engage the French. Lewis, now the King of France, rejected Pandulph's suit for peace. His claim was that officious Rome, having sent neither arms, men, nor money for France's cause in opposing John's hereticism and deviltry, should remain neutral.

Under the direction of Faulconbridge, the English made a strong stand against the French. The defaulting barons, advised by Melun, a dying French lord, that Lewis planned their execution if France won the victory, returned to the king and received his pardon for their disloyalty. John's graciousness to his barons and his new alliance with Rome, however, brought him only momentary happiness. He was poisoned at Swinstead Abbey and died after intense suffering.

After his death, Cardinal Pandulph was able to arrange a truce between the English and French. Prince Henry was named King of England. King Lewis returned home to France. Faulconbridge, brave, dashing, vainglorious, swore his allegiance to the new king. His and England's pride was expressed in his words that England had never been and would never be at a conqueror's feet, except when such a position might lead to future victories.

Critical Evaluation

An uneven product of William Shakespeare's early period and one of his first history plays, *King John* is neither as good as it might have been nor as bad as it has been considered. Written entirely in verse, the play sometimes fails to distinguish among the various characters in its portrayal of their speech—almost homogeneously filled with conceits and wordplays that, only in the case of Faulconbridge, fit the personality who speaks them. Its themes include the relationship between fortune and the individual's nature, the powerful finality of a king's words, the corrupt and conniving influence of the Church, and the degree of individual responsibility in the face of a leader's folly. This last is studied in Act IV, when John upbraids Hubert for taking him at his word in killing young Arthur; he tells Hubert that a king, too, has moods and his followers must protect him from his rash emotions. In general, as the brief abdication scene in the first part of Act V demonstrates, *King John* is generically a part of the *de casibus virorum illustrium* ("the fall of illustrious men") motif popular in medieval and Renaissance literature.

The play suffers from structural deficiencies that suggest Shakespeare had not yet mastered that peculiarly difficult combination of historical verisimilitude and artistic inspiration, that is, giving psychologically convincing motivation to actions that are "givens" of historical record. When Blanch and Lewis fall in love to order, when Pandulph enters as a *deus ex machina* to alter the course of events dramatically and unpredictably, when Faulconbridge carries Austria's head across the stage, when young Arthur whimsically decides to escape and kills himself, and when Lewis' rebuff to Pandulph goes unanswered, we suspect that Shakespeare nods. Yet Arthur's speech on his sadness, Hubert's mercy, Faulconbridge's touching pardon of his mother's folly, his saucy exchange with Austria, and Constance's speech about the fears of a queen, a woman, and a mother all contain the fertile seeds that would blossom into the full flower of Shakespeare's imagination.

For Further Study

Barroll, J. Leeds, ed. *Shakespeare Studies*. Vol. 1. Cincinnati, Ohio: University of Cincinnati, 1965. The first in a series of anthologies of Shakespearean criticism. "Shakespeare and the Double Image in *King John*," by John R. Elliot, is principally concerned with the historical and literary sources of the play.

Honigmann, E. A. J., ed. *The Arden Shakespeare: King John*. Cambridge, Mass.: Harvard University Press, 1962. In addition to the text of the play itself, this volume contains more than seventy pages of introductory material. The sources, the production history, and the text itself are considered. There are also appendices dealing with the sources and problems with the text.

Lloyd Evans, Gareth. *The Upstart Crow: An Introduction to Shakespeare's Plays.* London: J. M. Dent and Sons, 1982. A comprehensive discussion of the dramatic works of William Shakespeare. While the major emphasis is on critical reviews of the plays, there are also discussions of sources as well as material on the circumstances which surrounded the writing of the plays.

Pierce, Robert B. *Shakespeare's History Plays: The Family and the State.* Columbus: Ohio State University Press, 1971. A general discussion of Shakespeare's history plays. *King John* is considered as a transitional play between the early history plays and the later plays on Henry IV and V, which Pierce considers to be far greater works.

Ribner, Irving. *The English History Play in the Age of Shakespeare.* London: Methuen, 1965. A revised edition of the 1957 work first published in the United States by Princeton University Press. A discussion of history plays in the Elizabethan era of English drama, including a discussion of Shakespeare's contributions in the field. The development of the form through the period is discussed, and its sources are considered.

King Lear

Type of plot: Tragedy
Time of plot: First century B.C.E.
Locale: Britain
First performed: c. 1605-1606; first published, 1608

Principal characters

KING LEAR OF BRITAIN
KING OF FRANCE
DUKE OF CORNWALL
DUKE OF ALBANY
EARL OF KENT
EARL OF GLOUCESTER
EDGAR, Gloucester's legitimate son
EDMUND, Gloucester's illegitimate son
GONERIL,
REGAN, and
CORDELIA, Lear's daughters

The Story

King Lear, in foolish fondness for his children, decided to divide his kingdom among his three daughters. Grown senile, he scoffed at the foresight of his advisers and declared that each girl's statement of her love for him would determine the portion of the kingdom she received as her dowry. Goneril, his oldest daughter and the Duchess of Albany, spoke first. She said that she loved her father more than eyesight, space, liberty, or life itself. Regan, the Duchess of Cornwall, announced that the sentiment of her love had been expressed by Goneril, but that Goneril had stopped short of the statement of Regan's love. Cordelia, who had secretly confided that her love was more ponderous than her tongue, told her father that because her love was in her heart, not in her mouth, she was willing to sacrifice eloquence for truth. Lear angrily told her that truth alone should be her dowry and ordered that her part of the kingdom be divided between Goneril and Regan. Lear's disappointment in Cordelia's statement grew into a rage against the Earl of Kent, who tried to plead for Cordelia with the foolish king. Because of Kent's blunt speech, he was given ten days to leave the country. Loving his sovereign, he risked death by disguising himself and remaining in Britain to care for Lear in his infirmity.

When Burgundy and France came as suitors to ask Cordelia's hand in marriage, Burgundy, learning of her dowerless fate, rejected her. France, honoring Cordelia for her virtues, took her as his wife, but Lear dismissed Cordelia and France without his benediction. Goneril and Regan, wary of their father's vacillation in his weakened mental state, set about to establish their kingdoms against change.

Lear was not long in learning what Goneril's and Regan's claims of love for him really meant. Their caustic comments about the old man's mental and physical feebleness, furnished Lear's fool with many points for philosophical recriminations against the king. Realizing that his charity to his daughters had made him homeless, Lear cried in anguish against his fate. His prayers went unanswered, and his daughters' abuse hastened his derangement.

The Earl of Gloucester, like Lear, was fond of his two children. Edmund, a bastard, afraid that his illegitimacy would deprive him of his share of Gloucester's estate, forged a letter over Edgar's signature, stating that the sons should not have to wait for their fortunes until they were too old to enjoy them. Gloucester, refusing to believe that Edgar desired his father's death, was told by Edmund to wait in hiding and hear Edgar make assertions that could easily be misinterpreted against him. Edmund, furthering his scheme, told Edgar that villainy was afoot and that Edgar should not go unarmed at any time.

To complete his evil design, he later advised Edgar to flee for his own safety. After cutting his arm, he then told his father that he had been wounded while he and Edgar fought over Gloucester's honor. Gloucester, swearing that Edgar would not escape justice, had his son's description circulated so that he might be apprehended.

Edmund, meanwhile, allied himself with the dukes of Cornwall and Albany to defend Britain against the French army mobilized by Cordelia and her husband to avenge Lear's cruel treatment. Edmund won Regan and Goneril completely by his personal attentions to them and set the sisters against each other by arousing their jealousy.

Lear, wandering as an outcast on the stormy heath, was aided by Kent, disguised as a peasant. Seeking protection from the storm, they found a hut where Edgar, pretending to be a madman, had already taken refuge. Gloucester, searching for the king, found them there and urged them to hurry to Dover, where Cordelia and her husband would protect Lear from the wrath of his unnatural daughters.

Because he had attempted to give succor and condolence to the outcast Lear, Gloucester was blinded when Cornwall, acting on information furnished by Edmund, gouged out his eyes. While he was at his grisly work, a servant, rebelling against the cruel deed, wounded Cornwall. Regan killed the servant, but Cornwall died later as the result of his wound. Edgar, still playing the part of a madman, found his father wandering the fields with an old retainer. Edgar, who refrained from revealing his identity, promised to guide his father to Dover, where Gloucester planned to die by throwing himself from the high cliffs.

Goneril became bitterly jealous when widowed Regan was able to receive Edmund's full attention, who had been made Earl of Gloucester. She declared that she would rather lose the battle to France than lose Edmund to Regan. Goneril's hatred became more venomous when Albany, whom she detested because of his kindliness toward Lear and his pity for Gloucester, announced that he would try to right the wrongs done by Goneril, Regan, and Edmund.

Cordelia, informed by messenger of her father's fate, was in the French camp near Dover. When the mad old king was brought to her by the faithful Kent, she cared for her father tenderly and put him in the care of a doctor skilled in curing many kinds of ills. When he regained his reason, Lear recognized Cordelia, but the joy of their reunion was clouded by his repentance for having misunderstood and mistreated his only loyal daughter.

"More sinned against, than sinning"

King Lear, Act III, scene ii, line 60

The aging King Lear attempts to rid himself of the responsibilities of kingship by dividing his realm among his three daughters on condition that each daughter declare her love for him. The youngest daughter, Cordelia, refuses to indulge in this exercise, despite the effusive statements of love presented by her sisters, Goneril and Regan. Lear foolishly disinherits Cordelia, the only daughter who really loves him. He soon discovers his mistake when Regan puts Kent, the king's courtier, into stocks and Goneril refuses to assist the aged monarch. Lear calls his daughters "unnatural hags" and rushes into the stormy night. On the heath with his faithful jester, he cries out against the elements:

> *Lear.* Blow winds, and crack your cheeks. Rage, blow,
> You cataracts, and hurricanoes, spout
> Till you have drenched our steeples, drowned the cocks.
> You sulphurous and thought-executing fires,
> Vaunt-couriers of oak-cleaving thunderbolts,
> Singe my white head. And thou all-shaking thunder,
> Strike flat the thick rotundity o' th' world,
> Crack nature's moulds, all germens spill at once,
> That makes ingrateful man. . . .
> Let the great gods
> That keep this dreadful pother o'er our heads
> Find out their enemies now. . . .
> Close pent-up guilts,
> Rive your concealing continents, and cry
> These dreadful summoners grace. I am a man
> More sinned against, than sinning.

Edgar, protecting Gloucester, was accosted by Oswald, Goneril's steward, on his way to deliver a note to Edmund. In the fight that ensued, Edgar killed Oswald; he then delivered the letter to Albany, in which Goneril declared her love for Edmund and asked that he kill her husband. Gloucester died, feeble and broken-hearted after Edgar revealed himself to his father. Edmund, who commanded the British forces, took Lear and Cordelia prisoners. When they were taken off to prison, he sent along written instructions for how they were to be treated.

Albany, who was aware of Edmund's ambition for personal glory, arrested him on a charge of high treason. Regan interceded for her lover but was rebuffed by Goneril. Regan was suddenly taken ill and carried to Albany's tent. When Edmund, as was his right, demanded a trial by combat, Albany agreed. Edgar, still in disguise, appeared and in the fight mortally wounded his false brother. Goneril, learning from Albany that he knew of her plot against his life, was desperate. She went to their tent, poisoned Regan, and killed herself.

Edmund, dying, revealed that he and Goneril had ordered Cordelia to be hanged and her death to be announced as suicide because of her despondency over her father's plight. Edmund, fiendish and diabolical always, was also vain. As he lay dying, he looked upon the bodies of Goneril and Regan and expressed pleasure that two women were dead because of their jealous love for him.

Albany dispatched Edgar to prevent Cordelia's death, but he arrived too late. Lear refused all assistance when he appeared carrying her dead body in his arms. After asking forgiveness of heartbroken Kent, whom he recognized at last, Lear, a broken, confused old man, died in anguish. Edgar and Albany alone were left to rebuild a country ravaged by bloodshed and war.

Critical Evaluation

Despite the three-hundred-year-old debate regarding the lack of unity in the plot of *King Lear*, it is one of the most readable and gripping of William Shakespeare's dramas. The theme of filial ingratitude is presented clearly in the depiction of two families, whom circumstances eventually bring together as the two narrative lines converge. *King Lear* is not only an absorbing drama but a disturbing one as well. The beauty of diction and the overwhelming pathos of the treatment given to innocence and goodness add to the poignancy of the emotional play. Like all great tragic dramas, the story of Lear and his folly purges the emotions by terror and pity.

King Lear's first entrance in Act I is replete with ritual and ceremony. He is full of antiquity, authority, and assurance as he makes his regal way through the ordered court. When he reveals his intention to divide his kingdom into three parts for his daughters, he exudes the confidence generated by his long reign. The crispness and directness of his language suggest a power, if not imperiousness, that, far from senility, demonstrates the stability and certainty of long, unchallenged rule. From that point on, the play acts out the destruction of that fixed order and the emergence of a new, tentative balance.

In the opening scene, Lear speaks as king and father. The absolute ruler has decided to apportion his kingdom to his three heirs as a gift rather than bequest. In performing this act, which superficially seems both reasonable and generous, Lear sets in motion a chain of events that expose his vulnerabilities not only as a king and a father but also as a man. Shakespeare shows that it is foolish to divest oneself of power and responsibility and yet expect to retain the trappings of authority. This is exactly what Lear does when he relies with ill-placed confidence on the love of his daughters. He asks too much and he acts too precipitously, but he is punished by an inexorable universe out of all proportion to his errors in judgment.

When he asks his daughters for a declaration of love, as a prerequisite for a share

An early silent film version of King Lear *(1916) in a scene with Lear and his fool.* (Courtesy of The Museum of Modern Art, Film Stills Archive)

of the kingdom, he is as self-assured a parent as he is an overbearing monarch. He credits the facile protestations of love by Goneril and Regan because they are what he wants to hear and because they conform to the ceremonial necessities of the occasion. Cordelia's honest response, born of a greater love, are out of keeping with the occasion. Lear has not looked beneath the surface. He has let the ritual appearances replace the internal reality, in fact, he has refused to distinguish between the two.

The asseverations of Goneril and Regan soon emerge as the cynical conceits they really are, but by then Lear has banished Cordelia and the loyal Kent, who saw through the sham. Lear is successively and ruthlessly divested of all the accoutrements of kingship by his villainous daughters, who eventually reduce him to the condition of a ragged, homeless madman. Paradoxically, it is in this extremity on the heath with Edgar and the fool, that Lear comes to a knowledge of himself and his community with humanity that he had never achieved while enjoying the glories of power. Buffeted by the natural fury of the storm, which is symbolic of the chaos and danger that come with the passing of the old order, Lear through his madness sees the common bond that connects him to the rest of humanity.

The experience of Lear is, on a more manageable, human level, mirrored in the Gloucester subplot. Gloucester too suffers filial ingratitude but not one raised to a cosmic level. He too mistakes appearance for reality in trusting the duplicitous Edmund and disinheriting the honest Edgar, but his behavior is more clearly the outgrowth of an existing moral confusion, which is reflected in his ambivalent and unrepentant affection for his illegitimate son. His moral blindness leads to physical blindness when his faulty judgment makes him vulnerable to the villains. In his blindness, he finally sees the truth of his situation, but his experience remains that of a father and a man.

"As flies to wanton boys, are we to the gods"

King Lear, Act IV, scene i, line 38

The Earl of Gloucester has two sons. One, Edgar, is legitimate; the other, Edmund, is illegitimate, a bastard. Edmund conspires to turn the father against Edgar and deprive him of his birthright. Edgar flees into hiding, disguised as a madman named Tom. In the meantime, King Lear has been forced to wander on the stormy heath. Enraged, humbled, and pushed to the edge of madness, Lear and his jester stumble upon "Tom," the madman. Together, they are rescued by Gloucester, despite the daughters' injunctions not to aid the king. Regan and her husband, the Duke of Cornwall, discover Gloucester's defection and, in a rage, blind him. Turned loose to go where he wishes, Gloucester, led by an old man, encounters his son, Edgar, still disguised as Tom, the madman.

Gloucester. Is it a beggar man?
Old Man. Madman and beggar too.
Gloucester. He has some reason, else he could not beg.
   I' th' last night's storm, I such a fellow saw;
   Which made me think a man a worm. My son
   Came then into my mind, and yet my mind
   Was then scarce friends with him. I have heard more since.
   As flies to wanton boys, are we to the gods;
   They kill us for their sport.

Lear's experience parallels Gloucester's in that his figurative madness leads to a real madness in which he finally recognizes what he has lacked. He sees in the naked Edgar, himself a victim of Gloucester's moral blindness, the natural state of man, stripped of all external decoration, and he realizes that he has ignored the basic realities of the human condition. His experience finally transcends Gloucester's, however, because he is a king, preeminent among men. He not only represents the hazards of kingship but also the broadly human disposition to prefer pleasant appearances to troubling realities. Yet because of his position, Lear's failure brings the whole political and social order down with him.

Lear has violated nature by a culpable ignorance of it. The result is familial rupture, physical suffering, and existential confusion. Brought low, Lear begins to fashion a new salutary view of himself, human love, and human nature. In his insanity, Lear assembles a bizarre court of mad king, beggar, and fool that reasserts the common bonds of all men. Once he has achieved these realizations, the play's evil characters, so carefully balanced against the good in Shakespeare's precarious world, begin to kill each other off and succumb to the vengeance of regenerated justice.

It is however a mark of Shakespeare's uncompromising view of reality that there is no simple application of poetic justice to reward the good and punish the wicked. The good die too. Edgar finishes off his brother in a trial by combat, and the machinations of Goneril and Regan result in the destruction of both, but the redeemed Lear and Cordelia, the perfection of selfless love, also die. That Lear should die is perhaps no surprise. The suffering he has endured in his confrontation with the primal elements does not allow an optimistic return to normal life and prosperity. He has looked into the eye of nature and there is nothing left for him but to die.

The death of Cordelia is more troublesome because she is the perfectly innocent victim of the evil and madness that surround her. She dies gratuitously, not because of any internal necessity of the plot, but because the message to save her arrives too late. The dramatist has created his own inevitability to represent the ruthless consequences of the evil and chaos that have been loosed. When Lear enters with the dead Cordelia, he accomplishes the final expiation of his unknowing.

Out of these sufferings and recognitions comes a new moral stasis. Yet the purged world does not inspire great confidence that it will attain stability in the future. When Kent, who is old, refuses kingship, Edgar assumes authority but despite his rectitude there is an unsettling doubt that he has the force or stature to maintain the new order in this volatile world where evil and chaos always exist beneath the surface.

"Critical Evaluation" by Edward E. Foster

For Further Study

Booth, Stephen. *"King Lear," "Macbeth," Indefinition, and Tragedy*. New Haven, Conn.: Yale University Press, 1983. In part 1, "On the Greatness of *King Lear*," much of the discussion focuses on the repeated false endings of the play. Booth also has an important appendix on the doubling of roles in Shakespeare's plays, especially in *King Lear.*

Halio, Jay L. *Critical Essays on "King Lear."* New York: Twayne, 1995. Contains a selection of the best essays on *King Lear*, including several on the "two-text hypothesis," the play in performance, and interpretation. The introduction surveys recent trends in criticism.

Leggatt, Alexander. *King Lear*. Harvester New Critical Introductions. Hemel Hempstead, Hertfordshire, England: Harvester-Wheatsheaf, 1988. Includes a brief discussion of the stage history and critical reception, as well as a thorough discussion of the play's dramatic idiom and characters.

Mack, Maynard. *"King Lear" in Our Time*. Berkeley: University of California Press, 1965. Surveys the play's historical background, sources, and aspects of its staging. Also provides many perceptive critical comments on the action and its significance.

Rosenberg, Marvin. *The Masks of King Lear*. 1972. Reprint. Newark: University of Delaware Press, 1993. Rosenberg examines the significance of each scene and the "polyphony" of the characters, with extensive reference to the history of *King Lear* on the stage as of the earliest recorded performances. Also discusses the so-called Lear myth.

Love's Labour's Lost

Type of plot: Comedy
Time of plot: Sixteenth century
Locale: Navarre, Spain
First performed: c. 1594-1595; revised presentation, 1597; first published, 1598

Principal characters

FERDINAND, King of Navarre
BEROWNE,
LONGAVILLE, and
DUMAINE, lords of Navarre
DON ADRIANO DE ARMADO, a foolish Spaniard
COSTARD, a clown
THE PRINCESS OF FRANCE
ROSALINE,
MARIA, and
KATHARINE, ladies attending the princess
JAQUENETTA, a country wench

The Story

The King of Navarre had taken a solemn vow and forced three of his attending lords to take it also. This vow was that for three years they would fast and study, enjoy no pleasures, and see no ladies. None of the three noblemen wanted to take the vow; Berowne, in particular, felt that it would be impossible to keep his promise. He pointed out this fact to the king by reminding him that the princess of France was approaching the court of Navarre to present a petition from her father, who was ill. The king agreed that he would be compelled to see her, but he added that in such cases the vow must be broken by necessity. Berowne foresaw that "necessity" would often cause the breaking of their vows.

The only amusement the king and his lords would have was provided by Costard, a clown, and by Don Adriano de Armado, a foolish Spaniard attached to the court. Armado wrote the king to inform him that Costard had been caught in the company of Jaquenetta, a country wench of dull mind. Since all attached to the court had been under the same laws of abstinence from earthly pleasures, Costard was remanded to Armado's custody and ordered to fast on bran and water for one week. The truth was that Armado also loved Jaquenetta. He feared the king would learn of his love and punish him in the same manner.

The Princess of France arrived with her three attendants. All were fair, and they

184

expected to be received at the palace in the manner due their rank. The king, however, sent word that they would be housed at his lodge, since under the terms of his vow no lady could enter the palace. The princess, furious at being treated in this fashion, scorned the king for his bad manners. When she presented the petition from her father, she and the king could not agree because he vowed he had not received certain monies she claimed had been delivered to him.

At that first meeting, although each would have denied the fact, eight hearts were set to beating faster. The king viewed the princess with more than courteous interest. Berowne, Longaville, and Dumaine, his attendants, looked with love on the princess' ladies in waiting, Rosaline, Maria, and Katharine. A short time later Berowne sent a letter to Rosaline, with Costard as his messenger. Costard had also been given a letter by Armado, to be delivered to Jaquenetta. Costard, who was illiterate, mixed up the letters, giving Jaquenetta's to Rosaline and Rosaline's to the country wench.

Berowne had been correct in thinking the vow to leave the world behind would soon be broken. Hiding in a tree, he heard the king read aloud a sonnet that proclaimed his love for the princess. Later the king, in hiding, overheard Longaville reading some verses he had composed to Maria. Longaville, in turn, concealed himself and listened while Dumaine read a love poem inscribed to Katharine. Then each one in turn stepped out from hiding to accuse the others of breaking their vows. Berowne all that time had remained hidden in the tree. Thinking to chide them for their broken vows, he revealed himself at last and ridiculed them for their weakness, at the same time proclaiming himself the only one able to keep his vow. Costard and Jaquenetta then brought to the king the letter Berowne had written Rosaline, which Costard had mistakenly delivered to Jaquenetta.

All confessed that they had broken their vows. Berowne provided an excuse for all when he declared that one could learn much by studying women and the nature of love; thus, they were still devoting themselves to study. Having, in a fashion, saved face, the four determined to woo the ladies in earnest, and they made plans to entertain their loves with revels and dances.

Each lover sent his lady an anonymous token to wear in his honor. The ladies learned from a servant who the lovers were. The ladies played a joke on their suitors, who came in disguise to woo them. The women masked themselves and exchanged the tokens. The men arrived, also masked and disguised as Russians. Each man tried to make love to the lady wearing his token, but each was spurned and ridiculed. The ladies would not dance or sing, but would only mock the bewildered gentlemen.

Finally the suitors departed, hurt and indignant at the treatment they had received. Before long they returned in their own dress. The ladies, also unmasked, told of the lunatic Russians who had called on them. The men confessed their plot and forswore all such jokes forever, but the ladies did not stop teasing them. Since each man had made love to the wrong woman because of the exchange of tokens, the ladies pretended to be hurt that each man had broken his vows of love and constancy. The suitors suffered greatly for the sake of the ladies' merriment. Then the suitors learned that the ladies had anticipated the suitors' coming in disguise and thus had planned a joke of their own.

The king ordered a play presented for the entertainment of all. In the midst of the gaiety word came that the princess' father, the King of France, had died. She had to sail for home immediately, accompanied by her attendants. When the king and his lords pleaded with the ladies to stay in Navarre and marry them, the ladies refused to accept their serious protestations of love; they had jested too much to be believed. Each man vowed that he would remain faithful, only to be reminded of

The Princess of France (Lise Bruneau, standing) and Maria (Vilma Silva) are amused by their suitors in the Oregon Shakespeare Festival's 1996 production of Love's Labour's Lost. (David Cooper, courtesy of the Oregon Shakespeare Festival by permission of the Actors' Equity Association)

the former vows he had broken. Then each lady made a condition which, if met, would reward her lover a year hence. The king must retire for twelve months to a hermitage and there forsake all worldly pleasures. If at the end of that time he still loved the princess, she would be his. In the same fashion the other three lords must spend a year in carrying out the wishes of their sweethearts. Even the foolish Armado was included in the plan. He joined the others, announcing that Jaquenetta would not have him until he spent three years in honest work. Thus all the swains tried with jests and fair speech to win their ladies, but without success. Now as the price of their folly they had to prove in earnest that they deserved the hearts of their beloveds.

Critical Evaluation

The exuberant language of *Love's Labour's Lost* has made it, in the words of Anne Barton, "the most relentlessly Elizabethan of all Shakespeare's plays." At times the dazzling wordplays have been deemed too clever, complex, and convoluted to make for a play that translates well to a modern audience. Yet audiences continue to sense, if not always completely comprehend, the wit and consequent fun inherent in the language—and it is on the issues of language that appreciation of the play ultimately rests.

Several factors give the play a special status in the William Shakespeare canon. It is one of the few Shakespeare plays for which an original source has not been found. For a comedy, it is also unusual that in spite of at least five possible couplings, it does not end in the traditional marriage or multiple marriages. The happy ending is suspended and left to the future, with the agreement of the couples to meet a year later. It is highly unusual that death plays such a direct role in the outcome of the play. Given the artificial motivation for the beginning of the plot, however, as well as the heavily verbal middle, it is not surprising that it takes the extreme intrusion of death to jolt the characters back to reality.

Critical attention has focused largely on Shakespeare's satire of the men's behavior. The King of Navarre's plan is patently absurd. In wishing to take a vow to separate himself from women and from pleasure and to dwell only on study, Ferdinand is plainly rejecting life's realities. In his forcing his attendants to take the vow with him and in their agreeing to take it, the entire trustworthiness of vows is put at stake. The vows are, naturally, soon challenged by the intrusion into the king's withdrawn world of the princess of France and her attendants.

What follows largely justifies the complaints of those who find the plot weak. Little happens to move the story forward—love letters are misdirected and sonnets and verses are read. The games of words are followed by games of wooing, with some of the usual comic stage business of disguises and mistaken identities used to prolong the courtship. When the representatives of the outside world seem to have been thoroughly drawn into the king's artificial world of games, the startling news of the death of the King of France shatters this fragile and illusory world built on words. As a commentary on the insubstantiality of language, the play is strong. As drama, the vows of love from it are not as strong.

Love's Labour's Lost is often excused as an early play, suggesting but not itself exhibiting some of the greater characterizations that came later. The cynical Berowne and the quick-witted Rosaline, for example, seem to foreshadow Benedick and Beatrice in *Much Ado About Nothing* (c. 1598-1599). There is a hint of the substantial subplots so common in Shakespeare with the clowns and comic characters. Don Adriano de Armado, Costard, and Jaquenetta, for example, serve to reflect on the foolishness and self-deception of the main male characters.

"Heirs of all eternity"

Love's Labour's Lost, Act I, scene i, line 7

King Ferdinand of Navarre and his lords in attendance, Berowne, Longaville, and Dumaine, take an oath to forsake courtly pleasures and to devote three years to studying and fasting, thus making of Navarre "a little Academe." Ferdinand suggests that fame will defeat death's devouring disgrace and make of the scholars "heirs of all eternity."

> *King.* Let fame, that all hunt after in their lives,
> Live registered upon our brazen tombs,
> And then grace us, in the disgrace of death;
> When, spite of cormorant devouring Time,
> Th' endeavour of this present breath may buy
> That honour which shall bate his scythe's keen edge,
> And make us heirs of all eternity.
> Therefore, brave conquerors—for so you are,
> That war against your own affections,
> And the huge Army of the world's desires—
> Our late edict shall strongly stand in force.
> Navarre shall be the wonder of the world.
> Our court shall be a little Academe,
> Still and contemplative in living art.

With this play it may be helpful to remember that actual performances have often been comical and fun. A reading may be laborious, and some of the language difficult to grasp. The easygoing silliness of the play in performance, however, can be rewarding. The play may have been written specifically to be performed for a small, highly educated audience. Discussions about the precise dating of the play have relied on the numerous historical references in it. More than usual, Shakespeare seems to have chosen names that evoked real people of the time, a theatrical device that would appeal only to those in the know. Although not based on any specific sources, the play evokes the Petrarchan conventions and the exaggerated language of love so popular in the writings of courtiers of the time. *Love's Labour's Lost* is also remarkable for its large number of puns and other wordplay.

With this early play, Shakespeare seems to have fused form and content. In satirizing the unrealistic idealization of learning, in examining the reliability and trustworthiness of that fallible vehicle for expression—language—Shakespeare draws on his considerable stock of verbal tricks and games to make the point. Although all the labor that the men put into their verse and their trickery to express their love for the women seems lost at the end, it is a temporary loss. What the women ask for, ironically enough, is that the men fulfill the vows that they undertook in the first place. Words may be inadequate, but there are practically no other means, especially for a playwright, for expression. The unexpected ending, with its promise of fulfillment, seems to be a challenge to make the promise of words of love become true in deeds of love.

"Critical Evaluation" by Shakuntala Jayaswal

For Further Study

Barber, C. L. "The Folly of Wit and Masquerade in *Love's Labour's Lost.*" In *Shakespeare's Festive Comedy: A Study of Dramatic Form and Its Relation to Social Custom.* Princeton, N.J.: Princeton University Press, 1959. An influential study of the relationship between holiday rituals and the comedies. Sees the games in this play as providing necessary festive release.

Barton, Anne. Introduction to *Love's Labor's Lost.* In *The Riverside Shakespeare.* Boston: Houghton Mifflin, 1974. An introduction to the play's textual history and an explication of language and themes by a premier Oxonian Shakespeare scholar.

Carroll, William C. *The Great Feast of Language in "Love's Labour's Lost."* Princeton, N.J.: Princeton University Press, 1976. Argues that the play does not pit art against nature but rather shows their connection and interdependence. Includes a discussion of the songs at the play's end.

Gilbert, Miriam. *Love's Labour's Lost.* Manchester, England: Manchester University Press, 1993. Describes a select group of productions of the play. The variety of possible interpretations is revealed in the description of productions.

Roesen, Bobbyann. "*Love's Labour's Lost.*" *Shakespeare Quarterly* 4, no. 4 (October, 1953): 411-426. Examines the contrast between the artificial and the real in the play. Explains the movement toward reality as necessary for love.

Wilson, John Dover. "*Love's Labour's Lost:* The Story of a Conversion." In *Shakespeare's Happy Comedies.* Evanston, Ill.: Northwestern University Press, 1962. Explains how one's low opinion of the play may change after watching a performance. Compares the high spirits of the play to a Mozart opera and is an example of understanding the difference between reading and watching a play.

Macbeth

Type of plot: Tragedy
Time of plot: Eleventh century
Locale: Scotland
First performed: 1606; first published, 1623

Principal characters

MACBETH, a Scottish thane
LADY MACBETH, his wife
DUNCAN, the King of Scotland
MALCOLM, his son
BANQUO, a Scottish chieftain
MACDUFF, a rebel lord

The Story

On a lonely heath in Scotland, three weird witches sang their riddling runes and said that soon they would meet Macbeth. Macbeth, the noble thane of Glamis, had recently been victorious in a great battle against Vikings and Scottish rebels. For his brave deeds, King Duncan decided to confer upon him the lands of the rebellious thane of Cawdor.

On his way to see the king, Macbeth and his friend Banquo met the three witches on the dark moor. The wild and frightful women greeted Macbeth by first calling him thane of Glamis, then thane of Cawdor, and finally, King of Scotland. Finally, they prophesied that Banquo's heirs would reign in Scotland in years to come. When Macbeth tried to question the three hags, they vanished.

Macbeth thought very little about the strange prophecy until he met one of Duncan's messengers, who told him that he was now thane of Cawdor. This piece of news stunned Macbeth, but Banquo thought the witches' prophecy was an evil ruse to whet Macbeth's ambition and trick him into fulfilling the prophecy. Macbeth did not heed Banquo's warning; hearing the witches call him king had gone deep into his soul. He pondered over the possibility of becoming a monarch and set his whole heart on the attainment of this goal. If he could be thane of Cawdor, perhaps he could rule all of Scotland as well. As it was now, Duncan was king, and he had two sons who would rule after him. The problem was great. Macbeth shook off his dreams and accompanied Banquo to greet Duncan.

Duncan was a kind, majestic, gentle, and strong ruler; Macbeth was fond of him. When Duncan however mentioned that his son, Malcolm, would succeed him on the throne, Macbeth saw the boy as an obstacle in his own path; he hardly dared admit to himself how this impediment disturbed him. Duncan announced that he would spend one night of a royal procession at Macbeth's castle. Lady Macbeth, who was even more ambitious than her husband, saw Duncan's visit as a perfect opportunity for Macbeth to become king. She determined that he should murder Duncan and usurp the throne.

That night there was much feasting in the castle. After everyone was asleep, Lady Macbeth told her husband of her plan for the king's murder. Horrified, Macbeth at first refused to do the deed, but when his wife accused him of cowardice and dangled bright prospects of his future before his eyes, Macbeth finally succumbed. He stole into the sleeping king's chamber and plunged a knife into his heart.

The murder was blamed on two grooms whom Lady Macbeth had smeared with Duncan's blood while they were asleep. Yet suspicions were aroused in the castle. The dead king's sons fled—Malcolm to England and Donalbain to Ireland—and when Macbeth was proclaimed king, Macduff, a nobleman who had been Duncan's close friend, suspected him of the bloody killing.

Macbeth began to have horrible dreams; his mind was never free from fear. Often he thought of the witches' second prophecy, that Banquo's heirs would hold the throne, and the prediction tormented him. Macbeth was so determined that Banquo should never share in his own hard-earned glory that he resolved to murder Banquo and his son, Fleance.

Lady Macbeth and her husband gave a great banquet for the noble thanes of Scotland. At the same time, Macbeth sent murderers to waylay Banquo and his son before they could reach the palace. Banquo was slain in the scuffle, but Fleance escaped. Meanwhile, in the large banquet hall, Macbeth pretended great sorrow that Banquo was not present. Banquo was however present in spirit, and his ghost majestically appeared in Macbeth's own seat. The startled king was so frightened that he almost betrayed his guilt when he saw the apparition, but he was the only one to see it. Lady Macbeth quickly led him away and dismissed the guests.

More frightened than ever at the thought of Banquo's ghost having returned to haunt him and of Fleance who had escaped but might one day claim the throne, Macbeth determined to seek solace from the witches on the dismal heath. They assured Macbeth that he would not be overcome by man born of woman, nor until the forest of Birnam came to Dunsinane Hill. They also warned him to beware of Macduff. When Macbeth asked if Banquo's children would reign over the kingdom, the witches disappeared. The news they gave him had brought him cheer, however. Macbeth now felt he need fear no man, since all were born of women, and certainly the great Birnam forest could not be moved by human power.

Macbeth heard that Macduff was gathering a hostile army in England that was to be led by Duncan's son Malcolm, who was determined to avenge his father's murder. So terrified was Macbeth that he resolved to murder Macduff's wife and children in order to bring the rebel to submission. After this slaughter, however, Macbeth was more than ever tormented by fear; his twisted mind had almost reached the breaking point, and he longed for death to release him from his nightmarish existence.

Before long, Lady Macbeth's strong will broke as well. Dark dreams of murder and violence drove her to madness. The horror of her crimes and the agony of being hated and feared by all of Macbeth's subjects made her so ill that her death seemed imminent.

On the eve of Macduff's attack on Macbeth's castle, Lady Macbeth died, depriving her husband of all the support and courage she had been able to give him in the past. Rallying, Macbeth summoned strength to meet his enemy. Yet Birnam wood was moving, for Malcolm's soldiers were hidden behind cut green boughs, which from a distance appeared to be a moving forest. Macduff, enraged by the slaughter of his innocent family, was determined to meet Macbeth in hand-to-hand conflict.

Macbeth went out to battle filled with the false courage given him by the witches' prophecy that no man born of woman would overthrow him. Meeting Macduff, Macbeth began to fight him, but when he found out that Macduff had been ripped alive from his mother's womb, Macbeth fought with waning strength, all hope of victory gone. With a flourish, Macduff severed the head of the bloody King of Scotland. The prophecy was fulfilled.

"Out damned spot, out I say!"

Macbeth, Act V, scene i, line 38

Impatient and ambitious, Macbeth, with Lady Macbeth's help, murders King Duncan in his sleep. Macbeth escapes blame and is elected and crowned king. He becomes a bloody tyrant. Lady Macbeth, despite having pushed her husband into the murder, is superbly in command of herself during her waking hours. While she sleeps, however, her suppressed emotions and stifled conscience demand expression. Walking in her sleep, she cries out in anguish, reliving the night of the murder.

> *Lady Macbeth.* Out damned spot, out I say! One—two—why then
> 'tis time to do't. Hell is murky. Fie, my lord, fie! A soldier, and
> afeard? What need we fear who knows it, when none can call our
> power to account? Yet who would have thought the old man to
> have had so much blood in him? . . . Here's the smell of blood still.
> All the perfumes of Arabia will not sweeten this little hand. O, O,
> O! . . . Come, come, come, come, give me your hand. What's done
> cannot be undone. To bed, to bed, to bed.

Critical Evaluation

Not only is *Macbeth* by far the shortest of William Shakespeare's great tragedies, but it is also anomalous in some structural respects. Like *Othello* (1604) and only a very few other Shakespearean plays, *Macbeth* is without the complications of a subplot. Consequently, the action moves forward in a swift and inexorable rush. More significantly, the climax—the murder of Duncan—takes place very early in the play. As a result, attention is focused on the various consequences of the crime rather than on the ambiguities or moral dilemmas that had preceded and occasioned it.

In this, the play differs from *Othello*, in which the hero commits murder only after long plotting, and from *Hamlet* (1600-1601), in which the hero spends most of the play in moral indecision. It is more like *King Lear* (1605-1606), where destructive action flows from the central premise of the division of the kingdom. Yet *Macbeth* differs from that play, too, in that it does not raise the monumental, cosmic questions of good and evil in nature. Instead it explores the moral and psychological effects of evil in the life of one man. For all the power and prominence of Lady Macbeth, the drama remains essentially the story of the lord who commits regicide and thereby enmeshes himself in a complex web of consequences.

The three weird witches meeting Macbeth and Banquo, a woodcut appearing in the first edition of Raphael Holinshed's Chronicles of England, Scotland, and Ireland *(1577). Shakespeare is known to have consulted the unillustrated second edition (1587), so he may or may not have seen this woodcut.* (Reprinted by permission of The Folger Shakespeare Library)

When Macbeth first enters, he is far from the villain whose experiences the play subsequently describes. He has just returned from a glorious military success in defense of the crown. He is rewarded by the grateful Duncan, with preferment as thane of Cawdor. This honor, which initially qualifies him for the role of hero, ironically intensifies the horror of the murder Macbeth soon thereafter commits.

His fall is rapid, and his crime is more clearly a sin than is usually the case in tragedy. It is not mitigated by mixed motives or insufficient knowledge. Moreover, the sin is regicide, an action viewed by the Renaissance as exceptionally foul, since it struck at God's representative on earth. The sin is so boldly offensive that many have tried to find extenuation in the impetus given Macbeth by the witches.

However, the witches do not control behavior in the play. They are symbolic of evil and prescient of crimes which are to come, but they neither encourage nor facilitate Macbeth's actions. They are merely a poignant external symbol of the ambition that is already within Macbeth. Indeed, when he discusses the witches' prophecy with Lady Macbeth, it is clear that the possibility has been discussed before.

Nor can the responsibility be shifted to Lady Macbeth, despite her goading. In a way, she is merely acting out the role of the good wife, encouraging her husband to do what she believes to be in his best interests. She is a catalyst and supporter, but she does not make the grim decision, and Macbeth never tries to lay the blame on her.

"Life's but a walking shadow"

Macbeth, Act V, scene v, line 24

Lady Macbeth, initially strong in ambition, becomes weak from worry after the murder of King Duncan and finally suffers a complete mental and physical collapse, and dies. Macbeth receives word of her death while he watches the advance of an English army commanded by Malcolm, son of the murdered King Duncan. In one of the most famous speeches in all of Shakespeare, Macbeth comments on the brevity and futility of life as he sorrows for his dead queen:

> *Macbeth.* Tomorrow, and tomorrow, and tomorrow,
> Creeps in this petty pace from day to day,
> To the last syllable of recorded time;
> And all our yesterdays have lighted fools
> The way to a dusty death. Out, out, brief candle!
> Life's but a walking shadow, a poor player,
> That struts and frets his hour upon the stage,
> And then is heard no more. It is a tale
> Told by an idiot, full of sound and fury,
> Signifying nothing.

When Macbeth proceeds on his bloody course, there is little extenuation in his brief failure of nerve. He is an ambitious man overpowered by his high aspirations, yet Shakespeare is able to elicit feelings of sympathy for him from the audience. Despite the evil of his actions, he does not arouse the distaste audiences reserve for such villains as Iago and Cornwall. This may be because Macbeth is not evil incarnate but a human being who has sinned. Moreover, audiences are as much affected by what Macbeth says about his actions as by the deeds themselves. Both substance and setting emphasize the great evil, but Macbeth does not go about his foul business easily. He knows what he is doing, and his agonizing reflections show a man increasingly losing control over his own moral destiny.

Although Lady Macbeth demonstrated greater courage and resolution at the time of the murder of Duncan, it is she who falls victim to the physical manifestations of remorse and literally dies of guilt. Macbeth, who starts more tentatively, becomes stronger, or perhaps more inured, as he faces the consequences of his initial crime. The play examines the effects of evil on Macbeth's character and on his subsequent moral behavior. The later murders flow naturally out of the first. Evil breeds evil because Macbeth, to protect himself and consolidate his position, is forced to murder again. Successively, he kills Banquo, attempts to murder Fleance, and brutally exterminates Macduff's family. As his crimes increase, Macbeth's freedom seems to decrease, but his moral responsibility does not. His actions become more cold-blooded as his options disappear.

Shakespeare does not allow Macbeth any moral excuses. The dramatist is aware of the notion that any action performed makes it more likely that the person will perform other such actions. The operation of this phenomenon is apparent as Macbeth finds it increasingly easier to rise to the gruesome occasion. However, the dominant inclination never becomes a total determinant of behavior, so Macbeth does not have the excuse of loss of free will. It does however become ever more difficult to break the chain of events that are rushing him toward moral and physical destruction.

As he degenerates, he becomes more deluded about his invulnerability and more emboldened. What he gains in will and confidence is counterbalanced and eventually toppled by the iniquitous weight of the events he set in motion and felt

Macbeth (Orson Welles) stares at Banquo's ghost as an alarmed Lady Macbeth (Jeanette Nolan) and other members of the court look on, in the 1948 film version of Macbeth. (Courtesy of The Museum of Modern Art, Film Stills Archive)

he had to perpetuate. When he dies, he seems almost to be released from the imprisonment of his own evil.

"Critical Evaluation" by Edward E. Foster

For Further Study

Bradley, A. C. *Shakespearean Tragedy*. London: Macmillan, 1905. A classic study. Chapters on *Macbeth* deal with fundamental issues of evil, flawed nobility of character, and tragic choice; Bradley's eloquent prose helps the reader appreciate the grandeur of the subject.

Harbage, Alfred. *William Shakespeare: A Reader's Guide*. New York: Farrar, Straus & Giroux, 1963. An excellent introduction to Shakespeare's plays, accessible to the general reader while providing masterful analyses of selected plays. Discussion of *Macbeth* gives a scene-by-scene synopsis, illuminated by wide-ranging, sensitive, analytical commentary.

Holland, Norman. *The Shakespearean Imagination*. New York: Macmillan, 1964. Informative, readable discussions of Shakespeare's major plays based on a series of educational television lectures. Introductory chapters provide a good background to the beliefs and values of Shakespeare's times. The chapter on *Macbeth* discusses elements of the play such as theme, characterization, atmosphere, and imagery.

Long, Michael. *Macbeth*. Boston: Twayne, 1989. An excellent introduction to the play as well as original critical commentary. Includes chapters on stage history, literary counterparts and antecedents, and dramatic symbols, as well as scene-by-scene analysis. Long characterizes Macbeth's tragedy as both Christian and classical, a story of radical isolation from humanity.

Shakespeare, William. *Macbeth*. Edited by Alan Sinfield. Houndsmills, England: Macmillan, 1992. Contains a dozen articles on *Macbeth* that together provide a good idea of the intellectual issues, political concerns, and style of postmodernist criticism not only of this play but also of literature in general. Includes a useful introduction and summative chapter endnotes, plus an annotated bibliography.

Measure for Measure

Type of plot: Comedy: problem play
Time of plot: Sixteenth century
Locale: Vienna
First performed: c. 1604; first published, 1623

Principal characters

VINCENTIO, the Duke of Vienna
ANGELO, the lord deputy
ESCALUS, an ancient counselor
CLAUDIO, a young gentleman
LUCIO, his friend
ISABELLA, Claudio's sister
MARIANA, Angelo's former sweetheart
JULIET, Claudio's fiancée

The Story

The growing political and moral corruption of Vienna was a great worry to its kindly, temperate ruler, Duke Vincentio. Knowing that he himself was as much to blame for the troubles as anyone because he had been lax in the enforcement of existing laws, the duke tried to devise a scheme to revive the old discipline of civic authority.

Fearing that reforms instituted by himself might seem too harsh for his people to accept without protest, he decided to appoint a deputy governor and to leave the country for a while. Angelo, a respected and intelligent city official, seemed just the man for the job. The duke turned over the affairs of Vienna to Angelo for a certain length of time and appointed Escalus, a trustworthy old official, to be second in command. The duke then pretended to leave for Poland. In reality, he disguised himself as a friar and returned to the city to watch the outcome of Angelo's reforms.

Angelo's first act was to imprison Claudio, a young nobleman who had gotten his betrothed, Juliet, with child. Under an old statute, now revived, Claudio's offense was punishable by death. After being paraded through the streets in disgrace, the young man was sent to prison. He asked his rakish friend Lucio to go to the nunnery where Claudio's sister Isabella was a young novice about to take her vows and to ask her to plead with the new governor for his release. At the same time, Escalus, who had known Claudio's father well, begged Angelo not to execute the young man. The new deputy remained firm, however, in carrying out the duties of his office, and Claudio's well-wishers were given no reason to hope for their friend's release.

The duke, disguised as a friar, visited Juliet and learned that the young couple had been very much in love and had, in fact, been formally engaged; they would have been married but for the fact that Juliet's dowry had become a matter of legal dispute. There was no question of heartless seduction in the case at all.

Isabella, going before Angelo to plead her brother's case, met with little success at first, even though she had been thoroughly coached by the wily Lucio. Nevertheless, Angelo's cold heart was somewhat touched by Isabella's beauty. By the second interview, he had become so passionately aroused as to forget his reputation for saintly behavior. He told Isabella frankly that she could obtain her brother's release only by yielding herself to his lustful desires, otherwise Claudio would die. Isabella was shocked at these words from the deputy, but when she asserted that she would expose him in public, Angelo, amused, asked who would believe her story. At her wit's end, Isabella rushed to the prison where she told Claudio of Angelo's disgraceful proposition. When he first heard the deputy's proposal, Claudio was outraged, but the thought of death so terrified him that he finally begged Isabella to placate Angelo and give herself to him. Isabella, horrified by her brother's cowardly attitude, lashed out at him with a scornful speech, but she was interrupted by the disguised duke, who had overheard much of the conversation. He drew Isabella aside from her brother and told her that she would be able to save Claudio without shaming herself.

Left to right, actors Joel Colodner, Wayne Alexander, Laurie Walters, and Kelsey Grammer in a 1985 production of Measure for Measure *at Los Angeles's Mark Taper Forum.* (Jay Thompson, courtesy of the Mark Taper Forum)

The friar told Isabella that five years earlier Angelo had been betrothed to a high-born lady named Mariana. The marriage had not taken place, however. After Mariana's brother had been lost at sea with her dowry, Angelo had broken the engagement, hinting at supposed dishonor in the young woman. The friar suggested that Isabella plan a rendezvous with Angelo in a dark, quiet place and then let Mariana act as her substitute. Angelo would be satisfied, Claudio released, Isabella still chaste, and Mariana provided with the means to force Angelo to marry her.

Everything went as arranged, with Mariana taking Isabella's place at the assignation. Cowardly Angelo, however, fearing public exposure, broke his promise to release Claudio and instead ordered the young man's execution. Once again the good friar intervened. He persuaded the provost to hide Claudio and then to announce his death by sending Angelo the head of another prisoner who had died of natural causes.

On the day before the execution, a crowd gathered outside the prison. One of the group was Lucio, who accosted the disguised duke as he wandered down the street. Furtively, Lucio told the friar that nothing like Claudio's execution would have taken place if the duke had been ruler. Lucio went on confidentially to say that the duke cared as much for the ladies as any other man and also drank in private. In fact, said Lucio, the duke bedded about as much as any man in Vienna. Amused, the friar protested against this gossip, but Lucio angrily asserted that every word was true.

To arouse Isabella to accuse Angelo publicly of wrongdoing, the duke allowed her to believe that Claudio was dead. Then the duke sent letters to the deputy informing him that the royal party would arrive on the following day at the gates of Vienna and would expect to be welcomed. The command also ordered that anyone who had grievances against the government while the duke was absent should be allowed to make public pronouncement of them at that time and place.

Angelo grew nervous upon receipt of these papers from the duke. The next day, however, he organized a great crowd and a celebration of welcome at the gates of the city. At the prearranged time, Isabella and Mariana, heavily veiled, stepped forward to denounce Angelo. Isabella called him a traitor and violator of virgins; Mariana claimed that he would not admit her as his wife. The duke, pretending to be angry at these tirades against his deputy, ordered the women to prison and asked that someone apprehend the rascally friar who had often been seen in their company.

Then the duke went to his palace and quickly assumed his disguise as a friar. Appearing before the crowd at the gates, he criticized the government of Vienna severely. Escalus, horrified at the fanatical comments of the friar, ordered his arrest, seconded by Lucio, who maintained that the friar had told him only the day before that the duke was a drunkard and a frequenter of bawdy houses. At last, to display his own bravado, Lucio tore away the friar's hood. When the friar stood revealed as Duke Vincentio, the crowd fell back in amazement.

Angelo realized that his crimes would now be exposed, and he asked simply to be put to death without trial. The duke ordered him to marry Mariana first, and he told Mariana that Angelo's goods, once they were legally hers, would secure her a better husband. The duke was surprised when she begged for Angelo's pardon, in which entreaties she was joined by Isabella, but he relented. He did, however, send Lucio to prison. Claudio was released and married to Juliet. The duke himself asked Isabella for her hand.

"Some rise by sin, and some by virtue fall"

Measure for Measure, Act II, scene i, line 38

Angelo, having assumed command of Vienna upon Vincentio's supposed absence, has ordered strict compliance with laws which for many years have not been enforced. One such law requires capital punishment for getting a woman with child out of wedlock. Claudio, a young gentleman of the city, is arrested for this violation even though he stanchly asserts that Juliet "is fast my wife,/ Save that we do the denunciation lack/ Of outward order." In his new position of authority, Angelo refuses to exercise mercy, claiming that only a rigid application of the letter of the law will redeem the city from its dissolute behavior. When the new ruler is warned by Escalus, an old counselor who is second-in-command, that he himself is subject to certain vices he so peremptorily condemns, Angelo pompously replies "'Tis one thing to be tempted, Escalus,/ Another thing to fall." In the course of the action of the play, however, this deputy is to become a prime illustration of the fact that absolute power corrupts absolutely. When confronted by Isabella, Claudio's sister, who pleads for her brother's life, Angelo lusts for her and treacherously offers her brother's life for her own honor, a pledge he does not intend to fulfill once he has satisfied his pleasure. Escalus' reaction to Angelo's decree early in the play serves two primary purposes: It heightens the tension by foreshadowing the major conflict between Angelo and Isabella, and it suggests ironically that the extremes of indiscriminate virtue and vice are equally heinous in that each is motivated by self-gratification which disregards the welfare of others.

> *Angelo.* See that Claudio
> Be executed by nine tomorrow morning.
> Bring him his confessor, let him be prepared,
> For that's the utmost of his pilgrimage.
> *Escalus [Aside].* Well, Heaven forgive him, and forgive us all.
> Some rise by sin, and some by virtue fall.
> Some run from breaks of ice, and answer none,
> And some condemned for one fault alone.

Critical Evaluation

Measure for Measure is one of those troubled plays, like *All's Well That Ends Well* (c. 1602-1603) and *Troilus and Cressida* (c. 1601-1602), that William Shakespeare composed during the same years he was writing his greatest tragedies. Yet, though they are dark and often bitter, they are not straightforward tragedy or history or comedy. Although they have typically been grouped with the comedies, they have also been described as problem plays, which generally refers to plays that examine a thesis. The main concern in *Measure for Measure* is a grim consideration of the nature of justice and morality in both civic and psychological contexts.

The tone of this play, and of the other problem plays, is so gloomy and pessimistic that critics have tended to try to find biographical or historical causes for their bleakness. Some have argued that they reflect a period of personal disillusionment for the playwright, but there is no external evidence of this. Others have laid the blame on the decadence of the Jacobean period that followed Elizabeth's reign as queen of England. Although such dramatists as John Marston and Thomas Dekker did write similar plays around the same time, the historical evidence suggests that the period was, on the contrary, rather optimistic. What is clear is that Shakespeare has created a world as rotten as Denmark but without a tragic figure sufficient to purge and redeem it. The result is a threatened world, supported by comic remedies rather than purified by tragic suffering. Consequently, *Measure for Measure* remains a shadowy, ambiguous, and disquieting world even though it ends with political and personal resolutions.

The immediate source of the play seems to be George Whetstone's *History of Promos and Cassandra* (1578), which is based on a narrative and a dramatic version of the tale in Giambattista Giraldi Cinthio's *Hecatommithi* (1527), from whom Shakespeare also derived the plot of w (1604). However, Measure for Measure is such an eclectic amalgamation of items from a wide variety of literary and historical loci that a precise identification of sources is impossible. Indeed, the plot is essentially a conflation of three ancient folktales, which J. W. Lever has identified as the Corrupt Magistrate, the Disguised Ruler, and the Substituted Bedmate. Shakespeare integrates these with disparate other materials into a disturbing, indeterminate analysis of justice, morality, and integrity.

The title of the play comes from the scriptural text: "With what measure ye mete, it shall be measured to you again." As the play develops and expands on this quotation, it becomes clear that a simple but generous resolution "to do unto others what you would have them do unto you" will not suffice to resolve the situation. The play pursues its text so relentlessly that any easy confidence in poetic justice is undermined. In the final analysis, the action tends to support an admonition to "Judge not that ye be not judged," which can be either Christian charity or cynical irresponsibility.

Yet the play takes place in a world in which the civil authorities must judge others. Indeed, that is where the play begins. Vienna, as the duke himself realizes, is a moral morass, and bawdry and licentiousness of all sorts are rampant. The duke accepts responsibility for having been lax in enforcing the law. Corruption seethes throughout society from the nobility down to the base characters who are engaged less in a comic subplot than in a series of vulgar exemplifications of the pervasive moral decay.

The chilling paradox is that when Angelo, renowned for his probity and puritanical stringency, is made responsible for setting things right, he almost immediately falls victim to the sexual license he is supposed to eliminate. Claudio, whom Angelo condemns for making Juliet pregnant, had at least acted out of love and with a full intention to marry. Things do not turn out to be as they seemed. He who is responsible for justice yields to temptation while someone apparently guilty of vice is extenuated by circumstances.

Isabella, called on to intercede for her brother, is faced with an especially nasty dilemma, since her choice is between her honor and her brother's life. Neither is a noble alternative, and Claudio is not strong enough to offer himself up for her and turn the play into a tragedy. Unfortunately, when Claudio shows his reluctance, she behaves petulantly rather than graciously. True, her position is intolerable, but she spends more time speaking in defense of her virtue than in acting virtuously. For all her religious aspirations, which are eventually abandoned, she is not large enough to ennoble her moral context.

"Proud man, dressed in a little brief authority"

Measure for Measure, Act II, scene ii, lines 117-118

Arrested, Claudio sends to his sister, Isabella, for help. She, a novice in a convent, goes to Angelo, who holds power and enforces the strict law in Duke Vincentio's absence. She pleads for Claudio's life to no avail. As she gains confidence, however, she attacks man's presumptuous exercise of authority.

> *Isabella.* O, it is excellent
> To have a giant's strength; but it is tyrannous
> To use it like a giant.
> Merciful Heaven,
> Thou rather with thy sharp and sulphurous bolt
> Splits the unwedgeable and gnarled oak
> Than the soft myrtle. But man, proud man,
> Dressed in a little brief authority,
> Most ignorant of what he's most assured, . . .
> Plays such fantastic tricks before high heaven
> As makes the angels weep. . . .

Always lurking in the background is the duke, who watches developments and stands ready to intervene to avoid disaster. He seems slow to step in, but then if he had intervened earlier, or had never left in the first place, there would not have been a play that examines the ambiguities of guilt and extenuation, justice and mercy. The duke and Shakespeare allow the characters to act out the complex patterns of moral responsibility that are the heart of the play. When Angelo, thinking he is with Isabella, is in fact with Mariana, his act is objectively less evil than he thinks because he is really with the woman to whom he had earlier plighted his troth. Yet in intention he is more culpable than Claudio, whom he had imprisoned. Such are the intricate complications of behavior in the flawed world of *Measure for Measure*.

The justice that the duke finally administers brings about a comic resolution. Pardons and marriages unravel the complications that varying degrees of evil had occasioned, but no one in the play escapes untainted. The duke, after a period of moral spectatorship that borders on irresponsibility, restores order. Angelo loses his virtue and reputation but gains a wife. Isabella abandons her religious commitment but learns to be more human, for which she is rewarded with a marriage proposal. Everything works out, and justice, tempered with mercy, prevails. The audience is left, however, with an unsettled feeling that tendencies toward corruption and excess may be inextricably blended with what is best and most noble.

"Critical Evaluation" by Edward E. Foster

For Further Study

Bennett, Josephine Waters. *"Measure for Measure" as Royal Entertainment*. New York: Columbia University Press, 1966. A comprehensive discussion of the play, centering on the way it would have appeared to contemporary audiences. The author rejects earlier criticisms of the work as "dark comedy," and considers instead that in its historical context, it would have been viewed as high entertainment.

Lloyd Evans, Gareth. *The Upstart Crow: An Introduction to Shakespeare's Plays*. London: J. M. Dent and Sons, 1982. A comprehensive discussion of Shakespeare's dramatic works, including information on the plays' critical reviews and sources, as well as on the circumstances surrounding their gestation.

Muir, Kenneth, ed. *Shakespeare—The Comedies: A Collection of Critical Essays*. Englewood Cliffs, N.J.: Prentice-Hall, 1965. An anthology of essays that discuss Shakespeare's comedies from various points of view. The essay on *Measure for Measure*, by R. W. Chambers, emphasizes the violence in the play and its importance in furthering the plot.

Shakespeare, William. *Measure for Measure*. Edited by J. W. Lever. London: Methuen, 1965. In addition to the text of the play, this edition contains more than ninety pages of introductory material about the sources and a critical evaluation of the work. Also includes appendices with the original texts of Shakespeare's sources.

Wheeler, Richard P. *Shakespeare's Development and the Problem Comedies*. Berkeley: University of California Press, 1981. Discusses two of Shakespeare's comedies, *All's Well That Ends Well* and *Measure for Measure*. These two works are considered problem comedies because they do not fit the usual mold of Elizabethan comedy.

The Merchant of Venice

Type of plot: Comedy
Time of plot: Sixteenth century
Locale: Venice
First performed: c. 1596-1597; first published, 1600

Principal characters

SHYLOCK, a Jewish moneylender
PORTIA, a wealthy young woman
ANTONIO, an impoverished merchant, Shylock's enemy, who is championed by
     Portia
BASSANIO, Portia's husband and Antonio's friend
NERISSA, Portia's waiting-woman
GRATIANO, Nerissa's husband and Bassanio's friend
JESSICA, Shylock's daughter
LORENZO, Jessica's husband

The Story

Bassanio, meeting his wealthy friend Antonio, revealed that he had a plan for restoring the fortune he had carelessly spent and for paying the debts he had incurred. In the town of Belmont, not far from Venice, there lived a wealthy young woman named Portia, who was famous for her beauty. If he could secure some money, Bassanio declared, he was sure he could win her as his wife. Antonio replied that he had no funds at hand with which to supply his friend, as they were all invested in the ships he had at sea, but that he would attempt to borrow money for him in Venice.

Portia had many suitors for her hand. According to the strange conditions of her father's will, however, anyone who wished her for his wife had to choose correctly among three caskets of silver, gold, and lead that casket that contained the message that Portia was his. In case of failure, the suitors were compelled to swear never to reveal which casket they had chosen and never to woo another woman. Four of her suitors, seeing they could not win her except under the conditions of the will, had departed. A fifth, a Moor, decided to take his chances. The unfortunate man chose the golden casket, which contained only a skull and a mocking message. The Prince of Arragon was the next suitor to try his luck. He chose the silver casket, only to learn from the note it bore that he was a fool.

True to his promise to Bassanio, Antonio arranged to borrow three thousand ducats from Shylock, a wealthy Jew. Antonio was to have the use of the money for three months. If he found himself unable to return the loan at the end of that time, Shylock was given the right to cut a pound of flesh from any part of Antonio's body. Despite Bassanio's objections, Antonio insisted on accepting the terms, for he was sure his ships would return a month before the payment was due. He was confident that he would never fall into the power of the Jew, who hated Antonio because he often lent money to others without charging the interest Shylock demanded.

That night, Bassanio planned a feast and a masque. In conspiracy with his friend, Lorenzo, he invited Shylock to be his guest. Lorenzo, taking advantage of her father's absence, ran off with the Jew's daughter, Jessica, who took part of Shylock's fortune with her. Shylock was cheated not only of his daughter and his ducats but also of his entertainment, for the wind suddenly changed and Bassanio set sail for Belmont.

As the days passed, the Jew began to hear news of mingled good and bad fortune. In Genoa, Jessica and Lorenzo were lavishly spending the money she had taken with her. The miser flinched at the reports of his daughter's extravagance, but for compensation he had the news that Antonio's ships, on which his continuing fortune depended, had been wrecked at sea.

Portia, much taken with Bassanio when he came to woo her, would have had him wait before he tried to pick the right casket. Sure that he would fail as the others

Portia (Liisa Ivary), disguised as the lawyer Balthazar, reminds Shylock (Richard Elmore, right) that "the quality of mercy is not strained" in the Oregon Shakespeare Festival's 1991 production of The Merchant of Venice. *(Christopher Briscoe, courtesy of the Oregon Shakespeare Festival by permission of the Actors' Equity Association)*

had, she hoped to have his company a little while longer. Bassanio, however, was impatient to try his luck. Not deceived by the ornateness of the gold and silver caskets, and philosophizing that true virtue is inward virtue, he chose the lead box. In it was a portrait of Portia. He had chosen correctly. To seal their engagement, Portia gave Bassanio a ring. She declared he must never part with it, for if he did, it would signify the end of their love.

Gratiano, a friend who had accompanied Bassanio to Belmont, spoke up. He was in love with Portia's waiting-woman, Nerissa. With Portia's delighted approval, Gratiano planned that both couples should be married at the same time.

Bassanio's joy at his good fortune was soon blighted. Antonio wrote that he was ruined, all his ships having failed to return. The time for payment of the loan being past due, Shylock was demanding his pound of flesh. In closing, Antonio declared that he cleared Bassanio of his debt to him. He wished only to see his friend once more before his death. Portia declared that the double wedding should take place at once. Then her husband would be able to set out for Venice in an attempt to buy off the Jew with her dowry of six thousand ducats.

After Bassanio and Gratiano had departed, Portia declared to Lorenzo and Jessica, who had come to Belmont, that she and Nerissa were going to a nunnery, where they would live in seclusion until their husbands returned. She committed the charge of her house and servants to Jessica and Lorenzo.

Instead of taking the course she had described, however, Portia set about executing other plans. She gave her servant, Balthasar, orders to take a note to her cousin, Doctor Bellario, a famous lawyer of Padua, in order to secure a message and some clothes from him. She explained to Nerissa that they would go to Venice disguised as men.

The Duke of Venice, before whom Antonio's case was tried, was reluctant to exact the penalty in Shylock's contract. When his appeals to the Jew's better feelings went unheeded, he could see no course before him but to allow the moneylender his due. Bassanio tried to make Shylock relent by offering him the six thousand ducats, but, like the duke, he met only a firm refusal.

Portia, dressed as a lawyer, and Nerissa, disguised as her clerk, appeared in the court. Nerissa offered the duke a letter from Doctor Bellario, in which the doctor explained that he was very ill, but that Balthasar, his young representative, would present his opinion in the dispute.

When Portia appealed to the Jew's mercy, Shylock merely demanded the penalty. Portia then declared that the Jew, under the letter of the contract, could not be offered money in exchange for Antonio's release. The only alternative was for the merchant to forfeit his flesh.

Antonio prepared his bosom for the knife, for Shylock was determined to take his portion as close to his enemy's heart as he could cut. Before the operation could begin, however, Portia, examining the contract, declared that it contained no clause stating that Shylock could have any blood with the flesh. The Jew, realizing that he was defeated, offered at once to accept the six thousand ducats, but Portia declared that he was not entitled to the money he had already refused. She stated also that Shylock, an alien, had threatened the life of a Venetian citizen. For that crime

---

"The quality of mercy is not strain'd"

The Merchant of Venice, Act IV, scene i, line 184

Having borrowed three thousand ducats from Shylock with which to court the beautiful heiress, Portia, Antonio faces the day appointed to pay the debt without means to do so. According to his previous agreement with Shylock, he must give up one pound of his own flesh if he is unable to repay the money. The duke pleads for mercy from Shylock, and Bassanio offers twice the sum of the debt; but Shylock is adamant in demanding his pound of flesh. Portia, meanwhile, has disguised herself as a lawyer and now appears in the court.

> *Portia.* The quality of mercy is not strain'd,
> It droppeth as the gentle rain from heaven
> Upon the place beneath. It is twice blest:
> It blesseth him that gives, and him that takes. . . .
> It is an attribute to God himself;
> And earthly power doth then show likest God's
> When mercy seasons justice.

Antonio had the right to seize half of his property and the state the remainder.

Antonio refused that penalty, but it was agreed that one half of Shylock's fortune should go at once to Jessica and Lorenzo. Shylock was to keep the remainder, but it was to be willed to the couple after his death. In addition, Shylock was to undergo conversion. The defeated man had no choice but to agree to the terms.

Pressed to accept a reward, Portia took only a pair of Antonio's gloves and the ring that she herself had given Bassanio. Nerissa, likewise, managed to secure Gratiano's ring. Then Portia and Nerissa started back for Belmont, to be there when their husbands returned. They arrived home shortly before Bassanio and Gratiano appeared in company with Antonio. Pretending to discover that their husbands' rings were missing, Portia and Nerissa at first accused Bassanio and Gratiano of unfaithfulness. At last, to the surprise of all, they revealed their secret, which was vouched for by a letter from Doctor Bellario. For Jessica and Lorenzo, they had the good news of their future inheritance, and for Antonio a letter, secured by chance, announcing that some of his ships had arrived safely in port after all.

Critical Evaluation

Through the years, *The Merchant of Venice* has been one of William Shakespeare's most popular and most frequently performed plays. Not only does the work have an interesting and fast-moving plot; it also evokes an idyllic, uncorrupted world reminiscent of folktale and romance. From the opening description of Antonio's nameless sadness, the world is bathed in light and music. The insistently improbable plot is complicated only by the evil influence of Shylock, and he is disposed of by the end of Act IV. Yet Shakespeare uses this fragile vehicle to make significant points about justice, mercy, and friendship, three typical Renaissance virtues.

Although some critics have suggested that the play contains all of the elements of tragedy only to be rescued by a comic resolution, the tone of the whole play creates a benevolent world in which, despite some opposition, things will always work out for the best.

The story, which is based on ancient tales that could have been drawn from many sources, is actually two stories in one—the casket-plot, involving the choice by the suitor and his reward with Portia, and the bond-plot, involving the loan and the attempt to exact a pound of flesh. Shakespeare's genius is revealed in the way he combines the two. Although they intersect from the start in the character of Bassanio, who occasions Antonio's debt and is a suitor, they fully coalesce when Portia comes to Venice in disguise to make her plea and judgment for Antonio. At that point, the bond-plot is unraveled by the casket-heroine, after which the fifth act brings the celebratory conclusion and joy.

The most fascinating character to both audiences and critics has always been Shylock, the outsider, the anomaly in this felicitous world. Controversy rages over just what kind of villain Shylock is and just how villainous Shakespeare intended him to be. The matter has been complicated by the twentieth century desire to absolve Shakespeare of the common medieval and Renaissance vice of anti-Semitism. Some commentators have argued that in Shylock Shakespeare takes the stock character of the Jew—as personified in Christopher Marlowe's Barabas in his *The Jew of Malta* (1589)—and fleshes him out with complicating human characteristics. Some have gone so far as to argue that even in his villainy, Shylock is presented as a victim of the Christian society, the grotesque product of hatred and ostracism. Regardless of Shakespeare's personal views, the fact remains that in his treatment, Shylock becomes much more than a stock villain.

The more significant dramatic question is just what sort of character Shylock is and what sort of role he is being called upon to play. Certainly he is an outsider in both appearance and action, a stranger to the light and gracious world of Venice and Belmont. His language is full of stridency and materialism, which isolates him from the other characters. He has no part in the network of beautiful friendships that unites the others. He is not wholly a comic character, for despite often appearing ridiculous, he poses too much of a threat to be dismissed lightly. Yet he is too ineffectual and grotesque to be a villain as cold and terrifying as Iago or Edmund, or one as engaging as Richard III. He is a malevolent force, who is finally overcome by the more generous world in which he lives. That he is treated so harshly by the Christians is the kind of irony that ultimately protects Shakespeare from charges of mindless anti-Semitism. Still, on the level of the romantic plot, he is also the serpent in the garden, deserving summary expulsion and the forced conversion that is both a punishment and a charity.

The rest of the major characters have much more in common with each other as sharers in the common civilization of Venice. As they come into conflict with Shylock and form relationships with one another, they act out the ideals and commonplaces of high Renaissance culture. Antonio, in his small but pivotal role, is afflicted with a fashionable melancholy and a gift for friendship. It is his casually generous act of friendship that sets the bond-plot in motion. Bassanio frequently comments on friendship and knows how to accept generosity gracefully, but Bassanio is not just a model Renaissance friend but also a model Renaissance lover. He is quite frankly as interested in Portia's money as in her wit and beauty; he unself-consciously represents a cultural integration of love and gain quite different from Shylock's materialism. When he chooses the leaden casket, he does so for precisely the right traditional reason—a distrust of appearances, a recognition that the reality does not always correspond. Of course, his success as suitor is never really in doubt but is choreographed like a ballet. In any case, it is always the third suitor who is the successful one in folktales. What the ballet provides is another opportunity for the expression of the culturally correct sentiments.

Portia too is a heroine of her culture. She is not merely an object of love but a witty and intelligent woman whose ingenuity resolves the central dilemma. That she, too, is not what she seems to be in the trial scene is another example of the dichotomy between familiar appearance and reality. More important, she has the opportunity to discourse on the nature of mercy as opposed to strict justice and to give an object lesson that he who lives by the letter of the law will perish by it.

With Shylock safely, if a bit harshly, out of the way, the last act is an amusing festival of vindication of cultural values. The characters have had their opportunity to comment on the proper issues—love, friendship, justice, and the disparity between appearances and reality. Now all receive their appropriate reward in marriages and reunions or, in the case of Antonio, with the pleasantly gratuitous recovery of his fortune. There is no more trouble in paradise among the people of grace.

"Critical Evaluation" by Edward E. Foster

For Further Study

Bulman, James. *Shakespeare in Performance: The Merchant of Venice*. New York: St. Martin's Press, 1992. Provides a survey of nineteenth century productions and a critique of several major twentieth century productions, including a comparison of Jonathan Miller's stage version (featuring Laurence Olivier as Shylock) with the BBC-TV version he produced ten years later.

Danson, Lawrence. *The Harmonies of "The Merchant of Venice."* New Haven, Conn.: Yale University Press, 1978. An excellent full-length study of the play that treats everything from "The Problem of Shylock" to law and language, miracle and myth, love and friendship, and the "quality of mercy."

Gross, John. *Shylock: Four Hundred Years in the Life of a Legend*. London: Chatto & Windus, 1992. Gross traces Shylock's role and that of the play's in the history of anti-Semitism in the Western world. Also discusses the stage history of *The Merchant of Venice*, including several adaptations.

Levin, Richard A. *Love and Society in Shakespearean Comedy*. Newark: University of Delaware Press, 1985. Levin devotes one chapter to *The Merchant of Venice* and focuses on one of the play's central problems: the ambiguity of Shylock's conflicting motives in Act I, scene iii: the bond proposed may have been "a vicious and deceptive offer" or it may have been an incentive for better treatment from Antonio and others.

Rabkin, Norman. *Shakespeare and the Problem of Meaning*. Chicago: University of Chicago Press, 1981. In a superb essay on *The Merchant of Venice*, Rabkin notes the many significant inconsistencies and contradictions in the play and shows the impossibility of imposing easy, reductivist interpretation on it.

The Merry Wives of Windsor

Type of plot: Comedy
Time of plot: Sixteenth century
Locale: England
First performed: 1597; first published, 1602

Principal characters

SIR JOHN FALSTAFF, a rogue
FENTON, a young gentleman
SLENDER, a foolish gentleman
FORD and
PAGE, two gentlemen living at Windsor
DOCTOR CAIUS, a French physician
MISTRESS FORD, Ford's wife
MISTRESS PAGE, Page's wife
ANNE PAGE, the daughter of the Pages
MISTRESS QUICKLY, a servant of Doctor Caius

The Story

Sir John Falstaff was, without doubt, a rogue. True, he was fat, jolly, and in a way lovable, but he was still a rogue. His men robbed and plundered the citizens of Windsor, but he himself was seldom taken or convicted for his crimes. His fortunes being at low ebb, he hit upon a plan to remedy that situation. He had met Mistress Ford and Mistress Page, two good ladies who held the purse strings in their respective houses. Falstaff wrote identical letters to the two good ladies, letters protesting undying love for each of them.

The daughter of one of the ladies, Anne Page, was the center of a love triangle. Her father wished her to marry Slender, a foolish gentleman who did not love her or anyone else, but who would marry any girl that was recommended to him by his cousin, the justice. Mistress Page, on the other hand, would have her daughter married to Doctor Caius, a French physician then in Windsor. Anne herself loved Fenton, a fine young gentleman who was deeply in love with her. All three lovers paid the doctor's housekeeper, Mistress Quickly, to plead their cause with Anne, for Mistress Quickly had convinced each that she alone could persuade Anne to answer yes to a proposal. Mistress Quickly was, in fact, second only to Falstaff in her plotting and her trickery.

Unknown to poor Falstaff, Mistress Ford and Mistress Page compared the letters received from him, alike except for the lady's name. They decided to cure him of his knavery once and for all. Mistress Ford arranged to have him come to her house that night when her husband would not be there. Mistress Page wrote that she would meet him as soon as she could cautiously arrange it. In the meantime, two former followers of Falstaff had told the two husbands of that knave's designs on their wives. Page refused to believe his wife unfaithful, but Ford became jealous and planned to spy on his wife. Disguising himself as Mr. Brook, he called on Falstaff. His story was that he loved Mistress Ford but could not win her love, and he came to pay Falstaff to court her for him. His stratagem was successful; he learned from Falstaff that the knight already had a rendezvous with the lady that very night.

At the appointed time, having previously arranged to have several servants assist in the plot, the two ladies were ready for Falstaff. While Falstaff was trying to make love to Mistress Ford, Mistress Page rushed in and said that Ford was on his way home. Quickly the ladies put Falstaff in a clothesbasket and had him carried out by the servants, to be dumped into the Thames. Ford did arrive, of course, for, unknown to his wife, he knew Falstaff was to be there. After looking high and low without finding the rogue, he apologized to his wife for his suspicions. Mistress Ford did not know which had been the most sport, having Falstaff dumped into the river or listening to her husband's discomfited apologies.

The ladies had so much fun over their first joke played on Falstaff that they decided to try another. Mistress Ford then sent him another message, this one saying that her husband would be gone all of the following morning, and she asked Falstaff to call on her at that time so that she could make amends for the previous affair of the basket. Again Ford, disguised as Brook, called on Falstaff, and again he learned of the proposed assignation. He learned also of the method of Falstaff's previous escape and vowed the old roisterer should not again slip through his fingers.

When Mistress Ford heard from Mistress Page that Ford was returning unexpectedly, the ladies dressed Falstaff in the clothes of a fat woman whom Ford hated. Ford, finding the supposed woman in his house, drubbed the disguised knight soundly and chased him from the house. Again Ford searched everywhere for Falstaff, and again he was forced to apologize to his wife in the presence of the friends he had brought with him to witness her disgrace. The two ladies thought his discomfiture the funniest part of their joke.

Once more the wives planned to plague poor Falstaff, but this time they took their husbands into their confidence. When Mistress Page and Mistress Ford told about the letters they had received from Falstaff and explained the details of the two previous adventures, Ford felt very contrite over his former suspicions of his wife. Eagerly, the husbands joined their wives in a final scheme intended to bring Falstaff to public shame. The ladies would persuade Falstaff to meet them in the park at midnight. Falstaff was to be disguised as Herne the Hunter, a horned legendary huntsman said to roam the wintry woods each midnight. There he would be surrounded by Anne Page and others dressed as fairies and elves. After he had been frightened half to death, the husbands would accost him and publicly display his knavery.

A quite different event had also been planned for that night. Page plotted to have Slender seize Anne in her disguise as the fairy queen and carry her away to marry her. At the same time, Mistress Page arranged to have Doctor Caius find Anne and take her away to be married. Anne, however, had other plans. She and Fenton agreed to meet in the park and under cover of the dark and confusion flee her parents and her two unwelcome suitors.

All plans were put into effect. Falstaff, after telling the supposed Brook that on this night he would for a certainty win Mistress Ford for him, donned the horns of a stag and met the two ladies at the appointed place. Quickly the fairies and witches surrounded him, and the women ran to join their husbands and watch the fun. Poor

---

"The world's mine oyster"

The Merry Wives of Windsor, Act II, scene ii, line 3

This famous saying is associated with eager, ambitious, even arrogant youth. Today it usually refers to a young person who cannot wait to conquer the world. In the play, Pistol, a braggart follower of Sir John Falstaff, a self-fancied ladykiller, refuses to do Sir John a service the latter requests. Now, at the Garter Inn, Pistol asks a loan of Sir John, who indignantly refuses. Pistol, only half in jest, whips out his sword and compares the fat, round knight to the world and his purse to an oyster.

> *Falstaff.* I will not lend thee a penny.
> *Pistol.* Why then the world's mine oyster,
>   Which I with sword will open.
> *Falstaff.* Not a penny. . . .

Falstaff tried to pretend that he was asleep or dead, but the merry revelers burned his fingers with tapers they carried, and pinched him unmercifully. When Falstaff threw off his disguise, Ford and Page and their wives laid hold of him and soundly scolded him for his silly gallantry and bombast. The wives ridiculed his ungainly body and swore that none would ever have such a fool for a lover. Such was Falstaff's nature, however, that no one could hate him for long. After he had admitted his guilt and his stupidity, they all forgave him.

While all this merriment was going on, Anne and Fenton had stolen away to be married. They returned while the rest were busy with Falstaff. Page and his wife were in such good humor over all that had occurred that they forgave the young lovers and bestowed their blessing on them. Then the whole company, Falstaff included, retired to Page's house to laugh again over the happenings of that night.

Critical Evaluation

Under public pressure to bring back Sir John Falstaff after Prince Hal's arrogant dismissal of his boyhood friend in *Henry IV, Part II* (1597) and *Henry V* (1598-1599), Shakespeare reintroduces the fat knight in a slapstick romp, *The Merry Wives of Windsor*. On the one hand, the farce can be viewed as a ridiculous satire

Falstaff (Norman Foster) dances on the tavern table in a scene from a 1966 Austrian film version of Shakespeare's The Merry Wives of Windsor. *(Courtesy of The Museum of Modern Art, Film Stills Archive)*

of the London burghers, the Fords and the Pages, who successfully outwit the not-so-sly fox of an aristocrat, Falstaff, who is trying in his usual way to disrupt the pleasures and the comforts of the conventional.

Another way of approaching the play is by viewing it as a comic resolve of a story similar in some incidents to Shakespeare's earlier play, *Romeo and Juliet* (1594-1596). Unwittingly, Falstaff, in his buffoonery, performs the role of diverting the Pages from the elopement of their daughter, Anne, and Fenton, the comic Romeo. A potential tragedy thus averted, and love is allowed to flourish. Falstaff plays the same role which Shakespeare had assigned to him in the histories. As opposed to the deliberate Hal, who orders everything in his life, even his leisure with his cronies, Falstaff devotes his whole life to play, the gratification of the instincts, and the preservation of the self. His dalliance with the Mistresses Page and Ford may be a mockery of good burgher virtue, but he also pursues it with a good deal of pleasure, pleasure for its own sake. Everyone wins in the process. Anne is married to the man she loves, and the Pages, the Fords, and Sir John all have a thoroughly fine time in the romp. The only loser is respectability, which takes a back seat to the loud, vulgar guffaws of "Fat Jack" Falstaff.

For Further Study

Barton, Ann. "Falstaff and the Comic Community." In *Shakespeare's "Rough Magic": Renaissance Essays in Honor of C. L. Barber*, edited by Peter Erickson and Coppélia Kahn. Newark, N.J.: University of Delaware Press, 1985. An excellent study of Falstaff, the most controversial character in the play. Barton shows that Shakespeare was consciously trying to exclude such self-seeking epicureans from his plays; Falstaff in *The Merry Wives of Windsor* was the last time such a character received such prominence.

Green, William. *Shakespeare's "Merry Wives of Windsor."* Princeton, N.J.: Princeton University Press, 1962. This book follows the history of the play, from its composition to its first performance and audience.

Hemingway, Samuel B. "On Behalf of That Falstaff." *Shakespeare Quarterly* 3 (1952): 307-311. Hemingway attributes Falstaff's controversy to his presence in the *Henry IV* plays as well as in *The Merry Wives of Windsor*. Shakespeare's portrayal of him is different in each.

Roberts, Jeanne Addison. *Shakespeare's English Comedy: "The Merry Wives of Windsor" in Context.* Lincoln: University of Nebraska Press, 1979. Places the play into the context of the development of Shakespeare's career, arguing that the play provided Shakespeare's transition from writing histories to writing tragedies. Roberts also includes chapters on the text, date, sources, and genre.

Wells, Stanley, ed. *The Cambridge Companion to Shakespeare Studies.* Cambridge, England: Cambridge University Press, 1986. This is where all studies of Shakespeare should begin. It includes excellent chapters introducing the poet's biography, conventions and beliefs of Elizabethan England, and reviews of scholarship in the field.

A Midsummer Night's Dream

Type of plot: Comedy
Time of plot: Antiquity
Locale: Athens
First performed: c. 1595-1596; first published, 1600

Principal characters

THESEUS, Duke of Athens
LYSANDER and
DEMETRIUS, in love with Hermia
BOTTOM, a weaver
HIPPOLYTA, queen of the Amazons, fiancée of Theseus
HERMIA, in love with Lysander
HELENA, in love with Demetrius
OBERON, king of the fairies
TITANIA, queen of the fairies
PUCK, fairy page to Oberon

The Story

Theseus, the Duke of Athens, was to be married in four days to Hippolyta, queen of the Amazons, and he ordered his Master of the Revels to prepare suitable entertainment for the nuptials. Other lovers of ancient Athens, however, were not so happy as their ruler. Hermia, in love with Lysander, was loved also by Demetrius, who had her father's permission to marry her. When she refused his suit, Demetrius took his case to Theseus and demanded that the law be invoked. Theseus upheld the father; by Athenian law, Hermia must either marry Demetrius, be placed in a nunnery, or be put to death. Hermia swore that she would enter a convent before she would consent to become Demetrius' bride.

Faced with this awful choice, Lysander plotted with Hermia to leave Athens. He would take her to the home of his aunt and there marry her. They were to meet the following night in a wood outside the city. Hermia confided the plan to her good friend Helena. Demetrius had formerly been betrothed to Helena, and although he had switched his love to Hermia he was still desperately loved by the scorned Helena. Helena, willing to do anything to gain even a smile from Demetrius, told him of his rival's plan to elope with Hermia.

Unknown to any of the four young people, there were to be others in that same woods on the appointed night, Midsummer Eve. A group of Athenian laborers was to meet there to practice a play the members hoped to present in honor of Theseus and Hippolyta's wedding. The fairies also held their midnight revels in the woods. Oberon, king of the fairies, desired for his page a little Indian foundling, but Oberon's queen, Titania, had the boy. Loving him like a son, she refused to give him up to her husband. In order to force Titania to do his bidding, Oberon ordered his mischievous page, called Puck or Robin Goodfellow, to secure the juice of a purple flower once hit by Cupid's dart. This juice, when placed in the eyes of anyone sleeping, caused that person to fall in love with the first creature seen on awakening. Oberon planned to drop some of the juice in Titania's eyes and then refuse to lift the charm until she gave him the boy.

While Puck was on his errand, Demetrius and Helena entered the woods. Making himself invisible, Oberon heard Helena plead her love for Demetrius and heard the young man scorn and berate her. Demetrius had come to the woods to find the fleeing lovers, Lysander and Hermia, and Helena was following Demetrius. Oberon, pitying Helena, determined to aid her. When Puck returned with the juice, Oberon ordered him to find the Athenian and place some of the juice in his eyes so that he would love the woman who doted on him.

Puck went to do as he was ordered, while Oberon squeezed the juice of the flower into the eyes of Titania as she slept. Puck, coming upon Lysander and Hermia as they slept in the woods, mistook Lysander's Athenian dress for that of Demetrius and poured the charmed juice into Lysander's eyes. Lysander was awakened by Helena, who had been abandoned deep in the woods by Demetrius. The charm worked, although not as intended; Lysander fell in love with Helena. That poor woman, thinking that he was mocking her with his ardent protestations of love, begged him to stop his teasing and return to the sleeping Hermia. Lysander, pursuing Helena, who was running away from him, left Hermia alone in the forest. When she awakened she feared that Lysander had been killed, since she believed that he would never have deserted her otherwise.

Titania, in the meantime, awakened to a strange sight. The laborers, practicing for their play, had paused not far from the sleeping fairy queen. Bottom, the comical but stupid weaver who was to play the leading role, became the butt of another of Puck's jokes. The prankster clapped an ass's head over Bottom's own foolish pate and led the poor fool on a merry chase until the weaver was at the spot where Titania lay sleeping. Thus when she awakened she looked at Bottom, still with the head of an ass. She fell instantly in love with him and ordered the fairies to tend to his every want. This turn pleased Oberon mightily. When he learned of the mistake Puck had made in placing the juice in Lysander's eyes, however, he tried to right the wrong by placing love juice also in Demetrius' eyes, and he ordered Puck to have Helena close by when Demetrius awakened. His act made both women unhappy and forlorn. When Demetrius, who she knew hated her, also began to protest his ardent love to her, Helena thought that both men were taunting and ridiculing her. Poor Hermia, encountering Lysander, could not understand why he tried to drive her away, all the time protesting that he loved only Helena.

Again Oberon tried to set matters straight. He ordered Puck to lead the two men in circles until weariness forced them to lie down and go to sleep. Then a potion to remove the charm and make the whole affair seem like a dream was to be placed in Lysander's eyes. Afterward he would again love Hermia, and all the young people would be united in proper pairs. Titania, too, was to have the charm removed, for Oberon had taunted her about loving an ass until she had given up the prince to him. Puck obeyed the orders and placed the potion in Lysander's eyes.

The four lovers were awakened by Theseus, Hippolyta, and Hermia's father, who had gone into the woods to watch Theseus' hounds perform. Lysander again loved Hermia and Demetrius still loved Helena, for the love juice remained in his eyes. Hermia's father persisted in his demand that his daughter marry Demetrius, but since that young man no longer wanted her and all four were happy with their partners, he ceased to oppose Lysander's suit. Theseus gave them permission to marry on the day set for his own wedding to Hippolyta.

"True love never did run smooth"

A Midsummer Night's Dream, Act I, scene i, line 134

Hermia, daughter of Egeus, insists that regardless of her father's command that she marry Demetrius, she will instead marry Lysander, whom she loves. Theseus, Duke of Athens, insists that her only choice is to obey her father or to be put to death or forced into a nunnery. After delivering himself of this announcement according to Athenian law, the duke and all his attendants exit, leaving Hermia and her love Lysander together. Lysander then foolishly asks Hermia, "Why is your cheek so pale?/ How chance the roses there do fade so fast?" Then Lysander assures her that love has always traveled a rough road.

> *Lysander.* Ay me! For ought that I could ever read,
> Could ever hear by tale or history,
> The course of true love never did run smooth.

Titania also awakened and, like the others, thought that she had been dreaming. Puck removed the ass's head from Bottom and the bewildered weaver made his way back to Athens, reaching there just in time to save the play, since he was to play Pyramus, the hero. The Master of the Revels tried to dissuade Theseus from choosing the laborer's play for the wedding night. Theseus, however, was intrigued by a play that was announced as tedious, brief, merry, and tragic. So Bottom and his troupe presented an entertainingly awful *Pyramus and Thisbe*, much to the merriment of all the guests.

After the play all the bridal couples retired to their suites, and Oberon and Titania sang a fairy song over them, promising that they and all of their children would be blessed.

Critical Evaluation

A Midsummer Night's Dream marks the maturation of William Shakespeare's comic form beyond situation and young romantic love. One plot focuses on finding young love and on overcoming obstacles to that love. Shakespeare adds to the richness of comic structure by interweaving the love plot with a cast of rustic guildsmen, who are out of their element as they strive to entertain the ruler with a classic play of their own. The play also features a substructure of fairy forces, whose unseen antics influence the world of humans. With this invisible substructure of dream and chaos, *A Midsummer Night's Dream* not only explores the capriciousness and changeability of love (as the young men switch their affections from woman to woman in the blinking of an eye) but also introduces the question of the psychology of the subconscious.

Queen of the fairies Titania (Anita Louise), with Puck (Mickey Rooney) at her side, in the 1935 film version of A Midsummer Night's Dream. (Courtesy of The Museum of Modern Art, Film Stills Archive)

Tradition held that on midsummer night, people would dream of the one they would marry. As the lovers enter the chaotic world of the forest, they are allowed, with hilarious results, to experience harmlessly the options of their subconscious desires. By focusing in the last act on the play presented by the rustic guildsmen, Shakespeare links the imaginative world of art with the capacity for change and growth within humanity. This capacity is most laughingly realized in the play by the transformation of the enthusiastic actor, Bottom, into half-man, half-ass, an alteration that continues to delight audiences.

The play was originally performed at a marriage ceremony in 1595, and the plot is framed by the four-day suspension of ordinary life in Athens in expectation of the nuptial celebration of Theseus and his queen, Hippolyta. Both characters invoke the moon as they anticipate their union. The lunar spirit of nebulousness, changeability, and lunacy dominates much of the play's action.

A Midsummer Night's Dream is remarkable for its blending of diverse personages into an eventually unified whole. In addition to Theseus and Hippolyta, the cast includes three other categories of society, each distinguished by its own mode of discourse. Theseus and Hippolyta speak high blank verse, filled with leisurely confidence and classical allusion. The four young and mixed-up lovers—Hermia and Lysander, Helena and Demetrius—can also muster blank verse but are typified by rhyming iambic lines that indicate the unoriginal speech of those who woo. The rustic guildsmen are characterized by their prose speech, full of halts and stops, confusions, and malapropisms. The fairies for the most part speak a light rhymed tetrameter, filled with references to nature. Oberon and Titania, as king and queen of the fairies, speak a regal verse similar to that of Theseus and Hippolyta. The roles of the two kings and the two queens are often played by the same actors, since the characters are not on stage at the same time.

In the background of all the love matches is a hint of violence or separation. Theseus conquers Hippolyta. Oberon and Titania feud over a changeling boy. Pyramus and Thisbe, the lovers in the rustics' play, are kept apart by a wall. Demetrius stops loving Helena for no apparent reason and switches his affections to Hermia, who dotes on Lysander. The father of Hermia, supported by Theseus and Athenian law, would keep his daughter from marrying the man of her choosing and instead doom her to death or life in a nunnery.

"What fools these mortals be!"

A Midsummer Night's Dream, Act III, scene ii, line 115

Demetrius, who is in love with Hermia but who is loved by Helena, Hermia's good friend, is followed into the woods by Helena. He becomes angry with her for following him. Puck, fairy servant of Oberon, king of the fairies, is ordered to place on the eyelids of the sleeping Demetrius some of the juice of the magical flower love-in-idleness, so that when he awakes he will fall in love with Helena, whom he will see first. Puck, however, mistakes Lysander for Demetrius, and places the love juice on Lysander's eyelids. When he awakes, he sees first not his real love, Hermia, but Helena, to whom he professes his love. Helena thinks Lysander is making fun of her and resents his professions. Oberon discovers Puck's mistake and places some of the juice on Demetrius' eyes, then has Puck place Helena near so that she will be the first creature that Demetrius sees when he awakes. Puck is amused by all these happenings. He sums up his disdain for all concerned in this remark:

> *Puck.* Captain of our fairy band,
>   Helena is here at hand,
>   And the youth, mistook by me,
>   Pleading for a lover's fee.
>   Shall we their fond pageant see?
>   Lord, what fools these mortals be!

When Puck addresses the audience in the play's epilogue, he points to a major theme of the badly acted play-within-a-play: art requires an act of imaginative engagement on the part of those who experience it. Art can reveal alternatives, horrible or wonderful turns that life may take. Art's power to transform is only as effective as the audience's capacity to distinguish illusion from reality and to bring the possible into being.

"Critical Evaluation" by Sandra K. Fischer

For Further Study

Arthos, John. "The Spirit of the Occasion." In *Shakespeare's Use of Dream and Vision*. Totowa, N.J.: Rowman and Littlefield, 1977. Connects nature with the dream world and its dual potential of horror and bliss. Dreams stem from and inform the psyche, and they share a cognitive function with the world of art.

Brown, John Russell. *Shakespeare and His Comedies*. New York: Methuen, 1957. Focuses on Theseus' speech connecting the madman, the lover, and the poet. Reveals how the play negotiates and validates varying responses to the unknown.

Calderwood, James L. *A Midsummer Night's Dream*. New York: Twayne, 1992. Drawing on all the different theoretical approaches to literary interpretation, Calderwood organizes the experience of the play around the topics of patriarchal law, desire and voyeurism, marginality and threshold experiences, the power of naming, performativity, and the illusion of conciliation and unity. An excellent summary of the state of reading Shakespeare.

Patterson, Annabel. "Bottom's Up: Festive Theory." In *Shakespeare and the Popular Voice*. New York: Basil Blackwell, 1989. Reads the presentation of the lower class in political terms. Bottom's malapropisms represent a suppression of voice and class, yet his creative use of language points toward a more synthetic utopian society.

Welsford, Enid. *The Court Masque*. Cambridge, England: Cambridge University Press, 1927. Reads *A Midsummer Night's Dream* in light of the tradition of the court masque, which was a popular form at the time the play was presented. Focuses on the visual and aesthetic qualities of music and dance to try to interpret the play in its cultural context.

Much Ado About Nothing

Type of plot: Comedy
Time of plot: Thirteenth century
Locale: Italy
First performed: c. 1598-1599; first published, 1600

Principal characters

DON PEDRO, Prince of Arragon
DON JOHN, his bastard brother
CLAUDIO, a young lord of Florence
BENEDICK, a young lord of Padua
LEONATO, the governor of Messina
HERO, Leonato's daughter
BEATRICE, Leonato's niece
DOGBERRY, a constable

The Story

Don Pedro, Prince of Arragon, arrived in Messina accompanied by his bastard brother, Don John, and his two friends, the young Italian noblemen Claudio and Benedick. Don Pedro had vanquished his brother in battle. Now, reconciled, the brothers planned to visit Leonato before returning to their homeland. On their arrival in Messina, young Claudio was immediately smitten by the lovely Hero, daughter of Leonato. In order to help his faithful young friend in his suit, Don Pedro assumed the guise of Claudio at a masked ball and wooed Hero in Claudio's name. Then he gained Leonato's consent for Claudio and Hero to marry. The bastard Don John tried to cause trouble by persuading Claudio that Don Pedro meant to betray him and keep Hero for himself, but the villain was foiled in his plot and Claudio remained faithful to Don Pedro.

Benedick, the other young follower of Don Pedro, was a confirmed and bitter bachelor who scorned all men willing to enter the married state. No less opposed to men and matrimony was Leonato's niece, Beatrice. These two constantly sparred with one another, each trying to show intellectual supremacy over the other. Don Pedro, with the help of Hero, Claudio, and Leonato, undertook the seemingly impossible task of bringing Benedick and Beatrice together in matrimony in the seven days before the marriage of Hero and Claudio.

Don John, thwarted in his first attempt to cause disharmony, formed another plot. With the help of a servant, he arranged to make it appear as if Hero was being unfaithful to Claudio. The servant was to gain entrance to Hero's chambers when she was away. In her place would be her attendant, assuming Hero's clothes. Don John, posing as Claudio's true friend, would inform him of her unfaithfulness and lead him to Hero's window to witness her wanton disloyalty.

Don Pedro pursued his plan to persuade Benedick and Beatrice to stop quarreling and fall in love with each other. When Benedick was close by, thinking himself unseen, Don Pedro, Claudio, and Leonato talked of their great sympathy for Beatrice, who loved Benedick but was unloved in return. The three told one another of the love letters Beatrice wrote to Benedick and then tore up, and of the fact that Beatrice beat her breast and sobbed over her unrequited love for Benedick. At the same time, on occasions when Beatrice was nearby but apparently unseen, Hero and her maid told each other that poor Benedick pined and sighed for the heartless Beatrice. The two unsuspecting young people decided not to let the other suffer. Each would sacrifice principles and accept the other's love.

Just as Benedick and Beatrice prepared to admit their love for each other, Don John was successful in his base plot to ruin Hero. He told Claudio that he had learned of Hero's duplicity, and he arranged to take him and Don Pedro to her window that very night to witness her unfaithfulness. Dogberry, a constable, and the watch apprehended Don John's followers and overheard the truth of the plot, but in their stupidity the petty officials could not get their story told in time to prevent Hero's disgrace. Don Pedro and Claudio witnessed the apparent betrayal, and Claudio determined to allow Hero to arrive in church the next day still thinking herself beloved. Then, instead of marrying her, he would shame her before all the wedding guests.

All happened as Don John had hoped. Before the priest and all the guests, Claudio called Hero a wanton and forswore her love for all time. The poor girl protested her innocence, but to no avail. Claudio said that he had seen her foul act with his own eyes. Hero swooned and lay as if dead, but Claudio and Don Pedro left her with her father, who believed the story and wished his daughter really dead in her shame. The priest believed the girl guiltless, however, and he persuaded Leonato to believe in her too. The priest told Leonato to let the world believe Hero dead while they worked to prove her innocent. Benedick, also believing in her innocence, promised to help unravel the mystery. Then Beatrice told Benedick of her love for him and asked him to kill Claudio and so prove his love for her. Benedick challenged Claudio to a duel. Don John had fled the country after the successful outcome of his plot, but Benedick swore that he would find Don John and kill him as well as Claudio.

At last, Dogberry and the watch got to Leonato and told their story. When Claudio and Don Pedro heard the story, Claudio wanted to die and to be with his wronged Hero. Leonato allowed the two sorrowful men to continue to think Hero dead. In fact, they all attended her funeral. Leonato said that he would be avenged if Claudio would marry his niece, a girl who much resembled Hero. Although Claudio still loved the dead Hero, he agreed to marry the other girl so that Leonato should have his wish.

When Don Pedro and Claudio arrived at Leonato's house for the ceremony, all the women were masked. Leonato brought one young woman forward. After

Claudio promised to be her husband, she unmasked. She was, of course, Hero. At first Claudio could not believe his senses, but after he was convinced of the truth he took her to the church immediately. Then Benedick and Beatrice declared their true love for each other, and they too went to the church after a dance in celebration of the double nuptials to be performed. Best of all, word came that Don John had been captured and was being brought back to Messina to face his brother, Don Pedro, the next day. On that day, however, all was joy and happiness.

Beatrice (Emma Thompson, left) leads Hero (Kate Beckinsale) and the rest of the entourage in a merry romp in the 1993 film version of Much Ado About Nothing, *directed by Kenneth Branagh.* (Courtesy of The Museum of Modern Art, Film Stills Archive)

Critical Evaluation

William Shakespeare's *Much Ado About Nothing* has in fact very much to do with "noting" (an intended pun on "nothing") or half-seeing, with perceiving dimly or not at all. Out of a host of misperceptions arises the comedy of Shakespeare's drama. Indeed, if it can be said that one theme preoccupies Shakespeare more than any other, it is that of perception, which informs not only his great histories and tragedies but his comedies as well. An early history such as *Richard II* (1595-1596), for example, which also involves tragic elements, proceeds not only from the title character's inability to function as a king but also from his failure to apprehend the nature of the new politics. Both Othello and King Lear are perfect representatives of the tragic consequences of the inability to see. Hindered by their egos, they live in their own restricted worlds oblivious to reality. When they fail to take the real into account, whether it is the nature of evil or their own limitation, they must pay the cost.

Although the blindness of Leonato, Don Pedro, Claudio, and Benedick in *Much Ado About Nothing* very nearly results in tragedy, it is the comic implications of noting rather than seeing that Shakespeare is concerned with here. Yet if his mode is comic, his intention is serious. Besides the characters' inability to perceive Don John's villainy, their superficial grasp of love and their failure to understand the nature of courtship and marriage reveal their moral obtuseness. In fact, the whole society is shot through with a kind of civilized shallowness. The play begins as an unspecified war ends, and the audience is immediately struck by Leonato's and the messenger's lack of response to the casualty report. To the governor of Messina's question, "How many gentlemen have you lost in this action?" the messenger replies, "But few of any sort, and none of name." Leonato comments: "A victory is twice itself, when the achiever brings home full numbers." The heroes of the war, Don Pedro, Claudio, and Benedick, return in a high good humor, seemingly untouched by their experiences and now in search of comfort, games, and diversion.

Only Beatrice is unimpressed with the soldiers' grand entrance, for she knows what they are. Between their "noble" actions, they are no more than seducers, "valiant trenchermen," gluttons and leeches, or, like Claudio, vain young boys ready to fall in love on a whim. Even the stately Don Pedro is a fool who proposes to Beatrice on impulse after he has wooed the childish Hero for the inarticulate Claudio. In contrast to their behavior, Beatrice's initial cynicism—"I had rather hear my dog bark at a crow, than a man swear he loves me"—is salutary and seems like wisdom.

Yet Beatrice is as susceptible to flattery as is Benedick. Like her eventual lover and husband, she is seduced by Don Pedro's deception, the masque he arranges to lead both Beatrice and Benedick to the altar. Both of them, after hearing that they are adored by the other, pledge their love and devotion. To be sure, the scenes in which they are duped are full of innocent humor, but the comedy does not obscure Shakespeare's rather bitter observations on the foppery of human love and courtship.

Nor is their foppery and foolishness the end of the matter. Don John realizes that a vain lover betrayed is a cruel and indeed inhuman tyrant. With little effort he convinces Claudio and Don Pedro that the innocent Hero is no more than a strumpet. Yet rather than break off the engagement in private, they wait until all meet at the altar to accuse the girl of "savage sensuality." Without compunction they leave her in a swoon, believing her dead. Even the father, Leonato, would have her dead rather than shamed. It is this moment that reveals the witty and sophisticated aristocrats of Messina to be grossly hypocritical, for beneath their glittering and refined manners lies a vicious ethic.

In vivid contrast to the decorous soldiers and politicians are Dogberry and his watchmen, although they certainly function as no more than a slapstick diversion. Hilarious clowns when they attempt to ape their social betters in manners and speech, they are yet possessed by a common sense or—as one critic has observed—by an instinctual morality, which enables them to uncover the villainy of Don John's henchmen, Conrade and Borachio. As the latter says to the nobleman, Don Pedro, "I have deceived even your very eyes: what your wisdoms could not discover, these shallow fools have brought to light." Like the outspoken and bawdy

"Every one can master a grief but he that has it"

Much Ado About Nothing, Act III, scene ii, lines 28-29

The principal comic device of this play is an elaborate intrigue in which Don Pedro, Claudio, and Leonato attempt to provoke romantic interest between Benedick and Beatrice, two confirmed single people. By arrangement, each while eavesdropping overhears a declaration of the other's love, and each in turn feels all attraction for the other. One of the play's great comic moments occurs with this public admission. After all, they who were love's mockers are now love's victims. Benedick's friends await his arrival in anticipation, and when he appears for the first time since the eavesdropping scene, he is suddenly unable to compete in the verbal combat that has characterized both his and Beatrice's defenses against love:

> *Don Pedro.* I will only be bold with Benedick for his company, for
>   from the crown of his head to the sole of his foot, he is all mirth.
> *Benedick.* Gallants, I am not as I have been.
> *Leonato.* So say I, methinks you are sadder.
> *Claudio.* I hope he be in love.
> *Benedick.* I have the toothache.
> *Don Pedro.* Draw it.
> *Benedick.* Hang it.
> *Claudio.* You must hang it first, and draw it afterwards.
> *Don Pedro.* What? Sigh for the toothache?
> *Leonato.* Where is but a humour or a worm?
> *Benedick.* Well, every one can master a grief but he that has it.
> *Claudio.* Yet say I, he is in love.

Margaret, who knows that underlying the aristocrats' courtly manners in the game of love is unacknowledged lust, Dogberry and his bumbling followers immediately understand the issue and recognize villainy, though they may use the wrong words to describe it.

Shakespeare does not force the point home in the end. He is not dealing here with characters of great stature, and they could not bear revelations of substantial moral consequence. They may show compunction for their errors, but they exhibit no significant remorse and are ready to get on with the rituals of their class. It does not seem to matter to Claudio whether he marries Hero or someone who looks like her. Even Beatrice has apparently lost her maverick edge as she joins the strutting Benedick in the marriage dance. All ends well for those involved (with the exception of Don John), but through no great fault of their own.

"Critical Evaluation" by David L. Kubal

For Further Study

Bloom, Harold, ed. *William Shakespeare's "Much Ado About Nothing."* New York: Chelsea House, 1988. Contains eight significant articles from the 1970's and 1980's. See especially the essays by Richard A. Levin, who looks beneath the comedic surface to find unexpected, troubling currents, and Carol Thomas Neely, who contributes an influential feminist interpretation.

Evans, Bertrand. *Shakespeare's Comedies*. Oxford, England: Clarendon Press, 1960. Important critical study. Concludes that Shakespeare's comic dramaturgy is based on different levels of awareness among characters and between them and the audience. The comedy in *Much Ado About Nothing* reflects an intricate game of multiple deceptions and misunderstandings that the audience enjoys from a privileged position.

Hunter, Robert Grams. *Shakespeare and the Comedy of Forgiveness*. New York: Columbia University Press, 1965. Argues persuasively that the thematic core of several Shakespeare comedies derives from the tradition of English morality plays. In *Much Ado About Nothing*, Claudio sins against the moral order by mistrusting Hero and is saved by repentance and forgiveness.

Macdonald, Ronald R. *William Shakespeare: The Comedies*. New York: Twayne, 1992. Compact introduction to Shakespeare's comedy that is both critically sophisticated and accessible to the general reader. Essay on *Much Ado About Nothing* reveals various subtextual relationships of class and gender by probing the characters' semantically complex and ironic verbal behavior.

Ornstein, Robert. *Shakespeare's Comedies: From Roman Farce to Romantic Mystery*. London: Associated University Presses, 1986. Award-winning book by a major Shakespeare scholar. The chapter on *Much Ado About Nothing* offers a sensitive, graceful analysis of the play that focuses primarily on characterization, plot, and moral themes.

Othello, the Moor of Venice

Type of plot: Tragedy
Time of plot: Early sixteenth century
Locale: Venice and Cyprus
First performed: 1604; first published, 1622; revised, 1623

Principal characters

OTHELLO, the Moor of Venice
DESDEMONA, his wife
IAGO, a villain
CASSIO, Othello's lieutenant
EMILIA, Iago's wife

The Story

Iago, an ensign serving under Othello, Moorish commander of the armed forces of Venice, was passed over in promotion when Othello chose Cassio to be his chief of staff. In revenge, Iago and his follower, Roderigo, aroused from his sleep Brabantio, senator of Venice, to tell him that his daughter Desdemona had stolen away and married Othello. Brabantio, incensed that his daughter would marry a Moor, led his servants to Othello's quarters.

Meanwhile, the Duke of Venice had learned that armed Turkish galleys were preparing to attack the island of Cyprus, and in this emergency he had summoned Othello to the senate chambers. Brabantio and Othello met in the streets but postponed any violence in the national interest. Othello, upon arriving at the senate, was commanded by the duke to lead the Venetian forces to Cyprus. Then Brabantio told the duke that Othello had beguiled his daughter into marriage without her father's consent. When Brabantio asked the duke for redress, Othello vigorously defended his honor and reputation; he was seconded by Desdemona, who appeared during the proceedings. Othello, cleared of all suspicion, prepared to sail for Cyprus immediately. For the time being, he placed Desdemona in the care of Iago; Iago's wife, Emilia, was to be her attendant during the voyage to Cyprus.

A great storm destroyed the Turkish fleet and scattered the Venetians. One by one, the ships under Othello's command put into Cyprus until all were safely ashore and Othello and Desdemona once again united. Still intent on revenge, Iago told Roderigo that Desdemona was in love with Cassio. Roderigo, himself in love with Desdemona, was promised all of his desires by Iago if he would engage Cassio, who did not know him, in a personal brawl while Cassio was officer of the guard.

Othello declared the night dedicated to celebrating the destruction of the enemy, but he cautioned Cassio to keep a careful watch on Venetian troops in the city. Iago talked Cassio into drinking too much, so that when provoked by Roderigo, Cassio lost control of himself and fought with Roderigo. Cries of riot and mutiny spread through the streets. Othello, aroused by the commotion, demoted Cassio for permitting a fight to start. Cassio, his reputation all but ruined, welcomed Iago's promise to secure Desdemona's goodwill and through her have Othello restore Cassio's rank.

Cassio importuned Iago to arrange a meeting between him and Desdemona. While Cassio and Desdemona were talking, Iago enticed Othello into view of the pair, and spoke vague innuendoes. Afterward, Iago from time to time asked Othello questions in such a manner as to lead Othello to think there might have been something between Cassio and Desdemona before Desdemona married him. Once Iago had sown these seeds of jealousy, Othello began to doubt his wife.

When Othello complained to Desdemona of a headache, she offered to bind his head with the handkerchief that had been Othello's first gift to her. She dropped the handkerchief inadvertently, and Emilia picked it up. Iago, seeing an opportunity to further his scheme, took the handkerchief from his wife and hid it in Cassio's room. When Othello asked Iago for proof that Desdemona was untrue to him, threatening his life if he could not produce any evidence, Iago said that he had slept in Cassio's room and had heard Cassio speak sweet words in his sleep to Desdemona. He reminded Othello of the handkerchief and said that he had seen Cassio wipe his beard that day with that very handkerchief. Othello, completely overcome by passion, vowed revenge. He ordered Iago to kill Cassio, and he appointed the ensign his new lieutenant.

Othello asked Desdemona to account for the loss of the handkerchief, but she was unable to explain its disappearance. She was mystified by Othello's shortness of speech, and his dark moods. Goaded by Iago's continuing innuendoes, the Moor succumbed to mad rages of jealousy in which he fell into fits resembling epilepsy. In the presence of an envoy from Venice, Othello struck Desdemona, to the consternation of all. Emilia swore that her mistress was honest and true, but Othello, who in his madness could no longer believe anything good of Desdemona, reviled and insulted her with harsh words.

One night, Othello ordered Desdemona to dismiss her attendant and to go to bed immediately. That same night Iago persuaded Roderigo to waylay Cassio. When Roderigo was wounded by Cassio, Iago, who had been standing nearby, stabbed Cassio. In the scuffle Iago stabbed Roderigo to death as well, so as to be rid of his dupe, who might talk. Then a strumpet friend of Cassio came upon the scene of the killing and revealed to the assembled crowd her relationship with Cassio. Although Cassio was not dead, Iago hoped to use this woman to defame Cassio beyond all hope of regaining his former reputation. Pretending friendship, he assisted the wounded Cassio back to Othello's house. They were accompanied by Venetian noblemen who had gathered after the fight.

Othello entered his wife's bedchamber and smothered her, after telling her, mistakenly, that Cassio had confessed his love for her and had been killed. Then

Emilia entered the bedchamber and reported that Roderigo had been killed, but not Cassio. This information made doubly bitter for Othello his murder of his wife. Othello told Emilia that he had learned of Desdemona's guilt from Iago. Emilia could not believe that Iago had made such charges.

When Iago and other Venetians arrived at Othello's house, Emilia asked Iago to refute Othello's statement. Then the great wickedness of Iago came to light, and Othello learned how the handkerchief had come into Cassio's possession. When Emilia gave further proof of her husband's villainy, Iago stabbed her. Othello lunged at Iago and managed to wound him before the Venetian gentlemen could seize the Moor. Emilia died, still protesting the innocence of Desdemona. Mad with grief, Othello plunged a dagger into his own heart. The Venetian envoy promised that Iago would be tortured to death at the hands of the governor general of Cyprus.

"One that loved not wisely, but too well"

Othello, Act V, scene ii, line 344

This famous line describes a love affair between obviously unsuitable partners. In the play, Othello, a Moorish military commander in the service of Venice, has been victimized by Iago, his ancient (or ensign). The latter hates the Moor because he has made Cassio his lieutenant and not Iago. The ancient determines to destroy both of them. The evil Iago convinces Othello not only that his sweet bride Desdemona is unfaithful with Cassio but also that she must die. Othello smothers her in her bed (Act V, scene ii, lines 6-13):

> *Othello.* Yet she must die, else she'll betray more men.
> Put out the light, and then put out the light.
> If I quench thee, thou flaming minister,
> I can again thy former light restore,
> Should I repent me. But once put out thy light,
> Thou cunning'st pattern of excelling nature,
> I know not where is that Promethean heat
> That can thy light relume.

No sooner does he do so than Iago's entire plot is unraveled, and the Moor realizes that he has been diabolically duped. About to be removed to Venice for trial, he tries to exculpate himself:

> *Othello.* I pray you in your letters,
> When you shall these unlucky deeds relate,
> Speak of me, as I am. Nothing extenuate,
> Nor set down aught in malice. Then must you speak
> Of one that loved not wisely, but too well;
> Of one not easily jealous, but being wrought,
> Perplexed in the extreme; of one whose hand,
> Like the base Indian, threw a pearl away,
> Richer than all his tribe. . . .

Critical Evaluation

Although *Othello* has frequently been praised as William Shakespeare's most unified tragedy, many critics have found the central character to be the most unheroic of William Shakespeare's heroes. Some have found him stupid beyond redemption; others have described him as a passionate being overwhelmed by powerful emotion; still others have found him self-pitying and insensitive to the enormity of his actions. Yet all of these denigrations pale before the excitement and sympathy generated for the noble soldier in the course of the play.

As a "Moor," or black man, Othello would have been seen by Elizabethans as an exotic, a foreigner from a fascinating and mysterious land. Certainly he is a passionate man, but he is not devoid of sensitivity. Rather, his problem is that he is thrust into the unfamiliar context of Renaissance Italy, a land that had a reputation in the England of Shakespeare's time for connivance and intrigue. Shakespeare uses the racial difference to many effects: most obviously, to emphasize Othello's difference from the society in which he finds himself and to which he allies himself through marriage; more subtly and ironically to heighten his tragic stance against the white Iago, the embodiment of evil in the play. More than anything, Othello is natural man confronted with the machinations and contrivances of an overly civilized society. His instincts are to be loving and trusting, but he is cast into a society where these natural virtues would have made him extremely vulnerable.

The prime source of that vulnerability is personified in the figure of Iago, perhaps Shakespeare's consummate villain. Iago is so evil by nature that he does not even need any motivation for his antagonism toward Othello. He has been passed over for promotion, but that is clearly a pretext for a malignant nature whose hatred for Othello needs no specific grounds. It is Othello's candor, openness, and spontaneous, generous love that Iago finds offensive. His suggestion that Othello has seduced his own wife is an even flimsier fabrication to cover the essential corruption of his nature.

Iago sees other human beings only as victims or tools. He is the classical Renaissance atheist—an intelligent man, beyond moral scruple, who finds pleasure in the corruption of the virtuous and the abuse of the pliable. That he brings himself into danger is of no consequence, because he relies on his wit and believes that all can be duped and destroyed. There is no further purpose to his life. For such a manipulator, Othello, a good man out of his cultural element, is the perfect target.

More so than in any other Shakespeare play, one character, Iago, is the stage manager of the whole action. Once he sets out to destroy Othello, he proceeds by plot and by innuendo to achieve his goal. He tells others just what he wishes them to know, sets one character against another, and develops an elaborate web of circumstantial evidence to dupe the vulnerable Moor. Edgar Stoll has argued that the extraordinary success of Iago in convincing other characters of his fabrications is simply a matter of the conventional ability of the Renaissance villain. Yet there is more to the conflict than Iago's abilities, conventional or natural. Othello is the perfect victim because he bases his opinions and his human relationships on intuition rather than reason. His courtship of Desdemona is brief and his devotion absolute, as is his trust of his comrades, including Iago. It is not simply that Iago

Othello (James Earl Jones, left) listens to the false tales of Iago (Anthony Zerbe) that will eventually lead to tragedy in a production of Othello *mounted by the Mark Taper Forum.* (Courtesy of the Mark Taper Forum)

is universally believed. Ironically, he is able to fool everyone about everything except the subject of Desdemona's chastity. On that subject it is only Othello whom he is able to deceive. Roderigo, Cassio, and Emilia all reject Iago's allegations that Desdemona has been unfaithful. Only Othello is deceived, but that is because Iago is able to make him play a game with unfamiliar rules.

Iago entices Othello to use Venetian criteria of truth rather than the intuition on which he should rely. Iago plants doubts in Othello's mind, but his decisive success comes when he gets Othello to demand "ocular proof" before concluding that Desdemona is guilty. Although it seems that Othello is demanding conclusive evidence before jumping to the conclusion that his wife has been unfaithful, it is more important that he has accepted Iago's notion of what would constitute such concrete evidence. From that point on, it is easy for Iago to falsify evidence and create appearances that will lead to erroneous judgments. Othello betrays hyperemotional behavior in his rantings and his fits, but these are the result of his acceptance of what seems indisputable proof. It takes a long time, and a lot of falsifications, before Othello finally abandons his intuitive perception of the truth of his domestic situation. As Othello himself recognizes, he is not quick to anger, but, once angered, his natural passion takes over.

The crime that Othello commits is made to appear all the more heinous because of Desdemona's utter loyalty. It is not that she is naïve—indeed, her conversation reflects that she is sophisticated—but there is no question of her total fidelity to her husband. The evil represented by the murder is intensified by the audience's perception of the contrast between the victim's virtue and Othello's conviction that he is an instrument of justice. His chilling conviction reminds us of the essential probity of a man deranged by confrontation with an evil he cannot comprehend.

Critics such as T. S. Eliot have argued that Othello never comes to an understanding of the gravity of his crime—that he realizes his error but consoles himself in his final speech with cheering reminders of his own virtue. That does not, however, seem consistent with the valiant and honest military character who has thus far been depicted. Othello may have been grossly deceived, and he may be responsible for not clinging to the truth of his mutual love with Desdemona, but, in his final speech, he does face up to his error with the same passion with which he had followed his earlier misconception. Just as he had believed that his murder of Desdemona was divine retribution, he now believes that his suicide is a just act. His passionate nature believes it is meting out justice for the earlier transgression. There is a reference to punishment for Iago, but Shakespeare dismisses the obvious villain so as to focus on Othello's final act of expiation.

Edward E. Foster

For Further Study

Bloom, Harold, ed. *William Shakespeare's "Othello."* New York: Chelsea House, 1987. Seven essays that explore the issues of power and the difference between male and female roles and occupations. Holds that the play is at once tragic and comic. Includes helpful bibliography and Shakespeare chronology.

Calderwood, James L. *The Properties of "Othello."* Amherst: University of Massachusetts Press, 1989. Takes the theme of ownership as a starting point and provides an overview of Elizabethan property lines to set the stage for argument. Stretches the term property to include not only material and territorial possessions but racial, social, and personal identity.

Heilman, Robert B. *Magic in the Web: Action and Language in "Othello."* Lexington: University of Kentucky Press, 1956. Extensive discussion of Iago's manipulative rhetoric. Argues against Othello as a "victim," presenting him as responsible, if only in part, for his own actions. A good resource for both general readers and students.

Nevo, Ruth. *Tragic Form in Shakespeare*. Princeton, N.J.: Princeton University Press, 1972. Chapter on *Othello* describes the two primary ways of looking at the Moor of Venice: as a man blinded by love, and as a man blinded by his tainted vision of that love. Chronicles the events leading to the protagonist's downfall.

Vaughan, Virginia Mason, and Kent Cartwright, eds. *"Othello": New Perspectives*. Teaneck, N.J.: Fairleigh Dickinson University Press, 1991. A collection of twelve essays that examine different theoretical approaches. Goes beyond a discussion of good versus evil to reveal a variety of nuances in the play. Traces readings and misreadings from the first quarto to the present.

Pericles, Prince of Tyre

Type of plot: Romance or tragicomedy
Time of plot: Hellenistic period
Locale: Eastern Mediterranean Sea and its littorals
First performed: c. 1607-1608; first published, 1609

Principal characters

PERICLES, Prince of Tyre
THAISA, his wife
MARINA, their daughter
CLEON, governor of Tarsus
DIONYZA, his wife
LYSIMACHUS, governor of Mytilene
ANTIOCHUS, King of Antioch

The Story

In Syria, King Antiochus' wife died in giving birth to a daughter. When the child grew to lovely womanhood, King Antiochus conceived an unnatural passion for her. Her beauty attracted suitors to Antioch from far and wide, but King Antiochus, reluctant to give up his daughter, posed a riddle to each suitor. If the riddle went unanswered, the suitor was executed. Many men, hoping to win the princess, lost their lives in this way. Prince Pericles of Tyre went to Antioch to seek the hand of the beautiful princess. Having declared that he would willingly risk his life for the hand of the king's daughter, he read the riddle, the solution to which disclosed an incestuous relationship between King Antiochus and his daughter. Pericles understood but hesitated, prudently, to reveal his knowledge. Pressed by King Antiochus, he hinted that he had fathomed the riddle. King Antiochus, unnerved and determined to kill Pericles, invited the young prince to stay at the court for forty days, in which time he could decide whether he would forthrightly give the solution to the riddle. Pericles, convinced that his life was in great danger, fled. King Antiochus sent agents after him with orders to kill the prince on sight.

Pericles, back in Tyre, was fearful that King Antiochus would ravage Tyre in an attempt to take Pericles' life. After consulting with his lords, he decided that he could save Tyre by going on a journey to last until King Antiochus died. Thaliard, a Syrian lord who had come to Tyre to take Pericles' life, learned of Pericles' departure and returned to Antioch to report the prince's intention. Meanwhile, in the remote Greek province of Tarsus, Cleon, the governor, and his wife Dionyza grieved because there was famine in the land. As they despaired, it was reported that a fleet of ships stood off the coast. Cleon was sure that Tarsus was about to be invaded. Actually, the ships were those of Pericles, who had come to Tarsus with grain to succor the starving populace. Cleon welcomed the Tyrians, and his people invoked the Greek gods to protect their saviors from all harm.

Pericles received word from Tyre that King Antiochus' agents were relentlessly pursuing him, so that he was no longer safe in Tarsus. He thereupon took leave of Cleon and set sail. On the high seas the Tyrians met disaster in a storm. The fleet was lost; Pericles was the only survivor. Washed ashore in Greece, he was helped by simple fishermen. Fortunately, too, the fishermen took Pericles' suit of armor from the sea. With the help of the fishermen, Pericles went to Pentapolis, the court of King Simonides.

There a tournament was held to honor the birthday of Thaisa, the lovely daughter of King Simonides. Among the gallant knights he met, Pericles presented a wretched sight in his rusted armor. Even so, he defeated all antagonists and was crowned king of the tournament by Thaisa. At the banquet following the tourney Pericles, reminded of his own father's splendid court, lapsed into melancholy. Seeing his dejection, King Simonides drank a toast to him and asked him who he was. He disclosed that he was Pericles of Tyre, a castaway. His modesty and courteous deportment made an excellent impression on King Simonides and Thaisa.

Meanwhile, in Antioch, King Antiochus and his daughter, riding together in a chariot, were struck dead by a bolt of lightning. In Tyre, Pericles had been given up for dead, and the lords proposed that Helicanus, Pericles' deputy, take the crown. The old lord, confident that his prince was still alive, directed them to spend a year in search of Pericles. In Pentapolis, Thaisa, having lost her heart to Pericles, tricked her suitors into leaving by reporting that she would remain a maid for another year. Then she and Pericles were married.

A short time before Thaisa was to give birth to a child, Pericles was told that King Antiochus was dead and that Helicanus had been importuned to take the crown of Tyre. Free to go home, Pericles, with Thaisa and Lychorida, a nurse, took ship for Tyre. During the voyage the ship was overtaken by storms. Thaisa, seemingly dead after giving birth to a daughter, was placed in a watertight casket which was thrown into the raging sea. Pericles, fearful for the safety of his child, directed the seamen to take the ship into Tarsus, which was not far off.

The casket containing Thaisa having drifted ashore in Ephesus, the body was taken to Cerimon, a skilled physician. Cerimon, suspecting that Thaisa was not really dead, discovered by his skill that she was actually quite alive. Pericles, having reached Tarsus safely, remained there a year, at the end of which time he declared that Tyre had need of him. Placing little Marina, as he had named his daughter, in the care of Cleon and Dionyza, he set out for Tyre. In the meantime Thaisa, believing that her husband and child had been lost at sea, took the veil of a votaress to the goddess Diana. Years passed, while Pericles ruled in Tyre. As Marina grew, it was clear that she was superior in every respect to her companion, the daughter of Cleon and Dionyza. When Marina's nurse Lychorida died, Dionyza, jealous of the daughter of Pericles, plotted to have Marina's life, and she commissioned a servant to take Marina to a deserted place on the coast and kill her. As the servant threatened to take the girl's life, pirates frightened away the servant and took Marina aboard their ship. Taking her to Mytilene, they sold her to a brothel owner.

"The great ones eat up the little ones"

Pericles, Prince of Tyre, Act II, scene i, lines 31-32

Pericles, Prince of Tyre, has gone to the court of Antiochus, King of Antioch, to woo his daughter. However, the hand of the princess can be won only by the man who solves a riddle propounded by her father. Failure to do so brings death to the suitor. Pericles is able to solve the riddle, but in so doing he uncovers the terrible secret of incest between Antiochus and his daughter. The king knows that Pericles has discovered this secret and resolves upon the prince's death, but Pericles escapes from Antioch and returns to Tyre. Even in his own palace he is not safe from the vengeance of Antiochus, and he is advised by a faithful nobleman, Helicanus, to travel incognito until Antiochus either forgets his anger or dies. Pericles accepts the advice and starts on a voyage just in time to escape Thaliard, an agent sent by Antiochus to murder him. The prince stops for a while at Tarsus, but he is not safe even there, so he resumes his voyage. His ship is wrecked in a storm, and Pericles is the only survivor. As he wanders by the seashore, he meets three fishermen who are discussing the storm and the shipwreck and the dangers of the sea. Their comments on the struggle for survival among the fish form a satirical description of the struggle among men, even among such rulers as Antiochus and Pericles:

> *Patch-Breech.* . . . Master, I marvel how the fishes live in the sea.
> *First Fisherman.* Why, as men do a-land; the great ones eat up the
> little ones. I can compare our rich misers to nothing so fitly as to a
> whale; 'a plays and tumbles, driving the poor fry before him, and
> at last devours them all at a mouthful. Such whales have I heard on
> a th' land, who never leave gaping till they've swallowed the
> whole parish, church, steeple, bells and all.
> *Pericles.* A pretty moral.

In Tarsus, meanwhile, Dionyza persuaded the horrified Cleon that for their own safety against the rage of Pericles they must mourn the loss of Marina and erect a monument in her memory. When Pericles, accompanied by old Helicanus, went to Tarsus to reclaim his daughter, his grief on seeing the monument was so great that he exchanged his royal robes for rags, vowed never again to wash himself or to cut his hair, and left Tarsus.

In Mytilene, in the meantime, Marina confounded both the owners of the brothel and the customers by preaching the heavenly virtues instead of deporting herself wantonly. Lysimachus, the governor of Mytilene, went in disguise to the brothel. When Marina was brought to him, he quickly discerned her gentle birth, gave her gold, and assured her that she would soon be freed from her vile bondage.

Alarmed, the bawd put Marina in the hands of the doorkeeper. Marina shamed him, gave him gold, and persuaded him to place her as a teacher of the gentle arts. The money she earned by teaching singing, dancing, and needlework she gave to her owner, the bawd.

When Pericles, now a distracted wanderer, came to Mytilene, Lysimachus took a barge out to the Tyrian ship, but he was told that Pericles, grieved by the loss of both wife and daughter, would not speak to anyone. A Mytilene lord suggested that Marina, famous for her graciousness and charm, be brought. Marina came and revealed to Pericles that she knew a grief similar to his, for she had lost her father and mother. It soon became apparent to bewildered Pericles that his daughter stood before him. Rejoicing, he put aside his rags and dressed in regal robes. The goddess Diana then put him into a deep sleep, in which she directed him in a dream to go to Ephesus and to tell in the temple of Diana the loss of his wife.

Pericles hastened to Ephesus, where, in the temple, he revealed his identity to the votaries in attendance. Thaisa, overhearing him, fainted. Cerimon, who was also present, disclosed to Pericles that the votaress who had fainted was his wife. Pericles and Thaisa were joyfully reunited. Since Thaisa's father had died, Pericles proclaimed that he and Thaisa would reign in Pentapolis and that Lysimachus and Marina, as man and wife, would rule over Tyre. When the people of Tarsus learned of the evil done by Cleon and Dionyza, they burned the governor and his family alive in their palace.

Critical Evaluation

By scholarly consensus, it appears that in the case of *Pericles, Prince of Tyre*, William Shakespeare finished a play that someone else had been commissioned to write. Recent scholarship indicates that Shakespeare revised the entire play from an earlier version by another playwright, probably Thomas Heywood. The play was tremendously popular in its day and was the basis of a prose version by George Wilkins. *Pericles* is now considered to have been the first of the tragicomedies, or dark romances, that became so popular on the Jacobean stage. The play disregards consideration of time and place, delights in romantic improbabilities, and employs the obscure, compact style of Shakespeare's late plays. Probably it paved the way not only for *Cymbeline* (c. 1609-1610), *The Winter's Tale* (c. 1610-1611), and *The Tempest* (1611), but also for the plays of Francis Beaumont and John Fletcher.

Although seldom performed, *Pericles* does possess an interesting, romantic story and a certain sentimental beauty. It abounds in situations and surprises, although parts of its theme might be considered unpleasant. The similarities between it and Shakespeare's other late plays are striking. The likeness between Marina in *Pericles* and Perdita in *The Winter's Tale* is clear. The meeting between father and daughter, long separated, is suggestive of *Cymbeline*, and the reunion of Pericles and Thaisa anticipates that of Leontes and Hermione in *The Winter's Tale*. Pericles and Cerimon are wise and superior men in the manner of *The Tempest*'s Prospero. The themes of reunion after long division, reconciliation, and forgiveness seem to recur in all of these late plays, beginning with *Pericles*. Storms appear twice in the play, perhaps as a symbol of the storms of life; this resembles *The*

Tempest. In Shakespeare's last plays, there are children lost and found again, parents divided and reunited, a wife rejected and ill-used and restored again. The recurring myth of royalty lost and recovered apparently had some special significance for Shakespeare and his audience.

The play is heavy with symbols and is particularly concerned with the concept of lost authority or control, without which life cannot properly be conducted. It is possible that some allusion to the late Queen Elizabeth is intended, but the meaning may have been more personal to Shakespeare and may reflect a change or confu-

Pericles (Derrick Lee Weeden) shelters his newborn daughter from the storm in the Oregon Shakespeare Festival's 1989 production of Pericles, Prince of Tyre. (Christopher Briscoe, courtesy of the Oregon Shakespeare Festival by permission of the Actors' Equity Association)

sion in his life. The atmosphere, like that of *The Tempest*, is all sea and music. The brothel scenes are decidedly Shakespearean, with their joking references to disease. There is a hint of the attitudes of *Timon of Athens* (c. 1607-1608), namely, a certain anger and disgust with humanity in the midst of the poetry and music. Up to the third act, Shakespeare's revisions apparently were mostly confined to style, but comparison to the prose story based on the earlier version of the play suggests that with the fourth act he began to make extensive revisions in the plot as well. Certainly, the later scenes are superior in quality to the earlier ones. There is a subtlety and delicacy in the handling of certain scenes—such as when Pericles strikes Marina when she reproves him for his stubborn grief—that mark them as clearly from the hand of Shakespeare. *Pericles*, because of its uncertain place in the canon, has long been underrated as a play. Its importance, however, as the beginning of a new style for Shakespeare and other Jacobean playwrights cannot be overestimated.

For Further Study

Bergeron, David M. *Shakespeare's Romances and the Royal Family*. Lawrence: University Press of Kansas, 1985. Emphasizes the relationship of the masquelike elements of the play to the ceremonial forms predominant at the court of James I. One of the best historical analyses of *Pericles, Prince of Tyre*.

Fawkner, H. W. *Shakespeare's Miracle Plays*. Madison, N.J.: Fairleigh Dickinson University Press, 1992. This fascinating book does not condescend to *Pericles, Prince of Tyre* as so many Shakespeare studies do. Considers the play as a mature, complex, and achieved work of art.

Frye, Northrop. *A Natural Perspective: The Development of Shakespearean Comedy and Romance*. New York: Columbia University Press, 1965. In this work and in his earlier *Anatomy of Criticism*, Frye establishes a critical model of the Hellenistic romance by which the reader may better understand the plot and genre of *Pericles, Prince of Tyre*.

Knight, G. Wilson. *The Crown of Life*. New York: Oxford University Press, 1947. Knight was the first modern critic to take *Pericles, Prince of Tyre* seriously. Discusses the play's verbal beauty, its adventure, and its spiritual richness.

Neely, Carol Thomas. *Broken Nuptials in Shakespeare's Plays*. New Haven, Conn.: Yale University Press, 1985. The most important feminist analysis of *Pericles, Prince of Tyre*. Argues that the play affirms and subverts the conventional marriage plot of comedies.

Richard II

Type of plot: Historical
Time of plot: Fourteenth century
Locale: England
First performed: c. 1595-1596; first published, 1600

Principal characters

RICHARD II, the King of England
JOHN OF GAUNT, the Duke of Lancaster, Richard's uncle
EDMUND OF LANGLEY, the Duke of York, another uncle of Richard
HENRY BOLINGBROKE, the Duke of Hereford and the son of John of Gaunt
DUKE OF AUMERLE, son of the Duke of York
THOMAS MOWBRAY, the Duke of Norfolk
EARL OF NORTHUMBERLAND, a supporter of Bolingbroke

The Story

During the reign of Richard II, the two young dukes Henry Bolingbroke and Thomas Mowbray quarreled bitterly, and the king finally summoned them into his presence to settle their differences publicly. Although Bolingbroke was the oldest son of John of Gaunt, the Duke of Lancaster, and therefore a cousin of the king, Richard was perfectly fair in his interview with the two men and showed neither any favoritism.

Bolingbroke accused Mowbray, the Duke of Norfolk, of mismanaging military funds and of helping to plot the murder of the dead Duke of Gloucester, another of the king's uncles. These charges Mowbray forcefully denied. Richard decided that to settle the dispute the men should have a trial by combat at Coventry, and the court adjourned there to witness the tournament.

Richard, ever nervous and suspicious, grew uneasy as the contest began. Suddenly, just after the beginning trumpet sounded, the king forbade that the combat take place. Instead, he banished the two men from the country. Bolingbroke was to be exiled for six years and Mowbray for the rest of his life. At the same time Richard exacted their promise that they would never plot against him. Persisting in his accusations, Bolingbroke tried to persuade Mowbray to plead guilty to the charges before he left England. Mowbray, refusing to do so, warned Richard against Bolingbroke's cleverness.

Not long after his son had been banished, John of Gaunt, Duke of Lancaster, became ill and sent for Richard to give him advice. Although the Duke of York pointed out that giving advice to Richard was too often a waste of time, John of

Gaunt felt that perhaps a dying man would be heeded where a living one was not. From his deathbed he criticized Richard of extravagance and of mishandling the public funds and impoverishing the nation. John of Gaunt warned Richard also that the kingdom would suffer for his selfishness.

Richard paid no attention to his uncle's advice, and after John of Gaunt had died, the king seized his lands and wealth to back his Irish wars. The aged Duke of York, another of Richard's uncles, attempted to dissuade the king from his course, pointing out that Bolingbroke had influence among the people. York's fears were soon confirmed. Bolingbroke, hearing that his father's lands had been seized by the king's officers, used the information as an excuse to terminate his banishment. Gathering together troops and supplies, he landed in the north of England, where he was joined by other dissatisfied lords, including Lord Ross, Lord Willoughby, the Earl of Northumberland, and the earl's son, Henry Percy, known as Hotspur.

Richard, heedless of all warnings, had set off for Ireland to pursue his war, leaving his tottering kingdom in the hands of the weak Duke of York, who was no match for the wily Bolingbroke. When the exiled traitor reached Gloucestershire, the Duke of York visited him at his camp. Caught between loyalty to Richard and despair over the bankrupt state of the country, York finally yielded his troops to Bolingbroke. Richard, returning to England and expecting to find an army of Welshmen under his command, learned that after hearing false reports of his death they had gone over to Bolingbroke. Moreover, the strong men of his court—men like the Earl of Wiltshire, Bushy, and Green—had all been executed.

Destitute of friends and without an army, Richard took refuge in Flint Castle. Bolingbroke, using his usurped titles and estates as his excuse, took Richard prisoner and carried him to London. There Richard broke down. He showed little interest in anything and spent his time philosophizing on his downfall. When he was brought before Bolingbroke and the cruel and unfeeling Earl of Northumberland, Richard was forced to abdicate his throne and sign papers confessing his political crimes. Bolingbroke, assuming royal authority, ordered Richard imprisoned in the Tower of London.

During a quarrel among the young dukes of the court, the bishop of Carlisle announced that Mowbray had made a name for himself while fighting in the Holy Land and had then retired to Venice and died there. When Bolingbroke affected grief over the news, the bishop turned on him and denounced him for his part in ousting Richard. Bolingbroke, armed with the legal documents he had collected to prove his rights, prepared to assume the throne as Henry IV. Richard predicted to the Earl of Northumberland that Bolingbroke would soon come to distrust his old aide for his part in unseating a king. Soon after that, Richard was sent to the dungeons at Pomfret Castle and his queen was banished to France.

At the Duke of York's palace, the aging duke sorrowfully related to his duchess the details of the coronation procession of Henry IV. When the duke discovered that his son Aumerle and other loyal followers of Richard were planning to assassinate Henry IV at Oxford, York immediately started for the palace to warn the new monarch. The duchess, frantic at the thought of her son's danger, advised Aumerle to reach the palace ahead of his father, reveal his treachery to the king, and ask the royal pardon. She herself pleaded for her son before the king and won Aumerle's release.

Having punished the conspirators, Henry IV grew uneasy at the prospect of other treasonable activities, for while Richard lived there was always danger that he might be restored to power. Henry IV suggested casually to his faithful servant Sir Pierce Exton that he murder Richard at Pomfret.

Exton's plan worked. In his dungeon, Richard was provoked to quarrel with his guard and in the struggle that ensued the knight drew his sword and struck down his unhappy prisoner. He then placed Richard's body in a coffin, carried it to Windsor Castle, and there presented it to Henry IV. Distressed over the news of mounting insurrection in the country, King Henry pretended horror at the murder of Richard and vowed to make a pilgrimage to the Holy Land to atone for the death of his fallen cousin.

"This royal throne of kings, this sceptred isle"

Richard II, Act II, scene i, line 40

Richard II is approached by his uncle, John of Gaunt, and his uncle's son, Henry Bolingbroke (later King Henry IV), with accusations against Mowbray, Duke of Norfolk. Rather than have the accuser and the accused test the accusation by combat, Richard banishes both Bolingbroke and Mowbray from England. John of Gaunt protests the long banishment of his son, saying that by the time Bolingbroke returns he, Gaunt, will be dead. However, Richard will not revoke his decree. Gaunt later is carried in a chair to see Richard, and "a prophet new inspired/ And thus expiring do foretell of him,/ His rash fierce blaze of riot cannot last." Gaunt then comments on the nobility and greatness of England and prophesies its decline:

> *Gaunt.* This royal throne of kings, this sceptred isle,
>   This earth of majesty, this seat of Mars,
>   This other Eden, demi-Paradise, . . .
>   This happy breed of men, this little world,
>   This precious stone set in the silver sea, . . .
>   This blessed plot, this earth, this realm, this England, . . .
>   That England that was wont to conquer others,
>   Hath made a shameful conquest of itself.

Critical Evaluation

Part of William Shakespeare's second tetralogy of historical plays (with *Henry IV, Part I*, *Henry IV, Part II*, and *Henry V*), *Richard II* is also his second experiment in the *de casibus* genre of tragedy, dealing with the fall of an incompetent but not unsympathetic king. It is also part of the lyrical group of plays written between 1593 and 1596, in which Shakespeare's gradual transformation from poet to playwright can be traced. The sources of the play include the 1587 second edition of Raphael Holinshed's *Chronicles of England, Scotland, and Ireland* (1577); the chronicles of Jean Froissart and Edward Hall; George Ferrers and William Baldwin's *A Mirror for Magistrates* (1555); Samuel Daniel's verse epic on the Wars of the Roses, *The Civil Wars* (1595-1609); and a play by an unknown author, entitled *Thomas of Woodstock.*

Kelsey Grammer as King Richard II in the Mark Taper Forum's production of Richard II. (Jay Thompson, courtesy of the Mark Taper Forum)

The themes of the play are associated, in one way or another, with the question of sovereignty. Bolingbroke's challenge to Richard focuses on the divine right of kings and its historical basis and social implications. Connected with this is the matter of a subject's duty of passive obedience, especially as seen in the characters of Gaunt and York. Richard's arbitrariness in the opening scenes suggests the dangers of irresponsible despotism; throughout the play, Shakespeare follows his thoughts and strange behavior and contrasts those with the caginess and certainty of Bolingbroke, whose thoughts are revealed only in the way they are translated into action; Richard thus becomes a study of the complex qualities of the ideal ruler. In this respect, the play reflects the Renaissance fascination with optimal behavior in various social roles, as seen, for example, in Niccolò Machiavelli's *The*

Prince (1513), Roger Ascham's *The Schoolmaster* (1570), and Sir Thomas Elyot's *The Boke Named the Governour* (1531). Yet Shakespeare's psychological realism does not reach a falsely definitive conclusion, creating rather a tragic aura of uncertainty around Richard, which makes him a most attractive character. In many ways, the play is not so much a contest for power as a struggle within Richard himself to adjust to his situation.

This is the first of Shakespeare's plays with a central figure who is an introspective, imaginative, and eloquent man. It is, therefore, not surprising that the work includes some of his finest lyrical passages. *Richard II* is in fact the only play Shakespeare wrote entirely in verse, a verse supported by a regal formality of design and manner, and a profuse and delicate metaphorical base. Intricately interwoven throughout the play are image-patterns centered around the eagle, the lion, the rose, the sun (which begins with Richard but moves to Bolingbroke), the state as theater, the earth as a neglected or well-tended garden, and the rise and fall of fortune's buckets. The complicated imagery illustrates the subconscious workings of Shakespeare's imagination that will enrich the great tragedies to follow. As Henry Morley said, the play is "full of passages that have floated out of their place in the drama to live in the minds of the people." These passages include Gaunt's great apostrophe to England in Act II, scene i, York's description of "our two cousins coming into London," Richard's prison soliloquy in Act V, scene iv, and his monologues on divine right and on the irony of kingship.

So poetic is Richard II, that critics speculate Shakespeare may have written the part for himself. Richard, the lover of music, spectacle, domestic courtesy, and dignified luxury, would be the ideal host to Castiglione's courtier. His whimsical personality is balanced to great dramatic effect by his self-awareness. He seems fascinated with the contradictory flow of his own emotions; and this very fascination is a large part of his tragic flaw. Similarly, Richard's sensitivity is combined with a flair for self-dramatization that reveals only too clearly his ineptitude as a strong ruler. He plays to the wrong audience, seeking the approval of his court rather than that of the common people; he seems to shun the "vulgar crowd" in preference to the refined taste of a court that can appreciate his delicate character. The last three acts, in which Richard's charm as a man are emphasized, are obviously more central to the play's aesthetic than the first two, which reveal his weakness as a king. His sentimental vanity in the abdication scene is so effective that it was censored during Queen Elizabeth's lifetime. The alternation of courage and despair in Richard's mind determines the rhythm of the play; in the nineteenth century, Samuel Taylor Coleridge observed that "the play throughout is a history of the human mind."

When Richard speaks of "the unstooping firmness of my upright soul" we understand that he is compensating verbally for his inability to act. He insists on the sacramental nature of kingship, depending for his support on the formal, legal rituals associated with the throne; he is all ceremony and pathetically fatal pomp. Yet, from the outset, Richard contradicts even the logic of sovereign ceremony when he arbitrarily changes his decision, and banishes the two opponents in the joust. Bolingbroke is quick to note the king's weakness and steps into the power

"Tell sad stories of the death of kings"

Richard II, Act III, scene ii, line 157

Richard II comes back from Ireland to find his cousin, the banished Bolingbroke, back in the land and gaining power every minute. At first Richard's hopes are high in opposing Bolingbroke, but every messenger brings the report of the strength of Richard's opponent. One by one the king names his former adherents, only to have each name written off as dead or his forces dispersed. He has returned too late to save his kingdom. Finally realizing the extent of his helplessness, Richard sinks into despair and realizes that all his royal glory cannot, in the end, save him from death.

> *King Richard.* Let's talk of graves, of worms, and epitaphs,
> Make dust our paper, and with rainy eyes,
> Write sorrow on the bosom of the earth. . . .
> For God's sake let us sit upon the ground,
> And tell sad stories of the death of kings:
> How some have been depos'd, some slain in war,
> Some haunted by the ghosts they have deposed,
> Some poisoned by their wives, some sleeping kill'd,
> All murdered—for within the hollow crown
> That rounds the mortal temples of a king
> Keeps Death his court, and there the antic sits, . . .
> Comes at the last and with a little pin
> Bores through his castle wall, and farewell king!
> Cover your heads, and mock not flesh and blood,
> With solemn reverence; throw away respect,
> Tradition, form, and ceremonious duty,
> For you have but mistook me all this while.
> I live with bread like you, feel want,
> Taste grief, need friends; subjected thus,
> How can you say to me, I am a king?

vacuum it creates. Bolingbroke is the consummate actor who can be all things to all men by seeming so. He is impressed by the kingly power Richard wields: "Four lagging winters and four wanton springs/ End in a word: such is the breath of kings." He likes what he sees and, in deciding to imitate it, surpasses Richard. Even when Bolingbroke is ceremonious, as when he bows his knee to Richard before the abdication, he is acting. The difference is that he knows the most effective audience. Richard laments that he has seen Bolingbroke's courtship of the common people: "How he did seem to dive into their hearts." He recognizes the actor in Bolingbroke, and fears its power. It is not coincidental that York compares the commoners to the fickle theater audience. As in so many plays of Shakespeare, the theater itself becomes a central image; Richard's monologues are a stark contrast to Bolingbroke's speeches not only because they reveal internal states but also because they are narcissistically oriented. They reach inward, toward secrecy and communicative impotency; Bolingbroke speaks actively, reaching outward toward the audience he wishes to influence. His role can be compared usefully to that of Antony in *Julius Caesar* (1599-1600), Richard's to that of Brutus. The tension between the two styles of speaking, moreover, no doubt reflects the transformation in Shakespeare himself that will make the plays to follow more strikingly dramatic than sheerly poetic. The Bolingbroke of *Henry IV*, Parts I and II (1597-1598) is born in *Richard II*, his realistic, calculating, efficient, politically astute perform-ance directly antithetical to Richard's impractical, mercurial, meditative, and inept behavior. Bolingbroke is an opportunist, favored by fortune. A man of action and of few words, Bolingbroke presents a clear alternative to Richard when the two men appear together. If Richard is the actor as prima donna, Bolingbroke is the actor as director.

"Critical Evaluation" by Kenneth John Atchity

For Further Study

Evans, Gareth Lloyd. *The Upstart Crow: An Introduction to Shakespeare's Plays.* London: J. M. Dent and Sons, 1982. A comprehensive discussion of the dra-matic works of William Shakespeare. While the major emphasis is on critical reviews of the plays, there are also discussions of sources and information on the circumstances surrounding the writing of the plays.

Holderness, Graham, ed. *Shakespeare's History Plays: "Richard II" to "Henry V."* New York: St. Martin's Press, 1992. An anthology of critical works on Shake-speare's history plays. James L. Calderwood's "Richard II: Metadrama and the Fall of Speech" discusses the language used in the play and the power of that language as used by King Richard and his rival, Bolingbroke.

Leggatt, Alexander. *Shakespeare's Political Drama: The History Plays and the Roman Plays.* New York: Routledge, 1988. A discussion of the Shakespeare plays dealing with English history from the reign of King Henry II to that of Henry VIII, and with the three plays dealing with Roman history.

Pierce, Robert B. *Shakespeare's History Plays: The Family and the State.* Colum-bus: University of Ohio Press, 1971. A general discussion of Shakespeare's history plays. Pierce considers *Richard II* to be a direct forerunner of the plays on Henry IV and V.

Ribner, Irving. *The English History Play in the Age of Shakespeare.* 1957. Rev. ed. London: Methuen, 1965. A discussion of history plays in the Elizabethan era of English drama and Shakespeare's contributions in the field. Considers the development of the form and the sources.

Richard III

Type of plot: Historical
Time of plot: Fifteenth century
Locale: England
First performed: c. 1592-1593; first published, 1597; revised, 1623

Principal characters

EDWARD IV, the King of England
RICHARD, his brother, the Duke of Gloucester
GEORGE, his brother, the Duke of Clarence
QUEEN ELIZABETH, wife of Edward IV
LADY ANNE, the widow of the son of Henry VI and later the wife of Richard III
QUEEN MARGARET, the widow of Henry VI
EDWARD, the Prince of Wales and son of Edward IV
RICHARD, the Duke of York, another son of Edward IV
THE DUKE OF BUCKINGHAM, an accomplice of the Duke of Gloucester
LORD HASTINGS, a supporter of Prince Edward
LORD STANLEY, the Earl of Derby
SIR WILLIAM CATESBY, a court toady
HENRY TUDOR, the Earl of Richmond and later King Henry VII

The Story

After the conclusion of the wars between the houses of York and Lancaster, Edward IV was firmly restored to the throne. Before long, however, his treacherous brother Richard, the hunchbacked Duke of Gloucester, resumed his plans for gaining the throne. Craftily he removed one obstacle in his path when he turned the king against the third brother, the Duke of Clarence (whose given name was George) by telling the king of an ancient prophecy that his issue would be disinherited by one of the royal line whose name began with the letter G. Clarence was immediately arrested and taken to the Tower. Richard went to him, pretending sympathy, and advised him that the jealousy and hatred of Queen Elizabeth were responsible for his imprisonment. After promising to help his brother secure his freedom, Richard, as false in word as he was cruel in deed, gave orders that Clarence be stabbed in his cell and his body placed in a barrel of malmsey wine.

Hoping to make his position even stronger, Richard then made plans to marry Lady Anne, the widow of Prince Edward, the former Prince of Wales whose father was the murdered Henry VI. Edward had been slain by Richard and his brothers after the battles had ended, and Lady Anne and Henry's widow, Queen Margaret, were the only remaining members of the once powerful House of Lancaster still living in England. Intercepting Lady Anne at the funeral procession of Henry VI, Richard attempted to woo her. Although she hated and feared her husband's murderer, she was persuaded to accept an engagement ring when Richard insisted that it was for love of her that he had murdered her husband.

Richard went to the court, where Edward IV lay ill. There, he affected great sorrow and indignation over the news of the death of Clarence, thereby endearing himself to Lord Hastings and the Duke of Buckingham, who were friends of Clarence. He insinuated that Queen Elizabeth and her followers had turned the wrath of the king against Clarence, which brought about his death. Richard managed to convince everyone except Queen Margaret, who knew well what had really happened. Openly accusing him, she attempted to warn Buckingham and the others against Richard, but they ignored her.

Edward IV, ailing and depressed, tried to make peace among the factions in his realm, but he died before he could accomplish this end. His son, Prince Edward, was sent for from Ludlow to take his father's place. At the same time, Richard imprisoned Lord Grey, Lord Rivers, and Lord Vaughan, who were followers and relatives of the queen, and had them executed.

Terrified, Queen Elizabeth sought refuge for herself and her second son, the young Duke of York, with the archbishop of Canterbury. When Richard heard of the queen's action, he pretended much concern over the welfare of his brother's children and set himself up as their guardian. He managed to remove young York from the care of his mother and had him placed in the Tower along with Prince Edward. He announced that they were under his protection and that they would remain there only until Prince Edward had been crowned.

Learning from Sir William Catesby, a court toady, that Lord Hastings was a loyal adherent of the young prince, Richard contrived to remove that influential nobleman from the court by summoning him to a meeting ostensibly called to discuss plans for the coronation of the new king. Although Lord Stanley warned Hastings that ill luck awaited him if he went to the meeting, the trusting nobleman kept his appointment with Richard in the Tower. There, on the basis of trumped-up evidence, Richard accused Hastings of treason and ordered his immediate execution. Richard and Buckingham then dressed themselves in rusty old armor and pretended to the lord mayor that Hastings had been plotting against them; the lord mayor was convinced by their false protestations that the execution was justified.

Richard plotted to seize the throne for himself. Buckingham, supporting him, spoke in the Guildhall of the great immorality of the late King Edward and hinted that both the king and his children were illegitimate. Shocked, a citizens' committee headed by the lord mayor approached Richard and begged him to accept the crown. They found him in the company of two priests, with a prayer book in his hand. So impressed were they with his seeming piety, that they repeated their offer after he had hypocritically refused it. Pretending great reluctance, Richard finally accepted, after being urged by Buckingham, the lord mayor, and Catesby. Plans for an immediate coronation were made.

Lady Anne was interrupted during a visit to the Tower with Queen Elizabeth and the old Duchess of York and ordered to Westminster to be crowned Richard's queen. The three women heard with horror that Richard had ascended the throne; they were all the more suspicious of him because they had been prevented from seeing the young princes. Fearing the worst, they sorrowed among themselves and foresaw doom for the nation.

Soon after his coronation, Richard suggested to Buckingham that the two princes must be killed. When Buckingham balked at the order, Richard refused to consider his request to be elevated to the earldom of Hereford. Proceeding alone to secure the safety of his position, he hired Sir James Tyrrel, a discontented nobleman, to smother the children in their sleep. To make his position still more secure, Richard planned to marry Elizabeth of York, his own niece and daughter of

---

"The winter of our discontent"

Richard III, Act I, scene i, line 1

The great Samuel Johnson called this play "one of the most celebrated of our author's performances." Taken from Holinshed's *Chronicles*, this history play picks up where *Henry VI, Part III* leaves off. In that play, Richard, Duke of Gloucester, later King Richard III, stabbed King Henry VI, who in his dying breath predicted "more slaughter" for his murderer. With Richard's brother now installed as Edward IV, the physically malformed Richard (based on a description in Sir Thomas More's *History of King Richard the Third*, which Shakespeare is believed to have consulted) opens this play with a statement of triumph and with a revelation of his already-planned villainy. These famous lines play on the words "sun" and "son" as the badge of the House of York:

> *Richard.* Now is the winter of our discontent
> Made glorious summer by this sun of York;
> And all the clouds that low'r'd upon our house
> In the deep bosom of the ocean buried.
> Now are our brows bound with victorious wreaths,
> Our bruised arms hung up for monuments,
> Our stern alarums chang'd to merry meetings,
> Our dreadful marches to delightful measures,
> Grim-visag'd War hath smooth'd his wrinkled front;
> And now, in stead of mounting barbed steeds
> To fright the souls of fearful adversaries,
> He capers nimbly in a lady's chamber
> To the lascivious pleasing of a lute.
> But I, that am not shap'd for sportive tricks,
> Nor made to court an amorous looking-glass . . .
> I, that am curtail'd of this fair proportion,
> Cheated of feature by dissembling nature,
> Deform'd, unfinished, sent before my time
> Into this breathing world, scarce half made up, . . .
> I am determined to prove a villain. . . .

The 1995 film version of Richard III *sets Shakespeare's history play in the London of the 1930's. Here, King Richard (Ian McKellen, center) ascends to the throne.* (Courtesy of The Museum of Modern Art, Film Stills Archive)

the deceased Edward IV. Spreading the news that Queen Anne was mortally ill, he had her secretly murdered. He removed any threat from Clarence's heirs by imprisoning his son and by arranging a marriage for the daughter that considerably lowered her social status.

None of these precautions, however, could stem the tide of threats that were beginning to endanger Richard. In Brittany, Henry Tudor, the Earl of Richmond, gathered an army and invaded the country. When news of Richmond's landing at Milford reached London, Buckingham fled from Richard, whose cruelty and guilt were becoming apparent to even his closest friends and associates. Buckingham joined Richmond's forces, but shortly afterward Richard captured and executed him.

In a tremendous final battle, the armies of Richmond and Richard met on Bosworth Field. There, on the night before the encounter, all the ghosts of

Richard's victims appeared to him in his sleep and prophesied his defeat. They also foretold the Earl of Richmond's victory and success. The predictions held true. The next day, Richard, fighting desperately, was slain in battle by Richmond, after crying out the offer of his ill-gotten kingdom for a horse, his own having been killed under him. The earl mounted the throne and married Elizabeth of York, thus uniting the houses of York and Lancaster and ending the feud.

Critical Evaluation

Richard III is the last of a series of four plays that began with the three parts of *Henry VI*. These plays, though not strictly speaking a tetralogy, trace the bloody conflicts between the houses of Lancaster and York that came to be known as the Wars of the Roses and interpret the events leading up to the establishment of the Tudor dynasty. Despite Richard's painful experiences, the drama remains a history rather than a tragedy. Richard does not have the moral stature to be a tragic hero—who may murder, but only in violation of his own nature. Richard, by contrast, is a natural intriguer and murderer. Even as bloody a character as Macbeth contains within him an earlier, nobler Macbeth. Richard is too intelligent and self-aware, and too much in control of himself and those around him, to raise any of the moral ambiguities or dilemmas that are necessary to tragedy. Nor does Richard achieve any transcendent understanding of his actions.

Richard is, nevertheless, the dominating figure in the play and a fascinating one. All the other characters pale before him. The play is primarily a series of encounters between him and the opponents who surround him. Because Richard is physically small and has a humpback, many commentators have suggested that his behavior is a compensation for his physical deformity. Yet Richard is not a paranoid; everyone really does hate him. The deformity, a gross exaggeration of the historical reality, is more likely a physical representation of the grotesque shape of Richard's soul in a Renaissance world that took such correspondences seriously. In any case, Shakespeare created good theater by representing Richard as deformed, by which means his plots seem all the more grotesque.

Richard is also the master rhetorician in a play in which Shakespeare for the first time shows the full power of his language. Richard's speeches and the staccato exchanges among characters present the nervous energy that informs the more ambitious later plays. From his opening soliloquy, Richard fascinates not only with his language but also with his intelligence and candor. Until the very end, he is the stage manager of all that occurs. As a villain, he is unique in his total control and in the virtuosity of his performance. Even *Othello*'s Iago pales before him, for Richard, in soliloquies and asides, explains to the audience exactly what he is going to do and then carries it off.

In his opening speech, it is immediately clear that Richard will preside if not eventually prevail. He reveals not only his self-confident awareness of his own physical limitations and intellectual superiority but also a disarming perception of his own evil and isolation. His honest villainy is more total than Iago's both in the way that he is able to convince every character that he is his only friend and in the full step-by-step disclosure of his intentions to the audience. Since everyone is against him, he almost generates involuntary sympathy.

Shakespeare's plot is the relentless working out of Richard's schemes as they lead to his final destruction. His first confrontation, with Anne, is a model of Richard's abilities: The exchange begins with Anne's heaping abuse on her husband's murderer and ends with Richard extracting from her a promise of marriage. Anne is overwhelmed more by the brilliance and audacity of Richard's rhetorical wit than by the logic of his arguments. Yet the audience sees what an improbably

---

"My kingdom for a horse!"

Richard III, Act V, scene iv, line 7

Having won his way to the throne of England by a series of murders, Richard III finds himself brought to bay on Bosworth Field by Henry, Earl of Richmond, the future Henry VII. In the battle, Richard's horse is killed; he desperately seeks another, so that he can meet Richmond in hand-to-hand combat. In his anguish, shortly before his death at the hands of Richmond, he cries:

> *King Richard.* A horse, a horse, my kingdom for a horse!
> *Catesby.* Withdraw my lord, I'll help you to a horse.
> *King Richard.* Slave, I have set my life upon a cast,
>   And I will stand the hazard of the die.
>   I think there be six Richmonds in the field;
>   Five have I slain today instead of him.
>   A horse, a horse, my kingdom for a horse!

---

brief time Richard needs to be successful. It is part of the definition of this villain that he could succeed in such a wildly improbable adventure. Richard is frequently shown using those who hate him for his own benefit, in a perverse gratification of his ostensible desire for power and his submerged desire to be loved. Only his mother is able to see through to the total corruption of his heart.

Richard sees the path to kingship as being simply a matter of ingratiating himself with the right people and of murdering all those who stand in his way. He contracts the murder of Clarence in the tower amid a good bit of gallows humor, which sets the appropriately grim tone. Like a good Machiavel, he builds on past success and takes advantage of any fortuitous circumstances. He uses the death of Clarence to cast suspicion on Elizabeth and her party and to get the support of Buckingham, and he seizes on the death of Edward IV to have the influential nobles imprisoned and killed. Most events happen at Richard's instigation, and others he deftly turns to his own advantage. He efficiently removes all near claims to the throne by lies, innuendoes, and direct, vigorous action.

So appealing is his virtuosity and so faithful is he in informing the audience of his plans, that Shakespeare is even able to arouse sympathy for him when the tide of opposition to him swells under the leadership of Richmond. Shakespeare neatly figures the balance of power by setting up the opposing camps on opposite sides of the stage. The ominous appearances of the ghosts, to Richmond as well as Richard, portend that retribution is at hand. Although he is unnerved for the first time, Richard behaves with martial valor and struggles determinedly to the last. This last show of courage is the final complication of a consummate villain.

"Critical Evaluation" by Edward E. Foster

For Further Study

Farrell, Kirby. "Prophetic Behavior in Shakespeare's Histories." *Shakespeare Studies* 19 (1987): 17-40. Refers to historical prophecies in examining various kinds of prophecy in the play, both conscious and unconscious.

Hamel, Guy. "Time in Richard III." *Shakespeare Survey* 40 (1988): 41-49. Examines how time is used in the play and how Shakespeare constructs relationships between various references to time.

Hassel, R. Chris, Jr. *Songs of Death: Performance, Interpretation, and the Text of "Richard III."* Lincoln: University of Nebraska Press, 1987. Examines the play from various angles, including the theatrical and acting history of the play, the role of Providence, and the characters and their motives.

Miner, Madonne M. "'Neither Mother, Wife, nor England's Queen': The Roles of Women in *Richard III*." In *William Shakespeare's "Richard III,"* edited by Harold Bloom. New York: Chelsea House, 1988. The three sections of the essay examine the depth of characterization given to the women and their interactions. Also discusses the imagery of femaleness in the play.

Neill, Michael. "Shakespeare's Halle of Mirrors: Play, Politics, and Psychology in *Richard III*." In *William Shakespeare's "Richard III,"* edited by Harold Bloom. New York: Chelsea House, 1988. Examines the idea of theatricality in the play. Neill argues that Richard, like Hamlet, is an actor in the dramatic events that surround him.

Romeo and Juliet

Type of plot: Tragedy
Time of plot: Fifteenth century
Locale: Verona, Italy
First performed: c. 1595-1596; first published, 1597

Principal characters

ROMEO, son of the house of Montague
JULIET, daughter of the house of Capulet
FRIAR LAURENCE, a Franciscan
MERCUTIO, Romeo's friend
BENVOLIO, Romeo's friend
TYBALT, Lady Capulet's nephew
NURSE, in attendance on Juliet

The Story

In Verona, Italy, there lived two famous families, the Montagues and the Capulets. These two houses were deadly enemies, and their enmity did not stop at harsh words, but extended to bloody duels. Romeo, son of old Montague, thought himself in love with haughty Rosaline, a beautiful girl who did not return his affection. Hearing that Rosaline was to attend a great feast at the house of Capulet, Romeo and his trusted friend, Mercutio, donned masks and entered the great hall of their enemy as guests. Romeo was no sooner in the ballroom than he noticed the exquisite Juliet, Capulet's daughter, and instantly forgot his disdainful Rosaline. Romeo had never seen Juliet before, and in asking her name he aroused the suspicion of Tybalt, a fiery member of the Capulet clan. Tybalt drew his sword and faced Romeo. Old Capulet, coming upon the two men, parted them, and with the gentility that comes with age requested that they have no bloodshed at the feast. Tybalt, however, was angered that a Montague should take part in Capulet festivities and afterward nursed a grudge against Romeo.

Romeo went to Juliet, spoke in urgent courtliness to her, and asked if he might kiss her hand. She gave her permission, much impressed by this unknown gentleman whose affection for her was so evident. Romeo then begged to kiss her lips, and when she had no breath to object, he pressed her to him. They were interrupted by Juliet's nurse, who sent the young girl off to her mother. When she had gone, Romeo learned from the nurse that Juliet was a Capulet. He was stunned, for he was certain that this fact would mean his death. He could never give her up. Juliet, who had fallen instantly in love with Romeo, discovered that he was a Montague, the son of a hated house.

That night Romeo, too much in love to go home to sleep, stole to Juliet's house and stood in the orchard beneath a balcony that led to her room. To his surprise, he saw Juliet leaning over the railing above him. Thinking herself alone, she began to talk of Romeo and wished aloud that he were not a Montague. Hearing her words, Romeo could contain himself no longer, but spoke to her. She was frightened at first, and when she saw who it was she was confused and ashamed that he had overheard her confession. It was too late to pretend reluctance. Juliet freely admitted her passion, and the two exchanged vows of love. Juliet told Romeo that she would marry him and would send him word by nine o'clock the next morning to arrange for their wedding.

Romeo then went off to the monastery cell of Friar Laurence to enlist his help in the ceremony. The good friar was much impressed with Romeo's devotion. Thinking that the union of a Montague and a Capulet would dissolve the enmity between the two houses, he promised to marry Romeo and Juliet.

Early the next morning, while he was in company with his two friends, Benvolio and Mercutio, Romeo received Juliet's message, brought by her nurse. He told the old woman of his arrangement with Friar Laurence and bade her carry the word back to Juliet. The nurse gave her mistress the message. When Juliet appeared at the friar's cell at the appointed time, she and Romeo were married. Time was short, however, and Juliet had to hurry home. Before she left, Romeo promised that he would meet her in the orchard underneath the balcony after dark that night.

That same day, Romeo's friends, Mercutio and Benvolio, were loitering in the streets when Tybalt came by with some other members of the Capulet house. Tybalt, still holding his grudge against Romeo, accused Mercutio of keeping company with the hateful and villainous young Montague. Mercutio, proud of his friendship with Romeo, could not take insult lightly, for he was as hot-tempered when provoked as Tybalt. The two were beginning their heated quarrel when Romeo, who had just returned from his wedding, appeared. He was appalled at the situation because he knew that Juliet was fond of Tybalt, and he wished no injury to his wife's people. He tried in vain to settle the argument peaceably. Mercutio was infuriated by Romeo's soft words, and when Tybalt called Romeo a villain, Mercutio drew his sword and rushed to his friend's defense. Tybalt, the better swordsman, gave Mercutio a mortal wound. Romeo could try to settle the fight no longer. Enraged at the death of his friend, he rushed at Tybalt with drawn sword and killed him quickly. The fight soon brought crowds of people to the spot. For his part in the fray, Romeo was banished from Verona.

Hiding out from the police, he went, grief-stricken, to Friar Laurence's cell. The friar advised him to go to his wife that night, and then at dawn to flee to Mantua until the friar saw fit to publish the news of the wedding. Romeo consented to follow this advice. As darkness fell, he went to meet Juliet. When dawn appeared, heartsick Romeo left for Mantua.

Meanwhile, Juliet's father decided that it was time for his daughter to marry. Having not the slightest idea of her love for Romeo, the old man demanded that she accept her handsome and wealthy suitor, Paris. Juliet was horrified at her father's proposal but dared not tell him of her marriage because of Romeo's part in Tybalt's death. She feared that her husband would be instantly sought out and killed if her family learned of the marriage.

At first she tried to put off her father with excuses. Failing to persuade him, she went in dread to Friar Laurence to ask the good monk what she could do. Telling her to be brave, the friar gave her a small flask of liquid which he told her to swallow the night before her wedding to Paris. This liquid would make her appear to be dead for a certain length of time; her seemingly lifeless body would then be placed in an open tomb for a day or two, and during that time the friar would send for Romeo, who would rescue his bride when she awoke from the powerful effects of the draught. Then, together, the two would be able to flee Verona. Juliet almost lost courage over this desperate venture, but she promised to obey the friar. On the way home she met Paris and modestly promised to be his bride.

The great house of the Capulets had no sooner prepared for a lavish wedding than it became the scene of a mournful funeral. Juliet swallowed the strong liquid

---

"Star-crossed lovers"

Romeo and Juliet, Prologue, 1.6

This story of young love doomed to end in frustration and catastrophe has always been one of Shakespeare's most beloved works. Set in Italy during a hot summer, the play covers only one week in the lives of the feuding families, the Montagues and Capulets, and their two teenage children, Romeo, a Montague, and Juliet, a Capulet. In the Prologue that opens the play, a Chorus—similar to the choruses in classical Greek drama—sets the scene, the tragic action, and the consequence of the folly of the lovers' parents. The term "star-crossed" refers to another classical notion: that the "stars"—factors beyond the control of the two lovers—determined their tragic fate. However, when one considers that the lovers' fate is determined by all-too-human rivalry and hatred, is it possible that Shakespeare is calling this inevitability into question?

> *Chorus.* Two households both alike in dignity,
> In fair Verona, where we lay our scene,
> From ancient grudge break to new mutiny,
> Where civil blood makes civil hands unclean.
> From forth the fatal loins of these two foes,
> A pair of star-crossed lovers take their life;
> Whose misadventur'd piteous overthrows
> Doth with their death bury their parents' strife.
> The fearful passage of their death-marked love,
> And the continuance of their parents' rage,
> Which, but their children's end, naught could remove,
> Is now the two hours' traffic of our stage;
> The which if you with patient ears attend,
> What here shall miss, our toil shall strive to mend.

"What's in a name?"

Romeo and Juliet, Act II, scene ii, line 43

After meeting Juliet at a party and falling instantly in love, Romeo now stands in the dark beneath Juliet's window, enraptured at the sight of his beloved Juliet above him. She, unaware that he is listening, declares her love for Romeo and bewails the fact that he is a member of the rival Montague family. He feels that he should reveal his presence in the orchard but is too much bewitched. Instead of speaking to her, he debates with himself whether he should speak. While he remains silent, Juliet, pretending she is questioning Romeo, asks why her love should be victim to the mere accident of Romeo's family name.

> *Juliet.* 'Tis but thy name that is my enemy.
> Thou art thyself, though not a Montague.
> What's Montague? It is nor hand nor foot,
> Nor arm nor face, nor any other part
> Belonging to a man. O be some other name.
> What's in a name? That which we call a rose
> By any other word would smell as sweet;
> So Romeo would, were he not Romeo called,
> Retain that dear perfection which he owes
> Without that title. Romeo doff thy name,
> And for thy name, which is no part of thee,
> Take all myself.

and seemed lifeless. Her anguished family sadly placed her body in the tomb.

Meanwhile Friar Laurence wrote to Romeo in Mantua, telling him of the plan by which the lovers could make their escape together. These letters, however, failed to reach Romeo before word of Juliet's death arrived. He determined to go to Verona and take his last farewell of her as she lay in her tomb, and there, with the help of poison procured from an apothecary, to die by her side.

Reaching the tomb at night, Romeo was surprised to find a young man there. It was Paris, who had come to weep over his lost bride. Thinking Romeo a grave robber, he drew his sword. Romeo, mistaking Paris for a hated Capulet, warned him that he was desperate and armed. Paris, in loyalty to Juliet, fell upon Romeo, but Romeo killed him. By the light of a lantern, Romeo recognized Paris and, taking pity on one who had also loved Juliet, drew him into the tomb so that Paris too could be near her. Then Romeo went to the bier of his beautiful bride. Taking leave of her with a kiss, he drank the poison he had brought with him and soon died by her side.

It was near the time for Juliet to awaken from her deathlike sleep. The friar, hearing that Romeo had never received his letters, went himself to deliver Juliet from the tomb. When he arrived, he found Romeo dead. Juliet, waking, asked for her husband. Then, seeing him lying near her with an empty cup in his hands, she guessed what he had done. She tried to kiss some of the poison from his lips that she too might die, but failing in this, she unsheathed his dagger and without hesitation plunged it into her breast.

By this time a guard had come up. Seeing the dead lovers and the body of Paris, he rushed off in horror to spread the news. When the Capulets and Montagues arrived at the tomb, the friar told them of the unhappy fate which had befallen Romeo and Juliet, whose only sin had been to love. His account of their tender and beautiful romance shamed the two families, and over the bodies of their dead children they swore to end the feud of many years.

In Franco Zeffirelli's 1968 film production of Romeo and Juliet, *Romeo (Leonard Whiting, right) attempts to intercede as Tybalt (Michael York, left) duels with Mercutio (John McEnery, center) in a tragic skirmish between the Capulets and the Montagues that prefigures the deaths of the star-crossed lovers Romeo and Juliet.* (Courtesy of The Museum of Modern Art, Film Stills Archive)

Critical Evaluation

This story of star-crossed lovers is one of William Shakespeare's tenderest dramas. Shakespeare is sympathetic toward Romeo and Juliet, and in attributing their tragedy to fate, rather than to a flaw in their characters, he raised them to heights near perfection, as well as running the risk of creating pathos, not tragedy. They are both sincere, kind, brave, loyal, virtuous, and desperately in love, and their tragedy is greater because of their innocence. The feud between the lovers' families represents the fate which Romeo and Juliet are powerless to overcome. The lines capture in poetry the youthful and simple passion which characterizes the play.

One of the most popular plays of all time, *Romeo and Juliet* was Shakespeare's second tragedy (after *Titus Andronicus* of 1594, a failure). Consequently, the play shows the sometimes artificial lyricism of early comedies such as *Love's Labour's*

Lost (c. 1594-1595) and *A Midsummer Night's Dream* (c. 1595-1596), while its character development predicts the direction of the playwright's artistic maturity. In Shakespeare's usual fashion, he based his story on sources that were well known in his day: Masuccio Salernitano's *Novellino* (1476), William Painter's *The Palace of Pleasure* (1566-1567), and, especially, Arthur Brooke's poetic *The Tragical History of Romeus and Juliet* (1562). Shakespeare reduces the time of the action from the months it takes in Brooke's work to a few compact days.

In addition to following the conventional five-part structure of a tragedy, Shakespeare employs his characteristic alternation, from scene to scene, between taking the action forward and retarding it, often with comic relief, to heighten the dramatic impact. Although in many respects the play's structure recalls that of the *de casibus* genre concerning the fall of powerful men, its true prototype is tragedy as employed by Geoffrey Chaucer in *Troilus and Criseyde* (c. 1382)—a fall into unhappiness, on the part of more or less ordinary people, after a fleeting period of happiness. The fall is caused traditionally and in Shakespeare's play by the workings of fortune. Insofar as *Romeo and Juliet* is a tragedy, it is a tragedy of fate rather than of a tragic flaw. Although the two lovers have weaknesses, it is not their faults, but their unlucky stars, that destroy them. As the friar comments at the end, "A greater power than we can contradict/ Hath thwarted our intents."

"A plague on both your houses!"

Romeo and Juliet, Act III, scene i, line 102

The time is the day after the masked ball at which Romeo met and fell in love with Juliet. Mercutio and Benvolio, friends of Romeo, tease him about his whereabouts the night before. Benvolio is a quiet man, but Mercutio is hot-tempered. The three are walking on the street, and the day is hot, when suddenly they meet a group of young Capulets. A fight begins, and Romeo tries to stop it. Tybalt, a Capulet, strikes down Mercutio. Now dying, Mercutio curses the feuding houses of Montague and Capulet, describing the wound that will kill him:

> *Mercutio.* . . . 'tis not so deep as a well, nor so wide as a church door, but 'tis enough, 'twill serve. Ask for me tomorrow, and you shall find me a grave man. I am peppered, I warrant, for this world. A plague on both your houses!

Shakespeare succeeds in having the thematic structure closely parallel the dramatic form of the play. The principal theme is that of the tension between the two houses, and all the other oppositions of the play derive from that central one. Thus, romance is set against revenge, love against hate, day against night, sex against war, youth against age, and "tears to fire." Juliet's soliloquy in Act III, scene ii makes it clear that it is the strife between her family and Romeo's that has turned Romeo's love to death. If, at times, Shakespeare seems to forget the family theme in his lyrical fascination with the lovers, that fact only sets off their suffering all the more poignantly against the background of the senseless and arbitrary strife between the Capulets and Montagues. For the families, after all, the story has a classically comic ending; their feud is buried with the lovers—which seems to be the intention of the fate that compels the action.

The lovers never forget their families; their consciousness of the conflict leads to another central theme in the play, that of identity. Romeo questions his identity to Benvolio early in the play, and Juliet asks him, "Wherefore art thou Romeo?" At her request he offers to change his name and to be defined only as one star-crossed with her. Juliet, too, questions her identity, when she speaks to the nurse after Romeo's slaying of Tybalt. Romeo later asks the friar to help him locate the lodging of his name so that he may cast it from his "hateful mansion," bringing a plague upon his own house in an ironic fulfillment of Mercutio's dying curse. Only when they are in their graves, together, do the two lovers find peace from the persecution of being Capulet and Montague; they are remembered by their first names only, an ironic proof that their story had the beneficial political influence that the Prince, who wants the feud to end, wishes.

Likewise, the style of the play alternates between poetic gymnastics and pure and simple lines of deep emotion. The unrhymed iambic pentameter is filled with conceits, puns, and wordplay, presenting both lovers as very well-spoken young-sters. Their verbal wit, in fact, is not Shakespeare's rhetorical excess but part of their characters. It fortifies the impression the audience has of their spiritual natures, showing their love as an intellectual appreciation of beauty combined with physical passion. Their first dialogue, for example, is a sonnet divided between them. In no other early play is the imagery as lush and complex, making unforget-table the balcony speech in which Romeo describes Juliet as the sun, Juliet's nightingale-lark speech, her comparison of Romeo to the "day in night," which Romeo then develops as he observes, at dawn, "more light and light, more dark and dark our woes."

At the beginning of the play Benvolio describes Romeo as a "love-struck swain" in the typical pastoral fashion. He is, as the cliché has it, in love with love (Rosaline's name is not even mentioned until much later). He is youthful energy seeking an outlet; sensitive appreciation seeking a beautiful object. Mercutio and the friar comment on his fickleness. The sight of Juliet immediately transforms Romeo's immature and erotic infatuation to true and constant love. He matures more quickly than anyone around him realizes; only the audience understands the process, since Shakespeare makes Romeo introspective and articulate in his mono-logues. Even in love, however, Romeo does not reject his former romantic ideals. When Juliet comments, "You kiss by th' book," she is being astutely perceptive; Romeo's death is the death of an idealist, not of a foolhardy youth. He knows what he is doing, his awareness growing from his comment after slaying Tybalt, "O, I am Fortune's fool."

Juliet is equally quick-witted, and also has early premonitions of their sudden love's end. She is made uniquely charming by her combination of girlish innocence with a winsome foresight that is "wise" when compared to the superficial feelings expressed by her father, mother, and Count Paris. Juliet, moreover, is realistic as well as romantic. She knows how to exploit her womanly softness, making the audience feel both poignancy and irony when the friar remarks, at her arrival in the wedding chapel, "O, so light a foot/ Will ne'er wear out the everlasting flint!" It takes a strong person to carry out the friar's stratagem, after all; Juliet succeeds in the ruse partly because everyone else considers her weak in body and in will. She is a subtle actress, telling the audience after dismissing her mother and the nurse, "My dismal scene I needs must act alone." Her quiet intelligence makes the audience's tragic pity all the stronger when her "scene" becomes reality.

Shakespeare provides his lovers with effective dramatic foils in the characters of Mercutio, the nurse, and the friar. The play, nevertheless, remains forever that of "Juliet and her Romeo."

"Critical Evaluation" by Kenneth John Atchity

For Further Study

Battenhouse, Roy W. *Shakespearean Tragedy: Its Art and Its Christian Premises.* Bloomington: Indiana University Press, 1969. Argues that in *Romeo and Juliet*, Shakespeare shows a mistrust of carnal love, which leads the protagonists to suicide and damnation; the suicides in the tomb at the end of the play are an inversion of the Easter story.

Cartwright, Kent. *Shakespearean Tragedy and Its Double: The Rhythms of Audience Response.* University Park: Pennsylvania State University Press, 1991. Examines how audiences respond to Shakespeare's tragedies. Shows how an audience of *Romeo and Juliet* usually identifies strongly with the lovers, although the play compels detachment.

Evans, Robert. *The Osier Cage; Rhetorical Devices in "Romeo and Juliet."* Lexington: University Press of Kentucky, 1966. Explores the style of *Romeo and Juliet*, particularly Shakespeare's use of opposites such as love and violence, darkness and light, and appearance and reality.

Watts, Cedric. *Romeo and Juliet.* Boston: Twayne, 1991. One of the best starting places. Contains information on the history of the play and discusses its themes, sources, and characters.

Wells, Stanley, ed. *The Cambridge Companion to Shakespeare Studies.* Cambridge, England: Cambridge University Press, 1986. All studies of Shakespeare should begin with this book. Includes excellent chapters on the poet's life, the beliefs of Elizabethan England, and reviews of scholarship in the field.

The Taming of the Shrew

Type of plot: Comedy
Time of plot: Sixteenth century
Locale: Padua, Italy
First performed: c. 1593-1594; first published, 1623

Principal characters

BAPTISTA, a rich gentleman of Padua
KATHERINA, his shrewish daughter
BIANCA, another daughter
PETRUCHIO, Katherina's suitor
LUCENTIO, a student in love with Bianca
TRANIO, his servant
VINCENTIO, Lucentio's father
GREMIO and
HORTENSIO, Lucentio's rivals
A PEDANT

The Story

As a joke, a beggar was carried, while asleep, to the house of a noble lord and there dressed in fine clothes and waited on by many servants. The beggar was told that he was a rich man who, in a demented state, had imagined himself to be a beggar, but who was now restored to his senses. The lord and his court had great sport with the poor fellow, to the extent of dressing a page as the beggar's rich and beautiful wife and presenting the supposed woman to him as his dutiful and obedient spouse. The beggar, in his stupidity, assumed his new role as though it were his own, and he and his lady settled down to watch a play prepared for their enjoyment.

Lucentio and Tranio, his servant, had journeyed to Padua so that Lucentio could study in that ancient city. Tranio persuaded his master that life was not all study and work and that he should find pleasures also in his new residence. On their arrival in the city, Lucentio and Tranio encountered Baptista and his daughters, Katherina and Bianca. These three were accompanied by Gremio and Hortensio, young gentlemen both in love with gentle Bianca. Baptista, however, would not permit his younger daughter to marry until someone should take Katherina off of his hands. Although Katherina was wealthy and beautiful, she was such a shrew that no suitor would have her. Baptista, not knowing how to control his sharp-tongued daughter, announced that Gremio or Hortensio must find a husband for Katherina before either could woo Bianca. He charged them also to find tutors for the two girls, that they might be skilled in music and poetry.

Unobserved, Lucentio and Tranio witnessed this scene. At first sight, Lucentio also fell in love with Bianca and determined to have her for himself. His first act was to change clothes with Tranio, so that the servant appeared to be the master. Lucentio then disguised himself as a tutor in order to woo Bianca without her father's knowledge.

About the same time, Petruchio came to Padua. He was a rich and noble man of Verona, come to Padua to visit his friend Hortensio and to find for himself a rich wife. Hortensio told Petruchio of his love for Bianca and of her father's decree that she could not marry until a husband had been found for Katherina. Petruchio declared that the stories told about spirited Katherina were to his liking, particularly the account of her great wealth, and he expressed a desire to meet her. Hortensio proposed that Petruchio seek Katherina's father and present his family's name and history. Hortensio, meanwhile, planned to disguise himself as a tutor and thus plead his own cause with Bianca.

The situation grew confused. Lucentio was disguised as a tutor and his servant Tranio was dressed as Lucentio. Hortensio was also disguised as a tutor. Petruchio was to ask for Katherina's hand. Also, unknown to anyone but Katherina, Bianca loved neither Gremio nor Hortensio and swore that she would never marry rather than accept one or the other as her husband.

Petruchio easily secured Baptista's permission to marry his daughter Katherina, for the poor man was only too glad to have his older daughter finally wed. Petruchio's courtship was a strange one indeed, a battle of wits, words, and wills. Petruchio was determined to bend Katherina to his will, but Katherina scorned and berated him with a vicious tongue. Nevertheless, she had to obey her father's wish and marry him, and the nuptial day was set. Then Gremio and Tranio, the latter still believed to be Lucentio, vied with each other for Baptista's permission to marry Bianca. Tranio won because he claimed more gold and vaster lands than Gremio could declare. In the meantime, Hortensio and Lucentio, both disguised as tutors, wooed Bianca.

As part of the taming process, Petruchio arrived late for his wedding, and when he did appear he wore old and tattered clothes. Even during the wedding ceremony Petruchio acted like a madman, stamping, swearing, and cuffing the priest. Immediately afterward he dragged Katherina away from the wedding feast and took her to his country home, there to continue his scheme to break her to his will. He gave her no food and no time for sleep, while always pretending that nothing was good enough for her. In fact, he all but killed her with kindness. Before he was through, Katherina agreed that the moon was the sun, that an old man was a woman.

Bianca fell in love with Lucentio, whom she thought to be her tutor. In chagrin, Hortensio threw off his disguise and he and Gremio forswore their love for any girl so fickle. Tranio, still hoping to win her for himself, found an old pedant to act the part of Vincentio, Lucentio's father. The pretended father argued his son's cause with Baptista until that lover of gold promised his daughter's hand to Lucentio as he thought, but in reality to Tranio. When Lucentio's true father appeared on the scene, he was considered an impostor and almost put in jail for his deceit. The real

Lucentio and Bianca, meanwhile, had been secretly married. Returning from the church with his bride, he revealed the whole plot to Baptista and the others. At first Baptista was angry at the way in which he had been duped, but Vincentio spoke soothingly and soon cooled his rage.

Hortensio, in the meantime, had married a rich widow. To celebrate these weddings, Lucentio gave a feast for all the couples and the fathers. After the ladies had retired, the three newly married men wagered one hundred pounds each that his own wife would most quickly obey his commands. Lucentio sent first for Bianca, but she sent word that she would not come. Then Hortensio sent for his wife, but she too refused to obey his summons. Petruchio then ordered Katherina to appear, and she came instantly to do his bidding. At his request she also forced Bianca and Hortensio's wife to go to their husbands. Baptista was so delighted with his daughter's meekness and willing submission that he added another twenty thousand crowns to her dowry. Katherina told them all that a wife should live only to serve her husband and that a woman's heart and tongue ought to be as soft as her body. Petruchio had tamed the shrew forever.

Critical Evaluation

Although it is not possible to determine the dates of composition of William Shakespeare's plays with absolute certainty, it is generally agreed that the early comedy *The Taming of the Shrew* was probably written after *The Two Gentlemen of Verona* (c. 1594-1595) and before *A Midsummer Night's Dream* (c. 1595-1596).

Richard Burton as Petruchio and Elizabeth Taylor as Katherina in the 1967 film production of The Taming of the Shrew. *(Courtesy of The Museum of Modern Art, Film Stills Archive)*

Even at this early date, Shakespeare shows himself to be a master of plot construction. Disregarding the classical unity of action, which forbade subplots, for a more enlightened concept of unity, Shakespeare creates two distinct lines of action, each derived from a different source, and integrates them into a unified dramatic whole. A single source for the main plot of Petruchio's taming of Katherina has not been found. Misogynistic stories abounded in Shakespeare's time, stories of men exercising their "rightful" dominance over women. One in particular, a ballad entitled *A Merry Jest of a Shrewd and Curst Wife, Lapped in Morel's Skin* (printed c. 1550) tells the story of a shrewish wife who is beaten bloody by her husband and then wrapped in the salted skin of a plow horse named Morel. Like Katherina, this wife has a younger sister who is the favorite of their father. If Shakespeare used this ballad as a source for the main plot of this play, it is obvious that he toned it down greatly, substituting psychological tactics for physical brutality. Nevertheless, some stage versions of *The Taming of the Shrew* have emphasized Petruchio's physical mistreatment of Katherina. The eighteenth century English actor David Garrick as Petruchio threatened Katherina with a whip. Some critics today see in this play an unacceptable male chauvinism. One must remember that Shakespeare lived and wrote in a patriarchal world in which the father ruled the family and the husband ruled the wife. Much in this play reflects the patriarchal nature of Elizabethan society, but Katherina's strength of character may mitigate charges of male chauvinism against Shakespeare.

The source for the underplot, the wooing of Bianca by various suitors, is George Gascoigne's *Supposes* (1573). The heroine in Gascoigne's play is made pregnant by her lover, but she remains completely chaste in *The Taming of the Shrew*. Shakespeare also dispensed with the character of the bawdy Nurse of his source and modified the harsh satire that Gascoigne directed at Dr. Cleander, the pantaloon, who represents the degeneracy of "respectable" society. For this character Shakespeare substitutes Gremio, a wealthy old citizen of Padua who would marry Bianca but is thwarted by the young Lucentio. These changes are typical of Shakespeare, in whose plays sexual relationships are virtually always sanctified by marriage and in whose comedies satire is usually genial or at least counterbalanced by good humor.

The Taming of the Shrew is the only play by Shakespeare which has an "induction," or anterior section that introduces the main action. In the induction, which is set in Shakespeare's native Warwickshire, an unconscious drunken tinker is taken to the house of a lord, dressed in fine clothes, and made to think he is a lord who has been comatose for fifteen years. Convinced he is indeed a lord, Sly begins to speak in blank verse and agrees to watch a play performed by traveling players, namely *The Taming of the Shrew*. At the end of the first scene, Sly is already bored with the play and exclaims "Would 'twere done!" He is never heard from again.

This induction, which at first sight appears irrelevant, dramatizes a recurring theme in all of Shakespeare's comedies and the central theme of this play, namely the deceptiveness of appearances. Sly mistakes the opulence of his surroundings for his true reality and thinks he is a lord rather than a poor tinker of Burton-heath.

"Kill a wife with kindness"

The Taming of the Shrew, Act IV, scene i, line 211

Having married the shrewish Katherina and brought her home, Petruchio is determined to "tame" her. He acts abusively, cuffing his servants and complains about everything on the pretense that it is not good enough for his bride. Katherina protests that things are not as bad as he makes them out to be, but he continues his crazy behavior. Alone, he explains how his wife must "come, and know her keeper's call." He then discusses his plans for the taming of Katherina:

> *Petruchio.* Last night she slept not, nor tonight she shall not.
> As with the meat, some undeserved fault
> I'll find about the making of the bed;
> And here I'll fling the pillow, there the bolster,
> This way the coverlet, another way the sheets.
> Ay, and amid this burly I intend
> That all is done in reverent care of her;
> And in conclusion, she shall watch all night,
> And if she chance to nod, I'll rail and brawl,
> And with the clamour keep her still awake.
> This is a way to kill a wife with kindness.

In the play proper, many of the characters pose as people other than themselves and are responded to in guises not of their true nature. In the subplot, Lucentio, in order to woo Bianca, trades places with his servant Tranio and further takes on the role of Cambio, a schoolmaster hired by Gremio, to woo Bianca for himself. Hortensio, another suitor to Bianca, assumes the role of Litio, a music teacher, to gain access to her. Late in the action, a pedant is coerced to play the role of Vincentio, the father of Lucentio. When the true Vincentio appears on the scene, the disguises of the subplot are finally revealed.

In the major plot, the theme of illusion is not as literal but it is no less important. Katherina, the shrew, has played her part for so long that everyone believes she is an irritable and hateful woman. Conversely, Bianca, her sister, is universally regarded as sweet and of a mild disposition. Neither image is totally true. Bianca has to be told twice by her father to enter the house in the first scene, indicating that she is not as tractable as she is thought to be. Katherina, in her first meeting with Petruchio, does not protest when he tells her father that they will be married on Sunday. She remains silent, indicating that she has tacitly accepted him. In the final scene, the true natures of Katherina and Bianca come out for everyone to see. It is Bianca who is the disobedient wife. It is Katherina who gives a disquisition on the perfect Elizabethan wife. Whether her speech is to be taken at face value or as a statement of irony is debatable.

Petruchio has come "to wive it wealthily in Padua." He is a rip-roaring fortune hunter, who will wed any woman who is rich enough "Be she as foul as was Florentius's love/ As old as Sibyl, and as curst and shrewd/ As Socrates' Xanthippe." He is overwhelming in speech and manner and completely unintimidated by Katherina's reputation as a shrew. He annihilates her resistance by his outlandish actions. At his country house outside Padua, he mistreats his servants unconscionably, demonstrating to Katherina the kind of behavior that she has displayed. He then deprives her of sleep, food, and drink, as one would tame a falcon. Finally, he deprives her of fine clothing. By his example, she is led to see her own unreasonable behavior. She at last decides to submit to her husband's demands rather than persist in her perverse behavior. At the same time, however, some critics have pointed out that Katherina also "tames" Petruchio: In joining him in the marriage relationship, she wins his love and cooperation, and at the play's end, the contest to see "whose wife is most obedient" (Act V, scene ii, line 67) is won by Katherina and Petruchio in collusion against the other couples.

Regardless of whether one sees the play as chauvinistic or a tribute to the marriage partnership, *The Taming of the Shrew* remains a perennially popular stage production because its subject matter—the eternal issues surrounding relationships between men and women, and a strikingly "modern" concern with women's identities and roles—can be performed and interpreted in various ways depending on the inclinations of the play's directors.

"Critical Evaluation" by Robert G. Blake

For Further Study

Bloom, Harold, ed. *William Shakespeare's "The Taming of the Shrew": Modern Critical Interpretations.* New York: Chelsea House, 1988. Not for the fainthearted, this collection of essays is useful for indicating the trends of modern scholarship regarding the play. It contains a number of essays utilizing modern critical perspectives such as feminism and deconstruction.

Greenfield, Thelma N. "The Transformation of Christopher Sly." *Philological Quarterly* 33 (1954): 34-42. Greenfield argues that the importance of the Christopher Sly framing device lies in its establishment of the juxtaposition between reality and appearance evident also through the main action of the play.

Holderness, Graham. *Shakespeare in Performance: "The Taming of the Shrew."* Manchester, England: Manchester University Press, 1989. Holderness examines four different productions of the play, including the 1966 Franco Zeffirelli movie and the 1980 television adaptation starring John Cleese. The book is valuable in that it stresses the importance of the performance of Shakespeare's works.

Huston, J. Dennis. "'To Make a Puppet': Play and Play-Making in *The Taming of the Shrew.*" *Shakespeare Studies* 9 (1967): 73-88. Huston asserts that Shakespeare repeatedly shocks the audience by presenting a series of false starts (that of Christopher Sly being the first). This reflects Katherina's experience as she is tamed by Petruchio.

Wells, Stanley, ed. *The Cambridge Companion to Shakespeare Studies.* Cambridge, England: Cambridge University Press, 1986. This is where all studies of Shakespeare should begin. It includes excellent chapters introducing the poet's biography, conventions and beliefs of Elizabethan England, and reviews of scholarship in the field.

The Tempest

Type of plot: Romance or tragicomedy
Time of plot: Fifteenth century
Locale: An island in the sea
First performed: 1611; first published, 1623

Principal characters

PROSPERO, the rightful Duke of Milan
MIRANDA, his daughter
FERDINAND, son of the King of Naples
ARIEL, a spirit, Prospero's servant
CALIBAN, Prospero's slave
ALONSO, the King of Naples
SEBASTIAN, Alonso's brother
ANTONIO, the Duke of Milan, Prospero's brother
GONZALO, a philosopher, who saved the lives of Prospero and Miranda

The Story

Alonso, the King of Naples, was returning from the wedding of his daughter to a foreign prince when his ship was overtaken by a terrible storm. In his company were Duke Antonio of Milan and other gentlemen of the court. As the gale rose in fury and it seemed certain the vessel would split and sink, the noble travelers were forced to abandon ship and trust to fortune in the open sea.

The tempest was no chance disturbance of wind and wave. It had been raised by a wise magician, Prospero, when the ship sailed close to an enchanted island on which he and his lovely daughter, Miranda, were the only human inhabitants. Theirs was a sad and curious history. Prospero was the rightful Duke of Milan, but being devoted more to the study of philosophy and magic than to affairs of state, he had given much power to his ambitious brother, Antonio, who twelve years earlier had seized the dukedom with the aid of the crafty Neapolitan king. Prospero and his small daughter had been set adrift in a boat by the conspirators, and they would have perished miserably had not Gonzalo, an honest counselor, secretly stocked the frail craft with food, clothing, and some of the books Prospero valued most.

The exiles drifted at last to an island that had been the refuge of Sycorax, an evil sorceress. There Prospero found Caliban, her son, a strange, misshapen creature of brute intelligence, able only to hew wood and draw water. Also there were many good spirits of air and water who became obedient to Prospero's will when he freed

269

Anthony Hopkins as Prospero (right), with Stephanie Zimbalist as Miranda (left), Michael Bond as Caliban (center foreground), and Brent Carver as Ariel (center back), in a production of The Tempest *at Los Angeles's Mark Taper Forum.* (Nancy Hereford, courtesy of the Mark Taper Forum)

them from torments to which the sorceress Sycorax had condemned them. Chief among these was Ariel, a lively sprite.

Prospero, having used his magic arts to draw the ship bearing King Alonso and Duke Antonio close to his enchanted island, ordered Ariel to bring the whole party safely ashore, singly or in scattered groups. Ferdinand, King Alonso's son, was moved by Ariel's singing to follow the sprite to Prospero's rocky cell. Miranda, who did not remember ever having seen another human face than her father's bearded one, at first sight fell deeply in love with the handsome young prince, and he with her. Prospero was pleased to see the young people so attracted to each other, but he concealed his pleasure, spoke harshly to them, and, to test Ferdinand's mettle, commanded him to perform menial tasks.

Meanwhile Alonso, Sebastian, Antonio, and Gonzalo wandered sadly along the beach, the king in despair because he believed his son drowned. Ariel, invisible in the air, played solemn music, lulling to sleep all except Sebastian and Antonio. Drawing apart, they planned to kill the king and his counselor and make Sebastian tyrant of Naples. Watchful Ariel awakened the sleepers before the plotters could act.

"We are such stuff as dreams are made on"

The Tempest, Act IV, scene i, lines 156-157

Prospero, a magician, rules a mysterious island, commanding spirits of the air, including Ariel and other sprites and wonders. He has a lovely daughter named Miranda. The magician causes a tempest which drives a ship onto shore. All on it survive, but Prospero causes a handsome young prince, Ferdinand, to be separated from the others, and has Ariel lead Ferdinand to him. Ferdinand, enchanted, sees Miranda and falls in love with her, and she with him. Now, before his cell, Prospero presents a wedding pageant for them, enacted by spirits. Suddenly, he puts an end to this pageant with the famous speech which compares life to a dream or a play:

> *Prospero.* Our revels now are ended. These our actors,
> As I foretold you, were all spirits, and
> All melted into air, into thin air, . . .
> And like this insubstantial pageant faded
> Leave not a rack behind. We are such stuff
> As dreams are made on; and our little life
> Is rounded with a sleep.

On another part of the island, Caliban, carrying a load of wood, met Trinculo, the king's jester, and Stephano, the royal butler, both drunk. In rude sport they offered drink to Caliban. Tipsy, the loutish monster declared he would be their slave forever.

Like master, like servant. Just as Sebastian and Antonio had plotted to murder Alonso, so Caliban, Trinculo, and Stephano schemed to kill Prospero and become rulers of the island. Stephano was to be king, Miranda his consort, and Trinculo and Caliban would be viceroys. Unseen, Ariel listened to their evil designs and reported the plan to Prospero.

Miranda had disobeyed her father's injunction on interrupting Ferdinand in his task of rolling logs and the two exchanged lovers' vows, which were overheard by the magician. Satisfied with the prince's declarations of devotion and constancy, Prospero left them to their happy company. He and Ariel went to mock Alonso and his followers by showing them a banquet that vanished before the hungry castaways could taste the rich dishes. Then Ariel, disguised as a harpy, reproached them for their conspiracy against Prospero. Convinced that Ferdinand's death was punishment for his own crime, Alonso was moved to repentance for his cruel deed.

Returning to his cave, Prospero released Ferdinand from his task. While spirits dressed as Ceres, Iris, Juno, nymphs, and reapers entertained Miranda and the prince with a pastoral masque, Prospero suddenly remembered the schemes being entertained by Caliban and the drunken servants. Told to punish the plotters, after tempting them with a display of kingly garments, Ariel and his fellow spirits, now in the shapes of fierce hunting dogs, drove the plotters howling with pain and rage through bogs and brier patches.

Convinced that the King of Naples and his false brother Antonio had repented the evil deed they had done him years before, Prospero commanded Ariel to bring them into the enchanted circle before the magician's cell. With strange, beautiful music, Ariel lured the king, Antonio, Sebastian, and Gonzalo to the cell, where they were astonished to see Prospero in the appearance and dress of the wronged Duke of Milan. Prospero confirmed his identity, ordered Antonio to restore his dukedom, and severely warned Sebastian not to plot further against the king. Finally, he took the repentant Alonso into the cave, where he saw Ferdinand and Miranda playing chess. A joyful reunion followed between father and son, and the king was completely captivated by the beauty and grace of Miranda. During this scene of reconciliation and rejoicing, Ariel appeared with the master and boatswain of the wrecked ship, who reported the vessel safe and ready to continue the voyage. Ariel drove the three grotesque conspirators into the cell, where Prospero released them from their spell. Caliban was ordered to prepare food and set it before the guests, and Prospero invited his brother and the King of Naples and his entourage to spend the night in his cave.

Before he left the island, Prospero dismissed Ariel from his service, leaving that sprite free to wander as he wished. Ariel promised calm seas and auspicious winds for the voyage back to Naples and Milan, from where Prospero would journey to take possession of his lost dukedom and to witness the marriage of his daughter and Prince Ferdinand.

Critical Evaluation

Written toward the close of William Shakespeare's career, *The Tempest* is a work of fantasy and courtly romance, the story of a wise old magician, his beautiful, unworldly daughter, a gallant young prince, and a cruel, scheming brother. It contains all elements of a fairy tale in which ancient wrongs are righted and true lovers live happily ever after. The play is also one of poetic atmosphere and allegory. Beginning with a storm and peril at sea, it ends on a note of serenity and joy. None of Shakespeare's other dramas holds so much of the author's mature reflection on life itself.

Early critics of *The Tempest*, concerned with meaning, attempted to establish symbolic correlations between the characters Prospero, Ariel, Caliban, and Miranda and such qualities as imagination, fancy, brutality, and innocence. Others considered the play in terms of its spectacle and music, comparing it to the court masque or the Italian *commedia dell'arte*. Most critics read into Prospero's control and direction of all the characters—which climaxes with the famous speech in which he gives up his magic wand—Shakespeare's own dramatic progress and final farewell to the stage.

In the mid-twentieth century, criticism began to explore different levels of action and meaning, focusing on such themes as illusion versus reality, freedom versus slavery, revenge versus forgiveness, time, and self-knowledge. Some suggested that the enchanted island where the shipwreck occurs is a symbol of life itself: an enclosed arena wherein are enacted a range of human passions, dreams, conflicts, and self-discoveries. Such a wide-angled perspective satisfies both the casual reader wishing to be entertained and the serious scholar examining different aspects of Shakespeare's art and philosophy.

This latter view is consonant with one of Shakespeare's principal techniques, which he employs in all of his work: The analogy between microcosm and macrocosm. This Elizabethan way of looking at things simply meant that the human world mirrored the universe. In the major tragedies, this correspondence is shown in the pattern between order and disorder, usually with violent acts (the murder of Caesar, the usurpation of the throne by Richard III, Claudius' murder of Hamlet's father, Macbeth's killing of Duncan) correlated with a sympathetic disruption of order in the world of nature. Attendant upon such human events therefore are such natural and supernatural phenomena as earthquakes, strange beasts, unaccountable storms, voices from the sky, and witches.

The idea that the world is but an extension of the mind, and that the cosmic order in turn is reflected in human beings, gives validity to diverse interpretations of *The Tempest* and, as a matter of fact, encompasses many of them. The initial storm or "tempest" invoked by Prospero, which wrecks the ship, finds analogy in Antonio's long-past usurpation of Prospero's dukedom and his setting Prospero and Miranda

---

"O brave new world that has such people in it!"

The Tempest, Act V, sc i, 183-184

Prospero, former Duke of Milan and a magician who lives, with his daughter Miranda, on a magic island, foresees the arrival of his arch-enemies who usurped his power in Italy: his brother Antonio and the King of Naples, Alonso. After creating a storm in which these villains and their company are shipwrecked on the island, Prospero causes various misadventures to befall them and finally has everyone come to him. He reveals himself and forgives all. Miranda, who, for the first time in her life, is seeing people other than her father and the monster Caliban, is innocently delighted with the idea of a world with such inhabitants:

> *Miranda.* O wonder!
> How many goodly creatures are there here,
> How beauteous mankind is. O brave new world
> That has such people in it!
> *Prospero.* 'Tis new to thee.

adrift at sea in a storm in the hope they would perish. When, years later, the court party—Alonso, Sebastian, Antonio, and Ferdinand, along with the drunken Stephano and Trinculo—is cast upon the island, its "meanderings," pitfalls, and enchantments make it a place where everyone will go through a learning process and most come to greater self-knowledge.

Illusions on this island, which include Ariel's disguises, the disappearing banquet, and the line of glittering costumes that delude Stephano, Trinculo, and Caliban, find counterparts in the characters' illusions about themselves. Antonio has come to believe he is the rightful duke; Sebastian and Antonio, deluded by ambition, plan to kill Alonso and Gonzalo and make Sebastian tyrant of Naples. The drunken trio of court jester, butler, and Caliban falsely see themselves as future conquerors and rulers of the island. Ferdinand is tricked into believing that his father has drowned and that Miranda is a goddess. Miranda, in turn, nurtured upon illusions by her father, knows little of human beings and their evil. Even Prospero must come to see he is not master of the universe and that revenge is not the answer after all. He must move to a higher reality, in which justice and mercy have greater power.

It has been noted that the island holds different meanings for different characters. Here again is an illustration of the analogy between microcosm and macrocosm. The characters with integrity see it as a beautiful place; honest Gonzalo, for example, thinks it might be a utopia. Sebastian and Antonio, however, whose outlook is soured by their villainy, characterize the island's air as perfumed by a rotten swamp. Whether a character feels a sense of freedom or of slavery is conditioned not just by Prospero's magic but by the individual's view of the island and that individual's own makeup. The loveliest descriptions of the island's beauty and enchantment come from Caliban, the half-human, who, before his enslavement by Prospero, knew its offerings far better than anyone else.

In few of his other plays has Shakespeare created a closer relationship between the human and natural universes. In *The Tempest*, beauty and ugliness, good and evil, and cruelty and gentleness are matched with the external environment, and everything works toward a positive reconciliation of the best in both humans and nature. This harmony is expressed by the delightful pastoral masque Prospero stages for the young lovers, in which reapers and nymphs join in dancing, indicating the union of the natural with the supernatural. The coming marriage of Ferdinand and Miranda also foreshadows such harmony, as do the repentance and forgiveness demonstrated by the major characters.

It may be true, as Prospero states in Act V, that upon the island "no man was his own," but he also confirms that understanding has come like a "swelling tide," and he promises calm seas for the homeward journey, after which all will presumably take up the tasks and responsibilities of their respective station with improved perspective. As Prospero renounces his magic, Ariel is freed to return to the elements, and Caliban, true child of nature, is left to regain harmony with his world. Perhaps the satisfaction experienced by Shakespeare's audiences results from the harmony between humans and nature that illumines the close of the play.

"Critical Evaluation" by Muriel B. Ingham

For Further Study

French, Marilyn. *Shakespeare's Division of Experience*. New York: Summit Books, 1981. French sees the play as Shakespeare's attempt to synthesize themes from his earlier works and finally propound a theory of justice that satisfies the hierarchical imperatives he had previously set out. An examination of gender roles plays a significant part in her attempts to explicate Shakespeare's universe. Caliban is presented as representative of colonized peoples.

Kermode, Frank. *William Shakespeare: The Final Plays*. London: Longmans, Green, 1963. Kermode sees this play as the most classically unified of Shakespeare's late works, and finds a repetition of earlier themes including "guilt and repentance, the finding of the lost, forgiveness, the renewal of the world, [and] the benevolence of unseen powers."

Lindley, David. "Music, Masque and Meaning in *The Tempest*." *The Court Masque*. Manchester, England: Manchester University Press, 1984. Lindley examines the masque as a unique Renaissance art form and uncovers the role music plays in *The Tempest* to assert and deny power.

Peterson, Douglas L. *Time, Tide, and Tempest: A Study of Shakespeare's Romances*. San Marino, Calif.: Huntington Library, 1973. Places the play in the context of Shakespeare's romance plays. Explores the themes and motifs of redemption and natural order, which elaborated on Shakespeare's earlier vision.

Smith, Hallett Darius, ed. *Twentieth Century Interpretations of "The Tempest": A Collection of Critical Essays*. Englewood Cliffs, N.J.: Prentice-Hall, 1969. Provides viewpoints and interpretations of *The Tempest* by sixteen critics, including A. C. Bradley and Northrup Frye. Includes a chronology of important dates and a bibliography.

Timon of Athens

Type of plot: Tragedy
Time of plot: Fourth century B.C.E.
Locale: Athens and the nearby seacoast
Written: c. 1607-1608; first published, 1623

Principal characters

TIMON, an Athenian nobleman
FLAVIUS, his faithful steward
APEMANTUS, his philosophical and candid friend
ALCIBIADES, an Athenian general

The Story

The Athens house of Timon, a wealthy lord of the city, was the scene of much coming and going. Poets, artists, artisans, merchants, politicians, and well-wishers in general sought the friendship and favors of a man whose generosity knew no bounds. While waiting to speak to Timon, a poet disclosed his vision to an artist: Timon was depicted as the darling of Dame Fortune, and his friends and acquaintances spared no effort in admiring his favored position. The vision continued; Fortune turned and Timon tumbled into penury, his friends doing nothing to comfort him.

Timon joined the crowd of suitors in his reception chamber. When a messenger reported that Ventidius, his friend, had been jailed for a debt, Timon promised to pay the debt and to support Ventidius until he became solvent again. An old man complained that one of Timon's servants had stolen the heart of his only daughter. Timon promised to match the girl's dowry with an equal sum. Then he received the poet and the painter and the jeweler graciously, accepting their shameless flattery. Apemantus, a crudely candid friend, declared broadly that these flatterers and seekers of bounty were a pack of knaves. Alcibiades, a great military leader, came with a troop of followers to dine with Timon. As all prepared to feast at Timon's bounteous table, Apemantus cursed them roundly.

A great feast was served to the accompaniment of music. Ventidius, having been freed from jail, offered to repay the money spent in his behalf, but Timon declared that friendship would not allow him to accept Ventidius' money. When Apemantus warned Timon that men would readily slay the man whose food and drink they consume, Timon expressed his gratitude at having so many friends with which to share his generosity. He wished, however, that he might be poorer so that these good friends might know the joy of sharing their largess with him. Timon's eyes filled with tears, so overcome was he by the sentiments of friendship, as a group of costumed Athenian ladies presented lavish gifts to him from men of wealth. Timon then presented rich gifts to his departing friends. Flavius, his steward, observed that his master's infinite generosity had almost emptied his coffers. Timon told Apemantus that he would give him gifts, too, if he would cease railing at these felicities of friendship.

Before long Timon was reduced to insolvency and was near beggary. A senator to whom he owed a great sum of money sent his servant to collect. Other servants of Timon's creditors also gathered in front of his house. Timon, who had never given Flavius a chance to explain that he, Timon, had no more money, asked the steward the reason for the crowd outside. When Flavius told him the truth, Timon ordered the sale of all of his lands. Flavius disclosed that his lands were already sold or mortgaged. Refusing to share Flavius' alarm, Timon declared that he now had a chance to test his friends. He directed his servants to borrow money from Lucius, Lucullus, and Sempronius; the servants were then to go to the senators and borrow more. Flavius disclosed that he had already tried without success to borrow from these sources. Timon made excuses for them, however, and suggested that the servants try Ventidius, who had recently come into a large fortune.

The servant who went to Lucullus was told that times were difficult and that Timon's friendship alone was not sufficient security for a loan. When Lucullus offered the servant a bribe to say that he had been unable to see Lucullus, the horrified servant threw down the bribe money and departed in disgust. Lucius claimed that he, needing money, had hoped to borrow from Timon. A third servant went to Sempronius. Upon learning that Lucullus, Lucius, and even Ventidius had denied Timon loans, Sempronius pretended to be hurt that Timon had not sent to him first, and he also refused.

As Timon continued to be importuned by his creditors' servants, he went out in a rage and bade them cut out of his heart what he owed their masters. Still enraged, he directed Flavius to invite all of his creditors to a feast. Alcibiades, meanwhile, pled in the senate for the remission of the death sentence on a veteran soldier who had committed murder. The senators, deaf to arguments that the man had killed in self-defense, persisted in their decision. When Alcibiades continued to plea, the senators sentenced him, on pain of death, to be banished from Athens.

At Timon's house, tables were arranged as though for a great banquet. Apologizing profusely for being unable to honor his requests for money, Timon's guests appeared at his house expecting a lavish banquet. When Timon bade them eat, however, they discovered that the covered dishes were filled only with warm water. Timon then cursed them for what they were, threw the water in their faces, and drove them out of his house.

Now a confirmed misanthrope, Timon left Athens. For the moment he focused all of his hatred on Athens and its citizens, but he predicted that his curses would eventually encompass all humanity. Flavius, meanwhile, announced to his fellow servants that their service in Timon's house had come to an end. After sharing what little money he had with his fellows, Flavius pocketed his remaining money and declared his intentions of seeking out his old master.

One day Timon, who was living in a cave near the seashore, dug for roots and discovered gold. As he was cursing the earth for producing this root of all evil, Alcibiades appeared, accompanied by his two mistresses. Timon cursed the three and told them to leave him. When Alcibiades disclosed that he was on his way to besiege Athens, Timon gave him gold and wished him every success. He also gave the two women gold, after exhorting them to infect the minds and bodies of all men with whom they came in contact. When Alcibiades and his troops marched away, Timon continued to dig roots for his dinner.

"Men shut their doors against a setting sun"

Timon of Athens, Act I, scene ii, line 150

Timon is a generous and considerate patron of the arts and an extravagant, even lavish entertainer. He repays a kindness sevenfold and is well on his way to bankrupting himself. A Cynic philosopher named Apemantus, a plain-spoken fellow hated by everyone for his perceptive chiding, ridicules Timon's open-handedness and tries to warn him against his fairweather friends during a banquet and masque at Timon's house.

> *Apemantus.* We make ourselves fools, to disport ourselves,
> And spend our flatteries, to drink those men,
> Upon whose age we void it up again
> With poisonous spite and envy.
> Who lives, that's not depraved, or depraves?
> Who dies, that hears not one spurn to their graves
> Of their friends' gift?
> I should fear those that dance before me now
> Would one day stamp upon me. 'T has been done.
> Men shut their doors against a setting sun.

Apemantus appeared to rail at Timon for going to the opposite extreme from that which had caused his downfall. He declared that wild nature was as cruel as men, that Timon, therefore, would do well to return to Athens and flatter men who were still favored by fortune. After Apemantus left, a band of cutthroats, having heard that Timon possessed a great store of gold, went to the cave. When they told Timon that they were destitute, he threw gold at them and ordered them to practice their malign art in Athens. So bitter were Timon's words that they left him, determined to abandon all violence.

Flavius, finding the cave, wept at the pitiful state to which his master had fallen. Timon, at first rude to his faithful steward, was almost overcome by Flavius' tears. He gave Flavius gold, wished him well, and admonished him to succor only dogs.

After reports of Timon's newly found wealth reached Athens, the poet and the painter went to his cave. Timon greeted them sarcastically, praised them for their honesty, and gave them gold to use in destroying other sycophants and flatterers. Flavius returned, accompanied by two senators, who apologized for the great wrongs done to Timon and offered to lend him any amount of money he might desire. They also promised him command of the Athenian forces in the struggle against Alcibiades; Timon, however, cursed both Athens and Alcibiades. His prescription to the Athenians for ending their troubles was that they come to the shore and hang themselves on a tree near his cave. When he retreated into his cave, the senators, knowing their mission fruitless, returned to Athens.

In Athens, the senators begged Alcibiades to spare the city because its importance transcended the petty griefs of an Alcibiades or a Timon. Alcibiades agreed to spare Athens only on the condition that those who had offended Timon and him should be punished. As the city gates were opened to the besiegers, a messenger reported that Timon was dead. Alcibiades read Timon's epitaph, copied by the messenger. It reaffirmed Timon's hatred of humanity and expressed his desire that no one pause at his grave.

Critical Evaluation

One of William Shakespeare's most neglected plays, *Timon of Athens* was probably never performed during his lifetime, and it has only rarely been performed since. The reasons for its unpopularity include its strongly bitter tone and its lack of an emotionally satisfying ending. Further, the play has many elements that are uncharacteristic of Shakespeare's work: clashing themes, irregular verse passages, confused character names, and a shallow central character. For these reasons, scholars long suspected that *Timon of Athens* was a collaborative effort. Modern scholars, however, hold that the play's problems are due to the fact that Shakespeare wrote it by himself, but never polished it because he left it unfinished. His reasons for abandoning the play are not known, but reasonable inferences may be drawn from the play's curious nature.

Timon of Athens defies easy classification. As a bleak tale about a once kind man who dies a bitter misanthrope, the play appears to be a tragedy. What leads to Timon's financial ruin and ultimate destruction is, ironically, the generosity that permits him to rise high in Athenian society. His sudden and deep fall points up the fateful vulnerability of human existence—a nearly universal theme in tragedy. Despite this tragic motif, the play has many characteristics of traditional comedy. Because of its unusual blend of tragedy and comedy, it is now regarded not only as a curious experiment but also as an important transitional phase in Shakespeare's mature writing career.

There are several reasons for regarding *Timon of Athens* as a comedy. The play's savage depiction of greed, hypocrisy, and duplicity among the Athenian nobility constitutes the kind of social satire that became a dramatic staple in seventeenth century England. The immorality of the ruling classes was itself one of Shakespeare's own favorite themes. The theme is demonstrated here in the actions of the governors of Athens, who ruin Timon by cruelly calling in his debts. When they banish Alcibiades merely for seeking clemency for a deserving veteran, they expose Athens to the threat of his sacking the city. Later, after Timon is known again to have wealth, they hypocritically try to recruit him to defend the city against Alcibiades.

The play's satire is expressed most powerfully through the voice of Timon's friend Apemantus, who frequently utters crude jokes about wealthy men and government leaders. The sheer viciousness of his remarks is in itself often comical. Even more telling, however, is the play's use of a traditional device for ending comedies: reconciliation. However, it is not Timon himself who achieves a reconciliation, but Alcibiades—who gives up his plan to sack Athens. In rejecting vengeance, Alcibiades expresses the play's ultimate theme: that mercy is more valuable than justice. This strongly positive conclusion contrasts sharply with the harshly negative manner in which Timon ends his life.

After his fall, Timon (David Kelly) flees to the wilderness, and the cynical philosopher Apemantus (Tamu Gray) seeks him out, in the Oregon Shakespeare Festival's 1997 production of Timon of Athens. *(David Cooper, courtesy of the Oregon Shakespeare Festival by permission of the Actors' Equity Association)*

What makes this oddly ambiguous play most significant within Shakespeare's dramatic work is the timing of its composition. Hard evidence for dating the play is lacking, but Shakespeare most likely wrote it around 1606 to 1608. These years immediately followed the period in which he wrote the three dramas that have become known as his "problem plays"—*Troilus and Cressida* (c. 1601-1602), *All's Well That Ends Well* (1602-1604), and *Measure for Measure* (1604-1605). All three plays are unresolved examinations of psychological and sociological complications of life, sex, and death. *Timon of Athens* resembles them in its own ambiguities and its attention to the issues of atonement and reconciliation.

Shakespeare wrote many plays in the tradition of medieval morality plays, which combined comedy with moral lessons in order to educate audiences. The central lesson of *Timon of Athens* is that one cannot find happiness in leading a materialistic life, such as Timon lives until his downfall. While he is financially able to give great feasts and lavish expensive gifts on friends, he believes himself happy and well loved. Only after his money runs out does he realize the shallowness of his happiness. Even then, however, he still fails to recognize true friendship when it is offered by his faithful steward, Flavius. Thus, in contrast to traditional morality plays, *Timon of Athens* does not end with its hero's finding happiness by learning how to appreciate more spiritual values. Instead, Timon declines even deeper into despair and he dies miserably. The play thus begins with Timon symbolizing friendship and ends with him symbolizing misanthropy.

Whatever Shakespeare's intentions were when he began *Timon of Athens*, the play served him as an experiment in which to work out new themes. After abandoning it, he wrote the plays known as his romances: *Pericles, Prince of Tyre* (c. 1607-1608), *Cymbeline* (c. 1609-1610), *The Winter's Tale* (c. 1610-1611), and *The Tempest* (c. 1611). Like *Timon of Athens*, these plays explore such themes as exile and return, the absence of moral absolutes, and the transcendent quality of mercy.

For Further Study

Ellis-Fermor, Una. "Timon of Athens: An Unfinished Play." *The Review of English Studies* 18, no. 71 (July, 1942): 270-283. Discusses the controversy over the authorship of the play. Concludes that it is likely Shakespeare's work alone and that it is an unfinished play.

Knight, G. Wilson. "The Pilgrimage of Hate: An Essay on Timon of Athens." In *The Wheel of Fire: Interpretations of Shakespearian Tragedy*. Rev. ed. New York: Methuen, 1949. Interprets Timon as a noble figure, abused by a harsh world. Sees the play as a great tragedy.

Nowottny, Winifred M. T. "Acts IV and V of *Timon of Athens*." *Shakespeare Quarterly* 10, no. 4 (Autumn, 1959): 493-497. Interprets the play in a religious context. Sees the substitution of secular myths for Christian ones in the play.

Nuttall, A. D. *Timon of Athens*. Hemel Hempstead, England: Harvester Wheatsheaf, 1989. Provides a stage history, an account of the critical reception to the play, and a sustained analysis.

Soellner, Rolf. *Timon of Athens*. Columbus: Ohio State University Press, 1979. Critical analysis with reference to dramatic and cultural contexts. Discusses the merits of the play.

Titus Andronicus

Type of plot: Tragedy
Time of plot: Early Christian era
Locale: Rome and vicinity
First performed: 1594; first published, 1594

Principal characters

SATURNINUS, the emperor of Rome
BASSIANUS, his brother
TITUS ANDRONICUS, a Roman general
LAVINIA, his only daughter
MARCUS, his brother, a tribune
TAMORA, the queen of the Goths
AARON, her lover, a Moor
ALARBUS,
DEMETRIUS, and
CHIRON, her sons

The Story

Early in the Christian era, Saturninus and Bassianus, sons of the late emperor, contended for the crown of the Roman Empire. Both men were leaders of strong factions. Another candidate, a popular one, was Titus Andronicus, a Roman famed for his victories over the barbarian Goths to the north. Marcus Andronicus, brother of Titus, stated in the forum that Titus was the popular choice to succeed the late emperor. The sons, willing to abide by the desires of the populace, dismissed their factions.

As the prominent men of the city went into the senate house, Titus made his triumphant entry into Rome. He was accompanied by his surviving sons and by a casket containing the bodies of other sons. In his train also were Tamora, the queen of the Goths; her sons, Alarbus, Demetrius, and Chiron, and her lover, Aaron, a Moor. Before the senate house, Lucius, one of Titus' sons, demanded that a Gothic prisoner be sacrificed to appease the spirits of his dead brothers in the casket. When Titus offered as sacrifice the oldest son of Tamora, the queen pleaded for mercy, reminding Titus that her sons were as precious to her as his were to him. Titus paid her no heed. Alarbus was sacrificed, and the casket was then laid in the tomb of the Andronici. At that moment Lavinia, Titus' only daughter, appeared to greet her father and brothers and to pay her respects to her fallen brothers.

Marcus came out of the senate house, greeted Titus, and informed him that he was the choice of the people for the emperorship. Titus, unwilling to take on that responsibility at his age, persuaded the people to name Saturninus emperor instead. Saturninus, in gratitude, asked for and received the hand of Lavinia to become his queen. Bassianus, however, to whom Lavinia had given her heart, seized the maid with the help of Marcus and the sons of Titus and carried her away. Titus' son Mutius, who stayed behind to cover their flight, was killed by his father.

Saturninus, who begrudged Titus his popularity with the people, disavowed all allegiance and debt to the general and planned to take Tamora as his wife. Titus, deserted by his emperor, his brother, and his sons, was deeply shaken.

Marcus and Titus' sons returned and expressed the desire to bury Mutius in the family vault. Titus at first refused, saying that Mutius had been a traitor; then he relented after his brother and his sons argued effectively for proper burial. When Bassianus appeared with Lavinia, Saturninus vowed that he would avenge the stealing of the maid who had been given him by her father. Bassianus spoke in Titus' behalf, but Titus declared that he could plead his own case before the emperor. Tamora openly advised Saturninus to be gracious to Titus, but secretly she advised him to gain Titus' friendship only because Titus was so popular in Rome. She assured Saturninus that she would destroy Titus and his family for their having sacrificed one of her own sons. Saturninus therefore pardoned the Andronici and declared his intention of marrying Tamora. Believing their differences reconciled, Titus invited Saturninus to hunt with him the next day.

Aaron, contemplating Tamora's good fortune and the imminent downfall of Saturninus and of Rome as well, came upon Chiron and Demetrius, disputing and about to draw their swords over their chances of winning the favors of Lavinia. Advising the youths to contain themselves, he told them that both could enjoy Lavinia by seizing her in the forest during the hunt, which would be attended by the lords and ladies of the court.

Later, while the hunt was under way, Aaron hid a sack of gold at the foot of a large tree in the forest. He had previously arranged to have a pit dug near the tree; this pit he covered over with undergrowth. There Tamora found him and learned that both Bassianus and Lavinia would come to grief that day. Before Aaron left Tamora, he gave her a letter with directions that the message reach the hands of Saturninus. Bassianus and Lavinia approached and, seeing that the Moor and Tamora had been together, chaffed Tamora and threatened to tell Saturninus of her dalliance in the forest. Chiron and Demetrius came upon the scene. Informed by Tamora that Bassianus and Lavinia had insulted her, they stabbed Bassianus to death. When Tamora urged them to stab Lavinia they refused, saying that they would enjoy her first. Lavinia then appealed to Tamora to remember that Titus had spared her life. Tamora, recalling how Titus had ignored her pleas to spare her son from sacrifice, was determined that her sons should have their lustful pleasure. The brothers, after throwing the body of Bassianus into the pit, dragged Lavinia away to rape her.

Meanwhile, Aaron, on the pretext that he had trapped a panther, brought two of Titus' sons, Quintus and Martius, to the pit and left them there. Martius fell into the trap, where he recognized the murdered Bassianus by a ring he wore on his finger.

When Quintus tried to pull Martius out of the pit, he lost his balance and tumbled in to it. Aaron, returning with Saturninus, claimed that Titus' sons had murdered Bassianus. Tamora then gave Saturninus the letter that Aaron had given her. The letter, written ostensibly by one of the Andronici, outlined a plot to assassinate Bassianus, to bury him in a pit, and then to collect payment, which was a bag of gold hidden near the pit. When the bag of gold was found where Aaron had placed it, Saturninus was convinced of the brothers' guilt. Despite Titus' offer of his own person as security for his sons, Saturninus sentenced them to be tortured. Tamora assured Titus that she would speak to Saturninus on his behalf.

"The eagle suffers little birds to sing"

Titus Andronicus, Act IV, scene iv, line 83

Saturninus, the Roman emperor, has been under the influence of Tamora, queen of the Goths, who is leagued with her paramour Aaron and her sons, Alarbus, Demetrius, and Chiron, to wreck Titus and his family. Already Demetrius and Chiron, aided and abetted by Tamora, have raped Lavinia, Titus' daughter, and cut off her hands and tongue. Through Saturninus and the law, they have caused the death of two of Titus' sons. Now Lucius, another of Titus' sons, is approaching Rome at the head of an army intending revenge. Tamora, for her own purposes, tells Saturninus that he is an all-powerful emperor. The emperor, however, replies that the Roman citizens will revolt and join Lucius. Tamora continues to egg Saturninus on:

> *Tamora.* King, be thy thoughts imperious like thy name.
> Is the sun dimmed, that gnats do fly in it?
> The eagle suffers little birds to sing,
> And is not careful what they mean thereby,
> Knowing that with the shadow of his wings
> He can at pleasure sting their melody,
> Even so mayst thou the giddy men of Rome.

In another part of the forest, Chiron and Demetrius, their evil deed accomplished, cut off Lavinia's hands and tongue so that she would be able neither to write nor to tell of what had befallen her. Alone in the forest, Lavinia was joined at last by her uncle, Marcus, who led her to her father.

Later, in Rome, Titus recalled his years of faithful military service to the state and begged the tribunes to spare his sons, but they would not listen to him. Another son, Lucius, a great favorite with the people, attempted unsuccessfully to rescue his brothers. He was banished from the city. As Titus pleaded in vain, Marcus brought the ravished Lavinia to him. The sight of his daughter led Titus to wonder to what infinite depths of grief a man could come. Aaron announced to the grieving Andronici that Saturninus would release Martius and Quintus if one of the family would cut off his hand and send it to the court. Titus agreed to let Lucius and

Marcus decide between them; when they went to get an ax, Titus directed Aaron to cut off his hand. Later, a messenger brought Titus his hand and the heads of Martius and Quintus as well. Having suffered as much as a man could suffer, Titus vowed revenge. He directed the banished Lucius to raise an invading force among the Goths.

At his home, Titus appeared to be demented. Even so, it was clear to him one day that Lavinia was trying desperately to tell him something. She indicated in Ovid's *Metamorphoses* the section in which the story of Tereus' brutal rape of Philomela was recounted. Suddenly, it occurred to Marcus that he could, by holding a staff in his teeth and between his knees, write in the sand on the floor. Lavinia took the staff thus and wrote in the sand that Chiron and Demetrius were her violators.

Titus now sent his grandson Lucius with a bundle of weapons to present to Tamora's sons. The youths did not understand the message that Titus had attached to the gift, but Aaron quickly saw that Titus knew who Lavinia's ravishers were. As the brothers admired their gift, a blast of trumpets announced the birth of a child to Tamora. A nurse entered with the newborn baby, who was black, and stated that Tamora, fearful lest Saturninus see it, had sent the child to Aaron. Chiron and Demetrius, aware of their mother's shame, insisted that the infant be killed immediately. When they offered to do the murder, Aaron, the father, defied them. As a precaution, he killed the nurse, one of three women who knew the baby's color. Then he had a fair-skinned baby, newly born, taken to Tamora before he fled to the Goths.

Titus, now reputed to be utterly demented, wrote messages to the gods, attached them to arrows, and, with Marcus and his grandson, shot the arrows into the court. He persuaded a passing farmer to deliver a letter to Saturninus. The emperor was already disturbed because the messages carried by the arrows stated Titus' grievances against the state. When Saturninus threatened to execute justice on old Titus, Tamora, feeling her revenge complete, advised him to treat the distracted old soldier gently. The farmer, meanwhile, delivered Titus' letter. Enraged by its mocking message, Saturninus commanded that Titus be brought to him to be executed.

A messenger then brought word that the Goths, led by Lucius, threatened to sack Rome. Knowing Lucius' popularity with the Romans, Saturninus was fearful. Tamora, however, confident of her ability to save the city, directed the messenger to arrange a conference with Lucius at the house of Titus.

In the camp of the Goths, Aaron and his child were brought before Lucius. Aaron's captor disclosed that he had come upon the Moor in a ruined monastery and had heard him state aloud that the baby's mother was Tamora. At Lucius' promise to preserve the life of the child, Aaron confessed to his crimes against the Andronici. Lucius decreed that the Moor must die a horrible death.

Tamora, meanwhile, believing that Titus was demented beyond all reason, disguised herself as Revenge and with her sons, also disguised, presented herself to Titus. Although Titus recognized her, she insisted that she was Revenge, his friend. Titus, for his own purposes, pretended to be taken in by the disguises; he told Rapine and Murder, Revenge's cohorts, to seek out two such as themselves and destroy them. At Tamora's bidding, Titus directed Marcus to invite Lucius to a banquet, to which Saturninus and Tamora and her sons would also come.

Titus persuaded Chiron and Demetrius to stay with him while their companion, Revenge, went to perform other duties. He then called in his kinsmen, who seized and bound the brothers. Titus told them that he intended to kill them and feed to their mother a paste made of their bones and blood. Lavinia held a bowl between the stumps of her arms to catch their blood as Titus cut their throats.

Lucius, accompanied by a guard of Goths, came to his father's house, where he put Aaron in the charge of Marcus. Saturninus and Tamora made their appearance and were ushered to a banquet served by Titus, dressed as a cook. Titus, hearing from Saturninus that Virginius, in the legend, had done well to kill his ravished daughter, stabbed Lavinia. The startled Saturninus asked if Lavinia had been ravished and by whom. When Titus disclosed that Tamora's sons had done the evil deed, Saturninus asked to see the youths at once. Titus, declaring that Tamora was eating their remains, stabbed her. Saturninus stabbed Titus, and Lucius, in turn, stabbed Saturninus. A general fight ensued. Lucius and Marcus, with their followers, retired to a balcony to tell the people of Rome of the manifold evils wrought by Tamora, her sons, and Aaron. After the people had chosen him as their new emperor, Lucius sentenced Aaron to be buried waist deep and left to starve. He also decreed that Tamora's body be fed to wild beasts.

Critical Evaluation

Titus Andronicus, the first of William Shakespeare's ten tragedies, was written between 1589 and 1592, probably in 1590. The young writer was eager to establish himself as a commercially successful playwright, so he resorted to the traditionally accepted form of revenge tragedy for this play. Revenge tragedy is a particularly violent form of theater and had been used by Thomas Kyd in his spectacularly successful *The Spanish Tragedy* (c. 1585). Shakespeare, no doubt, had Kyd's success in mind as he created a play of unprecedented violence. In *Titus Andronicus,* eleven of the individually named characters are murdered, eight in view of the audience, and several are horribly mutilated. Lavinia's rape and mutilation represent the acme of brutality in the Elizabethan theater, and Shakespeare was unabashedly pandering to the Elizabethan audience's taste for blood and gore in his first attempt at tragedy. It is largely because of this excessive violence that many critics, from Shakespeare's fellow dramatist Ben Jonson to twentieth century poet T. S. Eliot, have censured this play as unworthy of Shakespeare. Some critics have even denied that Shakespeare wrote the play. Such condemnation fails to recognize that it is only when *Titus Andronicus* is considered in the light of Shakespeare's mature tragedies, which are among the greatest in the English language, that it falls short of the mark. It measures up very well when it is compared with *The Spanish Tragedy* or Christopher Marlowe's *The Jew of Malta* (1589), especially in regard to the important areas of characterization, language, and theme.

Although the characters in *Titus Andronicus* are clearly not as rich and subtle as are many of those in Shakespeare's later tragedies, some of them are still quite compelling and foreshadow several of Shakespeare's mature figures. Titus Andronicus is the first of Shakespeare's great Roman warriors who falls from high status because of a fatal flaw of character or intellect. In broad outline, his tragic downfall anticipates the destructive careers of Coriolanus, Julius Caesar, and Mark Antony. Even Othello's monumental rages recall Titus' propensity for impulsive violence. Titus is an outstanding example of Aristotle's conception of the tragic protagonist as a man who is greater than the ordinary and basically good, but who suffers from a deadly defect that destroys him. Titus' terrible suffering is a harrowing dramatic experience, and his character is an altogether remarkable creation for a twenty-six-year-old dramatist.

Tamora and Aaron also deserve particular mention. Tamora is the first of a small number of Shakespeare's malevolent women, some others being Goneril and Regan in *King Lear* (1605) and Lady Macbeth in *Macbeth* (1606). Like them, Tamora is seen in dramatic contrast to a benevolent female character, in this case Lavinia. Like the other villainesses, Tamora is crafty and manipulative, psychopathic and driven by a lust for power, but her animus against the Andronici is understandable in view of the sacrificial execution of her son Alarbus. She is perhaps ultimately less sympathetic than Lady Macbeth, who loses her mind because of her guilt, but she is clearly more human than Goneril and Regan, who are arguably the most malignant women in all of drama. Aaron is the first of Shakespeare's Machiavellian villains, the others being Richard III in *Richard III* (c. 1592-1593), Iago in *Othello* (1604), and Edmund in *King Lear*. Like the behavior of all villains of this type, Aaron's actions are scheming, sadistic, and psychopathic. He revels in doing evil, and his catalog of his life after his capture recalls the hateful braggadocio of Ithamore in Marlowe's *The Jew of Malta*, upon whom he is partially based.

The sheer excesses of his play run the risk of disgusting the audience, even one as fond of violence as the Elizabethan audience was. The shock of Lavinia's mutilations is reduced by the language which is used to describe her. It is the language of euphemism—"what stern ungentle hands/ Hath lopped and hewed and made thy body bare/ of her two branches" and "a crimson river of warm blood/ Like to a bubbling fountain stirred with wind/ Doth rise and fall between thy rosed lips"—and it creates a psychic distance between the fact of the violence and the audience's perception of it. References to classical myths involving physical dismemberment provide an imaginative context for the most grotesque outrages. Lavinia's rape and the removal of her tongue and hands to prevent disclosure of her persecutors recall the myth of Procne, Philomela, and Tereus, which is recorded in Ovid's *Metamorphoses* (c. 8) and which every Elizabethan would have known. The feast at which Tamora is served the baked bodies of her evil sons Chiron and Demetrius has a grim precedent in a Roman tragedy of Seneca. The language of euphemism and the language of myth buffer the shock of the most extreme episodes of violence in this play, rendering them more palatable to the audience.

Titus Andronicus is not without moral significance even though it obviously fails to achieve the catharsis of *Hamlet* (1600-1601) and *King Lear*. Revenge is shown to be unsatisfactory as a moral code of governance. Titus' obstinate sacrifice of Alarbus, a son of the captured Gothic queen Tamora, provides the motive for the subsequent outrages against his family. Avengers and victims become indistinguishable in the course of the play and are alike destroyed in the cruel and ultimately mindless bloodbath that follows Alarbus' execution. Titus, the once majestic leader, is reduced by the final act to a craftily insane murderer, not only of his enemies but also of his own daughter. Rome is in tatters until a semblance of order is restored at the end by the very Goths who were the original enemy. The play, then, is a powerful testament to the irrationality of revenge, or even of justice untempered by mercy, as a moral imperative.

"Critical Evaluation" by Robert G. Blake

For Further Study

Bessen, Alan C. *Shakespeare in Performance: "Titus Andronicus."* Manchester, England: Manchester University Press, 1989. Dessen follows the stage history of the play, noting that the watershed performance was the highly successful 1955 production by Peter Brook, starring Laurence Olivier and Vivien Leigh. Dessen also addresses the numerous staging problems involved in a production of *Titus Andronicus.*

Bowers, Fredson T. *Elizabethan Revenge Tragedy, 1587-1642.* Princeton, N.J.: Princeton University Press, 1940. Although somewhat old, this book is still useful and enjoyable. It traces the origins of the revenge tragedy to the plays of Seneca. Bowers shows how *Titus Andronicus* follows a pattern first formulated in English by Thomas Kyd in *The Spanish Tragedy.*

Hamilton, A. C. "*Titus Andronicus*: The Form of Shakespearean Tragedy." *Shakespeare Quarterly* 14 (1963): 201-213. Suggests that Titus' fault is in attempting to be godlike in the sacrifice of Alarbus. The rest of the play makes him increasingly human.

Rozett, Martha Tuck. *The Doctrine of Election and the Emergence of Elizabethan Tragedy.* Princeton, N.J.: Princeton University Press, 1984. Argues that the Calvinistic doctrine of predestination and election was influential upon Elizabethan tragedy.

Wells, Stanley, ed. *The Cambridge Companion to Shakespeare Studies.* Cambridge, England: Cambridge University Press, 1986. This is where all studies of Shakespeare should begin. Includes excellent chapters introducing the poet's biography, conventions and beliefs of Elizabethan England, and reviews of scholarship in the field.

Troilus and Cressida

Type of plot: Comedy: problem play
Time of plot: Antiquity
Locale: Troy
First performed: 1601-1602; first published, 1609

Principal characters

PRIAM, King of Troy
PARIS,
HELENUS,
HECTOR, and
TROILUS, his sons
AGAMEMNON,
ACHILLES,
ULYSSES,
AJAX, and
DIOMEDES, Greek commanders
PANDARUS, a Trojan lord
CRESSIDA, his niece
HELEN, wife of Greek king Menelaus

The Story

During the Trojan War, Troilus, younger son of Priam, King of Troy, fell in love with the lovely and unapproachable Cressida, daughter of Calchas, a Trojan priest who had gone over to the side of the Greeks. Troilus, frustrated by his unrequited love, declared to Pandarus, a Trojan lord and uncle of Cressida, that he would refrain from fighting the Greeks as long as there was such turmoil in his heart. Pandarus added to Troilus' misery by praising the incomparable beauty of Cressida; Troilus impatiently chided Pandarus, who answered that for all it mattered to him Cressida could join her father in the Greek camp.

Later, Pandarus overheard Cressida and her servant discussing Hector's anger at having received a blow in battle from Ajax, a mighty Greek warrior of Trojan blood. Pandarus extolled Troilus' virtues to Cressida, who was all but indifferent. As the two discoursed, the Trojan forces returned from the field. Pandarus praised the several Trojan warriors—Aeneas, Antenor, Hector, Paris, Helenus—as they passed by Cressida's window, all the while anticipating, for Cressida's benefit, the passing of young Troilus. When the prince passed, Pandarus was lavish in his praise, but Cressida appeared to be bored. As Pandarus left her to join Troilus,

Cressida soliloquized that she was charmed, indeed, by Troilus, but that she was in no haste to reveal the state of her affections.

In the Greek camp, meanwhile, Agamemnon, commander of the Greek forces in Ilium, tried to put heart into his demoralized leaders. Old Nestor declared that the seven difficult years of the siege of Troy had been a real test of Greek stamina. It was the belief of Ulysses that the difficulties of the Greeks lay in a lack of order and discipline, not in Trojan strength. He reminded his fellow Greek leaders that the disaffection of mighty Achilles and the scurrilous clowning of Patroclus, a Greek leader, had provoked disorder in the Greek ranks. Even Ajax, usually dependable, had become fractious, and his follower, deformed Thersites, embarrassed the Greeks with his taunts.

As the Greek leaders conferred, Aeneas delivered to them a challenge from Hector, who in single combat would defend the beauty and the virtue of his lady against a Greek champion. When the leaders went their several ways to announce the challenge to Achilles and to other Greeks, Ulysses and Nestor decided that the only politic action to take, the pride of Achilles being what it was, was to arrange somehow that Ajax be chosen to fight Hector. Ajax, Achilles, and Patroclus heard of the proclamation, but tended to disregard it. Their levity caused the railing Thersites to break with them.

In Troy, meanwhile, Hector was tempted to concede to a Greek offer to end hostilities if the Trojans returned Helen to her husband, King Menelaus. Troilus chided his brother and Helenus for their momentary want of resolution. As the brothers and their father, Priam, discussed the reasons for and against continuing the war, Cassandra, prophetess and daughter of Priam, predicted that Troy would be burned to the ground by the Greeks. Hector heeded her warning, but Troilus, joined by Paris, persisted in the belief that the war, for the sake of honor, must be continued. Hector, although aware of the evil the Trojans were committing in defending Paris' indefensible theft of Helen from her husband, conceded that for reasons of honor the fighting must continue.

The Greek leaders approached Achilles, who had kept to himself since his quarrel with Agamemnon. Refusing to confer with them, Achilles retired into his tent and sent his companion, Patroclus, to make his apologies. Achilles persisted in refusing to deal with the Greek commanders, who sought in him their champion against Hector. Ulysses played on the pride of Ajax with subtle flattery and convinced this Greek of Trojan blood that he should present himself as the Greek champion in place of Achilles.

In the meantime, Pandarus had prepared the way for a tryst between Troilus and Cressida by securing the promise of Paris and Helen to make excuses for Troilus' absence. He brought the two young people together in his orchard, where the pair confessed to each other their undying love. Cressida declared that if she were ever false, then all falsehood could forever afterward be associated with her name. Pandarus witnessed these sincere avowals of faith and himself declared that if Troilus and Cressida did not remain faithful to each other, then all go-betweens would be associated with his name. These declarations having been made, Pandarus led the young people to a bedchamber in his house.

In the Greek camp, Calchas, Cressida's father, persuaded Agamemnon to exchange Antenor, a Trojan prisoner, for Cressida, whose presence he desired. Diomedes, a Greek commander, was appointed to effect the exchange. Planning to ignore Achilles, the Greek leaders passed the warrior with only the briefest recognition. When he demanded an explanation of that treatment, Ulysses told him that fame was ephemeral and that great deeds were soon forgotten. Fearful for his reputation now that Ajax had been appointed Greek champion, Achilles arranged to play host to the unarmed Hector after the contest.

"'Tis mad idolatry to make the service greater than the god"

Troilus and Cressida, Act II, scene ii, lines 56-57

The Greeks offer to end the Trojan War. King Priam of Troy and his sons Hector, Troilus, Paris, and Helenus discuss the Greek condition of peace, which is the return of Helen. Formerly the wife of Menelaus, a Greek king, Helen fell in love with Prince Paris of Troy and fled with him, abandoning her husband and thus precipitating the war. Now Hector urges his father and brothers to accept the Greek offer. He argues that Troy's armies have been decimated and that the cause of it all is not worth the cost of her keeping.

> *Troilus.* What's aught but as 'tis valued?
> *Hector.* But value dwells not in particular will;
>   It holds his estimate and dignity
>   As well wherein 'tis precious of itself
>   As in the prizer. 'Tis mad idolatry
>   To make the service greater than the god. . . .

Diomedes returned Antenor to Troy, and, at dawn, he was taken to Pandarus' house to escort Cressida to the Greek camp. When Troilus and Cressida learned of Diomedes' mission, Troilus appealed unsuccessfully to the Trojan leaders to allow Cressida to remain in Troy. Heartbroken, he returned to Cressida and the young couple repeated their vows in their farewells. Troilus then escorted Cressida and Diomedes, who commented on Cressida's beauty, as far as the city gates. When Diomedes and Cressida encountered the Greek leaders outside the walls, Cressida was kissed by Agamemnon, Menelaus, Nestor, Patroclus, and others. Ulysses observed that she appeared wanton.

Warriors of both sides assembled to watch Hector and Ajax fight. The two companions clashed for only a moment before Hector desisted, declaring that he could not harm Ajax, his cousin. Ajax accepted Hector's magnanimity and invited the Trojan to join, unarmed, the Greek commanders at dinner. Hector, accompanied by Troilus, was welcomed among the Greeks with many warm compliments, but Achilles, meeting Hector, rudely mentioned that part of Hector's person in which he would one day inflict a mortal wound. Stung by Achilles' pride and lack of manners, Hector declared hotly that he would destroy all of Achilles at one stroke. The result was an agreement to meet in combat the next day. Ajax managed to calm heated tempers, however, and the feasting began.

Troilus, anxious to see his beloved Cressida, asked Ulysses where he might find Calchas, and Ulysses promised to be his guide. After the banquet, they followed Diomedes to Calchas' tent, where Cressida met him and, in affectionate overtures toward Diomedes, revealed to the hidden Troilus that she had already all but forgotten him. As she gave Diomedes, as a token of her love, a sleeve that had belonged to Troilus, compunction seized her for a moment. She quickly succumbed, however, to Diomedes' charms and promised to be his at their next meeting. Diomedes left, vowing to kill in combat the Trojan whose sleeve he would be wearing on his helmet. Troilus, unable to believe that Cressida was the woman whom he loved so passionately, returned to Troy. He vowed to take the life of Diomedes.

As the new day approached, Hector was warned by Andromache, his wife, and by his sister Cassandra not to do battle that day; all portents foretold disaster. When their words proved ineffectual, King Priam tried vainly to persuade Hector to remain within the walls. During the battle, Diomedes unhorsed Troilus and sent the horse as a gift to Cressida. Despite his overthrow, Troilus continued to fight heroically. Hector appeared to be, for his part, invincible. When Patroclus was severely wounded in the action, Achilles, enraged, ordered his followers, the Myrmidons, to stand ready. As the action subsided, and Hector was unarming himself at the end of the day, the Myrmidons, at Achilles' command, closed in on brave Hector and felled him with their spears.

Troilus announced to the retiring Trojan forces that Hector had been killed by treachery and that his body, tied to the tail of Achilles' horse, was being dragged around the Phrygian plain. As he made his way to the gates, he predicted general mourning in Troy and expressed his undying hatred for the Greeks. He encountered Pandarus, whom he abruptly dismissed as a cheap panderer, a man whose name would be infamous forever.

Critical Evaluation

In the Folio of 1623 *Troilus and Cressida* is described as a tragedy; in the Quarto it is called a history; in most structural respects it seems to be a comedy, though a very grim and bitter one. Critics have frequently classified it, with *Measure for Measure* (1604-1605) and *All's Well That Ends Well* (1602-1604), as a "problem play," perhaps as much because the play poses a problem in literary taxonomy as because it sets out to examine a problematic thesis. Probably written between *Hamlet* (1600-1601) and *Othello* (1604), during the period of the great tragedies, the play is so full of gloom and venom, so lacking in the playfulness and idealism of the earlier comedies, that critics have attributed its tone and manner either to a period of personal disillusionment in William Shakespeare's life or to his preoccupation at that time with tragic themes.

There is no external and little internal evidence for the biographical conclusion. It may be, however, that, in *Troilus and Cressida*, Shakespeare has been affected by the surrounding tragedies. It is as if he took the moral ambiguities and potential chaos of the worlds of the tragedies but ruled out the possibility of redemption and transcendence through heroic suffering. Instead, he peoples this tenuous world with blowhards, cynics, and poltroons and ruthlessly lets them muddle through for themselves. The world of *King Lear* (1605), for example, is on the brink of chaos, but at least there is the sublimity of Lear to salvage it. The world of *Troilus and Cressida* has no one to shore up its structure and challenge disintegration.

Although there were many contemporary versions of the relevant Homeric materials available to Shakespeare, it is clear that he was also familiar with the story as told by Chaucer in *Troilus and Criseyde* (c. 1382). Chaucer's world, however, was full of innocence, brilliance, and hope. If the medieval Criseyde behaves shabbily, it is only the result of feminine weakness and long importuning. If Chaucer's Troilus is naïve and a victim of courtly idealism, at least he can finally sort things out from an Olympian perspective. Shakespeare does not give his lovers, or the rest of the Greek heroes, this sympathy or opportunity but drags them through a drab and seamy degradation.

Shakespeare begins with characters traditionally honored for their nobility, but he does nothing to develop them even for a fall. He simply proceeds to betray them, to show them up, and thereby to represent the extreme precariousness of their world. The bloom of courtly love is gone as is the Christian optimism of the Middle Ages. Shakespeare seems to be reflecting not a personal situation but a late Renaissance malaise as he has his characters impotently preside at the dissolution of the revered old order.

In Chaucer, Troilus' love and woe had been instrumental in his maturation and, ultimately, in his salvation. Shakespeare's Troilus is more frankly sensual and his liaison is correspondingly sordid. He does not benefit from an ennobling passion, nor is he allowed to transcend his folly. He is not even accorded the dignity of a significant death. He fights on in pointless, imperceptive frenzy.

Cressida is also debased. She has fallen from courtly heroine to common whore. Perhaps Shakespeare borrowed her degradation from Robert Henryson's highly moralistic *Testament of Cresseid* (1532), in which the heroine sinks to prostitution. In any case, she does not have the initial austerity and later reserve which dignify the passion and fall of Chaucer's Criseyde. Her language, her every movement, suggests that she is more of a slut than a courtly heroine. Even as she enters the Greek camp, her promiscuous behavior betrays her, and her quick submission to Diomedes confirms what has been suspected all along. As if the lovers could not behave foully enough by themselves, Shakespeare provides them with Pandarus, as go-between and commentator, to further sully the relationship.

In Chaucer, the Trojan War had provided a fatalistic backdrop which enhanced the progress of the tragic love. In Shakespeare, the circumambient Homeric heroes serve only to discredit themselves and to amplify the chaos. Mark Van Doren has pointed out that, if Pandarus' role is to degrade the lovers, "the role of Thersites is to cheapen the heroes." They, however, do not need much help from their interlocutor. For example, when Ulysses gives his famous speech on order, one is more struck by the pointless bombast and strangulated rhetoric than by erudition. One is led to suspect that this world is out of touch with its ordering principles and that it is vainly trying to recapture them or to preserve their appearance with tortured language. Similarly, when Achilles delivers his set speech in Act III, it has all of the bitterness but none of the grace of Lear's corresponding speech. This Achilles is a petulant sybarite and the world is in trouble if he is its hero. The bombast, the irritability, and the inconsequentiality are all-pervasive. Agamemnon and Nestor are nothing more than windbags. When the Greeks meet to discuss plans, or the Trojans meet to discuss returning Helen, the conferences both quickly degenerate into pompous vacuity.

The moral and political disintegration is reflected in the shrill and strident language of the play. The diction, which is jawbreakingly full of inkhornisms, and the rhetorical excesses reinforce the notion that the characters are spinning out of control, no longer able to gain control of their language, no longer able to give even verbal order to their frustrations. The result is a play that can easily seem tedious. Consequently, *Troilus and Cressida* is rarely performed. It has, however, fascinated the critics. What all of this suggests is that the play is more interesting than appealing, more intriguing than satisfying, as it chronicles the demise of a world in which no one is left with the moral stature to make a last stand.

"Critical Evaluation" by Edward E. Foster

For Further Study

Barroll, J. Leeds, ed. *Shakespeare Studies VI*. Dubuque, Iowa: William C. Brown, 1970. Part of an annual series of Shakespearean review anthologies. "The Traditions of the Troy-Story Heroes and the Problem of Satire in *Troilus and Cressida*," by Mark Sacharoff, considers the story of the play and its earlier sources in light of previous criticism.

_____, ed. *Shakespeare Studies VIII*. New York: Burt Franklin, 1975. A later volume in the above-cited series. In "Cressida and the World of the Play," by Grant L. Voth and Oliver H. Evans, the role of Cressida is considered in terms of her calculating ways, which are seen as a direct response to Troilus' temporary infatuation.

Bullough, Geoffrey, ed. *Narrative and Dramatic Sources of Shakespeare*. Vol. 6. New York: Columbia University Press, 1966. Part of a six-volume series of critical essays concerning the sources of Shakespeare's plays. *Troilus and Cressida* is discussed in a forty-page introduction, which is followed by the actual texts and translations of the sources Shakespeare would have known.

Donaldson, E. Talbot. *The Swan at the Well: Shakespeare Reading Chaucer*. New Haven, Conn.: Yale University Press, 1985. A comparison between several of Shakespeare's plays and their sources in Chaucer's poems. There are two chapters dealing with *Troilus and Cressida*, comparing the play to its literary source, Chaucer's poem *Troilus and Criseyde*.

Lloyd Evans, Gareth. *The Upstart Crow: An Introduction to Shakespeare's Plays*. London: J. M. Dent and Sons, 1982. A comprehensive discussion of the dramatic works of William Shakespeare. Although the major emphasis is on critical reviews of the plays, there are also discussions of sources as well as material on the circumstances surrounding the writing of the plays.

Twelfth Night: Or, What You Will

Type of plot: Comedy
Time of plot: Sixteenth century
Locale: Illyria, a region on the east shore of the Adriatic Sea
First performed: c. 1600-1602; first published, 1623

Principal characters

VIOLA (CESARIO), Sebastian's twin sister and Orsino's lover
OLIVIA, a wealthy countess desired by Orsino
MARIA, her maid
SEBASTIAN, Viola's twin brother and Olivia's lover
ANTONIO, Sebastian's friend, a sea captain
ORSINO, the Duke of Illyria
SIR TOBY BELCH, Olivia's uncle
SIR ANDREW AGUECHEEK, Olivia's ancient suitor
MALVOLIO, Olivia's steward, a comic villain
FESTE, Olivia's jester

The Story

Viola and Sebastian, twin brother and sister who closely resembled each other, were separated when the ship on which they were passengers was wrecked during a great storm at sea. Each thought that the other was dead and set out alone with no hope of being reunited.

The lovely and charming Viola was cast upon the shores of Illyria, where she was befriended by a kind sea captain. They decided to dress Viola in men's clothing and have her take service as a page in the household of young Duke Orsino. Dressed in man's garb, Viola called herself Cesario and became the duke's personal attendant. Impressed by the youth's good looks and pert but courtly speech, Orsino sent "him" as his envoy of love to woo the Countess Olivia, who was mourning the death of her young brother.

The wealthy Olivia lived in a palace with her maid, Maria; her drunken old uncle, Sir Toby Belch; and her steward, Malvolio. Maria and Sir Toby were a happy-go-lucky pair who drank and caroused with Sir Andrew Aguecheek, an ancient nobleman who was much enamored of Olivia. In return for grog supplied by Sir Andrew, Sir Toby was supposed to press Sir Andrew's suit with Olivia. Actually, however, Sir Toby never stayed sober long enough to keep his part of the bargain. All these affairs were observed disapprovingly by Malvolio, Olivia's ambitious, narrow-minded steward, who could not tolerate jollity in those about him.

When Cesario arrived at the palace, Olivia was instantly attracted to the page—thinking her a man. She paid close attention to Orsino's message, but it was not love for Orsino that caused her to listen so carefully. When Cesario left, she sent Malvolio after her with a ring. It was a shock for Viola, who hitherto enjoyed playing the part of Cesario, to realize that Olivia had fallen in love with her in her male clothes.

The mourning Olivia (Bonnie Akimoto, left) unveils herself to a visitor, Viola (Robin Goodrin Nordli), disguised as the page Cesario, in the Oregon Shakespeare Festival's 1995 production of Twelfth Night. *(David Cooper, courtesy of the Oregon Shakespeare Festival by permission of the Actors' Equity Association)*

Meanwhile, Maria, Sir Toby, and Sir Andrew decided to stop Malvolio's constant prying into their affairs and devised a scheme whereby Malvolio would find a note, supposedly written by Olivia, in which she confessed her secret love for him and asked him to wear garish yellow stockings tied with cross garters and to smile continually in her presence. Overjoyed to receive this note, Malvolio soon appeared in his strange dress, capering and bowing before the startled countess. Olivia decided that Malvolio had lost his wits; to the amusement of the three conspirators, she had him confined to a dark room.

"If music be the food of love, play on"

Twelfth Night, Act I, scene i, line 1

The ruler of Illyria, Duke Orsino, is in love with Olivia, a young, beautiful, and very wealthy countess who is in mourning for a dead brother. The duke's affection is not requited by the countess, who will not admit his emissary or hear his protestations of love and pleads mourning for her brother as the reason she may not. At the beginning of the play, Duke Orsino is listening to melancholy music as he waits for his messenger, Valentine, to return with news from her.

> *Duke.* If music be the food of love, play on,
> Give me excess of it; that, surfeiting,
> The appetite may sicken, and so die.
> That strain again—it had a dying fall.
> O, it came o'er my ear, like the sweet sound
> That breathes upon a bank of violets,
> Stealing, and giving odour.

As the days passed, Viola fell in love with the duke, but the latter had eyes only for Olivia, with whom he pressed his page to renew his suit. When Cesario delivered another message from Orsino to Olivia, the countess openly declared her love for the young page. Cesario insisted, however, that his heart could never belong to any woman. So obvious were Olivia's feelings for Cesario that Sir Andrew became jealous. Sir Toby and Maria insisted that Sir Andrew's only course was to fight a duel with the page. Sir Toby delivered Sir Andrew's blustering challenge, which Cesario reluctantly accepted.

While these events were unfolding, Viola's twin brother, Sebastian, was being rescued by another sea captain, named Antonio, and the two became close friends. When Sebastian decided to visit the court of Duke Orsino at Illyria, Antonio decided to accompany him, even though he feared that he might be arrested there because he had once dueled with the duke. Upon arriving in Illyria, Antonio gave Sebastian his purse for safekeeping, and the two men separated for several hours.

While wandering about the city, Antonio chanced upon the duel between Cesario and Sir Andrew. Mistaking the disguised page for her brother, Antonio immediately went to the rescue of his supposed friend. When officers arrived on the scene, one of them recognized Antonio and arrested him in the name of the duke. Thinking that Viola was Sebastian, Antonio asked her to return his purse and was surprised and hurt when she disclaimed all knowledge of the captain's money. As Antonio was dragged away, he shouted invectives at "Sebastian" for not returning his purse, thereby alerting Viola to the fact that her brother was still alive.

Meanwhile, the real Sebastian was being followed by Sir Andrew, who never dreamed that this young man was not the same Cesario with whom he had just dueled. Prodded by Sir Toby and Maria, Sir Andrew engaged Sebastian in a new duel and was promptly wounded, along with Sir Toby. Olivia then interfered and had Sebastian taken to her home, thinking that he was Cesario. After sending for a priest, she married the surprised—but not unwilling—Sebastian.

As the officers escorted Antonio past Olivia's house, Orsino—accompanied by Cesario—appeared at her gates. Orsino recognized Antonio instantly and demanded to know why the sailor had returned to Illyria—a city filled with his enemies. Antonio explained that he had rescued and befriended the duke's present companion, Sebastian, and because of his deep friendship for the lad had accompanied him to Illyria despite the danger his visit involved. Pointing to Cesario, he sorrowfully accused the person he supposed to be Sebastian of violating their friendship by not returning his purse.

The duke was protesting against Antonio's accusation when Olivia appeared and saluted Cesario as her husband. Now the duke also began to think his page ungrateful, especially since he had told Cesario to press his own suit with Olivia. Just then Sir Andrew and Sir Toby arrived, looking for a doctor because Sebastian had wounded them. Seeing Cesario, Sir Andrew began to rail at him for his violence until Olivia dismissed the two old men. The real Sebastian then appeared and apologized for having wounded the old men.

Spying Antonio, Sebastian joyfully greeted his friend. Antonio and the rest of the amazed group, unable to believe what they saw, stared from Cesario to Sebastian. After Viola revealed her true identity and explained how she and her brother became separated, she and Sebastian greeted each other warmly. Seeing that the page of whom he had grown so fond was actually a woman, Duke Orsino declared that he would marry her.

After Malvolio was summoned, the plot against him was revealed. As he stormed off, vowing revenge, the others began celebrating the impending marriages of Viola and Orsino and of Sir Toby and Maria. Only Malvolio, unhappy in the happiness of others, remained peevish and disgruntled.

Critical Evaluation

William Shakespeare apparently wrote *Twelfth Night: Or, What You Will* to be performed on the twelfth feast day, the joyous climax of the Renaissance Christmas season; however, the feast day itself otherwise has nothing to do with the substance of the play. The play's subtitle suggests that it is a festive bagatelle to be lightly, but artfully, tossed off. Indeed, Shakespeare may have written the play earlier and revised it for the Christmas festival, for it contains many signs of revision.

The tone of *Twelfth Night* is consistently appropriate to high merriment. With nine comedies behind him when he wrote it, Shakespeare was at the height of his comic powers and in an exalted mood to which he never returned. Chronologically, the play immediately precedes Shakespeare's great tragedies and so-called problem plays. *Twelfth Night* recombines many elements and devices from earlier plays—particularly *The Two Gentlemen of Verona* (c. 1594-1595) and *The Comedy of Errors* (c. 1592-1594)—into a new triumph, unsurpassed in its deft execution.

"Some have greatness thrust upon 'em"

Twelfth Night, Act II, scene v, line 158

Malvolio is a self-loving, pompous steward in Countess Olivia's household. He nurses ridiculous aspirations for Olivia's affections and is disliked by Sir Toby Belch, Olivia's bibulous uncle, and Maria, Olivia's waiting woman. They, together with Sir Andrew Aguecheek, Sir Toby's friend and a hopeless suitor for the countess' hand, seek revenge on Malvolio because he has interfered with their merrymaking late one night. Maria prepares, in imitation of Olivia's handwriting and style, a love note to drop in Malvolio's way. He, walking in the garden, finds the note, recognizes the handwriting, breaks the seal, reads the contents, and in his pride and arrogance becomes convinced that the letter is from Olivia and is meant for him. Thus he is completely taken in by the tricksters' plan for revenge. Malvolio makes a fool of himself as he reads the letter aloud, unaware that the others are listening:

> *Malvolio [reads].* "If this falls into thy hand, revolve. In my stars I
> am above thee, but be not afraid of greatness. Some are born great,
> some achieve greatness, and some have greatness thrust upon
> 'em. . . . Be opposite with a kinsman, surly with servants; let thy
> tonge tang arguments of state; put thyself into the trick of
> singularity. She thus advises thee that sighs for thee. . . ." Daylight
> and champain discovers not more. This is open. I will be proud, I
> will read politic authors, I will baffle Sir Toby, I will wash off
> gross acquaintance. . . . Jove and my stars be prais'd!

It is a brilliant irony that Shakespeare's most joyous play should be compounded out of the sadnesses of its principal characters. Yet the sadnesses are, for the most part, those mannered sadnesses that the Elizabethans savored. Orsino, for example, particularly revels in a sweet melancholy reminiscent of that which afflicted Antonio at the beginning of *The Merchant of Venice* (c. 1596-1597). Orsino's opening speech—which has often been taken too seriously—is not a grief-stricken condemnation of love but rather owes much more to the Italian poet Petrarch. Orsino revels in the longings of love and in the bittersweet satiety of his romantic self-indulgence. He is in love with love.

On the other side of the city is the household of Olivia, which balances Orsino and his establishment. Although Olivia's sadness at her brother's death initially seems more substantial than Orsino's airy romantic fantasies, she, too, is a Renaissance melancholic who is wringing the last ounce of enjoyment out of her grief. Her plan to isolate herself for seven years of mourning is an excess, but one that provides an excellent counterbalance to Orsino's fancy; it also sets the plot in motion, since Orsino's love-longing is frustrated by Olivia's decision to be a recluse.

The point of contact between Orsino and Olivia—ferrying back and forth between the two—is Viola. As Cesario, she also is sad, but her sadness, like the rest of her behavior, is more direct and human. The sweet beauty that shines through her male disguise is elevated beyond a vulgar joke by Olivia's immediate, though circumstantially ridiculous, response to her human appeal. Viola's grief is not stylized and her love is for human beings rather than for abstractions. She seems destined to unite the two melancholy dreamers, but what the play instead accomplishes is that Viola, in her own person and in that of her alter ego, her brother, becomes part of both households. The ultimate outcome is a glorious resolution. It is, of course, immaterial to the dreamy Orsino that he gets Viola instead of Olivia—the romantic emotion is more important to him than is the specific person. Olivia, already drawn out of her seclusion by the disguised Viola, gets what is even better for her, Sebastian.

The glittering plot is reinforced by some of Shakespeare's best and most delicate dramatic poetry. Moreover, the drama is suffused with bittersweet music, and the idyllic setting in Illyria blends with language and imagery to create a most delightful atmosphere wholly appropriate to the celebration of love and the enjoyment of this world.

The one notable briar in the story's rose garden is Malvolio, the play's comic villain; however, he is easily the play's most interesting character. He is called a Puritan, but although he is not a type, he does betray the characteristics then associated with that austere Anglican sect. He is a self-important, serious-minded person with high ideals who cannot bear the thought of others being happy. As Sir Toby puts it to him, "Dost thou think because thou art virtuous, there shall be no more cakes and ale?" Malvolio suffers within a joyous world; it is against his will that he becomes part of the fun when he is duped and made to appear ridiculous. As a character, he represents a historical group, then growing in power, whose earnestness threatened to take the joy out of life (and, incidentally, to close England's theaters). Yet, Shakespeare does not indulge in a satire on Puritanism. He uses the critical powers of comedy in indirect ways.

Malvolio is ridiculous, but so are the cavaliers who surround him. The absurd Sir Andrew Aguecheek and the usually drunken Sir Toby Belch are the representatives, on the political level, of the old order that Malvolio's counterparts in the real world were soon to topple. Yet while these characters are flawed, they are certainly more engaging than the inflated Malvolio. Shakespeare does not set up the contrast as a political allegory, with right on one side and wrong on the other. Nevertheless, Malvolio is an intrusion into the otherwise idyllic world of the play. He cannot love; his desire for the hand of Olivia is grounded in an earnest will to get ahead. He cannot celebrate; he is too pious and self-involved. Nothing is left for him but to be the butt of a joke—his role in the celebration. Some critics have suggested that Malvolio is treated too harshly, but a Renaissance audience would have understood how ludicrous and indecorous it was for a man of his class to think, even for a moment, of courting Countess Olivia. His pompous and blustery language are the key to how alien he is to this festive context. When he has done his bit, Olivia casually mentions that perhaps he has been put upon, but this is the only sympathetic gesture he deserves. He is the force that threatens to destroy the celebration of all that is good and refined and joyful in Elizabethan society.

"Critical Evaluation" by Edward E. Foster

For Further Study

Berry, Ralph. *Shakespeare's Comedies: Explorations in Form*. Princeton, N.J.: Princeton University Press, 1972. A discussion of Shakespeare's comedies in which each chapter is devoted to a specific play. In the chapter "The Messages of *Twelfth Night*," Berry discusses the deceits and illusions in the play and concludes that it calls the very nature of reality into question.

Levin, Richard A. *Love and Society in Shakespearean Comedy*. Newark: University of Delaware Press, 1985. A critical study of three of Shakespeare's romantic comedies. Two chapters deal with *Twelfth Night*: "Household Politics in Illyria" discusses the acceptance of the various characters into society, while "Feste and the Antiromantic *Twelfth Night*" focuses on the discordant elements of the play.

Lloyd Evans, Gareth. *The Upstart Crow: An Introduction to Shakespeare's Plays*. London: J. M. Dent and Sons, 1982. Focuses mainly on critical reviews of Shakespeare's plays, as well as discussing sources and historical context and background.

Muir, Kenneth, ed. *Shakespeare—The Comedies: A Collection of Critical Essays*. Englewood Cliffs, N.J.: Prentice-Hall, 1965. An anthology of essays that discuss Shakespeare's comedies from various points of view. Harold Jenkins compares *Twelfth Night* with earlier plays by Shakespeare and others and concludes that it is the greatest of Shakespeare's romantic comedies.

Shakespeare, William. *Twelfth Night*. Edited by J. M. Lothian and T. W. Craik. London: Methuen, 1975. Includes more than eighty pages of introductory material and critical analysis, as well as the text of the play itself.

The Two Gentlemen of Verona

Type of plot: Comedy
Time of plot: Sixteenth century
Locale: Italy
First performed: c. 1594-1595; first published, 1623

Principal characters

VALENTINE and
PROTEUS, two young gentlemen
JULIA, the beloved of Proteus
SILVIA, the beloved of Valentine
THURIO, a man in love with Silvia
THE DUKE OF MILAN, Silvia's father
SPEED, Valentine's servant
LUCETTA, Julia's servant

The Story

Valentine and Proteus, two longtime friends, disagreed heartily on whether, as Valentine thought, the most important thing in life was to travel and learn the wonders of the world, or whether Proteus was right in believing nothing to be more important than love. The two friends parted for a time when Valentine traveled to Milan, to seek advancement and honor in the palace of the duke. He pleaded with Proteus to join him in the venture, but Proteus was too much in love with Julia to leave her side for even a short time. Julia was a noble and pure young girl, who had had many suitors. Proteus had at last won her heart and the two were happy in their love.

Valentine journeyed to Milan, and there he learned that his friend was right about the importance of love. For Valentine met the duke's daughter, Silvia, and fell instantly in love with her. Silvia returned his love, but her father wanted her to marry Thurio, a foolish man with no personal charms but much land and gold. Valentine longed for Silvia but saw no chance of persuading her father to consent to his suit. Then he learned that Proteus, whose father was ignorant of Proteus' love affair and wished his son to educate himself by travel, was soon to arrive in Milan.

The two friends had a joyful reunion, and Valentine proudly presented his friend to Silvia. To Proteus he praised the virtue and beauty of his beloved, and when they were alone, Valentine confided to Proteus that, since Sylvia's father refused to give her to anyone but Thurio, he planned to fashion a rope ladder and steal Silvia from her room and marry her. Valentine, asking his friend to help him in his plan, was too absorbed to notice that Proteus remained strangely silent. The truth was that Proteus, at the first sight of Silvia, had forgotten his solemn vows to Julia (sealed before he left her with the exchange of rings), had forgotten too his oath of friendship with Valentine, and that he was determined to have Silvia for his own. With protestations of self-hatred for betraying his friend, Proteus told the duke of Valentine's plan to escape with Silvia from the palace. The duke, forewarned, tricked Valentine into revealing the plot and banished him from Milan on penalty of his life.

While these events were taking place, Julia, thinking that Proteus still loved her and grieving over his absence, disguised herself as a page and traveled to Milan to see her love. She was on her way to Milan when Valentine was forced to leave that city. Valentine, not knowing that his onetime friend had betrayed him, believed Proteus' promise that he would carry letters back and forth between him and Silvia.

With Valentine out of the way, Proteus proceeded to get rid of Thurio as a rival. Thurio, foolish and gullible, was an easy man to trick. One night, Proteus and Thurio went to Silvia's window to serenade her in Thurio's name, but Proteus used the occasion to sing to her and make protestations of his love for her. Julia, in the disguise of a page, stood in the shadows and heard his betrayal of her, as well as Silvia's response that she would love no one but Valentine. She also accused him of playing false with Julia, for Valentine had told her of his friend's betrothal.

Calling herself Sebastian, Julia, still in the dress of a page, became employed by Proteus to carry messages to Silvia. One day, he gave her the ring that Julia herself had given him and told her to deliver it to Silvia. When Silvia refused the ring and sent it back to Proteus, Julia loved her rival and blessed her.

Valentine, in the meantime, had been captured by outlaws, once honorable men who had been banished for petty crimes and had taken refuge in the woods near Mantua. To save his life, Valentine had joined the band and soon became their leader. A short time later, Silvia, hoping to find Valentine, escaped from the palace and, with the help of an agent, arrived at an abbey near Milan. There she was captured by the outlaws. When her father heard of her flight, he took Thurio and Proteus to the abbey to look for her. Julia followed them. Proteus, arriving on the scene first, rescued her from the outlaws before they were able to take her to their leader. Again Proteus proclaimed his love for her. When she scornfully berated him, he seized her and tried to force himself on her. Valentine, who had overheard everything, sprang upon Proteus and pulled him away from her.

Valentine was more hurt by his friend's duplicity than by anything else, but such was his forgiving nature that when Proteus confessed his guilt and his shame over his betrayal, Valentine forgave him and received him again as his friend. In proof of his friendship, he was even prepared to give up his claim on Silvia. When she heard that, Julia, still disguised, fainted. Reviving, she pretended to hand over to Silvia the ring Proteus had ordered her to deliver, but instead she offered the ring Proteus had given her when they parted in Verona. Then Julia was recognized by all, and Proteus admitted that he still loved her.

The outlaws appeared with the duke and Thurio, whom they had captured in the forest. Thurio gave up all claim to Silvia, for he thought a girl who would run off into the woods to pursue another man much too foolish for him to marry. Her father, convinced at last of Valentine's worth, gave that young man permission to marry Silvia. During the general rejoicing Valentine begged one more boon. He asked the duke to pardon the outlaws, all brave men who would serve the duke faithfully if he would return them from exile. The duke granted the boon, and the whole party made its way back to Milan. There the two happy couples intended to share their wedding day and be happy in their mutual love and friendship.

"They do not love that do not show their love"

The Two Gentlemen of Verona, Act I, scene ii, line 31

Proteus, one of the two gentlemen of Verona, is in love with Julia. To further his suit, he sends a letter to her by the servant of Valentine (the other gentleman), Speed. Being deceived by Lucetta, Julia's waiting woman, into thinking that she is her mistress, Speed delivers the letter to her and reports to Proteus that the lady did not say anything about loving him. Julia, a maid ready and willing to fall in love with somebody, discusses her would-be suitors with Lucetta. Lucetta says that Proteus loves Julia best of all her suitors, but Julia does not believe the statement, because Proteus does not show his love. The two women disagree on how much love a lover displays.

> *Lucetta.* Fire that's closest kept burns most of all.
> *Julia.* They do not love that do not show their love.
> *Lucetta.* O, they love least that let men know their love.

Critical Evaluation

In *The Two Gentlemen of Verona*, William Shakespeare is learning the craft of playwriting, with plot elements, characters, and comic situations that will reappear in later plays. The work also mirrors the literary vogues of its time, particularly the popular prose romances of the day—forerunners of the later sentimental novel and the twentieth century psychological novel—that race the turbulencies of adolescence and youth. Some of Shakespeare's later comedies and his *Romeo and Juliet* (c. 1595-1596) reflect a similar concern. Himself then the father of a daughter approaching her teens, Shakespeare may have been especially sensitive to the problems of youth.

Proteus and Valentine are Italianates—young gentlemen sent abroad to acquire perfection at a foreign court. Proteus' name, a common Elizabethan label for the Italianate, further establishes that identification. Critics have made much of the geographical "inaccuracy" of Valentine's departure for Milan by boat, ignoring the fact that Shakespeare was too well read and too familiar with the geography of Europe not to know that travel from the real Verona to Milan would have had to have been by land. As in his other plays, Shakespeare uses place names for their connotations. Verona was the home of the lovers Romeo and Juliet, Milan the fashion center of Europe and the seat of the imperial court. With this Verona and this Milan he could retain the three worlds of his source, Jorge de Montemayor's prose romance *Diana* (c. 1559): the world of lovers subject to parental oversight, the sophisticated world of the court, and the green world of the forest.

In the first world, Proteus, like Felis in *Diana* and Euphues in John Lyly's romance *Euphues, the Anatomy of Wit* (1578-1580), goes through the wild emotional swings and naïve tentativeness of adolescence, and he submits tamely to his elders. He is in love with love and has an idealized vision of the court, where he hopes to achieve perfection.

Speed (Linda Alper) and Launce (Robert Vincent Frank) look to Crab (Bruiser, the dog) for answers to some of life's questions in the Oregon Shakespeare Festival's 1997 production of The Two Gentlemen of Verona. (David Cooper, courtesy of the Oregon Shakespeare Festival by permission of the Actors' Equity Association)

In the second world, the world of the court, Proteus is metamorphosed by self-interest and begins to assume poses. His desire for Valentine's Silvia leads him first to disloyalty to both his friend and Julia and eventually to outright treachery. At the end, rejected by Silvia after his final pose as a knight errant who has rescued her from outlaws, Proteus tries to take Silvia by force. Even the more stable Valentine changes at court, becoming adept at exaggerated expression; perfection for him becomes a matter of rhetorical skill—"A man is no man if with his tongue he cannot win a woman"—and a proficiency in conventional formulas and flattery. In fact, as Peter Lindenbaum has pointed out, Valentine's love affair is a reaction to his court experience.

"Who is Silvia?"

The Two Gentlemen of Verona, Act IV, scene ii, line 38

Valentine, one of the two gentlemen of Verona, has gone to Milan, where he has fallen in love with Silvia, the saucy and charming daughter of the Duke of Milan. The duke wants Silvia to marry Thurio, whom she detests. Informed by Proteus, the other gentleman of Verona (who has himself now abandoned Julia, his sweetheart of Verona, for Silvia), that Valentine means to elope with his daughter, the duke banishes Valentine from the country. Then he urges Thurio to press his suit. Thurio brings a group of musicians to the duke's palace to serenade Silvia. The song these musicians sing is one of Shakespeare's loveliest:

> *Song.* Who is Silvia? what is she,
>   That all our swains commend her?
> Holy, fair, and wise is she:
>   The heaven such grace did lend her,
>   That she might admired be.

Some critics have found fault with the way the play ends in the last of these worlds, the green world. Here, outlaws are readily pardoned, Proteus is forgiven his assault on Silvia, and Valentine temporarily resigns his claim on his beloved in favor of Proteus. Though Proteus' repentance seems sudden, it is plausible because it is preceded by the shock he received when his villainy was publicly exposed and he recognized his self-deception. With this recognition, the idealized picture of perfection that the Verona youth had envisioned for himself—hearing sweet discourse, conversing with noblemen, and being in the eye of every exercise worthy of a nobleman—suddenly gives way to the truth. The court produced this villain, and "shame and guilt confound him." Proteus recognizes not only his own imperfection but that of all humankind: "were man but constant, he were perfect."

To Valentine and the duke also comes discovery. The duke discovers the true nature of his favorite, Thurio, and of the despised "peasant" Valentine, and he learns to look at Valentine with new eyes and to consider him worthy of his daughter's love. He sees the outlaws as reformed men. The corrupting influence of the court has dissolved in the healing of the green forest. Even Julia, who dreamed of idealized love at the beginning of the play and then at court learned of the flaws in her beloved Proteus, discovers that she can still love him. Valentine, though he at first reacted with rage, feels the rekindling of his old feelings of friendship. The play thus ends with the regeneration of the protagonists, a conclusion required if the play is to remain faithful to the traditional endings of the prose romances that served as sources for the play.

Shakespeare does not go into much depth in portraying the characters in this play. In fact, some critics have suspected him of writing *The Two Gentlemen of Verona* primarily to mock the idealistic Renaissance romantic codes. It is more likely, however, that he is watching his characters with sympathetic amusement.

When Valentine is smitten with Silvia and confides his feelings to Speed, Speed mocks his impassioned behavior and comments, as Silvia enters, that he is now about to witness a puppet show. Even Silvia joins in the mockery, though more gently, when she stops Valentine's exaggerated praise and Petrarchan conventions with "I guess the sequel." Proteus' sentimental gift of a little dog, "Jewel," which Launce loses and replaces with the mongrel "Crab," is transformed from a gallant gesture into farce when the dog runs under the duke's table and lifts his leg against Silvia's farthingale. Just after Proteus' tender farewell to Julia, Launce parodies lovers' partings with his dog sitting in for the loved one; when Valentine laments his banishment from Silvia, Launce mimicks a lover's Petrarchan cataloging of his mistress' physical attributes.

The play also has moments of great charm. Shakespeare offers lyrical passages such as the well-known song "Who Is Silvia?," banter between characters, and the lighthearted antics of Speed and Launce.

"Critical Evaluation" by Thomas Amherst Perry

For Further Study

Leech, Clifford. Introduction to *The Two Gentlemen of Verona*, by William Shakespeare. London: Methuen, 1969. Concludes that the play is primarily concerned with mocking the idealistic pretensions of Renaissance codes of romantic love and friendship.

Lindenbaum, Peter. "Education in *The Two Gentlemen of Verona*." *Studies in English Literature* 15, no. 2 (Spring, 1975): 229-244. Concludes that the play is about the importance of penitence for past sins. The education of the "perfect man" envisioned at the beginning of the play takes the protagonists to the court and then to the green forest, where they will learn that they are imperfect because they are human.

Perry, Thomas A. "Proteus, Wry-Transformed Traveller." *Shakespeare Quarterly* 5, no. 1 (January, 1954): 33-40. Shows that to understand Proteus, one must first see him as a young Elizabethan Italianate in a passing phase; at the end of the play he is a chastened and regenerate youth.

Sargent, Ralph M. "Sir Thomas Elyot and the Integrity of *The Two Gentlemen of Verona*." *PMLA* 65, no. 2 (December, 1950): 1166-1180. Discusses the ways in which Proteus learns that he has violated the codes of masculine friendship and romantic love and how he is regenerated and reclaimed at the end of the play.

Stephenson, William E. "The Adolescent Dream-World of *The Two Gentlemen of Verona*." *Shakespeare Quarterly* 17, no. 2 (Spring, 1966): 165-168. Focuses on the fact that Proteus and Valentine are two very young gentlemen, sixteenth century adolescents still under parental authority. Their wild swings of emotion, naïveté, tentative behavior, tame submission to elders, and dreams and hallucinations of love are signs that they are just past the first changes of puberty. In the latter part of the play they are half-grown, and even the final denouement is a dream-action.

The Two Noble Kinsmen

Type of plot: Romance or tragicomedy
Time of plot: Antiquity
Locale: Athens and Thebes
First performed: c. 1612-1613; first published, 1634

Principal characters

THESEUS, Duke of Athens
HIPPOLYTA, his wife
EMILIA, her younger sister
PALAMON and
ARCITE, nephews of Creon, King of Thebes

The Story

During the marriage ceremony of Theseus, Duke of Athens, and Hippolyta, queen of the Amazons, three widowed queens begged Theseus' aid. Creon, King of Thebes, had slain their husbands in battle and would not permit their bodies to receive decent burial. Theseus commiserated with the queens, but provided small comfort for their grief when he directed that his nuptial ceremonies be continued. The queens persisting in their pleas, Theseus conceded to the extent of ordering an expeditionary force to be readied to march against Thebes. Not to be denied, the distracted queens finally persuaded him to champion their cause. He appointed Pirithous, an Athenian nobleman, to stand in his place for the remainder of the ceremony, kissed Hippolyta farewell, and led the queens away toward Thebes.

Meanwhile, in Thebes, the cousins Palamon and Arcite, nephews of Creon, found their uncle's tyranny unbearable and stultifying, and decided to leave Thebes. No sooner had they made this decision than they learned that Thebes was threatened by Theseus. The cousins, loyal to Thebes if not to Creon, deferred their departure in order to serve their city.

When the opposing forces met, Palamon and Arcite fought with great courage, but the Athenians were victorious in the battle. Theseus, triumphant, directed the three widowed queens to bury their dead in peace. Palamon and Arcite, having been wounded and left for dead on the battlefield, were taken by the Athenians. The cousins, healed of their wounds and finding themselves in a prison in Athens, impressed their jailers with their seeming unconcern at being incarcerated. In their cell, however, they sadly bemoaned their fate to each other. Resigned to spending the rest of their lives in prison, they recalled with grief the joys of battle and the hunt, and they grieved at the thought of a future without marriage. Even so, they

308

The King of the May (Michael J. Hume, left) and Lady Bright (Gina Daniels) tease Gerrold (Barry Kraft, seated) during a May Day celebration in the Oregon Shakespeare Festival's 1994 production of The Two Noble Kinsmen. *(David Cooper, courtesy of the Oregon Shakespeare Festival by permission of the Actors' Equity Association)*

made some attempt to reconcile themselves to imprisonment by declaring that in their cell they had each other's excellent company and that they were insulated from the evils that beset free men.

Emilia, Hippolyta's beautiful sister, entered the prison garden. Palamon saw her and fell in love at once. When Arcite beheld her, he too fell in love. Palamon declared that Arcite must not love her, but Arcite answered that Palamon, who had called her a goddess, might love her spiritually; he, Arcite, would love her in a more earthly manner. Palamon maintained that this goddess they had beheld was his to love because he had seen her first. Arcite, in turn, insisted that he too must love her because of the propinquity of the pair. Palamon, enraged, wished for liberty and weapons so that he and Arcite might decide the issue in mortal combat.

The jailkeeper, on orders, took Arcite to Theseus. Palamon, meanwhile, was filled with despair at the thought that Arcite was now free to win Emilia. The keeper returned to report that Arcite had been sent away from Athens and that Palamon must be moved to a cell in which there were fewer windows. Palamon writhed in the knowledge that Arcite now seemed certain to win the hand of Emilia.

Arcite, banished in the country near Athens, felt no advantage over his cousin. Indeed, he envied Palamon, who he believed could see Emilia every time she visited the prison garden with her maid. Desperate, he assumed a disguise and returned to Athens to participate in athletic games in honor of Emilia's birthday. Excelling in the games, he admitted that he was of gentle birth; but Theseus did not penetrate his disguise. Theseus, admiring Arcite's athletic prowess and his modesty, designated him to be a serving-man to Emilia.

In the meantime the daughter of the jailkeeper fell in love with Palamon and effected his escape. In the forest, where the court had gone a-Maying, Arcite came upon the escaped prisoner. In spite of Palamon's harsh words to him, Arcite promised to supply his cousin with food. Two days later he brought food and drink. When he left, he promised to return the next time with armor and weapons, that the two might decide their quarrel by combat.

Arcite having returned with armor and weapons, the two youths armed themselves and fought. At the same time Theseus and his party, hunting in the forest, came upon the struggling pair. Theseus condemned them to be executed straightway, one for having defied banishment, the other for having broken out of prison. Hippolyta, Pirithous, and Emilia begged Theseus for mercy. The duke then declared that they might live if they would forget Emilia. When both refused, Theseus resolved that the youths should go free, but that in a month they must return to Athens, both accompanied by three knights of their own choice, and resolve their problem in the lists. The victor would be awarded the hand of Emilia; the loser and his companions would be executed on the spot.

A month passed. As Emilia admired likenesses of Palamon and Arcite and despaired at her inability to choose one or the other as her favorite, the cousins, with six knights, returned to Athens. Arcite and his knight-companions invoked Mars, the god of war; Palamon and his cohorts invoked Venus, the goddess of love; Emilia, in her role as a priestess of Diana, invoked the goddess of chastity to bring victory to the youth who loved her best. In the tournament that followed Arcite was the victor.

Palamon lay his head on the block in anticipation of execution, but Pirithous interrupted the beheading to announce that Arcite had been thrown and mortally trampled by a black horse that Emilia had given him. Before he died, Arcite, brought before his cousin, relinquished his claim upon Emilia to Palamon. Palamon, reconciled with his cousin, observed sorrowfully that he had lost a great love in order to gain another.

Critical Evaluation

The Two Noble Kinsmen was a joint production of the aging Shakespeare and his protégé John Fletcher. Some specific scenes have been attributed, on the basis of stylistic traits, to each dramatist. That many scenes cannot be specifically assigned would suggest close collaboration. The main plot was taken from Giovanni Boccaccio's *Teseide* (1340-1345), which, in turn, was derived from Statius Caecilius' *Thebaid* (c. 219-166 B.C.E.). Shakespeare had already used the wedding of Theseus and Hippolyta in *A Midsummer Night's Dream* (c. 1595-1596). A century before, Sir Geoffrey Chaucer had used the story of Palamon and Arcite in "The Knight's Tale." The play is marked by a sentimentality that betokens the end of the golden age of Tudor and Stuart drama.

The Two Noble Kinsmen more closely resembles the tragicomedies of Francis Beaumont and Fletcher than it does Shakespeare's later plays, such as *Pericles* (1608), *Cymbeline* (1609), *The Winter's Tale* (1610-1611), and *The Tempest* (1611). Although the frame subplot of Theseus and Hippolyta recalls the same characters in *A Midsummer Night's Dream*, the mirthful, exuberant tone of Shakespeare's youthful comedy is replaced with one more serious, heroic, and formally stylized. For both authors, the main source of the play, as the Prologue mentions, is Chaucer's "The Knight's Tale" from his *Canterbury Tales* (1387-1400). Act I derives also from Sir Thomas North's translation of Plutarch's "Life of Theseus." the basis of both the play and Chaucer's narrative is the *Thebaid* of Statius, with which Shakespeare and Fletcher were probably familiar.

The major theme of the play, the tragic conflict between loyal friendship on the one hand and romantic passion on the other, is clearly but quite rigidly drawn. Palamon and Arcite, bound by noble comradeship and affection, turn at once into rivals and deadly enemies when they fall in love, nearly simultaneously and at first sight, with Emilia. Since their code is heroic, neither one compromises his claims for sole possession of the beloved. Instead of courting and winning the romantic prize, the kinsmen prepare to fight for her. Arcite, who calls upon Mars for assistance, wins the contest but loses his bride. Palamon wisely calls upon Venus to champion him. Thus, although he loses the contest he succeeds in love—which is the point of the play. When Sir William Davenant adapted *The Two Noble Kinsmen* in 1664 as *The Rivals*, he emphasized even more than did Shakespeare and Fletcher the code of heroic passion by which Palamon and Arcite live, a convention that would become exaggeratedly idealistic during the period of Cavalier drama.

In spite of its artificial conventions and sentimentality, *The Two Noble Kinsmen* is not without merit, particularly Shakespeare's limited part of the play. In Act I, for example, he introduces two themes that Fletcher fails to develop later: that of the intimate friendships between Theseus and Pirithous and between Emilia and Flavinia. Had the theme of these parallel friendships been advanced with greater complexity and psychological insight, the play would have surely engaged the modern reader's attention as something more than a curiosity in the history of seventeenth century drama.

For Further Study

Bertram, Paul. *Shakespeare and "The Two Noble Kinsmen."* New Brunswick, N.J.: Rutgers University Press, 1965. Discussion of the play, usually thought to be written by Shakespeare in collaboration with John Fletcher. Discussion of earlier critical works.

Donaldson, E. Talbot. *The Swan at the Well: Shakespeare Reading Chaucer.* New Haven, Conn.: Yale University Press, 1985. Compares several of Shakespeare's plays and their sources in Chaucer's poems. *"The Knight's Tale* and *The Two Noble Kinsmen"* compares Chaucer's story with Shakespeare's play.

Hillman, Richard. "Shakespeare's Romantic Innocents and the Misappropriation of the Romantic Past: The Case of *The Two Noble Kinsmen*." In *The Tempest and After*, edited by Stanley W. Wells. Cambridge, England: Cambridge University Press, 1991. Considers the characters' responses to their notions of romance.

Muir, Kenneth. *Shakespeare's Comic Sequence.* New York: Barnes & Noble Books, 1979. The essay on *The Two Noble Kinsmen* discusses the authorship of the play. There is also critical discussion of the play.

Waith, Eugene M. "Shakespeare and Fletcher on Love and Friendship." In *Shakespeare Studies: An Annual Gathering of Research, Criticism, and Reviews*, edited by J. Leeds Barroll. New York: Burt Franklin, 1986. Explores the conflict between love and friendship in the works of Shakespeare and Fletcher.

The Winter's Tale

Type of plot: Romance or tragicomedy
Time of plot: The legendary past
Locale: Sicilia and Bohemia
First performed: 1610-1611; first published, 1623

Principal characters

LEONTES, the King of Sicilia
HERMIONE, his queen
POLIXENES, the King of Bohemia
CAMILLO, Leontes' counselor
PERDITA, Leontes' daughter
FLORIZEL, Polixenes' son
PAULINA, Hermione's maid
AUTOLYCUS, a rogue

The Story

Polixenes, the King of Bohemia, was the guest of Leontes, the King of Sicilia. The two men had been friends since boyhood, and there was much celebrating and joyousness during the visit. At last Polixenes decided that he must return to his home country. Leontes urged him to extend his visit, but Polixenes refused, saying that he had not seen his young son for a long time. Then Leontes asked Hermione, his wife, to try to persuade Polixenes to remain. When Polixenes finally yielded to her pleas, Leontes became suspicious and concluded that Hermione and Polixenes must be lovers and that he had been cuckolded.

Leontes was generally of a jealous disposition, and he sought constant reassurance that his son Mamillius was his own offspring. Having now, out of jealousy, misjudged his wife and his old friend, Leontes became so angry that he ordered Camillo, his chief counselor, to poison Polixenes. All Camillo's attempts to dissuade Leontes from his scheme only strengthened the jealous man's feelings of hate. Nothing could persuade the king that Hermione was true to him. Eventually Camillo agreed to poison Polixenes, but only on condition that Leontes return to Hermione with no more distrust.

Polixenes had noticed a change in Leontes' attitude toward him. When he questioned Camillo, the sympathetic lord revealed the plot to poison him. Together, they hastily embarked for Bohemia.

Upon learning that Polixenes and Camillo had fled, Leontes was more than ever convinced that his guest and his wife had been guilty of carrying on an affair. He conjectured that Polixenes and Camillo had been plotting together all the while and planning his murder. Moreover, he decided that Hermione, who was pregnant, was in all likelihood bearing Polixenes' child and not his. Publicly he accused Hermione of adultery and commanded that her son be taken from her. She herself was imprisoned. Although his servants protested the order, Leontes was adamant.

In prison, Hermione gave birth to a baby girl. Paulina, her attendant, thought that the sight of the baby girl might cause Leontes to relent, so she carried the child to the palace. Instead of forgiving his wife, Leontes became more incensed and demanded that the child be put to death. He instructed Antigonus, Paulina's husband, to take the baby to a far-off desert shore and there abandon it. Although the lord pleaded to be released from this cruel command, he was forced to put out to sea for the purpose of leaving the child to perish on some lonely coast.

Leontes had sent two messengers to consult the Oracle of Delphi to determine Hermione's guilt. When the men returned, Leontes summoned his wife and the whole court to hear the verdict. The messengers read a scroll that stated that Hermione was innocent, as were Polixenes and Camillo, that Leontes was a tyrant, and that he would live without an heir until that which was lost was found.

The king, refusing to believe the oracle, declared its findings false, and again accused Hermione of infidelity. In the midst of his tirade a servant rushed in to say that young Mamillius had died because of sorrow and anxiety over his mother's plight. On hearing this, Hermione fell into a swoon and was carried to her chambers. Soon afterward, Paulina returned to announce that her mistress was dead. At this news Leontes, who had already begun to believe the oracle after news of his son's death, beat his breast with rage at himself. He reproached himself bitterly for the insane jealousy that had led to these unhappy events. In repentance, the king swore that he would have the legend of the deaths of his son and wife engraved on their tombstones and that he himself would do penance thereafter.

Meanwhile, Antigonus had taken the baby girl to a desert country near the sea. Heartsick at having to abandon her, the old courtier laid a bag of gold and jewels by her with instructions that she should be called Perdita, a name revealed to him in a dream. After he had done this, he was attacked and killed by a bear. Later, his ship was wrecked in a storm and all hands were lost. Although no news of the expedition reached Sicilia, the kind shepherd who found Perdita also saw the deaths of Antigonus and his men.

Sixteen years passed, bringing with them many changes. Leontes was a broken man, grieving alone in his palace. Perdita had grown into a beautiful and charming young woman under the care of the shepherd. So lovely was she that Prince Florizel, the son of Polixenes and heir to the throne of Bohemia, had fallen madly in love with her.

Unaware of the girl's background, and knowing only that his son was in love with a young shepherdess, Polixenes and Camillo, now his most trusted servant, disguised themselves and visited a sheep-shearing festival, where they saw Florizel, dressed as a shepherd, dancing with a lovely young woman. Although he realized that the shepherdess was of noble bearing, Polixenes in great rage forbade his son to marry her. Florizel thereupon made secret plans to elope with Perdita to a foreign country. Camillo, pitying the young couple, advised Florizel to embark for Sicilia and to pretend that he was a messenger of goodwill from the King of Bohemia. Camillo supplied the young man with letters of introduction to Leontes. It was part of Camillo's plan to inform Polixenes of the lovers' escape and travel to Sicilia to find them, thus taking advantage of the situation to return home once more.

"What's past help, should be past grief"

The Winter's Tale, Act III, scene ii, lines 223-224

Leontes, King of Sicilia, believes his wife, Queen Hermione, is guilty of adultery with his boyhood friend, Polixenes, King of Bohemia. He publicly proclaims her an adulteress, takes her small son, Mamillius, from her, and throws her into prison. She is pregnant and soon gives birth to a girl. Leontes disowns the child. Brought to trial, Hermione defends herself and declares her fidelity with dignity. Word is brought from the oracle of Delphi that convinces Leontes he has misjudged his wife and Polixenes. Before he can right the wrong, Mamillius, his son, dies of grief at his mother's sufferings. At the news, Hermione swoons and is removed from the court. Her waiting woman, Paulina, returns with the news that Hermione, too, is dead. Paulina rails at Leontes to effect—he is clearly distraught at the death of his wife. Rebuked by a lord, Paulina apologizes for her behavior.

> *Paulina.* I am sorry for't.
> All faults I make, when I shall come to know them,
> I do repent. Alas, I have showed too much
> The rashness of a woman; he [Leontes] is touched
> To the noble heart. What's gone, and what's past help,
> Should be past grief.

The poor shepherd, frightened by the king's wrath, decided to tell Polixenes how, years before, he had found the baby and a bag of gold and jewels by her side. Fate intervened, however, and the shepherd was intercepted by the rogue Autolycus and put aboard the ship sailing to Sicilia.

Soon Florizel and Perdita arrived in Sicilia, followed by Polixenes and Camillo. When the old shepherd heard how Leontes had lost a daughter, he described the finding of Perdita. Leontes, convinced that Perdita was his own abandoned infant, was joyfully reunited with his daughter. When he heard this, Polixenes immediately gave his consent to the marriage of Florizel and Perdita. The only sorrowful circumstance to mar the happiness of all concerned was the earlier tragic death of Hermione.

One day, Paulina asked Leontes to visit a newly erected statue of the dead woman in Hermione's chapel. Leontes, ever faithful to the memory of his dead wife—even to the point of promising Paulina never to marry again—gathered his guests and took them to view the statue. Standing in the chapel, amazed at the wonderful lifelike quality of the work, they heard strains of soft music. Suddenly the statue descended from its pedestal and was revealed as the living Hermione. She had spent the sixteen years in seclusion while awaiting some word of her daughter. The happy family was reunited, and Hermione completely forgave her repentant husband. He and Polixenes were again the best of friends, rejoicing in the happiness of Perdita and Florizel.

Critical Evaluation

Written after *Cymbeline* (1609-1610) and before *The Tempest* (1611), *The Winter's Tale* is as hard to classify generically as is the fully mature dramatic genius of its author. Partaking of the elements of tragedy, the play yet ends in sheer comedy, just as it mingles elements of realism and romance. William Shakespeare took his usual freedom with his source, Robert Greene's euphuistic romance *Pandosto: The Triumph of Time* (1588). Yet time remains the most crucial element in the play's structure, its clearest break with the pseudo-Aristotelian unities. The effect of time on Hermione, moreover, when the statue is revealed to be wrinkled and aged, heightens the pathos and credibility of the triumphant discovery and recognition scene. In order to allow that final scene its full effect, Shakespeare wisely has Perdita's discovery and recognition reported to the audience second-hand in Act V, scene ii. In keeping with the maturity of Shakespeare's dramatic talent, the poetic style of this play is clear, unrhetorical, sparse in its imagery, as well as metaphorically sharp. Verse alternates with prose as court characters alternate with country personages.

Mamillius tells his mother, who asks him for a story, that "a sad tale's best for winter." Ironically the little boy's story is never told; the entrance of Leontes interrupts it, and Hermione's son, his role as storyteller once defined, strangely disappears. In his place, the play itself takes over, invigorated by Mamillius' uncanny innocent wisdom, which reflects a Platonic view of childhood. The story that unfolds winds a multitude of themes without losing sight of any of them. It presents two views of honor, a wholesome one represented by Hermione and a demented one represented by Leontes. Like many of Shakespeare's plays, the narrative concerns the unholy power of kings who can be mistaken but whose power, however mistaken, is final. Yet the finality, here, is spared, the tragic ending avoided: The absolute goodness of Hermione, Paulina, Camillo, the shepherd, and Florizel proves to be enough to overcome the evil of Leontes. Moving from the older generation's inability to love to the reflowering of love in the younger, the play spins out into a truly comic ending, with the reestablishment of community, royal authority, and general happiness in a triple *gamos*. The balance of tension between youth and age, guilt and innocence, death and rebirth is decided in favor of life, and the play escapes the clutches of remorseless tragedy in a kind of ultimate mystical vision of human life made ideal through suffering.

Leontes is a most puzzling character. His antifeminism, as expressed in his cynical speech on cuckoldry, seems more fashionable than felt. In his determined jealousy, he resembles Othello, and in his self-inflicted insanity, Lear. In fact, the words of Lear to Cordelia resound in Leontes' great speech, beginning, "Is whispering nothing?" and concluding, "My wife is nothing; nor nothing have these nothings,/ If this be nothing." It is almost impossible to sympathize with him further when he condemns even his helpless child in the face of Paulina's gentle pleas; and it is not surprising that he at first even denies the oracle itself. Yet his

King Leontes (Mark Murphey) accuses his queen, Hermione (Lise Bruneau), of adultery in the Oregon Shakespeare Festival's 1996 production of The Winter's Tale. *(David Cooper, courtesy of the Oregon Shakespeare Festival by permission of the Actors' Equity Association)*

sudden recognition of culpability is no more convincing than his earlier, unmotivated jealousy. It is as if he changes too quickly for belief; perhaps this is the reason for Hermione's decision to test his penitence with time, until it ripens into sincerity. Certainly his reaction to his wife's swoon shows only a superficial emotion. Leontes is still self-centered, still regally assured that all can be put right with the proper words. Only after the years have passed in loneliness does he realize it takes more than orderly words to undo the damage wrought by disorderly royal commands. His admission to Paulina that his words killed Hermione paves the way for the happy ending.

Even the minor characters are drawn well and vividly. Camillo is the ideal courtier who chooses virtue over favor. Paulina, like the nurse Anna in Euripides' *Hippolytus* (428 B.C.E.), is the staunch helpmate of her mistress, especially in adversity, aided by magical powers that seem to spring from her own determined character. Her philosophy is also that of the classical Greeks: "What's gone and what's past help/ Should be past grief." This play does not have the tragic Greek ending, because Paulina preserves her mistress rather than assisting her to destroy herself. Even the rogue Autolycus is beguiling, with his verbal witticisms, his frank pursuit of self-betterment, and his lusty and delightful songs. His sign is Mercury, the thief of the gods, and he follows his sign like the best rascals in Renaissance tradition, Boccaccio's Friar Onion, Rabelais' Panurge, and Shakespeare's own Falstaff.

In Hermione and Perdita, Shakespeare achieves two of his greatest portraits of women. Hermione's speech reflects her personality, straightforward, without embroidery, as pure as virtue itself. Her reaction to Leontes' suspicion and condemnation is brief, but telling. "Adieu, my lord," she says, "I never wish'd to see you sorry; now/ I trust I shall." She combines the hardness of Portia with the gentleness of Desdemona; in fact, Antigonus' oath in her defense recalls the character of Othello's wife. Like Geoffrey Chaucer's patient Griselda, Hermione loses everything, but she strikes back with the most devastating weapon of all: time. Yet in the final scene of the play it is clear that her punishment of Leontes has made Hermione suffer no less. Perdita personifies, though never in a stereotyped way, gentle innocence: "Nothing she does or seems/ But smacks of something greater than herself/ Too noble for this place." Indeed, when Polixenes' wrath, paralleling Leontes' previous folly, threatens Perdita's life for a second time, the audience holds its breath because she is too good to be safe. When Shakespeare saves her, the play, sensing the audience's joy, abruptly ends on its highest note.

In its theme and structure, *The Winter's Tale* bears a striking resemblance to Euripides' *Alcestis* (438 B.C.E.). In both plays, the "death" of the queen threatens the stability and happiness of society and, in both, her restoration, which is miraculous and ambiguous, restores order to the world of the court. Shakespeare, however, widens the comic theme by adding the love of the younger generation. So *The Winter's Tale* defies the forces of death and hatred romantically as well as realistically. The sad tale becomes happy, as winter becomes spring.

"Critical Evaluation" by Kenneth John Atchity

For Further Study

Lloyd Evans, Gareth. *The Upstart Crow: An Introduction to Shakespeare's Plays.* London: J. M. Dent and Sons, 1982. A comprehensive treatment of the dramatic works of William Shakespeare, with major emphasis on critical reviews of the plays. Also discusses the sources from which Shakespeare drew and circumstances surrounding the writing of the plays.

Muir, Kenneth, ed. *Shakespeare—The Comedies: A Collection of Critical Essays.* Englewood Cliffs, N.J.: Prentice-Hall, 1965. An anthology of essays by a variety of authors, discussing Shakespeare's comedies from various points of view.

Derek Traversi's treatment of *The Winter's Tale* is mainly concerned with the later scenes of the play and includes an intensive discussion of the characters' motivations.

Overton, Bill. *The Winter's Tale*. Atlantic Highlands, N.J.: Humanities Press International, 1989. A critical evaluation of Shakespeare's play from a wide variety of points of view, including Marxism, feminism, and psychoanalysis. Also discusses previous critical studies of the play.

Sanders, Wilbur. *The Winter's Tale*. Boston: Twayne, 1987. A thorough critical evaluation of the play. Also includes information on the work's stage history and original reception by critics. Sanders also discusses the psychological factors of the play and the use of language.

Shakespeare, William. *The Winter's Tale*. Edited by J. H. P. Pafford. Cambridge, Mass.: Harvard University Press, 1963. A new edition of the play, containing more than eighty pages of introductory notes and twenty pages of appendices. Discusses the sources, the text itself, and the music and songs. Also includes an extensive critical evaluation of the play.

THE POETRY

A Lover's Complaint

Type of plot: Complaint
Time of plot: c. 1600
Locale: Unspecified
First published: 1609

Principal characters

I, the narrator
A MAID, abandoned by her lover
AN OLDER MAN, audience of her complaint
A YOUNG MAN, the seducer

The Story

The narrator lies down unseen to listen to a story being told by a pale woman who is tearing love letters and breaking rings. Though she at first appears to have lost all her beauty, vestiges remain. From a wicker basket she removes love tokens, which she tosses into the nearby stream.

An older man, once a city dweller, is grazing his cattle nearby. He sits down a proper distance from the woman and asks what troubles her. She replies that she would still appear young and beautiful if she had not yielded to the importunities of a handsome young man, as well-spoken as he was good-looking. He rode skillfully and dressed fashionably. Many women admired him, falling in love even with his picture.

The woman telling the story knew that he had been unfaithful to others. For a long time she had resisted him—until he began to woo her. He acknowledged that he had seduced others, but he claimed that the others sought their fate. Moreover, he had loved none of these women. They gave him jewels and locks of hair and sonnets to signify their love, all of which he offered to the woman, including a favor given him, he said, by a nun. He referred to this particular conquest perhaps to suggest that the lady was being too hesitant to return his affection when even a nun yielded at first sight. In his final argument he told the woman that he who had conquered so many was now himself defeated by her. Since the hearts of the seduced women depended on him for their happiness, and since he now depended on her for his, all relied on her to relieve their pain. His final word was "troth," implying fidelity and even marriage. Then he wept and she yielded to him.

The lady ends her complaint by stating that no woman could resist this man because women are good-natured, generous, and compliant. She herself, if he wooed her again, would yield once more even though she has reformed.

Critical Evaluation

A Lover's Complaint appeared at the end of Shakespeare's sonnets, published in 1609. For this poem Shakespeare drew on a long tradition of complaints by abandoned lovers, beginning with Dido in Vergil's *Aeneid* (19 B.C.)and Ovid's *Heroïdes* (before A.D. 8) and continuing through Geoffrey Chaucer, John Gower, and John Lydgate's *The Fall of Princes* (1431-1438). The third edition of *A Mirror for Magistrates* (1563) included Thomas Churchyard's poem about Jane Shore, who was mistress to Edward IV and whom Richard III "despoyled of all her goodes, and forced to do open penance." In 1578 the complaint of Elianor Cobham was added to the collection.

Samuel Daniel's "Complaint of Rosamond" echoes Jane Shore's lament; it tells of the seduction and eventual death of Rosamond Clifford, mistress to Henry II. Daniel's poem is written in rhyme royal, a seven-line stanza in iambic pentameter rhyming *ababbcc*, and it appears at the end of his "Delia" sonnets. Thomas Lodge published "The Complaint of Elstred" with his sonnet sequence *Philis* the following year. Edmund Spenser's *The Ruines of Rome* (c. 1591), another complaint of this period in rhyme royal, opens with a woman wailing by a stream and may have suggested the setting for Shakespeare's poem. Michael Drayton's 1594 *Matilda* and Thomas Middleton's *The Ghost of Lucrece* (1600) also use rhyme royal for their laments, as Shakespeare did for *The Rape of Lucrece* (1594). Thus the rhyme royal form of *A Lover's Complaint* and its publication at the end of a sonnet sequence are both conventional. Even the title may be borrowed from two poems in *The Arbor of Amorous Devices* (1597), bearing the same designation as Shakespeare's.

The language of *A Lover's Complaint* bears affinities with *Cymbeline* (c. 1609), suggesting that Shakespeare revised the poem shortly before publication. In language, character, situation, and theme, however, *A Lover's Complaint* is closer to *All's Well That Ends Well* (c. 1602) and *Measure for Measure* (1604). The opening of the poem and the first scene of *All's Well That Ends Well* are virtually identical. In the play Helena laments the departure of Bertram, whom she loves, though she has not yielded to him. Her audience, Parolles, is not silent, but Helena and he use the same kind of military metaphors as the lady in the poem to discuss virginity and its loss. Despite the harsh treatment Helena and the lady of the poem suffer, the former pursues and marries Bertram, and the lady would yield to her lover again. The lady of the poem also suggests Mariana in *Measure for Measure*, to whom Angelo plighted his troth but then "left her in her tears" (Act III, scene i, line 225). She continues to weep, but Angelo remains obdurate until the end of the play, when the duke forces Angelo to marry her.

The young man in the poem closely resembles Bertram. Both are young and lascivious, and each abandons a woman who loves him. Late in *All's Well That Ends Well*, Bertram thinks he seduces and then abandons Diana. The lady in the poem describes her lover as having "phoenix down" on his chin; Helena calls Bertram a phoenix. Both men have curly hair. The woman praises the young man's horsemanship, and Bertram in Italy becomes a cavalry general. The young man of the poem also bears a resemblance to Angelo, who appears to be just and chaste, punishing illicit fornication with death, yet seeks to sleep with Isabella. In the poem the lady says of her betrayer, "Where he most burnt in heart-wish'd luxury,/ He preach'd pure maid, and prais'd cold chastity."

In the two plays the men retain the love of the women they mistreat, and these works end in marriage. In *A Lover's Complaint* all does not end well; redemption through love does not occur. Here the mood is closer to that of the sonnets, in which again a Fair Youth repeatedly deceives and abuses the speaker, who continues to love him. In the later sonnets (after 126) a similar situation exists, though now the speaker is deceived by the Dark Lady. Helena, Mariana, the lady of *A Lover's Complaint*, and the speaker in the sonnets all demonstrate that true love does not alter "when it alteration finds" (Sonnet 116). In the plays this love triumphs; in the poems it remains unrequited.

Another possible connection among *All's Well That Ends Well*, the sonnets, and *A Lover's Complaint* is the model for the deceiving youth in each case: the third Earl of Southampton. Regarded by many scholars as the subject of the first 126 sonnets, he was lascivious, and he seduced and then abandoned Elizabeth Vernon, a maid of honor in Elizabeth's court. The speaker in *A Lover's Complaint* is several times called a maid, perhaps suggesting Elizabeth Vernon's post. Bertram and Southampton are both wards of the court, both refuse marriages proposed by their guardians, and both leave the country to become generals of cavalry. At last, like Bertram, Southampton married the woman he had abandoned.

In *A Lover's Complaint* the seducer has not returned, but the poem is a psychological study, not a completed drama. John Roe, in his 1992 Cambridge University Press edition of the poems, wrote that *A Lover's Complaint* shows the woman's inability to resist and the man's inability to desist. The poem also examines the consequences of that inability. How would Elizabeth Vernon have felt in the absence of Southampton? How do Helena and Mariana feel when their lovers reject them? In line 133 of *A Lover's Complaint* William Shakespeare may be punning on his own name, as he does in the sonnets: "Asked their own wills, and made their wills obey." Perhaps Shakespeare, too, is expressing his own sense of betrayal by the Fair Youth and Dark Lady. As *Troilus and Cressida*, another work of the early 1600's, illustrates, such sentiments are not the exclusive domain of women. The dark world of *A Lover's Complaint* is that of *Troilus and Cressida* and of *The Phoenix and the Turtle*, where "Truth may seem, but cannot be;/ Beauty brag, but 'tis not she:/ Truth and Beauty buried be" (*The Phoenix and the Turtle*, lines 62-64).

Joseph Rosenblum

For Further Study

Hieatt, A. Kent. "*Cymbeline* and the Intrusion of Lyric into Romance Narrative: Sonnets, *A Lover's Complaint*, Spenser's Ruins of Rome." In *Unfolded Tales: Essays on Renaissance Romance*, edited by George M. Logan and Gordon Teskey. Ithaca, N.Y.: Cornell University Press, 1989. The verbal links between *A Lover's Complaint* and *Cymbeline* suggest that Shakespeare revised the poem shortly before publication. Shakespeare therefore probably intended to publish the sonnets and the appended complaint, so the 1609 *Sonnets* was not a pirated work.

Muir, Kenneth. "*A Lover's Complaint:* A Reconsideration." In *Shakespeare, 1564-1964: A Collection of Modern Essays by Various Hands*, edited by Edward A. Bloom. Providence, R.I.: Brown University Press, 1964. Muir first addresses the question of authorship and then examines links between the poem and other works by Shakespeare. He sees the repeated use of military metaphors in the poem as reflecting the war between the sexes. Muir does not regard the poem as a masterpiece but concludes that "it is not without its own special music" (166).

Underwood, Richard Allan. *Shakespeare on Love: The Poems and the Plays. Prolegomena to a Variorum Edition of "A Lover's Complaint."* Salzburg, Austria: Institut für Anglistik und Amerikanistik, Universität Salzburg, 1985. An excellent study that begins with the history of complaint poetry and then turns to an analysis of Shakespeare's poem. Underwood draws useful parallels between *A Lover's Complaint* and *All's Well That Ends Well* and shows how both works reflect the behavior of the third Earl of Southampton.

Warren, Roger. "*A Lover's Complaint, All's Well,* and the Sonnets." *Notes and Queries* 17 (April 1970): 130-132. An early study connecting *A Lover's Complaint* to *All's Well That Ends Well*, particularly through a study of the language of the works.

The Passionate Pilgrim

Type of plot: Poetical miscellany
Time of plot: Mythical Cyprus to 1599
Locale: Cyprus and England
First published: 1599

Principal characters

VENUS, goddess of love
ADONIS, a youth beloved of Venus
A LADY, fickle and disdainful
A NARRATOR, a lover

The Story

The Passionate Pilgrim contains twenty poems. Five of these definitely are by Shakespeare: I (a version of Sonnet 138), II (a version of Sonnet 144), III (*Love's Labour's Lost*, Act IV, scene iii, lines 57-70), V (*Love's Labour's Lost*, Act IV, scene ii, lines 107-120, with a few variations, especially in the last two lines), and XVI (*Love's Labour's Lost*, Act IV, scene iii, lines 98-117). Four almost certainly are not by Shakespeare: VIII and XX are by Richard Barnfield, XI probably is by Bartholomew Griffin, and XIX is a composite of Christopher Marlowe's "The Passionate Shepherd to His Love" and Sir Walter Raleigh's "The Nymph's Reply to the Shepherd." The rest are of indeterminate authorship.

This collection does not seek to tell a story, but two narrative threads can be seen running through the first fourteen poems. In the second edition (1599), William Jaggard, the publisher of the work, added a separate title page, "Sonnets to Sundry Notes of Music," before poem XV, perhaps to imply a unity among the earlier pieces. One story that may unite the opening section is that of Venus and Adonis. Shakespeare's poem on this subject enjoyed great popularity in the 1590's. Jaggard may have sought to capitalize on the popularity of that work by arranging to have *The Passionate Pilgrim* sold by William Leake, at the sign of the Greyhound in St. Paul's Churchyard, where in 1599 a new edition of *Venus and Adonis* was being sold. Five of the poems (VII, X, XIII, XIV, and XVIII) use the same six-line stanza that Shakespeare employed in *Venus and Adonis*, and four of the poems specifically refer to the mythical lovers. In IV and XI Venus tries to seduce Adonis, but he flees. In VI she watches as he takes off his clothes to bathe. As soon as Adonis sees her, he leaps into the water, leaving her to wish that she were the brook. In IX Venus warns Adonis of the boar by showing him where another youth was wounded in the thigh. She reveals more than just her thigh, though, and once more Adonis runs away. In the third edition (1612) Jaggard explicitly linked *The Passionate Pilgrim* to Shakespeare's popular poem by adding as a subtitle "Certaine Amorous Sonnets, Between Venus and Adonis, Newly Corrected and Augmented."

Several of the other poems could appear to relate to Venus and Adonis. The speaker of Sonnet I refers to himself as "some untutor'd youth," like Adonis, and he speaks of lying "with love," which could mean Venus herself. The narrator in Sonnet II love's "a man (right fair)," who could be the Cyprian lad. In Sonnet III the speaker claims to love a goddess, perhaps Venus. The fifth poem in the collection offers no explicit reference to the mythical lovers, but the praise could be addressed by Venus to Adonis, or by Adonis to Venus, since the beloved is termed "celestial." Sonnet X laments a lover's death, as Venus mourned the slain Adonis. Praise of a youthful lover over an older one is the theme of Sonnet XII. Thomas Percy, in his *Reliques of Ancient English Poetry* (1765), argued that Venus here was rejecting her old husband, Vulcan, for the young Adonis. Sonnet XIII replies that beauty quickly fades, a view that either the scorned Vulcan or the scornful Adonis could espouse. Finally, in XIV, the male speaker hopes that his beloved will pay more attention to him tomorrow, thus echoing the sentiments of the spurned Venus.

One may also find in the first fourteen poems the emotions and experiences typical of other sonnet sequences popular in the 1590's. In the first poem the lovers are together. In II the lady proves unfaithful. Having apparently forsworn her as a consequence, the lover in III changes his mind and wants her back, a sentiment repeated in V. In VIII the lover again rejects his fickle lady. In X either she or their love is dead, leaving discontent as a legacy. The poems dealing with Venus and Adonis might serve as exempla. Thus, Adonis' flight from the too eager Venus could mirror a situation that occurred between the lovers. In XI the lover wishes that his lady would behave like Venus; if she did, he says, he certainly would not run away like Adonis.

Each of the final six poems tells its own story. In XV a lord's daughter loves both her tutor and a knight but chooses the scholar over the warrior. Poem XVI tells of Love's unfulfilled desire for a blossom, and XVII presents a shepherd's lament for his lost love. The speaker in XVIII advises a young man how to win a lady and tells him that a woman's disdain eventually will turn to consent. XIX repeats most of Marlowe's shepherd's attempt to win the love of a lady (lines 1-12 and 17-20 of the original twenty-four), followed by the first four lines of Raleigh's reply. The final piece comments on a nightingale's song. The speaker, hearing the bird, recognizes that both of them once had many apparent friends when Fortune smiled on them. Once hardship befell them, these same people vanished. This poem concludes with signs by which to distinguish "Faithful friend from flatt'ring foe."

Critical Evaluation

The Passionate Pilgrim serves as one of several measures of Shakespeare's popularity in 1598-1599 when Jaggard produced two editions of the work in quick succession. The two editions within a year reveal the demand for works bearing Shakespeare's name and suggest why Jaggard was eager to capitalize on what he expected would sell well. In 1598 *Love's Labour's Lost* had been published, the first of Shakespeare's printed plays to carry his name on the title page. Three of the five authentically Shakespearean pieces in *The Passionate Pilgrim* come from that play, though probably not from the printed text. Francis Meres' *Palladis Tamia: Wit's Treasury* of the same year praised Shakespeare as the greatest poet of the age and referred to Shakespeare's "sugared [eloquent] sonnets among his private friends," an allusion certain to spark curiosity. *Henry IV, Part I* and *Part II*, had recently been staged and had introduced to the public the beloved character Falstaff.

Jaggard must have come upon a commonplace book containing the poems in *The Passionate Pilgrim*. He may even have thought that these were all or mostly the work of Shakespeare, perhaps the "sugared sonnets" to which Meres had referred. (Jaggard's persistence in publishing *The Passionate Pilgrim* as Shakespeare's after the appearance of the sonnets in 1609 is harder to justify.) Whatever his thoughts, Jaggard almost certainly published the book without permission of the author. His printer for the book, Thomas Judson, led a checkered career; on February 4, 1600, Judson was forced to swear that he would leave the profession. Most of Jaggard's early productions were not listed in the Stationers' Register, an indication that they may have been pirated.

Despite the unsavory nature of the practice, Jaggard was not alone in capitalizing on a popular poet's name or in printing pieces without authority. In 1591 Richard Jones issued *Brittons Bowre of Delights* as the work of Nicholas Breton, though it was an anthology of works by various hands. Though Breton protested, in 1594 Jones published *The Arbor of Amorous Deuices*, "by N. B. Gent," when in fact only six or seven of the thirty poems were by Breton. In the 1612 edition of *The Passionate Pilgrim* Jaggard compounded his piracy by including nine poems from Thomas Heywood's *Troia Britanica*, which Jaggard had legitimately published three years earlier.

It is impossible to know the original order of the commonplace book that Jaggard used as his copy-text, but the publisher may have arranged the pieces to make the collection appear more Shakespearean than it was. Four of the first five poems are canonical, with III and V recognizably so since they had recently appeared in print. Dealing with Venus and Adonis, the early poems IV and VI would again suggest Shakespeare to the casual reader. The sonnet form of nine of the poems and the *Venus and Adonis* stanza-form of five more enhance the Shakespearean feeling, and XVIII parodies the advice of "W. S." printed in *Willobie His Avisa* (1594). This work is traditionally associated with Shakespeare.

If the casual reader in 1599 assumed that *The Passionate Pilgrim* was offering a sampling of Shakespearean verses, so did many eighteenth century Shakespeare scholars, and the authorship of the unassigned poems remains a matter of debate. The nineteenth century Shakespearean James Orchard Halliwell-Phillipps wrote of Sonnet XII, "Few persons would dream of assigning it to the pen of Shakespeare." Yet Arthur Quiller-Couch dreamed just that and could not imagine anyone else's writing that piece. Quiller-Couch called it "one of the loveliest lyrics in the language." Sir Sidney Lee, the preeminent Shakespearean at the beginning of the twentieth century, regarded Sonnets IV, VI, and IX as decidedly un-Shakespearean, whereas the poet John Masefield found in them Shakespeare's "freshest youthful manner."

Since Poem XI was included in Bartholomew Griffin's *Fidessa* (1596), perhaps all four Venus and Adonis poems are from his hand, though VI sounds much like the scene described in the induction to *The Taming of the Shrew* (scene ii, lines 51-53): "We will fetch thee straight/ Adonis painted by the running brook/ And Cytherea[Venus] all in sedges hid." Had Shakespeare originally planned to present the story of Venus and Adonis as a sonnet sequence, and were these poems part of that early effort? Did Griffin appropriate XI as his own? Sonnet XII appeared in Thomas Deloney's *Garland of Good Will*, in print by 1596, and XVII was included in Thomas Weelkes's *Madrigals* (1597). The earliest extant edition of Deloney's book, however, includes poems by other writers, and Weelkes probably wrote only the music, not the lyrics, to XVII.

Even the authentic Shakespeare poems pose problems because they differ to a greater or lesser extent from the accepted texts of these works. Line 11 of Sonnet 138 reads, "O, love's best habit is in seeming trust"; in the opening poem of *The Passionate Pilgrim* the line appears as "O, love's best habit's in a soothing tongue." Sonnet 138 concludes, "Therefore I lie with her, and she with me,/ And in our faults by lies we flattered be." *The Passionate Pilgrim* version ends, "Therefore I'll lie with love, and love with me,/ Since that our faults in love thus smother'd be." It is tempting to argue that Jaggard here offers an earlier draft of the sonnet printed in 1609 and so provides glimpses into Shakespeare's methods of composition and revision. Yet one finds that Sonnet XI and Song XIX also differ significantly from the texts printed elsewhere, so the anonymous creator of the commonplace book may have been responsible for the changes. Nor can one tell how many intermediaries intervened between the original poems and the copy Jaggard secured.

Hallet Smith concluded that "*The Passionate Pilgrim* adds nothing to our knowledge of Shakespeare's work, but it tells us something about his reputation and about the vagaries of publishers of his time." The book does more. While the little octavo printed on four sheets offers no solutions regarding Shakespeare's canon or writing habits, it continues to raise questions that tease us into thought.

Joseph Rosenblum

For Further Study

Adams, Joseph Quincy. *The Passionate Pilgrim*. New York: Charles Scribner's Sons for the Trustees of Amherst College, 1939. Adams reprints the first (1598 or 1599) and second (1599) editions of the collection. His lengthy preface analyzes the bibliographical history of the work to 1612 and compares the texts of the poems as printed by Jaggard with two manuscript miscellanies in the Folger Shakespeare Library.

Lee, Sidney. *The Passionate Pilgrim[,] Being a Reproduction in Facsimile of the First Edition 1599 from the Copy in the Christie Miller Library at Britwell[,] with Introduction and Bibliography by Sidney Lee*. Oxford: Clarendon Press, 1905. Actually reproduces the second edition; the first was not identified until

1920. Lee's introduction discusses the publication's history, the sources and content of *The Passionate Pilgrim*, and later editions. Still useful despite its age, and a beautiful example of bookmaking.

Roe, John, ed. *The Poems: "Venus and Adonis," "The Rape of Lucrece," "The Phoenix and the Turtle," "The Passionate Pilgrim," "A Lover's Complaint."* Cambridge, England: Cambridge University Press, 1992. This edition offers useful annotations and a succinct but informative introduction that traces the critical debates surrounding the work.

Roe, John. "*Willobie His Avisa* and *The Passionate Pilgrim*: Precedence, Parody, and Development." *Yearbook of English Studies* 23 (1993): 111-125. Poem XVIII of *The Passionate Pilgrim* resembles Canto XLVII of *Willobie His Avisa*. Through an examination of the connections between these two pieces Roe sheds light on Jaggard's poetical miscellany and helps date at least one of the pieces in the anthology.

The Phoenix and the Turtle

Type of plot: Elegy
Time of plot: Unspecified
Locale: Arabia
First published: 1601

Principal characters

PHOENIX, female bird
TURTLE, Phoenix's husband
REASON, speaker of the "Threnos"

The Story

The poem, written in heptasyllabic (with some octosyllabic) trochaic tetrameter, laments the death of the Phoenix and Turtle-dove, true lovers who perished together. In the opening five stanzas, each of four lines rhyming *abba*, an unnamed speaker summons the mourners. The first stanza invites "the bird of loudest lay," which may be the new phoenix because of the reference to the "sole Arabian tree," on which the phoenix traditionally sits. Another possibility is the crane. The speaker refers to the bird as "herald" and "trumpet," and Geoffrey Chaucer in "The Parlement of Foules" (c. 1377), a possible source for Shakespeare's poem, wrote of the crane "with his trompes soune" (with his trumpet's sound). The cock, lark, and nightingale have also been proposed.

Stanza 2 orders the screech owl, "shrieking harbinger," not to appear, and stanza 3 continues in this vein of interdiction, barring all birds of prey except the eagle, which is royal without being tyrannical. Stanzas 4 and 5 complete the guest list of mourners with the swan and crow. The swan's whiteness makes it the ideal priest, and its reputation for singing just before death links it to the dirge. Both the swan and the crow were regarded in the Renaissance as symbols of chastity and marital fidelity. The crow's sable hue also suits it to this occasion.

The following eight stanzas, also of four lines each with the *abba* rhyme scheme, shift from the imperative to the declarative mood as they praise the dead lovers. These lovers overcame the physical and metaphysical forces that would divide them to become one being, as indicated by the use of the singular verb in line 22 and the singular noun "simple" (meaning a compound and usually plural) in line 44.

Reason speaks the last fifteen lines, consisting of five three-line stanzas each with a single rhyme. Reason had listened to the praise of the lovers in stanzas 5-12 and had found the paradoxes puzzling. Reason's response accepts the excellence of the pair of birds, but the tone of the "Threnos" shifts from celebratory to elegiac. However remarkable these birds were, they now are dead, and with them have perished "Beauty, truth, and rarity." Reason concludes by urging those who survive to visit the urn containing the ashes of these lovers and "sigh a prayer" for them.

Critical Evaluation

Hyder Edward Rollins remarked that "The riddle of Shakespeare's poem has not been, probably never will be, solved to the satisfaction of all scholars." The only points of agreement are that Shakespeare wrote the piece (an issue that itself was long debated) and that it was published in 1601 as part of *Loves Martyr*, a collection of poems assembled by Robert Chester, who wrote most of the volume and who probably engaged the other contributors: Ben Jonson, John Marston, George Chapman, and William Shakespeare, as well as "Vatum Chorus" and "Ignoto," one or both of whom may also have been Jonson.

The subtitle states that *Loves Martyr* "allegorically shadow[s] the truth of Love." The nature of that allegory remains a matter of debate. Many writers have suggested that the female phoenix represents Elizabeth, the turtle-dove the Earl of Essex, whom Elizabeth loved but whose execution she ordered after his abortive rebellion in February, 1601, a few months before the publication of Chester's volume. Though Elizabeth was not yet dead, the loss of Essex was tantamount to her demise. Given the political risk of making such a statement, this interpretation has not found universal acceptance. Others agree that the phoenix is Elizabeth—the equation was a commonplace—but the turtle represents either some unnamed individual or England itself. The poem would thus celebrate the ties between ruler and ruled.

These interpretations ignore the fact that the poem is dedicated to Sir John Salusbury, whose knighting on June 14, 1601, by Elizabeth was the occasion for the publication of Chester's book. Carleton Brown, who edited the poems of Chester and Salusbury in 1914, sought to put Salusbury at the center of Shakespeare's poem by interpreting the turtle as the new-made knight, the phoenix as his wife, Ursula, the illegitimate daughter of Henry Stanley, fourth Earl of Derby, whose coat of arms depicts an eagle and child (hence the invitation of the eagle to the funeral). Still others treat Shakespeare as the subject of his poem and interpret the poem as mourning the death of the friendship between the poet and the third Earl of Southampton.

These varying interpretations affect the dating of the poem. E. A. J. Honigmann, who links the poem to the Stanleys, suggests that the work was composed in 1586, perhaps even before John Salusbury married. If the poem deals with Shakespeare's break with Southampton, the poem would have been composed in the mid-1590's; if it deals with the death of Essex, it must date from 1601.

Other debates concern the appropriateness of placing the second article in the title and the number of poems Shakespeare contributed. Vatum Chorus, Ignoto, Jonson, and Marston each contributed paired poems, while Chapman wrote one for the volume. Reason's five stanzas are headed "Threnos," and the rhyme scheme and stanza form differ from the rest of the verses. Thus, the separate title may indicate that *The Phoenix and the Turtle* is in fact two related but distinct poems. Critics cannot even agree on the tone of the piece. Robert Ellrodt found the poem "throughout funereal," whereas Peter Dronke thought it "exhilirating."

As these arguments suggest, the poem is enigmatic. Perhaps the best approach to the work is to accept the subtitle at face value: The poem is an allegory about love and its demise. While the occasion of the poem was the knighting of John Salusbury, the work need not therefore be occasional. Rather, Shakespeare sets out to demonstrate the various paradoxes that love embodies. The second stanza of the anthem (stanza 7 of the poem) claims that the lovers were both two and one. The language echoes the trinitarian three-in-one. Shakespeare, like John Donne, uses religious imagery to describe human love because both are forms of transcendence. The next stanza deals with another paradox: Love allows two bodies to occupy one space. In the following two stanzas Shakespeare offers the third paradox, the loss of identity as each lover becomes the other. These Neoplatonic ideas also inform Shakespeare's sonnets.

Reason, listening to these claims made by an unnamed speaker, finds them confusing and wonders in the final stanza of the anthem whether love can so reconcile opposites. Reason acknowledges here that the lovers appear to be one, but are they in fact? Reason's response is to acknowledge the assertions of the anthem but to add that, like the phoenix, these lovers were unique. They leave "no posterity," no successors who unite truth and beauty or who possess either quality in its absolute form. Some may claim to do so, but they are deceived (or attempting to deceive others). Those with a portion of the beauty or truth that the dead birds possess should go to the tomb of the deceased to pray.

Reason's elegiac tone and sense of a fallen world reflect the tragic mode of the plays Shakespeare was writing when *The Phoenix and the Turtle* was published and probably composed. It falls between *Hamlet*, in which the times are out of joint, and *Troilus and Cressida*, a dark satire on love. *Hamlet's* Ophelia and Cressida are both beautiful, but they are not trustworthy. One may see in *The Phoenix and the Turtle* an echo of *Romeo and Juliet* (c. 1595) and a foreshadowing of the deaths of Cordelia and Lear in *King Lear* (c. 1605) and Antony and Cleopatra in the play named for them (c. 1606). True love is rare, these works say, and it cannot endure in a postlapsarian world.

Joseph Rosenblum

For Further Study

Empson, William. "*The Phoenix and the Turtle*." *Essays in Criticism* 16 (1966): 147-153. Places Shakespeare's poem within the context of the other poems in *Loves Martyr*. John Marston's contribution immediately following Shakespeare's contradicts the statement that the lovers left no posterity.

Garber, Marjorie. "Two Birds with One Stone: Lapidary Re-inscription in *The Phoenix and Turtle*." *Upstart Crow* 5 (1984): 5-19. Interprets the poem as dealing with poetry. The work is a self-conscious artifact that combines elegy and epithalamion and renews itself, ending as it began with prayer. Like the phoenix, in its end is its beginning.

Matchett, William H. *"The Phoenix and the Turtle": Shakespeare's Poem and Chester's "Loues Martyr."* London: Mouton, 1965. Matchett argues that the poem deals with the love of Elizabeth and Essex. In the course of his discussion Matchett provides useful information about the historical context of the work and the poems that surround Shakespeare's in Chester's anthology.

Seltzer, Daniel. "'Their Tragic Scene': *The Phoenix and Turtle* and Shakespeare's Love Tragedies." *Shakespeare Quarterly* 12 (1961): 91-101. Links the poem to Shakespeare's tragedies in terms of language and theme. Seltzer concludes hat the poem is "a lyric statement of truths which the tragedies set forth dramatically."

Underwood, Richard Allan. *Shakespeare's "The Phoenix and Turtle": A Survey of Scholarship*. Saltzburg: Institut für Englische Sprache und Literatur, Universität Salzburg, 1974. The best survey of the various critical views of the poem from 1878, when Alexander B. Grosart edited *Loues Martyr* for the New Shakspere Society, to the 1960's. Includes generous excerpts of the criticism it analyzes.

The Rape of Lucrece

Type of plot: Tragedy
Time of plot: 500 B.C.E.
Locale: Rome
First published: 1594

Principal characters

COLLATINE, a Roman general
LUCRECE, his wife
TARQUIN, Collatine's friend and son of the Roman king

The Story

At Ardea, where the Romans were fighting, two Roman leaders, Tarquin and Collatine, spoke together one evening. Collatine described his beautiful young wife, Lucrece, in such glowing terms that Tarquin's passions were aroused. The next morning, Tarquin left the Roman host and journeyed to Collatium, where the unsuspecting Lucrece welcomed him as one of her husband's friends. As Tarquin told her many tales of Collatine's prowess on the battlefield, he looked admiringly at Lucrece and decided that she was the most beautiful woman in Rome.

In the night, while the others of the household were asleep, Tarquin lay restless. Caught between desire for Lucrece and dread of being discovered, to the consequent loss of his honor, he wandered aimlessly about his chamber. On the one hand, there was his position as a military man who should not be the slave of his emotions; on the other hand was his overwhelming desire. He feared the dreadful consequences that might be the result of his lustful deed. His disgrace would never be forgotten. Perhaps his own face would show the mark of his crimes and the advertisement linger on even after death. He thought for a moment that he might try to woo Lucrece but decided that such a course would be to no avail. She was already married and was not mistress of her own desires. Again he considered the possible consequences of his deed.

At last, emotion conquered reason. As Tarquin made his way to Lucrece's chamber, many petty annoyances deterred him. The locks on the doors had to be forced; the threshold beneath the door grated under his footstep; the wind threatened to blow out his torch; he pricked his finger on a needle. Tarquin ignored these omens of disaster. In fact, he misconstrued them as forms of trial that only made his prize more worth winning.

When he reached the chamber door, Tarquin began to pray for success. Realizing, however, that heaven would not countenance his sin, he declared that Love and

Fortune would henceforth be his gods. Entering the room, he gazed at Lucrece in sleep. When he reached forward to touch her breast, she awoke with a cry of fear. He told her that her beauty had captured his heart and that she must submit to his will. First he threatened Lucrece with force, telling her that if she refused to submit to him, he would not only kill her but also dishonor her name. His intention was to murder one of her slaves, place him in her arms, and then swear that he killed them because he had seen Lucrece embracing the man. If she yielded, however, he promised he would keep the whole affair secret. Lucrece began to weep and plead with Tarquin. For the sake of her hospitality, her husband's friendship, Tarquin's position as a warrior, he must pity her and refrain from this deed. Her tears serving only to increase his lust, Tarquin smothered her cries with the bed linen while he raped her.

Shame-ridden, he stole away, leaving Lucrece desolate. She, horrified and revolted, tore her nails and hoped the dawn would never come. In a desperate fury, she railed against the night; its darkness and secrecy had ruined her. She was afraid of the day, for surely her sin would be revealed. Still worse, through her fall, Collatine would be forever shamed. It was Opportunity that was at fault, she claimed, working for the wicked and against the innocent. Time, the handmaiden of ugly Night, was hand-in-hand with Opportunity, but Time could work for Lucrece now. She implored Time to bring misery and pain to Tarquin. Exhausted from her emotional tirade, Lucrece fell back on her pillow. She longed for a suicide weapon; death alone could save her soul.

As the dawn broke, she began to consider her death. Not until she had told Collatine the complete details of her fall would she take the step, however, for Collatine must revenge her on Tarquin. Lucrece called her maid and asked for pen and paper. Writing to Collatine, she asked him to return immediately. When she gave the messenger the letter, she imagined that he knew of her sin, for he gave her a sly, side glance. Surely everyone must know by now, she thought. Her grief took new channels. Studying a picture of the fall of Troy, she tried to find the face showing greatest grief. Hecuba, who gazed mournfully at Priam in his dying moments, seemed the saddest. Lucrece grieved for those who died in the Trojan War, all because one man could not control his lust. Enraged, she tore the painting with her nails.

Collatine, returning home, found Lucrece robed in black. With weeping and lamentations, she told him of her shame, but without naming her violator. After she had finished, Collatine, driven half-mad by rage and grief, demanded the name of the traitor. Before revealing it, Lucrece drew promises from the assembled soldiers that the loss of her honor would be avenged. Then, naming Tarquin, she drew a knife from her bosom and stabbed herself.

Heartbroken, Collatine cried that he would kill himself as well, but Brutus, his friend, stepped forward and argued that woe was no cure for woe; it was better to revenge Lucrece. The soldiers left the palace to carry the bleeding body of Lucrece through Rome. The indignant citizens banished Tarquin and all his family.

Critical Evaluation

The story of Tarquin's violation of Lucrece is an ancient Roman legend that has been presented in many versions other than in this poem by William Shakespeare. The Elizabethans were especially fond of this legend, so Shakespeare had numerous sources upon which to draw. Compared with his other writings, this poem is far more conventionally Elizabethan, yet its passages of great emotion and its consistently beautiful poetry rank it above other interpretations of the story known in his day.

The Rape of Lucrece was entered at the Stationers' Register on May 9, 1594. Like *Venus and Adonis*, which had been published the previous year, it was finely printed by Richard Field and dedicated to the Earl of Southampton. Both of these narrative poems had been written while the theaters were closed because of the plague, but these companion pieces are not the idle products of a dramatist during a period of forced inactivity. Rather, as the dedications and the care in publication indicate, they are efforts at what, in Shakespeare's day, was a more serious, more respectable type of composition than writing plays.

Longer and graver in tone than *Venus and Adonis*, *The Rape of Lucrece* was extremely popular, going through many editions, and was quoted frequently by contemporaries. The stern Gabriel Harvey, a Cambridge fellow and friend of Edmund Spenser, enthusiastically approved of the poem and paired it with *Hamlet* (1600-1601) for seriousness of intent. The poem may be the "graver labor" that Shakespeare promises Southampton in the dedication to *Venus and Adonis*. Whether or not Shakespeare intended to pair the poems, *The Rape of Lucrece* does provide a moralistic contrast to the view of love and sexuality expressed in the earlier poem.

The genre of *The Rape of Lucrece* is complaint, a form popular in the later Middle Ages and the Renaissance, and particularly in vogue in the late 1590's. Strictly speaking, the complaint is a monologue in which the speaker bewails his or her fate or the sad state of the world. Shakespeare, however, following the example of many contemporaries, took advantage of the possibilities for variety afforded by dialogue. The poem includes the long set speeches and significant digressions that had become associated with the complaint. The poetic style is the highly ornamented sort approved by sophisticated Elizabethan audiences.

The rhyme royal stanza may have been suggested by its traditional use in serious narrative or, more immediately, by Samuel Daniel's use of it in his popular *Complaint of Rosamond* (1592). Certainly *The Rape of Lucrece* shares with Daniel's poem the Elizabethan literary fascination with the distress of noble ladies. Despite the subject matter, the poem is not sensual, except in the lushness of its imagery. Even the passion of the rape scene is attenuated by a grotesquely extended description of Lucrece's breasts. The long, idealized description of the heroine is a rhetorical tour de force, not sexual stimulation. The theme of heroic chastity is always paramount, and readers are never distracted by action. Indeed, the prose "argument" that precedes the poem describes a story with enormous possibilities for action and adventure, but Shakespeare, consistent with his higher purpose, chooses to focus, reflectively and analytically, on the moral and psychological issues. Although the result is sometimes boring, there are occasional signs of Shakespeare's dramatic ability, especially in the exchanges before the rape.

The characters are static and stylized, but the revelation of the characters is skillfully done. As Tarquin's lust wrestles with his conscience, he is portrayed in an agony of indecision. The main medium of his internal conflict is the conventional theme of the antagonism of passion and reason. This section is a compendium of reflections on and rationalizations for the destructive power of lust. Tarquin thinks in terms of conventional images, but the contrasts and antitheses, as he is tossed back and forth between commonplaces, effectively represent his inner struggle. When he gives in, it is more a tribute to the potency of lust than a delineation or indictment of his character. When Lucrece appeals to the very concerns that have bedeviled Tarquin, there is a dramatic poignancy that most of the rest of the poem lacks. After the rape, the change in Tarquin's thoughts from lust to guilt and shame is striking.

Lucrece's complaint is also wholly conventional in substance, but contrast and antithesis again give a vitality to her grief as she rationalizes her suicide as not the destruction of her soul but the only way to restore her honor. The imagistic alternations from day to night, clear to cloudy, reflect her anguish and the difficulty of her decision.

The poem's structure suggests that the exploration and decoration of conventional themes concerning lust and honor are the main intent. *The Rape of Lucrece* centers on the mental states and moral attitudes of the characters immediately before and after the crucial action. The rape is a premise for the reflections, the suicide a logical result. The set speeches are reinforced by free authorial moralizing. Significant digressions, like the long physical description of Lucrece and her extended apostrophe to Opportunity, elaborate the main themes. The longest and most effective digression is Lucrece's contemplation of the Troy painting. The opportunities for finding correlatives are fully exploited. The city of Troy is apt, because it has been brought to destruction by a rape, and Paris is the perfect example of the selfishness of lust. Sinon, whose honest exterior belies his treachery, reminds Lucrece of the contrast between appearance and reality, nobility and baseness, that she had noted in Tarquin. The whole digression, which repeats by means of allusion, is ornamental rather than explanatory.

The severe paring of the plot further reveals Shakespeare's main concern. Collatine, the offended husband, appears only briefly, suffers silently, and does not even personally initiate the revenge; he does not intrude on the crucial issues. The bloodthirstiness of Lucrece's plea for revenge is another sign that elucidation of character is unimportant compared to the beautiful expression of moral imperatives. The revenge itself is, mysteriously, instigated by Brutus (an action that makes more sense in other versions of the tale) and is carried out perfunctorily in a few closing lines, because it is secondary to the themes of the poem.

Regardless of its moral earnestness and occasional tedium, *The Rape of Lucrece* is gorgeously ornamented with figures of speech, especially alliteration and assonance, and with figures of thought that please more for their brilliance of execution than their depth of conception. *The Rape of Lucrece* is, like *Venus and Adonis*, a rhetorical showpiece.

"Critical Evaluation" by Edward E. Foster

For Further Study

Bullough, Geoffrey. *Narrative and Dramatic Sources of Shakespeare.* Vol. 1. New York: Columbia University Press, 1957. Reprints the sources and analogues Shakespeare used, or may have used, in creating the poem; provides an intelligent introduction to how those sources pertain.

Donaldson, Ian. *The Rapes of Lucretia.* Oxford, England: Clarendon Press, 1982. Thorough study of the Lucretia story in Western art and literature. Describes how Shakespeare's version of the story redirects the meaning of the myth to apply to late sixteenth century English culture.

Kuhl, E. P. "Shakespeare's *Rape of Lucrece.*" *Philological Quarterly* 20, no. 3 (July, 1941): 352-360. A seminal article interpreting the poem as a political narrative to warn Shakespeare's patron, the Earl of Southampton, of the dangers of abusing power.

Prince, F. T., ed. Introduction to *The Poems*, by William Shakespeare. New York: Methuen, 1960. Classic introduction to the poem and its background, sources, and text. Although sometimes uncritical by contemporary standards, it remains a good starting point for study of the poem, especially for Prince's appreciation of the poem as poetry.

Stimpson, Catharine. "Shakespeare and the Soil of Rape." In *The Woman's Part: Feminist Criticism of Shakespeare*, edited by Carolyn Ruth Swift-Lenz, Gayle Greene, and Carol Thomas Nealy. Champaign: University of Illinois Press, 1980. Excellent introduction to feminist responses to the poem. Examines Lucrece's position in the patriarchy.

The Sonnets: An Overview

Although William Shakespeare's sonnets are generally considered to be among the most beautiful and most powerful poems in English literature, the attention of readers and scholars has more often centered on their possible biographical significance than on the literary qualities that give them their greatness. So little is known of the inner life of the poet, so little that helps to explain his genius, that it is not surprising to find critics minutely examining these lyrics that seem to reveal something of Shakespeare the man.

The sonnet sequence was one of the most popular poetic forms in the early 1590's; modeled originally on works by Dante Alighieri and Petrarch, the genre was developed in sixteenth century France and Italy and quickly reached England. Sir Philip Sidney's *Astrophil and Stella* (1591), written a few years before the poet's death in 1586, is a demonstration of how quickly the sonnet cycle achieved excellence in English. Edmund Spenser, Samuel Daniel, Michael Drayton, and many other well-known Elizabethan men of letters followed Sidney's example, paying tribute to the idealized ladies who inspired their almost religious devotion.

Shakespeare's poems, probably composed at intervals during the decade between 1590 and 1600, differ radically from the sonnets of his contemporaries in several ways. They are not based on the traditional Petrarchan theme of a proud, virtuous lady and an abject, scorned lover, and there is in them relatively little of the Platonic idealism that fills works like Spenser's *Amoretti* (1595), in which the poet's love for his lady lifts him above human weakness to contemplation of the divine. Shakespeare records a strangely ambiguous, tortured affection for a young nobleman; the emotions he expresses in his sonnets have a depth and complexity, an intensity, that can be encountered elsewhere only in the speeches of some of his greatest dramatic creations.

The narrative of Shakespeare's sequence is exceedingly sketchy. Scholars have, in fact, rearranged the poems many times in an attempt to produce a more coherent "plot" than appeared in the volume published, without the author's supervision, in 1609. It seems likely that the work as it now stands contains at least a few poems that were written as independent pieces, sonnets on popular Renaissance themes which have no real bearing on the subject of the sequence itself.

Three shadowy figures move through the reflections of the poet as he speaks in his sonnets. The most important is the "Fair Youth," the young nobleman. The fervor of the language with which Shakespeare speaks of his feelings for the youth has led to considerable discussion of the precise nature of the relationship. It must be remembered that the Renaissance regarded the friendship of man and man as the highest form of human affection, for within this relationship there could be

The youthful Henry Wriothesley, third Earl of Southampton, Shakespeare's patron and friend, often conjectured to have been the "Fair Youth" of the poet's sonnets. (Library of Congress)

complete spiritual and intellectual communication, unmarred by erotic entanglements.

The nobleman is initially idealized in much the same way that most poets envisioned their ladies, as the embodiment of beauty and virtue. Unlike the typical lady of more conventional sonnets, however, he proves to be false and deceptive, shifting his attention to a rival poet, whose identity has been the subject of much speculation. The sequence records the narrator-poet's despair at this betrayal and at the nobleman's affair with the "Dark Lady," the poet's mistress, who is, in a sense, his evil genius. It is not the loss of the lady he regrets, for he knows her character all too well, but the fact that his friend has yielded to her corruption. Throughout the sonnets the reader feels the poet's agonized sense that there is nothing lastingly beautiful or virtuous.

While it is customary to speak of the "I" of the sonnets as Shakespeare, it is dangerously misleading to overlook the possibility that these poems are dramatic, that "I" is as vividly conceived a creature of Shakespeare's mind as Hamlet, and that the poet is projecting himself into an imagined situation rather than describing a personal experience. Whether the speaker of the sonnets is Shakespeare or not, it does not alter the essential value of the poems themselves.

The greatness of the sonnets lies in their intellectual and emotional power, in Shakespeare's ability to find exactly the right images to convey a particular idea or feeling and in his magnificent gift for shaping the diction and rhythms of ordinary human speech into expressions of the subtlest and deepest human perceptions. He also developed his own sonnet form, the Shakespearian sonnet form, with which Thomas Wyatt and Henry Howard, Earl of Surrey had experimented earlier in the century. Almost all of Shakespeare's sonnets are divided into three quatrains, each with alternately rhyming lines, followed by a concluding couplet. This form is technically less complex than the Italian pattern, in which the first eight lines are built around two rhymes, rather than four. The technical requirements of the two forms determine to a degree their organization. The Italian sonnet generally breaks down into two sections, with the statement of a problem in the octave and its solution in the sestet, while the form used by Shakespeare lends itself to a tripartite exposition followed by a brief conclusion in the couplet. Shakespeare was, however, capable of varying his development of his subject in many different ways; a thought may run through twelve lines with a surprise conclusion or shift of emphasis in the couplet; it may break into the eight-line, six-line division of the Italian sonnet; or it may follow one of many other patterns.

The organization of the sequence seems somewhat haphazard. Within it are several groups of poems that clearly belong together, but they do not form an entirely satisfying narrative. Shakespeare uses his half-untold story as a basis for poems upon many familiar Renaissance themes: love, time, mutability, the conflict of body and soul, passion and reason. The first eighteen poems, all addressed to the nobleman, are variations on the theme of the transience of youth and beauty and the need for the youth to marry and beget children in order to preserve his virtues of face and mind in them. Shakespeare draws upon nature for images to convey his sense of the destruction that awaits all beauty, referring to "the violet past prime," "winter's ragged hand," "summer's green all girded up in sheaves." Youth becomes more precious and the preservation of beauty more important still when the poet considers that "everything that grows holds in perfection but a little moment."

Shakespeare's sense of the ravages of time leads him to a second important theme: Poetry, as well as heirs, can confer immortality. Sonnet 18 is one of the most beautiful and clearest expressions of this idea:

> Shall I compare thee to a summer's day?
> Thou are more lovely and more temperate:
> Rough winds do shake the darling buds of May,
> And summer's lease hath all too short a date;
> Sometime too hot the eye of heaven shines,
> And often is his gold complexion dimm'd;
> And every fair from fair sometime declines,
> By chance, or nature's changing course, untrimm'd:
> But thy eternal summer shall not fade,
> Nor lose possession of that fair thou ow'st,
> Nor shall Death brag thou wander'st in his shade,
> When in eternal lines to time thou grow'st;
>   So long as men can breathe or eyes can see,
>   So long lives this, and this gives life to thee.

The same idea forms the basis for another well-known sonnet, "Not marble nor the gilded monuments of princes," in which Shakespeare affirms the power of his verse to withstand the assaults of war, fire, and death. The sonnets making up the middle of the sequence deal with many aspects of the poet's feeling for the nobleman. Their tone is almost universally melancholy; the haunting language and clear visual images of Sonnet 73 make it perhaps the finest expression of this dominant mood:

> That time of year thou mayst in me behold
> When yellow leaves, or none, or few, do hang
> Upon those boughs which shake against the cold,
> Bare [ruin'd] choirs where late the sweet birds sang.
> In me thou see'st the twilight of such day
> As after sunset fadeth in the west,
> Which by and by black night doth take away,
> Death's second self, that seals up all in rest.
> In me thou see'st the glowing of such fire
> That on the ashes of his youth doth lie,
> As the death-bed whereon it must expire,
> Consum'd with that which it was nourish'd by.
>   This thou perceiv'st, which makes thy love more strong,
>   To love that well which thou must leave ere long.

The speaker pictures himself as a man aging, unworthy, despairing. Initially his friendship with the young nobleman provides his one comfort against the frustrations of his worldly state. At those moments, as in Sonnet 29, when he is most wretched:

Haply I think on thee; and then my state
(Like to the lark at break of day arising
From sullen earth) sings hymns at heaven's gate.
   For thy sweet love remember'd such wealth brings
   That then I scorn to change my state with kings.

A brilliantly conceived image, in Sonnet 33, communicates the impact of the poet's loss of confidence in the youth when the youth turns to the rival poet:

Full many a glorious morning have I seen
Flatter the mountain tops with sovereign eye,
Kissing with golden face the meadows green,
Gilding pale streams with heavenly alchemy;
Anon permit the basest clouds to ride
With ugly rack on his celestial face,
And from the forlorn world his visage hide,
Stealing unseen to west with this disgrace:
Even so my son one early morn did shine
With all triumphant splendour on my brow;
But out, alack! he was but one hour mine,
The region cloud hath mask'd him from me now.
   Yet him for this my love no whit disdaineth;
   Suns of the world may stain when heaven's sun staineth.

Many of the poems show the poet's attempts to accept the faithlessness, the fall from virtue, of the youth. While his betrayal cannot destroy the poet's affection ("Love is not love which alters when it alteration finds"), it represents the decay of all good, leaving the speaker filled with despair.

There are, toward the end of the sequence, approximately thirty poems addressed to or speaking of the Dark Lady. The lighter of these lyrics are witty commentaries on her brunette beauty—in the sonnet tradition, the lady is fair, as in Sonnet 132:

Thine eyes I love, and they as pitying me,
Knowing thy heart torment me with disdain,
Have put on black, and loving mourners be,
Looking with pretty ruth upon my pain.

The overworked Petrarchan metaphors about the charms of the sonneteer's mistress are parodied in another well-known poem, Sonnet 130:

My mistress' eyes are nothing like the sun;
Coral is far more red than her lips' red;
If snow be white, why then her breasts are dun;
If hairs be wires, black wires grow on her head.

Surrounding these relatively happy pieces are verses revealing the pain and conflict in the relationship between the poet and the lady. He knows that his feeling for her is primarily lustful and destructive; yet, as he says in Sonnet 129, he cannot free himself from her: "All this the world well knows; yet none knows well/ To shun the heaven that leads men to this hell."

Irony pervades the sonnets in which Shakespeare declares his full knowledge of her vices and her deceptions both of her husband and of him: "When my love swears that she is made of truth,/ I do believe her, though I know she lies." The poet's conflict is intensified by the lady's affair with the nobleman, and he tries to explain his reaction in the little morality play of Sonnet 144:

Two loves I have of comfort and despair,
Which like two spirits do suggest me still:
The better angel is a man right fair,
The worser spirit a woman colour'd ill.
To win me soon to hell, my female evil
Tempteth my better angel from my [side],
And would corrupt my saint to be a devil,
Wooing his purity with her foul pride.
And whether that my angel be turn'd fiend,
Suspect I may, yet not directly tell;
But being both from me, both to each friend,
I guess one angel in another's hell.
    Yet this shall I ne'er know, but live in doubt,
    Till my bad angel fire my good one out.

The tremendous appeal of Shakespeare's sonnets through the centuries rests essentially on the same qualities that have made his plays immortal, his phenomenal understanding of the workings of the mind and his incredible ability to distill many aspects of human experience into a few lines. The sonnets are, in many ways, dramatic poetry; the reader is constantly aware of the presence of the poet, the "I" of the sequence, who addresses the nobleman and the Dark Lady forcefully and directly, not as if he were musing in his study. A brief perusal of the opening lines of the sonnets shows a remarkable number of questions and commands that heighten the reader's sense of a dramatic situation:

That thou hast her, it is not all my grief,
And yet it may be said I lov'd her dearly . . .
Being your slave, what should I do but tend
Upon the hours and times of your desire?
Farewell! thou art too dear for my possessing,
And like enough thou know'st thy estimate.

The compression of language; the vivid images drawn from nature, commerce, the theater, and many other aspects of life; the wordplay; and the flexibility of rhythms of speech that characterize Shakespeare's blank verse—all contribute to the greatness of the sonnets as well. In these poems, as in his plays, he was able to transform traditional forms and raise them to new heights.

For Further Study

Crossman, Robert. "Making Love out of Nothing at All: The Issue of Story in Shakespeare's Procreation Sonnets." *Shakespeare Quarterly* 41, no. 4 (Winter, 1990): 470-488. Argues that a consistent story line unifies many of the sonnets, focusing especially on Sonnets 1 through 17. In this group, Crossman traces the progress of the sonnet speaker's friendship and warm affection for a fair young man.

Green, Martin. *Wriothesley's Roses: In Shakespeare's Sonnets, Poems, and Plays.* Baltimore: Clevendon Books, 1993. Links historical records with poetic context in various sonnets in an interesting attempt to establish the identities of Shakespeare's fair young man and of the rival poet who seems to compete with Shakespeare's speaker for the affections of the Dark Lady. Provides a good historical background.

Landry, Hilton. *Interpretation in Shakespeare's Sonnets.* Berkeley: University of California Press, 1963. Despite numerous more recent studies, this book remains an excellent introduction to the thematic analysis and interpretation of Shakespeare's sonnets.

Ramsey, Paul. *The Fickle Glass: A Study of Shakespeare's Sonnets.* New York: AMS Press, 1979. A clearly written scholarly examination of critical problems, poetic techniques, and meaning in the sonnets. Explores questions of authorship, order, and date of composition. Excellent discussion of metrical rules and Elizabethan rhetoric in the sonnets.

Smith, Hallet. *The Tension of the Lyre: Poetry in Shakespeare's Sonnets.* San Marino, Calif.: Huntington Library, 1981. General discussion of the sonnets, beginning with an exploration of poetic voice and audience, and including an overview of Shakespeare's world as it is reflected in the sonnets.

Weiser, David K. *Mind in Character: Shakespeare's Speaker in the Sonnets.* Columbia: University of Missouri Press, 1987. Thorough explication of the sonnets. Useful appendix classifies the sonnets by modes of address.

Sonnet 18

First published: 1609, in *Sonnets*

Shall I compare thee to a summer's day?
Thou art more lovely and more temperate:
Rough winds do shake the darling buds of May,
And summer's lease hath all too short a date;
Sometimes too hot the eye of heaven shines,
And often is his gold complexion dimm'd;
And every fair from fair sometime declines,
By chance, or nature's changing course untrimm'd:
But thy eternal summer shall not fade,
Nor lose possession of that fair thou ow'st,
Nor shall Death brag thou wand'rest in his shade,
When in eternal lines to time thou grow'st;
   So long as men can breathe or eyes can see,
   So long lives this, and this gives life to thee.

The Poem

This sonnet begins with a straightforward question in the first person, addressed to the object of the poet's attention: "Shall I compare thee to a summer's day?" After a direct answer, "Thou art more lovely and more temperate," the next seven lines of the poem develop the comparison with a series of objections to a summer day.

William Shakespeare develops the "temperate" elements of his comparison first, leaving the "lovely" qualities tor later consideration. His first criticism of summer is that in May rough winds shake the "darling" buds. This objection might seem trivial until one remembers that the poet is invoking a sense of the harmony implicit in classical concepts of order and form which writers of the Renaissance emulated. His use of the term "darling" extends the harmonious concept to include the vision of an orderly universe embracing its creations and processes with affection.

Such terms apply only to the ideal universe, however. In nature's corrupt state, after Adam's fall, all sublunary (earthly) forms and events fail to adhere to their primal harmony. Hence, rough winds shake the May buds and, as the next line indicates, summer is too short. Sometimes the sun is too hot; at other times the day becomes cloudy.

In lines 7 and 8, the poet summarizes his objections to the summer day by asserting that everything that is fair will be "untrimmed," either by chance or by a natural process. The most obvious meaning here is that everything that summer produces will become less beautiful over time. The word "fair," however, seems to mean more than merely beautiful to the eye and, like the words "lovely" and "darling," comprehends all desirable qualities. Here, too, the poet invokes the concept of sublunary corruption. Although he is apparently still discussing the disadvantages of a summer's day when compared to the person he is addressing, he is at the same time creating a transition to the next section of the poem by introducing the second element of his comparison, that comprehended in the word "lovely."

The last six lines of the sonnet detail the advantages of the person addressed, indicating no diminution in the durability or fairness of that individual. The reason lies in the "eternal lines to time" that Shakespeare creates in his sonnet, knowing that the poem in which the person is memorialized will last through all time.

Although in the concluding couplet Shakespeare gives a direct statement of the theme, he uses the pronoun "this" to carry the weight of meaning and gives no verbal referent to the pronoun. Yet in making the poem itself the referent, the poet creates the object that will transmit the immortality of its subject to eternity.

Forms and Devices

This poem is a sonnet, a poem consisting of fourteen lines in iambic pentameter, a form created by Petrarch, an Italian poet of the fourteenth century. A Petrarchan sonnet usually contains eight lines sketching a situation (the octave) and six lines applying it (the sextet). The form was modified by Sir Thomas Wyatt and Henry Howard, Earl of Surrey, appearing in poetic anthologies during the mid-sixteenth century. They and other poets created the English sonnet, consisting of three quatrains followed by a couplet, rhyming *abab, cdcd, efef, gg*. In this form, the eight-six division is occasionally maintained, as in Sonnet 18, but the concluding couplet summarizes the theme.

Taken as a whole, the sonnets of Shakespeare may be said to form a sonnet sequence: a series of sonnets, usually addressed to a woman for whom the poet has conceived a passion. From Petrarch's time on, the conventions of the "lover's complaint" pervaded the imagery of these sequences, but their originality of imagery and conceit generally transcends the limitations of the troubadour traditions from which they derive.

The women of these sequences have themselves become widely known: Petrarch's Laura, Sir Philip Sidney's Stella (Penelope Devereux), and Edmund Spenser's Elizabeth Boyle have achieved the kind of immortality that Shakespeare's Sonnet 18 contemplates. It is thus ironic that the object of Shakespeare's own sequence, now referred to as the Dark Lady, should be unknown. The sonnets themselves range over many topics, including the beauty and desirability of marriage for a young man, a love triangle, a "dark lad" and several philosophical and moral problems. They form a unique source of speculation on Shakespeare's life in addition to being poems of great power.

In Sonnet 18, Shakespeare sets up his comparison by rhetorically introducing the basis for a simile that will underlie the structure of the whole poem: the comparison between the person who is the object of the poet's attention and a summer's day. The first image, of rough winds shaking May's buds, is stated directly. In the next line, however, the poet uses the metaphor of summer's lease being too short, aptly indicating the transitory nature of a season and, by extension, a year, and a life.

The use of metonymy in "eye of heaven" (the sun) illustrates the power of that device: The eye is usually thought of as the agency for perception and character; here the central focus of the sky seems central to the concept of nature itself. Personification of this eye enhances the subject of the poem as a whole, for dimming his gold complexion implies hiding the beauty of the individual whom the poet addresses—something the poet intends to prevent.

The personification of death in line 11 curiously treats the word "shade," often used to describe those who have died. Here it seems to signify, instead, the atmosphere of death—the shadow that hovers over those who come within its influence, which the poet's lines are about to dispel.

Themes and Meanings

Like his plays, Shakespeare's sonnet introduces several themes reflecting Renaissance thought. The most important of those here is the belief that everything under the moon was corrupted by Adam's fall from grace. Thus, although the sun (the "eye of heaven") moved in an uncorrupted sphere above the moon, the earthly influence upon its shining could make it either too hot (line 5) or too hazy (line 6). A corollary of this fall was the consequent mutability of the sublunary creation. For Shakespeare the change was not lateral; rather, it involved a progressive degeneration of beauty, created by chance or by the influence of time on nature (lines 7, 8).

In Shakespeare's Sonnet 18, one may thus discern Renaissance beliefs about nature. One can also see remnants of medieval thinking. This combination appears most obviously in the poet's treatment of the Ovidian tradition. The Middle Ages had interpreted the Roman poet Ovid (43 B.C.E.-17 C.E.) as a moral poet whose *Metamorphoses* (c. 8 C.E.) contained a cosmology based on Greek and Roman myths. The Renaissance, on the other hand, saw him as an erotic poet whose *Amores* (c. 20 B.C.E.; *Loves*) and *Ars Amatoria* (c. 2 B.C.E.; *Art of Love*) provided the model for Petrarch and later sonneteers.

In Sonnet 18 one finds both the moral and erotic suggested in the words "lovely," "darling," and "fair." Emphasis on the physical beauty of the person addressed is tempered by hints that this beauty outshines that of the natural universe itself; through the poet's lines, it becomes one with Plato's eternal forms. Missing from this sonnet, however, is that part of the Petrarchan tradition that sees the lover complaining of his mistress' rejection and displaying his own despair or resolution resulting from it. In its place one finds the central theme of mutability, the imperfection and impermanence of the sublunary world, infusing the first eight lines and providing the foil for the rest of the poem.

In contrast to the mutability theme, the concluding sestet proclaims Shakespeare's art as the antidote to time and change. The poet's consciousness of his own genius, although placed here within a tradition maintained by several of his predecessors, transcends the limitations of the fallen world. *Ars longa, vita breve* (art is long, life is brief) becomes the underlying theme, arrayed in Shakespeare's unique and comprehensive poetic language.

Russell Lord

Sonnet 19

First published: 1609, in *Sonnets*

> Devouring Time, blunt thou the lion's paws,
> And make the earth devour her own sweet brood;
> Pluck the keen teeth from the fierce tiger's jaws,
> And burn the long-liv'd phoenix in her blood;
> Make glad and sorry seasons as thou fleet'st,
> And do what e'er thou wilt, swift-footed Time,
> To the wide world and all her fading sweets:
> But I forbid thee one most heinous crime,
> O, carve not with thy hours my love's fair brow,
> Nor draw no lines there with thine antique pen;
> Him in thy course untainted do allow,
> For beauty's pattern to succeeding men.
>   Yet do thy worst, old Time: despite thy wrong,
>   My love shall in my verse ever live young.

The Poem

Shakespeare's Sonnet 19 is a traditional English sonnet (traditional because Shakespeare made it so), consisting of a single stanza of fourteen lines, rhymed according to a standard format. Like the other 153 sonnets by Shakespeare, Sonnet 19 has no title.

In the first quatrain, the poet addresses time as a devourer, handing out a series of defiant invitations to time to perform its most destructive acts. First, time is instructed to "blunt" the "lion's paws," which gives the reader an image of enormous strength reduced to impotence. In line 2, the poet moves from the particular to the general, invoking time as a bully who forces the earth, seen as the universal mother, to consume all her beloved offspring. Line 3 echoes line 1, giving another image of the strongest of nature's creatures, this time the tiger, reduced to weakness. Time, seen as a fierce aggressor, will pluck out its teeth. In line 4, the poet moves to the mythological realm. He tells time to wreak its havoc by burning the "long-lived phoenix." The phoenix was a mythical bird that supposedly lived for five hundred years (or a thousand years, according to some versions of the legend) before being consumed in fire. The phoenix was also said to rise from its own ashes, but that is not a meaning that the poet chooses to develop here. The final phrase in the line, "in her blood," is a hunting term that refers to an animal in the full vigor of life.

The second quatrain begins with a fifth invitation to Time, couched in general rather than specific terms: "Make glad and sorry seasons as thou fleet'st." This takes the invocation of Time's destructive power to a more refined level, because it alludes to the human emotional response to the hurried passage of time: Seasons of gladness and seasons of sorrow form part of an ever-recurring cycle. Lines 6 and 7 seem to continue the poet's willingness to allow time full sway to do whatever it wants wherever it chooses.

In line 8, however, the argument begins to turn. Having built up a considerable sense of momentum, the poet checks it by announcing that there is one limit he wishes to place on Time. It transpires that all the concessions the poet has made to Time in lines 1 through 7 are one side of a bargain the poet wishes to strike. The terms are now forcefully announced, as the poet attempts to establish his authority over Time. He forbids Time, with its "antique pen," to make furrows on the brow of his beloved. The friend must be allowed to go through life untouched ("untainted") by the passage of Time. Anything less would be a crime, because the lover is an exceptional being who must represent to future ages the pattern of true beauty—an eternal beauty that stands outside the domain of Time.

In the final couplet, however, the poet seems to acknowledge the futility of his demand, yet he remains defiant. In spite of the wrongs that time inflicts, the poet's friend will forever remain young because he will live in the poet's verse.

Forms and Devices

The sonnet is a highly concentrated work of art in which the poet must develop and resolve his theme within the strict confines of the sonnet form. Sonnet 19, like all Shakespeare's sonnets, follows a standard pattern. It consists of three quatrains and a concluding couplet, and it follows the rhyme scheme *abab, cdcd, efef, gg*.

The meaning of the sonnet is reinforced by the variations Shakespeare makes in the meter. This takes the form of a subtle counterpoint between the regular metrical base, which is iambic pentameter, and the spoken rhythm—what one actually hears when the sonnet is read. For example, in the first quatrain, the theme of the destructiveness of time is brought out more forcefully by a series of metrical inversions.

In the third foot in the first line ("blunt thou"), a trochee is substituted for an iamb, resulting in a strong stress falling on the first syllable. This gives "blunt" a much stronger impact than it would otherwise have, especially as the rest of the line follows a regular iambic rhythm. In line 2, the last foot is a spondee rather than an iamb, resulting in two heavy stresses on "sweet brood." The emphasis on the "sweetness of what time destroys" makes the work of time seem even more harsh. Line 3 is a very irregular line, echoing the turbulence of the sense. There is a metrical inversion in the first foot (it is trochaic, not iambic) that serves to highlight the word "Pluck." This recalls, through assonance, the "blunt" of line 1. Both of these are forceful words that express the way in which time assaults the natural world. The second foot of line 3 is a spondee, and the assonance contained in "keen teeth" adds to its prominent impact in the line. The fourth foot of this line is also a spondee, making the "fierce tiger" very fierce indeed. Line 3 in particular, with its high number of stressed syllables, brings out the idea of time as an aggressive, fearsome warrior going to battle against all living things.

The meter of the second quatrain is more regular than the first. The speedy passage of the end of line 5 ("as thou fleet'st") echoes the sense, and this is emphasized again by the heavy stress on "swift" in line 6. In the third quatrain, the turbulent rhythm and harsh consonants of the earlier part of the sonnet vanish as the poet turns his attention to the beloved. The smooth and regular iambic rhythm of line 12, for example, "For beauty's pattern to succeeding men," suggests the perfection of his friend.

Time makes a forceful reappearance in the first line of the couplet, with the spondee, "old Time" prominently positioned immediately before the caesura. This makes the triumph of the last line, in which the poet obtains his victory through the power of his pen (a contrast to the seemingly all-powerful "antique pen" of Time), all the more striking and effective.

Themes and Meanings

In this sonnet, the poet faces up to one of the most fundamental facts of human existence: the transience of all things, even those of greatest power and beauty, including those most loved. In seizing on this theme, Shakespeare echoed a passage from the Roman poet Ovid's *Metamorphoses* (c. 8 C.E.), a source he turned to often: "Time, the devourer, and the jealous years that pass, destroy all things and, nibbling them away, consume them gradually in a lingering death."

The conflict between beauty and time, and the anguish of the lover who fears the touch of time on his beloved, is a major theme of the whole sonnet sequence. In Sonnet 16, for example, the friend is reproved for not making sufficient effort to "Make war upon this bloody tyrant Time." In sonnets 1 through 17, the poet proposes a solution. He enjoins his friend to marry and produce progeny, so that he will live again, achieving immortality through his offspring. Sonnet 12 states that nothing can stand against time "save breed." In Sonnet 19, however, this solution is implicitly abandoned because all of earth's "sweet brood" will be devoured by Time. Here "brood" recalls the "breed" of Sonnet 12, but the significance of the term has altered completely.

The battle against time is made more intense in this sonnet by the absolute value that the poet attaches to the friend. He is the very archetype of beauty, "beauty's pattern to succeeding men." Such an ideal view of the lover is repeated at other points in the sonnet sequence. Sonnet 106 states that all the beauty of past ages was only a prefiguring of what the friend now embodies. In Sonnet 14, the poet claims that the most fundamental values in existence are bound up in the life of his friend and cannot endure after his demise. Sonnet 104 reveals that future ages will not be able to produce anything to match the beauty the friend embodies. It might perhaps be said that the poet sees in the friend what William Blake would later describe as the "Divine Vision." This presence of an absolute, transcendental element in the relative world of time and change fuels the dramatic tension that gives Sonnet 19, and others, a stark and poignant power.

Bryan Aubrey

Sonnet 30

First published: 1609, in *Sonnets*

When to the sessions of sweet silent thought
I summon up remembrance of things past,
I sigh the lack of many a thing I sought,
And with old woes new wail my dear time's waste;
Then can I drown an eye (unus'd to flow)
For precious friends hid in death's dateless night,
And weep afresh love's long since cancell'd woe,
And moan th'expense of many a vanish'd sight;
Then can I grieve at grievances foregone,
And heavily from woe to woe tell o'er
The sad account of fore-bemoaned moan,
Which I new pay as if not paid before:
>   But if the while I think on thee, dear friend,
>   All losses are restor'd, and sorrows end.

The Poem

The opening lines of Shakespeare's Sonnet 30, "When to the sessions of sweet silent thought," evoke the picture of a man sweetly and silently reminiscing, living once again the pleasant (or "sweet") experiences of his past. The situation, however, soon shifts from silence to a sigh and from pleasantries to a lament for projects never completed, desires never fulfilled. This angst cannot be confined to the past but bursts into the poet's present consciousness. He suffers intense nostalgic pain for wasted time that can no longer be reclaimed. Old woes are reborn, reviving old hurts.

The second quatrain of the sonnet expands this idea, but the pain is heightened as the author thinks of the people who will never again come into his life. This brings tears into the eyes, as once again the pain of loss is relived. The vanished sights lamented are the faces of friends who have disappeared into death and the emptiness of love that is no more, but also suggested are places, possessions, and events that can never be reexperienced.

The third quatrain increases the weight and significance of the poem's central idea: The act of remembrance recalls old griefs into the present, where they become as painful in their rebirth as they were the first time they were experienced. It is as if the persona of the poem were caught in a psychological trap from which there is no escape and in which his mind, as if dragging chains, moves "heavily from woe to woe," unable to escape from the images that repeat "the sad account of fore-bemoaned moan." Though the account has been paid up in the past, the debt of pain is reopened and the poet must pay the entire amount again.

After twelve lines of bewailing the symptoms of his condition, the poet ends in a final couplet that moves abruptly to the solution. The cure is carefully coordinated with the disease, for just as the patient's woes were initiated by remembering the past, so are they dissipated by the thought of his current "dear friend," which restores all the lamented losses and ends all the reborn sorrows.

Forms and Devices

This sonnet is an "English" or "Shakespearean" sonnet—that is, it is composed of three quatrains and a couplet of iambic pentameter, rhymed *abab*, *cdcd*, *efef*, *gg*. What is different about the structure of this sonnet is that there is far less development from quatrain to quatrain than is usual for the overall collection. Shakespeare most often develops his sonnets by moving his argument in three quite distinct steps to its concluding couplet, or by developing three quite different images to be tied neatly together in the closing lines. This sonnet, however, has far more repetition than differentiation from quatrain to quatrain. The differences are subtle: The quatrains quietly move from wailing to weeping to grieving, a progression that is hardly noticed.

What makes this one of Shakespeare's most loved sonnets is not its structure but its music, achieved in part through the rhymes, but even more distinctively through the repetition of consonant sounds. In the first quatrain of the sonnet there are no less than twelve sibilant sounds, which, rather than hissing, evoke the music of the wind. The sound is repeated in the last line of the sonnet, surely an intended recapitulation to increase the feeling of completion. The fourth line of the poem introduces a series of alliterated *w* sounds: "And with old woes new wail my dear time's waste." These sounds introduce the rhythm of wailing, which is repeated in line 7, "And weep afresh love's . . . woe," and again in line 10, "from woe to woe." Repeated liquid sounds in line 7 add a languid sound to the line—"love's long since cancell'd woe"—and repeated *m*'s add both softness and length to lines 8 and 11: "And moan th'expense of many," and "fore-bemoaned moan." A lengthening of sound comes in the repetition of *fr*'s in "friends" and "afresh" in lines 6 and 7. The poem's alliteration enhances the meaning of the text and emphasizes both the standard iambic pulse and the variations from this standard in lines 1, 6, and 7.

Another device evident in this poem is what seems to be a calculated use of ambiguity. In the first line, the word "sessions" denotes a meeting of a legal court, but in context it also suggests a mere period of time. Thus "thought" could represent the judge presiding over the session or merely describe the activity of a designated period of time. Again the persona, the "I" of the poem, could be the judge, summoning his remembrances to stand trial. In the fourth line, the word "new" could be an adjective modifying "woes," which were once old and have now become new, or it could act as an adverb modifying "wail." It is not beyond possibility that "my dear" could be a noun of address, since the final couplet makes it clear that the sonnet was addressed to a "dear friend," though it seems more probable that "dear" is an adjective modifying either "time" or "waste."

"Time's waste" could be read as either the person having wasted his time or (more likely) as time, the destroyer, having laid waste to items and qualities of ultimate value to him. "Expense" in line 8 could be read in its most usual modern sense as cost, the money spent, or simply as loss: something that is spent is gone. "Foregone" in the ninth line probably means simply past, as having gone before, but could also carry the connotation of "given up" or "taken for granted." In the tenth line, "tell" could mean "to relate" but more likely has the older meaning of "count" or "tally." "Account" could mean a mere story, a financial account, or the final account-*ing* at the Last Judgment. This accumulation of ambiguity engages the reader's mind, focusing it on the form and keeping it from wandering; it also enriches the poem by suggesting alternative readings.

The dominant metaphor of the poem is the comparison of a period of reminiscing to the session of a court of law, but even so it is not meticulously carried out in the nature of an Elizabethan conceit. Words such as "cancell'd," "expense," "grievances," "account," and "losses . . . restored" may suggest court language, but the idea is not worked into the syntax. Other uses of figurative language enriching the poem are an eye "drowned" in tears, friends "hidden" in night, a woe "canceled" as if it were a debt, and an "account" of moans that needs to be settled.

Themes and Meanings

Shakespeare's Sonnet 30 is a beloved, often-remembered, often-quoted poem simply because it is an exquisite description of the pain of nostalgia, an experience which is common to most people. The human psyche does not want to let go of the experiences of its past, even when those experiences have been exceedingly painful, or perhaps especially because they were painful, since somehow the hurt has increased the meaning of the moment—certainly its intensity. The release which dissipates such remembered pain is also a welcome experience, and the reader of Shakespeare's sonnet experiences that release as the tension built up in the first twelve lines of the poem disappears in the recollection of a current, fulfilling friendship.

The poem is meaningful also because of its inclusion in the most famous collection of sonnets in the English language, if not in any language. Though almost no scholars believe that Shakespeare himself was responsible for the order in which the sonnets were printed, this poem does belong to the early group which were addressed to a young man. It also has a close relationship with the sonnet immediately preceding it and the one that follows, pointing to the probability that these were written together. Sonnet 29 has the same thought progression as Sonnet 30, as the poet laments the fact that Fortune has not been kind to him and wishes that he might change places with anyone a bit higher on her wheel. When the thought of his friend intrudes on this mediation, however, all is made right: The lark announces day, the earth sings, and he would change places with no one. Sonnet 31 is largely an explanation of the thirtieth. "Losses are restored" because those whom the author "supposed dead," whom he "thought buried," are alive in his friend, who contains all of their virtues. The friend is the grave containing all of their lives, "Hung with the trophies of my lovers gone,/ Who all their parts of me to thee did give." In this realization, the poet discovers a new, integrated personality, for what he used to find by dividing his love among many, he now finds in only one person who contains in himself all of those who have gone before. Though Shakespeare's Sonnet 30 stands alone, perfect in its own merits, that unity is more fully appreciated in the context of its neighbors.

Edward C. Adams

Sonnet 60

First published: 1609, in *Sonnets*

> Like as the waves make towards the pibbled shore,
> So do our minutes hasten to their end,
> Each changing place with that which goes before,
> In sequent toil all forwards do contend.
> Nativity, once in the main of light,
> Crawls to maturity, wherewith being crown'd,
> Crooked eclipses 'gainst his glory fight,
> And Time that gave doth now his gift confound.
> Time doth transfix the flourish set on youth,
> And delves the parallels in beauty's brow,
> Feeds on the rarities of nature's truth,
> And nothing stands but for his scythe to mow:
> > And yet to times in hope my verse shall stand,
> > Praising thy worth, despite his cruel hand.

The Poem

Sonnet 60, like all sonnets, is a fourteen-line poem of one stanza, rhymed according to a traditional scheme. As one of the 154 untitled sonnets by Shakespeare, it adheres to the form of what is referred to as the English, or Shakespearean, sonnet.

The first quatrain consists of an extended simile, comparing the passage of human life to the onward movement of waves rushing to the seashore. Each wave pushes the one in front of it and is, in turn, pushed by the one that follows it. Each following the other in close succession, the waves struggle forward.

The second quatrain introduces a new thought, more directly relating the passage of time to human life. The newborn baby, once it has seen the vast light of day, quickly begins to crawl. This is the first stage in its growth to adulthood. Once the human being is "crowned," however—that is, attains in adulthood its full stature as a royal king, the summit of the natural order—he is not allowed to rest and enjoy his status. The heavenly bodies, which have ruled his destiny since the day he was born, conspire against him to extinguish his glory. The same process that resulted in the gift of birth and growth is now responsible for change and decay.

The third quatrain develops the idea of time as destroyer, highlighting three lethal actions that time performs. First, time tears. It "doth transfix the flourish set on youth," which means that it pierces through the attractive outward appearance, the flower, of youth. Second, time imprints itself; it creates furrows ("delves the parallels") in the brow of the beautiful. Third, time is all-devouring. It consumes the most valuable and most prized things that nature produces. Nothing at all can stand against time, whose scythe will mow down everything.

It seems inevitable that time will be victorious, but in the final couplet the poet attempts to salvage what he can. He believes that at least one thing can survive the onslaught of time. In future times, his verse will "stand," if all else has fallen. At the same time, the poet reveals what has prompted his meditation on the destructive nature of time: his love for the youthful beauty of his friend. The poet's verse will always ring out in praise of this beauty, in spite of the devastation wrought by the "cruel hand" of time.

Forms and Devices

The frequent occurrence of *s* sounds (no fewer than seven) in the first two lines of Sonnet 60 suggests the sound of the incoming waves as they break on the shore. The final two *s* sounds, in "minutes hasten," are placed closer together than the others, and this suggests the increasing speed and urgency of the passage of time.

The sonnet's second quatrain is remarkable because it fuses three distinct sets of images: child, sun, and king. "Nativity" is at once the birth of a child and the rising of the morning sun. The child that "crawls to maturity" is also the ascending sun, and "crowned" suggests at once a king and the sun at its zenith in the sky. This thought would have come easily to an Elizabethan mind, at home with the idea of an intricate set of correspondences between the microcosmic world of humanity and the macrocosmic heavens. The same image occurs in Sonnet 33 and in Shakespeare's play *Richard II*.

At this point of maximum strength and power, the man-king-sun traces an assault on his position, as "Crooked eclipses 'gainst his glory fight." "Crooked" suggests the plotting of rivals to usurp his crown; "eclipses" is an astrological reference, suggesting an unfavorable aspect in the heavens that will bring about the inevitable downfall of the man-king, as well as ensuring the downward passage of the sun as it loses its glory over the western horizon. "Crawls" (line 6) and "Crooked" (line 7) are given added emphasis by the trochee at the beginning of each line and by alliteration, which also links them both to "crowned" at the end of line 6. The rising and falling rhythm of the final line of this quatrain, "And Time that gave doth now his gift confound," sums up the idea conveyed in the first three lines.

The third quatrain is introduced by a trochee, "Time doth," which gives notice that time is to be the direct subject of this part of the sonnet. Another trochee in the first foot of line 11 emphasizes the consuming aspect of Time, and Shakespeare again makes use of a trochaic foot, "Praising," in the first foot of the second line of the couplet. This paves the way for the defiant flourish with which the sonnet ends. The fact that the phrase "Praising thy worth" is followed by a caesura slows the line down and leaves this phrase echoing in the reader's mind, a magnificent counterpoint to the "cruel hand" of time that the sonnet has labored to convey. Labored is the appropriate word here, since the struggle of all sublunary things depicted in this sonnet is hard and unrelenting. Images of struggle begin in the first quatrain, as the waves "toil" and "contend" with each other. The slow struggle of the man upward is suggested by the caesura placed after "Crawls to maturity," and this struggle lasts far longer than his brief moment of glory, which dissolves after another fight.

Themes and Meanings

Sonnet 60 is closely related to Sonnets 63 through 65, and many others in the sonnet sequence, which also bemoan the inexorable advance of time and pose the question: How can beauty survive, given that all created things are transient and travel their allotted course to death? The theme of these sonnets was in part inspired by a passage from the Roman poet Ovid's *Metamorphoses* (c. 8 C.E.): "The baby, first born into the light of day, lies weak and helpless: after that he crawls on all fours, moving his limbs as animals do, and gradually, on legs as yet trembling and unsteady, stands upright, supporting himself by some convenient prop. Then he becomes strong and swift of foot, passing through the stage of youth till, having lived through the years of middle age also, he slips down the incline of old age, towards life's setting. Age undermines and destroys the strength of fonder years." This passage gave Shakespeare the image of "Nativity, once in the main of light,/ Crawls to maturity," and the passage that follows in Ovid, "Helen weeps . . . when she sees herself in the glass, wrinkled with age," may have suggested to Shakespeare the image of "delves the parallels in beauty's brow."

Shakespeare is not content to leave the world, or his friend, to mutability. The attempt in this sonnet to immortalize the friend through the poet's verse is a theme of many other Shakespearean sonnets as well, including Sonnets 19, 55, 63, 65, 100, 101, and 107. Some readers may find the resolution of the problem, which is accomplished in the final two lines of the poem, unsatisfactory. How can the hope expressed in the couplet somehow outweigh the remorseless pressure that has been built up in the first twelve lines? It might be argued that a poem about a beautiful person now dead is a poor substitute for the presence of the living person. The same argument might be applied to the solution proposed in Sonnets 1 through 17—that the friend should marry and produce offspring and thereby achieve a kind of immortality—but it should be pointed out that these are secular poems. The poet refuses to take refuge in any belief system that will soften or remove the effect of mutability. In this sonnet, as in others, there is no Christian heaven in which the lovers can look forward to another meeting, and the thought is not Neoplatonic; the friend is not described as a shadow or reflection of an eternal form, existing in an ideal world not subject to change. On the contrary, in this sonnet the human and the natural worlds are inextricably intertwined; the images of the devastating effects of time can be applied equally to both human and nonhuman realms. The poet thus works toward his triumph, limited though it may be, entirely in the terms that the natural order offers.

Bryan Aubrey

Sonnet 65

First published: 1609, in *Sonnets*

Since brass, nor stone, nor earth, nor boundless sea,
But sad mortality o'ersways their power,
How with this rage shall beauty hold a plea,
Whose action is no stronger than a flower?
O how shall summer's honey breath hold out
Against the wreckful siege of battering days,
When rocks impregnable are not so stout,
Nor gates of steel so strong, but Time decays?
O fearful meditation! where, alack,
Shall Time's best jewel from Time's chest lie hid?
Or what strong hand can hold his swift foot back?
Or who his spoil of beauty can forbid?
    O none, unless this miracle have might,
    That in black ink my love may still shine bright.

The Poem

The opening quatrain of Shakespeare's Sonnet 65 asks how beauty can resist that power in nature which destroys brass, stone, earth, and the sea, since beauty is less durable and powerful than any of those. The earth and sea together cannot withstand death, the dismal ("sad") state that overpowers everything in nature. In the third line, mortality becomes "this rage"—a violent anger, even a kind of madness, that opposes a most fragile supplicant, beauty. If the earth itself is no match for this force, beauty seems to have no hope of lasting, since its strength is no more than a flower's.

The second quatrain repeats the opening question, beauty now characterized by another of nature's insubstantial and temporary forms, "summer's honey breath," which the poet sees as the victim of an assault by a "wreckful siege" in the form of "battering days." The "earth" alluded to in the opening line is represented here as "rocks impregnable," and brass has been replaced by "gates of steel." Neither of these substantial forms can withstand time's battering and corrosive force. Though asking a question, the speaker implies that any resistance to time is doomed and, further, that natural things are in constant battle with a force that nothing survives, least of all something as evanescent as summer's breath.

The third quatrain begins with an expostulation that expresses the poet's feelings as he confronts the prospect of time's onslaught: "O fearful meditation!" Even flight is futile, for beauty, now represented as a jewel, cannot escape being encased finally and forever in "Time's chest." Time is then characterized as the swift runner

362

whose foot cannot be held back. No outside force—no "hand"—can or will reach out and rescue beauty from time's onward thrust. At the close of the third quatrain, beauty is not only a doomed supplicant but also a helpless victim of time's plundering. At this point, the poet appears to have accepted the inevitable annihilation of beauty by time's relentless onslaught.

The final couplet offers hope, however—the written word. Black ink, imbued with the poet's love, offers the only defense against Time's annihilating power, for the poet's words have the miraculous ability to reflect beauty's splendor in a timeless state.

Forms and Devices

The sonnet's fourteen lines form three quatrains and a concluding couplet, rhyming *abab, cdcd, efef, gg*. Known as the Shakespearean (or English) sonnet, this arrangement differs from the Italian (or Petrarchan) sonnet in adopting a different rhyme scheme and dividing the sestet (the final six lines) into a quatrain and couplet. The third quatrain addresses the poem's subject somewhat differently from the first two quatrains (which correspond to the octave of the Italian sonnet), and the couplet offers a final comment on, or a summary of, the foregoing argument. A typical line consists of five stresses, or ten syllables, called iambic pentameter: "Since brass, nor stone, nor earth, nor boundless sea." An extra syllable is occasionally added to the line, as in lines 2, 4, and 10. Within this highly patterned world, Sonnet 65 achieves myriad effects.

Wordplay creates much of the poem's irony by combining multiple meanings into one word. The "sad" in line 2 characterizes death personified as "mortality." Mortality is sad because it is his duty to destroy things. At the same time, "sad" expresses the poet's own feelings regarding this destructive force. In the third line, "this rage" ironically plays on the idea that mortality, usually thought of as a dormant state, is a violent passion, even a madness. Shakespeare twists the traditional conventions by assigning such a passion, not to the lover, but to the force that destroys beauty. Irony is implicit, too, in the reference to "boundless sea," which is nevertheless "bound" by "mortality." Though the tone of the sonnet may not be entirely serious—Shakespeare seems close to mocking the tradition of the forlorn lover in the line, "O fearful meditation! where, alack"—any playful spirit the poem may have is sobered by the ominous nature of the subject.

The poem's principal imagery focuses on the various forms given the chief antagonists, "Time" and beauty, though beauty is depicted in images that suggest insubstantial form (a mere "plea" and "summer's honey breath"), a passive hardness ("jewel"), and a helpless victim (Time's "spoil"). Time is personified variously, too, as a force that "decays," keeps jewelry in a chest, has a swift foot, and plunders his victims. When the poem wants to suggest the delicate, impermanent nature of beauty, imagery is deft—"flower . . . summer's honey breath." When the poem wants images of strength, it is prolific: "wreckful siege . . . battering days . . . rocks impregnable . . . gates of steel."

Numerous sound effects underscore the poem's doleful tone. Repetition of words (such as "nor" and "O") and structures (the five questions, for example) suggests the relentless assault of "this rage" as well as the urgency of the speaker's mingled hope and fear. Apt alliteration—"steel so strong" and "none, unless"—and vowel sounds reinforce the meaning. The sound of "brass" and "stone" suggests more durable qualities than those of a flower and honey breath, and the phrases "rocks impregnable" and "gates of steel" sound "harder" than the more mellifluous sounds of "miracle have might" and "my love."

Themes and Meanings

The central theme of Sonnet 65 is the opposition between the transitory, delicate nature of beauty and the devastating effect on beauty of mortality and its principal instrument, time. The opening questions seem rhetorical, indirectly arguing the poet's conviction that beauty is no match for aging and death. The final two lines dispel the gloomy predictions implicit in the questions, however, by pointing to the power of the written word to sustain its subject—in this case, beauty. As the poem advances through the first two quatrains, the changes in the images of time suggest an increase in the implacable strength of time, which only "o'ersways" in the second line but turns to a "rage" and then a "wreckful siege of battering days" attacking such impressive things as "rocks impregnable" and "gates of steel."

The final two lines, by opposing "black ink" with the light which the poet's love emits, leave the reader with the central conflict of the poet's vision: light (beauty) is opposed by darkness (black ink) and therefore utter annihilation. The balancing imagery of the final line suggests a resolution to this conflict, and so ends the poem on a bright note, literally on the word "bright" itself: The poet's love, expressed in this written sonnet, is the one force that can successfully oppose time and death. The word "still" in the last line introduces a paradox. If "my love" is "still," meaning lifeless, it cannot "shine," yet it does, or might; if it is indeed motionless, it cannot "still" be shining, yet it may, in "black ink," and in that form, it can forever oppose the destructive motion implicit in the phrase "this rage." The poet's skill is the only force that can reverse the effects of aging and stop time's forward motion, which carries all things to their death. The poet's hand becomes the "strong hand" (line 12) that can indeed hold time's "swift foot back." The surprise is that the strength is not physical but poetic.

A subtler surprise is that, while appearing to address what male lovers are expected to address, a beautiful woman, Shakespeare here focuses on beauty, perhaps in keeping with the poem's general air of indirection—rhetorical questions develop the poet's subject all the way to the final couplet in place of direct argument. The poem seems to suggest that to be any more direct, by addressing his beloved directly, he would "expose" her to time's onslaught. By remaining as "hidden" and insubstantial as "Time's best jewel," the object of his love may be saved. If the "black ink" of his poem draws a curtain of darkness before the face of his beloved, her beauty may nevertheless shine through the love that the poem expresses.

In keeping with the delicate indirection of the poem, the poet makes only slight references to the sexual aspect of his love, principally in the third quatrain, where "impregnable" subtly suggests where the poet's mind is going—time is a ravager of beautiful women, one way or another. Hints of ravishment continue as the poet references "gates of steel" and concludes in his using "spoil" (plundering) that beauty cannot "forbid."

The structure of the final line reflects brilliantly the poem's resolution, the inky blackness of annihilating time at one end of the line and, at the other, the redemptive light of the poet's love. Between these two states is the poet's "love," the fulcrum that forever separates and balances them.

Bernard E. Morris

Sonnet 73

First published: 1609, in *Sonnets*

That time of year thou mayst in me behold
When yellow leaves, or none, or few, do hang
Upon those boughs which shake against the cold,
Bare ruin'd choirs, where late the sweet birds sang.
In me thou seest the twilight of such day
As after sunset fadeth in the west,
Which by and by black night doth take away,
Death's second self, that seals up all in rest.
In me thou seest the glowing of such fire
That on the ashes of his youth doth lie,
As the death-bed whereon it must expire,
Consum'd with that which it was nourish'd by.
    This thou perceiv'st, which makes thy love more strong,
    To love that well, which thou must leave ere long.

The Poem

This fourteen-line poem, which is divided into three distinct quatrains (four-line stanzas) followed by a couplet (two lines), is addressed to the poet's lover and comments on the approach of old age in the speaker. As in all the Shakespearean sonnets, the voice is that of the poet. The lover has sometimes been interpreted as the unknown "Mr. W. H." to whom the first quarto edition was dedicated, although the nineteenth century poet and critic Samuel Taylor Coleridge surmised that the lover must be a woman.

The poet opens by stating that his lover must behold him at the time of life corresponding to late autumn, when almost no leaves remain on the trees and the birds have flown south. The poet's calling attention to his old age might seem incongruous, since many lovers might try to hide the fact from their companions. Yet, in this relationship, Shakespeare not only is being forthright but also seems to be seeking the sympathy of his dear friend.

In the second quatrain, the image shifts from the time of year to the time of day. He chooses twilight, the period between sunset and darkness, to reflect his state. "Twi" originally meant "half," so "half-light" signifies a period of diminished abilities and activities, again calling for the sympathy and understanding of the poet's friend. The second half of the quatrain brings forth more forcefully the associations of darkness with death and emphasizes the immanence of that mortal state in the poet's life.

The third quatrain moves from the world of seasons and time to the more restricted compass of natural phenomena—the way a fire burns itself to ashes and then is smothered by those ashes. As the magnitude of the image decreases, the force of its message concentrates, concluding with the very picture of a deathbed.

The concluding couplet sums up the purpose of Shakespeare's revelation of his decreasing powers: to request that his friend love more strongly because of the short time left to the poet. Critics have been concerned with the word "leave" in the last line, since it might be thought to indicate that the lover is the one to depart. Some have even commented that "lose" might better convey the idea. Certainly the death of the poet would cause a separation to occur, however, and the lover would be forced to "leave" him.

Forms and Devices

The sonnet form, consisting of fourteen lines of iambic pentameter, was created by Petrarch, an Italian poet of the fourteenth century. The classic Petrarchan (or Italian) sonnet usually consisted of eight lines (the octave) sketching a situation and six lines (the sestet) applying it. The form was modified by Sir Thomas Wyatt and Henry Howard, Earl of Surrey. They and other poets created the English sonnet, which consists ot three quatrains followed by a couplet, rhyming *abab*, *cdcd*, *efef*, *gg*. In this form, adopted by Shakespeare and frequently called the Shakespearean sonnet, the couplet summarizes the theme. Shakespeare's sonnets range over many topics, including the beauty of a young man, the desirability of his marriage, a love triangle, a "Dark Lady," and several philosophical and moral concerns. In addition to their poetic power, they remain a unique source of biographical speculation.

Sonnet 73 contains three distinct metaphors for the poet's progressive aging. The first of these is the implied comparison between his state and the time of year when a few yellow leaves, or none at all, remain on boughs shaking in the cold winds, deserted by the birds that usually inhabit them. One might be tempted to compare this directly with graying and loss of hair, but it is more probably to be taken generally as a reference to the aging process. The critic William Empson has pointed out manifold connotations of the "bare ruined choirs" in his *Seven Types of Ambiguity* (1930), evoking images of ruined monastery choir stalls made of wood and infused with the atmosphere of stained glass and choirboy charm, showing how that richness is unified by the way that the poet's subject relates to his narcissistic affection.

The second quatrain moves from the time of year to the time of day. Again there is a metaphor: The poet's likeness is that of a day fading in the west after sunset. Instead of the yellow of the first quatrain, there is the black of night's approach, a more sinister prospect. There follows a personification within the metaphor, naming night as death's second self, in essence creating a new metaphor within the first as it envisions night, which "seals up all in rest." The word "seals" suggests the permanent closing of a coffin lid, providing a finality that is only slightly relieved by the knowledge that the reader is actually seeing not death, but night. Some critics have suggested that the word "seals" suggests the "seeling" of the eyes of a falcon or hawk, a process of sewing the eyes of the bird so that it would obey the falconer's instructions more exactly. This suggests an even more forcible entry of death into the metaphor.

Structurally, this concept would close the octave of a Petrarchan sonnet, and although the English sonnet has ostensibly eliminated the eight-six division, the vestiges of a division remain, since the poet moves from his year-day metaphors to another kind of figure in his next quatrain. Here, the metaphor involves a complex process rather than a simple period of time. The afterglow of a fire gradually being choked by the ashes of its earlier burning becomes the description of Shakespeare's aging. The ashes of the fire's earlier combustion are the poet's own youthful dissipation, hinting an extravagance of which we know nothing biographically except the metaphorical statement made here. Although there is no specific color named, one senses the red of a glowing fire, enhancing the yellow and black of the previous descriptions. The concluding couplet moves from metaphor to direct statement, summarizing the purpose of the poet in revealing so frankly his approaching old age. After the richness of the preceding lines, it might appear almost anticlimactic, yet it is important to the structure of the form, lending finality to the whole.

Themes and Meanings

Like his plays, Shakespeare's sonnets introduce themes reflecting Renaissance thought. In order to understand them, one must realize what the term "Renaissance" implies. The word was introduced into art criticism by John Ruskin in *The Stones of Venice* (1851-1853), when he referred to a return to "pagan systems" in Italian painting and architecture during the fourteenth century. Essayist Walter Pater extended the meaning of the term to include all phases of intellectual life. Scholars have associated with the Renaissance such phenomena as Neoplatonism, humanism, and classicism. They have also deduced that medieval traditions were not utterly displaced from these developments; there was no sharp dividing line between the Middle Ages and the Renaissance.

Perhaps the most obvious theme in Sonnet 73 is that of mutability, deriving from Greek and Roman philosophers but strained through the theological thinkers of the Middle Ages and modified during the Renaissance. Basically, this theme sees all "sublunary" phenomena (those beneath the moon, thus corrupted) as subject to change. Thus they lack the permanence of both biblical perfection and Platonic ideals.

In this sonnet, Shakespeare's consciousness of himself and of his beloved friend remains rooted in mortality and mutability. Unlike the idealized relationship portrayed in earlier sonnets, here there is a strong consciousness of the changes that old age brings to the poet and to his relationships with others. Here is resignation in the face of the inevitability of death and his permanent separation from his beloved. Time becomes omnipotent. It controls all natural processes, and no expedient of art can resist it. The most one can do is to express a heightened affection for one who is soon to pass away.

If one examines the consistency with which Shakespeare has joined his three sets of images, one may glimpse something of the coherence created by the poet's genius. The words "bare ruin'd choirs" of the first quatrain are strengthened in the second into the words "Death's second self." In the third quatrain, what was previously merely a metaphor for sleep has become metaphorically a deathbed. The concluding couplet may be considered a further step still, since it translates metaphorical references to death into personal ones referring to the poet's own approaching end.

It has been shown that the poet uses a variety of colors within the quatrains of this sonnet: yellow, black, and red (glowing). These colors have suggested to other poets images of death and pestilence. Shakespeare uses them to describe metaphorically his approaching old age. Thus he maintains the theme of inevitable change and sublunary corruption throughout.

Russell Lord

Sonnet 76

First published: 1609, in *Sonnets*

Why is my verse so barren of new pride?
So far from variation or quick change?
Why with the time do I not glance aside
To new-found methods and to compounds strange?
Why write I still all one, ever the same,
And keep invention in a noted weed,
That every word doth almost tell my name,
Showing their birth, and where they did proceed?
O, know, sweet love, I always write of you,
And you and love are still my argument;
So all my best is dressing old words new,
Spending again what is already spent:
    For as the sun is daily new and old,
    So is my love still telling what is told.

The Poem

The first quatrain of Sonnet 76 consists of two questions that address a supposed problem with William Shakespeare's own verse—its utter conventionality, barrenness of thought, and monotony ("So far from variation"). A more ambitious or imaginative lover, he says, would express himself with variety and surprise ("quick change"). The second question implies that, in keeping with the fashion ("the time"), the poet should employ better "methods" and new "compounds." Besides being destitute of invention, it seems that he lacks a pleasing spirit of adventure.

The second quatrain questions the poet's motives or common sense in writing verses that are "ever the same" and have a familiar appearance ("noted weed"), since it can easily be known who wrote them and where they were sent ("did proceed"). In matters of love, the implication is, discretion is the soul of wit.

Having presented one side of love's coin in the first eight lines of the sonnet, the poet turns the coin over in the third quatrain, answering the implied charge of triteness and lack of imagination. Actually, he argues, by writing always of one subject, "you and love," he is being clever; instead of wasting his effort by trying always to invent new words, he devotes his "best" to simply dressing up the old and thereby finding continued use in what has already been used. Expressing his love in verse is in fact like spending money, and words are like coins. His subject, "you and love," enables him to give familiar words new meaning, to reuse those that have been used before. The benefits of this kind of recycling are too obvious to argue: less effort, less waste, greater efficiency.

Lest his beloved not be convinced by this curious way of looking at his verse, Shakespeare in his final couplet points out that his method is the very principle upon which the sun operates, returning again and again, ever the same yet always new. What better model can a poet have than the sun itself? His verse repeats what has already been written, or spoken, but like the sun, it brings with it a new look, the difference being the poet's "love."

Forms and Devices

Unlike the Italian (or Petrarchan) sonnet, the Shakespearean (or English) sonnet is divided into three quatrains and a couplet, rhyming *abab, cdcd, efef, gg*. The first two quatrains introduce and develop the subject of the poem at the end of the eighth line, where a pause occurs. The third quatrain addresses the subject from a somewhat different perspective, concluding the poet's argument in line 12. The couplet sums up the foregoing argument or, as in Sonnet 76, delivers a final statement that clenches the matter.

Each line of the sonnet regularly consists of five stresses, or ten syllables, called iambic pentameter. In Sonnet 76, lines 1, 3, 5, 8, and 12 are irregular. All these lines except line 1 combine iamb feet (in which the stress falls on the second syllable) with trochees, two-syllable feet whose stresses fall on the first syllable of each foot: "WHY with the TIME do I not GLANCE aSIDE," for example. The last four syllables in the first line vary the conventional line even further, placing the stresses and unstressed syllables in pairs (illustrated here within brackets): "so BAR[ren of NEW PRIDE]." These variations subtly contradict the poet's conceding that his verse is conventional.

Structurally, the poem develops as an argument. The first eight lines challenge the poet with three questions, which he answers in the third quatrain and final couplet with a witty rejoinder that demonstrates his skills as a noteworthy opponent. Within this debatelike format, Shakespeare's logic weaves a paradox, which ironically displays those very qualities and skills that the questions imply he lacks. His verse is deficient in "new-found methods" and "compounds strange," yet his poem is a compound of wit, logic, and sophisticated argument: By writing always of his "love" and "dressing old words new," the poet transforms old coin into new and in that way gives his "love" permanent currency ("still telling"). While seeming to admit his artistic failings through the first twelve lines, the poet's conceit—that writing and loving are like reusing the same words and spending money—cleverly demonstrates those skills he appears to admit not having.

The poem's rich wordplay is evident in simple puns, such as the use of "time" (line 3) to mean poetic meter and the time in which the poet lives; the double meaning of "O, know" (line 9); and the more subtle play on seed in "proceed" (line 8). Its more important role is developing at least three arguments simultaneously by playing on the various meanings of spending, telling, inventing, and arguing.

This wordplay is evident in how the poet suggests various roles for himself. As an actor, he might perform a "quick change" (line 2), develop a new style of acting ("new-found methods"), or stay with the familiar mode and dress ("noted weed"), performing his "best" by "dressing" old words in new ways. In this conceit, he ironically hints that his words are nothing more than memorized speech and that he is "acting" the part of the lover, ending with the ambiguous compliment of repeating ("telling") again and again "what is told" (line 14).

As a dealer in coin, on the other hand, he might make "quick change" or deal in new "compounds" (metals or coinages); his words, being coins (punning further on the notion that words are coined), reflect the value of his name, and he spends the word-coins that have been spent before (line 12). Finally, as the poet-logician, he debates the question of his method with a skillfully reasoned argument: His "love" and the words in which he expresses it are the same "coin" that he counts out and spends, making new currency out of the old or, like the sun, returning always the same but always new.

Themes and Meanings

The principal metaphor of the sonnet equates words with coins that the poet counts out, or spends, as he writes verse. Line 2 suggests that the poet's verse is unacceptable as currency, "far from . . . quick change." In line 7, "tell" plays on the idea of counting out the poet's name as if it were coin. The metaphor of spending continues in line 12 and concludes in the last line, where the twin actions of counting out ("telling") and being spent ("told") are brought together. Because "telling" also means revealing, the poet conducts a simultaneous argument, that to write verse is to reveal his love to the world, and he ends with a pun on "told," which conflates these two meanings and conclusively demonstrates the poet's skill in both writing and "spending," for he brings his argument to a close at the very point where it and his love are "told"—summed up, counted out, and revealed.

The idea that lovers should not let others know their secret runs through the puns already mentioned, especially the use of "tell," which suggests revealing a secret and hints at verbal indiscretion. The last line plays on this notion by asserting that the poet's "love," represented by this poem, continues to reveal publicly—so long as it is read—the fact of his love and its valued substance, which is already reckoned and revealed ("told"). If his verse is as repetitious as the sun, it is also as visible as the sun.

A third argument is evident from the first line, where "pride" suggests an animal in heat. This idea is continued in the reference to "birth" (line 8) and to spending and being spent (line 12), giving "new and old" (line 13) the additional meaning of generation. From old words come new life, as the old generation procreates the new.

The theme of the old producing the new unifies the various arguments of the poem. As an actor, Shakespeare is challenged to invent new "methods" instead of keeping "invention in a noted weed" that is "ever the same." His "best," however, is to dress "old words new." As a dealer in "coin," he is perhaps expected to make "quick change" and to seek "new-found methods" and "compounds strange" so as to avoid having "every word . . . tell" his name—that is, reveal its commonplace value. The third quatrain asserts the poet's superior value, the ability to spend "again what is already spent." Writing verse confers upon him a power, like the sun's, of continuously returning, by being read again and again, each time his verse shedding upon the world the brilliant light of his "love." The old generates new life by simply returning (being read or "told" again). The act of writing verse goes beyond even the procreative act, however, for the old is not replaced by the new; rather, the old and the new unite forever in the poem, which is "still" reckoning and revealing what has already been revealed and reckoned.

Bernard E. Morris

Sonnet 87

First published: 1609, in *Sonnets*

> Farewell, thou art too dear for my possessing,
> And like enough thou know'st thy estimate;
> The charter of thy worth gives thee releasing;
> My bonds in thee are all determinate.
> For how do I hold thee but by thy granting,
> And for that riches where is my deserving?
> The cause of this fair gift in me is wanting,
> And so my patent back again is swerving.
> Thyself thou gav'st, thy own worth then not knowing,
> Or me, to whom thou gav'st it, else mistaking,
> So thy great gift, upon misprision growing,
> Comes home again, on better judgment making.
>   Thus have I had thee as a dream doth flatter:
>   In sleep a king, but waking no such matter.

The Poem

Sonnet 87 opens with Shakespeare bidding a farewell to his beloved. The lady is too "dear" for the poet to have, he says; he does not deserve her, so his right of ownership reverts to her. The first four lines establish the "legal" justification for his giving up possession: the "charter of thy worth," a contract which grants its owner the right to be released of any "bonds" should the holder be found unworthy of maintaining possession of the property.

This legality established, the poet in the second quatrain argues the basis of his decision. The lady herself has granted him possession on the assumption that he was worthy of such a gift, yet he does not deserve "this fair gift," and according to a legally binding contractual agreement, he therefore must relinquish possession; his right ("patent") is hereby being returned ("back again is swerving").

The first eight lines of the poem soberly lay the legal foundation of the poet's ruling. The case is unarguable, since the "law" is clear on the matter of granting patents of ownership. Once the case has been decided, the poet pauses and, in the third quatrain, turns to events leading up to his decision. Originally, the lady—"fair" (line 7) probably refers to female beauty—gave herself to the poet because she was ignorant of her own value, or she overestimated the poet himself. As a result, her "great gift," increasing because of the misunderstanding ("misprision"), returns to the owner herself now that better judgment has been achieved. The final couplet appears to end the poem on self-effacement. The poet now realizes that he has been living a dream that both flatters and deludes him, for only

374

while sleeping is he a king deserving of such a gift (or made a king by the gift); awake, he discovers the dream to be a delusion and finds that he is not a king—"no such matter."

Forms and Devices

The sonnet's fourteen lines form three quatrains and a concluding couplet, rhyming *abab, cdcd, efef, gg.* In lines 1 and 3, "possessing" and "releasing" appear to be "near" rhymes, and "wanting" and "granting" (lines 5 and 7), sight rhymes. A typical Shakespearean sonnet line consists of five stressed and five unstressed syllables, called iambic pentameter. The first two quatrains, corresponding to the octave of the Italian sonnet, develop the poem's argument from one perspective. Whereas the Italian sonnet ends with a set of six lines, a sestet, Shakespeare divides his final six lines into a quatrain and a couplet. The third quatrain addresses the poem's subject differently from the previous two quatrains, and the couplet makes some kind of summary statement about the whole argument.

Sonnet 87 is unusual in that all but two of the lines (2 and 4) are irregular, containing an extra unstressed syllable at the end of the line. All but two of those syllables are *-ing*, the other two being *-er.* This attention-getting feature makes the reader wonder what the poet is up to. The "falling" syllable at the end of the line tends to weaken the effect of the rhyme, and collectively these rhymes may hint at a similar "weakness" on the part of the poet, either in his resolve or in his attitude toward his subject and himself. Perhaps the diffusion of structural force reflects a corresponding diffusion of spiritual force. The extra syllable may also reflect a corresponding "looseness" or excess in other areas of the poet's character and behavior.

By ending ten out of fourteen lines with the present progressive (such as "possessing," "releasing," "granting," "deserving"), Shakespeare focuses attention on the presentness of his actions. Though the poem speaks of past actions, the rhymes emphasize the ongoing nature of the poet's state of mind. The poet has given up possession of his "fair gift," but his feelings and thoughts continue to be occupied by the "matter" at hand. The opening "Farewell" focuses attention immediately on the present moment and sets up the "logic" of the progressive verb forms. In this way, the poet's structural peculiarities reflect, even underscore, not only his state of mind but also the principal ideas of his poem.

Typically, wordplay informs the sonnet throughout and enables the poet to develop multiple meanings simultaneously. For example, "bonds" (line 4) refers to the bonds of love and friendship as well as to legal documents. The lover's "how do I hold thee" refers to a physical act, but in figurative terms, legal possession is meant. Line 8 plays on the idea that a "patent" gives one a license to sell or manufacture something, but used in conjunction with "swerving," it has moral overtones while describing the course of a metaphorical ship.

Three principal metaphors control the contents of the poem. One is evident in the idea of the woman being a ship that has come to the poet's port and now is being returned to its own port ("back again is swerving" and "Comes home again"). The second metaphor is that of legal proceedings having to do with ownership, estimates, patents, charters, bonds, and so on. The poem becomes a courtroom where possession is returned to its owner once "judgment" (line 12) has been made. This perspective is reinforced by such words as "misprision," which is a legal term that means a wrong action or omission, specifically the failure of an official to do his duty, and "matter," which refers to something to be tried or proved. The third metaphor develops the idea that the lover "possesses" his beloved sexually, and if "this fair gift" (line 7) refers to her virginity, Shakespeare's argument is ironic, for one cannot return such a gift.

The puns and metaphors give the sonnet an air of a legal proceeding that on the surface seems playful, the poet cleverly displaying his verbal skills and wit. Upon closer scrutiny, however, the poem reveals something other than a flattering display of the poet's feelings for the person he addresses.

Themes and Meanings

The central focus of the poem is on the idea that in romantic and legal affairs alike, possession is granted upon a certain understanding of a thing's, or person's, value. The poet appears to be confessing that he is not good enough for the woman, and the sense of disappointment that pervades the poem from beginning to end appears to express the poet's sad discovery that he must give up possession of his "fair gift" according to the stipulations of his patent. Self-discovery and self-sacrifice are implicit, and they conclude with the poet's final stipulation—that he is in fact no "king," but far from it.

A darker side develops under the surface of this two-faced poem, however; the poet may be announcing to the lady that he is sending her away because she has lost value. In this light, the tone of the poem is sharpened to a cynical edge: Now that the poet has "had" the woman (line 13), her value is depreciated, and she must be returned. The matter is clear, and she "like enough" knows her "estimate" now that she has been possessed: She has given herself to a man too freely, without justification ("The cause of this fair gift in me is wanting"), so possession is forfeited. Indeed, he may not even want her now.

If one accepts the assumption that the "patent" guaranteed him a virgin or an unpregnant woman, his possessing her (sexually) has voided the contract. The statement "thy worth gives thee releasing" ironically refers to the woman's present condition, now debased because of her "misprision." The phrase "upon misprision growing" hints at a "mistake" that resulted in the woman's pregnancy—"swerving" in line 8 reinforces the idea that the lady has gone off course morally or otherwise. The poet's discovery that, awake, "no such matter" exists could therefore refer to his profound disappointment in finding that she is neither a "dream" nor "matter" fit for a king.

Couching his thoughts in legal terms may hint at the poet's underlying intent to pass judgment on the woman for her mistake, void their agreement, and send her packing. Shakespeare is careful to make clear who is responsible—she is the one who granted him possession of herself in the first place (line 5); "Thyself thou gav'st," he repeats (line 9), and she is guilty of poor judgment, which "better judgment" (line 12) must correct. He hints that the better judgment is his, and in the final two lines he suggests that all these errors have been occurring while he was asleep. The "dream" follows his having "had" the lady, and awaking and judging the matter, he sees her and the situation for what they are, not at all a dream. On sober judgment, he ends where he begins: "Farewell." This reading turns the poet's self-sacrifice into a cynical legal rescue.

Bernard E. Morris

Sonnet 91

First published: 1609, in *Sonnets*

> Some glory in their birth, some in their skill,
> Some in their wealth, some in their body's force,
> Some in their garments, though new-fangled ill,
> Some in their hawks and hounds, some in their horse;
> And every humor hath his adjunct pleasure,
> Wherein it finds a joy above the rest,
> But these particulars are not my measure,
> All these I better in one general best.
> Thy love is better than high birth to me,
> Richer than wealth, prouder than garments' cost,
> Of more delight than hawks or horses be;
> And having thee, of all men's pride I boast:
> > Wretched in this alone, that thou mayst take
> > All this away, and me most wretched make.

The Poem

Sonnet 91 is a relaxed work when compared to its predecessor, Sonnet 90 ("Then hate me when thou wilt, if ever, now"). The initial quatrain of Sonnet 91 is clear; it remarks that there are those who glory in birth, skill, wealth, strength, and worldly possessions.

The poet is establishing in the first quatrain a platform from which he will depart. The seemingly sardonic nature of this introduction becomes clear with the reference in line 3 to the "new-fangled ill," a description of clothes that are fashionable but ugly. The unattractiveness of material possessions serves as a metaphor that is related to the implicit ugliness of the other attributes mentioned. The second quatrain begins by excusing the vanities of those who prize the attributes listed in the first quatrain. The narrator simply says that each person's "humor"—personality or temperament—finds some joy that it particularly prizes. The quatrain ends, however, with the speaker turning to his own preferences. He interjects that none of those individual tastes suits him. Further, he states, he is able to do them all one better in "one general best."

That "general best" is named in the first line of the third quatrain, where the narrator identifies it as the love of his beloved. He then explicitly states that his love means more to him than high birth, skill, and material wealth or possessions. This idea separates him from those mentioned in the first quatrain, for he has put his love above all else. The narrator, however, omits a comparison with the strength that is prized by some in the first quatrain.

In the final couplet, Sonnet 91 abruptly assumes a paradoxical tone. The apparent adulation of the previous quatrain gives way to the narrator's recognition of the power that his lover holds over him and of the vulnerable, if not tenuous, position in which he has placed himself. The narrator admits that this love makes him "wretched" in one respect: He recognizes that his lover can take from him what he desires most—she herself. The end result of such an action would leave him even more wretched.

The departure in the last couplet from the initial quatrains illustrates the irony of love: One is wretched while in love and one is wretched when love has ended. The other attributes first mentioned and then disregarded by the narrator are all elements in which the possessors have some kind of control; they are all theirs to lose and cannot be taken from them. All those attributes either must be relinquished by neglect or bad decisions or must be willingly released. This is not the case with love. The final couplet of Sonnet 91 illustrates the vulnerability of one who succumbs to love. Once this has occurred, the lover is at the mercy of his beloved; it is the one whom he adores who holds his happiness. The narrator fears that he may one day lose the one thing he holds dearest.

Forms and Devices

The poem's form is that of a conventional Elizabethan sonnet. Each of its fourteen lines contains ten syllables. The poem consists of three distinct quatrains; the first two are complete sentences, and the third is directly linked to the concluding couplet. It begins with a series of images highlighted by the cadence which is produced by Shakespeare's steady use of anaphora in the first quatrain.

The extensive repetition of "some" (seven times in four lines) stresses the idea which will be refuted by the following two quatrains and couplet. This technique strongly links the lines of the initial quatrain. When this link is broken in the second and third quatrains, the isolation of the narrator is raised to a peak that climaxes in the final couplet.

The anaphora also seems to debase those who are primarily interested in things other than love. This attitude produces a certain irony in the poem's shift to the singular in the second and third quatrains, where an image of superiority is produced. The narrator, who seems to be deriding those who care so much for items and ideas that cannot reciprocate their affection, actually appears pompous by placing himself above the others.

This technique also produces an oxymoron that is as startling as it is ironic. Love should not be a wretched affair, yet the psychological realism of this emotion is often just that. Love does cause pain and concern as well as a feeling of contentedness. The usual practice of the sonneteer was to glorify love; the heights of this devotion could reach nearly absurd proportions. Shakespeare chooses to vary from this technique, and the result is a shocking revelation that clearly illustrates the point.

Shakespeare's use of surprise or negation in the closing couplet elaborates the nakedness a lover feels when he expounds his feelings for his beloved. The effect elicited by this negative couplet is in stark contrast to the usual pouring out of love and devotion found in the sonnets of Petrarch and others. It is the very twist of this conclusion, tying the sonnet into an organic whole, that makes the poem so effective. All the attributes mentioned in the initial quatrain parallel the emotions of the final quatrains and couplet.

As different as this conclusion may be, Sonnet 91 retains many of the elements which are traditionally included in the genre. The anaphora of the initial quatrain gives way to the expected love analogy. Certainly the narrator adores and idolizes his beloved. The explication of such emotions is the normal function of the sonnet form. It is the irony of the poem's shift in the closing couplet that differentiates it from more traditional sonnets.

Themes and Meanings

Shakespeare's Sonnet 91 exemplifies how vulnerable lovers become when they put their love above all else. Shakespeare has slightly altered the traditional Elizabethan sonnet from a form that glorifies love to one that exposes it as a deeply disturbing emotional experience. While countless Elizabethan poets employed the traditional techniques of composing sonnets, Shakespeare uses his control of language and images to twist the form and create an unusual and moving piece.

The pining and lamentation for lost or unrequited love, a theme prevalent in many traditional sonnets, is replaced by a psychological examination of the process of love. Further, Shakespeare has developed the first quatrain in such a way that it heightens the poem's surprise conclusion. This technique depends on several items, which the poem fails to explore, to present this viewpoint. Shakespeare never clearly produces facts that any of the scenarios noted in the first quatrain are to be shamed as excessive or covetous. Indeed, many of the traits are honorable: One's name is one's identity, for example, and it is paramount that artists be skilled. In retrospect, the elements listed in the initial quatrain are normal characteristics of life.

People become admired for certain values and scorned for others. Yet, in any society, high values are placed upon birth, wit, wealth, beauty, and material possessions. Those items do not seem to fit in a love poem, however, except to serve as grounds above which love can be elevated. Thus, it is expected that once those attributes are mentioned, they will be acknowledged as foolish, and the author will demonstrate that love is much better.

Shakespeare does follow this to a point, but then he breaks from tradition. The narrator claims that he is better off than others because he has obtained love. Yet love is not a measurable attribute; one may determine another's "worth" in terms of name, artistic ability, and sporting prowess, the elements mentioned in the opening quatrain and downplayed in the third. Moreover, love can be more decimating than those others when it is lost.

This raises the question of the value of love, which is answered by Shakespeare's omission of strength from the characteristics downplayed in the third quatrain. It is the strength of the feelings between the two lovers that creates both the thrill and the torment of love. The energy that exists between lovers clearly surpasses the power which comes from one's social standing, vocation, and sporting ability. It is love that bridges the gap between these characteristics, for it does not care about their value. Sonnet 91 demonstrates Shakespeare's superb ability to stray from the normal path and manipulate the language to express deep emotion in a way that ironically heightens the psychological trauma of love.

R. T. Lambdin

Sonnet 94

First published: 1609, in *Sonnets*

That they have pow'r to hurt, and will do none,
That do not do the thing they most do show,
Who moving others, are themselves as stone,
Unmoved, cold, and to temptation slow,
They rightly do inherit heaven's graces,
And husband nature's riches from expense;
They are the lords and owners of their faces,
Others but stewards of their excellence.
The summer's flow'r is to the summer sweet,
Though to itself it only live and die,
But if that flow'r with base infection meet,
The basest weed outbraves his dignity:
    For sweetest things turn sourest by their deeds;
    Lilies that fester smell far worse than weeds.

The Poem

Sonnet 94 is a typical English or Shakespearean sonnet: fourteen lines of iambic pentameter rhymed *abab*, *cdcd*, *efef*, *gg*. This rhyme scheme effectively divides the poem into three quatrains and a closing couplet, unlike the Italian or Petrarchan sonnet, which tends to be structured as an octave and sestet. In Sonnet 94, William Shakespeare's first-person voice of the lover extols the virtue of stoic restraint and suggests that acting on emotions corrupts the natural nobility of a person's character and, thus, compromises identity itself.

The first line opens the poem with a subject and a restrictive clause that describes the stoic character: Such persons have the power to act, to hurt others, but refuse to do so. The next three lines of the quatrain elaborate on this quality through a series of restrictive clauses: Though such persons may seem to threaten to act, they do not; they move others to act but are themselves unmoved, show little emotion, and restrain themselves from temptation.

Having defined the subject with these restrictive clauses, this rather long opening sentence finally arrives at the verb in line 5: "do inherit." Persons who can exercise such restraint are the proper recipients of grace (divine assistance or protection) and, in turn, protect the earthly manifestations of grace ("nature's riches") from waste. Those who can restrain their emotions and actions, moreover, are in control of their own identities—that is, they are not fickle or quick to change but constant. Such persons truly may be said to follow the advice voiced by

Polonius in *Hamlet*: "To thine own self be true." Others, the poem continues, rightly must be subservient to the virtues kept alive by such stoic characters.

In line 9, the formal "turn" in the sonnet, the poem shifts to a new conceit, that of the "summer's flow'r" as a metaphor for human identity. Though as an individual one recognizes one's value to oneself as self-evident in the fact of one's existence, one's life also has a value to the age and community in which one flourishes: The flowers of summer are "sweet" to the summer itself and contribute to making the summer the pleasant season it is. The speaker adds, however, that if that flower allows itself to be corrupted, then the value of that flower's identity—not simply to itself, but to its community as well—becomes lost, and, in that event, even weeds seem more dignified.

The couplet reiterates this point: Virtue may be corrupted by actions—"Sweetest things turn sourest by their deeds"—and such corrupted virtue is far more damaging to a community than the baseness and vices of individuals—"weeds"—who had no potential for beauty and virtue in the first place.

Forms and Devices

The most striking device in the opening five lines of Sonnet 94 is the repeated use of the word "do" in the sense of "perform" ("do none," line 1); as an intensifier ("do show," line 2); in both senses ("do not do," line 2); and finally, again, as an intensifier to emphasize the verb ("do inherit," line 5). Although the poem is about persons who restrain their actions, this repetition of the most basic word for performing an action, "to do," suggests that actions are being performed. In fact, though, if one looks at the grammar of this first sentence, one sees that all but one of these instances of the word are contained within restrictive clauses, and the main verb of the subject "they" is restrained, as it were, until the second quatrain: "do inherit" in line 5. The sentence thus echoes the sense that the "thing they most do show," like the appearance of grammatical action in "do," is restrained. When one does get to that main verb, moreover, it is a verb not of doing but of receiving, of inheriting.

The poem introduces its most significant metaphor in the second quatrain. The speaker compares this stoicism to legal inheritance and ownership of land, land that is then cultivated and made productive. Ownership of land was, in the sixteenth century, a traditional privilege of the nobility, although this rapidly was changing as members of the mercantile middle class accumulated more and more wealth. In lines 7 and 8, this metaphor depicts the relationship between the stoic personality and others in terms of social rank: The former is a lord for whom others are but servants. (It should be noted, however, that both types are, in effect, "stewards" with some serving the stoic's "excellence" and the stoic himself serving to protect "nature's riches.")

The third quatrain makes a surprising leap from these images of land and social rank to the image of the summer flower. The suddenness of this shift from one image to another, seemingly unrelated one is characteristic of Shakespeare's methods in the sonnets. It is also perhaps one reason that his contemporary, Ben Jonson, said of Shakespeare, *sufflaminandus erat*—that he needed to put on the brakes, to restrain his free ways with the language. One need not share, however, in Jonson's criticism of his illustrious friend. Instead, one should see this leap as a device that, like metaphor itself, leads one to new and surprising perspectives on its subject.

The natural beauty of the flower is also responsible to its environs, as the stoic is to nature's riches and as others are to the stoic himself: Additionally, its natural beauty, like the nobility of the stoic, can be so corrupted by "deeds" that it becomes inferior to those of less beauty or those of lower social rank—"weeds." The final rhyme of these two words, "deeds" and "weeds," makes emphatic the connection between unrestrained action and the corruption of personal identity and social responsibility.

Themes and Meanings

Shakespeare viewed nature in terms of its benefits to human society. On its own, nature produces wild, unweeded, overgrown fields and woods that neither please the aesthetic sense nor feed a community as effectively as the gardens and crops produced by horticulture, by "art." Nature, therefore, must be nurtured by human industry in order to be beneficial to society. In his poetry, too, Shakespeare's images of nature do not focus on the natural environment in its own right, but have ulterior poetic motives that refer the reader to human experience.

In one of his last plays, *The Tempest* (1611), Shakespeare uses gardening and careful husbandry as metaphors for political and romantic relationships: Friendship and marriage are means of nurturing natural sexual desires into a morally productive relationship; charity, forgiveness, and restraint are means of nurturing desires for political power and possession into an ethical and productive political state. In this play, too, the reader sees noble characters who, because they are unwilling to restrain their greed for power, seem less noble than their social inferiors who "seek for grace." These are the themes of Sonnet 94.

Nobility, as a political status, was passed through inheritance; its attendant personal virtues of honor, strength, and moral rectitude were, it was thought, genetic, passed through the blood. What Shakespeare suggests here is that true nobility is neither inherited nor inherent, but achieved. Political power that is beneficial to others is achieved by first having power over oneself, having the power to hurt, but having the restraint not to exercise such power.

Humans must first and foremost be "lords and owners of our faces." Conversely, if society is to be mutually beneficial, that responsibility for having control over one's own identity is not solely a responsibility to oneself, but also a responsibility to those with whom one lives. The flower produced by summer gives summer its character and has the potential, if corrupted, to make summer seem rank with decay rather than, as it should be, redolent of birth, growth, and life.

James Hale

Sonnet 106

First published: 1609, in *Sonnets*

When in the chronicle of wasted time
I see descriptions of the fairest wights,
And beauty making beautiful old rhyme
In praise of ladies dead and lovely knights,
Then in the blazon of sweet beauty's best,
Of hand, of foot, of lip, of eye, of brow,
I see their antique pen would have express'd
Even such a beauty as you master now.
So all their praises are but prophecies
Of this our time, all you prefiguring,
And for they look'd but with divining eyes,
They had not still enough your worth to sing:
    For we which now behold these present days
    Have eyes to wonder, but lack tongues to praise.

The Poem

In Shakespeare's Sonnet 106, the speaker calls upon the glories of the past to illustrate the present. He perceives that the beauty of his lover has been prophesied by the pens of past authors who are now long dead. The initial quatrain establishes the tone as one of courtly elegance. The references to "chronicle," "ladies," and "knights" all recall the glorified stereotypical image of a time long past, when a knight was obligated by the chivalric code to behave bravely in the battlefield and solicitously in the community.

This highly elevated rhetoric establishes the mood of Sonnet 106, yet the elegance seemingly gives way to irony in the juxtaposition of adjectives in line 4: "Ladies dead and lovely knights." The "beauty" of line 2 has been usurped by the truth of mutability: The ladies are literally dead; they live only as images created by the words of the old rhymes. Further, it seems that the adjectives describing the ladies and the knights have been willingly transposed. The common conception of the lady or mistress in the old poetry was of a fair and lovely creature of inspiration; it was the valiant knights who died for her.

The introductory octave continues with a shift in the second quatrain, where the narrator personifies beauty in the form of a coat of arms which accentuates the erotic images of his love's finest attributes: foot, lip, eye, and brow. These common physical, and even sexual, images initiate a change from the spiritual to the physical. The second quatrain concludes with a vivid image: The narrator visual-izes that the earlier poets would have expressed just such a beauty as his love. Thus the initial octave establishes the background from which the sestet will depart.

The sestet begins, in the third quatrain, by connecting the past with the present: The praises of the poets from an earlier age become actual prophecies. The narrator perceives that futuristic visions of his beloved provided the impetus for the old poets' works; however, this idea is quickly amended. Even though those authors were guided by divine inspiration, they were still unable to praise or describe the beauty of the narrator's lover adequately.

The concluding couplet emphasizes the futility of such an effort in the composition of love poems. It is clear that the authors of the past, now long dead, have transmitted their words along to the authors of the present. Yet their adoration remains an enigma; it is impossible for an author to describe his love truly by using mere words.

Forms and Devices

Sonnet 106 conforms to the Elizabethan fourteen-line stanzaic form. Each of the lines contains ten syllables, and the poem consists of two sentences. The first encompasses the initial octave, and the second, the final sestet. This form is similar to Shakespeare's Sonnets 32 and 47. The initial octave may be broken into two distinct quatrains. The first initiates the work with a "when" clause that, while syntactically logical, cannot stand alone.

The second quatrain counters the first with a "then" clause. Through this syntactical convention, logic is used first to divide and then to unite the initial octave. The final sestet similarly depends upon its syntactical sequence first to answer, then to expand upon, the logic conceived in the initial octave. Despite its unification, the sestet is composed of both a distinct quatrain and a concluding couplet.

The quatrain of the sestet begins a new sentence that remarks on the evidence put forward in the preceding sentence. It states that despite the worthy stature of the poets who composed the earlier works, their attempts at prophecy fall short: They were incapable of capturing the beauty of the narrator's beloved in words. The main point of the work, however, is the narrator's own seeming inability to put his love's beauty into words.

The sonnet uses alliteration, particularly of the *s* sound, throughout the poem. Shakespeare also creates effects by expanding or contracting the number of syllables that appear between certain repeated sounds. In the couplet, for example, a pulsating alliteration emphasizes the poem's conclusion; the "praise" of line 14 represents a compression of the *pr* and *ay* sounds previously heard in the "present days" of line 11. There is also an expanding alliterative pattern in the placement of *b* and *pr* sounds. In line 9, the pattern begins with "but prophecies." The sound is stretched in line 13—"behold these present"—and stretched even further in the final line: "but lack tongues to praise."

Sonnet 106 exhibits Shakespeare's uncanny ability to manipulate language into poetic form; the poem is not as simple and straightforward as it may appear. In line 3, the narrator refers to the "beautiful old rhyme" of bygone days, yet he is speaking a poem that both echoes and modifies those old rhymes, a poem that will one day take its place in the canon to which they belong.

Themes and Meanings

Sonnet 106 is in many ways a typical love poem filled with conventional techniques. While it does not offer significant insight into the many mysteries of the sonnets, it does provide a glimpse of an idea far too often overlooked in much criticism—that Shakespeare and other Elizabethan writers depended upon the authors of the past. It is often perceived that the literary works of Renaissance England rely solely upon the classical traditions or spring from an author's sudden burst of inspiration. Sonnet 106 proves that is not true, for it clearly displays Shakespeare's debt to medieval authors and their works.

Shakespeare was influenced by the work of Geoffrey Chaucer, whose "The Knight's Tale" from *The Canterbury Tales* (1387-1400) is a major source for the plot of *A Midsummer Night's Dream* (c. 1595-1596). While Shakespeare somewhat alters the myth surrounding the marriage of Hippolyta and Theseus, the Chaucerian influence is abundant. This type of borrowing is continued in Sonnet 106. In this poem, Shakespeare clearly reminds readers of his debt to the older works. He also shows an understanding of the themes of many of the ancient texts: ladies, knights, courtly love, and chivalry.

It is clear that perceiving beauty is one thing, while putting those visualizations into words is quite another. Thus, ironically, the narrator fails miserably in his quest—yet he is also successful to some degree. Despite his omission of any physical description, he has captured at least a part of his love's essence, and he is honoring her with a poem. Like the women who were glorified in literature long before her, she, too, has been given eternal life.

Sonnet 106 also has a consciousness of the theme implicit in the phrase "this our time" (line 10). The sonnet constantly reinforces the idea that what lovers can do is mandated by their particular era; what has previously occurred affects them, so they cannot ignore the past. Yet, after their death, they are doomed to become faint images for other authors to wonder about. At best, they can attempt an understanding of the ideals and the images of their present. This theme, introduced in Sonnet 106, is furthered in the more famous Sonnet 107 ("Not mine own fears, nor the prophetic soul"). The message of Sonnet 106 is clear, and its technique is conventional. It is of particular value because it shows an aspect of Shakespeare's work that is too often overlooked: its debt to medieval authors.

R. T. Lambdin

Sonnet 116

First published: 1609, in *Sonnets*

> Let me not to the marriage of true minds
> Admit impediments; love is not love
> Which alters when it alteration finds,
> Or bends with the remover to remove.
> O no, it is an ever-fixed mark
> That looks on tempests and is never shaken;
> It is the star to every wand'ring bark,
> Whose worth's unknown, although his highth be taken.
> Love's not Time's fool, though rosy lips and cheeks
> Within his bending sickle's compass come,
> Love alters not with his brief hours and weeks,
> But bears it out even to the edge of doom.
>> If this be error and upon me proved,
>> I never writ, nor no man ever loved.

The Poem

Sonnet 116 is generally considered one of the finest love poems ever written. In this sonnet, William Shakespeare raised the theme of romantic love to the status of high philosophy. At a time when love between man and woman was not often recognized as essentially other than a form of family obligation, Shakespeare spiritualized it as the motivator of the highest level of human action. Love of that kind has since become the most sought-after human experience.

The poem is a regular English sonnet of fourteen lines arranged in three quatrains and a concluding couplet. It begins by using the language of the Book of Common Prayer marriage service to make an explicit equation of love and marriage. It not only suggests that marriage is the proper end of love, but it also goes beyond to make love a necessary prerequisite. The quatrain continues by describing the essential constituents of the kind of love that qualifies. Such love does not change under changing circumstances; in fact, constancy is its first element. It continues even when unreciprocated or betrayed. Further, true love does not depend on the presence of the beloved but actually increases during absence.

The second quatrain uses a series of metaphors to flesh out the character of proper love. Its constancy is such that it not only endures threats but actually strengthens in adversity. Its attractive power secures the beloved from wandering, and it sets a standard for all other lovers. Although conspicuous and easily identifiable, its value is inestimable. Aspects of it can be measured, and many of its properties are tangible, but it resides in another dimension, unassessable by normal instruments in space and time.

The third quatrain considers the constancy of true love under the threats of time and aging. It declares that love is unaffected by time. To begin with, love far transcends such mundane physical characteristics as size, appearance, condition, and shape. For that reason, it ignores physical changes caused by age or health. It defies time and everything in its power, including death. True love operates in the realm of eternity. Not even death can part true lovers; their union endures forever. Because love has the capacity to raise human action to this exalted state, it alone enables humans to transcend temporal limitations. Humankind becomes godlike through love.

The sonnet ends with a simple couplet which transfers the focus from the ethereal region of eternal, transcendent love to the routine present of the poet-speaker. He merely observes that if he is ever proved wrong, then no man has ever loved. It seems a trivial conclusion, until one recognizes that this is exactly the feeling that allows men and women to continue to fall in love and to endow that feeling with meaning.

Forms and Devices

In spite of being one of the world's most celebrated short poems, Sonnet 116 uses a rather simple array of poetic devices. They include special diction, allusion, metaphor, and paradox. All work together to reinforce the central theme.

Shakespeare establishes the context early with his famous phrase "the marriage of true minds," a phrase that does more than is commonly recognized. The figure of speech suggests that true marriage is a union of minds rather than merely a license for the coupling of bodies. Shakespeare implies that true love proceeds from and unites minds on the highest level of human activity, that it is inherently mental and spiritual. From the beginning, real love transcends the sensual and physical. Moreover, the very highest level is reserved to "true" minds. By this he means lovers who have "plighted troth," in the phrasing of the marriage service—that is, exchanged vows to be true to each other. This reinforces the spirituality of loving, giving it religious overtones. The words "marriage" and "impediments" also allude to the language of the service, accentuating the sacred nature of love.

Shakespeare then deliberately repeats phrases to show that this kind of love is more than mere reciprocation. Love cannot be simply returning what is given, like an exchange of gifts. It has to be a simple, disinterested, one-sided offering, unrelated to any possible compensation. He follows this with a series of positive and negative metaphors to illustrate the full dimensions of love. It is first "an ever-fixed mark/ That looks on tempests and is never shaken." This famous figure has not been completely explained, although the general idea is clear. Love is equated with some kind of navigating device so securely mounted that it remains functional in hurricanes. It then becomes not a device but a reference point, a "star" of universal recognition but speculative in its composition; significantly, it is beyond human ken.

In "Love's not Time's fool," Shakespeare moves on to yet another metaphorical level. To begin with, love cannot be made into a fool by the transformations of time; it operates beyond and outside it, and hence cannot be subject to it. This is so although time controls those qualities which are popularly thought to evoke love: physical attractions. Shakespeare conjures up the image of death, the Grim Reaper with his "bending sickle," only to assert that love is not within his "compass"—which denotes both grip and reckoning and sweep of blade. Love cannot be fathomed by time or its extreme instrument, death. Love "bears it out"—perseveres in adversity—to the "edge of doom"—that is, beyond the grave and the worst phase of time's decay.

The final device is a conundrum in logic. It establishes an alternative—"If this be error"—then disproves it. What remains, and remains valid, is the other. It also bears a double edge. If this demonstration is wrong, Shakespeare says, "I never writ," which is an obvious contradiction. The only possible conclusion is that it is not wrong. He proceeds then to a corollary, "nor no man ever loved," which is as false as the previous statement.

Themes and Meanings

In Sonnet 116, Shakespeare presents an argument, forcing the double conclusion that love transcends normal human measures and that it represents the highest level of human activity. Yet, as a famous love poem, it is highly unusual: It is not a declaration of love but a definition and demonstration. It still accomplishes the object of a love poem, however, because the inspirer of this statement could not possibly be flattered more effectively.

Sonnet 116 develops the theme of the eternity of true love through an elaborate and intricate cascade of images. Shakespeare first states that love is essentially a mental relationship; the central property of love is truth—that is, fidelity—and fidelity proceeds from and is anchored in the mind. The objective tone and impersonal language of the opening reinforce this theme. This kind of love is as far removed from the level of mere sensation as any human activity could be. Like all ideal forms, it operates on the level of abstract intellect, or of soul. Hence it is immune to the physical, emotional, or behavioral "impediments" that threaten lesser loves. It is a love that fuses spirits intuitively related to each other.

The poem proceeds to catalog a number of specific impediments. The first involves reciprocation. Does true love persist in the face of rejection or loss of affection? Absolutely, even though those might be sufficient grounds for calling off a wedding. True love endures even the absence of the beloved: not that the "heart grows fonder" in the absence of the beloved, but that it operates independently of physical reminders. Such love stabilizes itself, as if possessing an instinctive self-righting mechanism. Shakespeare himself uses this kind of gyroscopic and autopilot imagery; like the navigational devices to which he alludes, true love serves as a standard for others, maintains its course under stress, and guarantees security against storm and turmoil.

This imagery duplicates the sequence of promises exchanged by true lovers in the marriage service that Shakespeare quotes in the opening of the poem. True love vows constancy regardless of better, worse, richer, poorer, sickness, health—all the vagaries of life and change. The simple series, however, seems to minimize the intensity of love necessary to do this. On the contrary, love is absolutely secure against external assault. In particular, it holds firm against the ravages of time. Since the poem begins by dissociating love from the limits of time, this should not be surprising, especially since the marriage service insists on the possibility of love surviving time and its consequence, change. So strong is the popular belief that love is rooted in physical attractiveness, however, that the poem is forced to repudiate this explicitly. It does it in the starkest way imaginable, by personifying time as the Grim Reaper and by bringing that specter directly before the eyes of the lover. This happens; the threat is real, but the true lover can face down even death.

The marriage service does that also, by asking the thinking lover to promise fidelity "until death us do part." Shakespeare's poem uses imagery to give form to this belief that true love has to be stronger than death, set as a seal upon the lover's heart.

James Livingston

Sonnet 129

First published: 1609, in *Sonnets*

> Th'expense of spirit in a waste of shame
> Is lust in action, and till action, lust
> Is perjur'd, murd'rous, bloody, full of blame,
> Savage, extreme, rude, cruel, not to trust,
> Enjoy'd no sooner but despised straight,
> Past reason hunted, and no sooner had,
> Past reason hated as a swallowed bait
> On purpose laid to make the taker mad:
> Mad in pursuit and in possession so,
> Had, having, and in quest to have, extreme,
> A bliss in proof, and prov'd, a very woe,
> Before, a joy propos'd, behind, a dream.
> > All this the world well knows, yet none knows well
> > To shun the heaven that leads men to this hell.

The Poem

Sonnet 129 is a typical Shakespearean sonnet in form, written in iambic pentameter with twelve lines rhymed *abab*, *cdcd*, *efef*, *gg*. Unlike the majority of Shakespeare's sonnets, however, it is not addressed to a particular individual but is directed to an audience, as a sermon is.

The first line is the only one that presents any difficulty in interpretation. Shakespeare sometimes compressed a large meaning into few words, creating an impressionistic effect. Although this opening line appears a bit garbled, it is easy enough to understand and well suited to the mood of the poem. It creates the impression of a mind overwhelmed by a whirlwind of bitter reflections. The poet is obviously talking about sexual lust. The first line states that lust is shameful and spiritually debilitating. The rest of the poem simply expands upon this idea.

The torrent of adjectives and short descriptive phrases that follows suggests the different ways in which sexual lust can lead to tragic outcomes. The reader may evoke specific illustrations from personal experience or from the world's literature which, from the Bible and Greek mythology to modern novels such as Vladimir Nabokov's *Lolita* (1955), is full of warnings against lust.

Each word or phrase in the opening lines suggests different scenarios. For example, the word "perjur'd" suggests the lies men tell women, the most common being "I love you" and "I want to marry you." Lust drives people to say many things they do not mean. The word "perjur'd" also suggests the humiliating experience of having to lie to the fiancé or spouse of one's lover, who might even be a personal friend.

The word "bloody" suggests even more serious outcomes of sexual lust. The outraged husband who discovers his wife in bed with another man may murder her, or him, or both. Lust also may lead to bloody abortions and suicides. "Full of blame" suggests the painful aftermath of many affairs based not on love but on lust. The woman blames the man for deceiving her; he blames her for leading him on, for allowing herself to become pregnant, or for confessing her adultery to her husband. "Full of blame" in Shakespeare's time probably suggested the great danger of contracting syphilis or gonorrhea, and in recent times it suggests the modern plague of acquired immunodeficiency syndrome (AIDS).

The closing couplet of the sonnet alights gracefully, with the juxtaposition of "well knows" and "knows well." The tone is like the calm after a storm. It is not a happy conclusion but a truthful one. Humanity repeats the same mistakes generation after generation. Sexual passion is hard to control and leads to much of the tragedy that human beings experience.

Forms and Devices

There are two important things to notice about the structure of this sonnet. One is that, except for the closing couplet, it consists of a single run-on sentence. The other is that it is built around a single simile, which takes up the seventh and eighth lines. The effect of crowding most of the poem into a single outburst is to leave the reader with a feeling of agitation mirroring the conflicting emotions that accompany sexual lust. Run-on sentences are often the targets of English teachers' red pencils, but at times such sentences can be extremely effective.

Shakespeare often filled his sonnets with metaphors and similes, as he did in his famous Sonnet 73, in which he compares his time of life to winter, to sunset, and to a dying fire. In other sonnets, however, he deliberately avoids metaphors and similes in order to obtain the maximum effect from a single striking image. This is the case in another of Shakespeare's most famous sonnets, Sonnet 29, which begins, "When in disgrace with fortune and men's eyes." After complaining at length about his miserable condition, the speaker changes his tone entirely and says that, should he happen to remember the friendship of the person he is addressing, his state, "Like to the lark at break of day arising/ From sullen earth, sings hymns at heaven's gate." These are two of the most beautiful lines in English poetry, and they are more effective because they are not competing with any other imagery in the sonnet.

In Sonnet 129, the dominant image is contained in the lines "Past reason hated as a swallowed bait/ On purpose laid to make the taker mad." After this—but without starting a new sentence—the poet launches into another tirade, echoing the word "Mad" at the beginning of the next line and rhyming it with "Had" at the beginning of the line after that. These devices arouse apprehension because it seems as if the speaker may actually be starting to rave.

People do not set out poisoned bait to kill human beings. The kind of bait Shakespeare is referring to is commonly used to kill rats: They are driven mad with thirst or pain and run out of the house to die. One of the reasons the image is so striking is that it implicitly compares people motivated by uncontrolled lust to the lowest, most detested animals. Sonnet 129 is unlike most of Shakespeare's other sonnets and in fact unlike most other Elizabethan sonnets, which are typically full of references to love, the moon, the stars, and other pleasant things. This strange sonnet on lust has a modern, experimental quality to it which foreshadows the cacophony and deliberately shocking ugliness of much twentieth century art.

Themes and Meanings

Shakespeare was not a deeply religious man. The moralistic tone of this poem seems so out of character that one distinguished Shakespearean scholar, A. L. Rowse, suggested that Shakespeare did not intend it to be taken seriously but wrote the sonnet as a sort of private joke for his circle of friends; yet its emotional effect is so powerful that it is hard to believe that Shakespeare was not writing with true feeling. It has also been suggested that Shakespeare wrote the sonnet after discovering that he had contracted syphilis from a liaison with a prostitute—or possibly from the mysterious "Dark Lady" mentioned in some of his other sonnets.

The theme is simple and clear. The poet is preaching a brief sermon on the dangers of sexual lust. These dangers have been a subject of literature since the stories of Samson and Delilah and of David and Bathsheba, recorded in the Old Testament. The Trojan War, which led to the destruction of a whole civilization and was described in both Homer's *Iliad* (c. 800 B.C.E) and Vergil's *Aeneid* (c. 29-19 B.C.E.), was reputedly caused by Paris' lust for Helen, the wife of Menelaus. In Shakespeare's own long poem *The Rape of Lucrece* (1594), the story is told of how the Etruscan rulers came to be driven out of Rome because of Sextus Tarquinius' rape of Lucrece and her subsequent suicide.

In Leo Tolstoy's novel *Anna Karenina* (1875-1877; English translation, 1886), the heroine throws herself under the wheels of a locomotive after she has left her husband and children and ultimately finds herself deserted by her faithless lover. In Henrik Ibsen's play *Gengangare* (1881; *Ghosts*, 1885), a promising young man dies because he inherited syphilis from his profligate father. In Anton Chekhov's best short story, "Dame s sobachkoi" (1899; "The Lady with the Dog," 1917), an adulterous relationship leads to endless mental torture for both parties involved. In Theodore Dreiser's novel *An American Tragedy* (1925), lust leads to murder and death in the electric chair. As Shakespeare wrote, the world well knows that sexual intercourse without love is often a grave disappointment and can lead to torment in a wide variety of forms. Unfortunately, many people have to learn this truth by bitter experience.

Finally, a political statement might be read into this sonnet. The fact that it departs from the norm and is not pretty and soothing might be taken to indicate a view that art should serve a higher purpose than merely helping the genteel elite to pass their leisure hours. Its denunciation of sexual lust might be read as an indictment of the aristocracy, whose favorite pastime, as shown by so many of the songs, poems, and paintings of the period, was playing at the game of love. Thus, it might be seen as foreshadowing views that led to the English Civil War, which began only twenty-six years after Shakespeare's death and changed the course of history.

Bill Delaney

Sonnet 130

First published: 1609, in *Sonnets*

My mistress' eyes are nothing like the sun;
Coral is far more red than her lips' red;
If snow be white, why then her breasts are dun;
If hairs be wires, black wires grow on her head.
I have seen roses damask'd, red and white,
But no such roses see I in her cheeks,
And in some perfumes is there more delight
Than in the breath that from my mistress reeks.
I love to hear her speak, yet well I know
That music hath a far more pleasing sound;
I grant I never saw a goddess go,
My mistress when she walks treads on the ground.
    And yet, by heaven, I think my love as rare
    As any she belied with false compare.

The Poem

Sonnet 130 is a "blazon"—a lyric poem cataloging the physical characteristics and virtues of the beloved. It is written in typical English or Shakespearean sonnet form, with three quatrains and a couplet in iambic pentameter rhymed *abab, cdcd, efef, gg*. The first-person voice of the poem should be understood as that of a dramatic persona; even if William Shakespeare means it to represent himself, he nevertheless has to create a distinct personality in the language, and from this distance, the reader has no way of knowing how accurately this might describe the man.

The speaker describes his beloved in comparison, or rather in contrast, to natural phenomena. In the love poem tradition, as it emerged in English poetry in imitation of the sonnets of fourteenth century Italian poet Petrarch, poets often compare their beloveds to the elements of nature. In this sonnet, Shakespeare takes the opposite tack by describing his beloved as "nothing like" the beautiful productions of nature or art.

Her eyes, the poet begins, do not shine like the sun; nor are her lips as red as coral. When compared to the whiteness of snow, his beloved's breasts seem "dun," a dull gray. The "wires" of line 4 refer to gold spun into golden thread, but his beloved's hair, if the metaphoric description of hairs as golden wires is valid, can only be seen as black, or tarnished beyond all recognition.

The damasked roses of the fifth line are variegated roses of red and white, and such, the poet continues, cannot be seen in his woman's face. Perfume, too, is an inaccurate simile for his lover's breath, since most perfumes are more pleasing. The word "reeks" in line 8 simply means "breathes forth" in Elizabethan English, although our modern sense of the word as denoting an offensive smell certainly emphasizes Shakespeare's point of contrast.

At the ninth-line "turn" (the formal point at which sonnets typically introduce an antithesis or redirect their focus), the speaker continues in the same vein, noting how music has a more pleasing sound than his lover's voice, though he also introduces an important point: None of these contrasts is to suggest that he finds his beloved any less pleasing. He loves her voice, as he does her other characteristics, but honestly he must acknowledge that music is, objectively speaking, more pleasing to the senses.

Lines 11 and 12 dismiss conventional descriptions of women as goddesslike. Who among mortal men has ever witnessed a goddess in order to make such similes in the first place? All this lover knows is what he sees, and his mistress is, like him, quite earthly and earthbound, walking on the ground.

The sonnet's couplet then explicates the point of the foregoing contrasts. The lover's objective comparisons of his beloved with nature and with the human artifacts of perfume and music, however unfavorable to the woman, do not change his subjective perception of her: She is as rare as any of those women whom poets describe with comparisons that exaggerate, and thus "belie," human beauty.

Forms and Devices

The effect of the formal division of the Shakespearean sonnet, the four quatrains and closing couplet, is to pile up examples of a single idea—that the beloved's beauty is really not comparable to the productions of nature and human art—so that by line 12, the reader wonders if there is anything at all about the woman that can be seen objectively as beautiful. The last two lines then provide a memorable explication of that idea: Objectivity and actual beauty are really no concern of the lover. While lines 11 and 12 dismiss comparisons to heavenly beauty as meaningless—mortals have no experience of the metaphysical world on which to base such similes—Shakespeare uses the mild expletive "by heaven" in line 13 to suggest in contrast that the impassioned subjectivity of the lover is itself metaphysical in origin, a kind of grace.

The speaker's attitude in this poem is strikingly antimetaphoric, and lines 3 and 4 subject two conventional metaphors to examination by deductive logic. Line 3 begins with a premise, "If snow be white," and concludes that the woman's breasts are "dun." In technical terms, the rhetorical device employed here is an "enthymeme," a syllogism in which one of the terms is left out and must be inferred by the reader. One may reconstruct the full syllogism thus: Snow is white; my lover's breasts are dull gray; therefore, my lover's breasts are not like snow. Since snow is in fact white, one can concur with the conclusion's logic and deny the validity of the simile "women's breasts are white like snow." Line 4 offers another enthymeme beginning with the premise "If hairs be wires" and concluding that the woman's hair is black, or tarnished, wire. The full syllogism here would read: Hairs are golden wires; my lover's hairs are black; therefore, my lover's hairs (wires) must be tarnished.

The conclusion follows logically, but the metaphoric premise is untrue: Hairs are not wires, and if the woman is judged on the basis of this premise, one can only conclude by denigrating the woman's physical characteristics as sullied examples of an ideal: tarnished gold. This is what Shakespeare means by "false compare"—unjust comparisons that not only ignore the possibility that the woman may be beautiful in her own right, but also miss the value of the beloved in the eyes of her lover: To him, she is, if not golden, at least as "rare." That the poet has his persona subject love and beauty to deductive logic at all tells the reader something important about the lover's attitude and about the overall meaning of the poem.

Themes and Meanings

The ostensible subject of this sonnet is the so-called Dark Lady of the later sonnets, a woman with whom the speaker of the poems is having a passionate sexual affair. The first 126 sonnets are addressed to a man, in whom the speaker denies having sexual interest. (See Sonnet 20, in which the speaker notes that the male beloved has "one thing to my purpose nothing.") These sonnets to and about the man attempt to consider the dimensions of platonic love, "the marriage of true minds" (Sonnet 116), without the compromising motive of sexual desire. In contrast, the sonnets addressed to the Dark Lady suggest that once sex enters into the relationship, the possibility of achieving a higher, platonic love is virtually lost. Indeed, the speaker and the Dark Lady engage in a sordid affair.

Although the poem focuses on this woman, its main subject is perception itself and the methods by which poets represent love. Poets often concern themselves with the nature of their art and, in creating new ways of seeing human experience, question the validity of the poetic conventions of their predecessors. This poem prompts some very fundamental questions about poetic devices. What does metaphor actually tell about the objects on which it focuses? If poetry attempts to bring one closer to what is true in the human experience, why is it that most poetic conventions are falsehoods? Love is not a rose, beloveds are not heavenly goddesses, lovers do not die from being rejected by their beloveds. As the character Rosalind, in Shakespeare's play *As You Like It*, remarks in response to the "poetic" language of her lover: "men have died from time to time, and worms have eaten them, but not for love."

In Sonnet 18, when the poet asks of the male beloved, "Shall I compare thee to a summer's day?" the answer, no, calls attention to the inadequacy of conventional metaphors and similes to describe accurately not the beloved, but the subjective nature of love. In the case of Sonnet 18, however, such comparisons are insufficient, the lover suggests, because they are not superlative enough. Here, he suggests the opposite: They are too superlative to give a realistic picture of his beloved. Such metaphors and similes are, after all, mere lies—poetic lies, perhaps, but lies nevertheless. Although clearly in love with the woman, this lover seems poignantly aware of the way she really looks, beyond his love-inspired subjectivity.

Sonnet 130 provides logic instead of metaphor, objectivity instead of hyperbole. In one very important sense, this focus on actual physical appearance seems appropriate to the affair between the speaker and the Dark Lady: Throughout the sonnets that represent this affair, Shakespeare continually stresses the point that their relationship is based primarily, almost exclusively, on physical appearance and physical attraction—on what Sonnet 129 calls "lust in action."

James Hale

Venus and Adonis

Type of plot: Erotic
Time of plot: Antiquity
Locale: Greece
First published: 1593

Principal characters

VENUS, goddess of love
ADONIS, a handsome youth loved by Venus

The Story

In all the world there was no more beautiful figure, no more perfectly made creature, than young Adonis. Although his beauty was a delight to the sun and to the winds, he had no interest in love. His only joy was in hunting and riding over the hills and fields after the deer and the fox. When Venus, the goddess of love, saw the beauty of young Adonis, she came down to Earth because she was filled with love for him.

Meeting him one morning in the fields as he rode out to the hunt, she urged him to dismount, tie his horse to a tree, and talk with her. Adonis had no desire to talk to any woman, even the goddess, but she forced him to do as she wished. Reclining by his side, she looked at him with caressing glances and talked passionately of the wonder and glory of love. The more she talked, the more she begged him for a kind look, a kiss, the more anxious he became to leave her and go on with his hunting. Venus was not easily repulsed, however; she told him how even the god of war had been a willing prisoner of her charms. She numbered all the pleasures she could offer him if he would accept her love. Blushing, Adonis finally broke from her arms and went to get his horse.

At that moment, his stallion heard the call of a jennet in a field nearby. Aroused, he broke the leather thong that held him and galloped to her. At first the jennet pretended to be cold to the stallion's advances, but when she perceived that Adonis was about to overtake his mount, she gave a neigh of affection and the two horses galloped away to another field. Adonis was left behind.

Dejected, he stood thinking of the hunt that he was missing because his horse had run away. Venus came up to him again and continued her pleas of love. For a while he listened to her, but in disgust he turned finally and gave her such a look of scorn that the lovesick goddess fainted and fell to the ground. Thinking he had killed her with his unkind look, Adonis knelt beside her, rubbed her wrists, and kissed her in hope of forgiveness. Venus, recovering from her swoon, asked him for one last kiss. He grudgingly consented before turning to leave. When Venus asked when they could meet the next day. Adonis replied that he would not see her, for he was to go boar hunting. Struck with a vision, the goddess warned the youth that he would be killed by a boar if he hunted the next day, and she begged him to meet her instead. She threw herself on the boy and carried him to the earth in her arms in a last attempt to gain his love. Adonis admonished the goddess on the difference between heavenly love and earthly lust. He left her alone and weeping.

The next morning found Venus wandering through the woods in search of Adonis. In the distance, she could hear the noise of the dogs and the voices of the hunters. Frantic because of her vision of the dead Adonis, she rushed through the forest trying to follow the sounds of the hunt. When she saw a wounded and bleeding dog, the fear she felt for Adonis became almost overpowering. Suddenly she came upon Adonis lying dead, killed by the fierce wild boar he had hunted. Venus' grief knew no bounds. If this love were taken from her, then never again should man love happily. Where love was, there also would mistrust, fear, and grief be found.

The body of Adonis lay white and cold on the ground, his blood coloring the earth and plants about him. From this soil there grew a flower, white and purple like the blood that spotted his skin. With a broken heart, Venus left Earth to hide her sorrow in the dwelling place of the gods.

Critical Evaluation

Venus and Adonis and *The Rape of Lucrece* (1594), two of William Shakespeare's most famous nondramatic works, were probably composed during the period between June, 1592, and May, 1594, while the theaters were temporarily closed because of the plague. *Venus and Adonis*, the earlier of the two poems, was entered at the Stationers' Register on April 18, 1593, and was printed shortly thereafter by Richard Field, who, incidentally, had originally come from Shakespeare's hometown, Stratford-on-Avon. *Venus and Adonis* was the first work of Shakespeare ever to be printed.

It should not be supposed from the date of composition that *Venus and Adonis* was merely a way of passing time while the theaters were closed. All indications are that Shakespeare thought of this poem as the public commencement of his serious literary work as distinct from his quotidian employment as a dramatist. Indeed, Shakespeare never bothered to see his plays into print, a fact that has proved the bane of editors ever since. *Venus and Adonis*, however, was handsomely printed with an ornate dedication to the Earl of Southampton in which Shakespeare speaks of the poem as his first serious literary effort. In subject and style, it is a kind of poetry that occupied most of Shakespeare's serious contemporaries.

Although the poem has been transmitted in only a few manuscripts, there is ample evidence that it was extremely popular in its own day. By 1600, it had become one of the most frequently quoted poems of the period, and many of Shakespeare's contemporaries referred to it with admiration. Even Gabriel Harvey, fellow of Cambridge and stern arbiter of critical taste, noted the great fame that the poem enjoyed among undergraduates, although he did add reservations about the erotic nature of the poem. In that eroticism, *Venus and Adonis* reflected a vogue for such poetry, which appeared in profusion in the 1590's. Like Shakespeare's, these narrative or reflective poems generally drew on classical or pseudo-classical sources.

Shakespeare derived the story of *Venus and Adonis* from Ovid's *Metamorphoses* (before 8 B.C.E.), the main difference being that in his poem Adonis becomes a coy and reluctant lover. This variation may be the result of accidental or intentional conflation of the tale with Ovid's story of Hermaphroditus and Salmacis or that of Narcissus. It could also be the result of the influence of stories in book 3 of Edmund Spenser's *Faerie Queene* (1590), in Thomas Lodge's *Scyllae's Metamorphosis* (1589), or in Christopher Marlowe's *Hero and Leander* (1598). In any case, the change brings it in line with other late sixteenth century

A contemporary depiction of Venus by the Italian artist Palma Giovane. (Archive Photos)

poems that stress male beauty. Regardless of the source, the substance of the poem is almost entirely conventional.

The few original additions that Shakespeare seems to have made—the digressive episode of the jennet and the stallion and the descriptions of the hunting of the fox and the hare, for example—are notable more for the conventional beauty of their style than for their narrative power. The entire poem is, in fact, an excellent example of stylistic decoration, an ornate work for a sophisticated audience more interested in execution than originality. The poetry is on the surface, in the ingenious handling of commonplaces and in brilliant flourishes of image and phrase.

Virtually nothing happens in the poem. The bulk of it is taken up with the amorous arguments of Venus interspersed with objections from Adonis. There is no forward movement, merely a debate that results in no conclusion. The characters do not develop; they simply are what they are and speak in accord with their stylized roles. The plot does not move from event to event by means of internal causality. Indeed, the only movement, that from the debate to the final scene in which Venus comes upon Adonis' body, is occasioned more by the emotional necessities of the poem than by demands of plot.

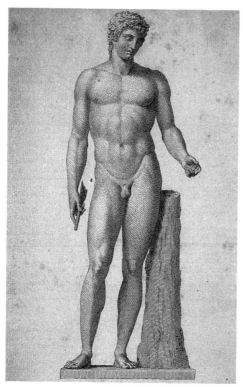

A statue of Adonis displayed at the Vatican in Rome. (Archive Photos)

It is tempting to see the poem, especially the debate, as a moral allegory in which Adonis represents rational control over sensual excess, while Venus represents not only passion but also the enduring love that can triumph over mutability. It is hard, however, to support this interpretation very far. Neither view prevails and the interdeterminacy suggests that the allegory is merely another ornament, not the heart of the poem. Moreover, the tone of the speeches and the tone of the narrator's commentary do not support moral earnestness. The many puns and erotic innuendos provide a suave distance, true both to Ovid and to Elizabethan taste.

The poem is a compendium of the themes that recurred in the amatory poems and sonnet sequences of the age. The arguments proposed by Venus, for example, are familiar appeals to the desire for immortality. The *carpe diem* ("seize the day") theme is prominent, as is the appeal to survival through procreation, and both are themes that Shakespeare exploited in his sonnets. Similarly, Adonis' rationalistic view of sex is reminiscent of Shakespeare's Sonnet 129 and many poems by Philip Sidney.

The poem is also a storehouse of the rhetorical figures and imagistic techniques of Elizabethan lyric style. Balance and antithesis, alliteration and assonance, produce a pleasing aural effect not so much to underline the meaning as to call attention to their own beauty. The imagery is sharply and brilliantly visual with bright reds and whites being the dominant, and highly conventional, colors. Images are there to embellish, not to explain, and even Adonis' fatal wound is gorgeous. The six-line stanza provides a supple medium for the gentle rhythms and sound patterns. The whole is an elegantly decorated blend of common themes into a pathetic-ironic showpiece.

"Critical Evaluation" by Edward E. Foster

For Further Study

Beauregard, David N. *"Venus and Adonis."* In *Shakespeare Studies*. Vol. 8. Edited by J. Leeds Barroll. New York: Burt Franklin, 1975. Considers critical studies of the story that range from classical interpretations of the original myth to twentieth century analyses of Shakespeare's poem.

Bullough, Geoffrey, ed. *Narrative and Dramatic Sources of Shakespeare*. New York: Columbia University Press, 1966. Part of a six-volume series of critical essays on the sources of Shakespeare's works. Included in the discussion of *Venus and Adonis* is a 1575 translation of Ovid's *Metamorphoses* by Arthur Golding.

Jahn, J. D. "The Lamb of Lust: The Role of Adonis in Shakespeare's *Venus and Adonis*." In *Shakespeare Studies*. Vol. 6. Edited by J. Leeds Barroll. Dubuque, Iowa: William C. Brown, 1970. An intense study of the personality of Adonis that Shakespeare creates in his poem.

Muir, Kenneth. "*Venus and Adonis*: Comedy or Tragedy?" In *Shakespearean Essays*. Vol. 2. Edited by Alwin Thaler and Norman Sanders. Knoxville: University of Tennessee Press, 1974. Considers the way in which the myth of Venus and Adonis has been interpreted by various authors and how Shakespeare's own audience might have interpreted the poem.

Prince, Frank Templeton. Introduction to *The Poems*, by William Shakespeare. London: Routledge, 1990. Provides more than forty pages of introductory material, in which Prince discusses the text and provides critical interpretations of the works. Also includes appendixes with information about the sources of Shakespeare's poems, with particular emphasis on *Venus and Adonis*.

A Brief History of Shakespeare Studies

The Jacobean playwright John Webster commended the "right happy and copious industry" of William Shakespeare; this industry has proved far less copious than that of Shakespeare's critics over the centuries. Whereas Shakespeare's works fit into one volume—admittedly large but still single—libraries have been written about them. The history of this criticism reveals not only the changing perceptions about and fortunes of the plays and poems but also the shifting *Zeitgeist*. As Bonamy Dobree observed in his review of E. M. W. Tillyard's *Shakespeare's Last Plays* (1938),

> The history of criticism is the history of general mental movements, even more so than is the history of "creative" literature; and this is especially true of the history of Shakespearean criticism, which reveals with a disturbing fidelity, not so much what people think of Shakespeare, but what they want of life. This is because in Shakespeare you can, with fatal ease, find anything you look for, not only by way of an "attitude towards life," but also by way of material for any literary or psychological theory which at the moment seems important (*Criterion* 17[1938]: 740-741).

The Beginnings

Even the first recorded criticism of Shakespeare, *Greene's Groatsworth of Wit* (1592), by the playwright and pamphleteer Robert Greene, reflects the truth of Dobree's assertion. Disillusioned with the theater, Greene on his deathbed attacked the rising star of the London stage, that transplant from Stratford whom Greene described as

> an upstart crow, beautified with our feathers, that with his *Tiger's heart wrapt in a player's hide*, supposes he is as well able to bombast out a blank verse as the best of you; and being an absolute *Johannes Factotum*, is in his own conceit the only Shake-scene in a country.

The comment anticipates much of what has been said of the dramatist since. It notes Shakespeare's use of others' plots and plays, implies that he lacks learning, reflects on his prosody, and argues, using a line from the playwright himself, that his reputation is undeserved. This hostile tone provoked responses even in the 1590's. Thomas Nashe and Henry Chettle condemned the tone of Greene's remarks, and in 1598 Francis Meres' *Palladis Tamia: Wit's Treasury* praised Shakespeare as extravagantly as Greene had condemned him: "As Plautus and Seneca are accounted the best for comedy and tragedy among the Latins, so Shakespeare among the English is the most excellent in both kinds for the stage."

As Samuel Schoenbaum notes in *Shakespeare's Lives*, the value of Meres' work as criticism or as a measure of Shakespeare's reputation is questionable, since *Palladis Tamia* offers a general panegyric to more than a hundred English authors, artists, and musicians, and it devotes more attention to Michael Drayton than to Shakespeare. Yet Shakespeare certainly had his admirers in his own day. Shortly after the playwright's death, William Basse wrote:

> Renowned Spenser, lye a thought more nye
> To learned Chaucer, and rare Beaumont lye
> A little neerer Spenser to make roome
> For Shakespeare in your threefold fourefold Tomb.

In any event, Edmund Spenser, Francis Beaumont, and Geoffrey Chaucer were not to be crowded by Shakespeare in Westminster Abbey's Poet's Corner, which would not house even a monument to Shakespeare until well into the eighteenth century. Ben Jonson, who "loved [Shakespeare] and [did] honor his memory on this side idolatry as much as any," maintained that Shakespeare needed no such recognition: "Thou art a monument without a tomb." Jonson also took issue with Beaumont's observation that Shakespeare's plays reveal "How far sometimes mortal man may go/ By the dim light of Nature." Greene's sneering at Shakespeare's lack of education has been turned by Beaumont—and later critics as well—into at least a modicum of praise, but for Jonson "a good poet's made as well as born." Jonson denied Shakespeare much learning, claiming that the dramatist had "small Latin and less Greek," though scholars have continued to debate this point. Yet Jonson maintained that whatever natural talent the dramatist possessed was supplemented with artistry and hard work:

> Who casts to write a living line must sweat
> (Such as thine are) and strike the second heat
> Upon the Muses' anvil, turn the same
> (And himself with it) that he thinks to frame.

Jonson's praise is probably sincere, as may be Thomas Walkley's in "The Stationer to the Reader" prefacing the 1622 quarto of *Othello*, which maintains that "the Author's name is sufficient to vent his work." Both Jonson and Walkley are, however, attempting to sell books, Jonson's lines serving as preface and puff to the 1623 First Folio. Perhaps a more just indication of where on Parnassus Shakespeare's Jacobean contemporaries placed him is John Webster's preface to *The White Devil* (1612), which ranks him with Thomas Dekker and John Heywood, below George Chapman, Jonson, Beaumont, and John Fletcher. Another measure is the sale of his works. The First Folio sold out within a decade, not a bad performance for an expensive book. Jonson's works, published in 1616, were not reprinted until 1640. Shakespeare's Second Folio (1632) satisfied demand for more than three decades, though, and by the 1640's Shakespeare's company, the King's Men, was producing three plays by Beaumont and Fletcher to one by Shakespeare.

In the latter half of the seventeenth century, Shakespeare continued to rank below Beaumont and Fletcher. When the theaters reopened in 1660 after eighteen years of the Puritans' official, if not totally successful, prohibition of stage plays,

Thomas Killigrew's company assumed the name and much of the repertoire of the King's Men. His patent granted him the rights to twenty of Shakespeare's plays, but the company produced only four. Three were staged in the spring of 1660, along with nine by Beaumont and Fletcher, three by James Shirley, and one each by Chapman, Jonson, Thomas Middleton, Sir William Davenant, and Killigrew. As patentee of the other licensed London theater, Davenant had the right to produce ten (later thirteen) of Shakespeare's plays. In 1660, he chose to stage only *Pericles*, probably because it mirrored in part the recent experiences of Charles II, a young ruler driven from his throne and then restored. Davenant put on eight works by Beaumont and Fletcher that first season. Commenting on the fare of the London theaters at the end of the 1660's, John Dryden observed that Beaumont and Fletcher "are now the most pleasant and frequent entertainments of the Stage; two of theirs being acted through the year for one of Shakespeare's or Jonson's." Samuel Pepys's *Diary* confirms this observation. In the 1660's, Pepys attended the theater some 350 times. He saw fifteen plays by Shakespeare, twenty-seven adaptations, and seventy-six performances of works by Beaumont and Fletcher.

It was Dryden who coined the phrase "the divine Shakespeare," but even for him the divinity was qualified. As Dryden wrote to explain his revision of *Troilus and Cressida*,

> It must be allowed to the present age, that the tongue in general is so much refined since Shakespeare's time, that many of his words, and more of his phrases, are scarce intelligible. And of those which are understood, some are ungrammatical, others coarse; and his whole style is so pestered with figurative expressions, that it is as affected as it is obscure.

With Davenant, Dryden adapted *The Tempest*; their version influenced performances for two centuries. *Antony and Cleopatra* became Dryden's *All for Love* (1678). Davenant's operatic *Macbeth* (1664) held the boards for eighty years. His *The Law Against Lovers* (1667) fused *Measure for Measure* and *Much Ado About Nothing*, and his *The Rivals* is based on *The Two Noble Kinsmen*. Nahum Tate gave *King Lear* a happy ending; he compensated by killing off Volumnia, Martius, Aufidius, and his new introduction, Nigridius, in his version of *Coriolanus*. John Lacy's *Sawny the Scot* (1667), a farcical version of *The Taming of the Shrew*, continued to be performed into the nineteenth century. As Pepys's diary indicates, Restoration audiences were thus more likely to see a Shakespeare adaptation than Shakespeare undefiled, but these new versions kept the plays alive. Folio editions of the works appeared in 1663-1664 and 1685, and individual plays were reprinted with some regularity. Five *Hamlet* quartos were published between 1676 and 1703.

As in the early 1600's, playgoers and readers alike continued to divide in their opinions. The eccentric Duchess of Newcastle praised Shakespeare after reading the Third Folio. Pepys called *Henry IV, Part I* "a good play" (June 4, 1661) but regarded *A Midsummer Night's Dream* as "the most insipid ridiculous play that ever I saw in my life" (September 29, 1662). He saw *Hamlet* five times and enjoyed it, perhaps because of the acting of Thomas Betterton, whose fine performances did much to enhance Shakespeare's reputation among theatergoers. *Romeo and*

Juliet, which Pepys saw on March 1, 1662, displeased him, but, again, the performers influenced his opinion; he claimed the piece was "the worst acted that ever I saw these people do." In 1689 Robert Gould remarked, "When e'er I *Hamlet*, or *Othello* read,/ My *Hair* starts up, and my *Nerves* shrink with dread." Thomas Rymer was less impressed, though like Greene his attacks on Shakespeare reflect hostility to the stage in general. In *A Short View of Tragedy* (1693), Rymer declared, "In the *Neighing* of an Horse, or in the *growling* of a Mastiff, there is a meaning, there is as lively expression, and, I may say, more humanity, than many times in the Tragical flights of Shakespear." Rymer singled out *Othello* for particular castigation:

> The moral, sure, of this fable is very instructive. First, this may be a caution to all maidens of quality how, without their parents' consent, they run away with blackamoors.
> Secondly, this may be a warning to all good wives, that they look well to their linen.
> Thirdly, this may be a lesson to husbands, that before their jealousy be tragical, the proofs may be mathematical.

Despite the absurdity of these comments, they anticipate two objections that would often be repeated in the next century: Shakespeare's vocabulary and his lack of poetical justice. Less dyspeptically, James Drake in 1699 observed that "Shakespeare . . . fell short of the Art of *Jonson*, and the conversation of *Beaumont* and *Fletcher*." Yet, in the same year that Rymer published his counterblast against Shakespeare, a Mr. Dowdall made the first recorded literary pilgrimage to Stratford.

The Eighteenth Century

In the eighteenth century, Shakespeare's fortunes rose. The University of Cambridge library admitted him to its shelves in 1715, acquiring a copy of the Fourth Folio (1685). In 1736-1737, a Shakespeare Ladies Club formed in London to promote revivals of Shakespeare's plays, and it succeeded: In the 1736-1737 season, about a fifth of the London repertory derived from Shakespeare. The Licensing Act of 1737 that imposed censorship on the theaters also helped Shakespeare because it drove much talented competition away from drama. A monument to Shakespeare was installed in Westminster Abbey in 1741, another sign of his growing reputation. David Garrick's great acting career did even more than Betterton's to advance Shakespeare's theatrical popularity. Though Garrick purged *Hamlet* of what he called "the tedious interruptions" and "its absurd digressions," he restored *Macbeth*, *Coriolanus*, *Cymbeline*, *The Tempest*, and *Antony and Cleopatra* to their pre-Restoration condition. Yet he, too, was not averse to adaptation, turning scenes into entertainments such as *Florizel and Perdita* (1756, based on *The Winter's Tale*) and *Catharine and Petruchio* (1756, derived from *The Taming of the Shrew*). Altogether, though, Garrick's influence was beneficial. During his management of Drury Lane Theatre, one of four tragedies and one of every six comedies staged were by Shakespeare. Even his rain-sodden Shakespeare Jubilee in 1769 further promoted popular interest in the playwright.

At the same time that audiences could see more (and more accurate) Shakespearean plays, texts, too, multiplied. Arthur Sherbo finds in the eighteenth century the birth of Shakespeare studies. In the seventeenth century, four editions of the collected works appeared; between 1709 and 1809 there were sixty-five, including the first American one (1795-1796). Lewis Theobald's *Shakespeare Restored* (1726) exemplifies the attention being devoted to textual matters. Rather than trying to revise the plays, as the Restoration had done, Theobald and his fellow (often rival) editors hoped to free the plays from corruption so that they could claim their place among the classics.

Like a classic, too, Shakespeare was now being collected. Garrick owned a number of early editions, and the botanist Richard Warner formed a Shakespeare library in anticipation of producing a new edition (preempted by George Steevens). An even greater sign of Shakespeare's popularity was the new phenomenon of Shakespeare forgeries. In the seventeenth century, publishers might attribute another author's play or poem to Shakespeare, but now authors hoped to capitalize on the dramatist's vogue by passing off their work as his. John Jordan of Stratford created a Shakespearean ballad about Sir Thomas Lucy, but this inventiveness paled before that of William Henry Ireland, who wrote an entire play, *Vortigern and Rowena*, staged at Drury Lane in 1796. Ireland also manufactured a manuscript of *King Lear* and many other items. The "Profession of Faith" that Ireland fathered on Shakespeare drew from Dr. Samuel Parr the declaration, "Sir, we have many very fine passages in our church service, and our litany abounds with beauties; but here, sir, here is a man who has distanced us all." Portraits of Shakespeare, no two alike, proliferated. The eighteenth century produced the first illustrated edition of Shakespeare (1709). Paintings based on the plays quickly found their way into the Royal Academy after it opened in 1769 and claimed equality with historical canvases (then regarded as the epitome of artistic achievement). In 1789, John Boydell opened his Shakespeare Gallery in Pall Mall; by 1800, it housed 160 pictures by the finest artists of the day, including Sir Joshua Reynolds, Benjamin West, Angelica Kauffmann, and George Romney.

Though appreciation for Shakespeare rose, critical commonplaces echoed those of the previous century. Nicholas Rowe, Shakespeare's first eighteenth century editor, commented that the playwright, ignorant of Aristotle's rules, "liv'd under a kind of mere light of Nature." Alexander Pope, who succeeded Rowe as editor of Shakespeare for Jacob Tonson, similarly observed that Shakespeare's characters "are so much Nature her self, that 'tis a sort of injury to call them by so distant a name as Copies of her." For them, as for John Milton, Shakespeare was still "Fancy's child,/ Warbling his native woodnotes wild."

Pleasing as these notes were, the wildness sometimes demanded refining. In the prologue to *The Invader of His Country*, formerly *Coriolanus*, John Dennis explained the need to bring order to the play, "Where Master-strokes in wild Confusion lye." Pope blamed the actors of Shakespeare's day and later for distorting the text, and he emended accordingly. Theobald sought to restore Shakespeare's text not only from Pope's efforts but also from earlier corruption. The apparent lack of poetic justice also continued to bother critics. Dennis lamented in 1712, "The good and the bad then perishing promiscuously in the best of Shakespearean tragedies, there can be either none or very weak instruction in them." Samuel Johnson echoed this concern, claiming that Shakespeare "sacrifices virtue to convenience, and is so much more careful to please than to instruct, that he seems to write without any moral purpose."

As long as neoclassical doctrines dominated critical thinking, Shakespeare's reputation remained subject to challenge. No English writer would have gone so far as Voltaire, who in 1748 called *Hamlet* "a piece gross and barbarous, that would not be approved by the lowest populace of France or Italy.... One would think that this work was the fruit of the imagination of a drunken savage." The English were less attached to rigid neoclassicism than were their counterparts across the Channel; moreover, Shakespeare represented English liberty opposed to French tyranny. During the Seven Years' War, *Henry V* was performed annually in London. Yet even Samuel Johnson, who appealed from rules to nature to defend Shakespeare's violation of the unities, the mingling of genres, and many of the plays' violations of decorum, objected to what he regarded as poorly constructed plots, hasty endings, anachronisms, and puns.

The Nineteenth Century

Romanticism removed theoretical impediments to the enjoyment of Shakespeare. August Wilhelm von Schlegel's *Course of Lectures in Dramatic Art and Literature*—delivered in Vienna in 1808, published in German (1809-1811), and then quickly translated into English by John Black (1815)—agreed with Dryden that Shakespeare was a giant before the Flood, a Gothic genius, but by 1800 Gothicism in literature as in architecture held equal status with the classical. To Schlegel, Shakespeare was the peer of Sophocles, indeed, his superior, as art of the Christian era surpassed that of the pagan. Johnson had to defend Shakespeare's mingling of genres; Schlegel celebrated it, claiming that art "delights in indissoluble mixtures."

Johnson pioneered another area of Shakespearean criticism that persisted into the twentieth century but is generally associated with Romanticism: the treatment of Shakespeare's characters as real people. Writing of Falstaff, Johnson proclaimed, "Unimitated, unimitable *Falstaff*, how shall I describe thee? Thou compound of sense and vice; of sense which may be admired but not esteemed, of vice which may be despised, but hardly detested." The popularity of this approach is evident in the very titles of works such as William Richardson's *A Philosophical Analysis and Illustration of Some of Shakespeare's Remarkable Characters* (1774), Maurice Morgann's *An Essay on the Dramatic Character of Sir John Falstaff* (1777), and Thomas Whateley's *Remarks on Some of the Characters of Shakespeare* (1785). A. C. Bradley's *Shakespearean Tragedy* (1904), with its focus on character, belongs to this tradition, which even L. C. Knights's "How Many Children Had Lady Macbeth?" (1933), an attack on this approach, could not counteract completely. Psychoanalytical studies such as Ernest Jones's *Hamlet and Oedipus* (1947) also derive from this line of investigation.

A number of Romantics went beyond Morgann or Bradley, identifying Shakespeare's characters with themselves. In a letter to Fanny Brawne dated August, 1820, John Keats wrote, "Hamlet's heart was full of such misery as mine is when he said to Ophelia, 'Go to a Nunnery, go, go!' Indeed I should like to give up the matter at once—I should like to die." Samuel Taylor Coleridge, too, likened himself to Hamlet, and William Hazlitt extended the equation to embrace all who fail to act or who seek in the theater diversion from the miseries of life.

In other ways, Romantic writers on Shakespeare refined earlier views. Though still speaking the language of nature, Shakespeare in the nineteenth century came to be regarded as a conscious artist, a view anticipated by Ben Jonson but then dropped in the neoclassical age. For Johann Wolfgang von Goethe, he was so great a poet that the stage was unworthy of him. Charles Lamb and Hazlitt repeated the view that the plays could not be represented accurately in the theater. With the many editions available—162 were published in the 1850's alone—the library replaced the theater as the place where most people encountered Shakespeare, and criticism increasingly focused on text rather than on performance. With a few notable exceptions such as Harley Granville-Barker, this tendency persisted into the late twentieth century and was even then only partially reversed.

Romantics also discovered in Shakespeare an ethical dimension. According to Coleridge, Shakespeare "never rendered that amiable which religion and reason taught us to detest; he never clothed vice in the garb of virtue." Henrietta Maria Bowdler and her brother Thomas produced *The Family Shakespeare* (1807; 2d ed., 1818) with the profanity removed, but they did not alter the plots. They thus found Shakespeare more moral than do many modern feminist critics, who see in the plays a defense of patriarchy and so condemn the author's stance. Others continue to find in the works the ethical outlook they themselves endorse, reading into the plays and poems orthodox or radical views on religion, war, women, politics, love, or commerce.

Less acceptable at the end of the twentieth century was the Romantics' biographical approach to the works. This effort to find the author in his writings enhanced the popularity of the sonnets, which had been excluded from the four folio editions of the seventeenth century and frequently omitted from eighteenth century editions as well: Rowe's and Pope's included them only in a supplementary volume. Not until 1780 did the great Shakespeare scholar Edmond Malone produce a carefully edited text that returned to the 1609 version. Ten years later Malone issued the *Plays and Poems*, which for the first time integrated the sonnets into the canon. Gary Taylor argues that Shakespeare's poems profited from the late eighteenth century vogue for Spenser and John Milton and the consequent resurgence of the sonnet form. Whatever their artistic appeal, though, Shakespeare's sonnets were read as revealing the life of their creator, about whom so little seemed to be known otherwise. Thus, Schlegel in his lectures maintained that "these sonnets paint most unequivocally the actual situation and sentiments of the poet." William Wordsworth in 1815 claimed that in the poems "Shakespeare expresses his own feelings in his own person," and in "Scorn Not the Sonnet" Wordsworth maintained that "with this key/ Shakespeare unlocked his heart."

Such biographical readings affected the perceived chronology of the plays. Because Leigh Hunt regarded *Twelfth Night* as genial, he claimed that it was Shakespeare's last play, the product of contented age. For Keats, *Hamlet* reflected

Shakespearean unhappiness in the playwright's middle years. This approach culminated in Edward Dowden's *Shakspere: A Critical Study of His Mind and Art* (1875). Using the plays, Dowden divided Shakespeare's life into four periods: "In the Workshop," "In the World," "Out of the Depths," and "On the Heights." These four periods correspond roughly to the romantic comedies, histories, tragedies, and late romances (a name that Dowden was the first to apply to these comedies). In this tradition, Frank Harris' *The Man Shakespeare and His Tragic Life Story* (1909) identifies Brutus with his creator, showing "his own sad heart and the sweetness which suffering had called forth in him." Gertrude and Cressida were avatars of the Dark Lady of the sonnets (whom Harris identified as Mary Fitton), who had betrayed the playwright. The success of the Ireland forgeries attests to the hunger for information that continues unabated. Oxfordians, Baconians, and all the other kooks and cranks who deny that William Shakespeare of Stratford wrote the plays and poems cannot accept the gaps in biographical knowledge, and even the learned and orthodox Stratfordian A. L. Rowse claims to have unriddled the sonnets.

Victorian and Later Criticism

As one of the first academic critics, Dowden heralded another change in Shakespearean studies. Shakespeare's first editors, John Heminge and Henry Condell, were men of the theater. In the eighteenth century, his editors and admirers were again not sheltered in academic bowers; Arthur Sherbo's *The Birth of Shakespeare Studies* (1986) illustrates how many people from all occupations contributed comments to the various editions that appeared between 1709 and 1821. Malone, the greatest English literary scholar of the eighteenth century, trained as a lawyer and held no academic post. In the Victorian period, Shakespeare moved into the university. Thus, between 1863 and 1866, William George Clark, John Glover, and William Aldis Wright, all from Cambridge, produced *The Works of William Shakespeare*, in nine volumes, published by Cambridge University Press and dedicated to the university's chancellor. Though nonacademics continued to contribute to scholarship—T. S. Eliot and Granville-Barker come at once to mind, and the publisher Robert Giroux's *The Book Known as Q* provides a fascinating analysis of the sonnets—criticism and editing have become largely the province of academics, who also constitute the primary audience for these writings, which have grown increasingly hermetic and esoteric. Like much modern literature, art, and music, late twentieth century criticism isolated itself from the public. William Wordsworth's famous definition of the poet as a man speaking to other men might be paraphrased to define the modern critic as a man (used generically) writing to himself and his colleagues. Yet the multiplicity of Shakespeare festivals—thirty-one in the United States alone in 1983—the popularity of movies based on the plays, and the British Broadcasting System (BBC) and Grenada television series suggest that the plays remain alive to greater audiences than ever.

In *Reinventing Shakespeare: A Cultural History, from the Restoration to the Present*, Gary Taylor argued that Dowden's fourfold division of Shakespeare's life reflects the Victorian belief in progress. The formation of the New Shakspere Society under F. J. Furnivall in 1873 similarly mirrors the age's faith in science.

The Reverend Frederick G. Fleay, one of the society's leading members, proclaimed,

> We must adopt every scientific method from other sciences applicable to our ends. From the mineralogist we must learn to recognize a chip of rock from its general appearance; from the chemist, to apply systematic tabulated tests to confirm our conclusions; from the botanist we must learn to classify; finally, from the biologist we must learn to take into account, not only the state of any writer's mind at some one epoch, but to trace its organic growth from beginning to end of his period of work. When these things are done systematically and thoroughly, then, and then only, may we expect to have a criticism that shall be free from shallow notions taken up to please individual eccentricities.

Dowden's anatomy of Shakespeare's life was a product of such thinking—Dowden was a charter member of the New Shakspere Society. Another product was Fleay's metrical tests to determine the chronology and authenticity of the plays. His results were not always happy: according to Fleay, *Henry VIII*, *Pericles*, *Timon of Athens*, *Macbeth*, *Julius Caesar*, and *The Taming of the Shrew* all showed signs of other authors. Most of his conclusions have been rejected by modern scholarship. Another member of the society, James O. Halliwell-Phillips, charged with writing the biography, stretched out his meager facts to a thousand pages that again portray an unlearned genius: "Residing with illiterate relatives in a bookless neighbourhood; thrown into the midst of occupations adverse to scholastic progress, it is difficult to believe that when he first left Stratford, he was not all but destitute of polished accomplishments." Modern scholarship finds a very different environment, a very different man.

Victorian sentimentality and belief in progress have not worn well in Shakespeare studies or anywhere else. The scientific method has fared somewhat better. The Hinman collator, developed by Charlton Hinman, greatly aided textual studies, and metrical tests, more sophisticated and aided by computers, continue to be applied to determine authorship, though this approach remains controversial. The twentieth century's belief in the social sciences was mirrored in Shakespearean criticism, with its sociological, anthropological, and psychological approaches. C. L. Barber's *Shakespeare's Festive Comedy* (1959), John Holloway's *The Story of the Night* (1961), and Northrop Frye's *A Natural Perspective* (1965) are products of this methodology. The rise of feminism finds its echo in essays such as Kathleen E. McLuskie's "The Patriarchal Bard" (1985) and Linda Bamber's *Comic Women, Tragic Men* (1982).

The Victorian concern with the past led to historically accurate productions and the creation of historically accurate texts. In 1838 William Macready offered Shakespeare's *The Tempest* rather than the Davenant/Dryden version, and Shakespeare's *King Lear* instead of Tate's. In 1877 Henry Irving abandoned Colley Cibber's *Richard III* for the original. F. R. Benson, William Poel, and Granville-Barker continued this practice, and Peter Hall's uncut versions demonstrate the vitality of the tradition. This nineteenth century new historicism benefitted criticism also. E. E. Stoll argued for seeing Shakespeare as a product of his time. Thus, he maintained that Shylock reveals the mentality of Shakespeare's audiences, their attitude toward Jews, misers, and moneylenders. This approach provides the background necessary to understand the works and offers a necessary corrective to those who fail to remember that Shakespeare was of his age as well as for all time. E. M. W. Tillyard's influential and controversial *The Elizabethan World Picture* (1943) is a product of this same concern for understanding the literary, intellectual, and cultural background of the works, as is new historicism. Yet no age is monolithic. Even if the majority of Shakespeare's audience hated Jews, Shylock need not be a clone of Barabas in Christopher Marlowe's *The Jew of Malta*. Though a majority of Elizabethans may have envisioned the world as Tillyard claims, Shakespeare may not have agreed. Artists in general, and great artists in particular, are antinomian; Shakespeare may have found other truths more appealing than the orthodoxies of his time.

In a revolt against the biographical-historical approach to literature, New Criticism turned to the texts as self-contained artifacts that would interpret themselves under proper investigation. Caroline F. E. Spurgeon tabulated Shakespeare's imagery, finding in *Macbeth*, for example, repeated references to clothes. The title character wears "borrow'd robes," "strange garments," and "a giant's robe/ Upon a dwarfish thief." Her study does not break completely with those of her predecessors: She hoped to use the imagery to understand the life of the creator, and her tables resemble those of Fleay's chemist. Still, she provided the impetus and much of the information that underlies the work of scholars such as Cleanth Brooks and Wolfgang Clemen. Deconstructionists, much as they claim to reject New Criticism, undertake the same close reading of the text. At its best, such interpretation has illuminated the plays, but it has also encouraged reading them as poems rather than as drama. Theater-based criticism has claimed, with some justice, that such approaches distort the works.

Joseph Rosenblum

Works Consulted

Benzie, William. *Dr. F. J. Furnival: A Victorian Scholar Adventurer*. Norman, Okla.: Pilgrim Books, 1983.

Eastman, Arthur M. *A Short History of Shakespearean Criticism*. New York: Random House, 1968.

Franklin, Colin. *Shakespeare Domesticated: The Eighteenth Century Editions*. Aldershot, England: Scolar Press, 1991.

Grebanier, Samuel. *The Great Shakespeare Forgery*. New York: W. W. Norton, 1965.

Halliday, F. E. *The Cult of Shakespeare*. New York: Thomas Yoseloff, 1957.

Marder, Louis. *His Exits and Entrances: The Story of Shakespeare's Reputation*. Philadelphia: J. B. Lippincott, 1963.

Munro, John, ed. *The Shakespeare Allusion-Book: A Collection of Allusions to Shakespeare from 1591 to 1700*. 2 vols. London: Oxford University Press, 1932.

Schoenbaum, Samuel. *Shakespeare's Lives*. 2d ed. New York: Oxford University Press, 1991.

Sherbo, Arthur. *The Birth of Shakespeare Studies: Commentators from Rowe (1709) to Boswell-Malone (1821)*. East Lansing, Mich.: Colleagues Press, 1986.

Taylor, Gary. *Reinventing Shakespeare: A Cultural History, from the Restoration to the Present*. New York: Weidenfeld and Nicolson, 1989.

Bibliography

This bibliography cites twentieth century criticism, particularly books, to suggest the range of materials on and approaches to Shakespeare and to provide a list of those works that students of Shakespeare are most likely to encounter and need. Though it has sought to include all the classic studies since the beginning of the twentieth century, the bibliography is weighted toward late twentieth century scholarship. The arrangement seeks to facilitate use. For example, the plays are listed alphabetically to avoid problems of chronology and classification. To avoid excessive repetition, entries appear under one heading only. Therefore, someone seeking material on *The Comedy of Errors* should look at the listings under "General Studies" and "Comedies" as well as under the play itself. Samuel Johnson observed that knowledge is of two kinds: Either one knows something, or one knows where to find the information. It is hoped that this bibliography contributes to the latter.

Joseph Rosenblum

EDITIONS OF SHAKESPEARE'S WORKS

Allen, Michael J. B., and Kenneth Muir, eds. *Shakespeare's Plays in Quarto: A Facsimile of Copies Primarily from the Henry E. Huntington Library.* Berkeley: University of California Press, 1981.

Barnet, Sylvan, ed. *The Complete Signet Classic Shakespeare.* New York: Harcourt Brace Jovanovich, 1972.

Bevington, David, ed. *The Complete Works of Shakespeare.* 4th ed. New York: HarperCollins, 1992.

Brockbank, Philip, ed. *The New Cambridge Shakespeare.* Cambridge, England: Cambridge University Press, 1984- .

Brooke, C. F. Tucker, ed. *The Shakespeare Apocrypha: Being a Collection of Fourteen Plays Which Have Been Ascribed to Shakespeare.* Oxford, England: Clarendon Press, 1918.

Brooks, Harold F., and Harold Jenkins, eds. *The New Arden Shakespeare.* Cambridge, Mass.: Harvard University Press, 1951- .

Evans, G. Blackmore, ed. *The Riverside Shakespeare.* Boston: Houghton Mifflin, 1974.

Furness, Horace Howard, et al., eds. *A New Variorum Edition of Shakespeare.* Philadelphia: J. B. Lippincott, 1871- .

Harbage, Alfred, ed. *William Shakespeare: The Complete Works.* New York: Penguin Books, 1977.

Harrison, G. B. *Shakespeare: The Complete Works*. New York: Brace & World, 1948.

Hinman, Charlton, ed. *The First Folio of Shakespeare: The Norton Facsimile*. New York: W. W. Norton, 1968.

Ribner, Irving, and George Lyman Kittredge, eds. *The Complete Works of Shakespeare*. Rev. ed. Waltham, Mass.: Ginn, 1971.

Wells, Stanley, and Gary Taylor. *William Shakespeare: The Complete Works*. London: Oxford University Press, 1986.

BIBLIOGRAPHIES

Bergeron, David Moore, and Geraldo U. de Sousa. *Shakespeare: A Study and Research Guide*. 2d and rev. ed. Lawrence: University Press of Kansas, 1987.

Berman, Ronald. *A Reader's Guide to Shakespeare's Plays*. Rev. ed. Glenview, Ill.: Scott, Foresman, 1973.

Bevington, David. *Shakespeare*. Arlington Heights, Ill.: AHM Publishing, 1978.

Champion, Larry S. *The Essential Shakespeare: An Annotated Bibliography of Major Modern Studies*. 2d ed. New York: G. K. Hall, 1993.

Ebisch, Walter, and Levin Schucking. *A Shakespeare Bibliography*. Oxford, England: Clarendon Press, 1931.

Godshalk, William, ed. *Garland Shakespeare Bibliographies*. New York: Garland, 1980-   .

Harris, Laurie L., et al., eds. *Shakespearean Criticism: Excerpts from the Criticism of William Shakespeare's Plays and Poetry, from the First Published Appraisals to Current Evaluations*. Detroit: Gale Research, 1984-   .

Howard-Hill, T. H. *Shakespearian Bibliography and Textual Criticism: A Bibliography*. Oxford, England: Clarendon Press, 1971.

McManaway, James G., and Jeanne Addison Roberts. *A Selective Bibliography of Shakespeare: Editions, Textual Studies, Commentary*. Charlottesville: University Press of Virginia, 1975.

Quinn, Edward, James Ruoff, and Joseph Grennen, eds. *The Major Shakespearean Tragedies: A Critical Bibliography*. New York: Free Press, 1973.

Sajdak, Bruce T., ed. *Shakespeare Index: An Annotated Bibliography of Critical Articles on the Plays, 1959-1983*. 2 vols. Millwood, N.Y.: Kraus, 1992.

Smith, Gordon Ross. *A Classified Shakespeare Bibliography, 1936-1958*. University Park: Pennsylvania State University Press, 1963.

Wells, Stanley, ed. *The Cambridge Companion to Shakespeare Studies*. Cambridge, England: Cambridge University Press, 1986.

_____, ed. *Shakespeare: A Bibliographical Guide*. New ed. London: Oxford University Press, 1990.

REFERENCE WORKS

Alexander, Marguerite. *A Reader's Guide to Shakespeare and His Contemporaries*. New York: Barnes & Noble Books, 1979.

Alexander, Peter. *Introductions to Shakespeare*. London: William Collins Sons, 1964.

Baker, Arthur Ernest. *A Shakespeare Commentary*. 2 vols. New York: Frederick Ungar, 1938.

Boyce, Charles. *Shakespeare A to Z*. New York: Facts on File, 1990.

Browning, D. C. *Everyman's Dictionary of Shakespeare Quotations*. London: J. M. Dent & Sons, 1953.

Campbell, Oscar James, ed., and Edward G. Quinn, assoc. ed. *The Reader's Encyclopedia of Shakespeare*. New York: Thomas Y. Crowell, 1966.

Clark, Sandra, and T. H. Long. *The New Century Shakespeare Handbook*. Englewood Cliffs, N.J.: Prentice-Hall, 1974.

DeLoach, Charles. *The Quotable Shakespeare: A Topical Dictionary*. Jefferson, N.C.: McFarland, 1988.

Evans, Gareth Lloyd, and Barbara Evans. *The Shakespeare Companion*. New York: Charles Scribner's Sons, 1978.

Fox, Levi, ed. *The Shakespeare Handbook*. Boston: G. K. Hall, 1987.

Gooch, Bryan N. S., and David Thatcher. *A Shakespeare Music Catalogue*. 5 vols. Oxford, England: Clarendon Press, 1990.

Halliday, Frank Ernest. *A Shakespeare Companion, 1564-1964*. Rev. ed. New York: Schocken Books, 1964.

Harbage, Alfred. *William Shakespeare: A Reader's Guide*. New York: Noonday Press, 1963.

Howard-Hill, T. H., ed. *Oxford Shakespeare Concordances*. Oxford, England: Clarendon Press, 1969-1973.

Lewis, William Dodge. *Shakespeare Said It: Topical Quotations from the Works of Shakespeare, Selected and Annotated*. Syracuse, N.Y.: Syracuse University Press, 1961.

Martin, Michael Rheta, and Richard C. Harrier. *The Concise Encyclopedic Guide to Shakespeare*. New York: Horizon Press, 1971.

Onions, C. T., and Robert D. Eagleson. *A Shakespeare Glossary*. Rev. ed. Oxford, England: Clarendon Press, 1986.

Partridge, Eric. *Shakespeare's Bawdy: A Scholarly, Fully Documented Examination of Shakespeare's Sexual Allusions*. 2d ed. London: Routledge & Kegan Paul, 1968.

Quennell, Peter, and Hamish Johnson. *Who's Who in Shakespeare*. New York: William Morrow, 1973.

Root, Robert Kilburn. *Classical Mythology in Shakespeare*. New York: Henry Holt, 1903.

Shaheen, Naseeb. *Biblical References in Shakespeare's Tragedies*. Newark: University of Delaware Press, 1987.

Spevack, Marvin. *A Complete and Systematic Concordance to the Works of Shakespeare*. 8 vols. Hildesheim, Germany: Georg Olms Verlagsbuchhandlung, 1968-1980.

Sugden, Edward H. *A Topographical Dictionary to the Works of Shakespeare and His Fellow Dramatists*. Manchester, England: Manchester University Press, 1925.

Zesmer, David M. *Guide to Shakespeare*. New York: Barnes & Noble Books, 1976.

GENERAL STUDIES

Sources

Bullough, Geoffrey, ed. *Narrative and Dramatic Sources of Shakespeare*. 8 vols. New York: Columbia University Press, 1957-1975.

Dessen, Alan C. *Shakespeare and the Late Moral Plays*. Lincoln: University of Nebraska Press, 1986.

Donaldson, E. Talbot. *The Swan at the Well: Shakespeare Reading Chaucer*. New Haven, Conn.: Yale University Press, 1985.

Gesner, Carol. *Shakespeare and the Greek Romance: A Study of Origins*. Lexington: University Press of Kentucky, 1970.

Hankins, John Erskine. *Shakespeare's Derived Imagery*. Lawrence: University of Kansas Press, 1953.

Hart, Alfred. *Shakespeare and the Homilies: And Other Pieces of Research into the Elizabethan Drama*. Melbourne, Australia: Melbourne University Press, 1934.

Hosley, Richard, ed. *Shakespeare's Holinshed: An Edition of Holinshed's Chronicles, 1587*. New York: G. P. Putnam's Sons, 1968.

Jones, Emrys. *The Origins of Shakespeare*. Oxford, England: Clarendon Press, 1977.

Martindale, Charles, and Michelle Martindale. *Shakespeare and the Uses of Antiquity: An Introductory Essay*. London: Routledge, 1990.

Muir, Kenneth. *The Sources of Shakespeare's Plays*. New Haven, Conn.: Yale University Press, 1978.

Noble, Richmond. *Shakespeare's Biblical Knowledge and Use of the Book of Common Prayer, as Exemplified in the Plays of the First Folio*. New York: Macmillan, 1935.

Potts, Abbie Findlay. *Shakespeare and "The Faerie Queene."* Ithaca, N.Y.: Cornell University Press, 1958.

Satin, Joseph. *Shakespeare and His Sources*. Boston: Houghton Mifflin, 1966.

Spencer, Terence J. B. *Shakespeare's Plutarch*. Harmondsworth, England: Penguin Books, 1964.

Thompson, Ann. *Shakespeare's Chaucer: A Study in Literary Origins*. New York: Barnes & Noble Books, 1978.

Thomson, J. A. K. *Shakespeare and the Classics*. London: George Allen & Unwin, 1952.

Whitaker, Virgil. *Shakespeare's Use of Learning: An Inquiry into the Growth of His Mind and Art*. San Marino, Calif.: Huntington Library, 1953.

The Text

Bartlett, Henrietta C., and Alfred W. Pollard. *A Census of Shakespeare's Plays in Quarto, 1594-1709*. Rev. and extended ed. New Haven, Conn.: Yale University Press, 1939.

Black, Matthew W., and Mathias A. Shaaber. *Shakespeare's Seventeenth-Century Editors, 1632-1685*. New York: Modern Language Association of America, 1937.

Burkhart, Robert E. *Shakespeare's Bad Quartos: Deliberate Abridgements Designed for Performance by a Reduced Cast*. The Hague: Mouton, 1975.

Feuillerat, Albert. *The Composition of Shakespeare's Plays: Authorship, Chronology*. New Haven, Conn.: Yale University Press, 1953.

Greg, Walter W. *The Editorial Problem in Shakespeare: A Survey of the Foundations of the Text*. 3d ed. Oxford, England: Clarendon Press, 1954.

_____. *The Shakespeare First Folio: Its Bibliographical and Textual History*. Oxford, England: Clarendon Press, 1955.

Hart, Alfred. *Stolne and Surreptitious Copies: A Comparative Study of Shakespeare's Bad Quartos*. Melbourne, Australia: Melbourne University Press, 1942.

Hinman, Charlton. *The Printing and Proof-Reading of the First Folio of Shakespeare*. 2 vols. Oxford, England: Clarendon Press, 1963.

Maguire, Laurie E. *Shakespearean Suspect Texts: The "Bad" Quartos and Their Contexts*. Cambridge: Cambridge University Press, 1996.

Pollard, Alfred W. *Shakespeare's Fight with the Pirates and the Problems of the Transmission of His Text*. London: A. Moring, 1917.

_____. *Shakespeare's Folios and Quartos: A Study in the Bibliography of Shakespeare's Plays, 1594-1685*. London: Methuen, 1909.

Prosser, Eleanor. *Shakespeare's Anonymous Editor: Scribe and Composition in the Folio Text of "2 Henry IV."* Stanford, Calif.: Stanford University Press, 1981.

Walker, Alice. *Textual Problems and the First Folio: "Richard III," "King Lear," "Troilus and Cressida," "Henry IV," "Hamlet," "Othello."* Cambridge, England: Cambridge University Press, 1953.

Walton, James Kirkwood. *The Quarto Copy for the First Folio of Shakespeare*. Dublin, Ireland: Dublin University Press, 1971.

Wells, Stanley, and Gary Taylor, with John Jowett and William Montgomery. *William Shakespeare: A Textual Companion*. Oxford, England: Clarendon Press, 1987.

Willoughby, Edwin Elliot. *The Printing of the First Folio*. Oxford, England: Oxford University Press, 1932.

Language

Baxter, John. *Shakespeare's Poetic Style: Verse into Drama*. London: Routledge & Kegan Paul, 1980.

Bevington, David. *Action Is Eloquence: Shakespeare's Language of Gesture*. Chicago: University of Chicago Press, 1984.

Burckhardt, Sigurd. *Shakespearean Meanings*. Princeton, N.J.: Princeton University Press, 1968.

Clemen, Wolfgang H. *The Development of Shakespeare's Imagery*. Cambridge, Mass.: Harvard University Press, 1951.

_____. *Shakespeare's Soliloquies*. Translated by Charity Scott Stokes. London: Methuen, 1987.

Colman, E. A. M. *The Dramatic Use of Bawdy in Shakespeare*. London: Longman, 1974.

Crane, Milton. *Shakespeare's Prose*. Chicago: University of Chicago Press, 1951.

Donawerth, Jane. *Shakespeare and the Sixteenth Century Study of Language*. Urbana: University of Illinois Press, 1984.

Evans, Benjamin Ifor. *The Language of Shakespeare's Plays*. London: Methuen, 1952.

Halliday, Frank Ernest. *The Poetry of Shakespeare's Plays*. London: Gerald Duckworth, 1954.

Hibbard, G. R. *The Making of Shakespeare's Dramatic Poetry*. Toronto: University of Toronto Press, 1981.

Hulme, Hilda M. *Explorations in Shakespeare's Language: Some Problems of Lexical Meaning in the Dramatic Text*. London: Longmans, Green, 1962.

Hussey, S. S. *The Literary Language of Shakespeare*. London: Longman Group, 1982.

Kennedy, Milton Boone. *The Oration in Shakespeare*. Chapel Hill: University of North Carolina Press, 1942.

Mahood, M. M. *Shakespeare's Wordplay*. London: Methuen, 1957.

Mariam, Joseph. *Shakespeare's Use of the Arts of Language*. New York: Columbia University Press, 1947.

Shirley, Frances A. *Swearing and Perjury in Shakespeare's Plays*. London: George Allen & Unwin, 1979.

Sipe, Dorothy L. *Shakespeare's Metrics*. New Haven, Conn.: Yale University Press, 1968.

Spurgeon, Caroline F. E. *Shakespeare's Imagery and What It Tells Us*. Cambridge, England: Cambridge University Press, 1935.

Vickers, Brian. *The Artistry of Shakespeare's Prose*. London: Methuen, 1968.

Willcock, Gladys D. *Shakespeare as a Critic of Language*. Oxford, England: Oxford University Press, 1934.

Wright, George T. *Shakespeare's Metrical Art*. Berkeley: University of California Press, 1988.

Yoder, Audrey. *Animal Analogy in Shakespeare's Character Portrayal*. New York: King's Crown Press, 1947.

Thematic and Topical Approaches

Alexander, Peter. *Alexander's Introductions to Shakespeare*. London: Collins, 1964.

Allman, Eileen Jorge. *Player-King and Adversary: Two Faces of Play in Shakespeare.* Baton Rouge: Louisiana State University Press, 1980.

Armstrong, Edward A. *Shakespeare's Imagination: A Study of the Psychology of Association and Inspiration.* London: Lindsay Drummond, 1946.

Arthos, John. *The Art of Shakespeare.* London: Bowes & Bowes, 1964.

──────────. *Shakespeare: The Early Writings.* Totowa, N.J.: Rowman & Littlefield, 1972.

Bamber, Linda. *Comic Women, Tragic Men: A Study of Gender and Genre in Shakespeare.* Stanford, Calif.: Stanford University Press, 1982.

Berger, Harry, Jr. *Imaginary Audition: Shakespeare on Stage and Page.* Berkeley: University of California Press, 1989.

Bevington, David, and Jay L. Halio, eds. *Shakespeare: Pattern of Excelling Nature.* Newark: University of Delaware Press, 1978.

Billington, Sandra. *Mock Kings in Medieval Society and Renaissance Drama.* Oxford, England: Clarendon Press, 1991.

Bilton, Peter. *Commentary and Control in Shakespeare's Plays.* New York: Humanities Press, 1974.

Birney, Alice Lotuin. *Satiric Catharsis in Shakespeare: A Theory of Dramatic Structure.* Berkeley: University of California Press, 1973.

Bowers, Fredson. *Hamlet as Minister and Scourge and Other Studies in Shakespeare and Milton.* Charlottesville: University Press of Virginia, 1989.

Bradshaw, Graham. *Shakespeare's Scepticism: Nature and Value in Shakespeare's Plays.* Brighton, England: Harvester, 1987.

Brissenden, Alan. *Shakespeare and the Dance.* Atlantic Highlands, N.J.: Humanities Press, 1981.

Brownlow, Frank Walsh. *Two Shakespearean Sequences: "Henry VI" to "Richard II" and "Pericles" to "Timon of Athens."* Pittsburgh: University of Pittsburgh Press, 1977.

Bryant, Joseph A., Jr. *Hippolyta's View: Some Christian Aspects of Shakespeare's Plays.* Lexington: University of Kentucky Press, 1961.

Bush, Geoffrey. *Shakespeare and the Natural Condition.* Cambridge, Mass.: Harvard University Press, 1956.

Calderwood, James L. *Shakespearean Metadrama: The Argument of the Play in "Titus Andronicus," "Love's Labour's Lost," "Romeo and Juliet," "A Midsummer Night's Dream," and "Richard II."* Minneapolis: University of Minnesota Press, 1971.

Campbell, Oscar James. *Shakespeare's Satire.* Oxford, England: Oxford University Press, 1943.

Chambers, Edmund Kerchever. *Shakespeare: A Survey.* London: Sedgwick & Jackson, 1925.

Clemen, Wolfgang H. *Shakespeare's Dramatic Art: Collected Essays.* London: Methuen, 1972.

Cook, Ann Jennalie. *Making a Match: Courtship in Shakespeare and His Society.* Princeton, N.J.: Princeton University Press, 1991.

Cook, Judith. *Women in Shakespeare.* London: Harrap, 1980.

Council, Norman. *When Honour's at the Stake: Ideas of Honour in Shakespeare's Plays*. London: George Allen & Unwin, 1973.

Craig, Hardin. *An Interpretation of Shakespeare*. New York: Dryden Press, 1948.

Cutts, John P. *The Shattered Glass: A Dramatic Pattern in Shakespeare's Early Plays*. Detroit: Wayne State University Press, 1968.

Dash, Irene G. *Wooing, Wedding, and Power: Women in Shakespeare's Plays*. New York: Columbia University Press, 1981.

Dawson, Anthony B. *Indirections: Shakespeare and the Art of Illusion*. Toronto: University of Toronto Press, 1978.

Dessen, Alan C. *Elizabethan Drama and Viewer's Eye*. Chapel Hill: University of North Carolina Press, 1977.

Dickey, Franklin M. *Not Wisely But Too Well*. San Marino, Calif.: Huntington Library, 1957.

Dollimore, Jonathan, and Alan Sinfield, eds. *Political Shakespeare: New Essays in Cultural Materialism*. Ithaca, N.Y.: Cornell University Press, 1985.

Drakakis, John, ed. *Alternative Shakespeares*. London: Methuen, 1985.

Dreher, Diane Elizabeth. *Domination and Defiance: Fathers and Daughters in Shakespeare*. Lexington: University Press of Kentucky, 1986.

Driscoll, James P. *Identity in Shakespearean Drama*. Lewisburg, Pa.: Bucknell University Press, 1983.

Dusinbere, Juliet. *Shakespeare and the Nature of Women*. New York: Barnes & Noble Books, 1975.

Eagleton, Terry. *William Shakespeare*. Oxford, England: Basil Blackwell, 1986.

Edwards, Philip. *Shakespeare and the Confines of Art*. London: Methuen, 1968.

Egan, Robert. *Drama Within Drama: Shakespeare's Sense of His Art in "King Lear," "The Winter's Tale," and "The Tempest."* New York: Columbia University Press, 1975.

Ellis-Fermor, Una. *The Frontiers of Drama*. London: Methuen, 1945.

_____. *The Jacobean Drama: An Interpretation*. London: Methuen, 1936.

Erickson, Peter. *Patriarchal Structures in Shakespeare's Drama*. Berkeley: University of California Press, 1985.

Farnham, Willard. *The Shakespeare Grotesque: Its Genesis and Transformation*. Oxford, England: Clarendon Press, 1971.

Ferguson, Margaret W., Maureen Quilligan, and Nancy J. Vickers, eds. *Rewriting the Renaissance: The Discourses of Sexual Difference in Early Modern Europe*. Chicago: University of Chicago Press, 1986.

Fergusson, Francis. *Shakespeare: The Pattern in His Carpet*. New York: Delacorte Press, 1970.

Fiedler, Leslie. *The Stranger in Shakespeare*. New York: Stein & Day, 1972.

Fitch, Robert E. *Shakespeare: The Perspective of Value*. Philadelphia: Westminster Press, 1969.

Foas, Ekbert. *Shakespeare's Poetics*. Cambridge, England: Cambridge University Press, 1981.

French, Marilyn. *Shakespeare's Division of Experience*. New York: Summit Books, 1981.

Frye, Roland Mushat. *Shakespeare and Christian Doctrine*. Princeton, N.J.: Princeton University Press, 1963.

Garber, Marjorie. *Coming of Age in Shakespeare*. London: Methuen, 1981.

——————. *Dream in Shakespeare: From Metaphor to Metamorphosis*. New Haven, Conn.: Yale University Press, 1974.

Girard, René. *A Theater of Envy: William Shakespeare*. New York: Oxford University Press, 1991.

Goldman, Michael. *Shakespeare and the Energies of Drama*. Princeton, N.J.: Princeton University Press, 1972.

Goldsmith, Robert Hillis. *Wise Fools in Shakespeare*. Liverpool, England: Liverpool University Press, 1955.

Granville-Barker, Harley. *Prefaces to Shakespeare*. 4 vols. Princeton, N.J.: Princeton University Press, 1963.

Grudin, Robert. *Mighty Opposites: Shakespeare and Renaissance Contrariety*. Berkeley: University of California Press, 1979.

Hallett, Charles, and Elaine Hallett. *Analyzing Shakespeare's Action: Scene vs. Sequence*. Cambridge, England: Cambridge University Press, 1991.

Hamilton, A. C. *The Early Shakespeare*. San Marino, Calif.: Huntington Library, 1967.

Hapgood, Robert. *Shakespeare the Theatre-Poet*. Oxford, England: Clarendon Press, 1988.

Harbage, Alfred. *As They Liked It: A Study on Shakespeare and Morality*. New York: Macmillan, 1947.

——————. *Shakespeare Without Words and Other Essays*. Cambridge, Mass.: Harvard University Press, 1972.

Hartwig, Joan. *Shakespeare's Analogical Scene: Parody as Structural Syntax*. Lincoln: University of Nebraska Press, 1983.

Henn, T. R. *The Living Image: Shakespearean Essays*. London: Methuen, 1972.

Hirsh, James E. *The Structure of Shakespearean Scenes*. New Haven, Conn.: Yale University Press, 1981.

Holderness, Graham, ed. *The Shakespeare Myth*. Manchester, England: Manchester University Press, 1988.

Holderness, Graham, Nick Potter, and John Turner. *Shakespeare: The Play of History*. Iowa City: University of Iowa Press, 1988.

Holland, Norman N. *Psychoanalysis and Shakespeare*. New York: McGraw-Hill, 1966.

——————. *The Shakespearean Imagination*. London: Macmillan, 1964.

Homan, Sidney. *When the Theater Turns to Itself: The Aesthetic Metaphor in Shakespeare*. Lewisburg, Pa.: Bucknell University Press, 1981.

Howard, Jean E. *Shakespeare's Art of Orchestration: Stage Technique and Audience Response*. Urbana: University of Illinois Press, 1984.

Howard, Jean E., and Marion F. O'Conner, eds. *Shakespeare Reproduced: The Text in History and Ideology*. London: Methuen, 1987.

Jochum, Klaus Peter. *Discrepant Awareness: Studies in English Renaissance Drama*. Frankfurt, Germany: Peter Lang, 1979.

Jorgensen, Paul A. *Shakespeare's Military World*. Berkeley: University of California Press, 1956.

Kahn, Coppélia. *Man's Estate: Masculine Identity in Shakespeare*. Berkeley: University of California Press, 1981.

Kastan, David Scott. *Shakespeare and the Shapes of Time*. Hanover, N.H.: University Press of New England, 1982.

Kernan, Alvin B. *The Playwright as Magician: Shakespeare's Image of the Poet in the English Public Theater*. New Haven, Conn.: Yale University Press, 1979.

Kirschbaum, Leo. *Character and Characterization in Shakespeare*. Detroit: Wayne State University Press, 1962.

Knight, G. Wilson. *The Crown of Life: Essays in Interpretation of Shakespeare's Final Plays*. 2d ed. London: Methuen, 1948.

_____. *The Shakespearean Tempest: With a Chart of Shakespeare's Dramatic Universe*. Oxford, England: Oxford University Press, 1932.

Knights, L. C. *Some Shakespearean Themes*. Stanford, Calif.: Stanford University Press, 1960.

Kott, Jan. *Shakespeare Our Contemporary*. Translated by Boleslaw Taborski. Garden City, N.Y.: Doubleday, 1964.

Laroque, François. *Shakespeare's Festive World: Elizabethan Seasonal Entertainment and the Professional Stage*. Translated by Janet Lloyd. Cambridge, England: Cambridge University Press, 1991.

Lenz, Carolyn, Ruth Swift, Gayle Greene, and Carol Thomas Neely, eds. *The Woman's Part: Feminist Criticism of Shakespeare*. Urbana: University of Illinois Press, 1980.

Levin, Harry. *Shakespeare and the Revolution of the Times: Perspectives and Commentaries*. New York: Oxford University Press, 1976.

Lewis, Percy Wyndham. *The Lion and the Fox: The Role of the Hero in the Plays of Shakespeare*. London: Grant Richards, 1927.

Long, John H. *Shakespeare's Use of Music: A Study of the Music and Its Performance in the Original Production of Seven Comedies*. Gainesville: University of Florida Press, 1955.

_____. *Shakespeare's Use of Music: The Final Comedies*. Gainesville: University of Florida Press, 1961.

_____. *Shakespeare's Use of Music: The Histories and Tragedies*. Gainesville: University of Florida Press, 1971.

McAlindon, Thomas. *Shakespeare and Decorum*. London: Macmillan, 1973.

McDonald, Russ, ed. *Shakespeare Reread: The Texts in New Contexts*. Ithaca, N.Y.: Cornell University Press, 1994.

Marienstras, Richard. *New Perspectives on the Shakespearean World*. Translated by Janet Lloyd. Cambridge, England: Cambridge University Press, 1985.

Masefield, John. *William Shakespeare*. New York: Barnes & Noble Books, 1954.

Murry, John Middleton. *Shakespeare*. London: Jonathan Cape, 1936.

Naylor, Edward W. *Shakespeare and Music*. 2d ed. London: J. M. Dent & Sons, 1931.

Neely, Carol Thomas. *Broken Nuptials in Shakespeare's Plays*. New Haven, Conn.: Yale University Press, 1985.

Nicoll, Allardyee. *Shakespeare: An Introduction*. New York: Oxford University Press, 1952.

Noble, Richmond. *Shakespeare's Use of Song: With the Text of the Principal Songs*. Oxford, England: Oxford University Press, 1923.

Novy, Marianne. *Love's Argument: Gender Relations in Shakespeare*. Chapel Hill: University of North Carolina Press, 1984.

Parker, M. D. H. *The Slave of Life: A Study of Shakespeare and the Idea of Justice*. London: Chatto & Windus, 1955.

Parker, Patricia, and Geoffrey Hartman, eds. *Shakespeare and the Question of Theory*. London: Methuen, 1985.

Pitt, Angela. *Shakespeare's Women*. Totowa, N.J.: Barnes & Noble Books, 1981.

Rabkin, Norman. *Shakespeare and the Common Understanding*. New York: Free Press, 1967.

——————. *Shakespeare and the Problem of Meaning*. Chicago: University of Chicago Press, 1981.

Raleigh, Walter. *Shakespeare*. London: Macmillan, 1907.

Righter, Anne. *Shakespeare and the Idea of the Play*. London: Chatto & Windus, 1962.

Rose, Mark. *Shakespearean Design*. Cambridge, Mass.: Harvard University Press, 1972.

Sanders, Wilbur. *The Dramatist and the Received Idea: Studies in the Plays of Marlowe and Shakespeare*. Cambridge, England: Cambridge University Press, 1968.

Schanzer, Ernest. *The Problem Plays of Shakespeare: A Study of "Julius Caesar," "Measure for Measure," and "Antony and Cleopatra."* London: Routledge & Kegan Paul, 1963.

Sen Gupta, S. C. *The Whirligig of Time: The Problem of Duration in Shakespeare's Plays*. Bombay, India: Orient Longman's, 1961.

Seng, Peter J. *The Vocal Songs in the Plays of Shakespeare: A Critical History*. Cambridge, Mass.: Harvard University Press, 1967.

Siegel, Paul N. *Shakespeare in His Time and Ours*. South Bend, Ind.: University of Notre Dame Press, 1968.

Skulsky, Harold. *Spirits Finely Touched: The Testing of Value and Integrity in Four Shakespearean Plays*. Athens: University of Georgia Press, 1976.

Smith, Marion Bodwell. *Dualities in Shakespeare*. Toronto: University of Toronto Press, 1966.

Soellner, Rolf. *Shakespeare's Patterns of Self-Knowledge*. Columbus: Ohio State University Press, 1972.

Spencer, Theodore. *Shakespeare and the Nature of Man*. New York: Macmillan, 1942.

Sternfeld, Frederick W. *Music in Shakespearean Tragedy*. London: Routledge & Kegan Paul, 1963.

Stirling, Brents. *The Populace in Shakespeare*. New York: Columbia University Press, 1949.

Summers, Joseph H. *Dreams of Love and Power: On Shakespeare's Plays*. Oxford, England: Clarendon Press, 1984.

Sundelson, David. *Shakespeare's Restorations of the Father*. New Brunswick, N.J.: Rutgers University Press, 1983.

Talbert, Ernest Williams. *Elizabethan Drama and Shakespeare's Early Plays: An Essay in Historical Criticism*. Chapel Hill: University of North Carolina Press, 1963.

Taylor, Mark. *Shakespeare's Darker Purpose: A Question of Incest*. New York: AMS Press, 1982.

Tennenhouse, Leonard. *Power on Display: The Politics of Shakespeare's Genres*. London: Methuen, 1986.

Thaler, Alwin. *Shakespeare and Our World*. Knoxville: University of Tennessee Press, 1966.

——————. *Shakespeare's Silences*. Cambridge, Mass.: Harvard University Press, 1929.

Turner, Frederick. *Shakespeare and the Nature of Time: Moral and Philosophical Themes in Some Plays and Poems of William Shakespeare*. Oxford, England: Clarendon Press, 1971.

Turner, Robert Y. *Shakespeare's Apprenticeship*. Chicago: University of Chicago Press, 1974.

Van den Berg, Kent T. *Playhouse and Cosmos: Shakespearean Theater as Metaphor*. Newark: University of Delaware Press, 1985.

Van Doren, Mark. *Shakespeare*. New York: Henry Holt, 1939.

Van Laan, Thomas F. *Role-Playing in Shakespeare*. Toronto: University of Toronto Press, 1978.

Wain, John. *The Living World of Shakespeare: A Playgoer's Guide*. New York: St. Martin's Press, 1964.

Watson, Robert N. *Shakespeare and the Hazards of Ambition*. Cambridge, Mass.: Harvard University Press, 1984.

Weiss, Theodore. *The Breath of Clowns and Kings: Shakespeare's Early Comedies and Histories*. New York: Atheneum, 1971.

West, Robert H. *Shakespeare and the Outer Mystery*. Lexington: University of Kentucky Press, 1968.

Women's Studies 9, nos. 1-2 (1981-1982).

Wright, George T. *Shakespeare's Metrical Art*. Berkeley: University of California Press, 1988.

Zeeveld, W. Gordon. *The Temper of Shakespeare's Thought*. New Haven, Conn.: Yale University Press, 1974.

Zukofsky, Louis. *Bottom: On Shakespeare, with Music to "Pericles" by Celia Zukofsky*. 2 vols. Austin: University of Texas Press, 1963.

Comedies

Anderson, Linda. *A Kind of Wild Justice: Revenge in Shakespeare's Comedies.* Newark: University of Delaware Press, 1987.

Barber, C. L. *Shakespeare's Festive Comedy: A Study of Dramatic Form and Its Relation to Social Custom.* Princeton, N.J.: Princeton University Press, 1959.

Bergeron, David M. *Shakespeare's Romances and the Royal Family.* Lawrence: University Press of Kansas, 1985.

Berry, Edward. *Shakespeare's Comic Rites.* Cambridge, England: Cambridge University Press, 1984.

Berry, Ralph. *Shakespeare's Comedies: Explorations in Form.* Princeton, N.J.: Princeton University Press, 1972.

Brown, John Russell. *Shakespeare and His Comedies.* 2d ed. London: Methuen, 1962.

Bryant, J. A., Jr. *Shakespeare and the Uses of Comedy.* Lexington: University Press of Kentucky, 1986.

Carroll, William C. *The Metamorphoses of Shakespearean Comedy.* Princeton, N.J.: Princeton University Press, 1985.

Champion, Larry S. *The Evolution of Shakespeare's Comedy: A Study in Dramatic Perspective.* Cambridge, Mass.: Harvard University Press, 1972.

Charlton, H. B. *Shakespearian Comedy.* London: Methuen, 1938.

Charney, Maurice, ed. *Shakespearean Comedy.* New York: New York Literary Forum, 1980.

Elam, Keir. *Shakespeare's Universe of Discourse: Language-Games in the Comedies.* Cambridge, England: Cambridge University Press, 1984.

Evans, Bertrand. *Shakespeare's Comedies.* Oxford, England: Clarendon Press, 1960.

Felperin, Howard. *Shakespearean Romance.* Princeton, N.J.: Princeton University Press, 1972.

Foakes, R. A. *Shakespeare: The Dark Comedies to the Last Plays, from Satire to Celebration.* Charlottesville: University Press of Virginia, 1971.

Frye, Northrop. *The Myth of Deliverance: Reflections on Shakespeare's Problem Comedies.* Toronto: University of Toronto Press, 1983.

——————. *A Natural Perspective: The Development of Shakespearean Comedy and Romance.* New York: Columbia University Press, 1965.

Hart, John A. *Dramatic Structure in Shakespeare's Romantic Comedies.* Pittsburgh: Carnegie-Mellon University Press, 1980.

Hartwig, Joan. *Shakespeare's Tragicomic Vision.* Baton Rouge: Louisiana State University Press, 1972.

Hassel, R. Chris, Jr. *Faith and Folly in Shakespeare's Romantic Comedies.* Athens: University of Georgia Press, 1980.

Hunt, Maurice. *Shakespeare's Romance of the Word.* Lewisburg, Pa.: Bucknell University Press, 1990.

Hunter, Robert G. *Shakespeare and the Comedy of Forgiveness.* New York: Columbia University Press, 1965.

Huston, J. Dennis. *Shakespeare's Comedies of Play*. New York: Columbia University Press, 1981.

Jensen, Ejner. *Shakespeare and the Ends of Comedy*. Bloomington: Indiana University Press, 1991.

Kay, Carol McGinnis, and Henry E. Jacobs, eds. *Shakespeare's Romances Reconsidered*. Lincoln: University of Nebraska Press, 1978.

Krieger, Elliot. *A Marxist Study of Shakespeare's Comedies*. London: Macmillan, 1979.

Lawrence, William Witherle. *Shakespeare's Problem Comedies*. Rev. ed. Harmondsworth, England: Penguin Books, 1969.

Leech, Clifford. *"Twelfth Night" and Shakespearean Comedy*. Halifax, Nova Scotia: Dalhousie University Press, 1965.

Leggatt, Alexander. *Shakespeare's Comedy of Love*. London: Methuen, 1973.

Lerner, Laurence, ed. *Shakespeare's Comedies: An Anthology of Modern Criticism*. Harmondsworth, England: Penguin Books, 1967.

Levin, Richard A. *Love and Society in Shakespearean Comedy: A Study of Dramatic Form and Content*. Newark: University of Delaware Press, 1985.

MacCary, W. Thomas. *Friends and Lovers: The Phenomenology of Desire in Shakespearean Comedy*. New York: Columbia University Press, 1985.

Macdonald, Ronald R. *William Shakespeare: The Comedies*. New York: Twayne, 1992.

McFarland, Thomas. *Shakespeare's Pastoral Comedy*. Chapel Hill: University of North Carolina Press, 1972.

Mowat, Barbara A. *The Dramaturgy of Shakespeare's Romances*. Athens: University of Georgia Press, 1976.

Muir, Kenneth, ed. *Shakespeare: The Comedies*. Englewood Cliffs, N.J.: Prentice-Hall, 1965.

_____. *Shakespeare's Comic Sequence*. Liverpool, England: Liverpool University Press, 1979.

Muir, Kenneth, and Stanley Wells, eds. *Aspects of Shakespeare's Problem Plays: "All's Well That Ends Well," "Measure for Measure," "Troilus and Cressida."* Cambridge, England: Cambridge University Press, 1982.

Nevo, Ruth. *Comic Transformations in Shakespeare*. London: Methuen, 1980.

Newman, Karen. *Shakespeare's Rhetoric of Comic Character: Dramatic Convention in Classical and Renaissance Comedy*. London: Methuen, 1985.

Ornstein, Robert. *Shakespeare's Comedies: From Roman Farce to Romantic Mystery*. Newark: University of Delaware Press, 1986.

Palmer, David, and Malcolm Bradbury, eds. *Shakespearean Comedy*. Stratford-upon-Avon Studies 14. New York: Crane, Russak, 1972.

_____, eds. *Shakespeare's Later Comedies: An Anthology of Modern Criticism*. Harmondsworth, England: Penguin Books, 1971.

Palmer, John Leslie. *Comic Characters of Shakespeare*. London: Macmillan, 1946.

Peterson, Douglas L. *Time, Tide, and Tempest: A Study of Shakespeare's Romances*. San Marino, Calif.: Huntington Library, 1973.

Pettet, E. C. *Shakespeare and the Romance Tradition*. London: Staples Press, 1949.

Phialas, Peter G. *Shakespeare's Romantic Comedies: The Development of Their Form and Meaning*. Chapel Hill: University of North Carolina Press, 1966.

Richman, David. *Laughter, Pain, and Wonder: Shakespeare's Comedies and the Audience in the Theater*. Newark: University of Delaware Press, 1990.

Riemer, A. P. *Antic Fables: Patterns of Evasion in Shakespeare's Comedies*. New York: St. Martin's Press, 1980.

Salinger, Leo G. *Shakespeare and the Traditions of Comedy*. Cambridge, England: Cambridge University Press, 1974.

Sen Gupta, S. C. *Shakespearean Comedy*. London: Oxford University Press, 1950.

Slights, Camille Wells. *Shakespeare's Comic Commonwealths*. Toronto: University of Toronto Press, 1993.

Smidt, Kristian. *Unconformities in Shakespeare's Early Comedies*. New York: St. Martin's Press, 1986.

Smith, Hallett. *Shakespeare's Romances: A Study of Some Ways of the Imagination*. San Marino, Calif.: Huntington Library, 1972.

Swinden, Patrick. *An Introduction to Shakespeare's Comedies*. London: Macmillan, 1973.

Thomas, Vivian. *The Moral Universe of Shakespeare's Problem Plays*. Totowa, N.J.: Barnes & Noble Books, 1987.

Tillyard, E. M. W. *Shakespeare's Early Comedies*. London: Chatto & Windus, 1965.

——————. *Shakespeare's Last Plays*. London: Chatto & Windus, 1938.

——————. *Shakespeare's Problem Plays*. Toronto: University of Toronto Press, 1949.

Toole, William B. *Shakespeare's Problem Plays: Studies in Form and Meaning*. The Hague: Mouton, 1966.

Traversi, Derek. *Shakespeare: The Last Phase*. Stanford, Calif.: Stanford University Press, 1955.

Uphaus, Robert W. *Beyond Tragedy: Structure and Experience in Shakespeare's Romances*. Lexington: University Press of Kentucky, 1981.

Weil, Herbert, Jr., ed. *Discussions of Shakespeare's Romantic Comedy*. Boston: D. C. Heath, 1966.

Westlund, Joseph. *Shakespearean Reparative Comedy: A Psychological View of the Middle Plays*. Chicago: University of Chicago Press, 1984.

White, R. S. *"Let Wonder Seem Familiar": Endings in Shakespeare's Romance Vision*. Atlantic Heights, N.J.: Humanities Press, 1985.

Williamson, Marilyn L. *The Patriarchy of Shakespeare's Comedies*. Detroit: Wayne State University Press, 1986.

Wilson, John Dover. *Shakespeare's Happy Comedies*. Evanston, Ill.: Northwestern University Press, 1962.

Young, David P. *The Heart's Forest: A Study of Shakespeare's Pastoral Plays*. New Haven, Conn.: Yale University Press, 1972.

Histories

Armstrong, William A., ed. *Shakespeare's Histories: An Anthology of Modern Criticism*. Harmondsworth, England: Penguin Books, 1972.

Berry, Edward. *Patterns of Decay: Shakespeare's Early Histories*. Charlottesville: University Press of Virginia. 1975.

Bloom, Harold, ed. *William Shakespeare: Histories and Poems*. New York: Chelsea House, 1986.

Blanpied, John W. *Time and the Artist in Shakespeare's English Histories*. Newark: University of Delaware Press, 1983.

Calderwood, James L. *Metadrama in Shakespeare's Henriad*. Berkeley: University of California Press, 1979.

Campbell, Lily Bess. *Shakespeare's "Histories": Mirrors of Elizabethan Policy*. San Marino, Calif.: Huntington Library, 1947.

Champion, Larry S. *"The Noise of Threatening Drum": Dramatic Strategy and Political Ideology in Shakespeare and the English Chronicle Plays*. Newark: University of Delaware Press, 1990.

——————. *Perspectives in Shakespeare's English Histories*. Athens: University of Georgia Press, 1980.

Coursen, Herbert R. *The Leasing Out of England: Shakespeare's Second Henriad*. Washington, D.C.: University Press of America, 1982.

Holderness, Graham. *Shakespeare's History*. New York: St. Martin's Press, 1985.

Hodgdon, Barbara. *The End Crowns All: Closure and Contradiction in Shakespeare's History*. Princeton, N.J.: Princeton University Press, 1991.

Jones, Robert C. *These Valiant Dead: Renewing the Past in Shakespeare's Histories*. Iowa City: University of Iowa Press, 1991.

Kelly, Henry A. *Divine Providence in the England of Shakespeare's Histories*. Cambridge, Mass.: Harvard University Press, 1970.

Ornstein, Robert. *A Kingdom for a Stage: The Achievement of Shakespeare's History Plays*. Cambridge, Mass.: Harvard University Press, 1972.

Pierce, Robert B. *Shakespeare's History Plays: The Family and the State*. Columbus: Ohio State University Press, 1971.

Porter, Joseph A. *The Drama of Speech Acts: Shakespeare's Lancasterian Tetralogy*. Berkeley: University of California Press, 1979.

Rackin, Phyllis. *Stages of History: Shakespeare's English Chronicles*. Ithaca, N.Y.: Cornell University Press, 1990.

Reed, Robert Rentoul, Jr. *Crime and God's Judgment in Shakespeare*. Lexington: University Press of Kentucky, 1984.

Reese, M. M. *The Cease of Majesty: A Study of Shakespeare's History Plays*. New York: St. Martin's Press, 1961.

Ribner, Irving. *The English History Play in the Age of Shakespeare*. Rev. ed. New York: Barnes & Noble Books, 1965.

Saccio, Peter. *Shakespeare's English Kings: History, Chronicle, and Drama*. London: Oxford University Press, 1977.

Sen Gupta, S. C. *Shakespeare's Historical Plays*. London: Oxford University Press, 1964.

Siegel, Paul N. *Shakespeare's English and Roman History Plays: A Marxist Approach*. Rutherford, N.J.: Fairleigh Dickinson University Press, 1986.

Smidt, Kristian. *Unconformities in Shakespeare's History Plays*. Atlantic Highlands, N.J.: Humanities Press, 1982.

Thayer, C. G. *Shakespearean Politics: Government and Misgovernment in the Great Histories*. Athens: Ohio University Press, 1983.

Tillyard, E. M. W. *Shakespeare's History Plays*. London: Macmillan, 1944.

Traversi, Derek. *Shakespeare from "Richard II" to "Henry V."* Stanford, Calif.: Stanford University Press, 1957.

Waith, Eugene M., ed. *Shakespeare, the Histories: A Collection of Critical Essays*. Englewood Cliffs, N.J.: Prentice-Hall, 1965.

Watson, Donald G. *Shakespeare's Early History Plays: Politics at Play on the Elizabethan Stage*. Athens: University of Georgia Press, 1990.

Wilders, John. *The Lost Garden: A View of Shakespeare's English and Roman Plays*. New York: Macmillan, 1978.

Winny, James. *The Player King: A Theme of Shakespeare's Histories*. New York: Barnes & Noble Books, 1968.

Tragedies

Battenhouse, Roy W. *Shakespearean Tragedy: Its Art and Its Christian Premises*. Bloomington: Indiana University Press, 1969.

Bayley, John. *Shakespeare and Tragedy*. London: Routledge & Kegan Paul, 1981.

Bloom, Harold, ed. *William Shakespeare: The Tragedies*. New York: Chelsea House, 1985.

Booth, Stephen. *"King Lear," "Macbeth," Indefinition, and Tragedy*. New Haven, Conn.: Yale University Press, 1983.

Bradbrook, Muriel C. *Themes and Conventions of Elizabethan Tragedy*. London: Cambridge University Press, 1935.

Bradley, Andrew C. *Shakespearean Tragedy*. London: Macmillan, 1904.

Brooke, Nicholas. *Shakespeare's Early Tragedies*. London: Methuen, 1968.

Brower, Reuben Arthur. *Hero and Saint: Shakespeare and the Greco-Roman Heroic Tradition*. New York: Oxford University Press, 1971.

Bulman, James C. *The Heroic Idiom of Shakespearean Tragedy*. Newark: University of Delaware Press, 1985.

Campbell, Lily B. *Shakespeare's Tragic Heroes: Slaves of Passion*. Cambridge, England: Cambridge University Press, 1930.

Cantor, Paul A. *Shakespeare's Rome: Republic and Empire*. Ithaca, N.Y.: Cornell University Press, 1976.

Champion, Larry S. *Shakespeare's Tragic Perspective*. Athens: University of Georgia Press, 1976.

Charlton, H. B. *Shakespearean Tragedy*. Cambridge, England: Cambridge University Press, 1948.

Charney, Maurice, ed. *Discussions of Shakespeare's Roman Plays*. Indianapolis: D. C. Heath, 1964.

_____. *Shakespeare's Roman Plays: The Function of Imagery in the Drama*. Cambridge, Mass.: Harvard University Press, 1961.

Coursen, Herbert R., Jr. *Christian Ritual and the World of Shakespeare's Tragedies*. Lewisburg, Pa.: Bucknell University Press, 1976.

Creeth, Edmund. *Mankynde in Shakespeare*. Athens: University of Georgia Press, 1976.

Danson, Lawrence. *Tragic Alphabet: Shakespeare's Drama of Language*. New Haven, Conn.: Yale University Press, 1974.

Evans, Bertrand. *Shakespeare's Tragic Practice*. Oxford, England: Clarendon Press, 1979.

Everett, Barbara. *Young Hamlet: Essays on Shakespeare's Tragedies*. Oxford, England: Clarendon Press, 1989.

Farnham, Willard. *Shakespeare's Tragic Frontier: The World of His Final Tragedies*. Berkeley: University of California Press, 1950.

Felperin, Howard. *Shakespearean Representation: Mimesis and Modernity in Elizabethan Tragedy*. Princeton, N.J.: Princeton University Press, 1977.

Foreman, Walter C., Jr. *The Music of the Close: The Final Scenes of Shakespeare's Tragedies*. Lexington: University Press of Kentucky, 1978.

Frye, Northrop. *Fools of Time: Studies in Shakespearean Tragedy*. Toronto: University of Toronto Press, 1967.

Goldman, Michael. *Acting and Action in Shakespearean Tragedy*. Princeton, N.J.: Princeton University Press, 1985.

Grene, Nicholas. *Shakespeare's Tragic Imagination*. New York: St. Martin's, 1992.

Harbage, Alfred, ed. *Shakespeare: The Tragedies, a Collection of Critical Essays*. Englewood Cliffs, N.J.: Prentice-Hall, 1964.

Harrison, George Bagshawe. *Shakespeare's Tragedies*. London: Routledge & Kegan Paul, 1951.

Heilman, Robert B., ed. *Shakespeare: The Tragedies, New Perspectives*. Englewood Cliffs, N.J.: Prentice-Hall, 1984.

Holloway, John. *The Story of the Night: Studies in Shakespeare's Major Tragedies*. London: Routledge & Kegan Paul, 1961.

Honigmann, E. A. J. *Shakespeare: Seven Tragedies, the Dramatist's Manipulation of Response*. London: Macmillan, 1976.

Hunter, Robert G. *Shakespeare and the Mystery of God's Judgments*. Athens: University of Georgia Press, 1976.

Jorgensen, Paul A. *William Shakespeare: The Tragedies*. Boston: Twayne, 1985.

Kirsch, Arthur. *The Passions of Shakespeare's Tragic Heroes*. Charlottesville: University Press of Virginia, 1990.

Knight, G. Wilson. *The Imperial Theme*. 3d ed. London: Methuen, 1951.

_____. *The Wheel of Fire*. Rev. ed. London: Methuen, 1949.

Lawlor, John. *The Tragic Sense in Shakespeare*. New York: Harcourt, Brace, 1960.

Leech, Clifford, ed. *Shakespeare: The Tragedies, a Collection of Critical Essays*. Chicago: University of Chicago Press, 1965.

Lerner, Laurence, ed. *Shakespeare's Tragedies: A Selection of Modern Criticism.* Harmondsworth, England: Penguin Books, 1963.

Long, Michael. *The Unnatural Scene: A Study in Shakespearean Tragedy.* London: Methuen, 1976.

McAlindon, Thomas. *Shakespeare's Tragic Cosmos.* Cambridge, England: Cambridge University Press, 1991.

MacCallum, Mungo W. *Shakespeare's Roman Plays and Their Background.* London: Macmillan, 1910.

McElroy, Bernard. *Shakespeare's Mature Tragedies.* Princeton, N.J.: Princeton University Press, 1973.

Mack, Maynard. *Everybody's Shakespeare: Reflections Chiefly on the Tragedies.* Lincoln: University of Nebraska Press, 1993.

Marsh, Derick R. C. *Passion Lends Them Power: A Study of Shakespeare's Love Tragedies.* Manchester, England: Manchester University Press, 1976.

Mason, Harold A. *Shakespeare's Tragedies of Love: An Examination of the Possibility of Common Readings of "Romeo and Juliet," "Othello," "King Lear," and "Antony and Cleopatra."* London: Chatto & Windus, 1970.

Mehl, Dieter. *Shakespeare's Tragedies: An Introduction.* Cambridge, England: Cambridge University Press, 1987.

Milward, Peter. *Biblical Influences in Shakespeare's Great Tragedies.* Bloomington: Indiana University Press, 1987.

Miola, Robert S. *Shakespeare's Rome.* Cambridge, England: Cambridge University Press, 1983.

Muir, Kenneth. *Shakespeare's Tragic Sequence.* London: Hutchinson University Library, 1972.

Nevo, Ruth. *Tragic Form in Shakespeare.* Princeton, N.J.: Princeton University Press, 1972.

Proser, Matthew N. *The Heroic Image in Five Shakespearean Tragedies.* Princeton, N.J.: Princeton University Press, 1965.

Rackin, Phyllis. *Shakespeare's Tragedies.* New York: Frederick Ungar, 1978.

Ribner, Irving. *Patterns in Shakespearean Tragedy.* New York: Barnes & Noble Books, 1960.

Rosen, William. *Shakespeare and the Craft of Tragedy.* Cambridge, Mass.: Harvard University Press, 1960.

Siegel, Paul N. *Shakespearean Tragedy and the Elizabethan Compromise.* New York: New York University Press, 1957.

Siemon, James R. *Shakespeare's Iconoclasm.* Berkeley: University of California Press, 1985.

Simmons, J. L. *Shakespeare's Pagan World: The Roman Tragedies.* Charlottesville: University Press of Virginia, 1973.

Smidt, Kristian. *Unconformities in Shakespeare's Tragedies.* New York: St. Martin's Press, 1990.

Snyder, Susan. *The Comic Matrix of Shakespeare's Tragedies: "Romeo and Juliet," "Hamlet," "Othello," and "King Lear."* Princeton, N.J.: Princeton University Press, 1979.

Speaight, Robert. *Nature in Shakespearean Tragedy*. London: Hollis & Carter, 1955.

Spivack, Bernard. *Shakespeare and the Allegory of Evil: The History of a Metaphor in Relation to His Major Villains*. New York: Columbia University Press, 1958.

Spurgeon, Caroline F. E. *Leading Motives in the Imagery of Shakespeare's Tragedies*. London: H. Milford, Oxford University Press, for the Shakespeare Association, 1930.

Stampfer, Judah. *The Tragic Engagement: A Study of Shakespeare's Classical Tragedies*. New York: Funk & Wagnalls, 1968.

Stirling, Brents. *Unity in Shakespearean Tragedy: The Interplay of Theme and Character*. New York: Columbia University Press, 1956.

Traversi, Derek. *Shakespeare: The Roman Plays*. Stanford, Calif.: Stanford University Press, 1963.

Whitaker, Virgil K. *The Mirror Up to Nature: The Technique of Shakespeare's Tragedies*. San Marino, Calif.: Huntington Library, 1965.

White, R. S. *Innocent Victims: Poetic Injustice in Shakespearean Tragedy*. 2d ed. London: Athlone Press, 1986.

Wilson, Harold S. *On the Design of Shakespearean Tragedy*. Toronto: University of Toronto Press, 1957.

Wilson, John Dover. *Six Tragedies of Shakespeare: An Introduction for the Plain Man*. London: Longmans, Green, 1929.

Young, David. *The Action to the Word: Structure and Style in Shakespearean Tragedy*. New Haven, Conn.: Yale University Press, 1990.

BIOGRAPHIES

Adams, Joseph Quincy. *A Life of Shakespeare*. Boston: Houghton Mifflin, 1923.

Bentley, Gerald Eades. *Shakespeare: A Biographical Handbook*. New Haven, Conn.: Yale University Press, 1961.

Bradbrook, M. C. *Shakespeare: The Poet in His World*. New York: Columbia University Press, 1978.

Burgess, Anthony. *Shakespeare*. New York: Alfred A. Knopf, 1970.

Burton, S. H. *Shakespeare's Life and Stage*. Edinburgh: W & R Chambers, 1989.

Chambers, Edmund Kerchever. *William Shakespeare: A Study of Facts and Problems*. 2 vols. Oxford, England: Clarendon Press, 1930.

Chute, Marchette. *Shakespeare of London*. New York: E. P. Dutton, 1949.

Fraser, Russell A. *Young Shakespeare*. New York: Columbia University Press, 1988.

Fraser, Russell. *Shakespeare: The Later Years*. New York: Columbia University Press, 1992.

Gurr, Andrew. *William Shakespeare: The Extraordinary Life of the Most Successful Writer of All Time*. New York: HarperPerennial, 1995.

Holland, Norman N., Sidney Homan, and Bernard J. Paris, eds. *Shakespeare's Personality*. Berkeley: University of California Press, 1989.

Honigmann, E. A. J. *Shakespeare: The Lost Years.* Totowa, N.J.: Barnes & Noble Books, 1985.

Levi, Peter. *The Life and Times of William Shakespeare.* New York: Henry Holt, 1989.

Quennell, Peter. *Shakespeare: A Biography.* Cleveland: World Publishing, 1963.

Reese, M. M. *Shakespeare: His World and His Work.* Rev. ed. New York: St. Martin's Press, 1980.

Rowse, A. L. *William Shakespeare.* New York: Macmillan, 1963.

Sams, Eric. *The Real Shakespeare: Retrieving the Early Years.* New Haven: Yale University Press, 1995.

Schoenbaum, Samuel. *Shakespeare's Lives.* New ed. New York: Oxford University Press, 1991.

—————. *William Shakespeare: A Documentary Life.* New York: Oxford University Press in association with Scolar Press, 1975.

—————. *William Shakespeare: Records and Images.* London: Scolar Press, 1981.

Thomson, Peter. *Shakespeare's Professional Career.* Cambridge: Cambridge University Press, 1992.

THE SHAKESPEAREAN STAGE

Adams, John Cranford. *The Globe Playhouse, Its Design and Equipment.* New York: Barnes & Noble Books, 1961.

Adams, Joseph Quincy. *Shakespearean Playhouses: A History of English Theaters from the Beginnings to the Restoration.* Boston: Houghton Mifflin, 1917.

Armstrong, William A. *The Elizabethan Private Theaters: Facts and Problems.* London: Society for Theatre Research, 1958.

Baldwin, Thomas Whitfield. *The Organization and Personnel of the Shakespearean Company.* Princeton, N.J.: Princeton University Press, 1927.

Barroll, Leeds. *Politics, Plague, and Shakespeare's Theater: The Stuart Years.* Ithaca, N.Y.: Cornell University Press, 1991.

Beckerman, Bernard. *Shakespeare at the Globe, 1599-1609.* New York: Macmillan, 1962.

Bentley, Gerald Eades. *The Profession of Player in Shakespeare's Time, 1590-1642.* Princeton, N.J.: Princeton University Press, 1984.

—————. *Shakespeare and His Theatre.* Lincoln: University of Nebraska Press, 1964.

Berry, Herbert, ed. *The First Public Playhouse: The Theatre in Shoreditch, 1576-1598.* Montreal: McGill-Queen's University Press, 1979.

—————. *Shakespeare's Playhouses.* New York: AMS Press, 1987.

Bradbrook, Muriel C. *Elizabethan Stage Conditions: A Study of Their Place in the Interpretation of Shakespeare's Plays.* Hamden, Conn.: Archon Books, 1962.

—————. *The Living Monument: Shakespeare and the Theatre of His Time.* Cambridge, England: Cambridge University Press, 1976.

_____. *The Rise of the Common Player: A Study of Actor and Society in Shakespeare's England*. Cambridge, England: Cambridge University Press, 1979.

Chambers, Edmund Kerchever. *The Elizabethan Stage*. 4 vols. Oxford, England: Clarendon Press, 1923.

Cohen, Walter. *Drama of a Nation: Public Theater in Renaissance England and Spain*. Ithaca, N.Y.: Cornell University Press, 1985.

Cook, Ann Jennalie. *The Privileged Playgoers of Shakespeare's London, 1576-1642*. Princeton, N.J.: Princeton University Press, 1981.

Dessen, Alan C. *Elizabethan Stage Conventions and Modern Interpreters*. Cambridge, England: Cambridge University Press, 1984.

Foakes, R. A. *Illustrations of the English Stage 1580-1642*. Stanford, Calif.: Stanford University Press, 1985.

Gair, Reavley. *The Children of Paul's: The Story of a Theatre Company, 1555-1608*. Cambridge, England: Cambridge University Press, 1982.

Greg, Walter Wilson, ed. *Dramatic Documents from the Elizabethan Playhouse*. 2 vols. Oxford, England: Clarendon Press, 1931.

Gurr, Andrew. *Playgoing in Shakespeare's London*. 2d ed. Cambridge: Cambridge University Press, 1996.

_____. *The Shakespearean Stage, 1574-1642*. 3d ed. Cambridge, England: Cambridge University Press, 1992.

Gurr, Andrew, with John Orrell. *Rebuilding Shakespeare's Globe*. London: Weidenfeld & Nicolson, 1989.

Harbage, Alfred. *Shakespeare's Audience*. New York: Columbia University Press, 1941.

Hattaway, Michael. *Elizabethan Popular Theatre: Plays in Performance*. London: Routledge & Kegan Paul, 1982.

Henslowe, Philip. *Henslowe's Diary*. Edited by R. A. Foakes and R. T. Rickert. Cambridge, England: Cambridge University Press, 1961.

Hillebrand, Harold Newcomb. *The Child Actors: A Chapter in Elizabethan Stage History*. University of Illinois Studies in Language and Literature 11, nos. 1 and 2. Urbana: University of Illinois Press, 1926.

Hodges, Cyril Walter. *The Globe Restored*. 2d ed. New York: W. W. Norton, 1973.

_____. *Shakespeare's Second Globe: The Missing Monument*. London: Oxford University Press, 1973.

Hodges, Cyril Walter, and Samuel Schoenbaum, eds. *The Third Globe: Symposium for the Reconstruction of the Globe Playhouse*. Detroit: Wayne State University Press, 1981.

Hotson, Leslie. *Shakespeare's Wooden O*. London: Rupert Hart-Davies, 1959.

Joseph, B. L. *Elizabethan Acting*. 2d ed. London: Oxford University Press, 1964.

Kernan, Alvin B. *Shakespeare, The King's Playwright: Theater in the Stuart Court, 1603-1613*. New Haven, Conn.: Yale University Press, 1995.

King, T. J. *Shakespearean Staging, 1599-1642*. Cambridge, Mass.: Harvard University Press, 1971.

Knutson, Roslyn Lander. *The Repertory of Shakespeare's Company: 1594-1613.* Fayetteville: University of Arkansas Press, 1991.

Linthicum, Marie Channing. *Costume in the Drama of Shakespeare and His Contemporaries.* Oxford, England: Clarendon Press, 1936.

Lomax, Marion. *Stage Images and Traditions: Shakespeare to Ford.* Cambridge, England: Cambridge University Press, 1987.

McMillin, Scott. *The Elizabethan Theatre and the Book of Sir Thomas More.* Ithaca, N.Y.: Cornell University Press, 1987.

Montrose, Louis A. *The Purpose of Playing: Shakespeare & the Cultural Politics of the Elizabethan Theatre.* Chicago: University of Chicago Press, 1996.

Mooney, Michael E. *Shakespeare's Dramatic Transactions.* Durham, N.C.: Duke University Press, 1990.

Nagler, Alois M. *Shakespeare's Stage.* Translated by Ralph Manheim. Enlarged ed. New Haven, Conn.: Yale University Press, 1981.

Orrell, John. *The Human Stage: English Theatre Design, 1567-1640.* Cambridge, England: Cambridge University Press, 1988.

_____. *The Quest for Shakespeare's Globe.* Cambridge, England: Cambridge University Press, 1983.

Parker, R. B., and Sheldon P. Zitner, eds. *Elizabethan Theater: Essays in Honor of S. Schoenbaum.* Newark: University of Delaware Press, 1996.

Reynolds, George Fulmer. *The Staging of Elizabethan Plays at the Red Bull Theater, 1605-1625.* London: Oxford University Press, 1940.

Rhodes, Ernest L. *Henslowe's Rose: The Stage and Staging.* Lexington: University Press of Kentucky, 1976.

Rutter, Carol Chillington, ed. *Documents of the Rose Playhouse.* Manchester, England: Manchester University Press, 1984.

Shapiro, Michael. *Children of the Revels: The Boy Companies of Shakespeare's Time and Their Plays.* New York: Columbia University Press, 1977.

Smith, Irwin. *Shakespeare's Blackfriar's Playhouse: Its History and Design.* New York: New York University Press, 1964.

_____. *Shakespeare's Globe Playhouse: A Modern Reconstruction.* New York: Charles Scribner's Sons, 1956.

Sturgess, Keith. *Jacobean Private Theatre.* London: Routledge & Kegan Paul, 1987.

Thomson, Peter W. *Shakespeare's Theatre.* London: Routledge, 1992.

Weimann, Robert. *Shakespeare and the Popular Tradition in the Theater: Studies in the Social Dimension of Dramatic Form and Function.* Edited by Robert Schwartz. Baltimore: The Johns Hopkins University Press, 1978.

Wickham, Glynne. *Early English Stages, 1300-1600.* 3 vols. London: Routledge & Kegan Paul, 1959-1981.

Wiles, David. *Shakespeare's Clown: Actor and Text in the Elizabethan Playhouse.* Cambridge, England: Cambridge University Press, 1987.

Yates, Frances A. *Theatre of the World.* Chicago: University of Chicago Press, 1969.

SHAKESPEARE IN PERFORMANCE

Agate, James E. *Brief Chronicles: A Survey of Plays by Shakespeare and the Elizabethans in Actual Performance, 1923-1942*. London: Jonathan Cape, 1943.

Ball, Robert Hamilton. *Shakespeare on Silent Film: A Strange Eventful History*. London: Allen & Unwin, 1968.

Bate, Jonathan, and Russell Jackson, eds. *Shakespeare: An Illustrated Stage History*. New York: Oxford University Press, 1996.

Beauman, Sally. *The Royal Shakespeare Company: A History of Ten Decades*. Oxford, England: Clarendon Press, 1982.

Berry, Ralph, ed. *On Directing Shakespeare: Interviews with Contemporary Directors*. New York: Barnes & Noble Books, 1977.

Brown, John Russell. *Shakespeare's Plays in Performance*. London: Edward Arnold, 1966.

Bulman, J. C., and H. R. Coursen, eds. *Shakespeare on Television: An Anthology of Essays and Reviews*. Hanover, N.H.: University Press of New England, 1988.

Byrne, M. St. Clare. "Fifty Years of Shakespearean Production: 1898-1948." *Shakespeare Survey* 2 (1949):1-20.

David, Richard. *Shakespeare in the Theatre*. Cambridge, England: Cambridge University Press, 1978.

Davies, Anthony. *Filming Shakespeare's Plays: The Adaptations of Laurence Olivier, Orson Welles, Peter Brook, and Akira Kurosawa*. Cambridge, England: Cambridge University Press, 1988.

Dawson, Anthony. *Watching Shakespeare: A Playgoer's Guide*. New York: St. Martin's Press, 1988.

Donaldson, Peter Samuel. *Shakespearean Films/Shakespearean Directors*. Boston: Unwin Hyman, 1990.

Eckert, Charles W., ed. *Focus on Shakespearean Films*. Englewood Cliffs, N.J.: Prentice-Hall, 1972.

Foulkes, Richard, ed. *Shakespeare and the Victorian Stage*. Cambridge, England: Cambridge University Press, 1986.

Jorgens, Jack J. *Shakespeare on Film*. Bloomington: Indiana University Press, 1977.

Leiter, Samuel L., ed. *Shakespeare Around the Globe: A Guide to Notable Postwar Revivals*. New York: Greenwood Press, 1986.

Manvell, Roger. *Shakespeare and the Film*. Rev. ed. San Diego: A. S. Barnes, 1979.

Odell, George C. D. *Shakespeare from Betterton to Irving*. 2 vols. New York: Charles Scribner's Sons, 1920.

Rothwell, Kenneth S., and Annabelle Henkin Melzer. *Shakespeare on Screen: An International Filmography and Videography*. New York: Neal-Schuman, 1990.

Salgado, Gamini. *Eyewitnesses to Shakespeare: Firsthand Accounts of Performances 1590-1890*. New York: Barnes & Noble Books, 1975.

Shattuck, Charles H. *Shakespeare on the American Stage*. 2 vols. Washington, D.C.: Folger Shakespeare Library, 1979-1987.

Speaight, Robert. *Shakespeare on the Stage: An Illustrated History of Shakespearean Performance*. Boston: Little, Brown, 1973.

Sprague, Arthur Colby. *Shakespeare and the Actors: The Stage Business in His Plays, 1660-1905*. Cambridge, Mass.: Harvard University Press, 1944.

——————. *Shakespearean Players and Performances*. Cambridge, Mass.: Harvard University Press, 1953.

Sprague, Arthur Colby, and J. C. Trewin. *Shakespeare's Plays Today: Some Customs and Conventions of the Stage*. Columbia: University of South Carolina Press, 1970.

Styan, J. L. *The Shakespeare Revolution: Criticism and Performance in the Twentieth Century*. Cambridge, England: Cambridge University Press, 1977.

Trewin, J. C. *Shakespeare on the English Stage*. London: Barrie & Rackliff, 1964.

Wells, Stanley. *Royal Shakespeare: Four Major Productions at Stratford-upon-Avon*. Greenville, S.C.: Furman University, 1976.

——————, ed. *Shakespeare Survey: An Annual Survey of Shakespearean Study and Production*. Vol. 39. Cambridge, England: Cambridge University Press, 1987.

Willes, Susan. *The BBC Shakespeare Plays: Making the Television Canon*. Chapel Hill: University of North Carolina Press, 1991.

Williams, Simon. *Shakespeare on the German Stage*. Vol. 1. Cambridge, England: Cambridge University Press, 1990.

THE PLAYS

All's Well That Ends Well

Bergeron, David. "The Mythical Structure of *All's Well That Ends Well*." *Texas Studies in Literature and Language* 14 (1972):559-568.

Bradbrook, Muriel C. "Virtue Is the True Nobility: A Study of the Structure of *All's Well That Ends Well*." *Review of English Studies* 1 (1950):289-301.

Cole, Howard C. *The "All's Well" Story from Boccaccio to Shakespeare*. Urbana: University of Illinois Press, 1981.

Dennis, Carl. "*All's Well That Ends Well* and the Meaning of *Agape*." *Philological Quarterly* 50 (1971):75-84.

Donaldson, Ian. "*All's Well That Ends Well*: Shakespeare's Play of Endings." *Essays in Criticism* 27 (1977):34-54.

Lawrence, William Witherle. "The Meaning of *All's Well That Ends Well*." *PMLA* 37 (1922):418-469.

Leggatt, Alexander. "*All's Well That Ends Well*: The Testing of Romance." *Modern Language Quarterly* 32 (1971):21-41.

Parker, R. B. "War and Sex in *All's Well That Ends Well*." *Shakespeare Survey* 37 (1984):95-113.

Price, Joseph G. *The Unfortunate Comedy: A Study of "All's Well That Ends Well."* Toronto: University of Toronto Press, 1968.

Smallwood, R. L. "The Design of *All's Well That Ends Well.*" *Shakespeare Survey* 25 (1972):45-61.

Styan, J. L. *"All's Well That Ends Well."* Manchester, England: Manchester University Press, 1984.

Antony and Cleopatra

Adelman, Janet. *The Common Liar: An Essay on "Antony and Cleopatra."* New Haven, Conn.: Yale University Press, 1973.

Barroll, J. Leeds. *Shakespearean Tragedy: Genre, Tradition, and Change in "Antony and Cleopatra."* Washington, D.C.: Folger Shakespeare Library, 1984.

Bono, Barbara J. *Literary Transvaluation: From Vergilian Epic to Shakespearean Tragicomedy.* Berkeley: University of California Press, 1984.

Fawkner, H. W. *Shakespeare's Hyperontology: "Antony and Cleopatra."* Rutherford, N.J.: Fairleigh Dickinson University Press, 1990.

Lamb, Margaret. *"Antony and Cleopatra" on the English Stage.* Rutherford, N.J.: Fairleigh Dickinson University Press, 1980.

Markels, Julian. *The Pillar of the World: "Antony and Cleopatra" in Shakespeare's Development.* Columbus: Ohio State University Press, 1968.

Riemer, A. P. *A Reading of Shakespeare's "Antony and Cleopatra."* Sydney, Australia: Sydney University Press, 1968.

Rose, Mark, ed. *Twentieth Century Interpretations of "Antony and Cleopatra."* Englewood Cliffs, N.J.: Prentice-Hall, 1977.

Scott, Michael. *"Antony and Cleopatra": Text and Performance.* London: Macmillan, 1983.

Steppat, Michael. *The Critical Reception of Shakespeare's "Antony and Cleopatra" from 1607-1905.* Amsterdam: Grxner, 1980.

Traci, Philip J. *The Love Play of Antony and Cleopatra: A Critical Study of Shakespeare's Play.* The Hague: Mouton, 1970.

As You Like It

Barber, C. L. "The Use of Comedy in *As You Like It.*" *Philological Quarterly* 21 (1942):353-367.

Bracher, Mark. "Contrary Notions of Identity in *As You Like It.*" *Studies in English Literature* 24 (1984):225-240.

Cirillo, Albert R. "*As You Like It*: Pastoralism Gone Awry." *ELH* 38 (1971):19-39.

Halio, Jay L., ed. *Twentieth Century Interpretations of "As You Like It": A Collection of Critical Essays.* Englewood Cliffs, N.J.: Prentice Hall, 1968.

Jamieson, Michael. *Shakespeare: "As You Like It."* London: Edward Arnold, 1965.

Morris, Harry. "*As You Like It*: Et in Arcadia Ego." *Shakespeare Quarterly* 26 (1975):269-275.

Palmer, D. J. "*As You Like It* and the Idea of Play." *Critical Quarterly* 13 (1971):234-245.

Shaw, John. "Fortune and Nature in *As You Like It.*" *Shakespeare Quarterly* 6 (1955):45-50.

Taylor, Michael. "*As You Like It*: The Penalty of Adam." *Critical Quarterly* 15 (1973):76-80.

Tolman, Albert H. "Shakespeare's Manipulation of His Sources in *As You Like It*." *Modern Language Notes* 37 (1922):65-76.

The Comedy of Errors

Arthos, John. "Shakespeare's Transformation of Plautus." *Comparative Drama* 1 (1967):239-253.

Baldwin, Thomas Whitfield. *On the Compositional Genetics of "The Comedy of Errors."* Urbana: University of Illinois Press, 1965.

—————. *William Shakespeare Adapts a Hanging*. Princeton, N.J.: Princeton University Press, 1931.

Barber, C. L. "Shakespearean Comedy in *The Comedy of Errors*." *College English* 25 (1964):493-497.

Brooks, Harold F. "Themes and Structure in *The Comedy of Errors*." In *Early Shakespeare*, edited by John Russell Brown and Bernard Harris. Stratford-upon-Avon Studies 3. London: Edward Arnold, 1961, 57-71.

Elliott, G. R. "Weirdness in *The Comedy of Errors*." *University of Toronto Quarterly* 9 (1939):95-106.

Grennan, Eamon. "Arm and Sleeve: Nature and Custom in *The Comedy of Errors*." *Philological Quarterly* 59 (1980):150-164.

Parker, Patricia. "Elder and Younger: The Opening Scene of *The Comedy of Errors*." *Shakespeare Quarterly* 34 (1983):325-327.

Sanderson, James L. "Patience in *The Comedy of Errors*." *Texas Studies in Literature and Language* 16 (1974-1975):603-618.

Williams, Gwyn. "*The Comedy of Errors* Rescued from Tragedy." *Review of English Literature* 5 (1964):63-71.

Coriolanus

Adelman, Janet. " 'Anger's My Meat': Feeding, Dependency, and Aggression in *Coriolanus*." In *Shakespeare: Pattern of Excelling Nature*, edited by David Bevington and Jay L. Halio. Newark: University of Delaware Press, 1978, 108-124.

Barton, Anne. "Livy, Machiavelli, and Shakespeare's *Coriolanus*." *Shakespeare Survey* 38 (1985):115-129.

Berry, Ralph. "The Metamorphoses of *Coriolanus*." *Shakespeare Quarterly* 26 (1975):172-183.

Brockman, B. A., ed. *"Coriolanus": A Casebook*. London: Macmillan, 1977.

Browning, I. R. "*Coriolanus*: Boy of Tears." *Essays in Criticism* 5 (1955):18-31.

Burke, Kenneth. "*Coriolanus*—and the Delights of Faction." *Hudson Review* 19 (1966):185-202.

Calderwood, James L. "*Coriolanus*: Wordless Meanings and Meaningless Words." *Studies in English Literature* 6 (1966):211-224.

Daniell, David. *"Coriolanus" in Europe*. London: Athlone Press, 1980.

Gurr, Andrew. "*Coriolanus* and the Body Politic." *Shakespeare Survey* 28 (1975):63-69.

Hofling, Charles K. "An Interpretation of Shakespeare's *Coriolanus.*" *American Imago* 14 (1957):407-435.

Holstun, James. "Tragic Superfluity in *Coriolanus.*" *ELH* 50 (1983):485-507.

Holt, Leigh. *From Man to Dragon: A Study of Shakespeare's "Coriolanus."* Salzburg, Austria: University of Salzburg Press, 1976.

Huffman, Clifford Chalmers. *Coriolanus in Context.* Lewisburg, Pa.: Bucknell University Press, 1971.

Hutchings, W. "Beast or God: The *Coriolanus* Controversy." *Critical Quarterly* 24 (Summer, 1982):35-50.

Lowe, Lisa. "'Say I Play the Man I Am': Gender and Politics in *Coriolanus.*" *Kenyon Review* 8 (Fall, 1986):86-95.

Meszaros, Patricia K. "'There Is a World Elsewhere': Tragedy and History in *Coriolanus.*" *Studies in English Literature* 16 (1976):273-285.

Oliver, H. J. "Coriolanus as Tragic Hero." *Shakespeare Quarterly* 10 (1959):53-60.

Phillips, James E., ed. *Twentieth Century Interpretations of "Coriolanus."* Englewood Cliffs, N.J.: Prentice-Hall, 1970.

Poole, Adrian. *Coriolanus.* Boston: Twayne, 1988.

Rabkin, Norman. "*Coriolanus*: The Tragedy of Politics." *Shakespeare Quarterly* 17 (1966):195-212.

Sicherman, Carol M. "*Coriolanus*: The Failure of Words." *ELH* 39 (1972):189-207.

Sprengnether, Madelon. "Annihilating Intimacy in *Coriolanus.*" In *Women in the Middle Ages and the Renaissance: Literary and Historical Perspectives*, edited by Mary Beth Rose. Syracuse, N.Y.: Syracuse University Press, 1986, 89-111.

Vetz, John W. "Cracking Strong Curbs Asunder: Roman Destiny and the Roman Hero in *Coriolanus.*" *English Literary Renaissance* 13 (1983):58-69.

Vickers, Brian. *Shakespeare: "Coriolanus."* London: Edward Arnold, 1976.

Cymbeline

Brockbank, J. P. "History and Histrionics in *Cymbeline.*" *Shakespeare Survey* 11 (1958):42-49.

Harris, Bernard. "What's Past Is Prologue: *Cymbeline* and *Henry VIII.*" In *Later Shakespeare*, edited by John Russell Brown and Bernard Harris. London: Edward Arnold, 1966, 203-233.

Hoeniger, F. David. "Irony and Romance in *Cymbeline.*" *Studies in English Literature* 2 (1962):219-228.

Hunt, Maurice. "Shakespeare's Empirical Romance: *Cymbeline* and Modern Knowledge." *Texas Studies in Language and Literature* 22 (1980):322-342.

Jones, Emrys. "Stuart *Cymbeline.*" *Essays in Criticism* 11 (1961):84-99.

Kirsch, A. C. "*Cymbeline* and Coterie Dramaturgy." *ELH* 34 (1967):285-306.

Lawrence, J. "Natural Bonds and Artistic Coherence in the Ending of *Cymbeline.*" *Shakespeare Quarterly* 35 (1984):440-460.

Schwartz, Murray M. "Between Fantasy and Imagination: A Psychological Exploration of *Cymbeline*." In *Psychoanalysis and Literary Process*, edited by Frederick C. Crews. Cambridge, Mass.: Winthrop, 1970, 219-283.

Swander, Homer. "*Cymbeline* and the 'Blameless Hero.'" *ELH* 31 (1964):259-270.

Taylor, Michael. "The Pastoral Reckoning in *Cymbeline*." *Shakespeare Survey* 36 (1983):97-106.

Thorne, William Barry. "*Cymbeline*: 'Lopp'd Branches' and the Concept of Regeneration." *Shakespeare Quarterly* 20 (1969):143-159.

Tinkler, F. C. "*Cymbeline*." *Scrutiny* 7 (1938/1939):5-20.

Warren, Roger. *Cymbeline*. Manchester, England: Manchester University Press, 1989.

Wickham, Glynne. "Riddle and Emblem: A Study in the Dramatic Structure of *Cymbeline*." In *English Renaissance Studies: Presented to Dame Helen Gardner in Honour of Her Seventieth Birthday*, edited by John Carey. Oxford, England: Clarendon Press, 1980, 94-113.

Edward III

Metz, G. Harold, ed. *Sources of Four Plays Ascribed to Shakespeare*. Columbia: University of Missouri Press, 1989.

Muir, Kenneth. "A Reconsideration of *Edward III*." *Shakespeare Survey* 6 (1953): 39-48.

Osterberg, V. "The 'Countess Scenes' of *Edward III*." *Shakespeare Jahrbuch* 65 (1929): 49-91.

Sams, Eric, ed. *Shakespeare's "Edward III": An Early Play Restored to the Canon*. New Haven, Conn.: Yale University Press, 1996.

Westersdorf, Karl P. "The Date of *Edward III*." *Shakespeare Quarterly* 16 (1965): 227-231.

Hamlet

Textual Studies

Clayton, Thomas, ed. *The "Hamlet" First Published (Q1, 1603): Origins, Form, Intertextualities*. Newark: University of Delaware Press, 1992.

Wilson, John Dover. *The Manuscript of Shakespeare's "Hamlet" and the Problems of Its Transmission: An Essay in Critical Bibliography*. 2 vols. New York: Macmillan, 1934.

Anthologies and Surveys of Criticism

Bevington, David, ed. *Twentieth Century Interpretations of "Hamlet."* Englewood Cliffs, N.J.: Prentice-Hall, 1968.

Brown, John Russell, and Bernard Harris, eds. *"Hamlet."* Stratford-upon-Avon Studies 5. London: Edward Arnold, 1963.

Burnett, Mark Thornton, and John Manning, eds. *New Essays on Hamlet.* New York: AMS, 1994.

Conklin, Paul S. *A History of "Hamlet" Criticism, 1601-1821.* New York: King's Crown Press, 1947.

Gottschalk, Paul. *The Meanings of "Hamlet": Modes of Literary Interpretation Since Bradley.* Albuquerque: University of New Mexico Press, 1972.

Hattaway, Michael. *"Hamlet."* Atlantic Highlands, N.J.: Humanities Press International, 1987.

Leavenworth, Russell E., ed. *Interpreting "Hamlet": Materials for Analysis.* San Francisco: Howard Chandler, 1960.

Muir, Kenneth, and Stanley Wells, eds. *Aspects of "Hamlet."* Cambridge, England: Cambridge University Press, 1979.

Price, Joseph G., ed. *"Hamlet": Critical Essays.* New York: Garland, 1986.

Sacks, Claire, and Edgar Whan, eds. *"Hamlet": Enter Critic.* New York: Appleton-Century-Crofts, 1960.

Williamson, Claude C. H., ed. *Readings on the Character of Hamlet.* London: George Allen and Unwin, 1950.

Source Studies

Gollancz, Israel, ed. *The Sources of "Hamlet": With Essays on the Legend.* London: Oxford University Press, 1926.

Hansen, William F. *Saxo Grammaticus and the Life of Hamlet: A Translation, History, and Commentary.* Lincoln: University of Nebraska Press, 1983.

Malone, Kemp. *The Literary History of Hamlet: The Early Tradition.* Heidelberg: Carl Winter, 1923.

Taylor, Marion A. *A New Look at the Old Sources of "Hamlet."* The Hague: Mouton, 1968.

General Studies

Aldus, P. J. *Mousetrap: Structure and Meaning in "Hamlet."* Toronto: University of Toronto Press, 1977.

Alexander, Nigel. *Poison, Play, and Duel: A Study in "Hamlet."* Lincoln: University of Nebraska Press, 1971.

Alexander, Peter. *Hamlet: Father and Son.* Oxford, England: Clarendon Press, 1955.

Calderwood, James L. *To Be and Not To Be: Negation and Metadrama in "Hamlet."* New York: Columbia University Press, 1983.

Charney, Maurice. *"Hamlet's" Fictions.* London: Routledge, 1988.

_____. *Style in "Hamlet."* Princeton, N.J.: Princeton University Press, 1969.

Cohen, Michael. *"Hamlet" in My Mind's Eye.* Athens: University of Georgia Press, 1989.

Cox, Lee Sheridan. *Figurative Design in "Hamlet": The Significance of the Dumb Show.* Columbus: Ohio University Press, 1973.

Davis, Arthur G. *"Hamlet" and the Eternal Problem of Man*. New York: St. John's University Press, 1964.

Davidson, Peter. *"Hamlet": Text and Performance*. London: MacMillan, 1983.

Dodsworth, Martin. *"Hamlet" Closely Observed*. London: Athlone Press, 1985.

Dollerup, Cay. *Denmark, "Hamlet," and Shakespeare: A Study of Englishmen's Knowledge of Denmark Towards the End of the Sixteenth Century with Special Reference to "Hamlet."* 2 vols. Salzburg, Austria: University of Salzburg Press, 1975.

Draper, John W. *The "Hamlet" of Shakespeare's Audience*. Durham. N.C.: Duke University Press, 1939.

Duthie, George Ian. *The "Bad" Quarto of "Hamlet": A Critical Study*. Cambridge, England: Cambridge University Press, 1941.

Erlich, Avi. *Hamlet's Absent Father*. Princeton, N.J.: Princeton University Press, 1977.

Fisch, Harold. *"Hamlet" and the Word: The Covenant Pattern in Shakespeare*. New York: Frederick Ungar, 1971.

Frye, Roland Mushat. *The Renaissance "Hamlet": Issues and Responses in 1600*. Princeton, N.J.: Princeton University Press, 1984.

Ghose, Zulfikar. *Hamlet, Prufrock, and Language*. New York: St. Martin's Press, 1978.

Grebanier, Bernard. *The Heart of "Hamlet": The Play Shakespeare Wrote*. New York: Thomas Y. Crowell, 1960.

Gurr, Andrew. *"Hamlet" and the Distracted Globe*. Edinburgh, Scotland: Sussex University Press, 1978.

Heilbrun, Carolyn. "The Character of Hamlet's Mother." *Shakespeare Quarterly* 8 (1957):201-206.

Hoff, Linda Kay. *Hamlet's Choice*. Lewiston, N.Y.: Edwin Mellen Press, 1988.

Jack, Adolphus Alfred. *Young Hamlet: A Conjectural Resolution of Some of the Difficulties in the Plotting of Shakespeare's Play*. Aberdeen, Scotland: Aberdeen University Press, 1950

Jones, Ernest. *Hamlet and Oedipus*. London: Gollancz, 1947.

Joseph, Bertram L. *Conscience and the King: A Study of "Hamlet."* London: Chatto & Windus, 1953.

King, Walter N. *Hamlet's Search for Meaning*. Athens: University of Georgia Press, 1982.

Kliman, Bernice W. *"Hamlet": Film, Television, and Audio Performance*. Rutherford, N.J.: Fairleigh Dickinson University Press, 1988.

Knights, L. C. *An Approach to "Hamlet."* Stanford, Calif.: Stanford University Press, 1961.

Levin, Harry. *The Question of "Hamlet."* New York: Oxford University Press, 1959.

Lidz, Theodore. *Hamlet's Enemy: Madness and Myth in "Hamlet."* New York: Basic Books, 1975.

Lundstrom, Rinda F. *William Poel's "Hamlets": The Director as Critic*. Ann Arbor, Mich.: UMI Research Press, 1984.

Mack, Maynard. "The World of *Hamlet.*" *Yale Review* 41 (1952):502-523.

Madariaga, Salvador de. *On "Hamlet."* London: Hollis & Carter, 1948.

Mander, Raymond, and Joe Mitchenson. *"Hamlet" Through the Ages: A Pictorial Record from 1709.* London: Macmillan, 1952.

McGee, Arthur. *The Elizabethan "Hamlet."* New Haven, Conn.: Yale University Press, 1987.

Mills, John A. *"Hamlet" on Stage: The Great Tradition.* Westport, Conn.: Greenwood Press, 1985.

Prosser, Eleanor. *"Hamlet" and Revenge.* London: Oxford University Press, 1967.

Quillian, William H. *"Hamlet" and the New Poetic: James Joyce and T. S. Eliot.* Ann Arbor, Mich.: UMI Research Press, 1975.

Rossi, Alfred. *Tyrone Guthrie Directs "Hamlet."* Berkeley: University of California Press, 1970.

Rowe, Eleanor. *"Hamlet": A Window on Russia.* New York: New York University Press, 1976.

Scofield, Martin. *The Ghosts of "Hamlet": The Play and Modern Writers.* Cambridge, England: Cambridge University Press, 1980.

Semper, I. J. *"Hamlet" Without Tears.* Dubuque, Iowa: Loras College Press, 1946.

Senelick, Lawrence. *Gordon Craig's Moscow "Hamlet": A Reconstruction.* Westport, Conn.: Greenwood Press, 1982.

Stoll, Elmer Edgar. *"Hamlet": An Historical and Comparative Study.* Minneapolis: University of Minnesota Press, 1919.

Todd, D. K. C. *I Am Not Prince Hamlet: Shakespeare Criticism Schools of English.* New York: Barnes & Noble Books, 1974.

Walker, Roy. *The Time Is Out of Joint: A Study of "Hamlet."* London: Andrew Dakers, 1948.

Warner, William Beatty. *Chance and the Text of Experience: Freud, Nietzsche, and Shakespeare's "Hamlet."* Ithaca, N.Y.: Cornell University Press, 1986.

Watkins, Ronald, and Jeremy Lemmon. *Hamlet.* Totowa, N.J.: Rowman & Littlefield, 1974.

Watts, Cedric. *"Hamlet."* Boston: Twayne, 1988.

Wilson, John Dover. *What Happens in "Hamlet."* 3d ed. Cambridge, England: Cambridge University Press, 1951.

Henry IV, Parts I and II

Aoki, Keiji. *Shakespeare's "Henry IV" and "Henry V": Hal's Heroic Character and the Sun-Cloud Theme.* Kyoto, Japan: Showa Press, 1973.

Bevington, David, ed. *"Henry the Fourth Parts I and II": Critical Essays.* New York: Garland, 1986.

Jenkins, Harold. *The Structural Problem in Shakespeare's "Henry the Fourth."* London: Methuen, 1956.

McLuhan, Herbert Marshall. *"Henry IV:* A Mirror for Magistrates." *University of Toronto Quarterly* 17 (1947):152-160.

Mitchell, Charles. "The Education of the True Prince." *Tennessee Studies in Literature* 12 (1967):13-21.

Morgan, Arthur Eustace. *Some Problems of Shakespeare's "Henry IV."* London: Oxford University Press, 1924.

Prosser, Eleanor. *Shakespeare's Anonymous Editors: Scribe and Compositor in the Folio Text of "Henry IV."* Stanford, Calif.: Stanford University Press, 1981.

Scoufos, Alice-Lyle. *Shakespeare's Typological Satire: A Study of the Falstaff--Oldcastle Problem.* Athens: Ohio University Press, 1979.

Wharton, T. F. *"Henry IV, Parts 1 and 2": Text and Performance.* London: Macmillan, 1983.

Wilson, John Dover. *The Fortunes of Falstaff.* Cambridge, England: Cambridge University Press, 1943.

Young, David P., ed. *Twentieth Century Interpretations of "Henry IV."* Englewood Cliffs, N.J.: Prentice-Hall, 1968.

Henry V

Battenhouse, Roy W. *"Henry V* as Heroic Comedy." In *Essays on Shakespeare and Elizabethan Drama in Honor of Hardin Craig*, edited by Richard Hosley. Columbia: University of Missouri Press, 1962.

Beauman, Sally, ed. *The Royal Shakespeare Company's Production of "Henry V" for the Centenary Season at the Royal Shakespeare Theatre.* Oxford, England: Pergamon Press, 1976.

Berman, Ronald, ed. *Twentieth Century Interpretations of "Henry V."* Englewood Cliffs, N.J.: Prentice-Hall, 1968.

Geduld, Harry M. *Filmguide to "Henry V."* Bloomington: Indiana University Press, 1973.

Hobday, C. H. "Imagery and Irony in *Henry V." Shakespeare Survey* 21 (1968):107-113.

Henry VI, Parts I, II, and III

Alexander, Peter. *Shakespeare's "Henry VI" and "Richard III."* Cambridge, England: Cambridge University Press, 1929.

Berman, Ronald S. "Fathers and Sons in the *Henry VI* Plays." *Shakespeare Quarterly* 13 (1962): 487-497.

Brockbank, J. P. "The Frame of Disorder: *Henry VI."* In *Early Shakespeare*, edited by John Russell Brown and Bernard Harris. London: Edward Arnold, 1961.

Dean, Paul. "Shakespeare's *Henry VI* Trilogy and Elizabethan 'Romance' Histories: The Origins of a Genre." *Shakespeare Quarterly* 33 (1982):34-48.

Henke, James T. *The Ego-King: An Archetype Approach to Elizabethan Political Thought and Shakespeare's "Henry VI" Plays.* Salzburg, Austria: Salzburg University Press, 1977.

Prouty, Charles Tyler. *The Contention and Shakespeare's "Henry VI": A Comparative Study.* New Haven, Conn.: Yale University Press, 1954.

Ricks, Don M. *Shakespeare's Emergent Form: A Study of the Structure of the "Henry VI" Plays*. Logan: Utah State University Press, 1968.

Riggs, David. *Shakespeare's Heroical Histories: "Henry VI" and Its Literary Tradition*. Cambridge, Mass.: Harvard University Press, 1971.

Henry VIII

Berman, Ronald. "*King Henry the Eighth*: History and Romance." *English Studies* 48 (1960):112-121.

Berry, Edward I. "*Henry VIII* and the Dynamics of Spectacle." *Shakespeare Studies* 12 (1979):229-246.

Cespedes, Frank V. "'We Are One in Fortunes': The Sense of History in *Henry VIII*." *English Literary Renaissance* 10 (1980):413-438.

Clark, Cumberland. *A Study of Shakespeare's "Henry VIII."* London: Golden Vista Press, 1931.

Kermode, Frank. "What Is Shakespeare's *Henry VIII* About?" *Durham University Journal*, n.s. 9 (1948):48-55.

Leggatt, Alexander. "*Henry VIII* and the Ideal England." *Shakespeare Survey* 38 (1985): 131-143.

McBride, T. "*Henry VIII* as Machiavellian Romance." *JEGP* 76 (1977):26-39.

Partridge, A. C. *The Problem of "Henry VIII" Re-opened: Some Linguistic Criteria for the Two Styles Apparent in the Play*. Cambridge, England: Bowes and Bowes, 1949.

Richmond, Hugh M. "Shakespeare's *Henry VIII*: Romance Redeemed by History." *Shakespeare Studies* 4 (1968):334-349.

Shirley, Frances A., ed. *"King John" and "Henry VIII": Critical Essays*. New York: Garland, 1988.

Wickham, Glynne. "The Dramatic Structure of Shakespeare's *Henry VIII*: An Essay in Rehabilitation." *Proceedings of the British Academy* 70 (1985):149-166.

Julius Caesar

Bonjour, Adrien. *The Structure of "Julius Caesar."* Liverpool, England: Liverpool University Press, 1958.

Daiches, David. *"Julius Caesar."* London: Edward Arnold, 1976.

Dean, Leonard F., ed. *Twentieth Century Interpretations of "Julius Caesar."* Englewood Cliffs, N.J.: Prentice-Hall, 1968.

Field, B. S., Jr. *Shakespeare's "Julius Caesar": A Production Collection*. Chicago: Nelson-Hall, 1980.

Foakes, R. A. "An Approach to *Julius Caesar*." *Shakespeare Quarterly* 5 (1954): 259-270.

Green, David C. *"Julius Caesar" and Its Source*. Salzburg, Austria: Salzburg University Press, 1979.

Greene, Gayle. "'The Power of Speech To Stir Men's Blood': The Language of Tragedy in Shakespeare's *Julius Caesar.*" *Renaissance Drama*, n.s. 11 (1980):67-93.

Hartstock, Mildred E. "The Complexity of *Julius Caesar.*" *PMLA* 81 (1966):56-62.

Ripley, John. *"Julius Caesar" on Stage in England and America, 1599-1973.* Cambridge, England: Cambridge University Press, 1980.

King John

Braunmuller, A. R. *"King John* and Historiography." *ELH* 55 (1988):309-332.

Burckhardt, Sigurd. *"King John*: The Ordering of This Present Time." *ELH* 33 (1966):133-153.

Curren-Aquino, Deborah T., ed. *"King John": New Perspectives.* Newark: University of Delaware Press, 1989.

Kastan, David Scott. "'To Set a Form upon That Indigest': Shakespeare's Fictions of History." *Comparative Drama* 17 (1983):1-16.

Shirley, Frances A., ed. *"King John" and "Henry VIII": Critical Essays.* New York: Garland, 1988.

Vaughn, Virginia Mason. "Between Tetralogies: *King John as Transition."* *Shakespeare Quarterly* 25 (1984):407-420.

Wixson, Douglas C. "'Calm Words Folded Up in Smoke': Propaganda and Spectator Response in Shakespeare's *King John.*" *Shakespeare Studies* 14 (1981):111-127.

King Lear

Textual Studies

Doran, Madeleine. *The Text of King Lear.* Stanford, Calif.: Stanford University Press, 1931.

Duthie, George Ian. *Elizabethan Shorthand and the First Quarto of "King Lear."* Oxford, England: Basil Blackwell, 1949.

Greg, Walter Wilson. *The Variants in the First Quarto of "King Lear": A Bibliographical and Critical Inquiry.* London: Printed for the Bibliographical Society, 1940 (for 1939).

Kirschbaum, Leo. *The True Text of "King Lear."* Baltimore: The Johns Hopkins University Press, 1945.

Stone, P. W. K. *The Textual History of "King Lear."* London: Scolar Press, 1980.

Taylor, Gary, and Michael Warren, eds. *The Division of the Kingdom: Two Versions of "King Lear."* New York: Oxford University Press, 1984.

Urkowitz, Steven. *Shakespeare's Revision of "King Lear."* Princeton, N.J.: Princeton University Press, 1980.

Anthologies of Criticism

Adelman, Janet, ed. *Twentieth Century Interpretations of "King Lear."* Englewood Cliffs, N.J.: Prentice-Hall, 1978.

Bonheim, Helmut, ed. *The "King Lear" Perplex.* Belmont, Calif.: Wadsworth, 1960.

Colie, Rosalie L., and F. T. Flahiff, eds. *Some Facets of "King Lear": Essays in Prismatic Criticism.* Toronto: University of Toronto Press, 1974.

Danson, Lawrence, ed. *On "King Lear."* Princeton, N.J.: Princeton University Press, 1981.

Muir, Kenneth. *"King Lear": Critical Essays.* New York: Garland, 1984.

General Studies

Bickersteth, G. L. *The Golden World of "King Lear."* Oxford, England: Oxford University Press, 1946.

Davis, Arthur G. *The Royalty of Lear.* New York: St. John's University Press, 1974.

Elton, William R. *"King Lear" and the Gods.* San Marino, Calif.: Huntington Library, 1966.

Fraser, Russell A. *Shakespeare's Poetics in Relation to "King Lear."* London: Routledge & Kegan Paul, 1962.

Gardner, Helen. *"King Lear."* London: Oxford University Press, 1967.

Goldberg, Samuel Louis. *An Essay on "King Lear."* Cambridge, England: Cambridge University Press, 1974.

Heilman, Robert B. *This Great Stage: Image and Structure in "King Lear."* Baton Rouge: Louisiana State University Press, 1948.

Jorgensen, Paul A. *Lear's Self-Discovery.* Berkeley: University of California Press, 1966.

Kozintsev, Grigori Mikhailovich. *"King Lear": The Space of Tragedy.* Berkeley: University of California Press, 1977.

Leggatt, Alexander. *"King Lear."* Boston: Twayne, 1988.

Lothian, John M. *"King Lear": A Tragic Reading of Life.* Toronto: Clark, Irwin, 1949.

Lusardi, James P., and June Schueter. *Reading Shakespeare in Performance: "King Lear."* Cranbury, N.J.: Associated University Presses, 1991.

Mack, Maynard. *"King Lear" in Our Time.* Berkeley: University of California Press, 1965.

Martin, William F. *The Indissoluble Knot: "King Lear" as Ironic Drama.* Lanham, Md.: University Press of America, 1987.

Muir, Kenneth. *"King Lear": A Critical Study.* Harmondsworth, England: Penguin Books, 1986.

Murphy, John L. *Darkness and Devils: Exorcism and "King Lear."* Athens: Ohio University Press, 1984.

Nameri, Dorothy E. *Three Versions of the Story of King Lear.* 2 vols. Salzburg, Austria: University of Salzburg Press, 1976.

Rosenberg, Marvin. *The Masks of "King Lear."* Berkeley: University of California Press, 1972.

Salgado, Gamini. *"King Lear": Text and Performance.* London: Macmillan, 1984.

Sewall, Richard B. *"King Lear."* In *The Vision of Tragedy.* New and enlarged ed. New Haven, Conn.: Yale University Press, 1980.

Thompson, Ann. *"King Lear."* Atlantic Highlands, N.J.: Humanities Press, 1988.

Wittreich, Joseph. *"Image of That Horror": History, Prophecy, and Apocalypse in "King Lear."* San Marino, Calif.: Huntington Library, 1984.

Zak, William F. *Sovereign Shame: A Study of "King Lear."* Lewisburg, Pa.: Bucknell University Press, 1984.

Love's Labour's Lost

Berman, Ronald. "Shakespearean Comedy and the Uses of Reason." *South Atlantic Quarterly* 63 (1964):1-9.

Bradbrook, Muriel C. *The School of Night: A Study of the Literary Relationships of Sir Walter Raleigh.* Cambridge, England: Cambridge University Press, 1936.

Carroll, William C. *The Great Feast of Language in "Love's Labour's Lost."* Princeton, N.J.: Princeton University Press, 1976.

Coursen, Herbert R., Jr. *"Love's Labour's Lost* and the Comic Truth." *Papers on Language and Literature* 6 (1970):316-322.

Ellis, Herbert A. *Shakespeare's Lusty Punning in "Love's Labour's Lost": With Contemporary Analogues.* The Hague: Mouton, 1973.

Hoy, Cyrus. *"Love's Labour's Lost* and the Nature of Comedy." *Shakespeare Quarterly* 13 (1962):31-40.

Montrose, Louis Adrian. *"Curious-Knotted Garden": The Form, Themes, and Contexts of Shakespeare's "Love's Labour's Lost."* Salzburg, Austria: University of Salzburg Press, 1977.

Taylor, Rupert. *The Date of "Love's Labour's Lost."* New York: Columbia University Press, 1932.

Yates, Frances A. *A Study of "Love's Labour's Lost."* Cambridge, England: Cambridge University Press, 1936.

Macbeth

Bartholomeusz, Dennis. *"Macbeth" and the Players.* Cambridge, England: Cambridge University Press, 1969.

Brown, John Russell, ed. *Focus on "Macbeth."* London: Routledge & Kegan Paul, 1982.

Calderwood, James L. *If It Were Done: "Macbeth" and Tragic Action.* Amherst: University of Massachusetts Press, 1986.

Clark, Arthur Melville. *Murder Under Trust: Or, The Topical "Macbeth" and Other Jacobean Matters.* Edinburgh: Scottish Academic Press, 1981.

Elliott, George Roy. *Dramatic Providence in "Macbeth": A Study of Shakespeare's Tragic Theme of Humanity and Grace.* Princeton, N.J.: Princeton University Press, 1958.

Fawkner, H. W. *Deconstructing "Macbeth": The Hyperontological View*. London: Associated University Presses, 1990.

Hunter, G. K. "*Macbeth* in the Twentieth Century." *Shakespeare Survey* 19 (1966):1-11.

Jorgensen, Paul A. *Our Naked Frailties: Sensational Art and Meaning in "Macbeth."* Berkeley: University of California Press, 1971.

    Long, Michael. *"Macbeth."* Boston: Twayne, 1989.

Muir, Kenneth, and Philip Edwards, eds. *Aspects of "Macbeth."* Cambridge, England: Cambridge University Press, 1977.

Paul, Henry N. *The Royal Play of "Macbeth": When, Why, and How It Was Written by Shakespeare*. New York: Macmillan, 1948.

Ramsey, Jarold. "The Perversion of Manliness in *Macbeth*." *Studies in English Literature* 13 (1973):285-300.

Rosenberg, Marvin. *The Masks of "Macbeth."* Berkeley: University of California Press, 1978.

Schoenbaum, Samuel, ed. *"Macbeth": Critical Essays*. New York: Garland, 1991.

Scott, William O. "Macbeth's—and Our—Self Equivocations." *Shakespeare Quarterly* 37 (1986):160-174.

Sinfield, Alan. "*Macbeth*: History, Ideology, and Intellectuals." *Critical Quarterly* 28 (1986):63-77.

Walker, Roy. *The Time Is Free: A Study of "Macbeth."* London: Andrew Dakers, 1949.

Willbern, David. "Phantasmagoric *Macbeth*." *English Literary Renaissance* 16 (1986):520-549.

Williams, Gordon. *"Macbeth": Text and Performance*. London: Macmillan, 1985.

Wills, Garry. *Witches and Jesuits: Shakespeare's Macbeth*. New York: Oxford University Press, 1994.

Measure for Measure

Bache, William B. *"Measure for Measure" as Dialectical Art*. Lafayette, Ind.: Purdue University Press, 1969.

Bennett, Josephine Waters. *"Measure for Measure" as Royal Entertainment*. New York: Columbia University Press, 1966.

Cox, John D. "The Medieval Background of *Measure for Measure*." *Modern Philology* 81 (1983):1-13.

Geckle, George L., ed. *Twentieth Century Interpretations of "Measure for Measure."* Englewood Cliffs, N.J.: Prentice-Hall, 1970.

Gless, Darryl J. *"Measure for Measure," the Law, and the Covenant*. Princeton, N.J.: Princeton University Press, 1979.

Hawkins, Harriet. *"Measure for Measure."* Boston: Twayne, 1987.

Lascelles, Mary. *Shakespeare's "Measure for Measure."* London: Athlone Press, 1953.

Leavis, F. R. "The Greatness of *Measure for Measure*." *Scrutiny* 10 (1942):234-247.

Miles, Rosalind. *The Problem of "Measure for Measure": A Historical Investigation*. New York: Barnes & Noble Books, 1976.

Nicholls, Graham. *"Measure for Measure": Text and Performance*. London: Macmillan, 1986.

Soellner, Rolf, and Samuel Bertsche, eds. *"Measure for Measure": Text, Source, and Criticism*. Boston: Houghton Mifflin, 1966.

Stevenson, David Lloyd. *The Achievement of "Measure for Measure."* Ithaca, N.Y.: Cornell University Press, 1966.

The Merchant of Venice

Barnet, Sylvan, ed. *Twentieth Century Interpretations of "The Merchant of Venice."* Englewood Cliffs, N.J.: Prentice-Hall, 1970.

Burckhardt, Sigurd. "*The Merchant of Venice*: The Gentle Bond." *ELH* 29 (1962):239-262.

Charlton, H. B. *Shakespeare's Jew*. Manchester, England: Manchester University Press, 1934.

Danson, Lawrence. *The Harmonies of "The Merchant of Venice."* New Haven, Conn.: Yale University Press, 1978.

Geary, Keith. "The Nature of Portia's Victory: Turning to Men in *The Merchant of Venice*." *Shakespeare Quarterly* 37 (1984):55-68.

Gollancz, Israel, Sir. *Allegory and Mysticism in Shakespeare: A Medievalist on "The Merchant of Venice."* London: G. W. Jones, 1931.

Grebanier, Bernard. *The Truth About Shylock*. New York: Random House, 1962.

Lelyveld, Toby. *Shylock on the Stage*. Cleveland: Western Reserve University Press, 1960.

Lyon, John. *"The Merchant of Venice."* Boston: Twayne, 1988.

Midgley, Graham. "*The Merchant of Venice*: A Reconsideration." *Essays in Criticism* 10 (1960):119-133.

Moody, A. D. *Shakespeare: "The Merchant of Venice."* London: Edward Arnold, 1964.

Overton, Bill. *"The Merchant of Venice."* Atlantic Highlands, N.J.: Humanities Press, 1987.

Silverman, Rita H. *Suffrance Is the Badge of All Our Tribe: A Study of Shylock in "The Merchant of Venice."* Lanham, Md.: University Press of America, 1981.

Spencer, Christopher. *The Genesis of Shakespeare's "Merchant of Venice."* Lewiston, N.Y.: Edwin Mellen Press, 1988.

The Merry Wives of Windsor

Barton, Anne. "Falstaff and the Comic Community." In *Shakespeare's "Rough Magic": Renaissance Essays in Honor of C. L. Barber*, edited by Peter Erickson and Coppélia Kahn. Newark: University of Delaware Press, 1985.

Bracey, William. *"The Merry Wives of Windsor": The History and Transmission of Shakespeare's Text*. Columbia: University of Missouri Press, 1952.

Carroll, William C. "'A Received Belief': Imagination in *The Merry Wives of Windsor*." *Studies in Philology* 74 (1977):186-215.

Green, William. *Shakespeare's "The Merry Wives of Windsor."* Princeton, N.J.: Princeton University Press, 1962.

Hotson, Leslie. *Shakespeare Versus Shallow*. Boston: Little, Brown, 1931.

Hunter, George K. "Bourgeoise Comedy: Shakespeare and Dekker." In *Shakespeare and His Contemporaries: Essays in Comparison*, edited by E. A. J. Honigmann. London: Manchester University Press, 1986.

Roberts, Jeanne Addison. *Shakespeare's English Comedy: "The Merry Wives of Windsor" in Context*. Lincoln: University of Nebraska Press, 1979.

A Midsummer Night's Dream

Briggs, Katherine M. *The Anatomy of Puck: An Examination of Fairy Beliefs Among Shakespeare's Contemporaries and Successors*. London: Routledge & Kegan Paul, 1959.

Dent, R. W. "Imagination in *A Midsummer Night's Dream*." *Shakespeare Quarterly* 15 (1964):115-129.

Fender, Stephen. *Shakespeare's "A Midsummer Night's Dream."* London: Edward Arnold, 1968.

Fisher, Peter F. "The Argument of *A Midsummer Night's Dream*." *Shakespeare Quarterly* 8 (1957):307-310.

Herbert, T. Walter. *Oberon's Mazed World: A Judicious Young Elizabethan Contemplates "A Midsummer Night's Dream" with a Mind Shaped by the Learning of Christendom Modified by the New Naturalist Philosophy and Excited by the Vision of a Rich, Powerful England*. Baton Rouge: Louisiana State University Press, 1977.

Olson, Paul A. "*A Midsummer Night's Dream* and the Meaning of Court Marriage." *ELH* 24 (1957):95-119.

Robinson, J. W. "'Palpable Hot Ice': Dramatic Burlesque in *A Midsummer Night's Dream*." *Studies in Philology* 61 (1964):192-204.

Robinson, James E. "The Ritual and Rhetoric of *A Midsummer Night's Dream*." *PMLA* 83 (1968):380-391.

Schanzer, Ernest. "The Moon and the Fairies in *A Midsummer Night's Dream*." *University of Toronto Quarterly* 24 (1955):234-246.

Selbourne, David. *The Making of A Midsummer Night's Dream: An Eye-Witness Account of Peter Brook's Production from First Rehearsal to First Night*. London: Methuen, 1982.

Warren, Roger. *"A Midsummer Night's Dream": Text and Performance*. London: Macmillan, 1983.

Weiner, Andrew D. "Multiforme Uniforme: *A Midsummer Night's Dream*." *ELH* 38 (1971):329-349.

Wiles, David. *Shakespeare's Almanac: "A Midsummer Night's Dream," Marriage, and the Elizabethan Calendar*. Rochester, N.Y.: Boydell & Brewer, 1993.

Young, David P. *Something of Great Constancy: The Art of "A Midsummer Night's Dream."* New Haven, Conn.: Yale University Press, 1966.

Much Ado About Nothing

Allen, John A. "Dogberry." *Shakespeare Quarterly* 24 (1973):35-53.

Berger, Harry L. "Against the Sink-a-Pace: Sexual and Family Politics in *Much Ado About Nothing.*" *Shakespeare Quarterly* 33 (1982):302-313.

Cook, Carol. "'The Sign and Semblance of Her Honor': Reading Gender Difference in *Much Ado About Nothing.*" *PMLA* 101 (1986):186-202.

Davis, Walter R., ed. *Twentieth Century Interpretations of "Much Ado About Nothing."* Englewood Cliffs, N.J.: Prentice-Hall, 1969.

Everett, Barbara. "*Much Ado About Nothing.*" *Critical Quarterly* 3 (1961):319-335.

King, Walter N. "*Much Ado About Nothing.*" *Shakespeare Quarterly* 15 (1964):143-155.

Mulryne, J. R. *Shakespeare: "Much Ado About Nothing."* London: Edward Arnold, 1965.

Prouty, Charles T. *The Sources of "Much Ado About Nothing": A Critical Study, Together with the Text of Peter Beverley's "Ariodanto and Ienerva."* New Haven, Conn.: Yale University Press, 1950.

Rose, Stephen. "Love and Self-Love in *Much Ado About Nothing.*" *Essays in Criticism* 20 (1970):143-150.

Stafford, T. J. "*Much Ado* and Its Satiric Intent." *Arlington Quarterly* 2 (1970):164-174.

Othello

Adamson, Jane. *"Othello" as Tragedy: Some Problems of Judgment and Feeling.* Cambridge, England: Cambridge University Press, 1980.

Calderwood, James L. *The Properties of "Othello."* Amherst: University of Massachusetts Press, 1989.

Draper, John W. *The "Othello" of Shakespeare's Audience.* Paris: Marcel Didier, 1952.

Elliott, George R. *Flaming Minister: A Study of "Othello" as a Tragedy of Love and Hate.* Durham, N.C.: Duke University Press, 1953.

Elliott, Martin. *Shakespeare's Invention of "Othello": A Study in Early Modern English.* New York: St. Martin's Press, 1988.

Flatter, Richard. *The Moor of Venice.* London: Heinemann, 1950.

Gardner, Helen. "*Othello*: A Retrospect, 1900-1967." *Shakespeare Survey* 21 (1968):1-11.

Grennan, Eamon. "The Women's Voice in *Othello*: Speech, Song, Silence." *Shakespeare Quarterly* 38 (1987):275-292.

Hankey, Julie, ed. *"Othello": Plays in Performance.* Bristol, England: Bristol Classical Press, 1987.

Heilman, Robert B. *Magic in the Web: Action and Language in "Othello."* Lexington: University of Kentucky Press, 1956.

Hyman, Stanley Edgar. *Iago: Some Approaches to the Illusion of His Motivation.* New York: Atheneum, 1970.

McLauchlan, Juliet. *Shakespeare: "Othello."* London: Edward Arnold, 1971.

Matteo, Gino J. *Shakespeare's "Othello": The Study and the Stage 1604-1904.* Salzburg, Austria: Salzburg University Press, 1974.

Rosenberg, Marvin. *The Masks of "Othello."* Berkeley: University of California Press, 1961.

Snyder, Susan, ed. *"Othello": Critical Essays.* New York: Garland, 1988.

Vaughan, Virginia M. *Othello: A Contextual History.* Cambridge, England: Cambridge University Press, 1994.

Vaughn, Virginia Mason, and Kent Cartwright, eds. *Othello: New Perspectives.* Rutherford, N.J.: Fairleigh Dickinson University Press, 1991.

Wine, Martin L. *"Othello": Text and Performance.* London: Macmillan, 1984.

Pericles, Prince of Tyre

Cutts, John P. "Pericles' 'Downright Violence.'" *Shakespeare Studies* 4 (1968):275-293.

Dunbar, Mary Judith. "'To the Judgement of Your Eye': Iconography and the Theatrical Art of *Pericles*." In *Shakespeare, Man of the Theatre*, edited by Kenneth Muir, Jay L. Halio, and D. J. Palmer. Newark: University of Delaware Press, 1983.

Ewbank, Inga-Stina. "'My Name Is Marina': The Language of Recognition." In *Shakespeare's Styles: Essays in Honour of Kenneth Muir*, edited by Philip Edwards, Inga-Stina Ewbank, and G. K. Hunter. Cambridge, England: Cambridge University Press, 1980.

Felperin, Howard. "Shakespeare's Miracle Play." *Shakespeare Quarterly* 18 (1967):363-374.

Flower, Annette C. "Disguise and Identity in *Pericles, Prince of Tyre*." *Shakespeare Quarterly* 26 (1975):30-41.

Greenfield, Thelma N. "A Re-Examination of the 'Patient' Pericles." *Shakespeare Studies* 3 (1967):51-61.

Hoeniger, F. David. "Gower and Shakespeare." *Shakespeare Quarterly* 33 (1982):461-479.

McIntosh, William A. "Musical Design in *Pericles*." *English Language Notes* 11 (1973):100-106.

Thorne, W. B. "*Pericles* and the 'Incest-Fertility' Opposition." *Shakespeare Quarterly* 22 (1971):43-56.

Welsh, Andrew. "Heritage in *Pericles*." In *Shakespeare's Last Plays: Essays in Honor of Charles Crow*, edited by Richard C. Tobias and Paul G. Zolbrod. Athens: Ohio University Press, 1974.

Richard II

Berger, Harry, Jr. *Imagining Audition: Shakespeare on Stage and Page.* Berkeley: University of California Press, 1989.

Cubeta, Paul M., ed. *Twentieth Century Interpretations of "Richard II."* Englewood Cliffs, N.J.: Prentice-Hall, 1971.

Hakola, Liisa. *In One Person Many People: The Image of the King in Three RSC Productions of William Shakespeare's "King Richard II."* Helsinki, Finland: Suomalainen Tiedeakatemia, 1988.

Hockey, Dorothy C. "A World of Rhetoric in *Richard II.*" *Shakespeare Quarterly* 15 (1964):179-191.

Humphreys, Arthur R. *Shakespeare: "Richard II."* London: Edward Arnold, 1967.

Page, Malcolm. *"Richard II": Text and Performance.* Atlantic Heights, N.J.: Humanities Press, 1987.

Phialas, Peter G. "*Richard II* and Shakespeare's Tragic Mode." *Texas Studies in Literature and Language* 5 (1963):344-355.

Reed, Robert Rentoul, Jr. *"Richard II": From Mask to Prophet.* University Park: Pennsylvania State University Press, 1968.

Talbert, Ernest W. *The Problem of Order: Elizabethan Commonplaces and an Example of Shakespeare's Art.* Chapel Hill: University of North Carolina Press, 1962.

Richard III

Textual Studies

Patrick, David Lyall. *The Textual History of "Richard III."* Stanford, Calif: Stanford University Press, 1936.

Smidt, Kristian. *Inurious Impostors and "Richard III."* New York: Humanities Press, 1964.

——————. *Memorial Transmission and Quarto Copy in "Richard III": A Reassessment.* New York: Humanities Press, 1970.

Walton, James Kirkwood. *The Copy for the Folio Text of "Richard III": With a Note on the Copy for the Folio Text of "King Lear."* Auckland, New Zealand: Auckland University College Press, 1955.

General Studies

Churchill, George B. *"Richard III" up to Shakespeare.* Berlin: Mayer and Muller, 1900.

Clemen, Wolfgang H. *A Commentary on Shakespeare's "Richard III."* Translated by Jean Bonheim. London: Methuen, 1968.

Garber, Marjorie. "Descanting on Deformity: Richard III and the Shape of History." In *Shakespeare's Ghost Writers: Literature as Uncanny Causality.* New York: Methuen, 1987.

Hankey, Julie, ed. *"Richard III": Plays in Performance*. London: Junction Books, 1981.

Hassel, R. Chris, Jr. *Songs of Death: Performance, Interpretation, and the Text of "Richard III."* Lincoln: University of Nebraska Press, 1987.

Richmond, Hugh M. *"King Richard III."* Manchester, England: Manchester University Press, 1989.

Wood, Alice I. P. *The Stage History of Shakespeare's "Richard III."* New York: Columbia University Press, 1909.

Romeo and Juliet

Cole, Douglas, ed. *Twentieth Century Interpretations of "Romeo and Juliet."* Englewood Cliffs, N.J.: Prentice-Hall, 1970.

Evans, Robert. *The Osier Cage: Rhetorical Devices in "Romeo and Juliet."* Lexington: University of Kentucky Press, 1966.

Hoppe, Henry R. *The Bad Quarto of "Romeo and Juliet": A Bibliographical and Textual Study*. Ithaca, N.Y.: Cornell University Press, 1948.

Kahn, Coppélia. "Coming of Age in Verona." *Modern Language Studies* 8 (1977-1978):5-22.

Levenson, Jill L. *"Romeo and Juliet": Shakespeare in Performance*. Manchester, England: Manchester University Press, 1987.

Moore, Olin H. *The Legend of Romeo and Juliet*. Columbus: Ohio State University Press, 1950.

Porter, Joseph A. *Shakespeare's Mercutio: His History and Drama*. Chapel Hill: University of North Carolina Press, 1988.

The Taming of the Shrew

Brooks, Charles. "Shakespeare's Romantic Shrews." *Shakespeare Quarterly* 11 (1960):351-356.

Daniell, David. "The Good Marriage of Katherine and Petruchio." *Shakespeare Survey* 37 (1984):23-31.

Greenfield, Thelma N. "The Transformation of Christopher Sly." *Philological Quarterly* 33 (1954):34-42.

Haring-Smith, Tori. *From Farce to Metadrama: A Stage History of "The Taming of the Shrew," 1594-1983*. Westport, Conn.: Greenwood Press, 1985.

Kehler, Dorothea. "Echoes of the Induction in *The Taming of the Shrew*." *Renaissance Papers* (1986):31-42.

Newman, Karen. "Renaissance Family Politics and Shakespeare's *The Taming of the Shrew*." *English Literary Renaissance* 16 (1986):86-100.

Roberts, Jeanne Addison. "Horses and Hermaphrodites: Metamorphoses in *The Taming of the Shrew*." *Shakespeare Quarterly* 34 (1983):159-171.

Seronsy, Cecil C. "'Supposes' as the Unifying Theme in *The Taming of the Shrew*." *Shakespeare Quarterly* 14 (1963):15-30.

Slights, Camille Wells. "The Raw and the Cooked in *The Taming of the Shrew.*" *JEGP* 88 (1989):168-189.

The Tempest

Brooks, Harold F. "*The Tempest*: What Sort of Play?" *Proceedings of the British Academy* 64 (1978):27-54.

Brown, John Russell. *Shakespeare: "The Tempest."* London: Edward Arnold, 1969.

Egan, Robert. "'This Rough Magic': Perspectives of Art and Morality in *The Tempest.*" *Shakespeare Quarterly* 23 (1972):171-182.

Hamilton, Donna B. *Virgil and "The Tempest": The Politics of Imitation.* Columbus: Ohio State University Press, 1990.

Hillman, Richard. "*The Tempest* as Romance and Anti-Romance." *University of Toronto Quarterly* 55 (1985/1986):141-160.

Hirst, David L. *"The Tempest": Text and Performance.* London: Macmillan, 1984.

Homan, Sidney R. "*The Tempest* and Shakespeare's Last Plays: The Aesthetic Dimensions." *Shakespeare Quarterly* 24 (1973):69-76.

Hunt, John Dixon. *A Critical Commentary on Shakespeare's "The Tempest."* London: Macmillan, 1968.

James, David Gwilyn. *The Dream of Prospero.* Oxford, England: Clarendon Press, 1967.

Jewkes, W. T. "'Excellent Dumb Discourse': The Limits of Language in *The Tempest.*" In *Essays on Shakespeare*, edited by Gordon Ross Smith. University Park: Pennsylvania State University Press, 1965.

Nuttall, Antony David. *Two Concepts of Allegory: A Study of Shakespeare's "The Tempest" and the Logic of Allegorical Expression.* New York: Barnes & Noble Books, 1967.

Schmidgall, Gary. *Shakespeare and the Courtly Aesthetic.* Berkeley: University of California Press, 1981.

Smith, Hallett, ed. *Twentieth Century Interpretations of "The Tempest."* Englewood Cliffs, N.J.: Prentice-Hall, 1969.

Sringley, Michael. *Images of Regeneration: A Study of Shakespeare's "The Tempest" and Its Cultural Background.* Uppsala, Sweden: Uppsala University, 1985.

Vaughn, Alden T., and Virginia Mason Vaughn. *Shakespeare's Caliban: A Cultural History.* Cambridge, England: Cambridge University Press, 1991.

Yachnin, P. "'If By Your Art': Shakespeare's Presence in *The Tempest.*" *English Studies in Canada* 14 (1988):119-134.

Timon of Athens

Bradbrook, Muriel C. *The Tragic Pageant of "Timon of Athens."* Cambridge, England: Cambridge University Press, 1966.

Brill, Lesley W. "Truth and *Timon of Athens.*" *Modern Language Quarterly* 40 (1979):17-36.

Butler, Francelia. *The Strange Critical Fortunes of "Timon of Athens."* Ames: Iowa State University Press, 1966.

Collins, A. S. "*Timon of Athens*: A Reconsideration." *Review of English Studies* 22 (1946):96-108.

Handelman, Susan. "*Timon of Athens*: The Rage of Disillusion." *American Imago* 36 (1979):45-68.

Merchant, W. M. "*Timon* and the Conceit of Art." *Shakespeare Quarterly* 6 (1955):249-257.

Muir, Kenneth. "*Timon of Athens* and the Cash Nexus." *Modern Quarterly Miscellany* 1 (1947):57-76.

Nuttall, A. D. "*Timon of Athens.*" Boston: Twayne, 1989.

Parrott, Thomas Marc. *The Problem of "Timon of Athens."* Oxford, England: Oxford University Press, 1923.

Soellner, Rolf. "*Timon of Athens*": *Shakespeare's Pessimistic Comedy*. Columbus: Ohio State University Press, 1979.

Walker, Lewis. "*Timon of Athens* and the Morality Tradition." *Shakespeare Studies* 12 (1979):159-177.

Titus Andronicus

Charney, Maurice. "*Titus Andronicus.*" Hemel Hempstead, England: Harvester Wheatsheaf, 1990.

Metz, G. Harold. "The Stage History of *Titus Andronicus*." *Shakespeare Quarterly* 28 (1977):154-169.

Palmer, D. J. "The Unspeakable in Pursuit of the Uneatable: Language and Action in *Titus Andronicus*." *Critical Quarterly* 14 (1972):320-339.

Parker, Douglas H. "Shakespeare's Use of Comic Conventions in *Titus Andronicus*." *University of Toronto Quarterly* 56 (1987):486-497.

Tricomi, Albert H. "The Aesthetics of Mutilation in *Titus Andronicus*." *Shakespeare Survey* 27 (1974):11-20.

Troilus and Cressida

Adamson, Jane. "*Troilus and Cressida.*" Boston: Twayne, 1987.

Campbell, Oscar James. *Comicall Satyre and Shakespeare's "Troilus and Cressida."* San Marino, Calif.: Huntington Library, 1938.

Foakes, R. A. "*Troilus and Cressida* Reconsidered." *University of Toronto Quarterly* 32 (1962-1963):142-154.

Greene, Gayle. "Language and Value in Shakespeare's *Troilus and Cressida*." *Studies in English Literature* 21 (1981):271-285.

Kimbrough, Robert. *Shakespeare's "Troilus and Cressida" and Its Setting*. Cambridge, Mass.: Harvard University Press, 1964.

McAlindon, Thomas. "Language, Style, and Meaning in *Troilus and Cressida*." *PMLA* 84 (1969):29-43.

Martin, Priscilla, ed. "*Troilus and Cressida*": *A Casebook*. London: Macmillan, 1976.

Oates, J. C. "The Ambiguity of *Troilus and Cressida.*" *Shakespeare Quarterly* 17 (1966):141-153.

Presson, Robert K. *Shakespeare's "Troilus and Cressida" and the Legends of Troy.* Madison: University of Wisconsin Press, 1953.

Twelfth Night

Draper, John W. *The "Twelfth Night" of Shakespeare's Audience.* Stanford, Calif.: Stanford University Press, 1950.

Everett, Barbara. "Or What You Will." *Essays in Criticism* 35 (1985):294-314.

Hartwig, Joan. "Feste's 'Whirligig' and the Comic Providence of *Twelfth Night.*" *ELH* 40 (1973):501-513.

Hollander, John. "*Twelfth Night* and the Morality of Indulgence." *Sewanee Review* 67 (1959):220-238.

Hotson, Leslie. *The First Night of "Twelfth Night."* New York: Macmillan, 1954.

Jenkins, Harold. "Shakespeare's *Twelfth Night.*" *Rice Institute Pamphlet* 45 (1959):1942.

Logan, Thad Jenkins. "*Twelfth Night*: The Limits of Festivity." *Studies in English Literature* 22 (1982):223-238.

Potter, Lois. "*Twelfth Night.*" London: Macmillan, 1985.

Salinger, Leo. "The Design of *Twelfth Night.*" *Shakespeare Quarterly* 9 (1958):117-139.

Tilley, Morris P. "The Organic Unity of *Twelfth Night.*" *PMLA* 29 (1914):550-566.

Wells, Stanley, ed. *"Twelfth Night": Critical Essays.* New York: Garland, 1986.

The Two Gentlemen of Verona

Brooks, H. F. "Two Clowns in a Comedy (To Say Nothing of the Dog): Speed, Launce (and Crab) in *The Two Gentlemen of Verona.*" *Essays and Studies*, n.s. 16 (1963):91-100.

Cole, Howard C. "The 'Full Meaning' of *The Two Gentlemen of Verona.*" *Comparative Drama* 23 (1989):201-227.

Danby, John F. "Shakespeare Criticism and *The Two Gentlemen of Verona.*" *Critical Quarterly* 2 (1960):309-321.

Holmberg, Arthur. "*The Two Gentlemen of Verona*: Shakespeare's Comedy as a Rite of Passage." *Queen's Quarterly* 90 (1989):33-44.

Kiefer, Frederick. "Love Letters in *The Two Gentlemen of Verona.*" *Shakespeare Studies* 18 (1986):65-85.

Rossky, William. "*The Two Gentlemen of Verona* as Burlesque." *English Literary Renaissance* 12 (1982):210-219.

Slights, Camille Wells. "*The Two Gentlemen of Verona* and the Courtesy Book Tradition." *Shakespeare Studies* 16 (1983):13-31.

Wells, Stanley. "The Failure of *The Two Gentlemen of Verona.*" *Shakespeare Jahrbuch* 99 (1963):161-173.

The Two Noble Kinsmen

Abrams, Richard. "Gender Confusion and Sexual Politics in *The Two Noble Kinsmen*." In *Drama, Sex, and Politics*. Vol. 7 in *Themes in Drama*. Cambridge, England: Cambridge University Press, 1985.

Bertram, Paul. *Shakespeare and "The Two Noble Kinsmen."* New Brunswick, N.J.: Rutgers University Press, 1965.

Edwards, Philip. "On the Design of *The Two Noble Kinsmen*." *Review of English Literature* 5 (October, 1964):89-105.

Frey, Charles H., ed. *Shakespeare, Fletcher, and "The Two Noble Kinsmen."* Columbia: University of Missouri Press, 1989.

Hart, Alfred. "Shakespeare and the Vocabulary of *The Two Noble Kinsmen*." *Review of English Studies* 10 (1934):274-287.

Holland, P. "Style at the Swan." *Essays in Criticism* 36 (1986):193-209.

Mincoff, M. "The Authorship of *The Two Noble Kinsmen*." *English Studies* 33 (1952):97-115.

Spencer, Theodore. "*The Two Noble Kinsmen*." *Modern Philology* 36 (1939):255-276.

The Winter's Tale

Bartholomeusz, Dennis. *"The Winter's Tale" in Performance in England and America, 1611-1976*. Cambridge, England: Cambridge University Press, 1982.

Battenhouse, Roy. "Theme and Structure in *The Winter's Tale*." *Shakespeare Survey* 33 (1980):123-138.

Bethell, S. L. *"The Winter's Tale": A Study*. London: Staples Press, 1947.

Bryant, Jerry H. *"The Winter's Tale* and the Pastoral Tradition." *Shakespeare Quarterly* 14 (1963):387-398.

Draper, R. P. *"The Winter's Tale": Text and Performance*. London: Macmillan, 1985.

Frey, Charles. *Shakespeare's Vast Romance: A Study of "The Winter's Tale."* Columbia: University of Missouri Press, 1980.

Gurr, Andrew. "The Bear, the Statue, and Hysteria in *The Winter's Tale*." *Shakespeare Quarterly* 34 (1983):420-425.

McDonald, Russ. "Poetry and Plot in *The Winter's Tale*." *Shakespeare Quarterly* 36 (1985):315-329.

Martz, Louis L. "Shakespeare's Humanist Enterprise: *The Winter's Tale*." In *English Renaissance Studies: Presented to Dame Helen Gardner in Honour of Her Seventieth Birthday*, edited by John Carey. Oxford, England: Clarendon Press, 1980.

Nuttall, A. D. *William Shakespeare: "The Winter's Tale."* London: Edward Arnold, 1966.

Overton, Bill. *"The Winter's Tale."* Atlantic Highlands, N.J.: Humanities Press, 1989.

Pyle, Fitzroy. *"The Winter's Tale": A Commentary on the Structure*. London: Routledge & Kegan Paul, 1969.

Sanders, Wilbur. *"The Winter's Tale."* Boston: Twayne, 1987.

Sokol, B. J. *Art and Illusion in "The Winter's Tale."* Manchester, England: Manchester University Press, 1994.

Williams, John A. *The Natural Work of Art: The Experience of Romance in Shakespeare's "The Winter's Tale."* Cambridge, Mass.: Harvard University Press, 1967.

THE POEMS

General Studies

Baldwin, T. W. *On the Literary Genetics of Shakespeare's Poems and Sonnets.* Urbana: University of Illinois Press, 1950.

Knight, G. Wilson. *The Mutual Flame: On Shakespeare's Sonnets and "The Phoenix and the Turtle."* London: Methuen, 1955.

The Phoenix and the Turtle

Buxton, John. "Two Dead Birds: A Note on *The Phoenix and Turtle.*" In *English Renaissance Studies: Presented to Dame Helen Gardner in Honour of Her Seventieth Birthday*, edited by John Carey. Oxford, England: Clarendon Press, 1980.

Copland, Murray. "The Dead Phoenix." *Essays in Criticism* 15 (1965):279-287.

Ellrodt, Robert. "An Anatomy of *The Phoenix and the Turtle.*" *Shakespeare Survey* 15 (1962):99-110.

Empson, William. *"The Phoenix and the Turtle."* *Essays in Criticism* 16 (1966):147-153.

Garber, Marjorie. "Two Birds with One Stone: Lapidary Re-inscription in *The Phoenix and Turtle.*" *Upstart Crow* 5 (1984):5-19.

Matchett, William H. *"The Phoenix and the Turtle": Shakespeare's Poem and Chester's "Loves Martyr."* The Hague: Mouton, 1965.

Underwood, Richard A. *Shakespeare's "The Phoenix and Turtle": A Survey of Scholarship.* Salzburg, Austria: Institut für Englische Sprache und Literatur, Universität Salzburg, 1974.

The Sonnets

Bermann, Sandra L. *The Sonnet over Time: A Study in the Sonnets of Petrarch, Shakespeare, and Baudelaire.* Chapel Hill: University of North Carolina Press, 1988.

Booth, Stephen. *An Essay on Shakespeare's Sonnets.* New Haven, Conn.: Yale University Press, 1969.

Bray, Denys, Sir. *The Original Order of Shakespeare's Sonnets.* London: Methuen, 1925.

Campbell, S. C. *Only Begotten Sonnets.* London: Bell & Hyman, 1978.

Duncan-Jones, Katherine. "Was the 1609 *Shake-Speare's Sonnets* Really Unauthorized?" *Review of English Studies*, n.s. 34 (1983):151-171.

Fineman, Joel. *Shakespeare's Perjured Eye: The Invention of Poetic Subjectivity in the Sonnets*. Berkeley: University of California Press, 1986.

Giroux, Robert. *The Book Known as Q: A Consideration of Shakespeare's Sonnets*. New York: Atheneum, 1982.

Hammond, Gerald. *The Reader and Shakespeare's Young Man Sonnets*. Totowa, N.J.: Barnes & Noble Books, 1981.

Hubler, Edward. *The Sense of Shakespeare's Sonnets*. Princeton, N.J.: Princeton University Press, 1952.

_____,et al. *The Riddle of Shakespeare's Sonnets*. New York: Basic Books, 1962.

Krieger, Murray. *A Window to Criticism: Shakespeare's "Sonnets" and Modern Poetics*. Princeton, N.J.: Princeton University Press, 1964.

Landry, Hilton. *Interpretations in Shakespeare's Sonnets*. Berkeley: University of California Press, 1963.

_____, ed. *New Essays on Shakespeare's Sonnets*. New York: AMS Press, 1976.

Leishman, J. B. *Themes and Variations in Shakespeare's Sonnets*. London: Hutchinson University Library, 1961.

Martin, Philip. *Shakespeare's Sonnets: Self, Love, and Art*. Cambridge, England: Cambridge University Press, 1972.

Melchiori, Giorgio. *Shakespeare's Dramatic Meditations: An Experiment in Criticism*. Oxford, England: Clarendon Press, 1976.

Muir, Kenneth. *Shakespeare's Sonnets*. London: George Allen & Unwin, 1979.

Padel, John. *New Poems by Shakespeare: Order and Meaning Restored to the Sonnets*. London: Herbert Press, 1981.

Peguiney, Joseph. *Such Is My Love: A Study of Shakespeare's Sonnets*. Chicago: University of Chicago Press, 1985.

Ramsey, Paul. *The Fickle Glass: A Study of Shakespeare's Sonnets*. New York: AMS Press, 1979.

Rowse, A. L. *Shakespeare's Sonnets: The Problems Solved*. New York: Harper & Row, 1973.

Schaar, Claes. *Elizabethan Sonnet Themes and the Dating of Shakespeare's Sonnets*. Lund, Sweden: C. W. K. Gleerup, 1962.

Smith, Hallett. *The Tension of the Lyre: Poetry in Shakespeare's Sonnets*. San Marino, Calif.: Huntington Library, 1981.

Stirling, Brents. *The Shakespeare Sonnet Order: Poems and Groups*. Berkeley: University of California Press, 1968.

Wait, R. J. C. *The Background of Shakespeare's Sonnets*. New York: Schocken Books, 1972.

Weiser, David K. *Mind in Character: Shakespeare's Speaker in the Sonnets*. Columbia: University of Missouri Press, 1987.

Wilson, Katherine M. *Shakespeare's Sugared Sonnets*. London: George Allen & Unwin, 1974.

Winny, James. *The Master-Mistress: A Study of Shakespeare's Sonnets*. London: Chatto & Windus, 1968.

Witt, Robert W. *Of Comfort and Despair: Shakespeare's Sonnet Sequence.* Salzburg, Austria: Institut für Anglistic und Amerikanistik, Universität Salzburg, 1979.

Narrative Poems

Allen, D. C. "Some Observations on *The Rape of Lucrece.*" *Shakespeare Survey* 15 (1962):89-98.

Donaldson, Ian. *The Rapes of Lucretia: A Myth and Its Transformations*. Oxford, England: Clarendon Press, 1982.

Keach, William. *Elizabethan Erotic Narrative: Irony and Pathos in the Ovidian Poetry of Shakespeare, Marlowe, and Their Contemporaries*. New Brunswick, N.J.: Rutgers University Press, 1977.

Levin, Richard. "The Ironic Reading of *The Rape of Lucrece* and the Problem of External Evidence." *Shakespeare Survey* 34 (1981):85-92.

Putney, Rufus. "*Venus and Adonis*: Amour with Humor." *Philological Quarterly* 20 (1941):533-548.

Simone, R. Thomas. *Shakespeare and "Lucrece": A Study of the Poem and Its Relation to the Plays*. Salzburg, Austria: Universitat Salzburg, 1974.

Sylvester, Bickford. "Natural Mutability and Human Responsibility: Form in Shakespeare's *Lucrece.*" *College English* 26 (1965):505-511.

Vickers, Nancy J. "The Blazon of Sweet Beauty's Best: Shakespeare's Lucrece." In *Shakespeare and the Question of Theory*, edited by Patricia Parker and Geoffrey H. Hartman. London: Methuen, 1985.

Walley, Harold R. "*The Rape of Lucrece* and Shakespearean Tragedy." *PMLA* 76 (1961):480-487.

Williams, Gordon. "The Coming of Age of Shakespeare's Adonis." *Modern Language Review* 78 (1983):769-776.

INDEXES

Character Index

Aaron (*Titus Andronicus*), 282
Achilles (*Troilus and Cressida*), 289
Adam (*As You Like It*), 83
Adonis (*Passionate Pilgrim*), 327
Adonis (*Venus and Adonis*), 399
Adriana (*Comedy of Errors*), 90
Aegeon (*Comedy of Errors*), 90
Aemilia (*Comedy of Errors*), 90
Agamemnon (*Troilus and Cressida*), 289
Agrippa, Menenius (*Coriolanus*), 96
Aguecheek, Sir Andrew (*Twelfth Night*), 295
Ajax (*Troilus and Cressida*), 289
Alarbus (*Titus Andronicus*), 282
Albany, Duke of (*King Lear*), 176
Alcibiades (*Timon of Athens*), 276
Alonso, King of Naples (*Tempest*), 269
Amiens (*As You Like It*), 83
Andronicus, Titus (*Titus Andronicus*), 282
Angelo (*Measure for Measure*), 197
Anne, Lady (*Richard III*), 248
Antiochus (*Pericles*), 235
Antipholus of Ephesus (*Comedy of Errors*), 90
Antipholus of Syracuse (*Comedy of Errors*), 90
Antonio (*Merchant of Venice*), 204
Antonio (*Twelfth Night*), 295
Antonio, Duke of Milan (*Tempest*), 269
Antony (*Antony and Cleopatra*), 76
Antony, Mark (*Julius Caesar*), 163
Apemantus (*Timon of Athens*), 276
Arcite (*Two Noble Kinsmen*), 308
Ariel (*Tempest*), 269
Armado, Don Adriano de (*Love's Labour's Lost*), 184
Arragon, Prince of (*Much Ado About Nothing*), 222
Arthur of Bretagne (*King John*), 171
Arviragus (*Cymbeline*), 103

Athens, Duke of (*Midsummer Night's Dream*), 216
Athens, Duke of (*Two Noble Kinsmen*), 308
Aufidius, Tullus (*Coriolanus*), 96
Aumerle, Duke of (*Richard II*), 241
Autolycus (*The Winter's Tale*), 313

Banquo (*Macbeth*), 190
Baptista (*Taming of the Shrew*), 263
Bassanio (*Merchant of Venice*), 204
Bassianus (*Titus Andronicus*), 282
Bastard of Orleans (*Henry VI, 1*), 138
Beatrice (*Much Ado About Nothing*), 222
Beaufort, Cardinal (*Henry VI, 2*), 145
Beaufort, Henry (*Henry VI, 1*), 138
Beaufort, John, Earl of Somerset (*Henry VI, 1*), 138
Bedford, Duke of (*Henry VI, 1*), 138
Belarius (*Cymbeline*), 103
Belch, Sir Toby (*Twelfth Night*), 295
Benedick (*Much Ado About Nothing*), 222
Benvolio (*Romeo and Juliet*), 255
Berowne (*Love's Labour's Lost*), 184
Bertram, Count of Rousillon (*All's Well*), 69
Bianca (*Taming of the Shrew*), 263
Blanch of Castile (*King John*), 171
Bohemia, King of (*The Winter's Tale*), 313
Bona, Lady (*Henry VI, 3*), 151
Bottom (*Midsummer Night's Dream*), 216
Britain, Queen of (*Cymbeline*), 103
Brutus, Junius (*Coriolanus*), 96
Brutus, Marcus (*Julius Caesar*), 163
Buckingham, Duke of (*Henry VIII*), 157
Buckingham, Duke of (*Richard III*), 248
Bullen, Anne (*Henry VIII*), 157

Cade, Jack (*Henry VI, 2*), 145
Caesar, Julius (*Julius Caesar*), 163

469

470

Quotation Index

Age cannot wither her, nor custom stale her infinite variety (*Antony and Cleopatra*, II, ii, 240-241), 78

All the world's a stage (*As You Like It*, II, vii, 139), 84

As flies to wanton boys, are we to the gods (*King Lear*, IV, i, 38), 181

Beware the ides of March (*Julius Caesar*, I, ii, 18), 164

Choked with ambition (*Henry VI, Part I*, II, v, 124), 140

Death will seize the doctor too (*Cymbeline*, V, v, 29-30), 105

Discretion is the better part of valor (*Henry IV, Part I*, V, iv, 122), 123

Eagle suffers little birds to sing, The (*Titus Andronicus*, IV, iv, 83), 284

Every one can master a grief but he that has it (*Much Ado About Nothing*, III, ii, 28-29), 226

Fling away ambition (*Henry VIII*, III, ii, 440), 159

Friends, Romans, countrymen, lend me your ears (*Julius Caesar*, III, ii, 78), 167

Great ones eat up the little ones, The (*Pericles, Prince of Tyre*, II, i, 31-32), 237

Heirs of all eternity (*Love's Labour's Lost*, I, i, 7), 188

I have immortal longings in me (*Antony and Cleopatra*, V, ii, 283-284), 80

If music be the food of love, play on (*Twelfth Night*, I, i, 1), 297

Kill a wife with kindness (*The Taming of the Shrew*, IV, i, 211), 267

Life's but a walking shadow (*Macbeth*, V, v, 24), 194

Like an eagle in a dovecote (*Coriolanus*, V, vi, 115), 98

Live we how we can, yet die we must (*Henry VI, Part III*, V, ii, 28), 153

Men shut their doors against a setting sun (*Timon of Athens*, I, ii, 150), 278

More sinned against than sinning (*King Lear*, III, ii, 60), 178

My kingdom for a horse! (*Richard III*, V, iv, 7), 253

O brave new world that has such people in it! (*The Tempest*, V, i, 183-184), 273

Once more unto the breach (*Henry V*, III, i, 1), 136

One that loved not wisely, but too well (*Othello*, V, ii, 344), 230

Our remedies oft in ourselves do lie, which we ascribe to heaven (*All's Well That Ends Well*, I, i, 231-232), 71

Out damned spot, out I say! (*Macbeth*, V, i, 38), 192

Plague on both your houses, A (*Romeo and Juliet*, III, i, 102), 260

Proud man, dressed in a little brief authority (*Measure for Measure*, II, ii, 117-118), 202

Quality of mercy is not strain'd, The (*The Merchant of Venice*, IV, i, 184), 207

Some have greatness thrust upon 'em (*Twelfth Night*, II, v, 158), 299

Some rise by sin, and some by virtue fall (*Measure for Measure*, II, i, 39), 200

Star-crossed lovers (*Romeo and Juliet*, Prologue, 1.6), 257

Tedious as a twice-told tale (*King John*, III, iv, 108), 173

Tell sad stories of the death of kings (*Richard II*, III, ii, 157), 246

There is something in the wind (*The Comedy of Errors*, II, i, 69), 92

Subject Index